The Commission on the

Intelligence Capabilities

of the

United States

Regarding

Weapons of
Mass Destruction

Report to the President of the United States

March 31, 2005

JUN 0 8 2005

Commission on the Intelligence Capabilities of the
United States Regarding Weapons of Mass Destruction
WASHINGTON, D.C. 20503

CO-CHAIRMEN:

THE HONORABLE
LAURENCE H. SILBERMAN

THE HONORABLE
CHARLES S. ROBB

March 31, 2005

Mr. President:

With this letter, we transmit the report of the Commission on the Intelligence Capabilities of the United States Regarding Weapons of Mass Destruction. Our unanimous report is based on a lengthy investigation, during which we interviewed hundreds of experts from inside and outside the Intelligence Community and reviewed thousands of documents. Our report offers 74 recommendations for improving the U.S. Intelligence Community (all but a handful of which we believe can be implemented without statutory change). But among these recommendations a few points merit special emphasis.

We conclude that the Intelligence Community was dead wrong in almost all of its pre-war judgments about Iraq's weapons of mass destruction. This was a major intelligence failure. Its principal causes were the Intelligence Community's inability to collect good information about Iraq's WMD programs, serious errors in analyzing what information it could gather, and a failure to make clear just how much of its analysis was based on assumptions, rather than good evidence. On a matter of this importance, we simply cannot afford failures of this magnitude.

After a thorough review, the Commission found no indication that the Intelligence Community distorted the evidence regarding Iraq's weapons of mass destruction. What the intelligence professionals told you about Saddam Hussein's programs was what they believed. They were simply wrong.

As you asked, we looked as well beyond Iraq in our review of the Intelligence Community's capabilities. We conducted case studies of our intelligence agencies' recent performance assessing the risk of WMD in Libya and Afghanistan, and our current capabilities with respect to several of the world's most dangerous state and non-state proliferation threats. Out of this more comprehensive review, we report both bad news and good news. The bad news is that we still know disturbingly little about the weapons programs and even less about the intentions of many of our most dangerous adversaries. The good news is that we have had some solid intelligence successes—thanks largely to innovative and multi-agency collection techniques.

Our review has convinced us that the best hope for preventing future failures is dramatic change. We need an Intelligence Community that is truly integrated, far more imaginative and willing to run risks, open to a new generation of Americans, and receptive to new technologies.

We have summarized our principal recommendations for the entire Intelligence Community in the Overview of the report. Here, we focus on recommendations that we believe only you can effect if you choose to implement them:

- *Give the DNI powers—and backing—to match his responsibilities.*

In your public statement accompanying the announcement of Ambassador Negroponte's nomination as Director of National Intelligence (DNI), you have already moved in this direction. The new intelligence law makes the DNI responsible for integrating the 15 independent members of the Intelligence Community. But it gives him powers that are only relatively broader than before. The DNI cannot make this work unless he takes his legal authorities over budget, programs, personnel, and priorities to the limit. It won't be easy to provide this leadership to the intelligence components of the Defense Department, or to the CIA. They are some of the government's most headstrong agencies. Sooner or later, they will try to run around—or over—the DNI. Then, only your determined backing will convince them that we cannot return to the old ways.

- *Bring the FBI all the way into the Intelligence Community.*

The FBI is one of the proudest and most independent agencies in the United States Government. It is on its way to becoming an effective intelligence agency, but it will never arrive if it insists on using only its own map. We recommend that you order an organizational reform of the Bureau that pulls all of its intelligence capabilities into one place and subjects them to the coordinating authority of the DNI—the same authority that the DNI exercises over Defense Department intelligence agencies. Under this recommendation, the counterterrorism and counterintelligence resources of the Bureau would become a single National Security Service inside the FBI. It would of course still be subject to the Attorney General's oversight and to current legal rules. The intelligence reform act almost accomplishes this task, but at crucial points it retreats into ambiguity. Without leadership from the DNI, the FBI is likely to continue escaping effective integration into the Intelligence Community.

- *Demand more of the Intelligence Community.*

The Intelligence Community needs to be pushed. It will not do its best unless it is pressed by policymakers—sometimes to the point of discomfort. Analysts must be pressed to explain how much they don't know; the collection agencies must be pressed to explain why they don't have better information on key topics. While policymakers must be prepared to credit intelligence that doesn't fit their preferences, no important intelligence assessment should be accepted without sharp questioning that forces the community to explain exactly how it came to that assessment and what alternatives might also be true. This is not "politicization"; it is a necessary part of the intelligence process. And in the end, it is the key to getting the best from an Intelligence Community that, at its best, knows how to do astonishing things.

- **Rethink the President's Daily Brief.**

The daily intelligence briefings given to you before the Iraq war were flawed. Through attention-grabbing headlines and repetition of questionable data, these briefings overstated the case that Iraq was rebuilding its WMD programs. There are many other aspects of the daily brief that deserve to be reconsidered as well, but we are reluctant to make categorical recommendations on a process that in the end must meet your needs, not our theories. On one point, however, we want to be specific: while the DNI must be ultimately responsible for the content of your daily briefing, we do not believe that the DNI ought to prepare, deliver, or even attend every briefing. For if the DNI is consumed by current intelligence, the long-term needs of the Intelligence Community will suffer.

* * *

There is no more important intelligence mission than understanding the worst weapons that our enemies possess, and how they intend to use them against us. These are their deepest secrets, and unlocking them must be our highest priority. So far, despite some successes, our Intelligence Community has not been agile and innovative enough to provide the information that the nation needs. Other commissions and observers have said the same. We should not wait for another commission or another Administration to force widespread change in the Intelligence Community.

Very respectfully,

Laurence H. Silberman
Co-Chairman

Charles S. Robb
Co-Chairman

Richard C. Levin   John McCain   Henry S. Rowen   Walter B. Slocombe

William O. Studeman   Patricia M. Wald   Charles M. Vest

Lloyd Cutler
(Of Counsel)

SUMMARY OF CONTENTS

APPENDICES

CONTENTS

PART TWO: LOOKING FORWARD

APPENDICES

INTRODUCTORY NOTE ON CLASSIFICATION

This unclassified report is derived from a 692-page classified report that was delivered to the President on March 31, 2005. We endeavored to write our classified report in a manner that allowed as much of its content as possible to be released—word for word—in this unclassified report. Because our mandate required us to review, and reach conclusions from, some of the more sensitive information in the possession of the United States Government, there was some information that we simply could not release in our unclassified report. Where the unclassified report omits substantive information that appears in the classified report, we make reference to the omission and, where possible, offer a general description of the omitted material.

We also note here that there are two chapters of our classified report that we could not include at all in our unclassified version. First, our classified report contained a chapter addressing the United States' intelligence capabilities with respect to two countries of proliferation concern, Iran and North Korea. Regrettably, even generalized statements about the state of the Intelligence Community's understanding of these countries are classified, and so we could not include our findings in this area in our unclassified report. Second, our classified report includes a short chapter on covert action which also is too sensitive to include in an unclassified format.

OVERVIEW OF THE REPORT

OVERVIEW OF THE REPORT

INTRODUCTION

On the brink of war, and in front of the whole world, the United States government asserted that Saddam Hussein had reconstituted his nuclear weapons program, had biological weapons and mobile biological weapon production facilities, and had stockpiled and was producing chemical weapons. All of this was based on the assessments of the U.S. Intelligence Community. And not one bit of it could be confirmed when the war was over.

While the intelligence services of many other nations also thought that Iraq had weapons of mass destruction, in the end it was the United States that put its credibility on the line, making this one of the most public—and most damaging—intelligence failures in recent American history.

This failure was in large part the result of analytical shortcomings; intelligence analysts were too wedded to their assumptions about Saddam's intentions. But it was also a failure on the part of those who collect intelligence—CIA's and the Defense Intelligence Agency's (DIA) spies, the National Security Agency's (NSA) eavesdroppers, and the National Geospatial-Intelligence Agency's (NGA) imagery experts.[*] In the end, those agencies collected precious little intelligence for the analysts to analyze, and much of what they did collect was either worthless or misleading. Finally, it was a failure to communicate effectively with policymakers; the Intelligence Community didn't adequately explain just how little good intelligence it had—or how much its assessments were driven by assumptions and inferences rather than concrete evidence.

Was the failure in Iraq typical of the Community's performance? Or was Iraq, as one senior intelligence official told the Commission, a sort of "perfect storm"—a one-time breakdown caused by a rare confluence of events that conspired to create a bad result? In our view, it was neither.

---

[*] While we have attempted to write this report in a way that is accessible to those not acquainted with the world of intelligence, we have included a primer on the U.S. Intelligence Community at Appendix C of this report for readers who are new to the subject.

The failures we found in Iraq are not repeated everywhere. The Intelligence Community played a key role, for example, in getting Libya to renounce weapons of mass destruction and in exposing the long-running A.Q. Khan nuclear proliferation network. It is engaged in imaginative, successful (and highly classified) operations in many parts of the world. Tactical support to counterterrorism efforts is excellent, and there are signs of a boldness that would have been unimaginable before September 11, 2001.

But neither was Iraq a "perfect storm." The flaws we found in the Intelligence Community's Iraq performance are still all too common. Across the board, the Intelligence Community knows disturbingly little about the nuclear programs of many of the world's most dangerous actors. In some cases, it knows less now than it did five or ten years ago. As for biological weapons, despite years of Presidential concern, the Intelligence Community has struggled to address this threat.

To be sure, the Intelligence Community is full of talented, dedicated people. But they seem to be working harder and harder just to maintain a *status quo* that is increasingly irrelevant to the new challenges presented by weapons of mass destruction. Our collection agencies are often unable to gather intelligence on the very things we care the most about. Too often, analysts simply accept these gaps; they do little to help collectors identify new opportunities, and they do not always tell decisionmakers just how limited their knowledge really is.

Taken together, these shortcomings reflect the Intelligence Community's struggle to confront an environment that has changed radically over the past decade. For almost 50 years after the passage of the National Security Act of 1947, the Intelligence Community's resources were overwhelmingly trained on a single threat—the Soviet Union, its nuclear arsenal, its massive conventional forces, and its activities around the world. By comparison, today's priority intelligence targets are greater in number (there are dozens of entities that could strike a devastating blow against the United States) and are often more diffuse in character (they include not only states but also nebulous transnational terror and proliferation networks). What's more, some of the weapons that would be most dangerous in the hands of terrorists or rogue nations are difficult to detect. Much of the technology, equipment, and materials necessary to develop biological and chemical weapons, for example, also has legitimate commercial applications. Biological weapons themselves can be built in small-scale facilities that are easy to conceal, and weapons-grade uranium can be effectively shielded from traditional detection techniques. At the same time, advances in technology have made the job of technical intelligence collection exceedingly difficult.

The demands of this new environment can only be met by broad and deep change in the Intelligence Community. The Intelligence Community we have today is buried beneath an avalanche of demands for "current intelligence"— the pressing need to meet the tactical requirements of the day. Current intelligence in support of military and other action is necessary, of course. But we also need an Intelligence Community with *strategic* capabilities: it must be equipped to develop long-term plans for penetrating today's difficult targets, and to identify political and social trends shaping the threats that lie over the horizon. We can imagine no threat that demands greater strategic focus from the Intelligence Community than that posed by nuclear, biological, and chemical weapons.

The Intelligence Community is also fragmented, loosely managed, and poorly coordinated; the 15 intelligence organizations are a "Community" in name only and rarely act with a unity of purpose. What we need is an Intelligence Community that is *integrated*: the Community's leadership must be capable of allocating and directing the Community's resources in a coordinated way. The strengths of our distinct collection agencies must be brought to bear together on the most difficult intelligence problems. At the same time we need a Community that preserves diversity of analysis, and that encourages structured debate among agencies and analysts over the interpretation of information.

Perhaps above all, the Intelligence Community is too slow to change the way it does business. It is reluctant to use new human and technical collection methods; it is behind the curve in applying cutting-edge technologies; and it has not adapted its personnel practices and incentives structures to fit the needs of a new job market. What we need is an Intelligence Community that is flexible—able to respond nimbly to an ever-shifting threat environment and to the rapid pace of today's technological changes.

In short, to succeed in confronting today's and tomorrow's threats, the Intelligence Community must be transformed—a goal that would be difficult to meet even in the best of all possible worlds. And we do not live in the best of worlds. The CIA and NSA may be sleek and omniscient in the movies, but in real life they and other intelligence agencies are vast government bureaucracies. They are bureaucracies filled with talented people and armed with sophisticated technological tools, but talent and tools do not suspend the iron laws of bureaucratic behavior. Like government bodies everywhere, intelligence agencies are prone to develop self-reinforcing, risk averse cultures that take outside advice badly. While laudable steps were taken to improve our intelligence agencies after September 11, 2001, the agencies have done less in response to the failures over Iraq, and we believe that many within those agencies do not accept the conclusion that we reached after our year of study: that the Community needs fundamental change if it is to successfully confront the threats of the 21st century.

We are not the first to say this. Indeed, commission after commission has identified some of the same fundamental failings we see in the Intelligence Community, usually to little effect. The Intelligence Community is a closed world, and many insiders admitted to us that *it has an almost perfect record of resisting external recommendations.*

But the present moment offers an unprecedented opportunity to overcome this resistance. About halfway through our inquiry, Congress passed the *Intelligence Reform and Terrorism Prevention Act of 2004*, which became a sort of a *deus ex machina* in our deliberations. The act created a Director of National Intelligence (DNI). The DNI's role could have been a purely coordinating position, with a limited staff and authority to match. Or it could have been something closer to a "Secretary of Intelligence," with full authority over the principal intelligence agencies and clear responsibility for their actions— which also might well have been consistent with a small bureaucratic super-structure. In the end, the DNI created by the intelligence reform legislation was neither of these things; the office is given broad responsibilities but only ambiguous authorities. While we might have chosen a different solution, we are not writing on a blank slate. So our focus has been in large part on how to make the new intelligence structure work, and in particular on giving the DNI tools (and support staff) to match his large responsibilities.

We are mindful, however, that there is a serious risk in creating too large a bureaucratic structure to serve the DNI: the risk that decisionmaking in the field, which sometimes requires quick action, will be improperly delayed. Balancing these two imperatives—necessary agility of operational execution and thoughtful coordination of intelligence activities—is, in our view, the DNI's greatest challenge.

In considering organizational issues, we did not delude ourselves that organizational structure alone can solve problems. More than many parts of government, the culture of the Intelligence Community is formed in the field, where organizational changes at headquarters are felt only lightly. We understand the limits of organizational change, and many of our recommendations go beyond organizational issues and would, if enacted, directly affect the way that intelligence is collected and analyzed. But we regret that we were not able to make such detailed proposals for some of the most important technical collection agencies, such as NSA and NGA. For those agencies, and for the many other issues that we could only touch upon, we must trust that our broader institutional recommendations will enable necessary reform. The DNI that we envision will have the budget and management tools to dig deep into the culture of each agency and to force changes where needed.

This Overview—and, in far more detail, the report that follows—offers our conclusions on what needs to be done. We begin by describing the results of our case studies—which include Iraq, Libya, Afghanistan, and others—and the lessons they teach about the Intelligence Community's current capabilities and weaknesses. We then offer our recommendations for reform based upon those lessons.

Three final notes before proceeding. First, our main tasks were to find out how the Intelligence Community erred in Iraq and to recommend changes to avoid such errors in the future. This is a task that often lends itself to hubris and to second-guessing, and we have been humbled by the difficult judgments that had to be made about Iraq and its weapons programs. We are humbled too by the complexity of the management and technical challenges intelligence professionals face today. We recommend substantial changes, and we believe deeply that such changes are necessary, but we recognize that other reasonable observers could come to a different view on some of these questions.

Second, no matter how much we improve the Intelligence Community, weapons of mass destruction will continue to pose an enormous threat. Intelligence will always be imperfect and, as history persuades us, surprise can never be completely prevented. Moreover, we cannot expect spies, satellites, and analysts to constitute our only defense. As our biological weapons recommendations make abundantly clear, all national capabilities—regulatory, military, and diplomatic—must be used to combat proliferation.

Finally, we emphasize two points about the scope of this Commission's charter, particularly with respect to the Iraq question. First, we were *not* asked to determine whether Saddam Hussein had weapons of mass destruction. That was the mandate of the Iraq Survey Group; our mission is to investigate the reasons why the Intelligence Community's pre-war assessments were so different from what the Iraq Survey Group found after the war. Second, we were not authorized to investigate how policymakers used the intelligence assessments they received from the Intelligence Community. Accordingly, while we interviewed a host of current and former policymakers during the course of our investigation, the purpose of those interviews was to learn about how the Intelligence Community reached and communicated its judgments about Iraq's weapons programs—not to review how policymakers subsequently used that information.

LOOKING BACK: CASE STUDIES IN FAILURE AND SUCCESS

Our first task was to evaluate the Intelligence Community's performance in assessing the nuclear, biological, and chemical weapons activities of three countries: Iraq, Afghanistan, and Libya. In addition, we studied U.S. capabilities against other pressing intelligence problems—including Iran, North Korea, Russia, China, and terrorism. We wanted a range of studies so we would not judge the Intelligence Community solely on its handling of Iraq, which was—however important—a single intelligence target. In all, the studies paint a representative picture. It is the picture of an Intelligence Community that urgently needs to be changed.

Iraq: An Overview

In October 2002, at the request of members of Congress, the National Intelligence Council produced a National Intelligence Estimate (NIE)—the most authoritative intelligence assessment produced by the Intelligence Community—which concluded that Iraq was reconstituting its nuclear weapons program and was actively pursuing a nuclear device. According to the exhaustive study of the Iraq Survey Group, this assessment was almost completely wrong. The NIE said that Iraq's biological weapons capability was larger and more advanced than before the Gulf War and that Iraq possessed mobile biological weapons production facilities. This was wrong. The NIE further stated that Iraq had renewed production of chemical weapons, including mustard, sarin, GF, and VX, and that it had accumulated chemical stockpiles of between 100 and 500 metric tons. All of this was also wrong. Finally, the NIE concluded that Iraq had unmanned aerial vehicles that were probably intended for the delivery of biological weapons, and ballistic missiles that had ranges greater than the United Nations' permitted 150 kilometer range. In truth, the aerial vehicles were not for biological weapons; some of Iraq's missiles were, however, capable of traveling more than 150 kilometers. The Intelligence Community's Iraq assessments were, in short, riddled with errors.

Contrary to what some defenders of the Intelligence Community have since asserted, these errors were *not* the result of a few harried months in 2002. Most of the fundamental errors were made and communicated to policymakers well before the now-infamous NIE of October 2002, and were not corrected in the months between the NIE and the start of the war. They were not isolated or random failings. Iraq had been an intelligence challenge at the forefront of U.S. attention for over a decade. It was a known adversary that had already fought one war with the United States and seemed increasingly likely to fight another. But, after ten years of effort, the Intelligence Community still had no good intelligence on the status of Iraq's weapons programs. Our full report examines these issues in detail. Here we limit our discussion to the central lessons to be learned from this episode.

The first lesson is that the Intelligence Community cannot analyze and disseminate information that it does not have. The Community's Iraq assessment was crippled by its inability to collect meaningful intelligence on Iraq's nuclear, biological, and chemical weapons programs. The second lesson follows from the first: lacking good intelligence, analysts and collectors fell back on old assumptions and inferences drawn from Iraq's past behavior and intentions.

The Intelligence Community had learned a hard lesson after the 1991 Gulf War, which revealed that the Intelligence Community's pre-war assessments had underestimated Iraq's nuclear program and had failed to identify all of its chemical weapons storage sites. Shaken by the magnitude of their errors, intelligence analysts were determined not to fall victim again to the same mistake. This tendency was only reinforced by later events. Saddam acted to the very end like a man with much to hide. And the dangers of underestimating our enemies were deeply underscored by the attacks of September 11, 2001.

Throughout the 1990s, therefore, the Intelligence Community assumed that Saddam's Iraq was up to no good—that Baghdad had maintained its nuclear, biological, and chemical technical expertise, had kept its biological and chemical weapons production capabilities, and possessed significant stockpiles of chemical agents and weapons precursors. Since Iraq's leadership had not changed since 1991, the Intelligence Community also believed that these capabilities would be further revved up as soon as inspectors left Iraq. Saddam's continuing cat-and-mouse parrying with international inspectors only hardened these assumptions.

These experiences contributed decisively to the Intelligence Community's erroneous National Intelligence Estimate of October 2002. That is not to say that its fears and assumptions were foolish or even unreasonable. At some point, however, these premises stopped being working hypotheses and became more or less unrebuttable conclusions; worse, the intelligence system became too willing to find confirmations of them in evidence that should have been recognized at the time to be of dubious reliability. Collectors and analysts too readily accepted any evidence that supported their theory that Iraq had stockpiles and was developing weapons programs, and they explained away or simply disregarded evidence that pointed in the other direction.

Even in hindsight, those assumptions have a powerful air of common sense. If the Intelligence Community's estimate and other pre-war intelligence had relied principally and explicitly on inferences the Community drew from Iraq's past conduct, the estimate would still have been wrong, but it would have been far more defensible. For good reason, it was hard to conclude that Saddam Hussein had indeed abandoned his weapons programs. But a central flaw of the NIE is that it took these defensible assumptions and swathed them in the mystique of intelligence, providing secret information that seemed to support them but was in fact nearly worthless, if not misleading. The NIE simply didn't communicate how weak the underlying intelligence was.

This was, moreover, a problem that was not limited to the NIE. Our review found that *after* the publication of the October 2002 NIE but *before* Secretary of State Colin Powell's February 2003 address to the United Nations, intelligence officials within the CIA failed to convey to policymakers new information casting serious doubt on the reliability of a human intelligence source known as "Curveball." This occurred despite the pivotal role Curveball's information played in the Intelligence Community's assessment of Iraq's biological weapons programs, and in spite of Secretary Powell's efforts to strip every dubious piece of information out of his proposed speech. In this instance, once again, the Intelligence Community failed to give policymakers a full understanding of the frailties of the intelligence on which they were relying.

Finally, we closely examined the possibility that intelligence analysts were pressured by policymakers to change their judgments about Iraq's nuclear, biological, and chemical weapons programs. The analysts who worked Iraqi weapons issues universally agreed that in no instance did political pressure cause them to skew or alter any of their analytical judgments. That said, it is hard to deny the conclusion that intelligence analysts worked in an environment that did not encourage skepticism about the conventional wisdom.

Other Case Studies: An Overview

Our remaining case studies present a more mixed picture. On the positive side, Libya is fundamentally a success story. The Intelligence Community assessed correctly the state of Libya's nuclear and chemical weapons programs, and the Intelligence Community's use of new techniques to penetrate the A.Q. Khan network allowed the U.S. government to pressure Libya into dismantling those programs. In counterterrorism, the Intelligence Community has made great strides since September 11, in particular with respect to tactical operations overseas. These successes stemmed from isolated efforts that need to be replicated in other areas of intelligence; in the case of Libya, from innovative collection techniques and, in the case of terrorism, from an impressive fusion of interagency intelligence capabilities.

But we also reviewed the state of the Intelligence Community's knowledge about the unconventional weapons programs of several countries that pose current proliferation threats, including Iran, North Korea, China, and Russia. We cannot discuss many of our findings from these studies in our unclassified report, but we can say here that we found that we have only limited access to critical information about several of these high-priority intelligence targets.

Lessons Learned from the Case Studies

Our case studies revealed failures and successes that ran the gamut of the intelligence process. Although each of these studies is covered in far greater detail in the report itself, we include here a summary of the central lessons we drew from them.

Poor target development: not getting intelligence on the issues we care about most. You can't analyze intelligence that you don't have—and our case studies resoundingly demonstrate how little we know about some of our highest priority intelligence targets. It is clear that in today's context the traditional collection techniques employed by individual collection agencies have lost much of their power to surprise our adversaries. The successful penetrations of "hard targets" that we did find were usually the result either of an innovative collection technique or of a creative integration of collection capabilities across agencies. In general, however, the Intelligence Community has not developed the long-term, coordinated collection strategies that are necessary to penetrate today's intelligence targets.

Lack of rigorous analysis. Long after the Community's assessment of Iraq had begun to fall apart, one of the main drafters of the NIE told us that, if he had to grade it, he would still give the NIE an "A." By that, he presumably meant that the NIE fully met the standards for analysis that the Community had set for itself. That is the problem. The scope and quality of analysis has eroded badly in the Intelligence Community and it must be restored. In part, this is a matter of tradecraft and training; in part, too, it is a matter of expertise.

Analytic "tradecraft"—the way analysts think, research, evaluate evidence, write, and communicate—must be strengthened. In many instances, we found finished intelligence that was loosely reasoned, ill-supported, and poorly communicated. Perhaps most worrisome, we found too many analytic products that obscured how little the Intelligence Community actually *knew* about an issue and how much their conclusions rested on inference and assumptions. We believe these tendencies must be reversed if decisionmakers are to have confidence in the intelligence they receive. And equally important, analysts must be willing to admit what they don't know in order to focus future collection efforts. Conversely, policymakers must be prepared to accept uncertainties and qualifications in intelligence judgments and not expect greater precision than the evaluated data permits.

Good "tradecraft" without expertise, however, will only get you so far. Our case studies identified areas in which the Community's level of expertise was far below what it should be. In several instances, the Iraq assessments rested on failures of technical analysis that should have been obvious at the time—failure to understand facts about weapons technology, for example, or failures to detect obvious forgeries. Technical expertise, particularly relating to weapons systems, has fallen sharply in the past ten years. And in other areas, such as biotechnology, the Intelligence Community is well behind the private sector.

But the problem of expertise goes well beyond technical knowledge. During the Cold War, the Intelligence Community built up an impressive body of expertise on Soviet society, organization, and ideology, as well as on the Soviet threat. Regrettably, no equivalent talent pool exists today for the study of Islamic extremism. In some cases, the security clearance process limits the Intelligence Community's ability to recruit analysts with contacts among relevant groups and with experience living overseas. Similarly, some security rules limit the ways in which analysts can develop substantive expertise. Finally, poor training or bad habits lead analysts to rely too much on secret information and to use non-clandestine and public information too little. Non-clandestine sources of information are critical to understanding societal, cultural, and political trends, but they are insufficiently utilized.

Lack of political context—and imagination. The October 2002 NIE contained an extensive technical analysis of Iraq's suspected weapons programs but little serious analysis of the socio-political situation in Iraq, or the motives and intentions of Iraqi leadership—which, in a dictatorship like Iraq, really meant understanding Saddam. It seems unlikely to us that weapons experts used to combing reports for tidbits on technical programs would ever have asked: "Is Saddam bluffing?" or "Could he have decided to suspend his weapons programs until sanctions are lifted?" But an analyst steeped in Iraq's politics and culture at least *might* have asked those questions, and, of course, those turn out to be the questions that could have led the Intelligence Community closer to the truth. In that respect, the analysts displayed a lack of imagination. The Iraq example also reflects the Intelligence Community's increasing tendency to separate regional, technical, and (now) terrorism analysis—a trend that is being exacerbated by the gravitational pull toward centers like the National Counterterrorism Center (NCTC).

Overemphasis on and underperformance in daily intelligence products. As problematic as the October 2002 NIE was, it was not the Community's biggest analytic failure on Iraq. Even more misleading was the river of intelligence that flowed from the CIA to top policymakers over long periods of time—in the President's Daily Brief (PDB) and in its more widely distributed companion, the Senior Executive Intelligence Brief (SEIB). These daily reports were, if anything, more alarmist and less nuanced than the NIE. It was not that the intelligence was markedly different. Rather, it was that the PDBs and SEIBs, with their attention-grabbing headlines and drumbeat of repetition, left an impression of many corroborating reports where in fact there were very few sources. And in other instances, intelligence suggesting the existence of weapons programs was conveyed to senior policymakers, but later information casting doubt upon the validity of that intelligence was not. In ways both subtle and not so subtle, the daily reports seemed to be "selling" intelligence—in order to keep its customers, or at least the First Customer, interested.

Inadequate information sharing. There is little doubt that, at least in the context of counterterrorism, information sharing has improved substantially since September 11. This is in no small part due to the creation of the Terrorist Threat Integration Center (now NCTC) and the increased practice of housing collectors and analysts together, which provides a real-world solution to some of the bureaucratic and institutional barriers that exist between the big intelligence-collecting agencies. But in the three and a half years since September 11, this push to share information has not spread to other areas, including counterproliferation, where sharing is also badly needed. Furthermore, even in the counterterrorism context, information sharing still depends too much on physical co-location and personal relationships as opposed to integrated, Community-wide information networks. Equally problematic, individual departments and agencies continue to act as though they own the information they collect, forcing other agencies to pry information from them. Similarly, much information deemed "operational" by the CIA and FBI isn't routinely shared, even though analysts have repeatedly stressed its importance. All of this reveals that extensive work remains yet to be done.

Poor human intelligence. When the October 2002 NIE was written the United States had little human intelligence on Iraq's nuclear, biological, and chemical weapons programs and virtually no human intelligence on leadership intentions. While classification prevents us from getting into the details, the picture is much the same with respect to other dangerous threats. We recognize that espionage is always chancy at best; 50 years of pounding away at the Soviet Union resulted in only a handful of truly important human sources. Still, we have no choice but to do better. Old approaches to human intelligence alone are not the answer. Countries that threaten us are well aware of our human intelligence services' *modus operandi* and they know how to counter it. More of the same is unlikely to work. Innovation is needed. The CIA deserves credit for its efforts to discover and penetrate the A.Q. Khan network, and it needs to put more emphasis on other innovative human intelligence methods.

Worse than having no human sources is being seduced by a human source who is telling lies. In fact, the Community's position on Iraq's biological weapons program was largely determined by sources who were telling lies— most notably a source provided by a foreign intelligence service through the Defense Intelligence Agency. Why DIA and the rest of the Community didn't find out that the source was lying is a story of poor asset validation practices and the problems inherent in relying on semi-cooperative liaison services. That the NIE (and other reporting) didn't make clear to policymakers how heavily it relied on a single source that no American intelligence officer had ever met, and about whose reliability several intelligence professionals had expressed serious concern, is a damning comment on the Intelligence Community's practices.

The challenge to traditional signals intelligence. Signals intelligence—the interception of radio, telephone, and computer communications—has historically been a primary source of good intelligence. But changes in telecommunications technology have brought new challenges. This was the case in Iraq, where the Intelligence Community lost access to important aspects of Iraqi communications, and it remains the case elsewhere. We offer a brief additional discussion of some of the modern challenges facing signals intelligence in our classified report, but we cannot discuss this information in an unclassified format.

Regaining signals intelligence access must be a top priority. The collection agencies are working hard to restore some of the access that they have lost; and they've had some successes. And again, many of these recent steps in the right direction are the result of innovative examples of cross-agency cooperation. In addition, successful signals intelligence will require a sustained research and development effort to bring cutting-edge technology to operators and analysts. Success on this front will require greater willingness to accept financial costs, political risks, and even human casualties.

Declining utility of traditional imagery intelligence against unconventional weapons programs. The imagery collection systems that were designed largely to work against the Soviet Union's military didn't work very well against Iraq's unconventional weapons program, and our review found that they aren't working very well against other priority targets, either. That's because our adversaries are getting better at denial and deception, and because the threat is changing. Again, we offer details about the challenges to imagery intelligence in our classified report that we cannot provide here.

Making the problem even more difficult, there is little that traditional imagery can tell us about chemical and biological facilities. Biological and chemical weapons programs for the most part can exist inside commercial buildings with no suspicious signatures. This means that we can get piles of incredibly sharp photos of an adversary's chemical factories, and we still will not know much about its chemical weapons programs. We can still see a lot—and imagery intelligence remains valuable in many contexts, including support to military operations and when used in conjunction with other collection disciplines—but too often what we can see doesn't tell us what we need to know about nuclear, biological, and chemical weapons.

Measurement and signature intelligence (MASINT) is not sufficiently developed. The collection of technologies known as MASINT, which includes a virtual grab bag of advanced collection and analytic methods, is not yet making a significant contribution to our intelligence efforts. In Iraq, MASINT played a negligible role. As in other contexts, we believe that the Intelligence Community should continue to pursue new technology aggressively— whether it is called MASINT, imagery, or signals intelligence. Innovation will be necessary to defeat our adversaries' denial and deception.

An absence of strong leadership. For over a year, despite unambiguous presidential direction, a turf battle raged between CIA's Counterterrorist Center (CTC) and the Terrorist Threat Integration Center (now NCTC). The two organizations fought over roles, responsibilities, and resources, and the Intelligence Community's leadership was unable to solve the problem. The intelligence reform act may put an end to this particular conflict, but we believe that the story reflects a larger, more pervasive problem within the Intelligence Community: the difficulty of making a decision and imposing the consequences on all agencies throughout the Community. Time and time again we have uncovered instances like this, where powerful agencies fight to a debilitating stalemate masked as consensus, because no one in the Community has been able to make a decision and then make it stick. The best hope for filling this gap is an empowered DNI.

LOOKING FORWARD: OUR RECOMMENDATIONS FOR CHANGE

Our case studies collectively paint a picture of an Intelligence Community with serious deficiencies that span the intelligence process. Stated succinctly, it has too little *integration* and too little *innovation* to succeed in the 21st century. It rarely adopts integrated strategies for penetrating high-priority targets; decisionmakers lack authority to resolve agency disputes; and it develops too few innovative ways of gathering intelligence.

This section summarizes our major recommendations on how to change this state of affairs so that full value can be derived from the many bright, dedicated, and deeply committed professionals within the Intelligence Community. We begin at the top, and suggest how to use the opportunity presented by the new intelligence reform legislation to bring better integration and management to the Intelligence Community. Our management recommendations are developed in greater detail in Chapter Six of our report. We next offer recommendations that would improve intelligence collection (Chapter 7) and analysis (Chapter 8). Then we examine several specific and important intelligence challenges—improving information sharing (Chapter 9); integrating domestic and foreign intelligence in a way that both satisfies national security imperatives and safeguards civil liberties (Chapter 10); organizing the Community's counterintelligence mission (Chapter 11); and a largely classified chapter on managing covert action (Chapter 12). We then devote a stand-alone chapter to examining the most dangerous unconventional weapons challenges the Intelligence Community faces today and offer specific prescriptions for improving our intelligence capabilities against these threats (Chapter 13).

Leadership and Management: Forging an Integrated Intelligence Community

A former senior Defense Department official described today's Intelligence Community as "not so much poorly managed as unmanaged." We agree. Everywhere we looked, we found important (and obvious) issues of inter-agency coordination that went unattended, sensible Community-wide proposals blocked by pockets of resistance, and critical disputes left to fester. Strong interagency cooperation was more likely to result from bilateral "treaties" between big agencies than from Community-level management. This ground was well-plowed by the 9/11 Commission and by several other important assessments of the Intelligence Community over the past decade.

In the chapter of our report devoted to management (Chapter 6), we offer detailed recommendations that we believe will equip the new Director of National Intelligence to forge today's loose confederation of 15 separate intelligence operations into a real, integrated Intelligence Community. A short summary of our more important management recommendations follows:

■ *Strong leadership and management of the Intelligence Community are indispensable.* Virtually every senior intelligence official acknowledged the difficulty of leading and managing the Intelligence Community. Along with acting as the President's principal intelligence advisor, this will be the DNI's main job. His success in that job will determine the fate of many other necessary reforms. We thus recommend ways in which the DNI can use his limited, but not insignificant, authorities over money and people. No matter what, the DNI will not be able to run the Intelligence Community alone. He will need to create a management structure that allows him to see deep into the Intelligence Community's component agencies, and he will need to work closely with the other cabinet secretaries—especially the Secretary of Defense—for whom several Intelligence Community agencies also work. New procedures are particularly needed in the budget area, where today's Intelligence Community has a wholly inadequate Planning, Programming, and Budgeting System.

■ *Organize around missions.* One of the most significant problems we identified in today's Intelligence Community is a lack of cross-Community focus on priority intelligence missions. By this, we mean that in most cases there is not one office, or one individual, who is responsible for making sure the Intelligence Community is doing all it can to collect and analyze intelligence on a subject like proliferation, or a country like Iran. Instead, intelligence agencies allocate their scarce resources among intelligence priorities in ways that seem sensible to them but are not optimal from a Community-wide perspective. The DNI needs management structures and processes that ensure a strategic, Community-level focus on priority intelligence missions. The specific device we propose is the creation of several "Mission Managers" on the DNI staff who are responsible for developing strategies for all aspects of intelligence relating to a priority intelligence target: the Mission Manager for China, for instance, would be responsible for driving collection on the China target, watching over China analysis, and serving as a clearinghouse for senior policymakers seeking China expertise.

■ *Establish a National Counter Proliferation Center.* The new intelligence legislation creates one "national center"—the National Counterterrorism Center (NCTC)—and suggests the creation of a second, similar center devoted to counterproliferation issues. We agree that a National Counter Proliferation Center (NCPC) should be established but believe that it should be fundamentally different in character from the NCTC. The NCTC is practically a separate agency; its large staff is responsible not only for conducting counterterrorism analysis and intelligence gathering but also for "strategic operational planning" in support of counterterrorism policy. In contrast, we believe that the NCPC should be a relatively small center (*i.e.*, fewer than 100 people); it should primarily play a *management and coordination* function by overseeing analysis and collection on nuclear, biological, and chemical weapons across the Intelligence Community. In addition, although we agree that government-wide strategic planning is required to confront proliferation threats, we believe that entities other than the NCPC— such as a Joint Interagency Task Force we propose to coordinate interdiction efforts—should perform this function.

■ *Build a modern workforce.* The intelligence reform legislation grants the DNI substantial personnel authorities. In our view, these authorities come none too soon. The Intelligence Community has difficulty recruiting and retaining individuals with critically important skill sets—such as technical and scientific expertise, and facility with foreign languages—and has not adapted well to the diverse cultures and settings in which today's intelligence experts must operate. We propose the creation of a new human resources authority in the Office of the DNI to develop Community-wide personnel policies and overcome these systemic shortcomings. We also offer specific proposals aimed at encouraging "joint" assignments between intelligence agencies, improving job training at all stages of an intelligence professional's career, and building a better personnel incentive structure.

■ *Create mechanisms for sustained oversight from outside the Intelligence Community—and for self-examination from the inside.* Many sound past proposals for intelligence reform have withered on the vine. Either the Intelligence Community is inherently resistant to outside recommendations, or it lacks the institutional capacity to implement them. In either case, sustained external oversight is necessary. We recommend using the new Joint Intelligence Community Council—which comprises the DNI and the cabinet secretaries with intelligence responsibilities—as a high-level "consumer council." We also recommend the President's Foreign Intelligence Advisory Board play a more substantial advisory role. Like others before us, we suggest that the President urge Congress to reform its own procedures to provide better oversight. In particular, we recommend that the House and Senate intelligence committees create focused oversight subcommittees, that the Congress create an intelligence appropriations subcommittee and reduce the Intelligence Community's reliance on supplemental funding, and that the Senate intelligence committee be given the same authority over joint military intelligence programs and tactical intelligence programs that the House intelligence committee now exercises. Finally—and perhaps most importantly—we recommend that the DNI create mechanisms to ensure that the Intelligence Community conducts "lessons learned" and after-action studies so that it will be better equipped to identify its *own* strengths and weaknesses.

Additional Leadership and Management Recommendations

In addition to those described above, Chapter Six of our report offers recommendations concerning:

■ How to build a coordinated process for "target development"—that is, the directing of collection resources toward priority intelligence subjects;

■ How to spur innovation outside individual collection agencies;

■ How the DNI might handle the difficult challenges of integrating intelligence from at home and abroad, and of coordinating activities and procedures with the Department of Defense; and

■ How the DNI might organize the office of the DNI to fit needed leadership and management functions into the framework created by the intelligence reform legislation.

Integrated and Innovative Collection

The intelligence failure in Iraq did not begin with faulty analysis. It began with a sweeping collection failure. The Intelligence Community simply couldn't collect good information about Iraq's nuclear, biological, or chemical programs. Regrettably, the same can be said today about other important targets, none of which will ever be easy targets—but we can and should do better.

Urging each individual collection agency to do a better job is not the answer. Where progress has been made against such targets, the key has usually been more integration and more innovation in collecting intelligence. As a result, we recommend the following:

■ *Create a new Intelligence Community process for managing collection as an "integrated enterprise."* In order to gather intelligence effectively, the Intelligence Community must develop and buy sophisticated technical collection systems, create strategies for focusing those systems on priority targets, process and exploit the data that these systems collect, and plan for the acquisition of future systems. Today, each of these functions is performed primarily within individual collection agencies, often with little or no Community-level direction or interagency coordination. We propose that the DNI create what we call an "integrated collection enterprise" for the Intelligence Community—that is, a management structure in which the Community's decentralized collection capabilities are harmonized with intelligence priorities and deployed in a coordinated way.

■ *Create a new Human Intelligence Directorate.* Both the Defense Department and the FBI are substantially increasing their human intelligence activities abroad, which heightens the risk that intelligence operations will not be properly coordinated with the CIA's human espionage operations, run by its Directorate of Operations (DO). The human intelligence activities of the Defense Department and the FBI should continue, but in the world of foreign espionage, a lack of coordination can have dangerous, even fatal, consequences. To address this pressing problem, we suggest the creation of a new Human Intelligence Directorate within the CIA, to which the present DO would be subordinate, to ensure the coordination of all U.S. agencies conducting human intelligence operations overseas. In addition to this coordination role, the Human Intelligence Directorate would serve as the focal point for Community-wide human intelligence issues, including helping to develop a national human intelligence strategy, broadening the scope of human intelligence activities, integrating (where appropriate) collection and reporting systems, and establishing Community-wide standards for training and tradecraft.

■ *Develop innovative human intelligence techniques.* The CIA's Directorate of Operations is one of the Intelligence Community's elite and storied organizations. However, the DO has remained largely wedded to the traditional model—a model that does not meet the challenges posed by terrorist organizations and nations that are "denied areas" for U.S. personnel. Accordingly, we recommend the establishment of an "Innovation Center" within the CIA's new Human Intelligence Directorate— but *not* within the DO. This center would spur the use of new and nontraditional methods of collecting human intelligence. In the collection chapter of our report, we also detail several new methods for collecting human intelligence that in our judgment should either be explored or used more extensively.

■ *Create an Open Source Directorate within the CIA.* We are convinced that analysts who use open source information can be more effective than those who don't. Regrettably, however, the Intelligence Community does not have an entity that collects, processes, and makes available to analysts the mass of open source information that is available in the world today. We therefore recommend the creation of an Open Source Directorate at the CIA. The directorate's mission would be to deploy sophisticated information technology to make open source information available across the Community. This would, at a minimum, mean gathering and storing digital newspapers and periodicals that are available only temporarily on the Internet and giving Intelligence Community staff easy (and secure) access to Internet materials. In addition, because we believe that part of the problem is analyst resistance, not lack of collection, we recommend that some of the new analysts allocated to CIA be specially trained to use open sources and then to act as open source "evange-analysts" who can jumpstart the open source initiative by showing its value in addressing particular analytic problems. All of this, we believe, will help improve the Intelligence Community's surprisingly poor "feel" for cultural and political issues in the countries that concern policymakers most. The Open Source Directorate should also be the primary test bed for new information technology because the security constraints—while substantial—are lower for open source than for classified material.

■ ***Reconsider MASINT.*** Measurements and signatures can offer important intelligence about nuclear, biological, and chemical weapons. But the tools we use to collect these measurements and signatures—tools collectively referred to within the intelligence community as "MASINT"— do not obviously constitute a single discipline. In a world of specialized collection agencies, there is reason to suspect that these orphaned technologies may have been under-funded and under-utilized. We recommend that the DNI take responsibility for developing and coordinating new intelligence technologies, including those that now go under the title MASINT. This could be done by a special coordinator, or as part of the DNI's Office of Science and Technology. The DNI's office does not need to directly control MASINT collection. Rather, we recommend that individual collection agencies assume responsibility for aspects of MASINT that fall naturally into their bailiwicks. At the same time, the DNI's designated representative would promote and monitor the status of new technical intelligence programs throughout the Intelligence

Community to ensure that they are fully implemented and given the necessary attention.

Additional Collection Recommendations

In addition to those described above, Chapter Seven of our report offers recommendations concerning:

- Developing new human and technical collection methods;

- Professionalizing human intelligence across the Intelligence Community;

- Creating a larger and better-trained human intelligence officer cadre;

- Amending the Foreign Intelligence Surveillance Act to extend the duration of certain forms of electronic surveillance against non-U.S. persons, to ease administrative burdens on NSA and the Department of Justice; and

- Improving the protection of sources and methods by reducing authorized and unauthorized disclosures.

Transforming Analysis

Integrated, innovative collection is just the beginning of what the Intelligence Community needs. Some of the reforms already discussed, particularly the DNI-level "Mission Managers," will improve analysis. But much more is needed. In particular, analytic expertise must be deepened, intelligence gaps reduced, and existing information made more usable—all of which would improve the quality of intelligence.

As an overarching point, however, the Intelligence Community must recognize the central role of analysts in the intelligence process. Needless to say, analysts are the people who analyze intelligence, put it in context, and communicate the intelligence to the people who need it. But in addition, analysts are the repositories for what the Intelligence Community *doesn't* know, and they must clearly convey these gaps to decisionmakers—as well as to collectors so that the Intelligence Community does everything it can to fill the holes. (Analysts will also play an increasingly prominent role in information security, as they "translate" intelligence from the most sensitive of sources to a variety of consumers, ranging from state and local first responders to senior policymakers.) To enable analysts to fulfill these roles, we recommend the following:

■ *Empower Mission Managers to coordinate analytic efforts on a given topic.* The Mission Managers we propose would serve as the focal point for all aspects of the intelligence effort on a particular issue. They would be aware of the analytic expertise in various intelligence agencies, assess the quality of analytic products, identify strategic questions receiving inadequate attention, encourage alternative analysis, and ensure that dissenting views are expressed to intelligence users. When necessary, they would recommend that the DNI use his personnel authorities to move analysts to priority intelligence topics. At the same time, Mission Managers should *not* be responsible for providing a single, homogenized analytic product to decisionmakers; rather, Mission Managers should be responsible for encouraging alternative analysis and for ensuring that dissenting views are expressed to intelligence customers. In sum, Mission Managers should be able to find the right people and expertise and make sure that the right analysis, including alternative analysis, is getting done.

■ *Strengthen long-term and strategic analysis.* The most common complaint we heard from analysts in the Intelligence Community was that the pressing demand for current intelligence "eats up everything else." Analysts cannot maintain their expertise if they cannot conduct long-term and strategic analysis. Because this malady is so pervasive and has proven so resistant to conventional solutions, we recommend establishing an organization to perform only long-term and strategic analysis under the National Intelligence Council, the Community's existing focal point for interagency long-term analytic efforts. The new unit could serve as a focal point for Community-wide alternative analysis, thereby complementing agency-specific efforts at independent analysis. And although some analysts in this organization would be permanently assigned, at least half would serve only temporarily and would come from all intelligence agencies, including NGA and NSA, as well as from outside the government. Such rotations would reinforce good tradecraft habits, as well as foster a greater sense of Community among analysts and spur collaboration on other projects.

■ *Encourage diverse and independent analysis.* We believe that diverse and independent analysis—often referred to as "competitive analysis"—should come from many sources. As we have just noted, we recommend that our proposed long-term research and analysis unit, as well as the National Intelligence Council, conduct extensive independent analysis. In some circumstances there is also a place for a "devil's advocate"—someone appointed to challenge the consensus view. We also think it important that a not-for-profit "sponsored research institute" be created *outside* the Intelligence Community; such an institute would serve as a critical window into outside expertise, conduct its own research, and reach out to specialists, including academics and technical experts, business and industry leaders, and representatives from the nonprofit sector. Finally, the Intelligence Community should encourage independent analysis throughout its analytic ranks. In our view, this can best be accomplished through the preservation of dispersed analytic resources (as opposed to consolidation in large "centers"), active efforts by Mission Managers to promote independent analysis, and Community-wide training that instills the importance of such analysis.

- *Improve the rigor and "tradecraft" of analysis.* Our studies, and many observers, point to a decline in analytic rigor within the Intelligence Community. Analysts have suffered from weak leadership, insufficient training, and budget cutbacks that led to the loss of our best, most senior analysts. There is no quick fix for tradecraft problems. However, we recommend several steps: increasing analyst training; ensuring that managers and budget-writers allot time and resources for analysts to actually *get* trained; standardizing good tradecraft practices through the use of a National Intelligence University; creating structures and practices that increase competitive analysis; increasing managerial training for Intelligence Community supervisors; enabling joint and rotational assignment opportunities; ensuring that finished intelligence products are sufficiently transparent so that an analyst's reasoning is visible to intelligence customers; and implementing other changes in human resource policies—such as merit-based-pay—so that the best analysts are encouraged to stay in government service.

- *Communicating intelligence to policymakers.* The best intelligence in the world is worthless unless it is effectively and accurately communicated to those who need it. The Iraq weapons of mass destruction case is a stark example. The daily reports sent to the President and senior policymakers discussing Iraq over many months proved to be disastrously one-sided. We thus offer recommendations on ways in which intelligence products can be enhanced, including how the President's Daily

Brief (PDB) might be improved. In this regard, we suggest the elimination of the inherently misleading "headline" summaries in PDBs and other senior policymaker briefs, and that the DNI oversee production of the PDB. To accomplish this, we recommend the DNI create an analytic staff too small to routinely undertake drafting itself, but large enough to have background on many of the issues that are covered by the PDB. The goal would be to enable the DNI to coordinate and oversee the process, without requiring him to take on the heavy—and almost over-whelming—mantle of daily intelligence support to the President. Critically, the DNI's staff would also ensure that the PDB reflects alternative views from the Community to the greatest extent feasible.

We also recommend that the DNI take responsibility, with the President's concurrence, for the three primary sources of intelligence that now reach the President: the PDB, the President's Terrorism Threat Report—a companion publication produced by the NCTC and focused solely on terror-ism-related issues—and the briefing by the Director of the FBI. We suggest that the DNI coordinate this intelligence in a manner that elimi nates redundancies and ensures that only material that is necessary for the President be included. We think this last point is especially important because we have observed a disturbing trend whereby intelligence is passed to the President (as well as other senior policymakers) not because it requires high-level attention, but because passing the information "up the chain" provides individuals and organizations with bureaucratic cover.

- **_Demand more from analysts._** We urge that policymakers actively probe and question analysts. In our view, such interaction is not "politiciza-tion." Analysts should expect such demanding and aggressive testing without—as a matter of principle and professionalism—allowing it to subvert their judgment.

Additional Analysis Recommendations

In addition to those described above, Chapter Eight of our report offers recom-mendations concerning:

- Developing technologies capable of exploiting large volumes of foreign language data without the need for human translations;

Additional Analysis Recommendations (Continued)

- Improving career-long analytical and managerial training;

- Creating a database for all finished intelligence, as well as adopting technology to update analysts and decisionmakers when intelligence judgments change;

- Improving the Intelligence Community's science, technology, and weapons expertise;

- Changing the way analysts are hired, promoted, and rewarded; and

- Institutionalizing "lessons learned" procedures to learn from past analytical successes and failures.

Information Sharing

While the new intelligence reform legislation correctly identifies information sharing as an area where major reforms are necessary, the steps it takes to address the problem raise as many questions as they answer. The legislation creates a new position—a "Program Manager" who sits outside of the Intelligence Community and reports directly to the President—responsible for creating an integrated, government-wide Information Sharing Environment for all "terrorism information." At the same time, the Director of National Intelligence is given responsibility for facilitating information sharing for *all* intelligence information *within* the Intelligence Community.

We believe that these two separate statutory information sharing efforts should be harmonized. We are less confident that any particular mechanism is optimal. Perhaps the least bad solution to this tricky problem—short of new legislation—is to require that the Program Manager report to the President *through* the DNI, and that the Information Sharing Environment be expanded to include all intelligence information, not just intelligence related to terrorism. In recommending this solution, however, we emphasize that information sharing cannot be understood merely as an Intelligence Community endeavor; whoever leads the effort to build the Information Sharing Environment must be sensitive to the importance of distributing necessary information to those who need it both in the non-intelligence components of the federal government, and to relevant state, local, and tribal authorities.

We also make specific recommendations concerning how best to implement the information sharing effort. Among these recommendations are: designating a single official under the DNI who will be responsible for both information sharing *and* information security, in order to break down cultural and policy barriers that have impeded the development of a shared information space; applying advanced technologies to the Information Sharing Environment to permit more expansive sharing with far greater security protections than currently exist in the Intelligence Community; and establishing clear and consistent Community-wide information sharing and security policies. Last but not least, we recommend that the DNI jettison the phrase "information sharing" itself, which merely reinforces the (incorrect) notion that information is the property of individual intelligence agencies, rather than of the government as a whole.

Finally, we believe it is essential to note the importance of protecting civil liberties in the context of information sharing. We believe that the intelligence reform act provides the framework for appropriate protection of civil liberties in this area, and that all information sharing must be done in accordance with Attorney General guidelines relating to "U.S. persons" information. At the same time, in our view the pursuit of privacy and national security is *not* a zero-sum game. In fact, as we describe in our report, many of the very same tools that provide counterintelligence protection can be equally valuable in protecting privacy.

Intelligence at Home: the FBI, Justice, and Homeland Security

Although the FBI has made strides in turning itself into a true collector and analyst of intelligence, it still has a long way to go. The Bureau, among other things, has set up Field Intelligence Groups in each of its 56 field offices and created an Executive Assistant Director for Intelligence with broad responsibility for the FBI's intelligence mission. Yet even FBI officials acknowledge that its collection and analysis capabilities will be a work in progress until at least 2010.

In our view, the biggest challenge is to make the FBI a full participant in the Intelligence Community. This is not just a matter of giving the Bureau new resources and new authority. It must also mean integrating the FBI into a Community that is subject to the DNI's coordination and leadership. Unfortunately, the intelligence reform legislation leaves the FBI's relationship to the

DNI especially murky. We recommend that the President make clear that the FBI's intelligence activities are to be fully coordinated with the DNI and the rest of the Community.

■ *Create a separate National Security Service within the FBI that includes the Bureau's Counterintelligence and Counterterrorism Divisions, as well as the Directorate of Intelligence.* The intelligence reform act empowers the DNI to lead the Intelligence Community, which includes the FBI's "intelligence elements." Although the statute leaves the term ambiguous, we believe that "elements" must include *all* of the Bureau's national security-related components—the Intelligence Directorate *and* the Counterterrorism and Counterintelligence Divisions. Anything less and the DNI's ability to coordinate intelligence across our nation's borders will be dangerously inadequate.

Simply granting the DNI authority over the Bureau's current Directorate of Intelligence is, we believe, insufficient. We say this because the Directorate of Intelligence has surprisingly little operational, personnel, and budgetary authority. Currently the directorate has no authority to initiate, terminate, or re-direct any collection or investigative operation in any of the FBI's 56 regional field offices that are scattered throughout the nation or within any of the four operational divisions (Counterintelligence, Counterterrorism, Cyber, and Criminal) at FBI Headquarters. Although the Directorate of Intelligence may "task" the field offices to collect against certain requirements, it has no direct authority to ensure that FBI resources actually carry out these requirements. Its "taskings" are really "askings." Nor does the directorate contain the great bulk of the FBI's intelligence analysts. And the directorate has no clear control over the Bureau's portion of the National Intelligence Program budget, which is largely spent by the Counterterrorism and Counterintelligence Divisions. In short, the intelligence directorate has few, if any, mechanisms for exercising direct authorities over FBI's intelligence collectors or analytic products. With a direct line of authority only to the Bureau's Directorate of Intelligence, the DNI cannot be ensured influence over the Bureau's national security functions, and the FBI will not be fully integrated into the Intelligence Community.

We therefore recommend the creation of a separate National Security Service *within the FBI* that has full authority to manage, direct, and control all Headquarters and Field Office resources engaged in counterintelligence, counterterrorism, and foreign intelligence collection, investigations, operations, and analysis. Critically, this division would then be subject to the same DNI authorities as apply to such Defense agencies as NSA and NGA. Of equal importance, this structure would maintain the Attorney General's oversight of the FBI's activities to ensure the Bureau's compliance with U.S. law. In this sense, the Attorney General's role would be similar to that of the Secretary of Defense, who—even with the appointment of the DNI—continues to oversee Defense Department agencies within the Intelligence Community, like NSA and NGA.

- *Ensure better mechanisms for coordination and cooperation on foreign intelligence collection in the United States.* The expansion of the FBI's intelligence collection and reporting activities over the past few years has engendered turf battles between the CIA and the FBI that have already caused counterproductive conflicts both within and outside of the United States. In particular, the two agencies have clashed over the domestic collection of foreign intelligence—an area in which they have long shared responsibilities. We see no reason to change the status quo dramatically or to expand the FBI's authority over foreign intelligence gathering inside the United States. If unanticipated conflicts emerge, both agencies should be instructed to take their differences to the DNI for resolution. The two agencies' capabilities should complement, rather than compete with, one another. We also expect that such an integrated approach would continue to rely on the existing Attorney General guidelines, which carefully limit the way both agencies operate within the United States, and with regard to U.S. persons overseas. We believe that strong CIA/FBI cooperation and clear guidelines are essential for protection of civil liberties as well as for effective intelligence gathering.

- *Reorient the Department of Justice.* Every agency that has major responsibility for terrorism and intelligence has been overhauled in the past four years. With one exception: at the Department of Justice, the famous "wall" between intelligence and criminal law still lingers, at least on the organization charts. On one side is the Office of Intelligence Policy and Review, which handles Foreign Intelligence Surveillance Court orders—those court orders that permit wiretaps and physical searches for national security reasons. On the other side are two separate sections of the Criminal Division (Counterterrorism and Counterespionage), reporting to two separate Deputy

Assistant Attorneys General. This organizational throwback to the 1990s scatters intelligence expertise throughout the Department and in some cases has contributed to errors that hampered intelligence gathering. A single office with responsibility for counterterrorism, counterintelligence, and intelligence investigations would ensure better communication and reduce the tendency to rebuild the wall along bureaucratic lines.

We recommend that these three components (perhaps joined by a fourth Justice Department component that coordinates issues related to transnational crimes) be placed together under the authority of an Assistant Attorney General for National Security who would, like the Assistant Attorney General for the Criminal Division, report either directly to the Deputy Attorney General, or to a newly created Associate Attorney General responsible for both the National Security and Criminal Divisions.

■ ***Strengthen the Department of Homeland Security's relationship with the Intelligence Community.*** The Department of Homeland Security is the primary repository of information about what passes in and out of the country—a critical participant in safeguarding the United States from nuclear, biological, or chemical attack. Yet, since its inception, Homeland Security has faced immense challenges in collecting information effectively, making it available to analysts and users both inside and outside the Department, and bringing intelligence support to law enforcement and first responders who seek to act on such information. We did not conduct a detailed study of Homeland Security's capabilities, but it is clear to us that the department faces challenges in all four roles it plays in the intelligence community—as collector, analyst, disseminator, and customer.

Among the obstacles confronting Homeland Security, we found during the course of our study that the Department's Immigration and Customs Enforcement still operates under an order inherited from the Treasury Department in the 1980s. The order requires high-level approval for virtually all information sharing and assistance to the Intelligence Community. We think this order should be rescinded, and we believe the DNI should carefully examine how Homeland Security works with the rest of the Intelligence Community.

Counterintelligence

Every intelligence service on the planet wants to steal secrets from the last remaining superpower. But as other nations increase their intelligence operations against the United States, U.S. counterintelligence has been in a defensive crouch—fractured, narrowly focused, and lacking national direction. This may change as a result of the President's newly announced counterintelligence strategy. The good ideas in the strategy must, however, still be put into practice.

CIA does counterintelligence abroad, but its capabilities are limited. The FBI's counterintelligence efforts within the United States are well-staffed, but hardly strategic in their nature. Finally, the Defense Department's counterintelligence capabilities lack effective cross-department integration and direction. To address these concerns, we recommend four steps to strengthen counterintelligence: the empowerment of the nation's chief counterintelligence officer, the National Counterintelligence Executive (NCIX); the development of a new CIA capability for enhancing counterintelligence abroad; the centralization of the Defense Department's counterintelligence functions; and, as suggested earlier, bringing the FBI into the Intelligence Community to ensure that its robust counterintelligence capabilities are employed in line with the DNI's priorities. Moreover, all of these efforts must focus greater attention on the technical aspects of counterintelligence, as our adversaries shift from human spying to attempting to penetrate our information infrastructure.

Covert Action

If used in a careful and limited way, covert action can serve as a more subtle and surgical tool than forms of acknowledged employment of U.S. power and influence. As part of our overall review of the Intelligence Community, we conducted a careful study of U.S. covert action capabilities. Our findings were included in a short, separate chapter of our classified report. Regrettably, this area is so heavily classified that we could not include a chapter on the subject in our unclassified report.

We will, however, state here—at a necessarily high level of generality—some of our overall conclusions on covert action. At the outset, we note that we found current covert action programs in the counterproliferation and counterterrorism areas to be energetic, innovative, and well-executed within the limits of their authority and funding. Yet some critically important programs are hobbled by lack of sustained strategic planning, insufficient commitment of resources on a long-term basis, and a disjointed management structure. In our classified report we suggest organizational changes that we believe would consolidate support functions for covert action and improve the management of covert action programs within the Intelligence Community; we are unable to provide further details on these recommendations, however, in this unclassified format.

Addressing Proliferation

So far, we have focused on improving the Intelligence Community writ large—on the theory that only a redesigned Community can substantially improve its performance in assessing the threat posed by weapons of mass destruction. But quite apart from the structural changes we have already recommended, the Intelligence Community also needs to change the way it approaches two of the greatest threats—biological weapons and new forms of nuclear proliferation.

Biological Weapons

The 2001 anthrax attacks on the United States killed five people, crippled mail delivery in several cities for a year, and imposed more than a billion dollars in decontamination costs. For all that, we were lucky. Biological weapons are cheaper and easier to acquire than nuclear weapons—and they could be more deadly. The threat is deeply troubling today; it will be more so tomorrow, when genetic modification techniques will allow the creation of even worse biological weapons. Most of the traditional Intelligence Community collection tools are of little or no use in tackling biological weapons. In our classified report, we discuss some of the specific challenges that confront our intelligence effort against the biological threat—but regrettably we cannot discuss them here.

Faced with a high-priority problem that does not yield to traditional methods, large parts of the Intelligence Community seem to have lowered their expectations and focused on other priorities. This is unacceptable. The Intelligence Community, and the government as a whole, needs to approach the problem with a new urgency and new strategies:

- *Work with the biological sciences community.* The Intelligence Community simply does not have the in-depth technical knowledge about biological weapons that it has about nuclear weapons. To close the expertise gap, the Community cannot rely on hiring biologists, whose knowledge and skills are extremely important, but whose depth and timeliness of expertise begins eroding as soon as they move from the laboratory to the intelligence profession. Instead, the DNI should create a Community Biodefense Initiative to institutionalize outreach to technical experts inside and outside of government. We describe specific components of this initiative in the body of our report.

- *Make targeted collection of biological weapons intelligence a priority within the Intelligence Community.* The Intelligence Community's collection woes starkly illustrate the need for more aggressive, targeted approaches to collection on biological threats. We recommend that the DNI create a deputy within the National Counter Proliferation Center who is specifically responsible for biological weapons; this deputy would ensure the implementation of a comprehensive biological weapons targeting strategy, which would entail gaining real-time access to non-traditional sources of information, filtering open source data, and devising specific collection initiatives directed at the resulting targets.

- *Leverage regulation for biological weapons intelligence.* The United States should look outside of intelligence channels for enforcement mechanisms that can provide new avenues of international cooperation and resulting opportunities for intelligence collection on biological threats. In the corresponding chapter of our report, we recommend encouraging foreign criminalization of biological weapons development and establishing biosafety and biosecurity regulations under United Nations Security Council Resolution 1540. We also propose extending biosecurity and biosafety regulations to foreign institutions with commercial ties to the United States.

Nuclear Weapons

The intelligence challenge posed by nuclear weapons continues to evolve. The Intelligence Community must continue to monitor established nuclear states such as Russia and China, and at the same time face newer and potentially more daunting challenges like terrorist use of a nuclear weapon. But the focus of the U.S. Intelligence Community has historically been on the capabilities of large nation states. When applied to the problem of terrorist organizations and smaller states, many of our intelligence capabilities are inadequate.

The challenges posed by the new environment are well-illustrated by two aspects of nuclear proliferation. The first is the continuing challenge of monitoring insecure nuclear weapons and materials, or "loose nukes"—mainly in the former Soviet Union but also potentially in other nations. The second aspect is the appearance of non-state nuclear "brokers," such as the private proliferation network run by the Pakistani scientist A.Q. Khan. In Khan's case, innovative human intelligence efforts gave the United States access to this proliferation web. However, not only does the full scope of Khan's work remain unknown, but senior officials readily acknowledge that the Intelligence Community must know more about the private networks that support proliferation. The Intelligence Community must adapt to the changing threat.

Intelligence Support to Interdiction

So far, the Intelligence Community has enjoyed a number of successes intercepting materials related to nuclear, biological, and chemical weapons (and their related delivery systems)—the process commonly referred to as "interdiction." But success has come at a cost. The Intelligence Community has focused so much energy on its own efforts that the Community shows less ambition and imagination in supporting other agencies that should play a large role in interdiction. Many other federal agencies could do more to interdict precursors, weapons components, and dangerous agents if they had effective intelligence support. We recommend several mechanisms to improve intelligence support to these agencies, most particularly the creation of a counterproliferation Joint Interagency Task Force modeled on similar entities that have proved successful in the counternarcotics context.

Moreover, since it may not be possible in all cases to identify proliferation shipments before they reach the United States, our last line of defense is detecting and stopping these shipments before they reach our border. Yet new sensor technologies have faced challenges. In the corresponding chapter of this report, we suggest how the Intelligence Community and Department of Homeland Security can work together on this issue.

Leveraging Legal and Regulatory Mechanisms

Intelligence alone cannot solve the proliferation threat. But it may not have to. Information that spies and eavesdroppers would spend millions for and risk their lives to steal can sometimes be easily obtained by the right Customs, Treasury, or export control officials. The industries that support proliferation are subject to a host of regulatory regimes. But the agencies that regulate industry in these areas—Treasury, State, Homeland Security, and Commerce—do not think of themselves as engaged in the collection of intelligence, and the Intelligence Community only rarely appreciates the authorities and opportunities presented by regulatory regimes.

Given the challenges presented by quasi-governmental proliferation, the United States must leverage all of its capabilities to flag potential proliferators, gain insight into their activities, and interdict them, where appropriate. We therefore recommend a series of possible changes to existing regulatory regimes, all designed to improve insight into nuclear, biological, or chemical proliferation and enhance our ability to take action. These changes include negotiating ship boarding agreements that include tagging and tracking provisions to facilitate the surveillance of suspect vessels, taking steps to facilitate greater coordination between the Commerce Department (and Immigrations and Customs Enforcement) and the Intelligence Community, using Commerce Department and Customs and Border Protection regulations to facilitate information sharing about suspect cargo and persons and to justify related interdictions, and expanding the Treasury Department's authority to block assets of proliferators.

CONCLUSION

The harm done to American credibility by our all too public intelligence failings in Iraq will take years to undo. If there is good news it is this: without actually suffering a massive nuclear or biological attack, we have learned how badly the Intelligence Community can fail in struggling to understand the most important threats we face. We must use the lessons from those failings, and from our successes as well, to improve our intelligence for the future, and do so with a sense of urgency. We already have thousands of dedicated officers and many of the tools needed to do the job. With that in mind, we now turn first to what went wrong in Iraq, then to other intelligence cases, and finally to our detailed recommendations for action.

PART ONE
LOOKING BACK

PART ONE:
LOOKING BACK

The President asked this Commission to perform two tasks: to assess the intelligence capabilities of the United States with respect to weapons of mass destruction "and related threats" of the 21st century, and to recommend ways to improve those capabilities. Part One of this report details our findings in connection with the first of these two objectives.

In order to assess the Intelligence Community's capabilities, we conducted a series of case studies that are reported in separate chapters of this report. Three of these case studies—Iraq, Libya, and Afghanistan—concern countries that were specified by the President. Each provided an opportunity that is all too rare in the uncertain world of intelligence: namely, to compare what the Intelligence Community believed about a country's unconventional weapons programs with the "ground truth." With respect to Iraq, the President asked us to compare the Intelligence Community's pre-war assessments about Iraq's weapons programs with the post-war findings of the Iraq Survey Group—and to analyze why the pre-war assessments were so mistaken. He also instructed us to perform similar "before and after" reviews of the Intelligence Community's performance in assessing the unconventional weapons programs of Libya before its government's decision to forfeit them, and of Afghanistan before the Operation Enduring Freedom military campaign. The first three chapters of this report detail our findings on each of these countries.

The Executive Order establishing this Commission also asked us to look for lessons beyond those provided by our reviews of these three countries, instructing us to examine the Intelligence Community's capabilities with respect to the threats posed by weapons of mass destructions in the hands of terrorists and in "closed societies." In response to these directives, we have examined the Intelligence Community's progress in improving its counterterrorism capabilities since the September 11 attacks. We also looked at the quality of our intelligence on the nuclear weapons programs of North Korea and Iran, although we regret that we are unable to discuss our findings in an unclassified format.

In sum, we include four of these case studies in this report—Iraq, Libya, Afghanistan, and Terrorism—and we draw heavily upon the lessons we learned from all of them in proposing recommendations for change in Part Two of this report. These case studies are not the only basis for our recommendations, however. We also reviewed the Intelligence Community's current capabilities with respect to other critical countries—such as China and Russia—and examined special challenges facing the Intelligence Community, such as that of integrating intelligence across the foreign-domestic divide, and of improving our counterintelligence capabilities. While our examination of these issues did not lead to separate written case studies, we use evidence gathered from these and other areas of our review of the Intelligence Community in explaining the recommendations we make in Part Two of this report.

CHAPTER ONE
CASE STUDY: IRAQ

INTRODUCTION

As war loomed, the U.S. Intelligence Community was charged with telling policymakers what it knew about Iraq's nuclear, biological, and chemical weapons programs. The Community's best assessments were set out in an October 2002 National Intelligence Estimate, or NIE, a summation of the Community's views.[1] The title, *Iraq's Continuing Programs for Weapons of Mass Destruction*, foretells the conclusion: that Iraq was still pursuing its programs for weapons of mass destruction (WMD). Specifically, the NIE assessed that Iraq had reconstituted its nuclear weapons program and could assemble a device by the end of the decade; that Iraq had biological weapons and mobile facilities for producing biological warfare (BW) agent; that Iraq had both renewed production of chemical weapons, and probably had chemical weapons stockpiles of up to 500 metric tons; and that Iraq was developing unmanned aerial vehicles (UAVs) probably intended to deliver BW agent.

These assessments were all wrong.

This became clear as U.S. forces searched without success for the WMD that the Intelligence Community had predicted. Extensive post-war investigations were carried out by the Iraq Survey Group (ISG). The ISG found no evidence that Iraq had tried to reconstitute its capability to produce nuclear weapons after 1991; no evidence of BW agent stockpiles or of mobile biological weapons production facilities; and no substantial chemical warfare (CW) stockpiles or credible indications that Baghdad had resumed production of CW after 1991. Just about the only thing that the Intelligence Community got right was its pre-war conclusion that Iraq had deployed missiles with ranges exceeding United Nations limitations.

How could the Intelligence Community have been so mistaken? That is the question the President charged this Commission with answering.[2]

We received great cooperation from the U.S. Intelligence Community. We had unfettered access to all documents used by the Intelligence Community in reaching its judgments about Iraq's WMD programs; we had the same access to all of the Intelligence Community's reports on the subject—including the articles in the President's Daily Brief that concerned Iraq's weapons programs. During the course of our investigation, we and our staff reviewed thousands of pages of documents—ranging from raw operational traffic produced by intelligence operators to finished intelligence products—and interviewed hundreds of current and former Intelligence Community officials.

We also drew on the labors of others. The Butler Commission report on the quality of British intelligence was an important resource for us, as was the work of Australian and Israeli commissions. The careful and well-researched July 2004 report of the Senate Select Committee on Intelligence on this topic was particularly valuable.

This report sets out our findings. For each weapons category, it tells how the Intelligence Community reached the assessments in the October 2002 NIE. It also offers a detailed set of conclusions. But before beginning, we offer a few broader observations.

An "Intelligence Failure"

Overall Commission Finding

The Intelligence Community's performance in assessing Iraq's pre-war weapons of mass destruction programs was a major intelligence failure. The failure was not merely that the Intelligence Community's assessments were wrong. There were also serious shortcomings in the way these assessments were made and communicated to policymakers.

For commissions of this sort, 20/20 hindsight is an occupational hazard. It is easy to forget just how difficult a business intelligence is. Nations and terrorist groups do not easily part with their secrets—and they guard nothing more jealously than secrets related to nuclear, biological, and chemical weapons. Stealing those secrets, particularly from closed and repressive regimes like Saddam Hussein's Iraq, is no easy task, and failure is more common than success. Intelligence analysts will often be forced to make do with limited, ambiguous data; extrapolations from thin streams of information will be the norm.

Indeed, defenders of the Intelligence Community have asked whether it would be fair to expect the Community to get the Iraq WMD question absolutely right. How, they ask, could our intelligence agencies have concluded that Saddam Hussein *did not* have weapons of mass destruction—given his history of using them, his previous deceptions, and his repeated efforts to obstruct

United Nations inspectors? And after all, the United States was not alone in error; other major intelligence services also thought that Iraq had weapons of mass destruction.

We agree, but only in part. We do not fault the Intelligence Community for formulating the hypothesis, based on Saddam Hussein's conduct, that Iraq had retained an unconventional weapons capability and was working to augment this capability. Nor do we fault the Intelligence Community for failing to uncover what few Iraqis knew; according to the Iraq Survey Group only a handful of Saddam Hussein's closest advisors were aware of some of his decisions to halt work on his nuclear program and to destroy his stocks of chemical and biological weapons. Even if an extraordinary intelligence effort had gained access to one of these confidants, doubts would have lingered.

But with all that said, we conclude that the Intelligence Community could and should have come much closer to assessing the true state of Iraq's weapons programs than it did. It should have been less wrong—and, more importantly, it should have been more candid about what it did not know. In particular, it should have recognized the serious—and knowable—weaknesses in the evidence it accepted as providing hard confirmation that Iraq had retained WMD capabilities and programs.

How It Happened

The Intelligence Community's errors were not the result of simple bad luck, or a once-in-a-lifetime "perfect storm," as some would have it. Rather, they were the product of poor intelligence collection, an analytical process that was driven by assumptions and inferences rather than data, inadequate validation and vetting of dubious intelligence sources, and numerous other breakdowns in the various processes that Intelligence Community professionals collectively describe as intelligence "tradecraft." In many ways, the Intelligence Community simply did not do the job that it exists to do.

Our review revealed failings at each stage of the intelligence process. Many past discussions of the Iraq intelligence failure have focused on intelligence analysis, and we indeed will have much to say about how analysts tackled the Iraq WMD question. But they could not analyze data that they did not have, so we begin by addressing the failure of the Intelligence Community to collect more useful intelligence in Iraq.

There is no question that collecting intelligence on Iraq's weapons programs was difficult. Saddam Hussein's regime had a robust and ruthless security system and engaged in sophisticated efforts to conceal or disguise its activities from outside intelligence services—efforts referred to within the Intelligence Community as "denial and deception." The United States had no Iraq embassy or official in-country presence; human intelligence operations were often conducted at a distance. And much of what we wanted to know was concealed in compartmented corners of the Iraqi regime to which few even at high levels in the Iraqi government had access.

Still, Iraq was a high-priority target for years, and the Intelligence Community should have done better. It collected precious little information about Iraq's weapons programs in the years before the Iraq war. And not only did the Community collect too little, but much of what it managed to collect had grave defects that should have been clear to analysts and policymakers at the time. Indeed, one of the most serious failures by the Intelligence Community was its failure to apply sufficiently rigorous tests to the evidence it collected. This failure touched all the most salient pieces of evidence relied on by our intelligence agencies, including the aluminum tubes, reporting on mobile BW, uranium from Niger, and assertions about UAVs.

One of the most painful errors, however, concerned Iraq's biological weapons programs. Virtually all of the Intelligence Community's information on Iraq's alleged mobile biological weapons facilities was supplied by a source, code-named "Curveball," who was a fabricator. We discuss at length how Curveball came to play so prominent a role in the Intelligence Community's biological weapons assessments. It is, at bottom, a story of Defense Department collectors who abdicated their responsibility to vet a critical source; of Central Intelligence Agency (CIA) analysts who placed undue emphasis on the source's reporting because the tales he told were consistent with what they already believed; and, ultimately, of Intelligence Community leaders who failed to tell policymakers about Curveball's flaws in the weeks before war.

Curveball was not the only bad source the Intelligence Community used. Even more indefensibly, information from a source who was *already known* to be a fabricator found its way into finished pre-war intelligence products, including the October 2002 NIE. This intelligence was also allowed into Secretary of State Colin Powell's speech to the United Nations Security Council, despite the source having been officially discredited almost a year earlier. This communications breakdown could have been avoided if the Intelligence Community had a uniform requirement to reissue or recall reporting from a source whose information turns out to be fabricated, so that analysts do not continue to rely on an unreliable report. In the absence of such a system, however, the Defense Intelligence Agency (DIA), which disseminated the report in the first place, had a responsibility to make sure that its bad source did not continue to pollute policy judgments; DIA did not fulfill this obligation.

Lacking reliable data about Iraq's programs, analysts' starting point was Iraq's history—its past use of chemical weapons, its successful concealment of WMD programs both before and after the Gulf War, and its failure to account for previously declared stockpiles. The analysts' operating hypothesis, therefore, was that Iraq probably still possessed hidden chemical and biological weapons, was still seeking to rebuild its nuclear weapons program, and was seeking to increase its capability to produce and deliver chemical and biological weapons. This hypothesis was not unreasonable; the problem was that, over time, it hardened into a presumption. This hard and fast presumption then contributed to analysts' readiness to accept pieces of evidence that, even at the time, they should have seen as seriously flawed.

In essence, analysts shifted the burden of proof, requiring evidence that Iraq did *not* have WMD. More troubling, some analysts started to disregard evidence that did not support their premise. Chastened by the effectiveness of Iraq's deceptions before the Gulf War, they viewed contradictory information not as evidence that their premise might be mistaken, but as evidence that Iraq was continuing to conceal its weapons programs.

The Intelligence Community's analysis of the high-strength aluminum tubes offers an illustration of these problems. Most agencies in the Intelligence Community assessed—incorrectly—that these were intended for use in a uranium enrichment program. The reasoning that supported this position was, first, that the tubes *could* be used in centrifuges and, second, that Iraq was good at hiding its nuclear program.

By focusing on whether the tubes could be used for centrifuges, analysts effectively set aside evidence that the tubes were better suited for use in rockets, such as the fact that the tubes had precisely the same dimensions and were made of the same material as tubes used in the conventional rockets that Iraq had declared to international inspectors in 1996. And Iraq's denial and deception capabilities allowed analysts to find support for their view even from information that seemed to contradict it. Thus, Iraqi claims that the tubes were for rockets were described as an Iraqi "cover story" designed to conceal the nuclear end-use for the tubes. In short, analysts erected a theory that almost could not be disproved—both confirming and contradictory facts were construed as support for the theory that the tubes were destined for use in centrifuges.

In the absence of direct evidence, premises and inferences must do. Analysts cannot be faulted for failures of collection. But they can be faulted for not telling policymakers just how little evidence they had to back up their inferences and how uncertain even that evidence itself was. The October 2002 NIE and other pre-war intelligence assessments failed to articulate the thinness of the intelligence upon which critical judgments about Iraq's weapons programs hinged.

Our study also revealed deficiencies in particular intelligence products that are used to convey intelligence information to senior policymakers. As noted above, during the course of its investigation the Commission reviewed a number of articles from the President's Daily Brief (PDB) relating to Iraq's WMD programs. Not surprisingly, many of the flaws in other intelligence products can also be found in the PDBs. But we found some flaws that were inherent in the format of the PDBs—a series of short "articles" often based on current intelligence reporting that are presented to the President each morning. Their brevity leaves little room for doubts or nuance—and their "headlines" designed to grab the reader's attention leave no room at all. Also, a daily drumbeat of reports on the same topic gives an impression of confirming evidence, even when the reports all come from the same source.

The Commission also learned that, on the eve of war, the Intelligence Community failed to convey important information to policymakers. After the October 2002 NIE was published, but before Secretary of State Powell made his address about Iraq's WMD programs to the United Nations, serious doubts became known within the Intelligence Community about Curveball, the aforementioned human intelligence source whose reporting was so critical to the Intelligence Community's pre-war biological warfare assessments. These doubts never found their way to Secretary Powell, who was at that time attempting to strip questionable information from his speech.

These are errors—serious errors. But these errors stem from poor tradecraft and poor management. The Commission found no evidence of political pressure to influence the Intelligence Community's pre-war assessments of Iraq's weapons programs. As we discuss in detail in the body of our report, analysts universally asserted that in no instance did political pressure cause them to skew or alter any of their analytical judgments. We conclude that it was the paucity of intelligence and poor analytical tradecraft, rather than political pressure, that produced the inaccurate pre-war intelligence assessments.

The Iraq Study

This case study proceeds in two parts. The study first details the stream of pre-war intelligence assessments, from the Gulf War to Operation Iraqi Freedom, and compares those to the post-war findings of the Iraq Survey Group. That comparison is provided for each weapons type—nuclear, biological, chemical, and their delivery systems—and also for the political context in Iraq during this time period. For each of these sections, the report also offers the Commission's findings, which often identify specific flaws that led to the inaccuracies in the assessments. The study then identifies the overarching conclusions about the collection, analysis, and dissemination of intelligence that we drew from our examination of the Intelligence Community's performance on the Iraq WMD question.

NUCLEAR WEAPONS

Nuclear Weapons Summary Finding

The Intelligence Community seriously misjudged the status of Iraq's alleged nuclear weapons program in the 2002 NIE and other pre-Iraq war intelligence products. This misjudgment stemmed chiefly from the Community's failure to analyze correctly Iraq's reasons for attempting to procure high-strength aluminum tubes.

The pre-war estimate of Iraq's nuclear program, as reflected in the October 2002 NIE *Iraq's Continuing Programs for Weapons of Mass Destruction*, was that, in the view of most agencies, Baghdad was "reconstituting its nuclear weapons program" and "if left unchecked, [would] probably…have a nuclear weapon during this decade," although it would be unlikely before 2007 to 2009.[3] The NIE explained that, in the view of most agencies, "compelling evidence" of reconstitution was provided by Iraq's "aggressive pursuit of high-strength aluminum tubes."[4] The NIE also pointed to additional indicators, such as other dual-use procurement activity, supporting reconstitution. The assessment that Iraq was reconstituting its nuclear program and could therefore have a weapon by the end of the decade was made with "moderate confidence."[5]

Based on its post-war investigations, the Iraq Survey Group (ISG) concluded—contrary to the Intelligence Community's pre-war assessments—that Iraq had not tried to reconstitute a capability to produce nuclear weapons after 1991.[6] Moreover, the ISG judged that Iraq's work on uranium enrichment, including development of gas centrifuges, essentially ended in 1991, and that its ability to reconstitute its enrichment program progressively decayed after that time.[7] With respect to the aluminum tubes, the ISG concluded that Iraq's effort to procure the tubes is "best explained by its efforts to produce 81-mm rockets," and the ISG uncovered no evidence that the tubes were intended for use in a gas centrifuge.[8]

The Community was, in brief, decidedly wrong on what many would view as the single most important judgment it made. The reasons why the Community was so wrong are not particularly glamorous—failures of analysts to question assumptions and apply their tradecraft correctly, errors in technical and factual analysis, a paucity of collection, and failure by the Community to authenticate relevant documents. But these seemingly workaday shortcomings collectively led to a major mis-estimation of a critical intelligence question.

This chapter details our review of the Intelligence Community's performance on the nuclear issue. Like the chapters that follow on the Community's assessments of other aspects of Iraq's weapons programs, this chapter is divided into three sections. First, we review the Intelligence Community's pre-war assessments of Iraq's nuclear program. We then summarize the findings of the ISG regarding Iraq's nuclear efforts and how those findings compare to the Intelligence Community's assessments. The final section contains our findings concerning the causes of the Intelligence Community's failures on the aluminum tubes issue and the now-infamous Niger story.

The Intelligence Community's Pre-War Assessments

The Intelligence Community's assessments of Iraq's pre-war nuclear program were not made in a vacuum. Rather, as the Intelligence Community later explained, its assessments were informed by its analysis of Iraq's nuclear ambitions and capabilities spanning the preceding fifteen years, as well as by "lessons learned from over a decade of dealing with Iraqi intransigence on this issue."[9] Thus the proper starting point for an evaluation of the Intelligence Community's assessments lies at the conclusion of the first Gulf War when the Intelligence Community reviewed the state of Saddam Hussein's nuclear programs and was surprised by what it found.

Post-Gulf War. Following the Gulf War, based on a variety of sources of intelligence including reporting from defectors, the Intelligence Community learned that Iraq's nuclear weapons program went "far beyond what had been assessed by any intelligence organization" in 1990-1991.[10] Before the Gulf War, in November 1990, the Community had assessed that, because analysts had not detected a formal, coordinated nuclear weapons program, Iraq likely would not have a nuclear weapon until the late 1990s.[11] Thus after the war the Intelligence Community was surprised to discover the breadth of Iraq's nuclear weapons program, including the wide range of technologies Iraq had been pursuing for uranium enrichment, which in turn indicated that Iraq "had been much closer to a weapon than virtually anyone expected."[12] This humbling discovery that Iraq had successfully concealed a sophisticated nuclear program from the U.S. Intelligence Community exercised a major influence on the Intelligence Community's assessments throughout the early 1990s and afterwards.

Iraq's subsequent and continuing attempts to evade and deceive international inspectors heightened analysts' concerns.[13] In a 1994 Joint Atomic Energy Intelligence Committee (JAEIC) assessment, *Iraq's Nuclear Weapons Program: Elements of Reconstitution*, the Intelligence Community agreed that the "Iraqi government is determined to covertly reconstitute its nuclear weapons program," and that, although Iraq had not yet begun reconstitution, it "would most likely choose the gas centrifuge route" and would "invest a great deal of time and effort" to "conceal its efforts from long-term monitoring."[14]

Mid-1990s. Still, through the mid-1990s, analysts continued to assess that Iraq had not yet reconstituted its nuclear program. Most agencies judged in a 1993 NIE that "if sanctions are lifted and especially if inspections cease, Baghdad will rapidly accelerate its effort" to produce nuclear weapons.[15] And all agencies agreed in a September 1994 JAEIC assessment that Iraq "still seems to be pursuing" its former program.[16] The Intelligence Community believed that if Iraq were able to mount a dedicated centrifuge program, it would probably take the Iraqis five to seven years to produce enough fissile material for a nuclear weapon.[17] This consensus was best reflected by an October 1997 assessment by the JAEIC, which reaffirmed its previous judgments that Iraq would need five to seven years to produce fissile material indigenously, assuming some availability of foreign technical assistance and supplies.[18] Whether that five to seven year clock had started to run, however, was unclear: this assessment noted that although there was "no firm evidence that reconstitution had begun, six years had passed since the Gulf War and the Community could not be certain whether the starting point for the five to seven year timeline was in the past or future."[19]

During this period, the lack of specific intelligence on the subject continued to complicate analysts' abilities to assess Iraq's ability to reconstitute its nuclear program. The Intelligence Community noted in a 1998 assessment, for instance, that there was limited and often contradictory human intelligence reporting on Iraqi nuclear efforts, with some human intelligence sources indicating that Iraq was continuing "low-level theoretical research for a weapons program" while other sources reported that "all nuclear-related activity [had been] halted."[20] The Intelligence Community acknowledged that it had an "incomplete picture of the Iraqi nuclear program."[21]

Post-1998. The end of international inspections in 1998, prompted by Saddam Hussein's preventing the inspectors from doing their work, increased concern among analysts that Iraq would use that opportunity to reconstitute its nuclear program. Accordingly, in 1999, the JAEIC noted that although it still had no specific evidence that reconstitution had begun, the absence of inspectors gave Iraq greater *opportunity* to conduct covert research and development.[22] As of December 2000, however, an Intelligence Community Assessment noted that Iraq still did not appear to have taken major steps toward reconstitution.[23] Thus, after the departure of inspectors, the Intelligence Community assumed that Iraq had the opportunity and the desire to jumpstart its covert nuclear weapons program; by the end of 2000, however, the Community had seen no firm evidence that this was actually happening.

This judgment began to shift in early 2001 as a result of a discovery that, in hindsight, was the critical moment in the development of the Intelligence Community's assessment of Iraq's nuclear program. In March 2001, intelligence reporting indicated that Iraq was seeking high-strength tubes made of 7075 T6 aluminum alloy.[24] The Intelligence Community obtained samples of the tubes when a shipment bound for Iraq was seized overseas.[25]

At this point, a debate began within the Intelligence Community about the reason why Iraq had procured the tubes. The CIA assessed that the tubes were most likely for gas centrifuges for enriching uranium and believed that the tubes provided compelling evidence that Iraq had renewed its gas centrifuge uranium enrichment program.[26] CIA subsequently identified possible non-nuclear applications for the tubes,[27] but continued to judge that the tubes were destined for use in Iraqi gas centrifuges[28]—even while acknowledging that the Intelligence Community had very little information on Iraq's WMD programs to corroborate this assessment.[29]

This judgment concerning the tubes' likely intended use was echoed by another expert technical entity within the Intelligence Community. Analysts from the National Ground Intelligence Center (NGIC), a component of the U.S. Army recognized as the national experts on conventional military systems, judged that while it could "not totally rule out the possibility" that the tubes could be used for rockets and thus were not destined for a nuclear-related use, the tubes were, technically speaking, poor choices for rocket bodies. NGIC's expert judgment was therefore that there was a very low probability the tubes were designed for conventional use in rockets.[30]

Because of NGIC's expertise on conventional weapons systems such as rockets, NGIC's view that the tubes were poor choices for rocket bodies gave CIA analysts greater confidence in their own judgment that the tubes were likely for use in centrifuges.[31]

Other entities took a different view, however. The Department of Energy (DOE), the U.S. government's primary repository of expertise on nuclear matters, assessed that the tubes—although they "could be used to manufacture centrifuge rotors"—were "not well-suited for a centrifuge application" and were more likely intended for use in Iraq's Nasser 81 millimeter Multiple Rocket Launcher (MRL) program.[32] The International Atomic Energy Agency (IAEA) agreed with DOE's assessment, concluding that the tubes were usable in a gas centrifuge application but that they were not directly suited to that use.[33]

Despite this disagreement, the CIA informed senior policymakers that it believed the tubes were destined for use in Iraqi gas centrifuges.[34] While noting that there was disagreement within the Intelligence Community concerning the most likely use for the tubes, the CIA pointed out that there was also interagency consensus that the tubes *could* be used for centrifuge enrichment.[35] This consensus on capability led many analysts at both CIA and DIA to think that the tubes supplied the evidence that Iraq was starting to "reconstitute" its nuclear program.[36]

Other streams of evidence also raised flags. At about the same time, analysts began to see indications that Iraq was seeking procurement of other dual-use items that would be consistent with a possible renewed effort at developing centrifuges.[37] This activity concerned even DOE, which had expressed skepticism that the intercepted tubes had centrifuge applications.[38] These concerns were affected by the Intelligence Community's history of underestimating Iraq's nuclear program; as the National Intelligence Council (NIC) would later observe, analysts became concerned during 2002 that "they may again be facing a surprise similar to the one in 1991."[39]

In the months before the October 2002 NIE, the CIA continued to assess that the tubes were intended for use in gas centrifuges, albeit with slight variations in the strength of that formulation, pointing out that Iraq's interest in the tubes was "key" to the assessment that Iraq was "reconstituting its centrifuge program."[40] CIA presented this view in an Intelligence Assessment, entitled

Iraq's Hunt for Aluminum Tubes: Evidence of a Renewed Uranium Enrichment Program, in which CIA concluded that the aluminum tubes "are most likely for gas centrifuges for enriching uranium" and that Iraq's pursuit of such tubes provided "compelling evidence that Iraq has renewed its gas centrifuge uranium enrichment program."[41] The assessment noted that "some" in the Intelligence Community believed conventional armament applications, such as multiple rocket launchers, were "more likely end-uses," but the assessment noted that NGIC, the "national experts on conventional military systems," had found such uses "highly unlikely."[42] At the same time, DOE disseminated a separate assessment arguing that, while the tubes could be modified for use as centrifuge rotors, "other conventional military uses [we]re more plausible."[43] The Department of State's Bureau of Intelligence and Research (INR) agreed with DOE's assessment.[44]

October 2002 NIE. The Intelligence Community judged in the NIE with moderate confidence that "Baghdad ha[d] reconstituted its nuclear weapons program."[45] Only INR dissented from this assessment, although INR judged in the President's Summary of the NIE that the overall evidence "indicates, at most, a limited Iraqi nuclear reconstitution effort."[46] By reconstitution, the Intelligence Community meant that Iraq was in the "process of restoring [its] uranium enrichment capability."[47] To the relevant CIA and DIA analysts, the pursuit of aluminum tubes provided "compelling evidence" of reconstitution.[48] In particular, the composition, dimensions, cost, and tight manufacturing tolerances for the tubes were assessed by CIA and DIA to exceed by far those needed for non-nuclear purposes, thus demonstrating that the tubes were intended for a nuclear-related use.[49] At the interagency coordination meeting for the NIE, both NSA and the National Geospatial-Intelligence Agency (NGA) agreed with the CIA/DIA position on the tubes.[50] DOE and INR dissented from the tubes judgment, assessing that the tubes were more likely for use in tactical rockets.[51]

The NIE stated that the conclusion that the tubes indicated reconstitution was bolstered by additional evidence that suggested Iraq could be rebuilding its nuclear program:

1. ***Other Dual-Use Procurements.*** Reporting indicated that Iraq was attempting to procure other dual-use items that would be required to build a gas centrifuge plant, such as magnets, "high-speed balancing machines," and machine tools.[52] These items are all dual-use materials,

however, and the reporting provided no direct indication that the materials were intended for use in a nuclear program, as indicated in the NIE.[53]

2. *Nuclear Cadre.* The NIE also pointed to evidence that Iraq was making efforts to preserve, and in some cases re-establish and enhance, its cadre of weapons personnel.[54] Reporting indicated that some scientists had been reassigned to the Iraqi Atomic Energy Commission (IAEC) and that Iraq had "reassembled" many scientists, engineers, and managers from Iraq's previous nuclear program.[55]

3. *Activity at Suspect Sites.* Sources indicated that Iraq was trying to procure a magnet production line in 1999-2001 and one report indicated the plant would be located at Al-Tahadi, where analysis suggested construction of buildings in late 2000 that could have housed a magnet production line.[56] Both sources indicated, however, that magnet procurements were likely affiliated with Iraq's missile program, rather than with nuclear applications, though some reporting noted that the cadre of scientists and technicians at the site formerly worked in the nuclear program.[57]

Uranium from Niger. Although the NIE did not include uranium acquisition in the list of elements bolstering its conclusion about reconstitution, it did note that Iraq was "vigorously trying to procure uranium ore and yellowcake" from Africa.[58] This statement was based largely on reporting from a foreign government intelligence service that Niger planned to send up to 500 tons of yellowcake uranium to Iraq.[59] The status of the arrangement was unclear, however, at the time of the coordination of the Estimate and the NIE therefore noted that the Intelligence Community could not confirm whether Iraq succeeded in acquiring the uranium.[60] Iraq's alleged pursuit of uranium from Africa was thus not included among the NIE's Key Judgments.[61] For reasons discussed at length below, several months after the NIE, the reporting that Iraq was seeking uranium from Niger was judged to be based on forged documents and was recalled.[62]

In short, all of the coordinating agencies, with the exception of INR, agreed that Iraq was reconstituting its nuclear program.[63] Of those agencies that agreed on reconstitution, all but DOE agreed that the tubes provided "compelling evidence" for that conclusion. DOE reaffirmed its previous assessments that, while the tubes could be modified for use in a gas centrifuge, they were poorly suited for such a function and were most likely designed for use in conventional rockets.[64] On the question of reconstitution, DOE believed that the other factors—the attempted procurement of magnets and balancing machines, efforts to reconstitute the nuclear cadre, activity at suspect sites, and evidence of Iraqi efforts to obtain uranium from Africa—justified the conclusion that Iraq was reconstituting its nuclear program.[65] None of the other agencies placed significant weight on reporting about attempts to procure uranium from Africa to support their conclusion of reconstitution.[66]

Post-NIE. The publication of the NIE did not settle the dispute about the aluminum tubes and so, in the period between the NIE and the invasion of Iraq, debate within the Intelligence Community over their significance continued. INR, for its part, continued to see "no compelling reason to judge that Iraq ha[d] entered" the timeframe of at least five to seven years that the Intelligence Community agreed Baghdad would need to produce sufficient fissile material for a nuclear weapon.[67] DOE, meanwhile, continued to believe that reconstitution was underway but that the "tubes probably were not part of the program," [68] assessing instead that the tubes were intended for use in conventional rockets.[69] On the other side of the dispute, NGIC and CIA continued to assess that the tubes were destined for use in gas centrifuges.[70] Outside the Intelligence Community, the IAEA, after inspections resumed in fall 2002, also weighed in on the dispute, concluding with DOE and INR that the tubes were likely intended for use in Iraq's 81 millimeter rocket program.[71]

During this time the CIA continued to explain to senior policymakers that the Intelligence Community was not of one view on the most likely use for the tubes,[72] but CIA offered its own view that the "alternative explanation" for the tubes' intended use—that they would be used for rockets—was likely an Iraqi "cover story."[73] The CIA also noted the overall paucity of information on Iraq's programs, but suggested that the lack of information was due in part to Iraq's successful efforts to hide its illicit activity.[74]

Other countries' intelligence agencies views of the tubes were, on balance, somewhat more circumspect than that of the majority in the NIE. For its part, the British Joint Intelligence Committee assessed, as did the NIE, that the aluminum tubes, with some modifications, would be suitable for use in a centrifuge, but noted that there was no definitive intelligence that the tubes were destined for the nuclear program.[75] The views of the Australian Office of

National Assessments on the relevance of the tubes to Iraq's nuclear program were "inconsistent and changeable."[76]

Post-War Findings of the Iraq Survey Group

The Iraq Survey Group concluded that Iraq had not tried to reconstitute a capability to produce nuclear weapons after 1991.[77] It concluded that Iraq's efforts to develop gas centrifuges for uranium enrichment ended in 1991, as did Iraq's work on other uranium enrichment programs, which Iraq had explored prior to the Gulf War.[78] The ISG also found no evidence that Iraq had taken steps to advance its pre-1991 work in nuclear weapons design and development.[79] Although the ISG did find indications that Saddam remained interested in reconstitution of the nuclear program after sanctions were lifted, it concluded that Iraq's ability to reconstitute its program progressively decayed after 1991.[80]

Not long after the start of the Iran-Iraq war in 1980, Iraq started to pursue formally a uranium enrichment program using a variety of uranium enrichment techniques.[81] By 1990, Iraq had built two magnetic-bearing centrifuges (with foreign assistance) using imported carbon fiber rotors and two oil-bearing centrifuges.[82] During the first Gulf War, however, nearly all of the key nuclear facilities in Iraq—those involved in the processing of nuclear material or weapons research—were bombed and many of the facilities were largely destroyed.[83]

After the Gulf War, Iraq initially chose not to disclose the extent of its nuclear program and instead sought to hide any evidence of it. Accordingly, the director of Iraq's Military Industrialization Commission, Hussein Kamil, ordered the collection of all inculpatory documents and equipment. The equipment and documentation were then moved to a variety of locations to hide them from the IAEA. Hussein Kamil ordered at least one set of all nuclear-related documents and some equipment to be retained by a senior scientist.[84]

Despite Iraqi efforts, in early summer 1991 the IAEA confronted Baghdad with evidence of uranium enrichment components during the course of its inspections. At that point Baghdad admitted to its large pre-war enrichment programs, but still did not fully declare the extent of its centrifuge program.[85]

Indeed, Iraq continued to resist more comprehensive disclosure of its pre-1991 nuclear program until after the defection of Hussein Kamil in 1995, when a large number of documents and equipment fell into the hands of UNSCOM and the IAEA. From this point forward, according to the ISG, the Iraqis appear to have been more cooperative and provided more complete information. For example, the Iraqis largely declared their pre-1991 centrifuge program, although a full set of documents obtained by Iraq from German engineers in the 1980s was not supplied to IAEA inspectors.[86]

Although the Iraqis did not make more comprehensive disclosures about their nuclear program until 1995, the Iraq Survey Group concluded that Iraq had actually ended its nuclear program in 1991. More specifically, the ISG assessed that Iraq's development of gas centrifuges essentially ended in 1991 and that Iraq did not continue work on any of the other pre-1991 enrichment methods it had explored, including electromagnetic isotope separation (EMIS).[87] The ISG did point out, however, that many of the former EMIS engineers and scientists continued to work for either the Iraqi Atomic Energy Commission or the Military Industrialization Commission in roles that could preserve their technical skills.[88]

Despite these efforts to preserve the skills and talent of the nuclear cadre, the intellectual capital underlying Iraq's nuclear program decayed in the years after 1991.[89] For example, starting around 1992, the Director of Iraq's Military Industrialization Commission transferred personnel from the former nuclear program to various military research and production facilities. Some of the work performed by these former nuclear scientists by its nature preserved for Iraq capabilities that would be needed for a reconstituted nuclear program. Still, the ISG noted that the overall decline of the Iraqi economy made it very difficult to retain scientists, many of whom departed for better prospects abroad.[90]

With the influx of funds from the Oil-for-Food program and later the suspension of cooperation with UNSCOM, Saddam began to pay renewed attention to former members of the Iraq nuclear program. In the late 1990s, for instance, he raised salaries for those in the Military Industrialization and Iraqi Atomic Energy Commissions, and new programs, such as joint programs with universities, were initiated to employ the talent of former nuclear program employees.[91] In the year before Operation Iraqi Freedom, Iraq's Military Industrialization Commission also took steps to improve capabilities that could have been applied to a renewed centrifuge program for uranium enrichment. But the ISG did not uncover information indicating that the technologies being pursued were intended to support such a program.[92]

With respect to Iraq's interest in procuring high-strength aluminum tubes, the ISG concluded that the Iraqi attempt to procure the tubes is best explained by Iraq's efforts to produce effective 81 millimeter rockets; the ISG uncovered no evidence that the tubes were intended for use in a gas centrifuge.[93] The ISG arrived at this conclusion only after investigating the key indicators that suggested a possible centrifuge end-use for the tubes—for example, the tubes' dimensions and tight manufacturing tolerances—and found no evidence of a program to design or develop an 81 millimeter aluminum rotor centrifuge.[94]

What the ISG found instead was that, with respect to the dimensions of the tubes, Iraqi nuclear scientists thought it was at best impractical for Iraq to have made a centrifuge with 81 millimeter rotors. For example, Ja'far Diya Ja'far, the head of Iraq's pre-1991 uranium enrichment program, stated in post-war debriefings that, while it was possible to make a rotor from the tubes, he thought it would be impractical to do so.[95] He also said that using 81 millimeter rockets as a "cover story" for a centrifuge project would not have been very useful, because Iraq had difficulty importing *any* goods.[96] Ja'far similarly did not consider it reasonable that Iraq could have pursued a centrifuge program based on 81 millimeter aluminum tubes, judging the technical challenges to doing so were too great.[97]

Conversely, the Iraq Survey Group investigation did uncover what it judged to be plausible accounts that linked the tubes to 81 millimeter rockets, and which answered questions about why the Iraqis had sought such tight manufacturing specifications for the tubes. For example, some sources indicated to the ISG that the tight tolerance requests were driven by a desire to improve the accuracy of the rockets. Inconsistencies among rockets had resulted in past variations in range and accuracy, according to these sources, and the Iraqis chose to address this problem by tightening specifications.[98] Another explanation was that the engineering drawings for the Iraqi 81 millimeter rocket, which was originally reverse-engineered from an Italian air-to-ground rocket (the Medusa), had undergone many ad hoc revisions over the years because the Iraqis were using their 81 millimeter rockets as ground-to-ground rockets. An Iraqi military committee was convened to return the design to the original Italian-based design, according to the ISG report, and that military committee then set new, and more strict, specifications.[99] The ISG also learned that misfires sometimes resulted from pitting in the tubes caused by improper storage and corrosion, a problem that could explain the requirement that the tubes be anodized and shipped carefully.[100]

Though ultimately concluding that the evidence did not show that the Iraqis intended a nuclear end-use for the tubes, the Iraq Survey Group did note some inconsistencies in the explanation that the tubes were intended for use in tactical rockets.[101] For example, the ISG found technical drawings that showed that Iraq's 81 millimeter rocket program had a history of using tubes that fell short of the strict manufacturing standards demanded in the procurement attempts before the war.[102] Also, the ISG found evidence that, in the months just before the war, the Iraqis accepted lower-quality, indigenously produced aluminum tubes for its 81 millimeter rockets, despite the continuing efforts to procure high-specification tubes from abroad.[103] Iraq also explored the possibility (about a year before the war) of using steel for the rocket bodies. This approach was rejected, however, because it would have required significant design modifications for the existing 81 millimeter rocket design.[104] The ISG noted that these efforts raise questions about whether high-specification tubes were really needed for rockets.[105]

The ISG reconciled this evidence by judging that Iraq's continued efforts to obtain tubes from abroad, even while simultaneously accepting some indigenously produced tubes for use in rockets, could be explained in large measure by bureaucratic inefficiencies and fear of senior officials in the ranks of the Iraqi government.[106] For example, Dr. Huwaysh, the head of the Military Industrialization Commission, "exhibited a rigid managerial style" and frequently made unreasonable production demands. The fear of being held responsible for rejected tubes or components affected the lead production engineer and he therefore decided to tighten specifications for the rocket program. Similarly, a report from the rocket program noted that some engineers requested tight specifications in order to appear effective in addressing problems. Also, because Huwaysh demanded results quickly, the engineers did not have time to attempt a detailed analysis of the causes for rocket scatter and inaccuracy; instead, the engineers simply tightened some specifications in the hope that that would improve accuracy.[107] Other factors influencing the continuing efforts to procure tubes from abroad included the "lack of sufficient indigenous manufacturing capabilities"—an effort that Iraq only began in 2002—the high costs of production, and the "pressure of the impending war."[108]

The ISG noted that one other factor that the Intelligence Community had cited as evidence that the tubes were intended for use in a centrifuge was that the potential supplier was asked to provide 84 millimeter tubes—a change that would have meant the tubes could *not* be used in an 81 millimeter rocket.[109] But the ISG found no clear indication that it was Iraq (or an Iraqi entity) that was making these inquiries about 84 millimeter tubes.[110] In any event, the ISG concluded that, although a larger diameter tube would be better for use in a centrifuge, Iraq already had 500 tons of 120 millimeter diameter aluminum shafts which it had imported before sanctions were imposed in 1990. And, furthermore, Iraq was using those shafts in the months before Operation Iraqi Freedom to support the flow-forming operations related to the 81 millimeter rocket program.[111]

With respect to alleged "high-level interest" in tubes by Iraqi leaders, the ISG concluded that such interest in the tubes appears to have focused on efforts to produce 81 millimeter rockets rather than on any element of a nuclear program.[112]

The Iraq Survey Group also found no evidence that Iraq sought uranium from abroad after 1991.[113] With respect to the reports that Iraq sought uranium from Niger, ISG interviews with Ja'far Diya Ja'far, the head of Iraq's pre-1991 enrichment programs, indicated that Iraq had only two contacts with the Nigerien government after 1998—neither of which was related to uranium.[114] One such contact was a visit to Niger by the Iraqi Ambassador to the Vatican Wissam Zahawie, the purpose of which Ja'far said was to invite the Nigerien President to visit Iraq (a story told publicly by Zahawie).[115] The second contact was a visit to Iraq by a Nigerien minister to discuss Nigerien purchases of oil from Iraq—with no mention of "any kind of payment, *quid pro quo*, or offer to provide Iraq with uranium ore, other than cash in exchange for petroleum."[116] The use of the last method of payment is supported by a crude oil contract, dated June 26, 2001, recovered by the ISG.[117]

The ISG found only one offer of uranium to Baghdad since 1991—an offer that Iraq appears to have turned down.[118] The ISG found a document in the headquarters of the Iraqi Intelligence Service that reveals that a Ugandan businessman had approached the Iraqi Embassy in Nairobi with an offer to sell uranium, reportedly from the Congo. The Iraqi Embassy in Nairobi, reporting back to Baghdad on the matter on May 20, 2001, indicated that the Embassy told the Ugandan that Iraq did not deal with "these materials" because of the sanctions.[119]

Finally, and on a broader plane, even if an order to reconstitute had been given, Iraq Survey Group interviews with former senior officials indicated that Iraq would not have been able to do so given the conditions inside the country in 2002.[120] Unsurprisingly, therefore, the ISG found no indication that Iraq had resumed fissile material or nuclear weapon research and development activities after 1991.[121]

Analysis of the Intelligence Community's Pre-War Assessments

This marked disjuncture between the Intelligence Community's assessments and the findings of the Iraq Survey Group about Iraq's purported nuclear weapons program was not solely the product of bad luck or the inherent difficulties of making intelligence judgments. It arose out of fundamental flaws in the way the Intelligence Community approached its business.

Above all, the Intelligence Community's failure on the nuclear issue was a failure of analysis. To be sure, the paucity of intelligence contributed to that failure. Although signals intelligence played a key role in some respects that we cannot discuss in an unclassified format, on the whole it was not useful. Similarly, though imagery intelligence showed some construction at a possible suspect nuclear site in or around 2000, imagery provided little helpful insight into the purpose of that activity and nothing beyond that. And, other than information on the alleged uranium deal that was later determined to be unreliable, very little human intelligence was available to provide insight into Iraq's intentions. The time pressures of the October 2002 NIE also may have hampered the normal thorough review before dissemination.[122]

But on the crucial question of whether the aluminum tubes were for use in a gas centrifuge or in tactical rockets—an analytical question—the Intelligence Community got it wrong.[123] And, notably, it was not one of the difficult and inherently speculative questions intelligence analysts often confront; it was not a question that required the Intelligence Community to make a prediction about future events or to draw conclusions about the state of the world based upon limited information. Rather, the critical question was, at bottom, largely a technical one, where the critical facts were known or knowable: namely, how well-suited were the aluminum tubes for tactical rockets and centrifuges, respectively? An even-handed assessment of the evidence should have led the Intelligence Community to conclude that the tubes were more likely destined for tactical rockets. This section examines this analytic failure and other issues uncovered by our review of the Intelligence Community's performance.

Nuclear Weapons Finding 1

The Intelligence Community's judgment about Iraq's nuclear program hinged chiefly on an assessment about Iraq's intended use for high-strength aluminum tubes it was seeking to procure. Most of the agencies in the Intelligence Community erroneously concluded these tubes were intended for use in centrifuges in a nuclear program rather than in conventional rockets. This error was, at the bottom, the result of poor analytical tradecraft—namely, the failure to do proper technical analysis informed by thorough knowledge of the relevant weapons technology and practices.

The judgment of most agencies that Baghdad's pursuit of aluminum tubes "provide[d] compelling evidence" that Iraq was reconstituting its weapons turned upon two separate but related analytical determinations.[124] The first was that the tubes would not have been well-suited for use in Iraq's conventional military arsenal—in particular, as a conventional rocket casing. The second was that the tubes *were* a suitable fit for centrifuges in a nuclear program.

This section addresses the soundness of each of these conclusions in turn. We find that the Intelligence Community—and in particular, conventional weapons analysts at the National Ground Intelligence Center (NGIC) in the Defense Department—got the first of these two questions completely wrong; the intercepted tubes were not only well-suited, but were in fact a precise fit, for Iraq's conventional rockets, and the Intelligence Community should have recognized as much at the time. The second question—whether the tubes would have been well-suited for centrifuge applications—was a closer one, but we conclude that certain agencies were more wedded to the analytical position that the tubes were destined for a nuclear program than was justified by the technical evidence. We also conclude that these misjudgments, while reflecting lapses in basic tradecraft, ultimately stemmed from a deeper source:

analysts' willingness to accept that a superficially enticing piece of evidence confirmed the prevailing assumption—that Iraq was attempting to reconstitute its nuclear program—was wrong. That CIA and DIA reached this conclusion was a product of, in our view, an effort to fit the evidence to the prevailing assumptions.

Suitability of the tubes for conventional rockets. The most egregious failure regarding the aluminum tubes was the inability of certain agencies to assess correctly their suitability for a conventional weapons system. While the CIA and DIA acknowledged that the tubes *could* be used for rockets, these agencies believed it was highly unlikely that the tubes had been intended for such a use.[125] But these agencies' basis for believing this was wrong. Iraq had been seeking tubes composed of a particular material—high-strength 7075-T6 aluminum—which CIA and DIA viewed as suggestive of a nuclear end-use.[126] But that material is wholly consistent with a non-nuclear end-use. This same material in fact has been used in rockets manufactured by Russia, Switzerland, and twelve other countries, according to Department of Defense rocket design engineers.[127] Indeed, *Iraq itself* had used this kind of aluminum in its Nasser 81 rocket program and had declared that use in its 1996 declaration to the IAEA.[128]

Yet NGIC, the national experts on conventional military systems, assessed in September 2002 that the material and tolerances of the tubes sought by Iraq were "highly unlikely" to be intended for rocket motor cases.[129] That assessment was clearly mistaken and should have been recognized as such at the time. NGIC later conceded, in written testimony to the Senate Select Committee on Intelligence, that "lightweight rockets, such as those originally developed for air-to-ground systems, typically use 7075-T6 aluminum for the motor casing."[130] As the experts on such systems, NGIC should have been aware of these facts. Similarly, although NGIC assessed that the tolerances of the tubes Iraq was seeking were "excessive" for rockets, NGIC was not aware at that time of the tolerances required for the Iraqi Nasser 81 rockets, for the Italian Medusa rocket on which the Nasser 81 was based, or for comparable U.S. rockets.[131]

NGIC also believed that the tubes would make poor choices for rocket motor bodies because the walls of the tubes were too thick.[132] But the tubes Iraq was seeking had precisely the same dimensions—including the same wall thickness—as the tubes that Iraq itself used in its Nasser 81 rockets in 1996.[133]

This fact also should not have come as a revelation to NGIC analysts, as DOE had published detailed assessments of the tubes used in the Nasser 81 rocket—including their dimensions—in August 2001, and as the IAEA had noted Iraq's use of the Nasser 81 rocket in its earlier catalogs of Iraq's weapons programs.[134] Yet the two primary NGIC rocket analysts said that they did not know the dimensions of the Nasser 81 rockets at that time. While these analysts assert that they had no access to IAEA information and did not receive the DOE reporting in question,[135] we believe that NGIC could and should have conducted a more exhaustive examination of the question. We agree with the conclusion of the Senate Select Committee on Intelligence that NGIC's performance represents a "serious lapse" in analytical tradecraft.[136]

CIA and DIA's confidence in their conclusions also led them to fail to pursue additional, easily obtainable data on the tubes that would have pointed them in the direction of conventional weapons applications. For example, though elements of the Intelligence Community were aware that the Nasser 81 millimeter rocket was likely reverse-engineered from the Italian Medusa air-to-ground rocket, neither DIA nor CIA—the two most vociferous proponents of a nuclear end-use—obtained the specifications for the Medusa rocket until well after the commencement of Operation Iraqi Freedom.[137] Indeed, CIA appears to have consciously bypassed attempts to gather this crucial data. A CIA officer had actually suggested that CIA track down the precise dimensions and specifications of the Medusa rocket in order to evaluate the possibility that the tubes Iraq was seeking were in fact intended for rockets. CIA rejected the request in early September 2002, however, on the basis that such information was not needed because CIA judged the tubes to be destined for use in centrifuges—a textbook example of an agency prematurely closing off an avenue of investigation because of its confidence in its conclusions.[138]

Suitability of tubes for nuclear centrifuges. As discussed above, a debate raged within the Intelligence Community in the months preceding the Iraq war on a second question as well: namely, whether the intercepted aluminum tubes were well-suited for use in nuclear centrifuges. According to both DOE and CIA centrifuge experts, the resolution of this issue depended primarily on the answer to two highly technical questions: first, whether the tubes had a sufficiently large internal diameter (and hence could allow the requisite gas flow) to enrich uranium effectively, and whether the walls of the tubes were too thick for use as centrifuge rotors.[139] While generally the analytical issue of the tubes' suitability for centrifuges was more technically complex than that of their fit for conventional rocket applications, the manner in which certain agencies answered these two technical questions about centrifuge-suitability suggests that their analysis was driven more by their underlying assumptions than by the available scientific evidence.

For example, to answer the first question, analysts from CIA's Weapons Intelligence, Non-Proliferation, and Arms Control Center (WINPAC) sought the assistance of the DOE National Laboratories—specifically, Oak Ridge National Laboratory—to test the tubes.[140] The Oak Ridge laboratory concluded that, while it was technically possible to enrich uranium using tubes of the diameter the Iraqis were seeking, it would be suboptimal to do so.[141] The prototype design unit that Iraq built before the Gulf War—which used carbon fiber rotors and was built with the assistance of German engineers using the European Urenco design—had a separative capability four to five times greater than would a centrifuge built using the 81 millimeter tubes for rotors.[142] Accordingly, to support a program that could produce one nuclear device per year, Iraq would need to manufacture and deploy 10,000 to 14,000 such machines.[143] The number of tubes Iraq was seeking, however, would be enough to manufacture 100,000 to 150,000 of these machines, which could produce 170-260 kg of highly enriched uranium per year (enough for 8-10 nuclear devices per year). But DOE pointed out that no proliferator has ever operated such a large number of centrifuges.[144] In other words, the tubes Iraq was seeking were so suboptimal for uranium enrichment that it would have taken many thousands of them to produce enough uranium for a weapon—and although Iraq was in fact seeking thousands of tubes, DOE assessed it would have been highly unlikely for a proliferator to choose a route that would require such a large number of machines.

With respect to the second suitability question—whether the walls of the tubes were too thick for centrifuge use—CIA's WINPAC sought the assistance of a contractor to perform separate tests (a "spin test") of the tubes in order to determine if they were strong enough to withstand the extremely high speeds at which centrifuge rotors must spin.[145] The initial test performed by the contractor was reported to have resulted in successfully spinning a tube at 60,000 revolutions per minute (rpm).[146] The NIE included these test results and explained that this test provided only a rough indication that the tubes were suitable as centrifuge rotors. The NIE noted, however, that additional tests would be performed at higher speeds to determine whether the tubes were suitable for operations under conditions that replicated gas centrifuge operations.[147]

Unfortunately, these subsequent tests—performed by CIA contractors in January 2003—only clouded an already murky picture. The contractors' initial findings gave the appearance that the tubes were of insufficient strength for use in centrifuge equipment. The CIA, however, questioned the methodology used by its contractors, asserting that the test results had failed to distinguish between the failures of the *tubes* and failures of the *test equipment* itself.[148] The contractors then provided a "correction" with new test data, which, the CIA believed, demonstrated that the tubes had sufficient strength to be spun at speeds of 90,000 rpm.[149] But DOE was unpersuaded by the corrected findings and argued that the CIA's conclusions were not supported by the test results.[150] At bottom, the ineptly handled spin tests did little more than deepen the divisions between CIA and DOE over the tubes' intended use; in the words of one former senior Intelligence Community official, the tests were "like throwing a lighted match into gasoline."[151]

In any event, the initial technical tests led all agencies to agree that the tubes *could* be used to build gas centrifuges for uranium enrichment.[152] DOE, however, did not believe that tubes were *intended* for such use, a view with which INR agreed. DOE's view was based on disagreement with CIA's view on both counts—DOE argued that the diameter of the tubes was too small and the walls were too thick for centrifuge use. The tubes, in DOE's judgment, were therefore "not favorable for direct use as centrifuge rotors."[153]

CIA countered that the dimensions of the tubes were "similar" to Iraq's prewar Beams gas centrifuge design and "nearly matched" the tube size used in another type of gas centrifuge, the Zippe design.[154] Nuclear analysts from WINPAC explained that prior to the Gulf War Iraq had pursued the development of a Beams centrifuge with aluminum rotors that had a wall thickness in excess of 3.0 millimeters, and that Iraq had built an oil centrifuge with aluminum rotors in excess of 6.0 millimeters. CIA also asserted that the unclassified document describing Zippe's design could be interpreted as using rotors with wall thicknesses that ranged from 1.0 millimeter to 2.8 millimeters.[155] WINPAC reasoned that, although these dated models for centrifuges were not ideal, Iraq was likely to build what it *could* rather than what would be the optimal design.[156] Specifically, old centrifuge designs using aluminum rotors were the only ones Iraq had successfully built in the past without extensive assistance from foreign experts.[157] Similarly, DIA assessed that "[a]lternative uses" for the tubes were "possible," but that such alternatives were "less likely because the specifications [of the tubes] are consistent with late 1980s Iraqi gas centrifuge rotor designs."[158]

DOE disputed this analysis on several grounds. From the outset, DOE believed that Iraq would pursue a more advanced design, such as the Urenco-style centrifuge that Iraq had pursued with the covert assistance of German engineers before the Gulf War.[159] DOE also disagreed with CIA's technical conclusion that the tubes were a plausible match for the Zippe design; it asserted that the optimum Zippe design required a wall thickness no greater than a certain figure (the figure itself is classified).[160] Finally, DOE noted that the Beams design had never been successfully used to enrich uranium—Beams himself could never get his design to work beyond pilot-plant operation.[161] As DOE subsequently explained, in DOE's view it was therefore irrelevant, and misleading, to point to similarities with this design as evidence the tubes were intended for use in a centrifuge.[162]

In sum, although even DOE agreed that the tubes *could* be used for centrifuges, DOE's assessment that such use was unlikely proved closer to the mark. DIA and CIA analysts overestimated the likelihood that the tubes were intended for use in centrifuges, an erroneous judgment that resulted largely from the unwillingness of many analysts to question—or rigorously test—the underlying assumption that Iraq would try to reconstitute its nuclear program.

The influence of assumptions on the analytical process. As we have seen, the majority of intelligence agencies—and in particular, CIA and DIA—were simply wrong on the question of whether the aluminum tubes were suitable for conventional rocket applications. A similar dynamic emerged during the intra-Community debate on whether the tubes were a good fit for centrifuge designs; while the judgments were in this case more defensible, CIA and DIA consistently construed quite ambiguous technical data as supporting the conclusion that the aluminum tubes were well-suited for use as centrifuges. A consistent pattern emerges: certain analysts, and certain agencies, were clearly inclined to view evidence—even exceedingly technical evidence—through the prism of their assumptions that Iraq was reconstituting its nuclear program.

This tendency is reflected in the way these analysts interpreted other information about the tubes as well. For instance, CIA and DIA assessed that the tight manufacturing tolerances that Iraq required for the tubes pointed towards centrifuge use, because of the increased cost and manufacturing challenges that would result from these stringent requirements.[163] But as DOE pointed out, although the specifications did seem excessive for use in conventional rockets, the tolerances were also a peculiar requirement if they were destined for centrifuges; the specifications were neither as tight as those previously used by Iraq for centrifuges nor as tight as those typically desired for high-speed rotating equipment.[164] Moreover, the tubes would have required substantial modifications to make them suitable for centrifuge use,[165] and the required modifications would have been inconsistent with the tight manufacturing tolerances demanded.[166] Finally, the tight specifications were not inconsistent with conventional rocket applications; as DOE pointed out to the Senate Select Committee on Intelligence, it is in fact quite common for inexperienced engineers to over-specify tolerances when trying to reverse-engineer equipment.[167]

The focus of certain intelligence agencies on the cost of the tubes offers another example of analysts straining to fit the data into their prevailing theories. The NIE cites reporting indicating that Iraq paid "up to" $17.50 for the tubes, and noted that the willingness to pay this "high" price was indicative of the high priority of the purchase—a fact which, it is suggested, supports the view that the tubes had nuclear application.[168] But in fact this price was not unusually elevated. DOE obtained a price quote from a U.S. manufacturer—without the tight tolerances—of $19.27 per tube.[169]

Adherence to prevailing assumptions also led analysts to discount contrary evidence. Both CIA and DIA were quick to dismiss evidence which tended to show that the tubes were intended for use in Iraq's rocket program, instead attributing such contrary evidence to Iraq's "deception" efforts. Analysts were well aware that Iraq historically had been very successful in "denial and deception"[170] activities, and that, at least in part because of such activities, the Intelligence Community had underestimated the scope of Iraq's pre-Gulf War nuclear program. So analysts, in order to ensure that they were not fooled again, systematically discounted the possibility that the tubes were for rockets.

Indeed, in some instances, analysts went even further, interpreting information that contradicted the prevailing analytical line as intentional deception, and therefore as *support* for the prevailing analytical view. For example, NGIC characterized the Iraqi claim that the tubes were for use in tactical rockets as "a poorly disguised cover story," reasoning that Iraq was claiming such an end-use for the tubes because Iraq was aware that its intentions to use the tubes in a nuclear centrifuge application "have been compromised."[171] CIA also noted in a Senior Executive Memorandum that Iraq "has established a cover story...to disguise the true nuclear end use" for the aluminum tubes, explaining that Iraq may be exploiting press reports regarding the disagreement within the Intelligence Community about the tubes.[172] In some quarters, then, the thesis that the tubes were destined for centrifuges took on the quality of a hypothesis that literally could not be disproved: both confirming and contradictory facts were construed as supporting evidence.[173]

The unwillingness to question prevailing assumptions that Iraq was attempting to reconstitute its nuclear program therefore resulted in faulty analysis of the aluminum tubes. While CIA analysts now agree with the ISG position that the tubes were most likely intended for use in rockets rather than in centrifuge applications,[174] as of March 2005, CIA had still not published a reassessment of its position on the tubes.[175]

Nuclear Weapons Finding 2

In addition to citing the aluminum tubes, the NIE's judgment that Iraq was attempting to reconstitute its nuclear weapons program also referred to additional streams of intelligence. These other streams, however, were very thin, and the limited value of that supporting intelligence was inadequately conveyed in the October 2002 NIE and in other Intelligence Community products.

Nuclear Weapons Finding 3

The other indications of reconstitution—aside from the aluminum tubes—did not themselves amount to a persuasive case for a reconstituted Iraqi nuclear program. In light of the tenuousness of this other information, DOE's argument that the aluminum tubes were not for centrifuges but that Iraq was, based on these other streams of information, reconstituting its nuclear program was a flawed analytical position.

Until now, this review has focused on flaws in the Intelligence Community's assessment concerning the likely uses of the aluminum tubes—the central basis for the overall judgment that Iraq was reconstituting. But the Intelligence Community also identified in the NIE other evidence to support this conclusion, including Iraq's attempts to procure other dual-use items needed for a gas centrifuge such as magnets and balancing machines, efforts to reconstitute its nuclear cadre, and activity at suspect sites. This evidence, however, was based on thin streams of reporting (and indeed, as will be shown, the NIE's recitation of this evidence was also marred by inaccuracies).[176] Analysts are of course often called upon to make judgments based on limited information, particularly on difficult targets such as Iraq's nuclear program. With that said, the NIE too often failed to communicate the paucity of intelligence supporting its assessments and also contained several inaccurate statements.

For example, the NIE indicated that according to sensitive reporting, Saddam Hussein was "personally interested in the procurement of aluminum tubes."[177] This sensitive reporting was a single report from a liaison service which reported that Saddam was "closely following" the purchase of the tubes.[178] Yet even this single report was under dispute. According to one CIA officer, it was the service's intelligence officer who said Saddam was following the purchase, although another CIA officer at the meeting remembered the exchange differently.[179] Even though fundamental doubts existed about the validity and ultimate source of this information, CIA was not able to clarify this point (which was understandable, given the uncertainties inherent in working with liaison services) and allowed the NIE to use the information without reflecting this uncertainty (which was not understandable).[180]

In other places, the NIE's assertions concerning Iraq's nuclear program were simply factually incorrect. First, the NIE pointed to Iraq's attempts to procure a permanent magnet production capability as evidence that Iraq was reconstituting its uranium enrichment program. It noted that "a large number of personnel for the new production facility worked in Iraq's pre-Gulf War centrifuge program."[181] This, however, was a mistake; the National Intelligence Officer (NIO) for Strategic and Nuclear Programs subsequently noted that the workers had not been associated with Iraq's centrifuge program but with the former EMIS program.[182] And the NIE misidentified a front company involved in procurement efforts and the items being procured; the company involved in the initial aluminum tube procurement was seeking high-speed spin testing machines, while another company, also involved in tube procurement, was seeking balancing machines.[183]

In light of this, DOE's position on Iraqi nuclear reconstitution appears rather dubious. DOE was alone in its view that these other procurement attempts, combined with the later-recalled reporting regarding uranium from Africa, provided sufficient evidence to conclude that Iraq was reconstituting. Leaving aside the factual errors noted above, there was no evidence that Iraq had actually obtained the dual-use items it was seeking, and DOE conceded that there was no evidence that the magnets Iraq was seeking were intended for the nuclear program.[184] With respect to the alleged uranium enrichment procurement efforts in Africa, DOE reasoned that any indication that Iraq was attempting to procure uranium covertly would be a significant indication of Iraq's intention to pursue a nuclear program.[185]

The gossamer nature of the evidence relied upon by DOE, and the doubts expressed about the attempts to procure uranium from Africa long before the reporting was recalled (more in a moment about this) had led senior officials in other agencies to question the substantive coherence of DOE's position. The former NIO for Strategic and Nuclear Programs, for one, said that he had not fully understood the logic supporting DOE's conclusion that Iraq was reconstituting despite specifically questioning DOE on this point during the NIE coordination meeting.[186] Similarly, a former senior intelligence officer remarked in November 2004 that DOE's position had "made sense politically but not substantively."[187] In fact, the DOE intelligence analyst who participated in the coordination meetings for the NIE—while maintaining that there was no political pressure on DOE, direct or indirect, to agree with the reconstitution conclusion at the NIE coordination meeting—conceded to this Commission that "DOE didn't want to come out before the war and say [Iraq] wasn't reconstituting."[188]

As mentioned above, DOE's position rested in part on a piece of evidence not relied upon by any of the other intelligence agencies in the NIE—that of Iraq's attempts to procure uranium from Niger.[189] This evidence was unconfirmed at the time of the NIE and subsequently shelved because of severe doubts about its veracity. As will be shown in the next section, the Intelligence Community was right to have its doubts about this story, and DOE was wrong to rely on it as an alternative piece of evidence confirming Iraq's interest in reconstitution.

Nuclear Weapons Finding 4

The Intelligence Community failed to authenticate in a timely fashion transparently forged documents purporting to show that Iraq had attempted to procure uranium from Niger.

Intelligence Community agencies did not effectively authenticate the documents regarding an alleged agreement for the sale of uranium yellowcake from Niger to Iraq. The President referred to this alleged agreement in his State of the Union address on January 28, 2003—evidence for which the Intelligence Community later concluded was based on forged documents.[190]

To illustrate the failures involved in vetting this information, some details about its collection require elaboration. The October 2002 NIE included the statement that Iraq was "trying to procure uranium ore and yellowcake" and that "a foreign government service" had reported that "Niger planned to send several tons" of yellowcake to Iraq.[191] The statement about Niger was based primarily on three reports provided by a liaison intelligence service to CIA in late 2001 and early 2002.[192] One of these reports explained that, as of early 1999, the Iraqi Ambassador to the Vatican planned to visit Niger on an official mission. The report noted that subsequently, during meetings on July 5-6, 2000, Niger and Iraq had signed an agreement for the sale of 500 tons of uranium.[193] This report stated that it was providing the "verbatim text" of the agreement.[194] The information was consistent with reporting from 1999 showing that a visit to Niger was being arranged for the Iraqi Ambassador to the Vatican.[195]

Subsequently, Vice President Cheney requested follow-up information from CIA on this alleged deal.[196] CIA decided to contact the former U.S. ambassador to Gabon, Ambassador Joseph Wilson, who had been posted to Niger early in his career and maintained contacts there, to see if he would be amenable to traveling to Niger. Ambassador Wilson agreed to do so and, armed with CIA talking points, traveled to Niger in late February 2002 and met with former Nigerien officials.[197]

Following the trip, CIA disseminated an intelligence report in March 2002 based on its debriefing of Ambassador Wilson.[198] The report carried the caveat that the individuals from whom the Ambassador obtained the information were aware that their remarks could reach the U.S. government and "may have intended to influence as well as to inform."[199] According to this report, the former Prime Minister of Niger said that he was not aware of any contracts for uranium that had been signed between Niger and any rogue states. He noted that if there had been such an agreement, he would have been aware of it.[200] He said, however, that in June 1999 he met with an Iraqi delegation to discuss "expanding commercial relations" between Niger and Iraq, which the Prime Minister interpreted as meaning the delegation wanted to discuss yellowcake sales. The Prime Minister let the matter drop, however, because of the United Nations sanctions on Iraq.[201]

The British Government weighed in officially on the Niger subject on September 24, 2002, when it disseminated a white paper on Iraq's WMD programs stating that "there is intelligence that Iraq has sought the supply of significant quantities of uranium from Africa."[202]

The story grew more complicated when, on October 9, 2002, several days after the NIE was published, an Italian journalist provided a package of documents to the U.S. Embassy in Rome, including documents related to the alleged agreement for the sale of uranium from Niger to Iraq.[203] The State Department passed these documents on to elements of the CIA. Although the documents provided to the Embassy by the Italian journalist related to the purported agreement, these elements of the CIA did not retain copies of the documents or forward them to CIA Headquarters because they had been forwarded through Embassy channels to the State Department.[204]

WINPAC analysts, for their part, only requested and obtained copies of the documents several months later—after State's INR had alerted the Intelligence Community in October 2002 that it had serious doubts about the authenticity of the documents.[205] And, even after this point, CIA continued to respond to policymakers' requests for follow-up on the uranium deal with its established line of analysis, without attempting to authenticate the documents and without noting INR's doubts about the authenticity of the information—despite not having looked at the documents with a critical eye.

For example, in mid-January 2003, the Chairman of the Joint Chiefs of Staff requested information—other than information about the aluminum tubes— about why analysts thought Iraq was reconstituting its nuclear program. In response, WINPAC published a current intelligence paper pointing to Iraqi attempts to procure uranium from several African countries, citing "fragmentary reporting," and making no reference to questions about the authenticity of the source documents.[206] Shortly thereafter, the National Security Council and Office of the Secretary of Defense requested information from the NIO for Strategic and Nuclear Programs and from DIA, respectively, on the uranium deal. The responses included information based on the original reporting, without any mention of the questions about the authenticity of the information.[207]

The CIA had still not evaluated the authenticity of the documents when it coordinated on the State of the Union address, in which the President noted that the "British government has learned that Saddam Hussein recently sought significant quantities of uranium from Africa."[208] Although there is some disagreement about the details of the coordination process, no one in the Intelligence Community had asked that the line be removed.[209] At the time of the State of the Union speech, CIA analysts continued to believe that Iraq probably was seeking uranium from Africa, although there was growing concern among some CIA analysts that there were problems with the reporting.[210]

The IAEA, after receiving copies of the documents from the United States, reviewed them and immediately concluded that they were forgeries.[211] As the IAEA found, the documents contained numerous indications of forgery— flaws in the letterhead, forged signatures, misspelled words, incorrect titles for individuals and government entities, and anomalies in the documents' stamps.[212] The documents also contained serious errors in content. For example, the document describing the agreement made reference to the legal authority for the agreement, but referenced an out-of-date statutory provision. The document also referred to a meeting that took place on "Wednesday, July 7, 2000" even though July 7, 2000 was a Friday.[213]

When it finally got around to reviewing the documents during the same time period, the CIA agreed that they were not authentic. Moreover, the CIA concluded that the original reporting was based on the forged documents and was thus itself unreliable.[214] CIA subsequently issued a recall notice at the beginning of April, 2003 for the three original reports, noting that "the foreign government service may have been provided with fraudulent reporting."[215] On June 17, 2003, CIA produced a memorandum for the Director of Central Intelligence (DCI) stating that "since learning that the Iraq-Niger uranium deal was based on false documents earlier this spring we no longer believe that there is sufficient other reporting to conclude that Iraq pursued uranium from abroad."[216] The NIO for Strategic and Nuclear Programs also briefed the Senate and House Intelligence Committees, on June 18 and 19, respectively, on the CIA's conclusions in this regard.[217]

Given that there were already doubts about the reliability of the reporting on the uranium deal, the Intelligence Community should have reviewed the documents to evaluate their authenticity as soon as they were made available in early October 2002, rather than waiting over six months to do so. The failure to review these documents caused the Intelligence Community to rely on dubious information when providing highly important assessments to policymakers about the likelihood that Iraq was reconstituting its nuclear program. The Community's failure to undertake a real review of the documents—even though their validity was the subject of serious doubts—was a major failure of the intelligence system.[218]

BIOLOGICAL WARFARE

Biological Warfare Summary Finding

The Intelligence Community seriously misjudged the status of Iraq's biological weapons program in the 2002 NIE and other pre-war intelligence products. The primary reason for this misjudgment was the Intelligence Community's heavy reliance on a human source—codenamed "Curveball"—whose information later proved to be unreliable.

The Intelligence Community assessed with "high confidence" in the fall of 2002 that Iraq "has" biological weapons, and that "all key aspects" of Iraq's offensive BW program "are active and that most elements are larger and more advanced than they were before the Gulf War."[219] These conclusions were based largely on the Intelligence Community's judgment that Iraq had "transportable facilities for producing" BW agents.[220] That assessment, in turn, was based largely on reporting from a single human source.

Contrary to the Intelligence Community's pre-war assessments, the ISG's post-war investigations concluded that Iraq had unilaterally destroyed its biological weapons stocks and probably destroyed its remaining holdings of bulk BW agent in 1991 and 1992.[221] Moreover, the ISG concluded that Iraq had conducted no research on BW agents since that time, although Iraq had retained some dual-use equipment and intellectual capital.[222] The ISG found no evidence of a mobile BW program.[223]

That Iraq was cooking up biological agents in mobile facilities designed to elude the prying eyes of international inspectors and Western intelligence services was, along with the aluminum tubes, the most important and alarming assessment in the October 2002 NIE. This judgment, as it turns out, was based almost exclusively on information obtained from a single human source—codenamed "Curveball"—whose credibility came into question around the time of the publication of the NIE and collapsed under scrutiny in the months following the war. This section discusses how this ultimately unreliable reporting came to play such a critical role in the Intelligence Community's pre-war assessments about Iraq's BW program. We begin by discussing the evolution of the Intelligence Community's judgments on this issue in the years preceding the second Iraq war; compare these pre-war assessments with what the ISG found; and, finally, offer our conclusions about the Intelligence Community's performance against the Iraqi BW target, focusing in particular on Curveball and the handling of his information by the Intelligence Community.

We note at the outset that this section includes new information about the failure of the Intelligence Community—and particularly of Intelligence Community management—to convey to policymakers serious concerns about Curveball that arose in the months preceding the invasion of Iraq. Although these findings are significant, we believe that other lessons about the Intelligence Community's assessments of Iraq's purported BW programs are the more critical ones. At bottom, the story of the Intelligence Community's performance on BW is one of poor tradecraft by our human intelligence collection agencies; of our intelligence analysts allowing reasonable suspicions about Iraqi BW activity to turn into near certainty; and of the Intelligence Community failing to communicate adequately the limited nature of their intelligence on Iraq's BW programs to policymakers, in both the October 2002 NIE and other contemporaneous intelligence assessments.

The Intelligence Community's Pre-War Assessments

The Intelligence Community's assessment of Iraq's BW program—like its judgments about Iraq's other WMD programs—evolved over time. The October 2002 NIE reflected a shift, however, in the Community's judgments about the state of Iraq's BW program. Previous Community estimates had assessed that Iraq *could* have biological weapons; the October 2002 estimate, in contrast, assessed with "high confidence" that Iraq "has" biological weapons. This shift in view, which began in 2000 and culminated in the October 2002 NIE, was based largely on information from a single source—Curveball—who indicated that Iraq had mobile facilities for producing BW agents.

Background. In the early 1990s, the Intelligence Community knew little about Iraq's BW program.[224] Prior to the Gulf War, the Intelligence Community judged that Iraq was developing several BW agents, including anthrax and botulinum toxin, at a number of facilities.[225] The Intelligence Community further assessed that Iraq might have produced up to 1,000 liters of BW agent, and that Iraq had used some of it to fill aerial bombs and artillery shells. At that time, however, the Community judged that it had insufficient information to make assessments about BW agent testing and deployment of filled munitions.[226] Between 1991 and 1995, the Intelligence Community learned little more about Iraq's BW program. However, there was some additional human intelligence reporting indicating that pre-Gulf War assessments of Iraq's BW program had substantially underestimated the quantities of biological weapons that Iraq had produced. Moreover, this reporting suggested that the Intelligence Community was unaware of some Iraqi BW facilities.[227]

It was not until 1995—when UNSCOM presented the Iraqis with evidence of continuing BW-related imports and Saddam Hussein's son-in-law, Hussein Kamil, defected—that Iraq made substantial declarations to the United Nations about its activities prior to the Gulf War, admitting that it had produced and weaponized BW agents.[228] These declarations confirmed that the Intelligence Community had substantially underestimated the scale and maturity of Iraq's pre-Desert Storm BW program. Iraq had, before the Gulf War, weaponized several agents, including anthrax, botulinum toxin, and aflatoxin; produced 30,165 liters of BW agent; and deployed some of its 157 bombs and 25 missile warheads armed with BW agents to locations throughout Iraq.[229] Following these declarations, the Intelligence Community estimated in 1997 that Iraq was still concealing elements of its BW program, and it assessed that Iraq would likely wait until either sanctions were lifted or the UNSCOM presence was reduced before restarting agent production. [230]

After 1998, the Intelligence Community found it difficult to determine whether activity at known dual-use facilities was related to WMD production. The departed inspectors had never been able to confirm what might be happening at Iraq's suspect facilities. Accordingly, the Intelligence Community noted that it had no reliable intelligence to indicate resumed production of biological weapons, but assessed that in the absence of inspectors Iraq *probably* would expand its BW activities.[231] These assessments were colored by the Community's earlier underestimation of Iraq's programs, its lack of reliable intelligence, and its realization that previous underestimates were due in part to effective deception by the Iraqis.[232] By 1999, the CIA assessed that there was some Iraqi research and development on BW and that Iraq could restart production of biological weapons within a short period of time. The 1999 NIE on Worldwide BW Programs judged that Iraq was "revitalizing its BW program" and was "probably continuing work to develop and produce BW agents."[233]

Growing concern. The Intelligence Community's concern about Iraq's BW program increased in early 2000, and the Community began to adjust upward its estimates of the Iraq BW threat, based on a "substantial volume" of "new information" regarding mobile BW facilities in Iraq.[234] This information came from an Iraqi chemical engineer, subsequently codenamed Curveball, who came to the attention of the Intelligence Community through a foreign liaison service. That liaison service debriefed Curveball and then shared the debriefing results with the United States. The foreign liaison service would not, however, provide the United States with direct access to Curveball. Instead, information about Curveball was passed from the liaison service to DIA's Defense HUMINT Service, which in turn disseminated information about Curveball throughout the Intelligence Community.

Between January 2000 and September 2001, DIA's Defense HUMINT Service disseminated almost 100 reports from Curveball regarding mobile BW facilities in Iraq.[235] These reports claimed that Iraq had several mobile production units and that one of those units had begun production of BW agents as early as 1997.[236]

Shortly after Curveball started reporting, in the spring of 2000, his information was provided to senior policymakers.[237] It was also incorporated into an update to a 1999 NIE on Worldwide BW Programs. The update reported that "new intelligence acquired in 2000…causes [the IC] to adjust our assessment upward of the BW threat posed by Iraq…The new information suggests that Baghdad has expanded its offensive BW program by establishing a large-scale, redundant, and concealed BW agent production capability."[238] In December 2000, the Intelligence Community produced a Special Intelligence Report that was based on reporting from Curveball, noting that "credible reporting from a single source suggests" that Iraq has produced biological agents, but cautioned that "[w]e cannot confirm whether Iraq has produced…biological agents."[239]

By 2001, however, the assessments became more assertive. A WINPAC report in October 2001, also based on Curveball's reporting about mobile facilities, judged "that Iraq continues to produce at least…three BW agents" and possibly two others. This assessment also concluded that "the establishment of mobile BW agent production plants and continued delivery system development provide Baghdad with BW capabilities surpassing the pre-Gulf War era."[240] Similar assessments were provided to senior policymakers.[241] In late

September 2002, DCI Tenet told the Senate's Intelligence and Armed Services Committees (and subsequently the Senate Foreign Relations Committee) that "we know Iraq has developed a redundant capability to produce biological warfare agents using mobile production units."[242]

October 2002 NIE. The October 2002 NIE reflected this upward assessment of the Iraqi BW threat that had developed since Curveball began reporting in January 2000. The October 2002 NIE reflected the shift from the late-1990s assessments that Iraq *could* have biological weapons to the definitive conclusion that Iraq "has" biological weapons, and that its BW program was larger and more advanced than before the Gulf War.[243] Information about Iraq's dual-use facilities and its failure to account fully for previously declared stockpiles contributed to this shift in assessments.[244] The information that Iraq had mobile BW production units, however, was instrumental in adjusting upward the assessment of Iraq's BW threat.[245] And for this conclusion, the NIE relied primarily on reporting from Curveball, who, as noted, provided a large volume of reporting through Defense HUMINT channels regarding mobile BW production facilities in Iraq.[246] Only in May 2004, more than a year after the commencement of Operation Iraqi Freedom, did CIA formally deem Curveball's reporting fabricated and recall it.[247] At the time of the NIE, however, reporting from three other human sources—who provided one report each on mobile BW facilities—was thought to have corroborated Curveball's information about the mobile facilities.[248] These three sources also proved problematic, however, as discussed below.

Another asylum seeker (hereinafter "the second source") reporting through Defense HUMINT channels provided one report in June 2001 that Iraq had transportable facilities for the production of BW.[249] This second source recanted in October 2003, however, and the recantation was reflected in a Defense HUMINT report in which the source flatly contradicted his June 2001 statements about transportable facilities.[250] Though CIA analysts told Commission staff that they had requested that Defense HUMINT follow-up with this second source to ascertain the reasons for his recantation, DIA's Defense HUMINT Service has provided no further information on this issue.[251] Nor, for that matter, was the report ever recalled or corrected.[252]

Another source, associated with the Iraqi National Congress (INC) (hereinafter "the INC source"), was brought to the attention of DIA by Washington-based representatives of the INC. Like Curveball, his reporting was handled by Defense HUMINT. He provided one report that Iraq had decided in 1996 to establish mobile laboratories for BW agents to evade inspectors.[253] Shortly after Defense HUMINT's initial debriefing of the INC source in February 2002, however, a foreign liaison service and the CIA's Directorate of Operations (DO) judged him to be a fabricator and recommended that Defense HUMINT issue a notice to that effect, which Defense HUMINT did in May 2002. Senior policymakers were informed that the INC source and his reporting were unreliable. The INC source's information, however, began to be used again in finished intelligence in July 2002, including the October 2002 NIE, because, although a fabrication notice had been issued several months earlier, Defense HUMINT had failed to recall the reporting.[254]

The classified report here discusses a fourth source (hereinafter "the fourth source") who provided a single report that Iraq had mobile fermentation units mounted on trucks and railway cars.

Post-NIE. After publication of the NIE in October 2002, the Intelligence Community continued to assert that Baghdad's biological weapons program was active and posed a threat, relying on the same set of sources upon which the NIE's judgments were based.[255] For example, a November 2002 paper produced by CIA's Directorate of Intelligence (DI) reiterated the NIE's assessment that Iraq had a "broad range of lethal and incapacitating agents" and that the "BW program is more robust than it was prior to the Gulf War."[256] The piece contended that Iraq was capable of producing an array of agents and probably retained strains of the smallpox virus. It further argued that technological advances increased the potential Iraqi BW threat to U.S. interests. And a February 2003 CIA Intelligence Assessment anticipated Iraqi options for BW (and CW) use against the United States and other members of the Coalition; the report stated that Iraq "maintains a wide range of…biological agents and delivery systems" and enumerated 21 BW agents which it judged Iraq could employ.[257]

Statements about biological weapons also appeared in Administration statements about Iraq in the months preceding the war. Secretary of State Colin Powell's speech to the United Nations Security Council on February 5, 2003, relied on the same human sources relied upon in the NIE.[258] Secretary Powell was not informed that one of these sources—the INC source—had been judged a fabricator almost a year earlier. And as will be discussed at length below, serious doubts about Curveball had also surfaced within CIA's Directorate of Operations at the time of the speech—but these doubts also were not communicated to Secretary Powell before his United Nations address.

Reliance on Curveball's reporting also affected post-war assessments of Iraq's BW program. A May 2003 CIA Intelligence Assessment pointed to the post-invasion discovery of "two probable mobile BW agent productions plants" by Coalition forces in Iraq as evidence that "Iraq was hiding a biological warfare program."[259] Curveball, when shown photos of the trailers, identified components that he said were similar to those on the mobile BW production facilities that he had described in his earlier reporting.[260]

Post-War Findings of the Iraq Survey Group

The Iraq Survey Group found that the Intelligence Community's pre-war assessments about Iraq's BW program were almost entirely wrong. The ISG concluded that "Iraq appears to have destroyed its undeclared stocks of BW weapons and probably destroyed remaining holdings of bulk BW agent" shortly after the Gulf War.[261] According to the ISG, Iraq initially intended to retain elements of its biological weapons program after the Gulf War. UNSCOM inspections proved unexpectedly intrusive, however, and to avoid detection, Saddam Hussein ordered his son-in-law and Minister of the Military Industrial Commission Hussein Kamil to destroy, unilaterally, Iraq's stocks of BW agents.[262] This took place in either the late spring or summer of 1991.[263] But Iraq retained a physical plant at Al-Hakam and the intellectual capital necessary to resuscitate the BW program.[264] Simultaneously, Iraq embarked on an effort to hide this remaining infrastructure and to conceal its pre-war BW-related activities.[265]

In early 1995, however, UNSCOM inspectors confronted Iraqi officials with evidence of 1988 imports of bacterial growth media in quantities that had no civilian use within Iraq's limited biotechnology industry.[266] This confrontation, followed by the defection of Hussein Kamil in August 1995, prompted Iraq to admit that it had produced large quantities of bulk BW agent before the Gulf War.[267] Iraq also released a large cache of documents and issued the first of several "Full, Final and Complete Declaration[s]" on June 22, 1996, further detailing its BW program. UNSCOM subsequently supervised the destruction of BW-related facilities at Al-Hakam in 1996.[268]

The Iraq Survey Group found that the destruction of the Al-Hakam facility effectively marked the end of Iraq's large-scale BW ambitions.[269] The ISG did judge that after 1996 Iraq "continued small-scale BW-related efforts" under the auspices of the Iraqi Intelligence Service, and also retained a trained cadre of scientists who could work on BW programs and some dual-use facilities capable of conversion to small-scale BW agent production.[270] Nevertheless, the ISG "found no direct evidence that Iraq, after 1996, had plans for a new BW program or was conducting BW-specific work for mili tary purposes."[271]

With respect to mobile BW production facilities, the "ISG found no evidence that Iraq possessed or was developing production systems on road vehicles or railway wagons."[272] The ISG's "exhaustive investigation" of the two trailers captured by Coalition forces in spring 2003 revealed that the trailers were "almost certainly designed and built exclusively for the generation of hydrogen." The ISG judged that the trailers "cannot … be part of any BW program."[273]

Analysis of the Intelligence Community's Pre-War Assessments

The Intelligence Community fundamentally misjudged the status of Iraq's BW programs. As the above discussion demonstrates, the central basis for the Intelligence Community's pre-war assessments about Iraq's BW program was the reporting of a single human source, Curveball. This single source, whose reporting came into question in late 2002, later proved to be a fabricator.

Our intelligence agencies get burned by human sources sometimes—it is a fact of life in the murky world of espionage. If our investigation revealed merely that our Intelligence Community had a source who later turned out to be lying, despite the best tradecraft practices designed to ferret out such liars, that would be one thing. But Curveball's reporting became a central part of the Intelligence Community's pre-war assessments through a serious breakdown in several aspects of the intelligence process. The Curveball story is at the same time one of poor asset validation by our human collection agencies; of a tendency of analysts to believe that which fits their theories; of inadequate communication between the Intelligence Community and the policymakers it serves; and, ultimately, of poor leadership and management. This section thus focuses primarily on our investigation of the Curveball episode, and the findings we drew from it.

Biological Warfare Finding 1

The DIA's Defense HUMINT Service's failure even to attempt to validate Curveball's reporting was a major failure in operational tradecraft.

The problems with the Intelligence Community's performance on Curveball began almost immediately after the source first became known to the U.S. government in early 2000. As noted above, Curveball was not a source who worked directly with the United States; rather, the Intelligence Community obtained information about Curveball through a foreign service. The foreign service would not provide the United States with direct access to Curveball, claiming that Curveball would refuse to speak to Americans.[274] Instead, the foreign intelligence service debriefed Curveball and passed the debriefing information to DIA's Defense HUMINT Service, the human intelligence collection agency of the Department of Defense.

The lack of direct access to Curveball made it more difficult to assess his veracity. But such lack of access does not preclude the Intelligence Community from attempting to assess the source's bona fides and the credibility of the source's reporting. Indeed, it is incumbent upon professional intelligence officers to attempt to do so, through a process referred to within the Intelligence Community as "vetting" or "asset validation."

Defense HUMINT, however, did not even attempt to determine Curveball's veracity. A Defense HUMINT official explained to Commission staff that Defense HUMINT believed that it was just a "conduit" for Curveball's reporting—that it had no responsibility for vetting Curveball or validating his information.[275] In Defense HUMINT's view, asset validation is solely the responsibility of analysts—in their judgment if the analysts believe the information is credible, then the source is validated.[276] This line echoes what Defense HUMINT officials responsible for disseminating Curveball's reporting told the Senate Select Committee on Intelligence; they told the Committee that it was not their responsibility to assess the source's credibility, but that it instead was up to the analysts who read the reports to judge the accuracy of the contents.[277]

The Senate Select Committee on Intelligence concluded that this view represents a "serious lapse" in tradecraft, and we agree.[278] Analysts obviously play a crucial role in validating sources by evaluating the credibility of their reporting, corroborating that reporting, and reviewing the body of reporting to ensure that it is consistent with the source's access. But analysts' validation can only extend to whether what a source says is internally consistent, technically plausible, and credible given the source's claimed access. The process of validation also must include efforts by the operational elements to confirm the source's bona fides (*i.e.*, authenticating that the source has the access he claims), to test the source's reliability and motivations, and to ensure that the source is free from hostile control.[279] To be sure, these steps are particularly difficult for a source such as Curveball, to whom the collection agency has no direct access. But human intelligence collectors can often obtain valuable information weighing on even a liaison source's credibility, and the CIA's DO routinely attempts to determine the credibility even of sources to whom it has no direct access. In light of this, we are surprised by the Defense HUMINT's apparent position that it had no responsibility even to *attempt* to validate Curveball.

As a footnote to this episode, while DIA's Defense HUMINT Service felt no obligation to vet Curveball or validate his veracity, it would later appear affronted that another agency— CIA—would try to do so. On February 11, 2003, after questions about Curveball's credibility had begun to emerge, an element of the DO sent a message to Defense HUMINT officials expressing concern that Curveball had not been vetted. The next day the Defense HUMINT division chief who received that message forwarded it by electronic mail to a subordinate, requesting input to answer CIA's query. In that electronic mail message, the Defense HUMINT division chief said he was "shocked" by CIA's suggestion that Curveball might be unreliable. The reply—which the Defense HUMINT official intended for Defense HUMINT recipients only but which was inadvertently sent to CIA as well— observed that "CIA is up to their old tricks" and that CIA did not "have a clue" about the process by which Curveball's information was passed from the foreign service.[280]

> ## Biological Warfare Finding 2
>
> Indications of possible problems with Curveball began to emerge well before the 2002 NIE. These early indications of problems—which suggested unstable behavior more than a lack of credibility—were discounted by the analysts working the Iraq WMD account. But given these warning signs, analysts should have viewed Curveball's information with greater skepticism and should have conveyed this skepticism in the NIE. The analysts' resistance to any information that could undermine Curveball's reliability suggests that the analysts were unduly wedded to a source that supported their assumptions about Iraq's BW programs.

As we have discussed, when information from Curveball first surfaced in early 2000, Defense HUMINT did nothing to validate Curveball's reporting. Analysts within the Intelligence Community, however, did make efforts to assess the credibility of the information provided by Curveball. In early 2000, when Curveball's reporting first surfaced, WINPAC analysts researched previous reporting and concluded that Curveball's information was plausible based upon previous intelligence, including imagery reporting, and the detailed, technical descriptions of the mobile facilities he provided.[281] As a WINPAC BW analyst later told us, there was nothing "obviously wrong" with Curveball's information, and his story—that Iraq had moved to a mobile capability for its BW program in 1995 in order to evade inspectors—was logical in light of other known information.[282]

At about the same time, however, traffic in the CIA's Directorate of Operations began to suggest some possible problems with Curveball.[283] The first CIA concerns about Curveball's reliability arose within the DO in May 2000, when a Department of Defense detailee assigned to the DO met Curveball. The purpose of the meeting was to evaluate Curveball's claim that he had been present during a BW accident that killed several of his coworkers by seeing whether Curveball had been exposed to, or vaccinated against, a BW agent.[284] Although the evaluation was ultimately inconclusive,[285] the detailee raised several concerns about Curveball based on their interaction.

First, the detailee observed that Curveball spoke excellent English during their meeting.[286] This was significant to the detailee because the foreign service had, on several earlier occasions, told U.S. intelligence officials that one reason a meeting with Curveball was impossible was that Curveball did not speak English. Second, the detailee was concerned by Curveball's apparent "hangover" during their meeting. The detailee conveyed these impressions of Curveball informally to CIA officials, and WINPAC BW analysts told Commission staff that they were aware that the detailee was concerned that Curveball might be an alcoholic.[287] This message was eventually re-conveyed to Directorate of Operations supervisors via electronic mail on February 4, 2003—literally on the eve of Secretary Powell's speech to the United Nations. The electronic mail stated, in part:

> I do have a concern with the validity of the information based on Curveball having a terrible hangover the morning of [the meeting]. I agree, it was only a one time interaction, however, he knew he was to have a [meeting] on that particular morning but tied one on anyway. What underlying issues could this be a problem with and how in depth has he been vetted by the [foreign liaison service]?[288]

By early 2001, the DO was receiving operational messages about the foreign service's difficulties in handling Curveball, whom the foreign service reported to be "out of control," and whom the service could not locate.[289] This operational traffic regarding Curveball was shared with WINPAC's Iraq BW analysts because, according to WINPAC analysts, the primary BW analyst who worked on the Iraq issue had close relations with the DO's Counterproliferation Division (the division through which the operational traffic was primarily handled).[290] This and other operational information was not, however, shared with analysts outside CIA.[291]

A second warning on Curveball came in April 2002, when a foreign intelligence service, which was also receiving reporting from Curveball, told the CIA that, in its view, there were a variety of problems with Curveball. The foreign service began by noting that they were "inclined to believe that a significant part of [Curveball's] reporting is true" in light of his detailed technical descriptions.[292] In this same message, however, the foreign service noted that it was "not convinced that Curveball is a wholly reliable source," and that "elements of [Curveball's] behavior strike us as typical of individuals we would normally assess as fabricators."[293] Even more specifically, the foreign service noted several inconsistencies in Curveball's reporting which caused the foreign service "to have doubts about Curveball's reliability."[294] It should be noted here that, like the handling foreign service, this other service contin-ued officially to back Curveball's reporting throughout this period.

Again, these concerns about Curveball were shared with CIA analysts work-ing on the BW issue.[295] But none of the expressed concerns overcame ana-lysts' ultimate confidence in the accuracy of his information. Specifically, analysts continued to judge his information credible based on their assess-ment of its detail and technical accuracy, corroborating documents, confirma-tion of the technical feasibility of the production facility designs described by Curveball, and reporting from another human source, the fourth source men-tioned above.[296] But it should be noted that during the pre-NIE period—in addition to the more general questions about Curveball's credibility discussed above—at least some evidence had emerged calling into question the sub-stance of Curveball's reporting about Iraq's BW program as well.[297]

Specifically, a WINPAC BW analyst told us that two foreign services had both noted in 2001 that Curveball's description of the facility he claimed was involved in the mobile BW program was contradicted by imagery of the site, which showed a wall across the path that Curveball said the mobile trailers traversed. Intelligence Community analysts "set that information aside," how-ever, because it could not be reconciled with the rest of Curveball's informa-tion, which appeared plausible.[298] Analysts also explained away this discrepancy by noting that Iraq had historically been very successful in "denial and deception" activities and speculated that the wall spotted by imag-ery might be a temporary structure put up by the Iraqis to deceive U.S. intelli-gence efforts.[299]

Analysts' use of denial and deception to explain away discordant evidence about Iraq's BW programs was a recurring theme in our review of the Com-munity's performance on the BW question.[300] Burned by the experience of being wrong on Iraq's WMD in 1991 and convinced that Iraq was restarting its programs, analysts dismissed indications that Iraq had actually abandoned its prohibited programs by chalking these indicators up to Iraq's well-known denial and deception efforts. In one instance, for example, WINPAC analysts described reporting from the second source indicating Iraq was filling BW warheads at a transportable facility near Baghdad. When imagery was unable to locate the transportable BW systems at the reported site, analysts assumed this was not because the activity was not taking place, but rather because Iraq was hiding activities from U.S. satellite overflights.[301] This tendency was best encapsulated by a comment in a memorandum prepared by the CIA for a senior policymaker: "Mobile BW information comes from [several] sources, one of whom is credible and the other is of undetermined reliability. We have raised our collection posture in a bid to locate these production units, but years of fruitless searches by UNSCOM indicate they are well hidden."[302] Again, the analysts appear never to have considered the idea that the searches were fruitless because the weapons were not there.

Biological Warfare Finding 3

The October 2002 NIE failed to communicate adequately to policymakers both the Community's near-total reliance on Curveball for its BW judgments, and the serious problems that characterized Curveball as a source.

The Community erred in failing to highlight its overwhelming reliance on Curveball for its BW assessments. The NIE judged that Iraq "has transportable facilities for producing bacterial and toxin BW agents" and attributed this judgment to multiple sources.[303] In reality, however, on the topic of mobile BW facilities Curveball provided approximately 100 detailed reports on the subject, while the second and fourth sources each provided a single report. (As will be discussed in greater detail below, the reporting of another source—the INC source—had been deemed a fabrication months earlier, but nonetheless found its way into the October 2002 NIE.)[304] The presentation of the material as attributable to "multiple sensitive sources," however, gave the impression that the support for the BW assessments was more broadly based than was in fact the case. A more accurate presentation would have allowed senior officials to see just how narrow the evidentiary base for the judgments on Iraq's BW programs actually was.

Other contemporaneous assessments about Iraq's BW program also reflect this problem. For example, the Intelligence Community informed senior policymakers in July 2002 that CIA judged that "Baghdad has transportable production facilities for BW agents...according to defectors."[305] Again, while three "defector" sources (Curveball, the second source, and the INC source) are cited in this report, Curveball's reporting was the overwhelmingly predominant source of the information.

And the NIE should not only have emphasized its reliance on Curveball for its BW judgments; it should also have communicated the limitations of the source himself. The NIE, for instance, described him as "an Iraqi defector deemed credible by the [Intelligence Community]."[306] The use of the term "credible" was apparently meant to imply only that Curveball's reporting was technically plausible. To a lay reader, however, it implied a broader judgment as to the source's general reliability. This description obscured a number of salient facts that, given the Community's heavy reliance upon his reporting, would have been highly important for policymakers to know—including the fact that the Community had never gained direct access to the source and that he was known at the time to have serious handling problems. While policymakers may still have credited his reporting, they would at least have been warned about the risks in doing so.

Biological Warfare Finding 4

Beginning in late 2002, some operations officers within the regional division of the CIA's Directorate of Operations that was responsible for relations with the liaison service handling Curveball expressed serious concerns about Curveball's reliability to senior officials at the CIA, but these views were either (1) not thought to outweigh analytic assessments that Curveball's information was reliable or (2) disregarded because of managers' assessments that those views were not sufficiently convincing to warrant further elevation.

After the NIE was published, but before Secretary Powell's speech to the United Nations, more serious concerns surfaced about Curveball's reliability. These concerns were never brought to Secretary Powell's attention, however. Precisely how and why this lapse occurred is the subject of dispute and conflicting memories. This section provides only a brief summary of the key events in this complicated saga.

The NIE went to press in early October 2002, but its publication did not end the need to scrutinize Curveball's reliability. To improve the CIA's confidence in Curveball, the CIA's Deputy Director for Operations (DDO), James Pavitt, sought to press the foreign intelligence service for access to Curveball.[307] Mr. Pavitt's office accordingly asked the chief ("the division chief") of the DO's regional division responsible for relations with the liaison service ("the division") to meet with a representative of the foreign intelligence service to make the request for access.[308] According to the division chief, he met with the representative in late September or early October 2002.[309]

At the lunch, the division chief raised the issue of U.S. intelligence officials speaking to Curveball directly. According to the division chief, the representative of the foreign intelligence service responded with words to the effect of "You don't want to see him [Curveball] because he's crazy." Speaking to him would be, in the representative of the foreign service's words, "a waste of time." The representative, who said that he had been present for debriefings of Curveball, continued that his intelligence service was not sure whether Curveball was actually telling the truth and, in addition, that he had serious doubts about Curveball's mental stability and reliability; Curveball, according to the representative, had had a nervous breakdown. Further, the representative said that he worried that Curveball was "a fabricator." The representative cautioned the division chief, however, that the foreign service would publicly and officially deny these views if pressed. The representative told the division chief that the rationale for such a public denial would be that the foreign service did not wish to be embarrassed.[310] According to the division chief, he passed the information to three offices: up the line to the office of CIA's Deputy Director for Operations;[311] down the line to his staff, specifically the division's group chief ("the group chief") responsible for the liaison country's region;[312] and across the agency to WINPAC.[313] At the time, the division chief thought that the information was "no big deal" because he did not realize how critical Curveball's reporting was to the overall case for Iraqi possession of a biological weapons program.[314] He assumed there were other streams of reporting to buttress the Intelligence Community's assessments. He could not imagine, he said, that Curveball was "it."[315]

Several months later, prompted by indications that the President or a senior U.S. official would soon be making a speech on Iraq's WMD programs, one of the executive assistants for the then-Deputy Director of Central Intelligence (DDCI) John McLaughlin[316] met with the group chief to look into the Curveball information.[317] This meeting took place on December 18, 2002.[318] Although the executive assistant did not specifically recall the meeting when he spoke with Commission staff,[319] an electronic mail follow-up from the meeting—which was sent to the division chief and the group chief—makes clear that the meeting was called to discuss Curveball and the public use of his information.[320]

As a result of this meeting, the division sent a message that same afternoon to the CIA's station in the relevant country again asking that the foreign intelligence service permit the United States to debrief Curveball.[321] The message stressed the importance of gaining access to Curveball, and noted the U.S. government's desire to use Curveball's reporting publicly. On December 20, the foreign service refused the request for access, but concurred with the request to use Curveball's information publicly—"with the expectation of source protection."[322]

By this point, it was clear that the division believed there was a serious problem with Curveball that required attention. A second meeting was scheduled on December 19 at the invitation of DDCI McLaughlin's same executive assistant.[323] According to the executive assistant, he called the meeting because it had become apparent to DDCI McLaughlin that Curveball's reporting was significant to the Intelligence Community's judgments on Iraq's mobile BW capability.[324] The invitation for the meeting stated that the purpose was to "resolve precisely how we judge Curveball's reporting on mobile BW labs," and that the executive assistant hoped that after the meeting he could "summarize [the] conclusions in a short note to the DDCI."[325] The meeting was attended by the executive assistant, a WINPAC BW analyst, an operations officer from the DO's Counterproliferation Division, and the regional division's group chief. Mr. McLaughlin, who did not attend this meeting, told this Commission that he was not given a written summary of the meeting and did not recall whether any such meeting was held.[326]

Although individuals' recollections of the meeting vary somewhat, there is little disagreement on the meeting's substance. The group chief argued that Curveball had not been adequately "vetted" and that his information should therefore not be relied upon. In preparation for the meeting, the group chief had outlined her concerns in an electronic mail to several officers within the Directorate of Operations—including Stephen Kappes, the then-Associate Deputy Director for Operations. The electronic mail opened with the following (in bold type):

> Although no one asked, it is my assessment that Curve Ball had some access to some of this information and was more forthcoming and cooperative when he needed resettlement assistance; now that he does not need it, he is less helpful, possibly because when hc was being helpful, he was embellishing, a bit. The [foreign service] ha[s] devel-

oped some doubts about him. We have been unable to vet him operationally and know very little about him. The intelligence community has corroborated portions of his reporting with open source information ...and some intelligence (which appears to confirm that things are where he said they were).[327]

At the meeting, the group chief stated that she told the attendees that the division's concerns were based on the foreign service representative's statements to the division chief, the CIA's inability to get access to Curveball, the significant "improvement" in Curveball's reporting over time, the decline of Curveball's reporting after he received the equivalent of a green card, among other reasons.[328] She also recalled telling the attendees the details of the foreign service representative's statements to the division chief.[329] In the group chief's view, she made it clear to all the attendees that the division did not believe that Curveball's information should be relied upon.[330]

With equal vigor, the WINPAC representative argued that Curveball's reporting was fundamentally reliable.[331] According to the WINPAC analyst, Curveball's information was reliable because it was detailed, technically accurate, and corroborated by another source's reporting.[332]

Both the group chief and the WINPAC analyst characterized the exchange as fairly heated.[333] Both of the two primary participants also recalled providing reasons why the other's arguments should not carry the day. Specifically, the group chief says she argued, adamantly, that the supposedly corroborating information was of dubious significance because it merely established that Curveball had been to the location, not that he had any knowledge of BW activities being conducted there. In addition, the group chief questioned whether some of Curveball's knowledge could have come from readily available, open source materials.[334] Conversely, the WINPAC BW analyst says that she questioned whether the group chief had sufficient knowledge of Curveball's reporting to be able to make an accurate assessment of his reliability.[335]

It appears that WINPAC prevailed in this argument. Looking back, the executive assistant who had called the meeting offered his view that the WINPAC BW analyst was the "master of [the Curveball] case," and that he "look[ed] to her for answers."[336] He also noted that the group chief clearly expressed her skepticism about Curveball during the meeting, and that she fundamentally took the position that Curveball's reporting did not "hold up."[337] The executive assistant further said that while the foreign service officially assessed that Curveball was reliable, they also described him as a "handling problem."[338] According to the executive assistant, the foreign service said Curveball was a handling problem because he was a drinker, unstable, and generally difficult to manage. In the executive assistant's view, however, it was impossible to know whether the foreign service's description of Curveball was accurate. Finally, the executive assistant said that he fully recognized Curveball's significance at the time of the meeting; that Curveball "was clearly the most significant source" on BW; and that if Curveball were removed, the BW assessment was left with one other human source, "but not much more."[339]

The following day, the executive assistant circulated a memorandum to the WINPAC BW analyst intended to summarize the prior day's meeting.[340] Perhaps in keeping with his reliance on the WINPAC BW analyst as the "master of the case," the executive assistant's "summary" of the draft of the memorandum, titled "Reliability of Human Reporting on Iraqi Mobile BW Capability," played down the doubts raised by the DO division:

> The primary source of this information is an Iraqi émigré (vice defector) …After an exhaustive review, the U.S. Intelligence Community—[as well as several liaison services]…judged him credible. This judgment was based on:
>
> ■ The detailed, technical nature of his reporting;
>
> ■ [Technical intelligence] confirming the existence/configuration of facilities he described (one Baghdad office building is known to house administrative offices linked to WMD programs);
>
> ■ UNSCOM's discovery of military documents discussing "mobile fermentation" capability;
>
> ■ Confirmation/replication of the described design by U.S. contractors (it works); and
>
> ■ Reporting from a second émigré that munitions were loaded with BW agent from a mobile facility parked[341] within an armaments center south of Baghdad.[342]

The memorandum then continued on to note that "[w]e are handicapped in efforts to resolve legitimate questions that remain about the source's veracity and reporting because the [foreign service] refuses to grant direct access to the source."[343] Later, in the "Questions/Answers" section, the memorandum stated:

> **How/when was the source's reliability evaluated**—[One foreign service] hosted a…meeting in 2001, over the course of which all the participating services judged the core reporting as "reliable." [One of the other services] recently affirmed that view—although the [service] ha[s] declined to provide details of sources who might provide corroboration. Operational traffic…indicates the [hosting foreign service] may now be downgrading its own evaluation of the source's reliability.[344]

It does not appear that this memorandum was circulated further; rather, the executive assistant explained that he would have used the memorandum to brief the DDCI at their daily staff meeting.[345]

Former DDCI McLaughlin, however, said that he did not remember being apprised of this meeting.[346] Mr. McLaughlin told the Commission that, although he remembered his executive assistant at some point making a passing reference to the effect that the executive assistant had heard about some issues with Curveball, he (Mr. McLaughlin) did not remember having ever been told in any specificity about the DO division's doubts about Curveball.[347] Mr. McLaughlin added that, at the same time, he was receiving assurances from the relevant analysts to the effect that Curveball's information appeared good.[348]

At about the same time, the division apparently tried another route to the top. Within a day or so after the December 19 meeting, the division's group chief said that she and the division chief met with James Pavitt (the Deputy Director for Operations) and Stephen Kappes (the Associate Deputy Director for Operations).[349] At this meeting, according to the group chief, she repeated the Division's concerns about Curveball.[350] But according to the group chief, Mr. Pavitt told her that she was not qualified to make a judgment about Curveball, and that judgments about Curveball should be made by analysts.[351]

When asked about this meeting by Commission staff, Mr. Pavitt said that although he knew there were handling problems with Curveball, he did not recall any such meeting with the division chief or the group chief.[352] Mr. Pavitt added, however, that he would have agreed that the call was one for the analysts to make. He also noted that he does not recall being aware, in December 2002, that Curveball was such a central source of information for the Intelligence Community's mobile BW judgments.[353] For his part, Mr. Kappes does not specifically recall this meeting, although he said that the concerns about Curveball were generally known within the CIA. He also said that he did not become aware of the extensive reliance on Curveball until after the war.[354]

That is where matters stood for about a month. But the issue arose once again in January 2003. During December and January, it became clear that the Secretary of State would be making an address on Iraq to the United Nations Security Council and that presenting American intelligence on Iraq's WMD programs would be a major part of the speech. In late January, the Secretary began "vetting" the intelligence in a series of long meetings at the CIA's Langley headquarters. In connection with those preparations, a copy of the speech was circulated so that various offices within CIA could check it for accuracy and ensure that material could be used without inappropriately disclosing sources and methods.[355] As part of that process, the group chief received a copy.[356] According to the group chief, she said that she "couldn't believe" the speech relied on Curveball's reporting, and immediately told the division chief about the situation.[357] The group chief also said that she edited the language in a way that made the speech more appropriate.[358]

According to the division chief, he was given the draft speech by an assistant, and he immediately redacted material based on Curveball's reporting. He then called the DDCI's executive assistant and asked to speak to the DDCI about the speech.[359] When interviewed by Commission staff, the executive assistant did not recall having any such conversation with the division chief, nor did he remember seeing a redacted copy of the speech.[360] However, another Directorate of Operations officer, who was responsible for evaluating the possible damage to DO sources from the release of information in the speech, remembers being approached during this time by the division chief. According to this officer, the division chief said he was concerned about the proposed inclusion of Curveball's information in the Powell speech and that the handling service itself thought Curveball was a "flake."

The DO officer responsible for sources and methods protection summarized these concerns in an electronic mail which he sent to another of the DDCI's aides for passage to the DDCI. The DO officer responsible for sources and methods did not recall that the division chief made any specific redactions of language from the draft.[361] The DDCI's executive assistant has no recollection of such an electronic mail or of any concerns expressed about Curveball.[362]

Later that afternoon, according to the division chief, he met with the DDCI to discuss the speech. The division chief recounted that he told the DDCI that there was a problem with the speech because it relied on information from Curveball, and that—based on his meeting with the foreign intelligence service representative—the division chief thought that Curveball could be a fabricator.[363] Although the division chief told the Commission that he could not remember the DDCI's exact response, he got the impression that this was the first time that the DDCI had heard of a problem with Curveball. Specifically, the division chief recalled that the DDCI, on hearing that Curveball might be a fabricator, responded to the effect of: "Oh my! I hope that's not true."[364] It was also at this time, according to the division chief, that he (the division chief) first learned that Curveball provided the primary support for the Intelligence Community's judgments on BW.

The group chief provided indirect confirmation of the exchange; she remembered the division chief telling her about this exchange shortly after it occurred.[365] Similarly, former DDO James Pavitt told the Commission that he remembered the division chief subsequently relating to him that the division chief had raised concerns about Curveball to the DDCI around the time of the Secretary of State's speech.[366]

By contrast, former DDCI McLaughlin told the Commission that he did not remember any such meeting with the division chief. Specifically, the former DDCI said that he was not aware of the division chief contacting his (Mr. McLaughlin's) executive assistant to set up a meeting about Curveball; there was no such meeting on his official calendar; he could not recall ever talking to the division chief about Curveball; and he was not aware of any recommended redactions of sections of the draft speech based on Curveball's reporting. Moreover, Mr. McLaughlin told the Commission that the division chief never told him that Curveball might be a fabricator.[367] The former DDCI added that it is inconceivable that he would have permitted information to be used in Secretary Powell's speech if reservations had been raised about it.[368]

On January 24, 2003, the CIA sent another message to the CIA's relevant station asking for the foreign intelligence service's "transcripts of actual questions asked of, and response given by, Curveball concerning Iraq's BW program not later than …COB [close of business], 27 January 2003." The message further noted that the CIA had "learned that [the President] intend[ed] to refer to the Curveball information in a planned United Nations General Assembly (UNGA) speech on 29 January 2003." According to the division chief, this message was sent on behalf of the DCI's office, but was "released" by the group chief.[369]

Three days later, on January 27, 2003, the relevant station responded and said that they were still attempting to obtain the transcripts. The message then noted:

> [The foreign liaison service handling Curveball] has not been able to verify his reporting. [This foreign service] has discussed Curveball with US [and others], but no one has been able to verify this information.… The source himself is problematical. Defer to headquarters but to use information from another liaison service's source whose information cannot be verified on such an important, key topic should take the most serious consideration.[370]

Shortly after these messages were exchanged with the relevant station, the division chief told the DDCI's executive assistant that the foreign service would still not provide the CIA with access to Curveball.[371] The division chief also sent an electronic mail—the text of which was prepared by the group chief—to the DDCI's executive assistant from the DO, which noted (in part):

> In response to your note, and in addition to your conversation with [the division chief], we have spoken with [the relevant] Station on Curve Ball:
>
> ■ We are not certain that we know where Curve Ball is...
>
> ■ Curve Ball has a history of being uncooperative. He is seeing the [handling foreign service soon] for more questions. The

[handling foreign service] cannot move the meeting up, we have asked.

- [The foreign service] ha[s] agreed to our using the information publicly, but do[es] not want it sourced back to them. Neither the [foreign service] nor, per [the foreign service's] assessment, Curve Ball, will refute their information if it is made public and is not attributed. Per Station, and us, we should be careful to conceal the origin of the information since if Curve Ball is exposed, the family he left in Iraq will be killed.

- The [handling foreign service] cannot vouch for the validity of the information. They are concerned that he may not have had direct access, and that much of what he reported was not secret. (per WINPAC, the information they could corroborate was in open source literature or was imagery of locations that may not have been restricted.)

- [A magazine says that the handling foreign service has] intelligence information on the mobile poison capabilities of the Iraqis, but that they will not share it.[372]

As a result, according to the division chief, the executive assistant told the division chief that the DDCI would speak to the analysts about the issue.[373] Although the executive assistant did not remember such a conversation, former DDCI McLaughlin told the Commission that he remembered talking to the WINPAC BW analyst responsible for Iraq about Curveball in January or February 2003.[374] Mr. McLaughlin said that he received strong assurances from the WINPAC analyst that the reporting was credible.[375]

By this time, there was less than a week left before Secretary Powell's February 5 speech, and the vetting process was going full-bore.[376] On February 3, 2003, the DDCI's executive assistant who had previously participated in meetings about Curveball sent a memorandum titled "[Foreign service] BW Source" to the division chief.[377] The memorandum, addressed to the division chief, read:

[T]his will confirm the DDCI's informal request to touch base w/ the [relevant] stations once more on the current status/whereabouts of the émigré who reported on the mobile BW labs. A great deal of effort is being expended to vet the intelligence that underlies SecState's upcoming UN presentation. Similarly, we want to take every precaution against unwelcome surprises that might emerge concerning the intel case; clearly, public statements by this émigré, press accounts of his reporting or credibility, or even direct press access to him would cause a number of potential concerns. The DDCI would be grateful for the [Chief of Station's] view on the immediate 'days-after' reaction in [the handling foreign service country] surrounding source of this key BW reporting.[378]

Preparations for the United Nations address culminated with Secretary Powell, Director of Central Intelligence George Tenet, and support staff going to New York City prior to the speech, which was to be delivered on February 5, 2003.[379] Until late in the night on February 4, Secretary Powell and Mr. Tenet continued to finalize aspects of the speech.[380]

According to the division chief, at about midnight on the night before the speech, he was called at home by Mr. Tenet. As the division chief recalls the conversation, Mr. Tenet asked whether the division chief had a contact number for another foreign intelligence service (not the service handling Curveball) so Mr. Tenet could get clearance to use information from a source of that service.[381] The division chief told the Commission that he took the opportunity to ask the DCI about the "[foreign service country] reporting" from the liaison service handling Curveball. Although he did not remember his exact words, the division chief says that he told Mr. Tenet something to the effect of "you know that the [foreign service] reporting has problems."[382] According to the division chief, Mr. Tenet replied with words to the effect of "yeah, yeah," and that he was "exhausted."[383] The division chief said that when he listened to the speech the next day, he was surprised that the information from Curveball had been included.[384]

In contrast to the division chief's version of events, Mr. Tenet stated that while he had in fact called the division chief on the night before Secretary Powell's speech to obtain the telephone number (albeit in the early evening as opposed to midnight) there had been no discussion of Curveball or his reporting.[385] Nor was there any indication that any information in the speech might be suspect. Mr. Tenet noted that it is inconceivable that he would have failed to raise with Secretary Powell any concerns about information in the speech about which Mr. Tenet had been made aware.[386] Moreover, he noted that he had never been made aware of any concerns about Curveball until well after the cessation of major hostilities in Iraq.

In sum, there were concerns within the CIA—and most specifically the Directorate of Operations' division responsible for relations with the handling liaison service—about Curveball and his reporting. On several occasions, operations officers within this division expressed doubts about Curveball's credibility, the adequacy of his vetting, and the wisdom of relying so heavily on his information.

These views were expressed to CIA leadership, including at least the Associate Deputy Director for Operations and the executive assistant to the Deputy Director of Central Intelligence, and likely the Deputy Director for Operations and even—to some degree—mentioned to the Deputy Director of Central Intelligence himself. It would appear, however, that the criticism of Curveball grew less pointed when expressed in writing and as the issue rose through the CIA's chain of command. In other words, although we are confident that doubts about Curveball were expressed in one way or another to the Deputy Director for Central Intelligence, it is less clear whether those doubts were accompanied by the full, detailed panoply of information calling into question Curveball's reliability that was presented to more junior supervisors. We found no evidence that the doubts were conveyed by CIA leadership to policymakers in general—or Secretary Powell in particular.

As the discussion above illustrates, it is unclear precisely how and why these serious concerns about Curveball never reached Secretary Powell, despite his and his staff's vigorous efforts over several days in February 2003 to strip out every dubious piece of information in his proposed speech to the United Nations. It is clear, however, that serious concerns about Curveball were widely known at CIA in the months leading up to Secretary Powell's speech. In our view, the failure to convey these concerns to senior management, or, if such concerns were in fact raised to senior management, the failure to pass that information to Secretary Powell, represents a serious failure of management and leadership.

Biological Warfare Finding 5

CIA management stood by Curveball's reporting long after post-war investigators in Iraq had established that he was lying about crucial issues.

A team of Intelligence Community analysts was dispatched to Iraq in early summer 2003 to investigate the details of Iraq's BW program. The analysts were, in particular, investigating two trailers that had been discovered by Coalition forces in April and May 2003, which at the time were thought to be the mobile BW facilities described by Curveball. As the summer wore on, however, at least one WINPAC analyst who had traveled to Iraq, as well as some DIA and INR analysts, became increasingly doubtful that the trailers were BW-related.[387]

The investigation also called into question other aspects of Curveball's reporting. According to one WINPAC BW analyst who was involved in the investigations, those individuals whom Curveball had identified as having been involved in the mobile BW program "all consistently denied knowing anything about this project."[388] Furthermore, none of the supposed project designers even knew who Curveball was, which contradicted Curveball's claim that he had been involved with those individuals in developing the mobile BW program.[389]

Additional research into Curveball's background in September 2003 revealed further discrepancies in his claims. For example, WINPAC analysts interviewed several of Curveball's supervisors at the government office where he had worked in Iraq. Curveball had claimed that this office had commenced a secret mobile BW program in 1995. But interviews with his supervisors, as well as friends and family members, confirmed that Curveball had been fired from his position in 1995.[390] Moreover, one of Curveball's family members noted that he had been out of Iraq for substantial periods between 1995 and 1999, times during which Curveball had claimed he had been working on BW projects.[391] In particular, Curveball claimed to have been present at the site of a BW production run when an accident occurred in 1998, killing 12 workers.[392] But Curveball was not even in Iraq at that time, according to information supplied by family members and later confirmed by travel records.[393]

By the end of October 2003, the WINPAC analysts conducting these investigations reported to the head of the ISG that they believed Curveball was a fabricator and that his reporting was "all false." But other WINPAC analysts, as well as CIA headquarters management, continued to support Curveball.[394] By January 2004, however, when CIA obtained travel records confirming that Curveball had been out of Iraq during the time he claimed to have been working on the mobile BW program, most analysts became convinced that Curveball had fabricated his reporting.[395]

Mr. Tenet was briefed on these findings on February 4, 2004. CIA management, however, was still reluctant to "go down the road" of admitting that Curveball was a fabricator.[396] According to WINPAC analysts, CIA's DI management was slow in retreating from Curveball's information because of political concerns about how this would look to the "Seventh Floor," the floor at Langley where CIA management have their offices, and to "downtown." CIA's Inspector General, in his post-war Inspection Report on WINPAC, concluded that "the process [of retreating from intelligence products derived from Curveball reporting] was drawn out principally due to three factors: (1) senior managers were determined to let the ISG in Iraq complete its work before correcting the mobile labs analysis; (2) the CIA was in the midst of trying to gain direct access to Curveball; and (3) WINPAC Biological and Chemical Group (BCG) management was struggling to reconcile strong differences among their BW analysts." Senior managers did not want to disavow Curveball only to find that his story stood up upon direct examination, or to find that "the ISG uncovered further evidence that would require additional adjustments to the story."[397]

Any remaining doubts, however, were removed when the CIA was finally given access to Curveball himself in March 2004. At that time, Curveball's inability to explain discrepancies in his reporting, his description of facilities and events, and his general demeanor led to the conclusion that his information was unreliable.[398] In particular, the CIA interviewers pressed Curveball to explain "discrepancies" between his aforementioned description of the site at Djerf al-Naddaf,[399] which he had alleged was a key locus for transportable BW, and satellite imagery of the site which showed marked differences in layout from that which Curveball described.[400] Specifically, there was a six foot high wall that would have precluded mobile BW trailers from moving into and out of the facility as Curveball had claimed. Curveball was completely unable or unwilling to explain these discrepancies. The CIA concluded that Curveball had fabricated his reporting, and CIA and Defense HUMINT recalled all of it.[401]

The CIA also hypothesized that Curveball was motivated to provide fabricated information by his desire to gain permanent asylum.[402] Despite speculation that Curveball was encouraged to lie by the Iraqi National Congress (INC), the CIA's post-war investigations were unable to uncover any evidence that the INC or any other organization was directing Curveball to feed misleading information to the Intelligence Community.[403] Instead, the post-war investigations concluded that Curveball's reporting was not influenced by, controlled by, or connected to, the INC.[404]

In fact, over all, CIA's post-war investigations revealed that INC-related sources had a minimal impact on pre-war assessments.[405] The October 2002 NIE relied on reporting from two INC sources, both of whom were later deemed to be fabricators. One source—the INC source—provided fabricated reporting on the existence of mobile BW facilities in Iraq. The other source, whose information was provided in a text box in the NIE and sourced to a "defector," reported on the possible construction of a new nuclear facility in Iraq. The CIA concluded that this source was being "directed" by the INC to provide information to the U.S. Intelligence Community.[406] Reporting from these two INC sources had a "negligible" impact on the overall assessments, however.[407]

Biological Warfare Finding 6

In addition to the problems with Curveball, the Intelligence Community—and, particularly, the Defense HUMINT Service—failed to keep reporting from a known fabricator out of finished intelligence on Iraq's BW program in 2002 and 2003.

Another serious flaw affecting the Intelligence Community's pre-war assessments was its inability to keep reporting from a known fabricator out of finished intelligence. Specifically, the INC source, handled by DIA's Defense HUMINT Service, provided information on Iraqi mobile BW facilities that was initially thought to corroborate Curveball's reporting. The INC source was quickly deemed a fabricator in May 2002, however, and Defense

HUMINT issued a fabrication notice but did not recall the reporting on mobile BW facilities in Iraq. Despite the fabrication notice, reporting from the INC source regarding Iraqi mobile BW facilities started to be used again several months later in finished intelligence—eventually ending up in the October 2002 NIE and in Secretary Powell's February 2003 speech to the United Nations Security Council.[408]

This inability to prevent information known to be unreliable from making its way to policymakers was due to flawed processes at DIA's Defense HUMINT Service. Specifically, Defense HUMINT did not have in place a protocol to ensure that once a fabrication notice is issued, all previous reporting from that source is reissued with either a warning that the source might be a fabricator or a notice that the report is being recalled.[409] Though a fabrication notice was sent out, the reporting was never recalled, nor was the fabrication notice electronically attached to the original report. Analysts were thus forced to rely on their memory that a fabrication notice was issued for that source's reporting—a difficult task especially when they must be able to recognize that a particular report is from that source, which is not always obvious from the face of the report.[410]

Some steps have been taken to remedy this procedural problem. First, DIA's Defense HUMINT Service has now taken steps to ensure that reporting from a fabricating source is reissued with either the fabrication notice or recall notice electronically attached, rather than simply issuing a fabrication notice.[411] Second, the Director of the Central Intelligence Agency is currently working to establish Community-wide procedures to ensure that the information technology system links original reports, fabrication notices, and any subsequent recalls or corrections.[412] Unfortunately, however, the Intelligence Community continues to lack a mechanism that electronically tracks the sources for finished intelligence materials or briefings. This makes "walking back" intelligence papers or briefings to policymakers difficult, as there is no way to know which pieces relied upon what information.[413]

This failure properly to inform others that the INC source's reporting was not valid, however, was not merely a technical problem. DIA's Defense HUMINT Service also allowed Secretary Powell to use information from the INC source in his speech to the United Nations Security Council—even though a Defense HUMINT official was present at the coordination session at CIA held before the speech. A Defense HUMINT Division Chief, who was aware of the fabrication notice on the INC source, attended both of the February 2 and 3 coordination meetings for the Powell speech yet failed to alert the Secretary that one of the sources the speech relied upon was a fabricator.[414] That Defense HUMINT official said that he was not aware that the information being discussed came from the INC source, indicating that Defense HUMINT had not adequately prepared itself for the meeting by reviewing the information Secretary Powell was considering using in the speech.[415]

Conclusion

This section has revealed that Intelligence Community management was remiss in not taking action based on expressed concerns about Curveball's reliability. In retrospect, we conclude that the Intelligence Community's leadership should have more aggressively investigated Curveball's bona fides, rather than seeing the confidence of the analysts and the responsible liaison service as sufficient reason to dismiss the rival concerns of the operators and other liaison services. These leaders also should have pushed harder for access to Curveball—even at the cost of significant inter-liaison capital—given that the source's reporting was so critical to the judgment that Iraq was developing a mobile BW capability. After the NIE, CIA leadership should have paid closer heed to mounting concerns from the DO and, at the very least, informed senior policymakers about these concerns.

This said, the Community's failure to get the Iraq BW question right was not at its core the result of these managerial shortcomings. We need more and better human intelligence, but all such sources are inherently uncertain. Even if there had not been—as there was—affirmative reason to doubt Curveball's reporting, it is questionable whether such a broad conclusion (that Iraq had an active biological weapons production capability) should have been based almost entirely on the evidence of a single source to whom the U.S. Intelligence Community had never gained access. The Intelligence Community's failure to get the BW question right stemmed, first and foremost, from the strong prevailing assumptions about Iraq's intentions and behavior that led the Intelligence Community to conclude that Curveball's reporting was sufficient evidence to judge with "high confidence" that Iraq's offensive BW program was active and more advanced than it had been before the first Gulf War. The Intelligence Community placed too much weight on one source to whom the Community lacked direct access—and did so without making clear to policymakers the extent of the judgment's reliance on this single, unvetted source.

CHEMICAL WARFARE

Chemical Warfare Summary Finding

The Intelligence Community erred in its 2002 NIE assessment of Iraq's alleged chemical warfare program. The Community's substantial overestimation of Iraq's chemical warfare program was due chiefly to flaws in analysis and the paucity of quality information collected.

In the fall of 2002, the Intelligence Community concluded with "high confidence" that Iraq had chemical warfare agents (CW), and further assessed that it had "begun renewed production of mustard, sarin, GF (cyclosarin), and VX."[416] Although the NIE cautioned that the Intelligence Community had "little specific information on Iraq's CW stockpile," it estimated that "Saddam probably [had] stocked at least 100 metric tons (MT) and possibly as much as 500 MT of CW agents."[417] The Community further judged that "much of" Iraq's CW stockpiles had been produced in the past year, and that Iraq had "rebuilt key portions of its CW infrastructure." [418]

After the war, the ISG concluded—contrary to the Intelligence Community's pre-war assessments—that Iraq had unilaterally destroyed its undeclared CW stockpile in 1991 and that there were no credible indications that Baghdad had resumed production of CW thereafter.[419] The ISG further found that Iraq had not regained its pre-1991 CW technical sophistication or production capabilities. Further, the ISG found that pre-war concerns of Iraqi plans to use CW if Coalition forces crossed certain defensive "red lines" were groundless; the "red lines" referred to conventional military planning only.[420] Finally, the ISG noted that the only CW it recovered were weapons manufactured before the first Gulf War, and that after 1991 only small, covert labs were maintained to research chemicals and poisons, primarily for intelligence operations.[421] The ISG did conclude, however, that "Saddam never abandoned his intentions to resume a CW effort when sanctions were lifted and conditions were judged favorable," and that Iraq's post-1995 infrastructure improvements "would have enhanced Iraq's ability to produce CW" if it chose to do so.[422]

The Intelligence Community's errors on Iraq's chemical weapons were, not unlike its errors on Iraq's nuclear and biological programs, heavily influenced by a single factor. In the case of chemical weapons, the factor was the Community's over-reliance on dubious imagery indicators. At the same time, the Community's chemical weapons assessment was further led astray by breakdowns in communication between collectors and analysts and a paucity of supporting human and signals intelligence. All of this played a part in leading the Community to assess, incorrectly, that Iraq was stockpiling and producing chemical agents. And while a chemical warfare program is difficult to distinguish from a legitimate chemical infrastructure, the roots of the Community's failures reached well beyond such difficulties.

This section opens with a careful look at the Intelligence Community's assessments of Iraq's chemical program dating back to the end of the first Gulf War and reaching forward to the beginning of Operation Iraqi Freedom. The chapter then shifts to a detailed summary of the findings of the ISG regarding Iraq's alleged chemical warfare program. It then offers the Commission's findings from its in-depth study of the performance of the Intelligence Community on this subject, focusing especially on over-reliance on faultily-used imagery indicators and on the poverty of human and signals intelligence.

The Intelligence Community's Pre-War Assessments

The Intelligence Community's assessment of Iraq's CW programs and capabilities remained relatively stable during the 1990s, judging that Iraq retained a modest capability to restart a chemical warfare program. The October 2002 NIE therefore marked a shift from previous assessments in that it concluded that Iraq had actually begun renewed production of chemical agents on a sizable scale.[423] This shift was based primarily on imagery, although analysts also saw support for their assessment in a small stream of human and signals intelligence on Iraq's CW capabilities. [424]

Background. For more than ten years, the Intelligence Community believed that Iraq retained the capability to jumpstart its CW program. After Operation Desert Storm in 1991, the Community judged that Iraq retained CW munitions and CW-related materials; the Community based these judgments primarily on accounting discrepancies between Iraq's declarations about its chemical weapons program and what UNSCOM had actually discovered.[425] As with assessments of Iraq's nuclear and biological weapons programs, the conclusion that Iraq still had CW munitions was "reinforced by Iraq's continuing efforts to frustrate" United Nations inspectors.[426] Encapsulating this line of reasoning, in 1995 the CIA judged that Iraq could "begin producing [chemical] agent in a matter of weeks after a decision to do so," based on the assessment that Iraq had "sequestered ...at least some tens of metric tons" of CW precursors.[427] This assessment cautioned, however, that building Iraq's "CW program to its previous levels" would require two to three years.[428]

Mid-1990s: Growing concern. The Intelligence Community's understanding of Iraq's CW program was altered with the defection in August 1995 of Hussein Kamil, the head of Iraq's Military Industrialization Committee and, as such, the head of Iraq's WMD programs. Among a host of damning revelations, Kamil released details previously unknown to the U.S. Intelligence Community about Iraq's pre-1991 production and use of VX nerve gas. More specifically, Iraq subsequently admitted that it had worked on in-flight mixing of binary CW weapons before the Gulf War, produced larger amounts of VX agent than previously admitted, and perfected long-term storage of a VX precursor. These admissions about Iraqi work on VX—a potent nerve agent and an advanced chemical weapon—all played an important role in shaping subsequent Intelligence Community assessments about Iraq's CW program.[429]

Two further revelations about the extent of Iraq's pre-1991 CW efforts also markedly influenced the Community's view of Iraq's CW programs. First, in June 1998, U.S. tests of warhead fragments from an Iraqi al-Hussein missile yielded traces of degraded VX.[430] This finding was noteworthy to Community analysts because it established beyond any doubt (in analysts' eyes) that Iraq, before 1991, had successfully weaponized VX—a technical advance that Iraq refused to admit in its United Nations declarations both before and after the United States became aware of the test results.[431]

Second, in July 1998, weapons inspectors found documents—now commonly known as the "Air Force Documents"—that detailed Iraqi CW use in the Iran-Iraq War.[432] This finding was significant because the documents indicated Iraq had expended far fewer CW munitions in the Iran-Iraq War than previously thought, thus suggesting that Iraq possessed more *unexpended* CW munitions than analysts believed. Analysts lent additional credence to the information because Iraqi officials refused to let inspectors actually keep the relevant document, which suggested to analysts that the documents were incriminating and important.[433] Though both of these revelations concerned Iraq's pre-1991 CW effort, analysts saw them as lending support to the assessment that Iraq was continuing its deliberate efforts to obscure elements of its CW capabilities.

By 1998, the Intelligence Community was continuing to assess that Baghdad retained "key elements of its CW program including personnel, production data, and hidden stocks of production equipment and precursor chemicals" and that "Iraq could begin limited CW agent production within weeks after United Nations sanctions are lifted and intrusive inspections cease."[434] The Community noted, however, that it lacked "reporting to confirm whether [CW] production [was] taking place."[435]

2001-2002: Little change. The Community continued through 2001 to note that there was no evidence that Iraq had started large-scale production of CW.[436] Though analysts continued to believe that Iraq's *capability* to produce CW was increasing, primarily through the development of an indigenous chemical industry, and that Iraq might have engaged in small-scale production,[437] the Community continued to assess that Iraq had not restarted large-scale production.[438] Even after the terrorist attacks of September 11, 2001— when the Intelligence Community detected what it determined to be the dispersal of Iraqi military units in anticipation of U.S. military strikes[439]—the CIA found no evidence that the munitions Iraq was moving were CW-related.[440] And additional reporting during this time did not reveal whether certain suspect sites were actively engaged in CW weapons production— although it remained impossible to determine whether dual-use precursor chemicals were being produced for illicit purposes.[441]

With respect to possible CW stockpiles, as of 2002 the Community assessed that Iraq possessed between 10 and 100 metric tons of CW agent and that it might have had sufficient precursors to produce an additional 200 metric tons.[442] This estimated stockpile was smaller than the stockpiles Iraq possessed before the Gulf War, as an early 2002 Senior Executive Memorandum noted.[443] But according to a CIA analyst's mid-2002 briefing to senior officials, Iraq could restart CW production in a matter of days by using dual-use facilities and hidden precursors.[444] These assessments, however, did not go so far as to conclude that Iraq had restarted production or, relatedly, had sizable CW stockpiles.

The October 2002 NIE. The October 2002 NIE reflected a shift in the Intelligence Community's judgment about Iraq's CW program in two ways: (1) the NIE assessed that Iraq had large stockpiles of CW; and (2) the NIE unequivocally stated that Iraq had restarted CW production.[445]

Regarding stockpiles, the NIE stated that "[a]lthough we have little specific information on Iraq's CW stockpile, Saddam probably has stocked at least 100 metric tons and possibly as much as 500 metric tons of CW agents—much of it added in the last year."[446] This judgment represented a significant increase in the Intelligence Community's estimate of the size of Iraq's CW stockpile.

This stockpile estimate rested primarily on Iraqi accounting discrepancies, Iraq's CW production capacity, estimates of Iraqi precursor stocks, and—at the upper limit (500 metric tons)—on practical considerations such as the size of pre-Gulf War stockpiles and Iraq's limited delivery options.[447] This calculation was also informed by the Intelligence Community's assessments of Iraqi military requirements, ammunition demand, and possible changes in Iraqi use doctrine.[448]

The lower end of this stockpile range (100 metric tons) was premised on the aforementioned 1999 estimate that Iraq possessed between 10 and 100 metric tons of CW agents and that Iraq "could" produce an additional 200 tons of agents "using unaccounted-for precursor chemicals."[449] This 1999 estimate was itself premised on previous Iraqi CW accounting irregularities.[450] The Community assessments of the range of Iraq's CW stockpile thus rested largely on what analysts estimated Iraq could do with unaccounted-for precursors and production capabilities.

In addition to assessing the size of the Iraqi CW stockpile, the NIE judged that "much" of the CW stockpile had been "added in the last year."[451] This latter assessment, in turn, rested on the NIE's second major CW conclusion: that Baghdad had "begun renewed production of mustard, sarin, GF (cyclosarin), and VX."

The NIE's judgment that Iraq had restarted CW production was based primarily on imagery intelligence.[452] As analysts subsequently explained, this imagery showed trucks transshipping materials to and from ammunition depots, including suspect CW sites, in Iraq. These transshipments began in March 2002 and continued until early 2003.[453] At approximately 11 sites, imagery analysts saw a number of "indicators" in the imagery that suggested to them that some of the trucks were possibly moving CW munitions; then, because imagery analysts observed evidence of numerous such shipments, CW analysts in turn assessed that Iraq was moving significant volumes of CW munitions and therefore that Iraq had restarted CW production.[454] These indicators included the presence of "Samarra-type" trucks—a distinctive type of tanker truck—which were regularly associated with CW shipments in the late 1980s and during the Gulf War; atypical security patterns "associated with" the Special Republican Guard, which was believed to be responsible for protecting parts of Iraq's WMD programs; at least at one site, the grading of the topsoil, which likewise suggested to analysts deliberate concealment of suspect activity; and other indicators.[455]

Although the NIE's judgment that Iraq had restarted CW production was based primarily on imagery, that judgment was also supported by small streams of human and signals intelligence. The NIC subsequently explained in its Statement for the Record that this human intelligence reporting consisted of "a number of specific reports alleging that Iraq had resumed large-scale production of CW agents."[456] None of these reports was considered "highly reliable," however, and only six were deemed "moderately reliable." [457]

Of these reports, Community analysts identified to us several as having been most significant, although subsequent analysis of the reports revealed—in some cases—serious flaws in the reporting. The key reports were: one involving a foreign source in 1999 who reported that two Iraqi companies were involved in the production of nerve gas;[458] reporting concerning a factory for the production of castor oil that could be used to make "sarin";[459] information from an Iraqi defector, who claimed to be an expert in VX production, describing the production of "tons" of nerve agents in mobile labs;[460] reporting from a source with "good but historical access" asserting that, as of 1998, mustard and binary chemical agents were being produced in Iraq;[461] a source who reported that Iraq was producing a binary compound and mustard as of fall 2001;[462] and reporting on the production of CW at dual-use facilities.[463]

Finally, a liaison service reported in September 2002 that a senior Iraqi official had indicated that Iraq was producing and stockpiling chemical weapons.[464] Although this report was distributed to a very small group of senior officials prior to the publication of the NIE—including to the NIE's principal author—it was not made available to most analysts.[465] In any event, as described below, the senior Iraqi official later denied having made such statements.

In addition to these imagery indicators of transshipment activity and human intelligence, the NIE also drew upon a handful of additional pieces of information—

based largely on other Intelligence Community reporting—to support the assessment that Baghdad had restarted CW production. This information suggested suspect activity at dual-use sites and included: indications that Iraq was expanding its indigenous chemical industry in ways that were deemed unlikely to be for civilian purposes, specifically by increasing the indigenous production capacity for chlorine—despite the fact that Iraq's civilian chlorine needs were met through United Nations-permitted imports;[466] the "management" of key chemical facilities by "previously identified CW personnel";[467] attempted procurement of nuclear, biological, and chemical weapons defensive materials; and the attempted procurement of dual-use materials associated with CW.[468] Although the NIE noted that the Intelligence Community could not "link definitively Iraq's procurement of CW precursors, technology, and specialized equipment from foreign sources directly" to its CW program,[469] it nevertheless assessed that "Iraq's procurements have contributed to the rebuilding of dual-use facilities that probably are adding to Iraq's overall CW agent capability."[470] In drawing this conclusion, the NIE drew particular attention to Iraq's attempts to obtain necessary precursors for nerve agents.[471]

Finally, reporting on other aspects of Iraq's unconventional weapons programs also influenced some analysts' CW-related conclusions. Specifically, reporting on the existence of Iraqi mobile BW production facilities—namely, reports from Curveball—buttressed some analysts' certainty in their CW judgments. As one CIA analyst put it, "much of the CW confidence [in the pre-war assessments] was built on the BW confidence."[472] In other words, although some CW analysts at times questioned the existence of significant Iraqi CW stockpiles, the reports that Iraq had a hidden, mobile BW program pushed the analysts "in the other direction" and helped convince them of their ultimate conclusion: that Iraq was hiding a CW program.[473]

Post-October 2002 NIE reports. In November 2002, the NIC published a Memorandum to Holders of the October NIE entitled *Iraq's Chemical Warfare Capabilities: Potential for Dusty and Fourth-Generation Agents*.[474] The Memorandum warned that Iraq might possess dusty agent[475] and that it had the technical expertise to develop fourth-generation agents[476] that could be extremely lethal. Identifying the "Key Intelligence Gaps" on Iraq's CW program, the Memorandum observed that although the Intelligence Community "assess[ed]" that Iraq was producing blister and nerve agents, the Intelligence Community had not "identified key production facilities" and did "not know the extent of indigenous production or procurement of CW precursors."[477]

But just as the NIE had cautioned that the Intelligence Community had "little specific information on Iraq's CW stockpile," the Memorandum stated that the Intelligence Community had "almost no information on the size, composition, or location of Iraq's CW stockpile."[478] In a separate NIE published in January 2003, however, the Community reiterated its estimate that Iraq "ha[d] 100 to 500 metric tons of weaponized bulk agent."[479]

In December 2002, CIA's WINPAC published a coordinated Intelligence Community paper that reiterated its belief that "Iraq retain[ed] an offensive CW program," but it did not specifically describe the extent of any CW stockpiles.[480] In addition, the CIA reported the Intelligence Community had "low confidence" in its ability to monitor the Iraqi CW program due to "stringent operational security" and "successful denial and deception practices."[481]

Post-War Findings of the Iraq Survey Group

The Iraq Survey Group's findings undermined both the Intelligence Community's assessments about Iraq's pre-war CW program and, indeed, the very fundamental assumptions upon which those assessments were based. The ISG concluded—contrary to the Intelligence Community's pre-war assessments— that Iraq had actually unilaterally destroyed its undeclared CW stockpile in 1991 and that there were no credible indications that Baghdad resumed production of CW thereafter.[482] Iraq had not regained its pre-1991 CW technical sophistication or production capabilities prior to the war. Further, pre-war concerns of Iraqi plans to use CW if Coalition forces crossed certain defensive "red lines" were groundless; the "red lines" referred to conventional military planning only.[483] Finally, the only CW the Iraq Survey Group recovered were weapons manufactured before the first Gulf War; the ISG concluded that, after 1991, Iraq maintained only small, covert labs to research chemicals and poisons, primarily for intelligence operations.[484] However, "Saddam never abandoned his intentions to resume a CW effort when sanctions were lifted and conditions were judged favorable," and Iraq's post-1996 infrastructure improvements "would have enhanced Iraq's ability to produce CW" if it had chosen to do so.[485]

Despite having "expended considerable time and expertise searching for extant CW munitions,"—the vaunted stockpiles—the ISG concluded with "high confidence that there are no CW present in the Iraqi inventory."[486] The ISG specifically investigated 11 sites that were associated with suspected CW transshipment activity, conducting an in-depth inspection of two of the sites, which were "assessed prior to war to have the strongest indicators of CW movement."[487] Neither of these sites revealed any CW munitions.[488] Further, the ISG's "review of documents, interviews, intelligence reporting, and site exploitations revealed alternate, plausible explanations" for pre-war transshipment activity that the Intelligence Community judged to have been CW-related.[489]

Regarding Iraq's dual-use chemical infrastructure and personnel, the Iraq Survey Group found no direct link to a CW program. Instead, investigators found that, though Iraq's chemical industry began expanding after 1996, in part due to the influx of funds and resources from the Oil-for-Food program, the country's CW capabilities remained less than those which existed prior to the Gulf War.[490] The ISG also interviewed 30 of the approximately 60 "key" Iraqi CW scientists, all of whom denied having been involved in any CW activity since 1990 and the vast majority of whom denied having any knowledge of any CW activity occurring.[491]

The ISG also cited a number of reasons why Iraq's expansion of its chlorine capacity was not, contrary to the NIE's assessment, capable of being diverted to CW production.[492] Specifically, Iraq experienced a "country-wide chlorine shortage," and Iraq's chlorine plants "suffered from corroded condensers and were only able to produce aqueous chlorine."[493] Further, "[t]echnical problems and poor maintenance of aging equipment throughout the 1990s resulted in many chemical plants, including ethylene and chlorine production plants, operating at less than half capacity despite the improvements to the chemical industry."[494]

In sum, the Iraq Survey Group found no direct link between Iraq's dual-use infrastructure and its CW program. However, "concerns" about some aspects of the infrastructure[495] arising out of "an extensive, yet fragmentary and circumstantial body of evidence" suggested Saddam intended to maintain his CW capabilities by preserving CW-related assets and expertise.[496]

Regarding Iraqi decisionmaking about its CW program after 1991, the ISG concluded that, in the aftermath of the Gulf War, "Iraq initially chose not to fully declare its CW" in anticipation that inspections would be short-lived and ineffective. This position changed after a particularly invasive search in late June 1991, after which Iraq destroyed its hidden CW and precursors while retaining some documents and dual-use equipment. Iraq kept these latter items for the next five years, but did not renew its CW efforts out of fear that such a move would imperil its effort to have sanctions lifted. In August 1995, however, after the defection of Hussein Kamil, Saddam relented and revealed to inspectors extensive VX research and other, more advanced, technologies.[497]

Overall, although the vast majority of CW munitions had been destroyed, the Iraq Survey Group recognized that questions remained relating to the disposition of hundreds of pre-1991 CW munitions.[498] Still, given that, of the dozens of CW munitions that the ISG discovered, all had been manufactured before 1991, the Intelligence Community's 2002 assessments that Iraq had restarted its CW program turned out to have been seriously off the mark.[499]

Finally, on two ancillary issues the ISG found little or no evidence to support indications of Iraqi CW efforts. First, with respect to a "red line" defense of Baghdad, the ISG found no information that such a defense—which amounted to a multi-ring conventional defense of the city—called for the use of CW.[500] According to a senior Iraqi military officer, the "red line" was simply the line at which Iraqi military units would no longer retreat.[501] At the same time, both generals and high-level defense officials believed that a plan for CW use existed, even though they themselves knew nothing about it.[502]

Second, with respect to CW work by the Iraqi Intelligence Service, there was "no evidence" of CW production in clandestine labs, other than the Service's laboratory effort to develop substances to kill or incapacitate targeted individuals.[503]

Analysis of the Intelligence Community's Pre-War Assessments

As the foregoing comparison illustrates, the Intelligence Community's pre-war assessments of Iraq's CW program were well off the mark. Iraq did not have CW stockpiles; it was not producing CW agent; and its chemical infrastructure was in far worse shape than the Intelligence Community believed. It is a daunting task in any circumstance to distinguish a normal chemical infrastructure and conventional military establishment on the one hand from a chemical warfare program on the other. But the Community made more difficult the challenges of identifying a CW program in Iraq by latching on to ambiguous imagery indicators and by failing to collect enough good intelligence to keep analytic judgments tethered to reality.

There are several reasons for the significant gap between the Intelligence Community's pre-war assessment of Iraq's CW program and the Iraq Survey Group's findings. Chief among these was the over-reliance on a single, ambiguous source (the Samarra-type tanker trucks) to support multiple judgments. Less central, although still significant, were the failure of analysts to understand fully the limitations of technical collection; the lack of quality human intelligence sources; the lack of quality signals intelligence; and, on a broader plane, the universal difficulty of establishing the existence of a CW program in light of the prevalence of dual-use technology.

Chemical Warfare Finding 1

The Intelligence Community relied too heavily on ambiguous imagery indicators identified at suspect Iraqi facilities for its broad judgment about Iraq's chemical warfare program. In particular, analysts leaned too much on the judgment that the presence of "Samarra-type" trucks (and related activity) indicated that Iraq had resumed its chemical weapons program.

As noted, the pre-war assessment that Iraq had restarted CW production relied primarily on CW analysts' assessments of imagery intelligence.[504] This imagery showed trucks transshipping materials to and from ammunition depots, including suspect CW-sites, in Iraq.[505] In the late spring of 2002, analysts started to believe that these shipments involved CW munitions.[506] This belief was based on the aforementioned "indicators" seen on the imagery— that is, activity and circumstances surrounding the shipments that were thought to be indicative of CW activity. The most important of these indicators was the presence of "Samarra-type" trucks—a distinctive type of tanker truck—which had been regularly associated with Iraqi CW shipments in the late 1980s and during the Gulf War.[507] Based on the assessment that the presence of these Samarra-type trucks (in combination with the other indicators) suggested CW shipments, CW analysts then judged that the frequency of such transshipments pointed to the assessment that "CW was already deployed with the military logistics chain," which, in turn, indicated to these analysts that Iraq had added to its CW stockpile in the last year. That assessment, in turn, indicated to analysts that Iraq had restarted CW production.

In short, the key pre-war assessments about Iraq's CW program—that Iraq was actively producing CW and had increased its stockpile of CW—rested on the following evidence and associated reasoning:

- Imagery revealed the presence of Samarra-type trucks at suspect weapons sites;

- The presence of Samarra-type trucks indicated CW activity;

- The scale of the Samarra-type trucks' involvement demonstrated Iraq had already deployed CW with their forces; and

- For CW to be deployed with Iraqi forces, Iraq had to have restarted CW production within the past year—the period during which analysts had seen Samarra-type trucks.

As this logic train illustrates, the final conclusion regarding restarted CW production was, therefore, fundamentally grounded on the single assessment that the Samarra-type trucks seen on imagery were in fact CW-related.[508] This assessment, however, proved to be incorrect—thereby eliminating the crucial pillar on which the Community's judgment about Iraq's CW program rested.

Post-war investigation revealed how the Intelligence Community ran astray. After the war, NGA "reassessed" the imagery from one of the sites thought to bear the strongest indications of CW activity—the Al Musayyib Barracks—by incorporating information from ISG inspections and debriefings of key personnel.[509] Contrary to pre-war assessments, NGA concluded that the activity represented "conventional maintenance and logistical activity rather than chemical weapons."[510] NGA analysts drew this conclusion in part after reexamining imagery and in part on ISG debriefs of former commanders of the Al Musayyib site.[511]

More detailed analysis of other imagery intelligence—in particular, surface grading—also revealed the absence of a clear link to CW.[512] NGA assessed that grading could be associated with innocuous, routine activities.[513] The rationales behind that assessment are discussed in the classified report.

The story is much the same with respect to pre-war assessments of other imagery evidence regarding certain security patterns.[514] Post-war analysis by

NGA could not confirm pre-war assessments that these security patterns were indicative of Special Republican Guard activity associated with security at CW-related sites. Indeed, at least one human source debriefed after the war said the security activity in question was not related to the Special Republican Guard and that it was actually related to the performance of miscellaneous jobs associated with the ammunition depot.[515]

Finally, post-war debriefings suggested that other CW-related imagery evidence was also innocuous, although this suggestion was neither definitively confirmed nor refuted by the imagery reassessment.[516] And NGA notes that it is generally not possible to determine from imagery whether some activities, such as certain safety measures, are intended to support the training of offensive or defensive chemical warfare troops. And NGA has noted that imagery, when used alone, may not definitely determine the intended purpose of an adversary's activity.

The Community's over-reliance on ambiguous imagery indicators thus played a pivotal role in its ultimate misjudgment that Iraq had restarted CW production and had increased its CW stockpiles. In our view analysts relied too heavily on the presence of Samarra tanker trucks—backed by other, even more ambiguous imagery indicators—to support multiple, interdependent, and wide-ranging judgments about Iraq's chemical warfare program. And the Community did so despite the truism about which NGA itself has cautioned: imagery alone can neither prove nor disprove a CW association.[517]

Building one assessment upon another in this fashion—without carrying forward the uncertainty of each "layer" of assessment—results in a false impression of certainty for analysts' ultimate judgment. We believe, therefore, that at a minimum analysts must communicate the uncertainty of their judgments, and the degree to which they rely on narrow assessments about specific indicators. Moreover, avoiding the pitfalls of such layering requires careful consideration of alternative hypotheses, such as, in this case, the possibility that the shipments involved conventional weapons and that the trucks were for water supply or fire suppression.

We do not discount the fact that analysts must sometimes focus on seemingly mundane indicators. But at the same time analysts must always recognize, and communicate to decisionmakers, the tenuous quality of their reasoning.

Chemical Warfare Finding 2

Analysts failed to understand, and collectors did not adequately communicate, the limitations of imagery collection. Specifically, analysts did not realize that the observed increase in activity at suspected Iraqi chemical facilities may have been the result of increased imagery collection rather than an increase in Iraqi activity.

Analytical flaws in assessing the significance of the imagery indicators were not the only factors leading to the misassessment of the imagery intelligence. In addition, analysts may have misperceived the significance of the imagery on Iraq's supposed CW program because they did not fully understand—and the collectors did not fully explain—the scope and nature of imagery collection against the target. Indeed, we cannot rule out the possibility that the analytic judgment that Iraq had added to its CW stockpile in the preceding year rested, at least in part, on a simple increase in *collection* and reporting rather than any rise in Iraqi *activity*.

Pre-war, analysts relied upon imagery to detect transshipment activity at suspected CW sites, and beginning in March 2002, analysts believed that they were seeing an "increase" in such activity.[518] In reality, however, the "increase" in transshipment activity that analysts saw starting in March 2002 may have been due, at least in part, to an increased volume of imagery *collected* by U.S. satellites rather than to any increased activity by the Iraqis. To only somewhat oversimplify the matter, it wasn't that the Iraqis were using Samarra trucks more often in 2002—it was that in 2002 the United States was taking more pictures of places where the Samarra trucks were being used. And this failure to distinguish between *actual* increased activity at suspect CW sites and the *appearance* of increased activity due to increased imaging likely contributed to the mistaken assessment that Iraq was ramping up CW production in 2002.

This error sprung from the fact that not all Community analysts were fully cognizant of a major change in NGA collection that occurred in the spring of

2002.[519] Until 2000, imagery collection on Iraq had been oriented primarily toward supporting military operations associated with the no-fly zones.[520] But in 2001 and 2002, imagery collection against Iraq WMD more than doubled, prompted by recommendations that more attention be given to the target.[521] Most significantly, the United States began "expanded imagery collection over Baghdad [and] suspect WMD sites" in March 2002—not coincidentally the same time that analysts began to "see" new activity they associated with CW transshipments.[522]

Thus, in drawing their conclusions about the state of Iraq's CW production based on increased transshipment activity, analysts did not realize the necessity of distinguishing between the "new" activity they saw, on the one hand, at sites that had been previously imaged on a regular basis (e.g., suspect WMD sites) and, on the other, at sites that had not been previously imaged on a regular basis (e.g., ammunition depots that had not been previously associated with WMD).[523] Whereas increased activity at the former could be attributed to changes in Iraqi behavior (since the United States had been photographing the sites prior to March 2002), the same could not be said for the latter category (since there was no "baseline" of activity with which to compare levels of activity seen from March 2002 on).[524]

This problem extended to one of the sites that was key to analysts' conclusions about Iraqi CW production—the Al Musayyib Barracks. According to NGA, Al Musayyib had not been regularly imaged prior to the March 2002 imaging blitz because it had not been previously associated with Iraq's chemical or biological weapons programs.[525] Unaware of this important fact, analysts confidently assessed that the Iraqis had expanded transshipment activity at Al Musayyib, as well as other sites, when they began to see more images of Samarra-type truck activity. In short, analysts attributed what they saw to nefarious Iraqi activity when it could just as easily have been attributed to changes in U.S. collection priorities. In our view, this failure is the direct result of poor communication between analysts and collectors about a crucial change in the scope and nature of collection against a vital target.

Chemical Warfare Finding 3

Human intelligence collection against Iraq's chemical activities was paltry, and much has subsequently proved problematic.

Analysts were not alone in contributing to a flawed assessment about a resuscitant Iraqi CW program. Collectors, too, were involved—but mostly by their conspicuous absence. Against Iraq's program, Intelligence Community collectors failed to produce much either in terms of quantity or, worse, validity, thus making analysts' jobs considerably harder, and influencing analysts to place more weight on the imagery intelligence than it could logically bear.

A small quantity of human source reporting supplied the bulk of the narrow band of intelligence supplementing the imagery intelligence. And the most striking fact about reporting on Iraq's CW program was, as with other elements of Iraq's weapons programs, its paucity. Yet there was more than just scarcity, for—as with sources on Iraq's supposed BW program—many of the CW sources subsequently proved unreliable. Indeed, perhaps even more so that with the BW sources, Community analysts should have been more cautious about using the CW sources' reporting, as much of it was deeply problematic on its face. In our view, prior to the war, analysts should have viewed at least three human sources more skeptically than they did. In addition, post-war, questions about the veracity of two other human sources have also surfaced.

Sources Whose Reliability Should Have Been Questioned Prior to the NIE

One source, an Iraqi defector who had worked as a chemist in Iraq through the 1990s, reported information that made its way into the NIE.[526] This happened even though, from the start of his relations with the U.S. Intelligence Community, the Community had deemed aspects of his reporting not credible. His information survived, despite these indications that he might be an unreliable source, because analysts simply rejected those parts of his reporting that seemed implausible and accepted the rest. For example, he claimed that Iraq had produced a combined nuclear-biological-chemical weapon, a claim that analysts recognized at the time as absurd.[527] Analysts were also skeptical of his claim that Iraq had begun producing "tons" of VX in 1998 in mobile labs, because such labs would be very unlikely to have the capacity to produce such large amounts of agent.[528]

Despite these highly suspect claims, analysts credited the source's reporting that Iraq had successfully stabilized VX.[529] As one analyst reviewing his reporting after the war said of it, "half seems credible and half seems preposterous."[530] Yet at the time the NIE was written, with substantial skepticism about the validity of much of his information, analysts nevertheless judged his reporting to be "moderately credible."[531] In our view, given that important parts of his information were simply unbelievable and recognized as such by analysts, the Community should have approached him and his intelligence with more caution—and certainly should have been more skeptical about using selections from his reporting in the authoritative NIE.

Indeed, analytic skepticism about the source's claims was later confirmed by revelations about his operational history, revelations that led to the Intelligence Community deeming him a fabricator and recalling his reporting, although not all of his reporting was recalled until almost one year after the war started.[532] He had initially come to the CIA's attention via a foreign intelligence service, which asked for the CIA's assistance after he had approached them.[533] In March 2003, however, the CIA terminated contact with him, after administering an examination in February 2003 during which he was deceptive. CIA had also learned that he had—before approaching this foreign service—already been debriefed by two other intelligence services, indicating that he was something of an "information peddler."[534] Moreover, one of these two services had concluded that although his pre-1991 information was credible, his post-1991 information was both not credible and possibly "directed" by a hostile service.[535] CIA started to recall his reporting in March 2003, but did not recall all of it until February 2004.[536]

Another source, who was described as a contact with "good but historical access" but lacking "an established reporting record," reported in July 2002 that, as of 1998, Iraq was producing mustard and binary chemical agents.[537] At the same time, he also reported on a "wide range of disparate subjects," including on Iraq's missile program and nuclear and biological weapons programs.[538] Such broad access, on its face, was inconsistent with what analysts understood to be Iraq's well-known tendency towards compartmentation of sensitive weapons programs.[539] Yet because of the Community's *own* compartmentation—working-level analysts saw reporting on *their* area but not on others—they did not realize at the time that one source was reporting on a range of topics for which he was unlikely to have access.[540] Moreover, although analysts did not know it at the time, the source obtained his information from unknown and undescribed sub-sources.[541]

Finally, a third source provided information that was technically implausible on its face. His reporting claimed that Iraq had constructed a factory for the production of castor oil that could be used for the production of sarin.[542]

Although castor beans can be used to make ricin, not sarin—a fact that analysts readily understood—analysts did not discount the information.[543] Instead, they interpreted it in a way that would cure the technical difficulty, reading it as indicating that the facility could produce *both* sarin and ricin.[544] But in so doing, analysts were consciously compensating for technical errors in the reporting. This exercise of "compensating for errors" in the reporting may well be appropriate in some instances, as when the source of the report may not have the competence to report accurately on a given technical subject.[545] But such speculative interpretation must be carefully balanced with a healthy skepticism, especially when, as in the case of Iraq's CW program, the intelligence as a whole on the subject is weak and analysts' underlying assumptions are strong. An untethered "compensating for errors" runs the risk of skewing the analysis in the direction of those assumptions, as, unfortunately, happened here.

Sources Whose Reliability Has Been Questioned After the NIE

The remaining human intelligence sources relied upon to support the conclusion that Iraq had restarted CW production, while not so problematic on the surface as the sources just described, have become questionable in hindsight.

One liaison source, details about whom cannot be disclosed at this level of classification, reported on production and stocks of chemical and biological weapons and agents, based on what he learned from others in his circle of high-level contacts in Baghdad.[546] While this source provided general information on Iraq's CW program, he provided few details. In our view, the bottom line on this source was that he had no personal knowledge of CW and provided few details of CW capabilities—factors that should have prompted caution in using his reporting as significant evidence that the Iraqis had restarted CW production.

One other human source—while unlikely to have affected the NIE because his reporting dissemination was so limited—was also called into question after the start of the war. In September 2002, a liaison service reported that a senior Iraqi official had said that Iraq was producing and stockpiling chemical weapons.[547] The source of the information claimed to have spoken with this senior official on this topic. CIA was able to confirm at the time of the report that the senior official had been in contact with the source. After the start of the war, however, when CIA officers interviewed the senior official, he denied ever making such comments. Although the CIA's Directorate of Operations requested liaison assistance in clarifying this issue, as of March 2005 the issue remained unresolved.

Chemical Warfare Finding 4

Signals intelligence collection against Iraq's chemical activities was minimal, and much was of questionable value.

Signals intelligence provided only minimal information regarding Iraq's chemical weapons programs and, due to the nature of the sources, what was provided was of dubious quality and therefore of questionable value. Although the Intelligence Community originally cited more than two dozen such intelligence reports as supporting the proposition that Iraq was attempting to reconstitute its chemical weapons program, a subsequent review revealed that only a handful of the reports provided any usable information for analysis. It is not readily apparent what caused this discrepancy, but we think it plain that the Intelligence Community should have conducted a far more careful and thoughtful pre-war analysis of this signals intelligence information and treated it with greater skepticism.

Conclusion

Similar to its assessments about Iraq's nuclear and biological efforts, the Intelligence Community's mistaken assessments about Iraq's chemical weapons program can be traced in large part to a single point of failure—the Community's over-reliance on ambiguous imagery indicators. But the Community's bottom line on Iraq's chemical weapons capabilities was further influenced by a breakdown in communication between imagery collectors and analysts; a basic paucity of quality intelligence, particularly quality signals intelligence; and the fact that much of the human and signals intelligence that was collected was bad.

It is, however, understandable that analysts assessed—as they did throughout the 1990s—that Iraq retained a chemical warfare capability. Iraq's pre-Gulf War chemical weapons stockpile was large and relatively sophisticated. Nor did Saddam's uncooperative and secretive behavior after the war encourage confidence that he had converted from the CW path. The Community's failure on CW was therefore not in thinking that Iraq had such a capability—that was, in many ways, the only sensible conclusion, given the evidence. Rather, analysts erred in their assessment—based largely on ambiguous imagery indicators that could not logically support the judgment—that Iraq had in fact resumed producing and stockpiling significant quantities of CW.

DELIVERY SYSTEMS

Delivery Systems Summary Finding 1

The Intelligence Community incorrectly assessed that Iraq was developing unmanned aerial vehicles for the purpose of delivering biological weapons strikes against U.S. interests.

Delivery Systems Summary Finding 2

The Intelligence Community correctly judged that Iraq was developing ballistic missile systems that violated United Nations strictures, but was incorrect in assessing that Iraq had preserved its Scud missile force.

The Intelligence Community assessed in the October 2002 NIE that Iraq was developing small Unmanned Aerial Vehicles (UAVs) capable of autonomous flight, which most agencies assessed were "probably" intended to deliver biological warfare agents.[548] The Intelligence Community also judged that these UAVs could threaten the U.S. homeland.[549] This latter assessment was based on an Iraqi attempt to procure commercially available civilian U.S. mapping software for its UAVs. That attempted procurement, the Intelligence Community assessed, "strongly suggest[ed] that Iraq [was] investigating the use of these UAVs for missions targeting the United States."[550]

By January 2003, however, the Intelligence Community had pulled back from its view that Iraq intended to target the United States.[551] This re-assessment reflected a belief among CIA analysts that the Iraqi attempt to procure U.S. mapping software may have been inadvertent.[552] As a result, the Intelligence Community assessed in January 2003 that while the mapping software could provide the *capability* to target the United States, the purchasing attempt did not necessarily indicate an intent to do so.[553] By early March 2003, CIA had further retreated from the view that the purchase of the mapping software evidenced an intent to target the United States and, in early March 2003, on the eve of the invasion of Iraq, CIA advised senior policymakers that it was an open question whether the attempted software procurement evinced the intent to target the United States at all.[554]

Following its exhaustive investigation in Iraq, the Iraq Survey Group concluded that Iraq had indeed been developing small UAVs, but found no evidence that the UAVs had been designed to deliver biological agent.[555] Instead, the ISG concluded that Iraq had been developing and had flight tested a small, autonomous UAV intended for use as a reconnaissance platform,[556] and had developed a prototype for another small UAV for use in electronic warfare missions.[557] Although both UAVs had the range, payload, guidance, and autonomy necessary to deliver a biological agent, the ISG found no evidence that Iraq intended to use them in such a way.[558] With respect to the mapping software, Iraqi officials told ISG investigators that the software in question had been included as part of a package deal with autopilots they had purchased for the UAVs; the Iraqis, the ISG judged, had not actually intended to buy the mapping software.[559]

The October 2002 NIE had also examined whether Iraq was deploying missiles capable of reaching beyond the 150 kilometer limit imposed by the United Nations. The NIE assessed that Iraq was deploying two types of short-range ballistic missiles capable of flying beyond the United Nations-authorized range limit.[560] The NIE also assessed, based largely on Iraqi accounting discrepancies and incomplete records and record keeping, that Iraq retained a covert force of up to a few dozen Scud-variant missiles in defiance of United Nations resolutions.[561] The ISG concluded—consistent with this assessment—that Iraq had been developing and deploying ballistic missiles that exceeded United Nations restrictions, although the ISG also found, contrary to pre-war assessments, that Iraq had not retained Scud or Scud-variant missiles after 1991.[562]

The Intelligence Community's assessments of Iraq's delivery systems developments offered both a bright and a dark spot on its Iraq record. While far from perfect (which can never be reasonably expected in intelligence work), the Community's judgments about the progress of Iraq's ballistic missile programs were substantively accurate. As the ISG discovered, the Iraqis were indeed violating United Nations strictures by working on missiles that exceeded the 150 kilometer range limit. But on the issue of whether Iraq was developing UAVs to deliver biological agent against U.S. targets—including the U.S. homeland—the Community erred, once again attributing more to spotty intelligence than that information could bear.

This section describes the Community's analysis of Iraq's work on delivery systems between the first Gulf War and Operation Iraqi Freedom, as well as the ISG's findings concerning the same. The Commission then offers its findings based on a thorough investigation into the Community's efforts on Iraqi delivery systems, concentrating particularly on the analytical flaws apparent from the Community's products on the uses of Iraqi UAVs.

The Intelligence Community's Pre-War Assessments

As with other aspects of Iraq's WMD programs, the Intelligence Community's assessment of Iraq's delivery systems evolved over the course of many years and was heavily influenced by Iraq's past actions and intransigence.

Background. Before the Gulf War Iraq had been in the early stages of a project to convert the MiG-21 jet aircraft into UAVs for BW delivery.[563] In addition, Iraq had experimented in 1990 on a BW spray system, designed to be used with the MiG-21 UAV.[564] Iraq admitted to this program in 1995, after the defection of Hussein Kamil.[565] Subsequent UNSCOM inspections discovered video showing the spray-system experiments.[566] Also, analysts in the early 1990s had observed continued activity at Salman Pak—Iraq's primary BW research and development facility prior to the Gulf War—where, UNSCOM reported, work continued on modified commercial crop sprayers for BW delivery and the presence of UAV program personnel.[567] Iraq claimed that, because of the war, it had abandoned the MiG-21 UAV project after conducting only one experiment in 1991, but UNSCOM inspections could not confirm this claim.[568] In the mid-1990s Iraq also began testing another modified jet aircraft, the L-29, as a UAV, that analysts believed was a follow-on to the converted MiG-21 program.[569]

These discoveries also cast new light, in analysts' minds, on UNSCOM's earlier discovery of 11 small-to-medium sized UAV drones at the Salman Pak compound in 1991.[570] Although Iraq denied having developed these UAVs for BW delivery, Iraq's later admission—after an initial denial—that the MiG-21 program was for the purpose of delivering biological agents led analysts to believe, given Iraqi deception, that Iraq's small UAVs had a similar purpose.[571] Analysts also focused on Iraqi admissions—in their 1996 declaration to the United Nations—that, in the late 1980s, senior Iraqi officials had met to discuss the feasibility of using small UAVs as BW delivery vehicles.[572]

This history, along with evidence that Iraq had flight-tested small and medium-sized UAVs, led most Intelligence Community analysts to conclude consistently from the late 1990s through 2002 that Iraq was maintaining its UAV program for BW and CW delivery.[573] Briefings and written products to senior policymakers in mid-2002 reflected this assessment.[574] As with the other elements of Iraq's purported weapons programs, however, intelligence on UAVs in the years preceding 2002 was partial and ambiguous. While it was clear that Iraq did have a UAV program, the key question— whether that program was meant to be a delivery system—remained unanswered. Therefore, analysts' judgments again depended heavily upon assumptions based on Iraq's earlier behavior and Community views about Iraq's sophisticated denial and deception activities.[575]

With respect to ballistic missiles, the Intelligence Community judged in 1992 that Iraq's ballistic missile programs were more advanced than the Community had assessed before the Gulf War.[576] Iraq was further along in its production capability for Scud and Scud-derivative missiles and had produced more components indigenously than the Intelligence Community had assessed before the Gulf War.[577] By 1995, the Intelligence Community judged that Iraq was developing liquid-propellant missiles with an expected range of about 150 kilometers.[578] In 1998, the Community assessed that these missiles, named the al-Samoud, were capable of flying farther than the 150 kilometer limit imposed by the United Nations and that Iraq was also developing solid-propellant missiles.[579] By early 2002, the Intelligence Community judged that Iraq probably still retained a small force of Scud missiles and that both its liquid-propellant and solid-propellant missiles were capable of flying over 150 kilometers.[580]

October 2002 NIE. The October 2002 NIE judged, with a dissent from the Director of Air Force Intelligence, that Iraq was developing small UAVs "probably" for BW delivery which could be used against U.S. forces and allies in the region.[581] In addition, the NIE mentioned the concern of most agencies about the possible intent to use UAVs as delivery systems against the U.S. homeland.[582] This possible use was based on the attempted procurement of U.S. mapping software by an Iraqi procurement agent.[583]

As noted, the Director of Air Force Intelligence dissented from the majority view. In contrast to other organizations, the Air Force judged that Iraq was developing UAVs "primarily for reconnaissance rather than [as] delivery platforms for [CW or BW] agents."[584] The Air Force further noted that CW or BW delivery is "an inherent capability of UAVs but probably is not the impetus for Iraq's recent UAV programs."[585]

Analysts' judgments that Iraq's small UAVs were intended for BW delivery were based on the following logic: the Iraqis had admitted that the MiG-21 program was intended for BW delivery, and analysts judged that the L-29 program, for which there was some evidence of a BW-delivery mission, was the successor to the MiG-21 program. Because the L-29 program had suffered set-backs in late 2000 after a crash, analysts then deduced that Iraq's new, small UAVs may have been designed to replace the L-29 effort, and that they were therefore also intended to deliver BW agents.[586]

There was very little reporting, however, to support the conclusion that the small UAVs were "probably" intended for BW delivery. Only one human intelligence report indicated that small UAVs were intended for CW or BW delivery.[587] Given the dearth of reporting on the purpose for the small UAVs, analysts instead deduced their intended purpose from Iraq's previous admissions and from what was assessed about the characteristics of Iraq's other UAV programs.

For example, analysts pointed to several human intelligence reports that suggested that Iraq's L-29 UAV program could be used to deliver CW or BW agents.[588] Only one of those reports, however, stated explicitly that the L-29 UAV was intended for biological or chemical weapon delivery, and that early 1998 report was based on a report of unknown reliability.[589] Analysts believed, though, that this conclusion was reinforced by separate reporting indicating that Iraq was prepared to use modified L-29 UAVs against U.S. forces in the Persian Gulf area; these UAVs, the reasoning went, would have been useless for delivery of conventional weapons and BW was therefore a likelier function.[590]

But there were other indications that the UAVs were *not* intended for BW delivery. Iraq's 1996 declaration to the United Nations indicated that the drones discovered in 1991 were actually intended for reconnaissance and aerial targeting—not BW delivery.[591] Intelligence reporting supported this view; Iraq was attempting to procure equipment for its small UAVs, which suggested the UAVs' purpose was reconnaissance. [592] Finally, as noted in the Air Force dissent, the small UAVs were not ideally suited for BW or CW delivery; the Air Force assessed instead that "the small size of Iraq's new UAV strongly suggests a primary role of reconnaissance, although chemical/biological weapons (CBW) delivery is an inherent capability."[593] Although CIA's WINPAC had published an Intelligence Assessment in 2001 that discussed these possible non-BW delivery missions for Iraq's UAVs, such alternative missions were not emphasized in the October 2002 NIE because WINPAC's "focus [in] the NIE was WMD delivery systems and not the Iraqi UAV program as a whole."[594]

In sum, the evidentiary basis for the pre-war assessment that Iraq was developing UAVs "probably intended" for BW delivery was based largely on the BW focus of Iraq's pre-1991 UAV programs and a thin stream of (primarily human intelligence) reporting that hinted at such a function for post-1991 UAVs.[595]

As noted above, the NIE also judged that Iraq's UAVs "could threaten...the U.S. Homeland."[596] This assessment was based on two streams of reporting: first, intelligence reporting indicating that the UAVs had a range of over 500 kilometers and could be launched from a truck; and, second, reporting that an Iraqi procurement agent was attempting to buy U.S. mapping software for its small UAVs.[597] The latter piece of information was, however, the only evidence that supported Iraq's *intent* to target the United States. Based on this stream of reporting, the NIE reasoned that, because the mapping software would be useless outside the United States, its procurement "strongly suggest[ed]" Iraq was interested in using the UAVs to target the United States.[598]

The procurement effort revealed by the reporting was spearheaded by an Iraqi procurement agent who had been involved in the pre-Gulf War Iraqi UAV program ("the procurement agent"). The procurement agent had subsequently emigrated to another country where he ran an illicit procurement network for Iraq.[599] In late 2000 or early 2001, the procurement agent received a "shopping list" from an Iraqi general associated with the UAV program that included autopilots and gyroscopes. To fill this request, the procurement agent researched potential suppliers for these items, and in May 2001 he submitted requests for price quotes to a manufacturer and a distributor for the requested items, which included autopilots and gyroscopes but also included "Map Source" mapping software. The distributor responded with a price quote for the autopilot package, which included "Garmin 50 State" topographic mapping software, also sold as "Map Source." After consulting with Baghdad and soliciting a final price quote, in early 2002 the procurement agent submitted a final procurement list, which included the Garmin 50 State mapping software, to the distributor.[600]

Although the distributor had been assured by the procurement agent that the end-user was "legitimate," the distributor remained concerned about the procurement agent's interest in these items and contacted its own country's authorities in March 2002. The distributor also removed the mapping software from its website.[601]

Following the attempted procurement, several analytical assessments were published regarding the attempted procurement of the mapping software. An Intelligence Community Assessment titled *Current and Future Air Threats to the US Homeland*, published July 29, 2002, noted that Iraq was seeking route planning software and an associated topographic database "likely intended to use with its UAVs" and "almost certainly relate[d] to the United States."[602] CIA's Office of Near Eastern and South Asian Analysis also disseminated an intelligence assessment on August 1, 2002, observing that the mapping software would "provide precise guidance, tracking, and targeting in the United States." [603]

A liaison intelligence service subsequently approached the procurement agent to question him about the attempted procurement.[604] In these discussions, the procurement agent claimed that he had not intended to purchase mapping software of the United States. Although he admitted that the software he had ordered had not been "bundled" with other items he ordered, he explained that he had not well understood all of the elements of the package and had not wanted to miss out on an important piece of software. He said he had been concerned that the other system pieces might not work if he did not purchase the mapping software; it was cheap; and he had thought the system would allow the user to scan maps and program them into a GPS. Asked by the liaison service to submit to a thorough examination, the procurement agent refused.[605] Thus, by fall 2002, the CIA was still uncertain whether the procurement agent was lying.

While the October 2002 NIE was being coordinated, a CIA analyst interviewed the procurement agent in an effort to determine if his attempted procurement of the U.S. mapping software had in fact been inadvertent, as he claimed. The analyst initially concluded that the procurement agent was lying because a review of the website showed that, contrary to the procurement agent's claims, the option to purchase the mapping software was not on the page with the autopilots and gyroscopes. After further research, however, the analyst determined that the version of the website that the procurement agent had accessed in early 2001 had in fact contained the configuration and software option that the procurement agent described. This discovery led the analyst to believe that the purchase order may have indeed been inadvertent.[606]

Although the CIA was now beginning to obtain indications that the procurement agent's attempted purchase of the U.S. mapping software may in fact have been inadvertent as the procurement agent claimed, CIA remained uncertain whether the procurement agent was lying.[607] As the National Foreign Intelligence Board was convening to review and approve the NIE, several CIA analysts expressed concern about its use of the words "strongly suggests" and recommended that the language be toned down. But these concerns did not reach the DCI himself until the Board process had concluded.[608] With the lengthy Board meeting finished, the DCI concluded that the word "strongly" would remain in the NIE because the coordination process was complete at that point and the new information had not been confirmed.[609]

As noted, the NIE also stated that gaps in accounting suggested that Iraq retained a small covert Scud force, and the NIE assessed that Iraq was deploying missiles capable of flying farther than the United Nations limit of 150 kilometers.[610]

Post-NIE. The Intelligence Community's assessment that the UAVs were "probably" for BW delivery remained unchanged in the run-up to the war.[611] In a paper sent to the National Security Council in January 2003, the CIA noted that an Iraqi Ministry of Defense official had indicated that Iraq considered its UAVs to be an important strategic weapon.[612] And in testimony before the Senate Select Committee on Intelligence in early February 2003, DCI Tenet stated that "[w]e are concerned that Iraq's UAVs can dispense chemical and biological weapons."[613]

The Intelligence Community did, however, begin to retreat from its assessment that Iraq intended to target the U.S. homeland, though not quickly enough to prevent the charge's inclusion in the President's speech in Cincinnati in October 2002. In the immediate aftermath of the publication of the October 2002 NIE, CIA increasingly believed that the attempted purchase of the mapping software—on which this judgment was based—may have been inadvertent.[614] Accordingly, at least one CIA analyst recommended that a reference to the UAVs targeting the United States be deleted from a draft Presidential speech. Because of persistent uncertainty within the analytical ranks about the significance of the mapping software, however, CIA and the Intelligence Community's official position remained unchanged from the NIE. The President's speech, which was delivered on October 7, 2002 in Cincinnati, therefore expressed concern "that Iraq is exploring ways of using these UAVs for missions targeting the United States."[615]

Subsequent analytical products did begin to reflect the uncertainty over the significance of the mapping software, though. An NIE addressing the UAV question, entitled *Nontraditional Threats to the US Homeland Through 2007*, which was approved by the National Foreign Intelligence Board in November 2002, was not published for two months because of disagreement over whether the order for the U.S. mapping software indicated Iraqi intent to target the U.S. homeland.[616] The *Nontraditional Threats* NIE ultimately addressed the UAV issue in terms of capabilities rather than intent. That is, that NIE phrased the first judgment like the October 2002 Iraq NIE, noting that Iraqi UAVs "could strike the US Homeland if transported to within a few hundred kilometers," but phrased the software judgment only in terms of capability, noting that this "[route planning] software...could support [the] programming of a UAV autopilot for operation in the United States." For their parts, the Air Force, DIA, and the Army assessed that the purpose of the acquisition was to obtain generic mapping capability and that that goal was "not necessarily indicative of an intent to target the US homeland."[617]

By early March 2003, days before the March 19 invasion of Iraq, the CIA had further pulled back from its October NIE view, concluding in a memorandum to the Chairman of the House Permanent Select Committee on Intelligence that it was an open question whether the attempted procurement of the mapping software had been the result of a specific request from Baghdad or had been inadvertent.[618] CIA also advised senior policymakers of this change in view. In the memorandum, the CIA stated that it "[had] no definite indications that Baghdad [was] planning to use WMD-armed UAVs against the U.S. mainland....[Although] we cannot exclude the possibility that th[e] purchase [of mapping software] was directed by Baghdad, information acquired in October suggests that it may have been inadvertent."[619]

With respect to ballistic missiles, CIA's position remained unchanged after the NIE.[620] Subsequent to the NIE, the Intelligence Community confirmed from Iraq's December 2002 declaration to the United Nations that Iraq had two versions of the al-Samoud missile, as described in the NIE. The longer-range version was inefficiently designed and did not go as far as the NIE had postulated, but it did have a range in excess of 150 kilometers.[621]

Post-War Findings of the Iraq Survey Group

The Iraq Survey Group concluded that, although Iraq had pursued UAVs as BW delivery systems in the past, Iraq's pre-Operation Iraqi Freedom program to develop small, autonomous-flight UAVs had actually been intended to fulfill reconnaissance and airborne electronic warfare missions. The ISG found no evidence suggesting that Iraq had, at the time of the war, any intent to use UAVs as BW or CW delivery systems.[622]

The ISG concluded that Iraq's purpose in converting a MiG-21 into a Remotely Piloted Vehicle (RPV) in early 1991 had been to create a CBW delivery system.[623] After the MiG-21 RPV program failed, Iraq in 1995 resumed efforts to convert manned aircraft into RPVs, this time with an L-29 jet trainer.[624] The ISG, however, was unable to establish whether the L-29 had an intended CBW role, although the ISG did obtain some indirect evidence that the L-29 RPV may have been intended for CBW delivery.[625] The ISG also concluded that Iraq had the capability to develop chemical or biological spray systems for the L-29, but found no evidence of any work along these lines.[626] The L-29 program ended in 2001.[627]

After several crashes of the L-29s, Iraq began to pursue long-range UAV options, probably at some point in 2000.[628] The ISG assessed, however, that these small UAVs had *not* been intended for use as chemical or biological delivery systems.[629] Specifically, although these small UAVs had the range, payload, guidance, and autonomy necessary to be used as BW delivery platforms, the ISG found no evidence that Iraq had intended to use them for such a purpose, had a suitable dispenser available, or had conducted research and development activity associated with use as a BW delivery system.[630]

The more advanced of Iraq's two UAV programs, the Al-Musayara-20, had actually been developed for use as a reconnaissance platform, according to a senior Iraqi official.[631] An interview with an Iraqi military official after Operation Iraqi Freedom revealed that many general officers had been shot down on helicopter reconnaissance missions during the Iran-Iraq war and therefore the military was interested in developing a UAV to perform such missions.[632] According to another official, although the Al-Musayara-20 was developed for a reconnaissance role, other roles, such as for the delivery of high explosives, were also considered.[633]

A competing program to the Al-Musayara, the Al Quds UAV program, had been less advanced but had included prototypes of varying sizes and weights.[634] The ISG concluded that the Al Quds program had been intended as an airborne electronic warfare platform.[635] Like the Al-Musayara, the Al Quds UAV had the range, autonomous guidance, and payload to enable it to deliver CBW.[636] The ISG uncovered no evidence, however, that Iraq had been developing a dispenser or had the intent to use the UAV as a BW delivery system. The Al Quds UAV was still in development when the war started.[637]

According to the Iraq Survey Group, Iraqi officials denied deliberately seeking to acquire mapping software for the United States, but did say they received mapping software that came as part of the package with the autopilots they purchased.[638] An official claimed to have received several autopilots for UAVs through the procurement agent, but asserted that these autopilots were never installed because they arrived on the eve of the war. The official was unaware of the current location of the autopilots.[639]

Regarding missile systems, the Iraq Survey Group concluded that Iraq had been developing and deploying ballistic missiles that exceeded United Nations restrictions.[640] The ISG concluded that Iraq had not possessed Scud or Scud-variant missiles after 1991, having by then either expended or unilaterally destroyed its stockpile.[641]

Analysis of the Intelligence Community's Pre-War Assessments

The Iraq Survey Group's uncovering of ballistic missile work that violated United Nations' restrictions affords a bright spot for the Intelligence Community's record of assessments on Iraq's unconventional weapons programs. The NIE accurately assessed that Iraq was deploying ballistic missiles with ranges exceeding United Nations restrictions.[642] And although the NIE did not assess accurately the status of Iraq's Scud missile force, we are not especially troubled by this inaccuracy in light of the NIE's clear statement that this assessment was based merely on accounting discrepancies.[643]

The record of the Intelligence Community's performance on the UAVs is more mixed (in part because the Intelligence Community's assessments themselves shifted during the pre-war period). While these assessments accurately described the Iraqi UAVs technical *capability* to deliver BW, the Intelligence Community's assessments that the UAVs were intended for this purpose—or that Iraq intended to strike the United States—were not borne out by the ISG's findings.

It is worth considering why the Intelligence Community's assessments were more correct in this area than they were with respect to other aspects of Iraq's arsenal. One possible answer is that—unlike the status of Iraq's BW and CW stockpiles—certain questions about Iraq's delivery systems—especially missiles—could be answered through technical means that operate from outside of the denied area, and which are generally less subject to questions about reliability. The intentions of a closed regime, however, are difficult to penetrate, and the reliability of any such information is difficult to determine. In areas of analysis that turn largely on intent, therefore, such as whether a regime is producing BW or intends to use its UAVs for BW delivery, the quality of the analysis will be largely dependent on the quality of the available human intelligence and on the ability of signals intelligence to penetrate communications. This highlights the imperative for analysts to explain the premise of their judgments, particularly when the ultimate judgment may rest on a very thin stream of information or on a chain of assumptions about intent.

With that said, the pre-war assessments on Iraq's delivery systems reflect significant shortcomings in analysis.

Delivery Systems Finding 1

The Intelligence Community made too much of an inferential leap, based on very little hard evidence, in judging that Iraq's unmanned aerial vehicles were being designed for use as biological warfare delivery vehicles and that they might be used against the U.S. homeland.

The NIE went beyond what one could reasonably conclude from the intelligence by judging that Iraq's UAVs were "probably intended to deliver biological warfare agents." Although past Iraqi interest in UAVs as BW vehicles was a reasonable indicator that the interest may have continued, the paucity of subsequent evidence should have led to a more nuanced statement in the NIE—such as that BW delivery was a possible use, but not necessarily an intended one. That the NIE did not discuss in any detail other possible missions for the UAVs only compounded this problem.[644] Moreover, most analysts discounted specific reporting indicating that Iraq was seeking equipment suited to a reconnaissance mission for its UAVs.

The Intelligence Community's assessments about the purpose of Iraq's UAV programs rested largely on inferences drawn from the inherent capabilities of such UAVs and knowledge about Iraq's past UAV programs, as discussed above. The conclusion that the UAVs were probably intended for BW delivery, however, reached beyond what the intelligence would reasonably bear.

Similarly, the single stream of reporting that the Iraqi procurement agent was attempting to purchase U.S. mapping software was insufficient to justify the NIE's statement that this interest "strongly suggest[ed]" that Iraq was investigating ways to target the U.S. homeland with UAVs. While certain analysts took the proper steps to push the Intelligence Community back from this judgment after doubts about this reporting emerged, the Intelligence Community as a whole was slow to assimilate this new information—particularly given its critical importance.

Delivery Systems Finding 2

The Intelligence Community failed to communicate adequately to policymakers the weak foundations upon which its conclusions were based.

Whether or not any statement about attacking the U.S. homeland merited inclusion in the NIE, it is clear that the rather thin foundation for these assessments was not clearly communicated to policymakers. And the NIE's assessment that the UAVs were "probably intended" for BW delivery did not make clear that this conclusion rested largely on analytical assumptions about Iraqi intent based on the history of Iraq's UAV programs and on the UAVs' inherent capabilities. Nor did the NIE explain why it focused only on a possible weapons-related role for UAVs. A WINPAC analyst subsequently explained that the NIE's purpose was to discuss Iraq's WMD programs, and that accordingly the UAV section addressed the UAVs' use as a BW delivery platform and not their other possible uses. The failure to explain that reasoning in the NIE, however, leaves the impression that other possible uses for the UAV had been rejected rather than simply not discussed.[645]

Delivery Systems Finding 3

The Intelligence Community failed to give adequate consideration to other possible uses for Iraq's UAVs or to give due credence to countervailing evidence.

Finally, once again, the UAV episode reflects the tendency of Intelligence Community analysts to view data through the lens of its overall assumptions about Saddam Hussein's behavior. As noted, the NIE itself did not discuss other possible purposes for the UAVs or explain why the Estimate focused only on a weapons-related purpose. In addition, however, the Intelligence Community was too quick to characterize evidence that contradicted the theory that UAVs were intended for BW delivery as an Iraqi "deception" or "cover story." And a Senior Executive Memorandum warned that Iraq "probably will assert that UAVs are intended as target drones or reconnaissance platforms" to counter the claim in the British and U.S. "white papers" that the UAVs have a BW delivery role.[646]

Delivery Systems Finding 4

The Intelligence Community was generally correct in assessing that Iraq was continuing ballistic missile work that violated United Nations restrictions, but erred in many of the specifics.

We commend the Intelligence Community for correctly assessing that Iraq was working on ballistic missile programs that violated United Nations strictures. As the ISG's findings demonstrate, however, many of the Community's specific estimates were off the mark. The Community judged, for instance, that Iraq retained a force of "up to a few dozen Scud-variant SRBMs [short-range ballistic missiles]."[647] The ISG concluded, however, that Iraq did not have any Scud missiles after 1991.[648] Similarly, the Community stated in the NIE that "in January 2002, Iraq flight-tested an extended-range version of the al-Samoud that flew beyond the 150-km range limit." The Community subsequently learned that it had misidentified the missile and had incorrectly deduced the missile's range; in actuality, the missile, while it had a range that exceeded 150 kilometers, did not exceed that limit by as much as analysts initially thought because the engine was less effective than they estimated.[649]

In short, while the Community was technically correct that Iraq's missile systems violated United Nations strictures, it erred significantly in degree.

Conclusion

As has proven the case with other pre-war Intelligence Community judgments about Iraq's unconventional weapons programs, the assumptions held by Iraq analysts about Saddam Hussein's behavior were not unreasonable ones. These assumptions, however, drove the Intelligence Community to make overly inferential leaps about Iraq's UAV program based on thin evidence, and to fail to communicate this thin evidentiary basis to policymakers. While we fully understand that, in the wake of September 11, the Community felt obliged to report even relatively unlikely threats against the United States, the Community should have at a minimum explained more fully the uncertainties underlying its assessments.

REGIME DECISIONMAKING

Regime Decisionmaking Summary Finding

The Intelligence Community, because of a lack of analytical imagination, failed even to consider the possibility that Saddam Hussein would decide to destroy his chemical and biological weapons and to halt work on his nuclear program after the first Gulf War.

The Intelligence Community failed to examine seriously the possibility that domestic or regional political pressures or some other factors might have prompted Saddam Hussein to destroy his stockpiles and to forswear active development of weapons of mass destruction after the first Gulf War.[650] The Community was certainly aware of the overall political dynamics that underpinned Saddam Hussein's regime—that he was a brutal dictator who ruled Iraq through a combination of violence, secrecy, mendacity, and fear—but the Community did not seriously consider the range of possible decisions that Saddam might make regarding his weapons programs given his idiosyncratic decisionmaking processes.

Though the likelihood that one of those possible decisions was to destroy his weapons seemed very remote to almost all outside observers, it was one that Community analysts at least should have seriously considered. In truth, any assessment of the effect of Saddam's political situation on his decisions about WMD in the years from 1991 to 2003 would more likely than not have resulted—and, in point of fact, did result—in the conclusion that Saddam retained his WMD programs.[651] But whether or not it was extraordinarily difficult (if not effectively impossible) for the Intelligence Community to have discerned Saddam Hussein's true intentions, the Community's lack of imagination about the range of strategies and tactics Saddam might adopt left the Community with an incomplete analytical picture.

Having gained access to Iraq and its leaders, the Iraq Survey Group concluded that the unlikely course of voluntary abandonment by Saddam Hussein of his weapons of mass destruction was, in fact, the reality. According to the ISG, Saddam's regime, under severe pressure from United Nations sanctions, reacted by unilaterally destroying its WMD stockpiles and halting work on its WMD programs.[652] Saddam decided to abandon his weapons programs because the economy and infrastructure of Iraq were collapsing under the weight of the sanctions. Saddam therefore ordered the unilateral destruction of biological and chemical weapons stockpiles in 1991 and chose to focus on securing sanctions relief before resuming WMD development.[653] At the same time, in an attempt to project power—both domestically as well as against perceived regional threats such as Iran and Israel—Iraq chose to obfuscate whether it actually possessed WMD.[654] As a result, the U.S. Intelligence Community—and many other intelligence services around the world— believed that Iraq continued to possess unconventional weapons in large part because Iraqis were acting as if they *did* have them.

Like previous chapters, this section begins with a brief description of how the Intelligence Community assessed Baghdad's decisionmaking before the war and then compares that with the ISG's findings. We then describe the Community's lack of creative thinking about Saddam's motives that led to the failure even to consider the possibility that Saddam Hussein had decided to abandon his banned weapons programs.

The Intelligence Community's Pre-War Assessments

The Intelligence Community's assessments of Saddam's thought processes in the decade before Operation Iraqi Freedom are reflected in two broad lines of analysis: the threats to Saddam's regime and his threat to regional security. Throughout both these areas, one aspect remained relatively constant—the Intelligence Community emphasized repeatedly that it lacked "solid information about the activities and intentions of major players in Iraq" and was, in the words of one senior intelligence official, "flying blind" on the subject.[655]

Regime stability and decisionmaking. The Intelligence Community early on identified sanctions as a significant threat to Saddam's regime, but never assessed whether Saddam might address that threat by destroying his WMD. Immediately after the Gulf War, for example, the Intelligence Community prepared a Special National Intelligence Estimate assessing Saddam's prospects for survival in power.[656] That assessment noted that economic vulnerabilities presented a threat to Saddam's regime and that the "lifting of sanctions…would provide relief to the regime and would strengthen Saddam's prospects for survival."[657] The Special Estimate therefore assessed that Saddam would concentrate on getting sanctions eased or removed.[658]

Through the mid-1990s, the Intelligence Community continued to judge that the sanctions were a threat to the regime, but that Saddam "probably believe[d]" he could "outlast" them.[659] For example, in December 1993, the Intelligence Community produced another NIE on Saddam's prospects for survival, judging that the United Nations sanctions were "Saddam's Achilles' heel" because of their debilitating effect on the Iraqi economy.[660] The NIE did not consider the possibility that Iraq would actually comply with United Nations resolutions. In fact, the Estimate identified as one of the assumptions underlying the analysis that "Saddam Husayn would not fully comply with U.N. Resolutions."[661]

By June 1995, as living conditions and the economy continued to decline, the Intelligence Community assessed that Saddam's overall strategy was to seek a lifting of sanctions with the lowest possible level of compliance with UNSCOM's demands for a full accounting of Iraq's WMD programs.[662] Laying out Saddam's options, a June 1995 Special Estimate judged that in the short term Saddam was "likely to make a gesture to UNSCOM...by providing limited additional information on Iraq's BW program."[663] If that gesture failed to achieve relief from sanctions within three months, however, Saddam "probably [would] return to a confrontational mode."[664] Such a "confrontational mode" included suspending cooperation with UNSCOM, sabotaging or obstructing UNSCOM monitoring, and expelling or taking hostage United Nations personnel.[665] In short, the Intelligence Community judged that Saddam would choose confrontation over greater cooperation with the United Nations as a way to end sanctions.[666]

Throughout the remainder of the 1990s, the Intelligence Community continued to assess that sanctions threatened Saddam's regime, but also that "Saddam [was] determined to maintain elements of his WMD programs and probably calculate[d] he [could] stonewall UNSCOM while wearing down the Security Council's will to maintain sanctions."[667] Saddam's success in undermining international support for the sanctions and in repressing internal dissent also gave him greater confidence and resolve.[668] But more importantly, the commerce allowed under the Oil-for-Food program fueled international perceptions that sanctions had weakened.[669] This weakening, combined with the failure of UNSCOM to "uncover tangible proof of Iraqi concealment of weapons of mass destruction," bolstered domestic and international perceptions of the regime's strength.[670]

At the same time, by the end of the decade the Community assessed that Saddam "appear[ed] to have made a strategic decision that confrontation would be necessary to gain an end to the sanctions."[671] Saddam felt "that putting pressure on UNSCOM and the Security Council [was] the only way to achieve his goal of ending sanctions," according to the Intelligence Community, because Saddam did "not intend to fully comply with relevant Security Council resolutions."[672]

The Intelligence Community viewed Iraq's behavior vis-à-vis the United Nations inspections during this time against the backdrop of these assessments and of Iraq's history of concealing its WMD programs.[673] Accordingly, the Community judged that Iraq would continue to obstruct inspections "to the degree they believe[d] the inspections [would] undermine the security apparatus or uncover proscribed materials."[674] Thus, when Iraq agreed to the resumption of inspections in 2002, the Intelligence Community judged that Iraq did so in part because of confidence in its ability to hide its weapons-related activities.[675] The Community also assessed that Saddam was motivated to reengage with the United Nations in order to avoid U.S. military intervention.[676] If such delaying tactics failed to divert an attack, Iraq "could make a tactical retreat by acceding to some United Nations and U.S. demands and then reneg[ing] on them at the earliest opportunity."[677] Although Iraq had tried to open several back channels to the United States seeking improved relations, the Community viewed these moves as public relations efforts and did not consider as an option the possibility that Iraq would actually comply with United Nations resolutions.[678]

Still, analysis of Saddam's thinking and motivations remained largely speculative. In addition to the simple lack of information on Saddam's plans and intentions, the nature of Saddam's decisionmaking process, which the Intelligence Community assessed as highly centralized and therefore difficult to penetrate, compounded analysts' difficulties.[679] Saddam made "all key policy decisions" with little input from the bureaucracy, and he usually acted quickly and decisively.[680] He could also be "impulsive and deceptive" about his decisions.[681] Moreover, the Intelligence Community judged that Saddam "rule[d] primarily by fear," using his control over the military, security, and intelligence services to "impose his absolute authority and crush resistance."[682] Saddam reinforce[d] this control through "prominent members of his Tikriti clan who occup[ied] key leadership positions."[683] As a result, "all major decisions [were] made by Saddam and a few close relatives and associates."[684]

The Intelligence Community noted that these characteristics of Saddam's leadership style made it very difficult to read his intentions.[685]

Regional security and decisionmaking. The Intelligence Community assessed that regional supremacy for Iraq remained Saddam Hussein's fundamental goal from 1991 through 2003.[686] The Community judged, though, that to achieve that goal Saddam would need to rebuild Iraq's military might— including weapons of mass destruction.[687]

But, according to the Intelligence Community, Iraq's conventional military capabilities had deteriorated significantly during this time. By 1999, after four more years of sanctions and damage inflicted by U.S. military operations, Saddam's military was "smaller and much less well-equipped than it was on the eve of his 1990 invasion of Kuwait."[688] By 2002, the Community assessed that "Iraqi military morale and battlefield cohesion [were] more fragile today than in 1991."[689]

With respect to WMD capabilities, on the other hand, the Community's assessments that Iraq "retain[ed] residual chemical and biological weapons of mass destruction" remained constant.[690] Although cautioning that reading Saddam's intentions was difficult and that "critical factors important in shaping his behavior [we]re largely hidden from us," the Community nonetheless assessed that Saddam was "determined to retain elements of his WMD programs so that he [would] be able to intimidate his neighbors and deter potential adversaries such as Iran, Israel, and the United States."[691] Given Iraq's history with WMD, its desire for regional dominance, and the weaknesses in its conventional military forces, the Community did not consider the possibility that Saddam would try to achieve such intimidation and deterrence while bluffing about his possession of WMD.[692]

Post-War Findings of the Iraq Survey Group

The Iraq Survey Group concluded that Saddam Hussein unilaterally destroyed his WMD stocks in 1991. Saddam apparently concluded that economic sanctions posed such a threat to his regime that, although he valued the possession of WMD, he concluded that he had to focus on sanctions relief before resuming WMD development.

Background. Iraq's successful use of CW to repel human-wave attacks in the Iran-Iraq war had convinced Saddam Hussein of the importance of WMD and it became an "article of faith" for Saddam that WMD and theater ballistic missiles were necessary to secure Iraqi national security.[693] Saddam also believed that Iraq's possession of WMD and Iraq's willingness to use it "contributed substantially to deterring the United States from going to Baghdad in 1991."[694]

The destruction of WMD. After the Gulf War, however, the United Nations passed resolutions explicitly linking the removal of economic sanctions with Iraq's WMD disarmament.[695] Saddam Hussein initially judged that the sanctions would be short-lived, that Iraq could weather them by making a few limited concessions, and that Iraq could successfully hide much of its pre-existing weaponry and documentation.[696] Accordingly, Iraq declared to the United Nations part of its ballistic missile and chemical warfare programs, but not its biological or nuclear weapons programs.[697] But after initial inspections proved much more thorough and intrusive than Baghdad had expected, Saddam became concerned. In order to prevent discovery of his still-hidden pre-1991 WMD programs, Saddam ordered Hussein Kamil to destroy large numbers of undeclared weapons and related materials in July 1991.[698]

According to the Iraq Survey Group, Saddam's decision to destroy Iraq's WMD stockpiles in 1991 was likely shared with only a handful of senior Iraqi officials, a decision that would have important and lasting consequences.[699] Saddam so dominated the political structure of the Iraqi regime that his strategic policy and intent were synonymous with the regime's strategic policy and intent.[700] Moreover, in addition to dominating the regime's decisionmaking, Saddam also maintained secrecy and compartmentalization in his decisions, relying on a few close advisors and family members.[701] And Saddam's penchant for using violence to ensure loyalty and suppress dissent encouraged a "culture of lying" and discouraged administrative transparency.[702] As a result, the ISG concluded that instructions to subordinates were rarely documented and often shrouded in uncertainty.[703] The decision to destroy the WMD stockpiles was therefore confined to a very small group of people at the top of the Ba'ath pyramid.

The sanctions bind. By the mid-1990s, United Nations sanctions were taking a serious toll; removing them therefore became Saddam's first priority, according to the ISG.[704] Iraq's failure to document its unilateral destruction of WMD, however, complicated this effort. Also complicating Saddam's goal of sanctions removal was his continuing concern with regional threats to his security. Although he had destroyed his militarily significant WMD stocks, his "perceived requirement to bluff about WMD capabilities made it too dangerous to clearly reveal" Iraq's lack of WMD to the international community, especially Iran.[705] Saddam was therefore in a bind, on the one hand wanting to avoid being caught in a violation of United Nations sanctions but, on the other, not wanting his rivals to know of his weakness.

Saddam decided to strike the balance between these competing objectives, according to the ISG, by preserving Iraq's ability to reconstitute his WMD while simultaneously seeking sanctions relief through the appearance of cooperation with the IAEA, UNSCOM, and, later, the United Nations Monitoring Verification and Inspection Commission (UNMOVIC).[706] Iraq's behavior under the sanctions reflects that the Iraqis "never got the balance right."[707] Though Saddam repeatedly told his ministers not to participate in WMD-related activity, he at the same time was working to preserve the capability eventually to reconstitute his unconventional weapons programs.[708] And the Iraqis continued to conceal proscribed materials from United Nations inspectors.[709] Moreover, even when there was nothing incriminating to hide, the Iraqis did not fully cooperate with the inspectors, judging that an effective United Nations inspection process would expose Iraq's lack of WMD and therefore expose its vulnerability, especially vis-à-vis Iran.[710]

The regime's decision to disclose long-concealed WMD documents in the wake of Hussein Kamil's defection in 1995 further eroded confidence in the credibility of Iraqi declarations. The ISG concluded that the release of these documents served only to validate UNSCOM concerns that Iraq was still concealing its WMD programs.[711]

Suspending cooperation with the United Nations. Angered by the continuing sanctions, inspections, and military attacks such as Operation Desert Fox, Saddam Hussein in a secret meeting in 1998 unilaterally abrogated Iraqi compliance with all United Nations resolutions, though, according to the ISG, it is unclear if anything concrete followed from this decision.[712] Meanwhile, Iraq continued to take advantage of the Oil-for-Food Program to augment regime revenue streams. Saddam Hussein used much of Iraq's growing reserves of hard currency to invest in Iraq's military-industrial complex, to procure dual-use materials, and to initiate military research and development projects. Sanctions remained in place, however.[713]

With international scrutiny bearing down on Iraq in late 2002, Saddam Hussein finally revealed to his senior military officials that Iraq had no weapons of mass destruction.[714] His generals were "surprised" to learn this fact, because Saddam's "boasting" had led many to believe Iraq had some hidden WMD capacity and because Saddam's secretive decisionmaking style fostered uncertainty.[715] In fact, senior officials were still convinced that Iraq had WMD in March 2003 because Saddam had assured them that if the United States invades, they need only "resist one week" and then Saddam would "take over."[716]

Analysis of the Intelligence Community's Pre-War Assessments

Saddam Hussein's decisionmaking process was, as the Intelligence Community assessed before the war and the Iraq Survey Group confirmed, secretive and highly centralized. And in this sense, the Intelligence Community cannot be faulted for failing to penetrate this process. But we believe the Community is open to criticism for failing to appreciate the full range of Saddam's strategic and tactical decisionmaking options regarding his weapons programs. At the very least, the Community should have *considered* the possibility that Saddam had halted active pursuit of his WMD programs after 1991.

Saddam and his regime repeatedly insisted that all of Iraq's banned weapons had been destroyed and that there were no active programs to reconstitute the capability. The United Nations inspectors, after 1996, found no conclusive evidence that these claims were wrong. In retrospect, as found by the ISG, it is clear that the stockpiles and programs were not there to be found. The question therefore arises of why the Intelligence Community did not discover that fact before the war, or at least consider the possibility that, however improbably, Saddam was telling the truth.

As discussed above, the Intelligence Community made multiple—and avoidable—errors in concluding "with high confidence" that Saddam retained WMD stockpiles and programs. It is a separate question why the Community failed to conclude affirmatively that he did *not* have them.

In large part the explanation lies in Saddam's own behavior. He *had* concealed crucial facts about his WMD efforts. He *did* repeatedly and continually obstruct the inspectors, to the point, in 1998, of completely terminating cooperation and forcing the inspectors to conclude that they could no longer do their work. When someone acts like he is hiding something, it is hard to entertain the conclusion that he really has nothing to hide.

The failure to conclude that Saddam had abandoned his weapons programs was therefore an understandable one.[717] And even a human source in Saddam's inner circle, or intercepts of conversations between senior Iraqi leaders, may not have been sufficient for analysts to have concluded that Saddam ordered the destruction of his WMD stockpiles in 1991—and this kind of intelligence is extremely difficult to get. According to Charles Duelfer, the Special Advisor to the Director of Central Intelligence for Iraq's Weapons of Mass Destruction and head of the Iraq Survey Group, only six or seven senior officials were likely privy to Saddam's decision to halt his WMD programs.[718] Moreover, because of Saddam's secretive and highly centralized decisionmaking process, as well as the "culture of lies" within the Iraqi bureaucracy, even after Saddam informed his senior military leaders in December 2002 that Iraq had no WMD, there was uncertainty among these officers as to the truth, and many senior commanders evidently believed that there were chemical weapons retained for use if conventional defenses failed.[719]

That it would have been very difficult to get such evidence is, however, not the end of the story. Failing to conclude that Saddam had ended his banned weapons programs is one thing—not even considering it as a possibility is another. The Intelligence Community did not even evaluate the possibility that Saddam would destroy his stockpiles and halt work on his nuclear program. The absence of such a discussion within the Intelligence Community is, in our view, indicative of the rut that the Community found itself in throughout the 1990s. Rather than thinking imaginatively, and considering seemingly unlikely and unpopular possibilities, the Intelligence Community instead found itself wedded to a set of assumptions about Iraq, focusing on intelligence reporting that appeared to confirm those assumptions.

Over the course of 12 years the Intelligence Community did not produce a single analytical product that examined the possibility that Saddam Hussein's desire to escape sanctions, fear of being "caught" decisively, or anything else would cause him to destroy his WMD.[720] The National Intelligence Officer for Near East and South Asia noted that such a hypothesis was so far removed from analysts' understanding of Iraq that it would have been very difficult to get such an idea published even as a "red-team" exercise.[721] An intellectual culture or atmosphere in which certain ideas were simply too "unrespectable" and out of synch with prevailing policy and analytic perspectives pervaded the Intelligence Community. But much of the conventional wisdom that led analysts to reject even the consideration of this alternative hypothesis was itself based largely on assumptions rather than derived from analysis of hard data.[722] In our view, rather than relying on inherited assumptions, analysts need to test favored hypotheses even more rigorously when the paucity of intelligence forces analysts to rely, not on specific intelligence, but on a country's history, politics, and observed behavior.[723]

Conclusion

Iraq's decision to abandon its unconventional weapons programs while simultaneously hiding this decision was, at the very least, a counterintuitive one. And given the nature of the regime, the Intelligence Community can hardly be blamed for not penetrating Saddam's decisionmaking process. In this light, it is worth noting that Saddam's fellow Arabs (including, evidently, his senior military leadership as well as many of the rest of the world's intelligence agencies and most inspectors) also thought he had retained his weapons programs, thus responding to charges that the Community was projecting Western thinking onto a product of a foreign culture.

What the Intelligence Community *can* be blamed for, however, is not considering whether Saddam might have taken this counterintuitive route. Community analysts should have been more imaginative in contemplating the range of options from which Saddam might select. While such imaginative analysis would not necessarily or even likely have ultimately led analysts to the right conclusion, serious discussion of it in finished intelligence would have at least warned policymakers of the range of possibilities, a function that is critically important in the inherently uncertain arena of political analysis.

CAUSES FOR THE INTELLIGENCE COMMUNITY'S INACCURATE PRE-WAR ASSESSMENTS

The Intelligence Community fundamentally misjudged the status of Iraq's nuclear, biological, and chemical programs. While the Intelligence Community did accurately assess certain aspects of Iraq's programs, the Community's central pre-war assessments—that Iraq had biological and chemical weapons and was reconstituting its nuclear weapons program—were shown by the post-war findings to be wrong.[724] The discrepancies between the pre-war assessments and the post-war findings can be, in part, attributed to the inherent difficulties in obtaining information in denied areas such as Iraq. But the Intelligence Community's inaccurate assessments were also the result of systemic weaknesses in the way the Community collects, analyzes, and disseminates intelligence.

Collection

The task of collecting meaningful intelligence on Iraq's weapons programs was extraordinarily difficult. Iraq's highly effective denial and deception program (which was employed against all methods of U.S. collection), the absence of United Nations inspectors after 1998, and the lack of a U.S. diplomatic presence in-country all contributed to difficulties in gathering data on the Iraqi regime's purported nuclear, biological, and chemical programs. And these difficulties were compounded by the challenge of discerning regime intentions.

Nonetheless, we believe the Intelligence Community could have done better. We had precious little human intelligence, and virtually no useful signals intelligence, on a target that was one of the United States' top intelligence priorities. The preceding sections, which have focused on the Intelligence Community's assessments on particular aspects of Iraq's weapons programs, have tended to reflect shortcomings in what is commonly referred to as "tradecraft"; the focus has been on questions such as whether a critical human source was properly validated, or whether analysts drew unduly sweeping inferences from limited or dubious intelligence. But it should not be forgotten why these tradecraft failures took on such extraordinary importance. They were important because of how little additional information our collection agencies managed to provide on Iraq's weapons programs.

This was a problem the Intelligence Community saw coming. As early as September 1998, the Community recognized its limited collection on Iraq.[725] The National Intelligence Council noted these limits in 1998, the specifics of which cannot be discussed in an unclassified forum.[726] Yet the Intelligence Community was still unwilling—or unable—to take steps necessary to improve its capabilities after late 1998. In short, as one senior policymaker described it, the Intelligence Community after 1998 "was running on fumes," depending on "inference and assumptions rather than hard data."[727]

This section examines and assesses the performance of each of the collection disciplines on Iraq's weapons programs.

Human Intelligence

Human intelligence collection in Iraq suffered from two major flaws: too few human sources, and the questionable reliability of those few sources the Intelligence Community had. After 1998, the CIA had no dedicated unilateral sources in Iraq reporting on Iraq's nuclear, biological, and chemical programs; indeed, the CIA had only a handful of Iraqi assets in total as of 2001.[728] Furthermore, several of the liaison and defector sources relied upon by the Intelligence Community, most prominently Curveball, proved to be fabricators. Several systemic impediments to effective collection contributed to this dearth of human intelligence.

Conclusion 1

Saddam Hussein's Iraq was a hard target for human intelligence, but it will not be the last that we face. When faced with such targets in the future, the United States needs to supplement its traditional methodologies with more innovative approaches.

There are several reasons for the lack of quality human sources reporting on Iraqi weapons programs. At the outset, and as noted above, Iraq was an uncommonly challenging target for human intelligence. And given the highly compartmented nature of Saddam Hussein's regime, it is unclear whether even a source at the highest levels of the Iraqi government would have been able to provide true insight into Saddam's decisionmaking. The challenges revealed by the Iraq case study suggest some inherent limitations of human intelligence collection.

But these difficulties also point to the need, not only for improving traditional human source collection, but also for exploring new methods to approach such targets. Although CIA's Directorate of Operations has a well-developed methodology for recruiting and running assets in denied areas, the nature of the WMD target, particularly as aspects of it may migrate away from centralized, state-run programs, indicates that current methodologies should be supplemented with alternative approaches. In particular, when we want information about procurement networks or non-state run proliferation activities of interest, then we may need to use non-traditional platforms. The technical complexity of the WMD target also suggests that it may require a cadre of case officers with technical backgrounds or training. We discuss the possibilities—and the limitations—of some of these new approaches in Chapter Seven (Collection).

The Iraq case study also reveals the importance of liaison relationships for exploiting human sources in denied areas. Reliance on liaison sources, without any knowledge of the identity of the source or subsource(s), can be problematic, as the Curveball episode most painfully demonstrates. But liaison services can provide invaluable access to targets the U.S. Intelligence Community may find it difficult, if not impossible, to recruit or penetrate. It is thus critical to enhance our intelligence from liaison services.

Conclusion 2

Rewarding CIA and DIA case officers based on how many assets they recruit impedes the recruitment of *quality* assets.

This case study also suggests that current internal promotion and incentive structures are impediments to recruitment of quality assets. In practice, both CIA's Directorate of Operations (DO) and DIA's Defense HUMINT Service reward case officers based largely on the quantity rather than quality of their recruitments.[729] While this is in part because quality is inherently difficult to measure, the "numbers game" encourages officers to focus their recruitment efforts on assets who are easier to recruit—often individuals who are themselves several steps removed from information of intelligence value. Other activities that may enhance the long-term ability to recruit quality assets—language or WMD-related technical training, for example—are also often discouraged because of the significant amount of time such training takes out of the officer's career.

Finding the right personnel incentive structures is a perennial concern, and CIA's DO has taken some positive steps in recent years. But much more needs to be done. In Chapters Six (Management) and Seven (Collection) of our report, we offer several recommendations aimed at improving the personnel system within the Intelligence Community.[730]

Conclusion 3

The CIA, and even more so the DIA, must do a better job of testing the veracity of crucial human sources.

Another problem was the questionable reliability of the few human sources the Community had. As the Curveball and Niger experiences illustrate, asset validation and authentication are crucial to the Intelligence Community's ability to produce reliable intelligence. Although the CIA has an established asset validation system in place, the system and its use are not without flaws. As practiced, asset validation can sometimes become an exercise in "checking the boxes" rather than a serious effort to vet and validate the source.

On the other hand, at least the CIA understands the importance of asset validation. With respect to Curveball—the primary source of our intelligence on Iraq's BW program—the Defense HUMINT Service disclaimed any *responsibility* for validating the asset, arguing that credibility determinations were for analysts and that the collectors were merely "conduits" for the reporting.[731] This abdication of operational responsibility represented a serious failure in tradecraft.[732]

Although lack of direct physical access to the source made vetting and validating Curveball more difficult, it did not make it impossible. While Defense HUMINT neglected its validation responsibilities, elements of the CIA's DO understood the necessity of validating Curveball's information and made efforts to do so; indeed, they found indications that caused them to have doubts about Curveball's reliability.[733] The system nonetheless "broke down" because of analysts' strong conviction about the truth of Curveball's information and because the DO's concerns were not heard outside the DO.

In that regard, although CIA was alert to the need to assess Curveball's credibility, CIA was insufficiently diligent in following up on concerns that surfaced regarding his reliability. When what had been "handling" concerns became issues that reflected more directly on Curveball's veracity, working-level CIA officials did not press these concerns early enough or with sufficient vigor to the senior-most levels of CIA and senior leaders did not pay enough attention to those concerns that were expressed.

For its part, these senior-most levels of management at CIA—including the Deputy Director for Operations and the Deputy Director of Central Intelligence—were remiss in not raising concerns about Curveball with senior policymakers before the war. Even though these concerns may not have been raised with sufficient passion to indicate a serious problem, CIA management should at a minimum have alerted policymakers that such concerns existed.

While the DO made some efforts to try to validate Curveball, its failure to authenticate the Niger reporting also reflected a tradecraft error. The CIA made no effort to authenticate the documents on which those reports were based—even though one of those reports was a "verbatim" text of a document, and even though there were doubts emerging about their authenticity.

This said, we of course do not suggest that reliance on human intelligence reporting should be limited only to those sources who have been fully vetted and validated. The Intelligence Community does, however, need to ensure that consumers of intelligence have better visibility into the Community's assessment of the integrity of a given source.

Conclusion 4

Iraq's denial and deception efforts successfully hampered U.S. intelligence collection.

Iraq's well-developed denial and deception efforts also hampered the Intelligence Community's ability to collect reliable intelligence. On the human intelligence front, for instance, by the early 1990s the Community had identified significant Iraqi efforts to manipulate U.S. human intelligence operations. The Iraqis sought to saturate U.S. intelligence collection nodes with false and misleading information.[734] Furthermore, Iraq's pervasive security and counterintelligence services rendered attempts to recruit Iraqi officials extremely difficult.[735]

Iraq's denial and deception capabilities also frustrated U.S. signals and imagery collection due to Iraq's excellent security practices. The specifics of these capabilities are discussed in the classified report.

Conclusion 5

In the case of Iraq, collectors of intelligence absorbed the prevailing analytic consensus and tended to reject or ignore contrary information. The result was "tunnel vision" focusing on the Intelligence Community's existing assumptions.

At the same time, the knowledge that Iraq's denial and deception techniques had been so successful in the past hampered efforts to develop quality human sources. For example, several human sources asserted before the war that Iraq did not retain any WMD.[736] And one source, who may have come closer to the truth than any other, said that Iraq would never admit that it did *not* have WMD because it would be tantamount to suicide in the Middle East.[737] But the pervasive influence of the conventional wisdom—that Iraq had WMD and was actively hiding it from inspectors—created a kind of intellectual "tunnel vision" that caused officers to believe that information contradicting the conventional wisdom was "disinformation."[738] Potential sources for alternative views were denigrated or not pursued by collectors.[739] Moreover, collectors were often responding to requirements that were geared toward supporting or confirming the prevailing analytical line.[740] The reliance on prevailing assumptions was not just an analytical problem, therefore, but affected both the collection and analysis of information.

Technical Intelligence Collection

Technical intelligence was able to provide very little in the way of conclusive intelligence about Iraq's purported WMD programs. This deficiency stemmed from several causes.

Conclusion 6

Intercepted communications identified some procurement efforts, but such intelligence was of only marginal utility because most procurements were of dual-use materials.

In the late 1990s, the Intelligence Community focused on targeting procurement networks. This approach was problematic, in part because much of the equipment and precursor materials required to produce biological and chemical weapons, and to a lesser extent nuclear weapons, can also serve other legitimate purposes. Also, attempted procurements cannot be equated with an actual weapons capability. Although evidence that a country such as Iraq was procuring dual-use items can of course be useful, such procurement activity will rarely provide unequivocal evidence of weapons activity. As such, information that Iraq was procuring industrial chemicals provided little insight into Iraq's CW programs because such purchases were consistent with the development of an indigenous chemical industry. This inherent problem was compounded by the Intelligence Community's tendency to exaggerate the nefariousness of Iraq's dual-use procurement efforts.

Conclusion 7

Signals intelligence against Iraq was seriously hampered by technical barriers.

The National Security Agency's (NSA's) lack of access was largely the result of technical barriers to collection. As a result, NSA was unable to exploit those communications that would be most likely to provide insights into Iraq's WMD programs.[741] The technical barriers to accessing these communications are substantial, and NSA and other signals intelligence collectors must

continue efforts to develop technical solutions to such challenges. The classified report discusses these technical barriers in greater detail.

Conclusion 8

Other difficulties relating to the security and counterintelligence methods of
the Iraqi regime hampered NSA collection.

The classified report discusses further reasons why signals intelligence collection against Iraq was so challenging.

Conclusion 9

Traditional imagery intelligence has limited utility in assessing chemical and
biological weapons programs.

Imagery intelligence is also limited in what it can reveal about a nation's
WMD programs. Imagery intelligence will rarely, if ever, provide insight into
intent regarding WMD—particularly CW or BW programs. Flawed conclusions drawn from imagery of suspected Iraqi CW sites before the war, for
instance, demonstrate that even precise and high-quality photographs of a target may yield little of value or, worse, positively mislead.[742] While imagery
will be a valuable tool for the Community in developing a full picture of a target country's infrastructure and overt movements, without credible human or
signals intelligence imagery is of limited utility with regard to BW and CW.
This said, imagery will nevertheless remain critical for satisfying requirements such as intelligence support to military operations, helping to cue other
forms of collection by providing overhead images, and providing methods for
corroborating or disproving information from other collection methods.

As the National Geospatial-Intelligence Agency's (NGA's) has conceded, the
inherent nature of chemical and biological weapons facilities means that the
infrastructure and activities of suspect WMD programs are difficult to assess
even with sophisticated and expensive U.S. satellites. Imagery analysts must
therefore look for "signatures" of suspicious activity. These signatures hold
open the possibility of identifying suspect activity but are susceptible to error
and denial and deception. As such, to answer the question whether a facility is

intended for the production of biological or chemical weapons, imagery analysis must be supplemented with other kinds of intelligence.

Beyond these straightforward difficulties, suspect activity can also be deliberately concealed from overhead reconnaissance.[743] Iraq—like many other countries with aspirations to develop nuclear, biological, and chemical weapons programs—was well aware of U.S. overhead collection capabilities and practices, and took steps to avoid detection.[744] Imagery intelligence will therefore remain only one piece of the collection effort against WMD, and will have to be used in conjunction with information from other sources.[745]

Despite these inherent limitations, the pre-war assessments of Iraq's chemical warfare program relied very heavily on imagery. For example, the NIE assessed that "much of" Iraq's estimated stockpile of 100 to 500 metric tons of CW was "added in the last year."[746] Analysts explained that this assessment—which indicated not only that Iraq had large stockpiles but that it was actively producing CW agents—was based largely on imagery showing "transshipment" activity that analysts judged to be the movement of CW munitions.[747] Post-war "reassessments" by the National Geospatial-Intelligence Agency, however, revealed that this transshipment activity was likely related to conventional maintenance and logistical activity.[748] Because of the dearth of solid reporting from signals or human intelligence on Iraq's chemical warfare program, imagery of "transshipments" was asked to carry more weight than it could logically bear.[749]

Measurement and signature intelligence (MASINT). MASINT played a negligible role in intelligence collection against the Iraqi WMD target. There were several reasons for this.

Conclusion 10

MASINT collection was severely hampered by problems similar to those faced by other intelligence methods. Analysts' lack of familiarity with MASINT also reduced its role in analysts' assessments of Iraq's WMD programs.

MASINT collection was hampered by practical problems stemming from the difficulties inherent in collecting intelligence against a regime such as Saddam's Iraq.[750] Furthermore, information from other intelligence collection methods is important to cue MASINT collection.[751] The difficulties described above, which are described in greater detail in the classified report, rendered MASINT collection an even more difficult task than usual.

Second, in part because of a lack of collection and in part because of a general lack of understanding among analysts about MASINT and its capabilities, very little MASINT actually factored into Community assessments. There was MASINT reporting on WMD—the National Intelligence Collection Board noted that from June 2000 through January 2003 MASINT sources produced over 1,000 reports on Iraqi WMD (none of which provided a definitive indication of WMD activity).[752] But the reporting did not play a significant role in forming assessments about Iraq's WMD programs.[753] This lack of reliance was no doubt due in part to the tendency among analysts to discount information that contradicted the prevailing view that Iraq had WMD. But it was also due in part to unfamiliarity with, and lack of confidence in, MASINT.[754]

Collection Management

Conclusion 11

Recognizing that it was having problems collecting quality intelligence against Iraq, the Intelligence Community launched an effort to study ways to improve its collection performance. This process was hampered by haphazard follow-up by some agencies; in particular, NSA failed to follow-up promptly on the Intelligence Community's recommendations.

Our study of Iraq not only reveals shortcomings in (and inherent limitations of) specific collection disciplines; it also highlights the Intelligence Community's inability to harmonize and coordinate the collection process *across* collection systems. There are many reasons for the Community's inability to do so, including resource and personnel management issues. But another reason for the difficulty may be the simple fact that there is no institutionalized process above the various collection agencies that oversees the whole of collection. It was not until 1998 that a collection management system was established that was dedicated to "examin[ing] the [Intelligence Community]'s most intractable intelligence problems and develop[ing] new ways to improve collection."[755] That entity, the Collection Concepts Development Center (CCDC), was established by the Assistant DCI for Collection. When the CCDC tackled the problem of collection on Iraq—in 2000—it set out a coordinated approach that sought to optimize the available collection resources. For example, the CCDC study recommended a shift of imagery collection away from military targets such as the no-fly zones and towards suspect WMD sites. The study also recommended ways for NSA to try to penetrate Iraq's communications, as discussed below. But the CCDC effort is sustained only through the force of the Assistant DCI for Collection's individual efforts. Our report will offer recommendations as to the best way that such an effort can be institutionalized within the Intelligence Community.

Such an institutionalized process would also ensure that new collection strategies are implemented by individual collection agencies. For example, as noted, the 2000 CCDC study addressed the problem presented by NSA's inability to exploit certain critical Iraqi communications. The CCDC recommended that NSA collect signals from a certain source to assess whether that source was being used for WMD-related communications.[756] NSA failed to pursue this recommendation vigorously.[757] Instead, NSA acknowledged that "NSA did not discover that the Iraqis had this mode of communications...until late 2002," at which time "NSA's limited resources were fully engaged with other priorities."[758] This anecdote highlights the imperative for a well-managed collection system, to ensure that we do not miss valuable collection opportunities in the future.

A related problem—that of the poor quality of interagency communication—is illustrated by imagery analysis of increased collection of suspected Iraqi CW sites in 2002. In this instance, analysts fundamentally misunderstood how imagery was collected, a significant breakdown in a crucial communication link between collectors and analysts. Until 2000, imagery intelligence collection had been largely oriented toward supporting military operations such as patrolling the no-fly zones.[759] Imagery collection operations against the Iraq WMD target more than doubled from 2001 through 2002, however, prompted largely by the aforementioned CCDC study, which recommended that more resources be focused on that target.[760] The increased coverage included images of ammunition depots that had not previously been imaged on a regular basis.[761] Analysts, however, were not aware of the degree to which imaging was increased during this period nor of the specifics of NGA's targeting changes.[762] As a result, analysts interpreted this imagery as reflecting new and increased activity—when, in reality, much of the "increase" in activity may have been simply an increase in the volume of imagery collected. [763]

Analysis

Intelligence analysis is a tricky business. Analysts are often forced to make predictions in the absence of clear evidence—and then are pilloried after twenty-twenty hindsight reveals that they failed to paint a full picture from conflicting and scattered pieces of evidence. As we have seen, assessing the scope of an adversary's nuclear, biological, and chemical weapons programs poses an especially formidable challenge in this regard; extrapolations from past experience and thin streams of reporting are usually necessary.

Even the best analytical practices, therefore, will sometimes result in assessments that later prove inaccurate. But given the difficulties inherent in analyzing WMD programs—and the serious consequences for judging the capabilities and intentions of such programs incorrectly—it is imperative that the analysis on which such judgments are based be as rigorous, thorough, and candid as possible. In the case of Iraq, the analytical community fell short of this standard.

Analysts have indicated that their starting point for evaluating Iraq's WMD programs was Iraq's past. Analysts' assumptions were formed based on Iraq's history of producing CW and BW, its use of CW, its history of effectively concealing its nuclear program before the Gulf War, and the regime's failure to account for its previously declared stockpiles.[764] Thus, the analysts operated from the premise that Iraq very likely still possessed CW and BW, was still hiding it from inspectors, and was still seeking to rebuild its nuclear weapons program. The analytical flaw was not that this premise was unreasonable (for it was not); rather, it was that this premise hardened into a presumption, and analysts began to fit the facts to the theory rather than the other way around.

Conclusion 12

Analysts skewed the analytical process by requiring proof that Iraq did not have WMD.

One consequence of this tendency was that analysts effectively shifted the burden of proof, requiring proof that Iraq did *not* have active WMD programs rather than requiring affirmative proof of their existence. Though the U.S. *policy* position was that Iraq bore the responsibility to prove that it did not have banned weapons programs, the Intelligence Community's burden of proof should have been more objective. CIA's WINPAC nuclear analysts explained that, given Iraq's history of successful deception regarding the state of its nuclear program and evidence that Iraq was attempting to procure components that *could* be used in a uranium enrichment program, they could not envision having reached the conclusion that Iraq was *not* reconstituting its nuclear program. The analysts noted that they could have reached such a conclusion only if they had specific information from a very well-placed, reliable human source.[765] By raising the evidentiary burden so high, analysts artificially skewed the analytical process toward confirmation of their original hypothesis—that Iraq had active WMD programs.

Conclusion 13

Analysts did not question the hypotheses underlying their conclusions, and tended to discount evidence that cut against those hypotheses.

Indeed, it appears that in some instances analysts' presumptions were so firm that they simply *disregarded* evidence that did not support their hypotheses. As we saw in several instances, when confronted with evidence that indicated Iraq did not have WMD, analysts tended to discount such information. Rather than weighing the evidence independently, analysts accepted information that fit the prevailing theory and rejected information that contradicted it.[766] While analysts must adopt some frame of reference to interpret the flood of data they see, their baseline assumptions must be flexible enough to permit revision by discordant information. The analysts' frame of reference on Iraq's WMD programs—formed as it was by Iraq's previous use of such weapons, Iraq's continued efforts to conceal its activities, and Iraq's past success at hiding such programs—was so strong, however, that contradictory data was often discounted as likely false.

Analysts' discounting of contradictory information reflected, in part, an awareness of Iraq's sophisticated denial and deception efforts and of Iraq's past success in hiding the extent of its WMD programs. Reacting to that lesson, analysts understandably (if not wholly defensibly) began to view the absence of evidence of WMD as evidence of Iraq's ability to deceive the United States about its existence. For example, both CIA and the National Ground Intelligence Center simply assumed that Iraq's claims that the aluminum tubes were for rockets was a "cover story" designed to deflect attention from Iraq's nuclear program. Similarly, analysts had imagery intelligence from 2001 that contradicted Curveball's information about mobile BW facilities, but analysts believed that this discrepancy was attributable to Iraq's denial and deception capabilities.[767]

The disciplined use of alternative hypotheses could have helped counter the natural cognitive tendency to force new information into existing paradigms. Alternative hypotheses are particularly important for assessing WMD programs, which can be easily concealed under the guise of dual-use activity. With the aluminum tubes, the "transshipment" activity at ammunition depots, and the development of small UAVs, analysts did not fully consider the alternative (and non-WMD related) explanations. Analysts set aside evidence indicating a reconnaissance mission for the UAVs, and did not fully explore the possibility that the transshipment activity involved only conventional munitions. And with respect to the aluminum tubes, CIA and DIA analysts concluded that the tubes were destined for use in a gas centrifuge largely because they *could* be used for such a purpose, in the process discounting evidence that the tubes were in many respects better suited for use in rockets. [768]

The widely recognized need for alternative analysis drives many to propose organizational solutions, such as "red teams" and other formal mechanisms. Indeed, the *Intelligence Reform and Terrorism Prevention Act* mandates the establishment of such mechanisms to ensure that analysts conduct alternative analysis. Any such organs, the creation of which we encourage, must do more than just "alternative analysis," though. The Community should institute a formal system for competitive—and even explicitly *contrarian*—analysis. Such groups must be licensed to be troublesome. Further, they must take contrarian positions, not just ones that take a harder line (a flaw with the Team B exercise of the 1970s).[769]

The Iraq case shows, however, that alternative analysis mechanisms offer, at best, an incomplete solution to the problem. In addition to testing fully-developed judgments with formal red team exercises, analysts must incorporate the discipline of alternative hypotheses into the foundation of their analytical tradecraft, testing and weighing each piece of evidence. It would be unrealistic to "zero-base" every assessment, or to ignore history when forming analytical judgments. But the conventional wisdom must be tested throughout the analytical process to ensure that a position is not adopted without rigorous questioning. We offer a variety of approaches to this problem in Chapter Eight (Analysis) of our report.

Competitive analysis must also take place at the institutional level. In other words, the need for individual analysts to question their hypotheses and challenge the conventional wisdom also applies to the Intelligence Community as a whole, and suggests the need to strengthen competitive analysis among agencies in the Intelligence Community.[770]

After September 11, the Intelligence Community was criticized for its failure to communicate and share information across agency lines. That failure prevented analysts from "connecting the dots" because information known to one agency was not put together with information known to another. With each agency holding one or two pieces of the puzzle, none could see the whole picture. The logical response, therefore, was to recommend the formation of centers to bring all the relevant information together. The Iraq story, however, presents a different set of problems. As discussed, the strength of the prevailing assumptions about Iraq presented a distinct picture to analysts and pieces of the puzzle that did not fit that picture were either made to fit awkwardly or discarded. The problem, therefore, was not that analysts lacked awareness of what other analysts were thinking; rather, the problem was that most analysts were thinking the same thing.

Strengthening competitive analysis among components of the Intelligence Community could help alleviate that problem. There *was* of course some competitive analysis on Iraq—the NIE contained dissenting positions from State's Bureau of Intelligence and Research (INR), DOE, and the Air Force.[771] And those dissenting positions were at least somewhat closer to the truth than the majority position. Although reasonable minds can differ as to how significant the dissents were (at least in the cases of INR and DOE),[772] such competitive analyses in general encourage the consideration of alternative views and ensure that those independent views reach policymakers.

Conclusion 14

The Community made serious mistakes in its technical analysis of Iraq's unconventional weapons program. The National Ground Intelligence Center in particular displayed a disturbing lack of diligence and technical expertise.

The problem of discounting contrary evidence was compounded by inexcusable analytical lapses. One reason that CIA analysts were confident in their conclusion that the aluminum tubes were for use in centrifuges and not rockets was that the "rocket experts" in the Intelligence Community, the National Ground Intelligence Center (NGIC), assessed that the tolerances of the tubes Iraq was seeking were "excessive" for rockets. But NGIC rocket analysts told Commission staff that at the time they made that assessment they were not aware of the tolerances required for the Iraqi Nasser 81 rockets, for the Italian Medusa rocket on which the Nasser 81 was based, or for comparable U.S. rockets.[773] NGIC should have been aware of these facts.

The reasons for this failure of technical analysis were not particularly grand. Rather, analysts in NGIC, used to focusing almost exclusively on Soviet weapons systems, simply did not do their homework in tracking down information about Iraqi and U.S. weapons that would have shed light on the question whether the aluminum tubes could be used in conventional rockets. CIA analysts, for their part, were too quick to see confirmation of their hypothesis—that Iraq would seek to reconstitute its nuclear program at the first opportunity—based on somewhat dubious technical evidence.

Conclusion 15

Analysis of Iraqi weapons programs was also flawed by "layering," with one individual assessment forming the basis for additional, broader assessments that did not carry forward the uncertainties underlying each "layer."

A related concern is the problem of layering of analysis: the building of one judgment upon another without carrying forward the uncertainties of the earlier judgments.[774] The judgment in the October 2002 NIE that Iraq was reconstituting its weapons programs was built on previous assessments about Iraq's weapons programs. These earlier assessments, however, were based on relatively thin streams of reporting, yet the cumulative level of uncertainty was not reflected in the Key Judgments nor in some of the NIE's discussions. In brief, previous assessments based on uncertain information formed, through repetition, a relatively unquestioned baseline for the analysis in the pre-war assessments.

The NIE's CW assessments offer an example of the phenomenon. The NIE's estimates that Iraq had up to 500 metric tons of chemical weapons were based largely on accounting discrepancies and Iraq's CW production capacity rather than positive evidence.[775] Although the NIE conceded that "we have little specific information on Iraq's CW stockpile," it did not make clear that the baseline assumption rested largely on Iraqi accounting discrepancies. Because that baseline assumption was not made clear, the NIE gave the impression of greater certainty about the actual existence and size of stockpiles than was warranted. Similarly, the assessment that "much" of that stockpile was "added in the last year" was based largely on imagery evidence of "transshipment" in the spring of 2002.[776] Analysts assessed that Iraq had added to its CW stockpile in the previous year because the level of transshipment activity seen on imagery indicated that "CW is already deployed with the military logistics chain."[777] But that assessment in turn rested on whether the activity seen on imagery was CW-related. As the post-war reassessment by NGA concluded, it was not. By building one assessment on top of another without carrying forward the uncertainty from the first layer, the NIE gave the impression of greater certainty about its judgments than was warranted.[778]

This "layering" phenomenon occurred not only with respect to one line of analysis over time, but it also occurred across analytical lines. For example, a senior CW analyst related that he and other CW analysts had been "drifting" in the direction of concluding that Iraq did *not* have much of a CW program. The appearance of Curveball's reporting on BW, however, "pushed [CW analysts] the other way." The analyst explained that if Iraq was producing and hiding BW, then it was probably also producing and hiding CW. In other words, "much of the CW confidence was built on the BW confidence." [779]

Conclusion 16

Analysis of Iraq's weapons programs took little account of Iraq's political and social context. While such a consideration would probably not have changed the Community's judgments about Iraq's WMD, the failure even to *consider* whether Saddam Hussein had elected to abandon his banned weapons programs precluded that possibility.

Another shortcoming of the pre-war assessments of Iraq's WMD programs was the failure to analyze the state of these programs within the context of

Iraq's overall political, social, cultural, and economic situation.[780] In short, the Intelligence Community did not sufficiently understand the political dynamics of Saddam Hussein's Iraq, and as a consequence did not understand the political and economic pressures that led to his decision to destroy his WMD stockpiles while continuing to obfuscate about Iraq's possession of WMD.

As the Iraq Survey Group found, Saddam was facing two opposing pressures—the need to get relief from sanctions and the need to project strength at home and abroad. Saddam reacted to these pressures, according to the ISG, by destroying his WMD stockpiles after the Gulf War and focusing on sanctions relief before resuming WMD development. At the same time, Saddam continued to hinder the inspectors and sow confusion about Iraq's WMD programs.[781]

Yet the weapons analysts did not consider how the political situation might have affected Baghdad's decisions regarding its weapons programs. To be sure, it is doubtful that such consideration would have changed the analytical outcome—the regional analysts were also operating under certain assumptions about Saddam's regime, and those assumptions did not allow for the possibility that Saddam would destroy his CW and BW stocks and halt work on his nuclear programs, as the ISG found. But the failure even to *consider* how the political dynamics in Iraq might have affected Saddam's decisions about his WMD programs was a serious shortcoming that resulted in an incomplete analytical picture.[782] The failure by the Intelligence Community to entertain the possibility that Saddam was actually telling the truth also inclined analysts to accept deeply problematic evidence that might have been more rigorously questioned if the Community had actually considered the possibility that Saddam had abandoned his banned programs.

Several related problems contribute to the lack of context in analytical products. One, there is not yet an institutionalized, effective method to exploit open source resources that would have allowed a better understanding of developments in Iraq. Two, analysts are rarely assigned to one substantive account for any length of time (with the exception of INR analysts) and cannot therefore develop the requisite expertise to evaluate contextual influences. (Of course, longevity on one account can exacerbate the problem of over-reliance on past judgments.) And three, the pressure to respond to current intelligence needs as opposed to long-term research efforts degrades the overall level of expertise on all accounts. Given limited analytical resources, the demand for current intelligence suffocates long-term research and therefore largely precludes development of the kind of in-depth knowledge that such research fosters.[783] A related aspect of this problem is the current system of incentives for analysts, which rewards analysts for the quantity of finished intelligence pieces produced, and therefore encourages analysts to focus on current intelligence. CIA's Directorate of Intelligence is exploring ways to provide incentives for long-term research. Also, the Directorate's creation of a Senior Analytical Service to enable analysts to continue at the working-level (instead of moving into management) and still be promoted should help build expertise. We address these and other related issues in Chapter Eight (Analysis).

Conclusion 17

The Community did not adequately communicate uncertainties about either its sources or its analytic judgments to policymakers.

More generally, the pre-war assessments highlight the importance of correct presentation of material to consumers, particularly regarding the uncertainties of given judgments and how these judgments were made. While finished intelligence needs to offer a bottom line to be useful to the policymaker, it should also clearly spell out how and from what its conclusions were derived. In the case of WMD programs in hard target nations like Iraq, this means that policymakers must be made aware when—as will often necessarily be the case—many of the Community's estimates rely largely on inherently ambiguous indicators such as capabilities assessments, indirect reports of intentions, deductions based on denial and deception efforts associated with suspect WMD sites, and on ambiguous or thin pieces of "confirmatory" evidence. For example, the fact that the evidence for Iraq's biological weapons program relied largely on reporting from a single source, and that the evidence for Iraq's chemical weapons program derived largely from limited signature-based evidence of "transshipment" activity, should have been more transparent.

Such context is largely absent from the daily products provided to senior policymakers, however, and the daily dose of such products may provide a cumulative level of "certainty" that is unwarranted. Moreover, with respect to NIEs, the "confidence measures" used to describe the level of certainty in the judgments are not well-explained or understood. A more detailed description, explanation, and/or display of what those confidence measures mean should be incorporated. And those measurements should be rigorously and consistently applied.

Ironically, the NIE did contain numerous caveats, but their impact was diminished by their presentation. For example, as noted, the NIE stated that "[t]oday we have less direct access and know even less about the current status of Iraq's nuclear program than we did before the Gulf War."[784] Yet that caveat came on page 13 of the NIE, after it had twice stated that Iraq was reconstituting its program and could have enough fissile material for a nuclear weapon in the next several years.

Conclusion 18

The Community failed to explain adequately to consumers the fundamental assumptions and premises of its analytic judgments.

The fundamental assumptions and logical premises on which analytical judgments are based should be clearly explained. Analysts noted that the "impending war" influenced their approach to the pre-war assessments of Iraq's WMD programs, particularly the October 2002 NIE. That is, with the knowledge that U.S. troops would soon have to face whatever WMD capabilities Iraq had, analysts adopted more of a worst-case-analysis approach.[785] Yet that approach was not identified or explained to the reader of the NIE. By contrast, when the CIA's Counterterrorism Center prepared a paper on possible links between Iraq and al-Qa'ida, it clearly identified the analysis underlying that paper as of the aggressive, "dot-connecting" sort.[786]

Although too many qualifications can lead to equivocal analysis, when the evidence is equivocal, the conclusion must be as well. This must especially be the case when the results of debate about intelligence data or analysis will influence important policy decisions. Flagging the logical premises and baseline assumptions for the ultimate judgment would produce a better understanding by policymakers of the possible logical weaknesses in the assessment. It also would likely improve the analytic process as well, by forcing analysts themselves to articulate clearly their operative assumptions. Similarly, analysis that relies heavily on a single source, such as on Curveball's reporting and on the presence of Samarra-type trucks to support the conclusions that Iraq had BW and CW, respectively, should be highlighted.

Information Sharing

In addition to illuminating shortcomings in intelligence collection and analysis, our study of Iraq also highlighted a familiar challenge: that of ensuring effective sharing of information. In the Iraq case, the information sharing problem manifested itself in three specific ways: intelligence was not passed (1) from the collectors to the analysts; (2) from the analysts to the collectors; and (3) from foreign liaison services to the Intelligence Community.

Conclusion 19

Relevant information known to intelligence collectors was not provided to Community analysts.

The lack of an effective system for information sharing between collectors and analysts is a well-known systemic problem, but one that has proven highly resistant to resolution. Intelligence Community collectors retain a strong institutional bias against sharing operational information with analysts—CIA's Directorate of Operations is often reluctant to share relevant operational information with CIA's Directorate of Intelligence, let alone with the rest of the Community or with policymakers. Similarly, NSA is reluctant to share raw data with anyone outside of NSA.[787] Both NSA and the DO have legitimate concerns for the protection of sources and methods, and this concern must be weighed carefully when determining whether, and in what form, to share information across the Community or even across directorates.

Our review of the Intelligence Community's performance on Iraq identified several specific shortcomings in the way that collectors share intelligence with analysts. First, the source descriptions on raw human source reporting often provided insufficient detail and clarity to allow analysts adequate insight into the source's reliability. For example, the CIA report on the alleged uranium deal that was sourced to Ambassador Wilson described him (unhelpfully) as "a contact with excellent access who does not have an established reporting record."[788] Source descriptions that provide more explicit information on the context in which the information was obtained can significantly improve analysts' ability to gauge the credibility of that information. In September 2004, the CIA's DO implemented new source descriptions that are designed to provide additional such contextual detail.[789] This is an important step in the right direction, but more needs to be done.

Second, with CIA reporting, analysts were often unable to determine whether a series of raw human intelligence reporting came from the same source. For most reporting, there is currently no way to determine from the face of the CIA report whether a series of reports represents one source reporting similar information several times or several different sources independently providing the same information. For obvious reasons, it is important to distinguish corroboration from repetition. The improved source descriptions should help alleviate this problem, as will increased dialogue between collectors and analysts.

Finally, analysts often obtain insufficient insights into the operational details bearing on the reliability of sources.[790] Such information sharing is not an end in itself, of course. In the case of Curveball, for example, the DO *did* share operational information with DI analysts—including information that indicated possible problems with the source's reliability—but analysts' belief in Curveball's information remained unshaken. Increased dialogue, rather than simply sharing traffic, may help bridge these gaps.

It must be acknowledged that sharing operational details presents a great threat to the protection of sources and methods. Accordingly, any information sharing protocol must therefore be carefully tailored. The CIA recently conducted a DI-DO information sharing pilot program, which addressed the operational as well as technical barriers to effective information sharing within CIA.[791] Such pilot programs, however, are of little use if the recommended protocols are not implemented across the board.

A separate, but related problem is the lack of a mechanism to ensure that information calling into question a prior piece of intelligence is swiftly communicated to those analysts (and policymakers) who received the intelligence. This problem was most acutely demonstrated in the case of the Iraqi National Congress source, in which Defense HUMINT failed to reissue the reporting (either with the fabrication notice or recall notice attached)—a failure that led analysts and senior policymakers to accept the reporting months after it was known to be worthless. Defense HUMINT has taken steps to ensure that fabricated reporting is recalled, and the Director of the CIA is currently working to establish Community-wide standards to ensure that the original reporting, the fabrication notice, and the recalled reporting are electronically linked. It remains to be seen, however, whether the information-technology hurdles involved in linking related reporting can be overcome.

Conclusion 20

Relevant information known to intelligence analysts was not provided to Community collectors.

The systemic lack of effective information sharing occurs in the other direction as well, however. For example, the DO was not aware that the DI was relying so heavily on reporting from Curveball in its pre-war assessments of Iraq's BW program.[792] Similarly, although Defense HUMINT participated in the coordination sessions for Secretary Powell's speech, the Defense HUMINT participant said that he was not aware that the information being discussed came from the same Iraqi National Congress source who was known to be a fabricator.[793]

The National Intelligence Council has taken steps to address this problem. For example, the DO and Defense HUMINT will now directly participate in the NIE coordination process and will do so from the initial stages of that process, giving the collectors a better window into the sources relied upon and therefore an enhanced opportunity to bring to the fore any concerns about those sources. Also, a new National Intelligence Officer for "Intelligence Assurance" has been established to oversee these quality control measures.[794] Although it is still too early to tell, we hope that these steps address previous shortcomings in the NIE process.

Conclusion 21

Inability to obtain information from foreign liaison services hampered the Community's ability to assess the credibility of crucial information.

The information sharing problem is compounded with respect to foreign liaison. Although the Intelligence Community has been criticized for over-reliance on liaison sources,[795] such criticism is to some extent overstated.

Liaison reporting can play a valuable role in opening up avenues of collection the United States would not be able to approach on its own; indeed, at times it is the only information we have. The key to its usefulness, however, is the ability to assess its reliability. That determination hinges on several factors, including effective information sharing with the liaison service.

Information sharing between intelligence services is dependent upon many factors, including diplomatic and policy factors that are beyond the Intelligence Community's ability to control. Despite constant requests from the CIA, the handling foreign service refused to provide direct access to Curveball until spring of 2004, which seriously undermined the ability to determine his reliability. And in at least two instances—the inability of the Intelligence Community to learn the identity of the individual who provided the fourth BW source's information or the identity of the source of the corroborating information the liaison service claimed for the Niger deal—the foreign liaison services refused to share crucial information with the United States because of fear of leaks.[796] Until *that* systemic problem can be addressed, increased information sharing with liaison is unlikely to improve markedly. We discuss the issue of unauthorized disclosures in more detail and offer recommendations in Chapters Six (Leadership and Management) and Seven (Collection).

A cautionary note: the increased sharing of intelligence *reporting* among liaison services—without sharing the sourcing details or identity of the source—may lead to unwitting circular reporting. When several services unknowingly rely on the same sources and then share the intelligence production from those sources, the result can be false corroboration of the reporting. In fact, one reason for the apparent unanimity among Western intelligence services that Iraq posed a more serious WMD threat than proved to be the case was the extensive sharing of intelligence information, and even analysis, among liaison services. Such sharing of information, without sharing of source information, can result in "groupthink" on an international scale.

Dissemination

The collection, analysis, and dissemination of finished intelligence is a cycle, and many of the issues related to collection and analysis also affect dissemination of the product. But at least one issue merits separate discussion. The interface between the Intelligence Community and the policymaker—the way that intelligence analysis is conveyed to the consumer—needs reexamination.

Conclusion 22

The President's Daily Brief likely conveyed a greater sense of certainty about analytic judgments than warranted.

As part of its investigation, this Commission was provided access, on a limited basis, to a number of articles from the President's Daily Brief (PDB) relating to Iraq's WMD programs. Although we saw only a limited cross-section of this product, we can make several observations about the art form. In short, many of the same problems that occurred with other intelligence products occurred with the PDBs, only in a magnified manner. For instance, the PDBs often failed to explain, or even signal, the uncertainties underlying their judgments. Information from a known fabricator was used in PDBs, despite the publication of a fabrication notice on that source months earlier. PDB articles discounted information that appeared to contradict the prevailing analytical view by characterizing, without justifications, such information as a "cover story" or purposeful deception. The PDBs attributed information to multiple sources without making clear that the information rested very heavily on only one of those sources. And the titles of PDB articles were sometimes more alarmist than the text would support.

In addition to the problems it shares with other intelligence products, the PDB format presents some unique problems as well. As discussed above, the emphasis on current intelligence can adversely affect the distribution of analytical resources and can reduce the level of expertise needed for contextual analysis. But the focus on current intelligence may also adversely affect the consumers of intelligence. In particular, the daily exposure to current intelligence products such as the PDB may create, over time, a greater perception of certainty about their judgments than is warranted. And the way these products are generated and disseminated may actually skew the way their content is perceived. For example, when senior policymakers are briefed with the President's Daily Brief or a similar product, they often levy follow-up questions on the briefer. The response to those questions is then typically disseminated in the same format. Therefore, if one policymaker has an intense interest in one area and actively seeks follow-up, that questioning can itself generate numerous PDBs or Senior Executive Memoranda. A large volume of reporting on one topic can result, and that large volume may skew the sense among other policymakers as to the topic's importance.

Conclusion 23

The National Intelligence Estimate process is subject to flaws as well, and the Iraq NIE displays some of them. The length of the NIE encourages policymakers to rely on the less caveated Key Judgments. And the language of consensus ("most agencies believe") may obscure situations in which the dissenting agency has more expertise than the majority.

Long-term products such as the NIE bear reexamination as well. With respect to the October 2002 NIE on Iraq, some of the weaknesses in that product are attributable to anomalies in this particular NIE process, including the unusually short timeframe for publication (discussed further below), while others are attributable to inherent weaknesses in the NIE process itself.

One criticism of NIEs in general is that they are too long, read poorly, and are not popular with consumers.[797] The October 2002 NIE, at 90 pages, is almost twice as long as the average NIE.[798] One consequence of the length of the NIE—aside from discouraging its readers to look beyond the Key Judgments—is that its sheer heft suggests that there was a surfeit of evidence supporting those Key Judgments. That impression may encourage reliance on the Key Judgments alone. To the extent that intelligence judgments are often questions of degree (*e.g.*, the *likelihood* that an adversary has BW), however, short summaries and Key Judgments run a serious risk of misleading readers. Moreover, to the extent that daily intelligence products to senior policymakers may have conveyed a high level of confidence on Iraq WMD previous to the publication of the NIE, policymakers may have understood the confidence levels in the NIE to be higher than actually intended. At a minimum, therefore, NIEs must be carefully caveated and the degree of uncertainty in the judgments clearly communicated.

Another criticism of the NIE process is that it is inappropriately democratic—as the Assistant DCI for Analysis and Production described it, the "FBI has the same vote as the DOE" even when one agency clearly has greater expertise on the relevant subject matter.[799] The quest for consensus in NIEs—and the democratic process applied to reach that consensus—can produce confusing results.

For example, on the question whether Iraq was reconstituting its nuclear program, the position of CIA and DIA (with NGA and NSA in agreement) was that the tubes were for use in centrifuges, and therefore that the procurement of these tubes, along with some other procurement activity, indicated that Iraq was reconstituting its nuclear weapons program. The position of CIA and DIA was that they would not have reached a judgment of reconstitution *without* the tubes. DOE, on the other hand, believed that the tubes were *not* for centrifuges but that the other activity was sufficient to conclude that Iraq was reconstituting. While it is true that CIA and DOE agreed on the ultimate conclusion— reconstitution was underway—their respective bases for that conclusion were fundamentally at odds. The "most agencies believe" formulation glossed over this fundamental problem. A straightforward presentation of each agency's views might have better exposed the logical incompatibility of the CIA and DOE positions.[800] Moreover, the "democratic" process diminished the weight of DOE's "expert" opinion on nuclear technology.

Finally, the Iraq story revealed another inherent weakness of the NIE. The Iraq NIE, we now know, relied to a large extent on unreliable human source reporting. Although there were many contributing factors to this problem, one significant failing was that those involved in the coordination process were not aware of the degree to which the BW assessments relied on a single source or that another source had already been deemed a fabricator. This problem is currently being addressed. Newly-instituted National Intelligence Council procedures require the collecting agency to review and verify the reliability of its sources used in the NIE.[801]

> ### Conclusion 24
>
> The Iraq NIE was produced to meet a very short deadline. The time pressure was unfortunate and perhaps avoidable, but it did not substantially affect the judgments reached in the NIE.

To understand the unusual nature of the Iraq NIE process, it is necessary to understand how the National Intelligence Estimate process usually works. NIEs are produced under the auspices of the National Intelligence Council and are the "Intelligence Community's most authoritative written judgments on national security issues."[802] NIEs are primarily "estimative," that is, they "make judgments about the likely course of future events and identify the implications for U.S. policy."[803] Because of this "estimative" quality, NIEs are generally produced over the course of several months.[804] In the usual process, an NIE is requested by the NIC or by senior policymakers. The first step after the NIE is requested and authorized is the preparation of the Terms of Reference, which define precisely the question the NIE will address.[805] The National Intelligence Officer with responsibility for that subject area will generally take responsibility for overseeing the research and drafting of the NIE and its coordination. The individual agencies will appoint senior-level officers to serve as representatives for coordination sessions. These representatives will not be the drafters of the NIE but will speak for their agencies at the coordination meetings.[806]

The drafting and coordination of a National Intelligence Estimate is an iterative process. After a draft NIE is produced and reviewed by the NIC, the draft is circulated to the individual agencies for review. Comments on the draft are discussed at the interagency coordination meetings and changes are incorporated. If consensus is not possible on certain points, the dissenting agency is free to draft a dissent for inclusion in the NIE. The coordinated draft is submitted to a panel of outside readers for their review.[807] The draft is then submitted to NIC management for review and approval.[808] The final step is review and approval by the National Foreign Intelligence Board, which is chaired by the Director of the CIA.[809] Substantive changes occasionally are made to the NIE at this level.[810]

Once a draft is written, the review and coordination process alone takes at least one month, according to the NIO for Strategic and Nuclear Programs. Therefore, the NIO noted that a normal timeframe to draft, coordinate, and disseminate an NIE on a topic such as Iraq's WMD programs would be "several" months.[811]

The October 2002 NIE on Iraq, however, was requested on September 9, 2002, in a letter from Senator Richard Durbin of the Senate Select Committee on Intelligence (SSCI), for publication within three weeks.[812] This short deadline significantly truncated the usual NIE process. Although the NIOs and the working-level analysts involved in drafting the NIE agree that this short time frame probably did not affect the overall judgments in the NIE, the rushed schedule had consequences that may have affected the quality of the product.[813]

One consequence was that the Joint Atomic Energy Intelligence Committee (JAEIC), which often provides "expert" input on estimates involving nuclear issues, did not convene an interagency meeting to discuss the dispute over the aluminum tubes in the weeks immediately preceding the NIE coordination sessions, despite several attempts to do so.[814] Whether input from the JAEIC would have altered the judgments in the NIE is of course an open question. The opportunity for the JAEIC to review the points of contention between the CIA and DOE on the aluminum tubes, however, may have at a minimum resulted in a clearer exposition of that debate. The short timeframe may also have compromised the quality of the overall exchange of views during the coordination process. Normally, there might be several rounds of coordination at the interagency level. In the October 2002 NIE, however, there was one marathon coordination session. According to one DOE analyst who attended the coordination meeting, the short deadline reduced the chances that the various agencies could succeed in harmonizing their positions.[815]

The Intelligence Community might well have avoided the need to produce the NIE in such a short timeframe, however. On July 22, 2002, the Chairman of the Senate Select Committee on Intelligence sent a letter to DCI Tenet requesting that the NIC prepare a National Intelligence Estimate on covert action, to include an assessment of Iraq's WMD efforts. The CIA's Office of Congressional Affairs, however, did not pass this request to the NIOs responsible for global WMD activities. According to the NIO for Strategic and Nuclear Programs, the SSCI was informed orally that covert action activities were not a proper subject for NIEs and that such an NIE would not be prepared.[816] A formal response was not sent to the SSCI until September 25, 2002, at which time the DCI reiterated this position but also added that he had "directed the preparation of a new NIE on Iraq's weapons of mass destruction" in response to the September 9, 2002 request from Senator Durbin. The NIO for Strategic and Nuclear Programs noted that if he had been alerted in July about the Senate Select Committee's interest in an NIE on Iraq's weapons of mass destruction, he could have started the process at that point and avoided much unnecessary time pressure.[817]

Another anomaly in the October 2002 NIE process contributed to some of the inconsistencies between the text of the NIE on the one hand and the Key

Judgments and the unclassified NIE on the other. According to the NIO for Strategic and Nuclear Programs, under normal procedures the National Intelligence Council prepares the classified NIE and then derives the unclassified summary from that NIE. In the case of Iraq, however, the NIC accepted an assignment from the White House in May 2002 to prepare an unclassified "White Paper" on Iraq WMD, without first preparing a classified NIE.[818] When the Senate requested a classified NIE (and an unclassified version of the NIE) in September 2002, the NIO noted that the National Intelligence Council should have then folded the "White Paper" project into the NIE project, by deriving the unclassified product from the classified version. The two projects continued on parallel tracks, however. Accordingly, when attempts were later made to harmonize the two papers, caveats such as "we assess" were dropped from the Key Judgments, communicating a greater sense of certainty than was warranted.[819]

In short, the inherent flaws in the NIE process were compounded in this situation by the particular circumstances surrounding production of the Iraq NIE.

Conclusion 25

The shortened NIE coordination process did not unfairly suppress the National Ground Intelligence Center's slightly more cautious estimates of Iraq's CW stockpile.

Though the National Intelligence Estimate process in general, and the 2002 Iraq NIE process in particular, suffer from numerous flaws, in this case that process was not responsible for unduly suppressing agency views, as some have suggested. At least two analysts from one agency—NGIC—believe that NGIC's views on Iraq's CW program were not accurately represented in the October 2002 NIE.[820] These two NGIC analysts expressed the belief that this omission was not inadvertent but was consciously and unfairly omitted by the NIO for Strategic and Nuclear Programs.[821] While we have much to criticize about the NIE process, this is not one of them and is not supported by the facts.

According to the NGIC analysts, NGIC disagreed with the NIE's assessment that Iraq had restarted CW production and therefore could have increased its stockpiles to between 100 and 500 metric tons.[822] NGIC believed that Iraq's stockpiles therefore remained within the previously assessed 10 to 100 metric ton range.[823] Yet, apparently to NGIC's dismay, the 100 to 500 metric tons figure was eventually published in the NIE without an indication that NGIC disagreed with the Estimate's conclusions about Iraq's CW production and existing CW stockpiles.[824]

NGIC's claim that its dissenting views were purposefully suppressed by the NIO is not, however, borne out by the facts. According to NGIC's line edits on the NIE draft, NGIC did indeed suggest softening the language in some places—for example, to say that Iraq had begun production of mustard agent and *possibly* nerve agents, and to say that Iraq was *attempting* to procure various chemicals and equipment covertly. NGIC also suggested that, rather than saying that Iraq had *as much as* 500 metric tons of CW stockpiled, the NIE should say that Iraq had *up to* 500 metric tons stockpiled.[825] Even accepting that these views represented a meaningful dissenting position, NGIC's views were not purposefully suppressed. NGIC had several opportunities to make its dissent known (through DIA), including at the NIE coordination meeting on September 25, 2002; on a number of drafts of the NIE; or at the Military Intelligence Board meeting on September 30, 2002.[826] If NGIC (or DIA, as NGIC's representative) had wanted to insert a footnote reflecting a different view, it had the opportunity to do so at that point. Yet it did not.

In fact, DIA concurred with the language in the NIE regarding the size of Iraq's CW stockpile because the language "was sufficiently caveated to indicate DIA's uncertainty in the size of the stockpile."[827] Nor did NGIC subsequently take the opportunity between the NIE and the opening of the war to publish its dissenting view in finished intelligence.[828]

In sum, the National Ground Intelligence Center's serious accusation that its views on Iraq's CW program were purposefully excluded from the NIE is not supported by the available evidence.

Politicization

Many observers of the Intelligence Community have expressed concern that Intelligence Community judgments concerning Iraq's purported WMD programs may have been warped by inappropriate political pressure.[829] To discuss whether those judgments were "politicized," that term must first be defined.

Conclusion 26

The Intelligence Community did not make or change any analytic judgments in response to political pressure to reach a particular conclusion, but the pervasive conventional wisdom that Saddam retained WMD affected the analytic process. [830]

The Commission has found no evidence of "politicization" of the Intelligence Community's assessments concerning Iraq's reported WMD programs. No analytical judgments were changed in response to political pressure to reach a particular conclusion.[831] The Commission has investigated this issue closely, querying in detail those analysts involved in formulating pre-war judgments about Iraq's WMD programs.

These analysts universally assert that in no instance did political pressure cause them to change any of their analytical judgments. Indeed, these analysts reiterated their strong belief in the validity and soundness of their pre-war judgments at the time they were made.[832] As a former Assistant Secretary of State for Intelligence and Research put it, "policymakers never once applied any pressure on coming up with the 'right' answer on Iraq."[833] Moreover, the CIA's Ombudsman for Politicization conducted a formal inquiry in November 2003 into the possibility of "politicization" with respect to assessments of Iraqi WMD. That inquiry involved the (perceived) delay in CIA's reassessment of its position on WMD in Iraq. The Ombudsman also found no evidence, based on numerous confidential interviews with the analysts involved, that political pressure had caused any analyst to change any judgments.[834]

The Commission also found no evidence of "politicization" even under the broader definition used by the CIA's Ombudsman for Politicization, which is not limited solely to the case in which a policymaker applies overt pressure on an analyst to change an assessment. The definition adopted by the CIA is broader, and includes any "unprofessional manipulation of information and judgments" by intelligence officers to please what those officers perceive to be policymakers' preferences.[835] But the definition retains the idea that circumstantial pressure to produce analysis quickly is not politicization—there must be some skewing of analytical judgments, either deliberately or unintentionally.[836] The Ombudsman noted that in his view, analysts on Iraq worked under more "pressure" than any other analysts in CIA's history, in terms of their being required to produce so much, for so long, for such senior decisionmakers. But that circumstantial pressure did not cause analysts to alter or skew their judgments.[837] We have found no evidence to dispute that conclusion.

There is also the issue of interaction between policymakers and other customers on the one hand and analysts on the other.[838] According to some analysts, senior decisionmakers continually probed to assess the strength of the Intelligence Community's analysis, but did not press for changes in the Intelligence Community's analytical judgments. We conclude that good-faith efforts by intelligence consumers to understand the bases for analytic judgments, far from constituting "politicization," are entirely legitimate. This is the case even if policymakers raise questions because they do not like the conclusions or are seeking evidence to support policy preferences. Those who must use intelligence are entitled to insist that they be fully informed as to both the evidence and the analysis.

Nor is pressure to work more quickly than is ideal or normal "politicization." Iraq WMD analysts insisted to Commission staff that they faced tremendous pressure to produce finished intelligence and to respond promptly to policymakers' questions, but that such "pressure" was generated by time and analytical resource limitations, not by efforts to alter the analysts' judgments. And according to the National Intelligence Officers responsible for drafting the NIE on Iraq WMD in the fall of 2002, there was no communication with policymakers about the Estimate's conclusions beyond pressure to complete the paper within a short three-week timeframe.[839] Furthermore, all of the Iraqi WMD analysts interviewed by the Commission staff stated that they reached their conclusions about Iraq's pursuit of WMD independently of policymaker pressure, based on the evidence at hand.[840] In fact, given the body of evidence available, many analysts have said that they could not see how they could have reached any other conclusions about Iraq's WMD programs.[841]

However, there is no doubt that analysts operated in an environment shaped by intense policymaker interest in Iraq. Moreover, that analysis was shaped—and distorted—by the widely shared (and not unreasonable) assumption, based on his past conduct and non-cooperation with the United Nations, that Saddam retained WMD stockpiles and programs. This strongly-held assumption contributed to a climate in which the Intelligence Community was too willing to accept dubious information as providing confirmation of that assumption. Neither analysts nor users were sufficiently open to being told that affirmative, specific evidence to support the assumption was, at best, uncertain in content or reliability.

Some analysts were affected by this "conventional wisdom" and the sense that challenges to it—or even refusals to find its confirmation—would not be welcome. For example, the National Intelligence Officer for Near East and South Asia described a "*zeitgeist*" or general "climate" of policymaker focus on Iraq's WMD that permeated the analytical atmosphere.[842] This "climate" was formed in part, the NIO claimed, by the gathering conviction among analysts that war with Iraq was inevitable by the time the NIE was being prepared.[843] But this "*zeitgeist*," he maintained, did not dictate the prevailing analytical view that Iraq had CW and BW and was reconstituting its nuclear program—in fact, the NIO said he did not see how analysts could have come up with a different conclusion about Iraq's WMD based on the intelligence available at the time.[844] Similarly, the DOE analysts who participated in the NIE coordination meeting stated that there was no political pressure on DOE, direct or indirect, to agree with the NIE's conclusion that Iraq was "reconstituting" its nuclear program. At the same time, however, he said that "DOE did not want to come out before the war and say [Iraq] wasn't reconstituting."[845]

Even in the absence of politicization, distortion can creep into the analytical product, not only through poor tradecraft, but through poor management and reliance on conventional wisdom. The general assumption that Saddam retained WMD and the backdrop of impending war, particularly in the wake of September 11, affected the way analysts approached their task of predicting the threat posed by Iraq's WMD programs. For example, this atmosphere contributed to analysts' use of a worst-case-scenario or heightened-burden-of-proof approach to analysis. This overall climate, we believe, contributed to the too-ready willingness to accept dubious information as supporting the conventional wisdom and to an unwillingness even to consider the possibility that the conventional wisdom was wrong.

But while some of the poor analytical tradecraft in the pre-war assessments was influenced by this climate of impending war, we have found no evidence to dispute that it was, as the analysts assert, their own independent judgments—flawed though they were—that led them to the conclusion that Iraq had active WMD programs.

As described above, the pre-war assessments of Iraq's WMD programs suffered from numerous other analytical failures. Primary among those analytical flaws was a failure to question assumptions or to keep an open mind about the significance of new data. Such failures are more likely if management within the Intelligence Community does not foster, or at least tolerate, dissenting views. Yet one systemic problem within the Intelligence Community works to frustrate expressions of dissent. As the former Assistant Secretary of State for Intelligence and Research described the problem, the senior leadership of the Intelligence Community is faced with an inevitable conundrum—the head of the Intelligence Community must be close to the President in order for the intelligence product to have relevance, but such closeness also risks the loss of objectivity.[846] When this balance tips too far toward the desire for the Intelligence Community to be "part of the [Administration] team," analysts may be dissuaded from offering dissenting opinions.[847]

The failure to pursue alternative views in forming the pre-war assessments of Iraq's WMD, however, was likely due less to the political climate than to poor analytical tradecraft, a failure of management to actively foster opposition views, and the natural bureaucratic inertia toward consensus. In the case of pre-war assessments of Iraqi WMD, working-level WINPAC analysts described an environment in which managers rewarded judgments that fit the consensus view that Iraq had active WMD programs and discouraged those that did not.[848] To the degree that analysts judged—as we believe some of them did—that "non-consensus" conclusions would not be welcomed, vigorous debate in the analytic process was made much more difficult.

Yet these analysts insisted that they genuinely believed that consensus view, based on the evidence at hand, and we have found no evidence that this was not the case. Moreover, to the extent management at CIA or elsewhere in the government created a climate of conformity, it was not unique to the Iraq situation. For example, an employee survey in April 2004 revealed that 17 percent of WINPAC analysts said they worked "in an atmosphere in which some managers who hold strong views make it difficult to publish opposing points of views."[849] In surveys of the CIA's Directorate of Intelligence as a whole, however, 23 percent reported working in such an environment.[850]

> ## Conclusion 27
>
> The CIA took too long to admit error in Iraq, and its Weapons Intelligence, Nonproliferation, and Arms Control Center actively discouraged analysts from investigating errors.

A related problem is bureaucratic resistance to admitting error. Just as the Intelligence Community has an obligation to consumers to provide unvarnished intelligence assessments that are free from politicization, the Community also has an obligation to inform consumers when it learns that information on which previous judgments were based is unreliable. The Iraq experience demonstrates that the Intelligence Community is reluctant to confess error, and is even reluctant to encourage the pursuit of information that may reveal such error. In this respect, the infamous case of Curveball offers an excellent example.

After the initial phase of the war, two WINPAC analysts who had traveled to Iraq began to have doubts about the foundation of their assessments, particularly the BW assessments. Yet CIA management was resistant to this new information.[851] The reaction of CIA management in this instance demonstrates at best a lack of encouragement for dissenting views. As described above, when analysts traveled to Iraq in the summer and fall of 2003 and began to investigate Curveball's bona fides, serious doubts arose about his truthfulness. The WINPAC BW analyst who had conducted the investigations in Iraq brought his concerns to WINPAC management. He argued that Curveball was a fabricator because he had lied about his access (in particular covering up that he had actually been fired from his government job in 1995), lied about being present during a BW accident when he had actually been out of the country at that time, and lied about the purpose for the trailers found by Coalition forces.[852] According to the analyst, however, management was hostile to the idea of publishing a reassessment or retreating from Curveball's information, since other analysts still believed in his veracity.

By January 2004, however, travel records confirmed that Curveball had not even been in Iraq during the time he claimed to have been present at a BW facility, and this discrepancy convinced most analysts that Curveball was a fabricator. By March 2004, when CIA was able to interview Curveball and he could not explain imagery that contradicted his reporting, "any remaining doubts" about Curveball's reliability were removed, according to the former WINPAC BW analyst.[853]

CIA management, however, was still reluctant to "go down the road" of admitting that Curveball was a fabricator. According to the former WINPAC analyst, Directorate of Intelligence management was slow in retreating from Curveball's information because of concerns about how this would look to the "Seventh Floor" and to "downtown." When Curveball's reporting was finally recalled in May 2004, the CIA alerted senior policymakers to that fact, but CIA did not publish a reassessment of its position on Iraq's BW program.[854]

As noted, the CIA's Inspector General, in a review of WINPAC's performance finished in November 2004, concluded that "the process [of retreating from intelligence products derived from Curveball reporting] was drawn out principally due to three factors: (1) senior managers were determined to let the ISG in Iraq complete its work before correcting the mobile labs analysts; (2) the CIA was in the midst of [trying] to gain direct access to Curveball; and (3) WINPAC Biological and Chemical Group (BCG) management was struggling to reconcile strong differences among their BW analysts."[855] The report went on to say that senior managers did not want to disavow Curveball only to find that his story stood up upon direct examination or to find that "the ISG uncovered further evidence that would require additional adjustments to the story."[856]

But CIA had gained direct access to Curveball in March 2004 and his reporting had been recalled in May 2004. After May 2004, therefore, two of the Inspector General's reasons were no longer valid, and the third—waiting for the Iraq Survey Group report—would delay any reassessment for six months *after* the Intelligence Community had already conceded that the primary source for its pre-war BW assessment had fabricated his reporting. In any event, as of March 2005 WINPAC has still not published a reassessment of Iraq's BW program.

Moreover, the analysts who raised concerns about the need for reassessments were not rewarded for having done so but were instead forced to leave WINPAC.[857] One analyst, after presenting his case in late 2003 that Curveball had fabricated his reporting, was "read the riot act" by his office director, who accused him of "making waves" and being "biased."[858] The analyst told Commission staff that he was subsequently asked to leave WINPAC. Similarly, a WINPAC CW analyst who pressed to publish a reassessment of Iraq's CW program in late 2003 was also, according to the analysts, "told to leave" WINPAC.[859] Although managers must be able to overrule subordinates once an issue has been debated, managers must also create an atmosphere in which such debate is encouraged rather than punished.[860]

In sum, there was no "politicization" of the intelligence product on Iraq. Poor tradecraft, exacerbated by poor management, contributed to the erroneous assessments of Iraq's WMD programs. These problems were further exacerbated by the reluctance of Intelligence Community management to foster and consider dissenting views. Finally, the Intelligence Community was unwilling to identify the errors underlying its intelligence assessments, admit those errors, and explain to consumers how those errors affected previous judgments.

Accountability

Recommendation

The Director of National Intelligence should hold accountable the organizations that contributed to the flawed assessments of Iraq's WMD programs.

Numerous failures within the Intelligence Community contributed to the flawed estimates on Iraq. Many of these failures are systemic—flaws in the way the Intelligence Community is managed, organized, and structured. Part Two of this report contains dozens of recommendations for systemic reform based on the lessons learned from Iraq and other case studies. But reform requires more than changing the Community's systems; it also requires accountability.

Individuals. There are unfortunately a number of examples in the Iraq assessments of individuals whose conduct fell short of what the Intelligence Community has a right to expect. Among these is the handling of Curveball's reporting on mobile BW. In late January of 2003, the Secretary of State was engaged in an intense personal effort to explore every flaw in the intelligence he was about to present to the United Nations Security Council. By then, a division in the CIA's Directorate of Operations had spent months pointing out

Curveball's flaws with some persistence. Yet the Secretary of State never learned of those doubts.

A number of individuals stood between the two and could have made the connection. Some acknowledge knowing about Curveball's problems but did not understand that he was the key to the entire BW assessment. Others knew how central Curveball was to the BW case but deny knowing about Curveball's problems. Still others—particularly in CIA's WINPAC—were aware of both sides of the issue and did not present the doubts to the Secretary or other policymakers. Finally, the most senior officials of the Agency insist the serious concerns expressed about Curveball's reliability were never conveyed to them—despite assertions to the contrary.

This Commission was not established to adjudicate personal responsibility for the intelligence errors on Iraq. We are not an adjudicatory body, nor did we take testimony under oath. We were not authorized or equipped to assign blame to specific individuals, particularly when there are disputes about critical facts. We are, however, equipped to address the question of *organizational* accountability.

Organizations. Almost every organization in the Intelligence Community—collectors, analysts, and management—performed poorly on Iraq. But there are differences among the agencies, both in their initial performance and in how they responded when their mistakes became clear. The National Intelligence Council, for example, faltered badly in producing the flawed NIE on Iraq's WMD programs. But it also learned from its errors. It now brings the collection agencies into the NIE process to evaluate their sources, and its recent estimates are more candid about intelligence gaps, weak sources, and divergent viewpoints.

For some organizations, however, problems run deeper. Three agencies made such serious errors, or resisted admitting their errors so stubbornly, that questions may fairly be raised about the fundamental culture or capabilities of the organizations themselves.

1. The performance of the National Ground Intelligence Center (NGIC) in assessing the aluminum tubes was a gross failure. NGIC got completely wrong the question of the tubes' suitability for conventional rockets—a question that is at the core of NGIC's assigned area of exper-

tise. And NGIC was not aware of, and did not pursue, basic information that was critical to its assessments.[861]

2. The Defense HUMINT Service inexcusably failed to recall reporting from a known fabricator, and compounded that error by failing to notice when its discredited reporting crept into Secretary Powell's speech. Defense HUMINT also bears heavy responsibility for the Curveball episode. Defense HUMINT disseminated Curveball's reporting while taking little or no responsibility for checking the accuracy of his reports. In fact, Defense HUMINT still calls itself merely a "conduit" for Curveball's information and resists the idea that it had any real responsibility to vet his veracity.[862]

3. CIA's Weapons Intelligence, Nonproliferation, and Arms Control Center (WINPAC) is the Intelligence Community's center for all-source analysis on weapons of mass destruction. As such, it was at the heart of many of the errors discussed earlier, from the mobile BW case to the aluminum tubes. Just as bad, some WINPAC analysts—and WINPAC as an institution—showed great reluctance to correct these errors, even long after they had become obvious.[863] Creating an intelligence center always carries some risk that alternative views will be sacrificed in pursuit of consensus, and we fear that a culture of enforced consensus has infected WINPAC as an organization.

In short, we have doubts that the broad reforms described in Part Two will be enough to change the organizational culture of NGIC, Defense HUMINT, and WINPAC. Yet the cultures of each contributed crucially to the Iraq WMD debacle. We therefore recommend that the Director of National Intelligence give serious consideration to whether each of these organizations should be reconstituted, substantially reorganized, or made subject to detailed oversight.

ENDNOTES

[1] NIEs, produced under the auspices of the National Intelligence Council (NIC), contain the coordinated judgments of the Intelligence Community and are the DCI's most authoritative written judgments concerning national security issues. CIA website, http://www.cia.gov.nic/NIC_about/html.

[2] Executive Order 13328, which established this Commission, did not authorize us to investigate how policymakers used the intelligence they received from the Intelligence Community on Iraq's weapons programs. As a result, while we interviewed several policymakers, the purpose of those interviews was to obtain information about how the Intelligence Community reached and communicated its judgments about Iraq's weapons programs, and not to review policymakers' use of intelligence information.

[3] NIC, National Intelligence Estimate, *Iraq's Continuing Programs for Weapons of Mass Destruction* (NIE 2002-16HC) (Oct. 2002) (hereinafter "NIE") at pp. 5, 6. The Intelligence Community is composed of the Central Intelligence Agency (CIA), the Department of State's Bureau of Intelligence and Research (INR), the Department of Energy (DOE), the Department of the Treasury, the Federal Bureau of Investigation (FBI), the Department of Homeland Security (DHS), the National Reconnaissance Office (NRO), the National Security Agency (NSA), the National Geospatial-Intelligence Agency (NGA), the Defense Intelligence Agency (DIA), and Army Intelligence, Navy Intelligence, Coast Guard Intelligence, Air Force Intelligence, and Marine Corps Intelligence. Not all of these elements coordinate on all NIEs, however. The October 2002 NIE on Iraq WMD was coordinated among CIA, INR, DOE, NSA, NGA (then known as the National Imagery and Mapping Agency (NIMA)), DIA, and all the military intelligence components. NIC, *How the Intelligence Community Arrived at the Judgments in the October 2002 NIE on Iraq's WMD Programs* (March 2004) (hereinafter "DCI Statement for the Record") at Introduction, p. 1 n. 1. This was the DCI's Statement for the Record prepared by the NIC and approved by the principals of the National Foreign Intelligence Board. The assessment that Iraq was reconstituting was expressed as the view of "most agencies" to reflect that INR, among the agencies coordinating on the NIE, did not agree with that assessment. Interview with National Intelligence Officer for Strategic and Nuclear Programs (hereinafter "NIO/SNP") (Sept. 20, 2004).

[4] *Id.* at p. 16. Although DOE agreed that Iraq was reconstituting its nuclear program, it based that conclusion on factors other than the aluminum tubes. DOE assessed that the tubes were more likely for use in tactical rockets, a view adopted by INR. The details of the discussion are addressed further below.

[5] NIE at p. 9.

[6] Iraq Survey Group (ISG), *Comprehensive Report of the Special Advisor to the DCI on Iraqi WMD*, Volume II, "Nuclear" (Sept. 30, 2004) at p. 7 (hereinafter "ISG Report, Nuclear").

[7] *Id.* at pp. 1, 7, 8.

[8] *Id.* at p. 21.

[9] DCI Statement for the Record at Tab 1, p. 4.

[10] *Id.* at p. 7.

[11] *Id.* at p. 4 (citing November 1990 study by the Joint Atomic Energy Intelligence Committee).

[12] *Id.* at p. 7. Iraq had pursued multiple uranium enrichment technologies, including a centrifuge program and the outdated Electromagnetic Isotope Separation (EMIS) process, before the Gulf War. *Id.* at pp. 7, 11.

[13] *Id.* at pp. 7-8.

[14] Joint Atomic Energy Intelligence Committee (JAEIC), *Iraq's Nuclear Weapons Program: Elements of Reconstitution* (JAEIC 94-004) (Sept. 1994) at p. v. The JAEIC is a DCI committee charged with analyzing technical nuclear issues. DCI Statement for the Record at Tab 1, p. 4.

[15] DCI Statement for the Record at Tab 1, p. 9.

[16] *Id.*

[17] *See, e.g.*, CIA, *Iraq: WMD Programs: The Road to Reconstruction* (OSWR) (Feb. 3, 1995).

[18] JAEIC, *Reconstitution of Iraq's Nuclear Weapons Program: An Update* (JAEIC 97-004) (Oct. 1997); *see also* DCI Statement for the Record at Tab 1, p. 14.

[19] JAEIC, *Reconstitution of Iraq's Nuclear Weapons Program: An Update* (JAEIC 97-004) (Oct. 1997) at p. iii.

[20] NIC, *Current Iraqi WMD Capabilities* (NICM 1848-98) (Oct. 1998) at p. 2.

[21] *Id.*

[22] JAEIC, *Reconstitution of Iraq's Nuclear Weapons Program: Post Desert Fox* (JAEIC 99-003) (June 1999); *see also* DCI Statement for the Record at Tab 1, p. 17.

[23] NIC, *Iraq: Steadily Pursuing WMD Capabilities* (ICA 2000-007 HCX) (Dec. 2000) at pp. 7-8.

[24] Classified intelligence report (March 2001); *see also* DCI Statement for the Record at Tab 1, pp. 18-19.

[25] NIE at p. 75 (tubes seized in June 2001); *see also* DCI Statement for the Record at Tab 1, p. 19.

[26] Interview with CIA WINPAC nuclear analysts (Oct. 8, 2004). Iraq was prohibited from possessing tubes composed of 7075 T6 aluminum alloy with outer diameters exceeding 75mm under Annex III to United Nations Security Council Resolution 687 because of their potential use in gas centrifuges. DOE Office of Intelligence, Technical Intelligence Note, *Iraq's Gas Centrifuge Program: Is Reconstitution Underway?* (TIN 000064) (Aug. 17, 2001) at pp. 7-8. In the gas centrifuge process, a feed of uranium hexafluoride (UF_6) gas is enriched in a rapidly spinning rotor within a vacuum chamber. The uranium isotopes are separated by the combined effects of centrifugal force and countercurrent circulation; as the rotor spins, the heavier isotopes are concentrated preferentially at the rotor's wall and are then convected upwards, where they can be scooped out. To be able to spin at such high-speeds, the rotors must be constructed from high-strength material, such as carbon-fiber, maraging steel, or high-strength aluminum such as the 7075 T6 alloy. U.S. Congress, Office of Technology Assessment, *Technologies Underlying Weapons of Mass Destruction* (OTA-BP-ISC-115) (1993).

[27] *See, e.g.*, CIA, *Iraq's Current Nuclear Capabilities* (June 20, 2001) (noting that although the tubes are "more consistent" with a centrifuge application, "we are also considering non-nuclear applications for the tubes"); Senior Executive Memorandum, *What We Knew About Iraq's Centrifuge-Based Uranium Enrichment Program Before and After the Gulf War* (Nov. 24, 2001) (noting that there are "divergent views" about the intended use of the tubes).

[28] *See, e.g.,* Senior Executive Memorandum, *The Iraqi Threat* (Dec. 15, 2001) ("[W]e believe a shipment of...tubes...[are] destined for use in Iraqi gas centrifuges."); Senior Publish When Ready, Title Classified (June 30, 2001) (noting that Iraq is likely to argue that the tubes are for conventional or civilian use, a use "that cannot be discounted," but also noting that the specifications for the tubes "far exceed any known conventional weapons application, including rocket motor casings for 81mm" MRLs).

[29] *See, e.g.,* Senior Executive Memorandum, *The Status of Iraq's Nuclear Program* (Jan. 11, 2002) (noting that the "Intelligence Community has less access to Saddam's nuclear intent and activities today than before the Gulf War").

[30] Electronic mail from NGIC to WINPAC (Aug. 13, 2001); Interview with CIA Iraq WMD Review Group analyst (Sept. 9, 2004) (describing assessment provided by NGIC to CIA/DI analysts in November 2001; the CIA Iraq WMD Review Group was an entity established within CIA in August 2003 to provide an evaluation to the DCI of the pre-war intelligence assessments of Iraq's WMD programs). NGIC's assessment was shortly thereafter incorporated into a DIA Military Intelligence Digest supplement. *See* DIA, Military Intelligence Digest Supplement, *Iraq: Procuring Possible Nuclear-Related Gas Centrifuge Equipment* (MID-227-01-SCI) (Nov. 30, 2001).

[31] Interview with CIA WINPAC nuclear analysts (Oct. 8, 2004).

[32] DOE Office of Intelligence, Technical Intelligence Note, *Iraq's Gas Centrifuge Program: Is Reconstitution Underway?* (TIN 000064) (Aug. 17, 2001). Although DOE judged that the dimensions and specifications of the tubes were not well suited for centrifuge use, DOE stressed that "none of the factors" that led to that conclusion "precluded Iraq's use (or, at a minimum, attempted use) of the tubes for centrifuge rotor manufacture." Among these factors, DOE noted that the inside diameter and wall thickness were not favorable for use as centrifuge rotors. At the same time, DOE noted that the dimensions of the tubes precisely matched those of Iraq's Nasser-81 mm rockets. *Id.* at pp. 8-9; *see also* DOE, Daily Intelligence Highlight, *Iraq: High Strength Aluminum Tube Procurement* (April 11, 2001) (tubes "could be used to manufacture gas centrifuge rotor cylinders for uranium enrichment" but the tubes "more likely" are intended to support a different application, such as rocket casings).

[33] Department of State, UNVIE Vienna 001337 (July 27, 2001) (cable from the U.S. Mission to the United Nations in Vienna describing IAEA conclusions regarding the aluminum tubes); *see also* UNVIE Vienna 001134 (July 25, 2002) (reiterating previous assessment).

[34] Senior Executive Memorandum, *The Iraq Threat* (Dec. 15, 2001).

[35] Senior Executive Memorandum, *What We Knew About Iraq's Centrifuge-Based Uranium Enrichment Program Before and After the Gulf War* (Nov. 24, 2001); Senior Executive Memorandum, *The Iraq Threat* (Dec. 15, 2001); DCI Statement for the Record at Tab 1, p. 19. As noted, while DOE believed the tubes were not "well-suited" for centrifuge applications, they "could be used" for that purpose. DOE, Office of Intelligence, Technical Intelligence Note, *Iraq's Gas Centrifuge Program: Is Reconstitution Underway?* (TIN 000064) (Aug. 17, 2001) at p. 4, and DOE Daily Intelligence Highlight, *Iraq: High Strength Aluminum Tube Procurement* (April 11, 2001) at p. 1. Although DOE assessed that the tubes' dimensions were not "favorable" for centrifuge use, it noted that the tubes "could be modified" for that use. DOE Office of Intelligence, Technical Intelligence Note, *Iraq's Gas Centrifuge Program: Is Reconstitution Underway?* (TIN 000064) (Aug. 17, 2001) at pp. 8-9; DOE Office of Intelligence, Technical Intelligence Note, *Iraq: Recent Aluminum Tube Procurement Efforts* (TIN 000108) (Sept. 13,

2002) at p. 1; DOE, Daily Intelligence Highlight, *Iraq: Gas Centrifuge Program Recounted* (Nov. 8, 2002) at p. 1 (noting that "DOE continues to assess that the high-strength aluminum tubes Iraq has been attempting to acquire... could be modified for centrifuge use but that the more likely end-use is the fabrication of motor cases for tactical rockets").

[36] DCI Statement for the Record at Tab 1, p. 19.

[37] Classified intelligence report (noting that a front company had received the specification for a vertical spin testing machine from an individual believed to be in Iraq); *see also* DCI Statement for the Record at Tab 1, pp. 21-22 (noting reporting indicating that Iraq was making efforts to preserve its cadre of weapons personnel, and imagery reporting of construction at Al-Tahadi, where analysts thought a magnet production line was to be built).

[38] DOE Office of Intelligence, Technical Intelligence Note, *Iraq's Gas Centrifuge Program: Is Reconstitution Underway?* (TIN 000064) (Aug. 17, 2001) at pp. 4, 8-9; DOE, Daily Intelligence Highlight, *Iraq: High Strength Aluminum Tube Procurement* (April 11, 2001) at p. 1; DOE Office of Intelligence, Technical Intelligence Note, *Iraq: Recent Aluminum Tube Procurement Efforts* (TIN 000108) (Sept. 13, 2002) at p. 1; DOE, Daily Intelligence Highlight, *Iraq: Gas Centrifuge Program Recounted* (Nov. 8, 2002) at p. 1 (noting that "DOE continues to assess that the high-strength aluminum tubes Iraq has been attempting to acquire... could be modified for centrifuge use but that the more likely end-use is the fabrication of motor cases for tactical rockets").

[39] DCI Statement for the Record at Tab 1 at p. 22. DOE was also becoming concerned that this activity could indicate "preliminary steps" to support a "gas centrifuge program restart." DOE Office of Intelligence, Technical Intelligence Note, *Iraq's Gas Centrifuge Program: Is Reconstitution Underway?* (TIN 000064) (Aug. 17, 2001).

[40] Senior Executive Memorandum, *The Status of Iraq's Nuclear Program* (Jan. 11, 2002) ("[T]he recent aluminum tube procurement effort, which CIA assesses to be an integral part of Iraq's centrifuge program"); Senior Executive Memorandum, *The Status of Iraq's Uranium Enrichment Program* (March 12, 2002) (the tubes are "suitable" for use as gas centrifuges); CIA, *Iraq: Expanding WMD Capabilities Pose Growing Threat* (Aug. 1, 2002) (the tubes are "best suited for use" in a gas centrifuge; text box indicates CIA considered other uses, but does not describe other agencies' views); Senior Executive Memorandum, *Details About Our Assessments on Iraq's Nuclear Program Since 1991* (Sept. 16, 2002) ("Reporting on Iraq's persistent interest in high-strength aluminum tubes—complemented by magnet production and machine tool and balancing machine procurement efforts—is key to our current assessment that Baghdad is reconstituting its centrifuge program."); Senior Executive Memorandum, *Questionable Dual-Use Items That Countries Have Sold to Iraq in the Past Five Years* (Sept. 27, 2002) (listing of dual-use items lists application of aluminum tubes as "rockets/nuclear applications" but assessment is that the tubes are "destined for use" in a uranium enrichment program). *See also* CIA, Talking Points prepared for the Deputy DCI for a Principals Committee Meeting on Iraq WMD (Aug. 28, 2002) (noting tubes are "destined for a gas centrifuge program" and their procurement shows "clear intent to produce weapons-capable fissile material") (described in Interview with CIA Iraq WMD Review Group analyst (Sept. 9, 2004)).

[41] CIA, *Iraq's Hunt for Aluminum Tubes: Evidence of a Renewed Uranium Enrichment Program* (WINPAC IA 2002-051HCX) (Sept. 30, 2002) at pp. i, 1.

[42] *Id.* at pp. 3, 7.

[43] DOE Office of Intelligence, Technical Intelligence Note, *Iraq: Recent Aluminum Tube*

Procurement Efforts (TIN 000108) (Sept. 13, 2002) at p. 1. During this timeframe, the Intelligence Community briefed the relevant congressional committees on the aluminum tubes issue, with DOE, INR, and CIA presenting their respective views. Interview with CIA Iraq WMD Review Group analyst (Sept. 9, 2004).

[44] Interview with CIA Iraq WMD Review Group analyst (Sept. 9, 2004) (citing testimony of INR in Intelligence Community briefing to the Senate Select Committee on Intelligence on Sept. 17, 2002).

[45] NIE at p. 16.

[46] *Id.* at pp. 14, 16; NIC, President's Summary, NIE, *Iraq's Continuing Programs for Weapons of Mass Destruction* (PS/NIE 2002-16HC) (Oct. 2002).

[47] DCI Statement for the Record at Tab 1, p. 23; *see also* Interview with NIO/SNP (Sept. 20, 2004). Although the NIE does use the phrase "has reconstituted" on page 16, the NIE also more accurately reflects the idea that reconstitution is a process elsewhere in the draft. NIE at p. 16 ("reconstitution is underway").

[48] NIE at p. 16; Interview with NIO/SNP (Sept. 20, 2004).

[49] NIE at p. 17. The NIE also drew support for its conclusion that the tubes were destined for a nuclear program from indications that Saddam Hussein was "personally interested in the procurement of aluminum tubes." *Id.* at p. 16. The NIE relied for this point on one human intelligence report from a liaison service, which reported that Saddam was "closely following" the purchase of the tubes. Classified intelligence report and cable traffic (Sept. 2002). According to the relevant station, however, it was the intelligence officer who said Saddam was following the purchase. At least one CIA officer at the meeting, however, remembered the exchange differently. Interview with CIA Iraq WMD Review Group analyst (Sept. 20, 2004). CIA efforts to obtain clarification on this point were unsuccessful, and the sourcing for this report remains unclear as of early 2005. *Id.*

[50] Interview with NIO/SNP (Sept. 20, 2004); Interview with DOE intelligence analyst (Oct. 27, 2004) (confirming that NSA and NGA agreed with the CIA/DIA position at the NIE coordination meetings); Interview with DOE intelligence analyst (Oct. 27, 2004) (same). An NSA official represented to the Commission in July 2004 that NSA had taken no position on the tubes issue at the NIE coordination. Interview with NSA official (July 14, 2004). As those who attended the NIE coordination meeting described it, however, NSA and NGA agreed to support the CIA/DIA position, and neither NSA nor NGA raised any objection when their positions were recorded as such. Interview with NIO/SNP (Sept. 20, 2004); Interview with DOE intelligence analyst (Oct. 27, 2004).

[51] NIE at pp. 81-85.

[52] *Id.* at p. 18. The NIE's reference to "high speed balancing machines" erroneously combines two separate pieces of equipment; it should have mentioned high-speed spin testing machines and balancing machines. DCI Statement for the Record at Tab 1, p. 32; *see also* Interview with NIO/SNP (Sept. 20, 2004).

[53] NIE at pp. 12-13; *see, e.g.*, Classified intelligence reporting (reflecting procurement attempts and noting that the items could be used in a nuclear program but providing no evidence they were intended for such a purpose); Senate Select Committee on Intelligence, *Report on the U.S. Intelligence Community's Prewar Intelligence Assessments on Iraq* (July 7, 2004) at pp. 119-120, 140 (noting no direct evidence of intended use in a nuclear program)

(hereinafter "SSCI").

[54] NIE at pp. 6, 19, 21.

[55] *See, e.g.,* Classified intelligence report (March 2000) (including assessment that as of December 1998 Iraq had the personnel and organizational resources to rapidly restart its nuclear program); Classified intelligence report (Nov. 1995) (assessment of a foreign liaison service that Iraq's scientific and technical staff has remained intact); Department of Defense, Classified intelligence report (April 2001) (construction activity indicates effort to restart nuclear research program); *see also* DCI Statement for the Record at Tab 1, pp. 21-22.

[56] Classified intelligence report (April 2002); Classified intelligence report (Nov. 2000).

[57] Classified intelligence report (April 2002); Classified intelligence report (Nov. 2000); *see also* SSCI at p. 124; Comments from NGA (March 3, 2005). With respect to the NIE's statement that "activity" at suspect sites had "increased" (NIE at p. 23), the NIO and CIA analysts told the SSCI that there was no new activity taking place at the suspect sites; the "activity" referred to in the NIE was the continuing work of personnel at these sites. SSCI at p. 124. The NIE also mentioned in a text box that defector reporting indicated that Iraq may have constructed another, new nuclear facility. NIE at p. 20. This assessment was based on reporting from a joint CIA-DIA source, all of whose reporting was disseminated by DIA. After the war, CIA attempted to verify the location of facilities in Iraq that the source had described and was unable to do so; further investigation led CIA to conclude that the source was "directed" by the Iraqi National Congress. Interview with CIA counterintelligence official (Dec. 8, 2004). As of March 3, 2005, however, the DIA had not recalled the source's reporting. Comments from CIA/DO (March 3, 2005).

[58] NIE at p. 25.

[59] *Id.*

[60] *Id.* Yellowcake is uranium ore concentrate, produced during the milling process of uranium ore.

[61] *Id.* at pp. 5-8.

[62] Interview with NIO/SNP (Sept. 20, 2004). In addition to recalling the reporting, CIA briefed the congressional intelligence committees in June 2003 that, given the recall of the earlier reporting, there was insufficient evidence to conclude that Iraq had recently sought uranium from Africa. *Id.* Further details regarding the forged documents are discussed below.

[63] As noted, in the President's Summary of the NIE, INR's position was more equivocal; INR judged that the overall evidence "indicates, at most, a limited Iraqi nuclear reconstitution effort." NIC, President's Summary, NIE, *Iraq's Continuing Programs for Weapons of Mass Destruction* (PS/NIE 2002-16HC) (Oct. 2002).

[64] *Id.* at pp. 81-83; *see also* DCI Statement for the Record at Tab 1, p. 28. INR agreed with DOE's assessment of the tubes. NIE at pp. 84-85. The President's Summary of the NIE reflected the NIE's conclusions, noting that "[m]ost agencies judge that Iraq is reconstituting its nuclear weapons program." The Summary explained that "[m]ost agencies judge" that Iraq's pursuit of aluminum tubes was "related to a uranium enrichment effort." Finally, the Summary also explained that "INR and DOE believe that the tubes more likely are intended for conventional weapon uses." NIC, President's Summary, NIE, *Iraq's Continuing Programs for Weapons of Mass Destruction* (PS/NIE 2002-16HC) (Oct. 2002). The unclassified version of the NIE repeats the bottom-line assessment from the NIE that "if left unchecked, [Iraq] probably will

have a nuclear weapon during this decade." The unclassified NIE also noted the disagreement over the tubes, explaining that "[m]ost intelligence specialists assess" that the tubes were intended for use in a centrifuge program, "but some believe that these tubes [were] probably intended for conventional weapons programs." NIC, *Iraq's Weapons of Mass Destruction Programs* (Oct. 2002) (unclassified NIE) at p. 1.

[65] Interview with DOE intelligence analyst (Oct. 27, 2004); *see also* DOE, Daily Intelligence Highlights, *Iraq: Nuclear Reconstitution Efforts Underway?* (July 22, 2002); DOE Office of Intelligence, Technical Intelligence Note, *Iraq: Recent Aluminum Tube Procurement Efforts* (TIN 000108) (Sept. 13, 2002) (judging that these other indicators collectively indicate intention to rejuvenate Iraq's nuclear weapons program). DOE stated its reliance on these factors, with the exception of its reliance on evidence of Iraqi efforts to obtain uranium from Africa, in the NIE. NIE at p. 6.

[66] Interview with NIO/SNP (Sept. 20, 2004).

[67] DCI Statement for the Record at Tab 1, p. 28; INR, *Iraq: Quest for Aluminum Tubes* (Oct. 9, 2002) at p. 1 (noting that INR accepted DOE's technical assessment of the tubes).

[68] *Id.*; *see also* Interview with DOE intelligence analyst (Oct. 27, 2004).

[69] DOE, Daily Intelligence Highlights, *Iraq: Gas Centrifuge Program Recounted* (Nov. 8, 2002) at p. 1 (reaffirming earlier assessments that while the tubes could be modified for centrifuge use their more likely end use is fabrication of motor cases for tactical rockets).

[70] NGIC, Assessment, *Iraq: Specialty Aluminum Tubes Are an Exercise in Deception* (Nov. 25, 2002) at p. 1 (noting the tube specifications are excessive for disposable rocket application and suggest probable application in a nuclear centrifuge); Interview with CIA WINPAC nuclear analysts (Oct. 8, 2004).

[71] Department of State, UNVIE Vienna 001134 (July 25, 2002); UNVIE Vienna 000240 (March 4, 2003) (Iraq explanation that tubes are for 81 mm rocket program is "credible").

[72] Senior Executive Memorandum, *Questions on Why Iraq is Procuring Aluminum Tubes and What the IAEA Has Found to Date* (Jan. 10, 2003) (noting that CIA, DIA, NGA, and NSA all assess that the tubes are most likely for centrifuges, while DOE intelligence and INR believe that the tubes are for the rocket program).

[73] Senior Executive Memorandum, Title Classified (Feb. 1, 2003); Senior Executive Memorandum, *What We Think of the IAEA's Analysis of Iraq's Attempt to Purchase Aluminum Tubes* (Dec. 26, 2002) (Iraqi claims that the tubes are for rockets may be "subterfuge" since the disagreement within the Intelligence Community regarding the tubes has appeared in the press); *see also* NGIC, Assessment, *Iraq: Specialty Aluminum Tubes Are an Exercise in Deception* (Nov. 25, 2002) (noting that Iraqi middlemen started to claim the tubes were for rockets after press reports revealed the dispute within the U.S. government on their intended use).

[74] *See, e.g.*, Senior Executive Memorandum, *Key Milestones in Our Assessments of Iraq's Nuclear Program* (Sept. 14, 2002) (noting the debate over the tubes' intended use but also the fact that "Iraq's denial and deception programs and the lack of human intelligence have resulted in intelligence gaps"); Senior Publish When Ready, *Evidence of Iraq's Nuclear Weapons Program Other Than the Aluminum Tube Procurement Effort* (Jan. 17, 2003) ("We have less access to information on Saddam's nuclear weapons intent and activities today than before the Gulf War, a time when significant nuclear developments escaped our detection.").

[75] Committee of Privy Counsellors, Chairman the Rt. Hon The Lord Butler of Brockwell,

KG GCB CVO, Chairman, *Review of Intelligence on Weapons of Mass Destruction* (July 14, 2004) at p. 132 (noting March 2002 Joint Intelligence Committee assessment) (hereinafter "Butler Report"). The British Government's unclassified dossier of September 2002 assessed that "the present Iraqi programme is almost certainly seeking an indigenous ability to enrich uranium to the level needed for a nuclear weapon." The dossier noted that while there was "no definitive intelligence" that the aluminum tubes were destined for a nuclear program, the tubes have "potential application in the construction of gas centrifuges" used to enrich uranium. *Id.*

[76] Australian Parliamentary Joint Committee on ASIO, ASIS and DSD, *Intelligence on Iraq's Weapons of Mass Destruction* (Dec. 2003) at p. 61; *see also* Government of the Commonwealth of Australia, *Report of the Inquiry into Australian Intelligence Agencies* (July 2004).

[77] ISG Report, Nuclear, at p. 7.

[78] *Id.* at pp. 7-8.

[79] *Id.* at p. 8.

[80] *Id.* at pp. 1, 8-9.

[81] *Id.* at pp. 3-4.

[82] *Id.* at pp. 7, 30. After the invasion of Kuwait and the embargo, Iraq undertook a "crash program" to produce a nuclear weapon. This program required the diversion of IAEA-safeguarded research reactor fuel at Tuwaitha. Iraq planned to further enrich some reactor fuel by building a centrifuge. The program encountered many obstacles, however, and never got off the ground. *Id.* at p. 4.

[83] *Id.* at pp. 4, 7.

[84] *Id.* at pp. 4-5. The ISG Report noted that since Operation Iraqi Freedom began, two scientists from Iraq's pre-1991 nuclear weapons program have emerged to provide the ISG with uranium enrichment technology and components, which they had kept hidden from inspectors. These scientists kept uranium enrichment documentation and technology in anticipation of renewing these efforts—actions that they contend were officially sanctioned. *Id.* at pp. 8, 73. Specifically, one former EMIS scientist hid EMIS-related material and equipment near his home. The former head of Iraq's pre-1991 centrifuge program also hid centrifuge components and a complete set of workable centrifuge blueprints at his home in 1991, for the purpose of reconstituting the program once sanctions were lifted. *Id.* at pp. 73-74.

[85] *Id.* at p. 5.

[86] *Id.*

[87] *Id.* at pp. 7-8. The ISG noted that significant looting and damage have occurred since the beginning of Operation Iraqi Freedom (OIF) at most of the dual-use manufacturing facilities that supported the pre-1991 EMIS program. Accordingly, the ISG has not been able to confirm that the Iraqi regime attempted to preserve the EMIS technology, although one scientist with the pre-1991 program kept documents and components that would be useful in restarting such an effort, as noted above. *Id.* at p. 8.

[88] *Id.* at p. 9.

[89] *Id.* at p. 5.

[90] *Id.* Iraq tried various means to retain scientists, including restricting foreign travel and preventing scientists from seeking other jobs. *Id.* Iraq later also tried to restore some of the incentives that scientists working in the nuclear program had previously enjoyed, as discussed below. *Id.* at pp. 5-6.

[91] *Id.* Saddam Hussein raised salaries for employees in the MIC and IAEC in the late 1990s, reinstituting the pay differential that former nuclear personnel enjoyed under Hussein Kamil and that had been cut after his defection. *Id.*

[92] *Id.* at pp. 35-36. These technologies—which included projects to acquire a magnet production line at Al Tahadi, carbon fiber filament winding equipment for missile fabrication, and machines for rotary balancing and spin testing—were intended to improve specific military or commercial products, according to the ISG. *Id.*

[93] *Id.* at p. 21.

[94] *Id.*

[95] *Id.* at pp. 22-23. Ja'far explained that the diameter of the tubes would cause the enrichment output to be far lower than the centrifuge design Iraq had pursued before 1991. *Id.*

[96] *Id.*

[97] *Id.*

[98] *Id.* Other sources, however, indicated the range and accuracy problems were caused by other factors, such as poor quality propellant. *Id.* at p. 25.

[99] *Id.*

[100] *Id.* at pp. 25-26.

[101] *Id.* at p. 21. The ISG based its findings regarding the tubes on interviews with both nuclear and rocket experts. *Id.*

[102] *Id.*

[103] *Id.* at pp. 21, 27.

[104] *Id.* at p. 28.

[105] *Id.* at pp. 27-28.

[106] *Id.* at p. 29.

[107] *Id.*

[108] *Id.* at p. 21.

[109] *Id.* at p. 30; *see also* NIE at p. 78.

[110] ISG Report, Nuclear at p. 30. Iraqi procurement agents customarily relied on intermediaries so as to disguise Iraq as the end-user. But because such efforts are disguised, it is often difficult to determine on whose behalf a procurement request is made. Interview with CIA Iraq WMD Review Group analyst (Sept. 9, 2004). In this instance, the ISG did not find a clear connection linking the procurement request to Iraq. ISG Report, Nuclear at p. 30. Also, it was not clear whether the request for a larger tube was inadvertent. Interview with CIA WINPAC nuclear analysts (Oct. 8, 2004); Interview with CIA Iraq WMD Review Group analyst (Sept. 9, 2004).

[111] ISG Report, Nuclear at p. 30.

[112] *Id.* at p. 22.

[113] *Id.* at p. 9. Coalition forces found 16 barrels of material in May 2003 that were associated with the yellowcake plant Iraq had at al Qaim—material that ISG believes is associated with the pre-1991 nuclear program. Known Iraqi holdings of yellowcake were accounted for by the Coalition and the IAEA in June 2004. *Id.* at pp. 9-13.

[114] *Id.* at pp. 4, 9.

[115] Raymond Whitaker, "Niger Timebomb: The Diplomat, the Forgery, and the Suspect Case for War," *The Independent on Sunday* (Aug. 10, 2003) at p. 8.

[116] ISG Report, Nuclear at p. 9.

[117] *Id.* at pp. 9-11.

[118] *Id.* at p. 11.

[119] *Id.*

[120] *Id.* at pp. 7-8. As noted, two scientists retained documents and components that could have the potential to contribute to a restart of the program, but this activity was isolated. *Id.* at pp. 8-9, 73.

[121] *Id.* at p. 6.

[122] Part of that thorough review would include input from experts, such as input from the Joint Atomic Energy Intelligence Committee (JAEIC)—a DCI committee operating under the auspices of the National Intelligence Council that is charged with analyzing technical nuclear issues. DCI Statement for the Record at Tab 1, p. 4. The JAEIC offered to convene an inter-agency meeting to discuss the issue in the spring and again in the summer of 2002, but no such meeting was held. JAEIC, *Letter Responding to Written Questions From Commission Staff* (Jan. 5, 2005). The meeting was not held, according to the JAEIC, because the CIA informed the JAEIC staff in early August 2002 that CIA was not ready to discuss its position. *Id.* The JAEIC did not convene after the NIE was requested in early September 2002 because the JAEIC member agencies could not support both efforts at the same time on the compressed time scheduled for the NIE, according to the JAEIC. *Id.* According to CIA, on the other hand, CIA had proposed in August that the JAEIC prepare an assessment of the tubes, but that assessment was not completed before Congress requested the NIE. Comments from CIA WINPAC (March 3, 2005). And the JAEIC did not convene a discussion after the NIE was published because the NIE had already set forth the differing positions of the various Intelligence Community agencies. JAEIC, *Letter Responding to Written Questions From Commission Staff* (Jan. 5, 2005). Whether the JAEIC could have produced a consensus opinion on the tubes is an open question, but because the dispute did not turn solely on technical issues—all agencies agreed that the tubes *could* be used to build centrifuges—they differed only on whether they *would* be used for centrifuges. *See also* DOE, *Letter from Director DOE Intelligence Responding to Written Questions* (Dec. 30, 2004) (noting that all agencies agreed tubes could be used for centrifuges and that the dispute was whether they would be used for that purpose).

[123] As discussed above, the Intelligence Community was not of one mind on the significance of the tubes for Iraq's nuclear program. CIA, DIA, NSA, and NGA agreed that the tubes were for use in a gas centrifuge program, while DOE and INR believed the tubes were more likely for use in tactical rockets. In any event, the majority position of the Intelligence Community, as presented to the policymakers before Operation Iraqi Freedom, was that Iraq was reconstituting its nuclear program and that the aluminum tubes were "compelling evidence" of that effort.

[124] NIE at p. 16.

[125] DIA, Military Intelligence Digest Supplement, *Iraq: Procuring Possible Nuclear-Related Gas Centrifuge Equipment* (MID-227-01-SCI) (Nov. 30, 2001); DIA, Defense Intelligence Assessment, *Iraq's Reemerging Nuclear Weapon Program* (DI-1610-93-02-SCI) (Sept. 2002); CIA, *Iraq's Hunt for Aluminum Tubes* (WINPAC IA 2002-051HCX) (Sept. 30, 2002).

[126] DIA, *Iraq's Reemerging Nuclear Weapon Program* (DI-1610-93-02-SCI) (Sept. 2002); CIA, *Iraq's Hunt for Aluminum Tubes* (WINPAC IA 2002-051HCX) (Sept. 30, 2002).

[127] SSCI at p. 100.

[128] DCI Statement for the Record at Tab 1, p. 27 & n. 100. CIA analysts explained that the IAEA inspection result from 1996 did not carry more weight in their analysis because the inspection reporting raised questions about whether the tubes found by the IAEA really were of the right high-strength alloy needed for centrifuges. Interview with CIA WINPAC nuclear analysts (Oct. 8, 2004). For its part, DOE believed that there was no plausible reason for Iraq to have *overstated* its declaration to claim that the tubes were made of 7075 T6 aluminum –an item Iraq was proscribed from possessing under United Nations Security Council resolutions— if the tubes were actually made of something else. Interview with DOE intelligence analyst (Oct. 27, 2004). In any event, the IAEA subsequently tested the tubes in early February 2003 and confirmed that they were in fact 7075 T6 aluminum. Interview with CIA WINPAC nuclear analysts (Oct. 8, 2004).

[129] CIA, *Iraq's Hunt for Aluminum Tubes* (WINPAC IA 2002-051HCX) (Sept. 30, 2002) (text box with NGIC's position) at p. 7. NGIC states that it did not receive the 1996 Iraqi declaration to the IAEA. Interview with NGIC officials (Dec. 7, 2004).

[130] SSCI at p. 100. Iraq's Nasser 81 mm rocket is reverse-engineered from the Italian Medusa air-to-ground rocket. NGIC, *Iraq: Specialty Aluminum Tubes are an Exercise in Deception* (Nov. 25, 2002) at p. 2.

[131] Interview with NGIC analysts (Dec. 7, 2004); DIA, Military Intelligence Digest Supplement, *Iraq: Procuring Possible Nuclear-Related Gas Centrifuge Equipment* (MID-227-01-SCI) (Nov. 30, 2001). The U.S. Mark 66 2.75-inch rocket uses a 7075 T6 aluminum case, and has manufacturing specifications "roughly comparable" to the Iraq tubes. NGIC, *Iraq: Specialty Aluminum Tubes are an Exercise in Deception* (Nov. 25, 2002) at pp. 1-2; Interview with NGIC analysts (Dec. 7, 2004).

[132] DIA, Military Intelligence Digest Supplement, *Iraq: Procuring Possible Nuclear-Related Gas Centrifuge Equipment* (MID-227-01-SCI) (Nov. 30, 2001).

[133] DCI Statement for the Record at Tab 1, p. 27 & n.100.

[134] DOE Office of Intelligence, Technical Intelligence Note, *Iraq's Gas Centrifuge Program: Is Reconstitution Underway?* (TIN 000064) (Aug. 17, 2001) at p. 6; IAEA Inspection Report, Nassr GE (Sept. 22, 1996).

[135] Interview with NGIC analysts (Dec. 7, 2004).

[136] SSCI at p. 133.

[137] NGIC, *Iraq: Specialty Aluminum Tubes Are an Exercise in Deception* (Nov. 25, 2002) at p. 2 (noting that efforts to obtain specifications for the Medusa had to that point been unsuccessful).

[138] Classified cable traffic (Sept. 2002); Interview with CIA Iraq WMD Review Group analyst (Sept. 9, 2004). Many months later, CIA finally obtained and disseminated information from the Italians on the Medusa specifications. Classified intelligence report (Nov. 2003). The specifications were slightly less stringent than those sought by Iraq, but slightly more stringent than those of comparable U.S. rockets. The differences were minimal, however. NGIC, Assessment, *Iraq: Specialty Aluminum Tubes Are an Exercise in Deception* (Nov. 25, 2002) at p. 2; *see also* Interview with NGIC analysts (Dec. 7, 2004).

[139] Interview with CIA WINPAC nuclear analyst (Oct. 8, 2004); Interview with DOE intelligence analyst (Oct. 27, 2004).

[140] Interview with CIA WINPAC nuclear analyst (Oct. 8, 2004). DOE Office of Intelligence, Technical Intelligence Note, *Iraqi Gas Centrifuge Program: Is Reconstitution Underway?* (TIN 000064) (Aug. 17, 2001) (providing technical assessment of how such tubes might perform in a centrifuge application)

[141] *Id.*; Interview with DOE intelligence analyst (Oct. 27, 2004); *see also* DOE, Daily Intelligence Highlights, *Iraq High-Strength Aluminum Tube Procurement* (April 11, 2001) (noting that the small tube diameter would pose "various design and operational problems and limitations"); DOE Office of Intelligence, Technical Intelligence Note, *Iraq's Gas Centrifuge Program: Is Reconstitution Underway?* (TIN 000064) (Aug. 17, 2001) at p. 9 (same).

[142] DOE Office of Intelligence, Technical Intelligence Note, *Iraq: Seeking Additional Aluminum Tubes* (TIN 000084) (Dec. 17, 2001) at p. 3; DOE Office of Intelligence Technical Intelligence Note, *Iraqi Gas Centrifuge Program: Is Reconstitution Underway?* (TIN 000064) (Aug. 17, 2001) at p. 8.

[143] DOE Office of Intelligence Technical Intelligence Note, *Iraqi Gas Centrifuge Program: Is Reconstitution Underway?* (TIN 000064) (Aug. 17, 2001) at p. 11.

[144] *Id.* at pp. 4, 11.

[145] Interview with CIA WINPAC nuclear analysts (Oct. 8, 2004). WINPAC analysts contacted the technical group within the CIA/DO's Counter Proliferation Division (CPD) for assistance in testing the tubes; CPD recommended a contractor to perform the tests. DOE did not assist with these tests, and DOE never performed any tests of its own on the tubes.

[146] Interview with CIA WINPAC nuclear analyst (Oct. 8, 2004).

[147] NIE at p. 76. This initial spin test was done without first balancing the tubes, "a critical step required for full-speed operation." *Id.*

[148] Interview with CIA WINPAC nuclear analyst (Oct. 8, 2004).

[149] *Id.*; *see also* Classified intelligence report (June 2003) (reissuing earlier report on spin-test results; that report had been issued in January 2003 and reissued once previously with corrections in May 2003).

[150] DOE Office of Intelligence, Technical Intelligence Note, *Technical Evaluation of CIA Spin Tests of Iraqi Aluminum Tubes* (TIN 000127) (May 2003); *see also* Interview with DOE intelligence analyst (Oct. 27, 2004).

[151] Interview with former Assistant Secretary of State for Intelligence and Research (Nov. 1, 2004). This official noted that INR and DOE viewed the CIA's reliance on the tubes as a "forced argument" designed to support the pre-conceived conclusion of reconstitution. *Id.*

[152] NIE at p. 17.

[153] DOE Office of Intelligence, Technical Intelligence Note, *Iraq's Gas Centrifuge Program: Is Reconstitution Underway?* (TIN 000064) (Aug. 17, 2001) at p. 9. DOE's view was that the tubes were "too thick for the design we assess that Iraq is most likely to be pursuing." DOE Office of Intelligence, Technical Intelligence Note, *Iraq: Recent Aluminum Tube Procurement Efforts* (TIN 000108) (Sept. 13, 2002) at p. 3. DOE also viewed the tubes as "too thick for *favorable* use as rotor tubes." DOE Office of Intelligence, Technical Intelligence Note, *Iraq's Gas Centrifuge Program: Is Reconstitution Underway?* (TIN 000064) (Aug. 17, 2001) at p. 9 (emphasis added). DOE noted that the tubes "could be modified" for use in centrifuge rotors.

DOE explained that "we can conceive of various workable schemes to modify the tubes for favorable centrifuge rotor use," including machining the inner and outer surfaces, which DOE judged to be within the Iraqis' capabilities if they had the proper tools. The modifications envisioned by DOE were "up to and including re-melting the tubes and restarting…[the] fabrication process." DOE Office of Intelligence, Technical Intelligence Note, *Iraq's Gas Centrifuge Program: Is Reconstitution Underway?* (TIN 000064) (Aug. 17, 2001) at pp. 8-10. If the tubes were used *without* thinning the walls, modifications to other parts of the centrifuge system would require "significant additional research and development." DOE Office of Intelligence, Technical Intelligence Note, *Iraq: Seeking Additional Aluminum Tubes* (TIN 000084) (Dec. 17, 2001) at p. 2. A DOE analyst told Commission staff that DOE did not rule out the possibility that the tubes could be used in gas centrifuges until after the commencement of OIF. Interview with DOE intelligence analyst (Oct. 27, 2004).

[154] NIE at p. 77; CIA, *Iraq's Hunt for Aluminum Tubes: Evidence of a Renewed Uranium Enrichment Program* (WINPAC IA 2002-051HCX) (Sept. 30, 2002) at p. 4. The Zippe and Beams-type gas centrifuges are based on declassified designs from the early 1960s that were instrumental in the early Russian and U.S. centrifuge programs. NIE at p. 77.

[155] NIE at p. 79, n. 7. A CIA WINPAC nuclear analyst explained that the Zippe design does not explicitly state a wall thickness for the rotors, and that a range of workable thicknesses can be arithmetically derived from other design specifications. Interview with CIA WINPAC nuclear analyst (Oct. 8, 2004).

[156] Interview with CIA WINPAC nuclear analyst (Oct. 8, 2004).

[157] NIE at p. 78.

[158] DIA, *Iraq's Reemerging Nuclear Weapon Program* (DI-1610-93-02-SCI) (Aug. 7, 2002) at p. 9.

[159] CIA WINPAC analysts noted, however, that the Urenco designs used rotors made of carbon fiber or maraging steel that Iraq was incapable of making itself. Interview with CIA WINPAC nuclear analyst (Oct. 8, 2004).

[160] DOE Office of Intelligence, Technical Intelligence Note, *Iraq: Seeking Additional Aluminum Tubes* (TIN 000084) (Dec. 17, 2001) at p. 3. DOE told the SSCI that Zippe's designs "had wall thicknesses" of a figure different than that indicated in the NIE's chart, and that DOE had "explained" this to CIA analysts "several times." SSCI at p. 110. But, as noted, according to CIA analysts a range of wall thicknesses can be arithmetically derived from Zippe's design. In fact, DOE later conceded that Zippe built at least one rotor with a thicker wall, according to the NIO/SNP. The NIO noted that the Senate Select Committee on Intelligence dropped DOE's concession from the final SSCI report when DOE conceded that Zippe had, in fact, made a thicker tube. According to the NIO, this revelation was contrary to a statement DOE made in the NIE (at p. 77) and in subsequent discussions until the SSCI was finalizing its report and DOE recognized its error. Interview with NIO/SNP (Sept. 20, 2004). DOE, for its part, disputes that it ever made the concession that Zippe built at least one rotor with a thicker wall. Comments from DOE (March 3, 2005). In interviews with Commission staff, a DOE analyst would only reiterate that a former DOE official had spoken to Mr. Zippe and that Mr. Zippe himself used a design with a thinner wall. The DOE analyst conceded, however, that the Zippe report, which is the only insight into the Zippe design that Iraq was likely to have, does not specify a wall thickness. Interview with DOE intelligence analyst (Oct. 27, 2004).

[161] Interview with DOE intelligence analyst (Oct. 27, 2004).

[162] *Id.*

[163] NIE at pp. 17, 78; *see also* CIA, *Iraq's Hunt for Aluminum Tubes: Evidence of a Renewed Uranium Enrichment Program* (WINPAC IA 2002-051HCX) (Sept. 30, 2002) at p. 4; NGIC, *Iraq: Specialty Aluminum Tubes Are an Exercise in Deception* (NGIC-1143-7184-03) (Nov. 25, 2002) at pp. 1-2.

[164] DOE Office of Intelligence, Technical Intelligence Note, *Iraq: Seeking Additional Aluminum Tubes* (TIN 000084) (Dec. 17, 2001) at pp. 2, 4; DOE Office of Intelligence, Technical Intelligence Note, *Iraq's Gas Centrifuge Program: Is Reconstitution Underway?* (TIN 000064) (Aug. 17, 2001) at p. 9; *see also* SSCI at p. 104.

[165] DOE Office of Intelligence, Technical Intelligence Note, *Iraq's Gas Centrifuge Program: Is Reconstitution Underway?* (TIN 000064) (Aug. 17, 2001) at p. 9 (noting tubes could be used if the walls were thinned); DOE Office of Intelligence Technical Intelligence Note, *Iraq: Seeking Additional Aluminum Tubes* (TIN 000084) (Dec. 17, 2001) at p. 2 (if tubes used without thinning the walls, modifications to other parts of the centrifuge system would require "significant additional research and development"); *see also* Butler Report at pp. 130-131; NIE at p. 77 (NIE assessment that the 900 mm tubes would have to be cut to make two 400 mm rotors); NIE at pp. 81-84 (noting views of DOE, INR, and IAEA that tubes would require other modifications before being used in centrifuge rotors).

[166] Butler Report at pp. 130-131.

[167] SSCI at p. 103. In fact, IAEA interviews with Iraqi engineers in early 2003 indicated that Iraq may have over-specified the tubes for use in rockets because of engineering inexperience. Interview with DOE intelligence analyst (Oct. 27, 2004).

[168] NIE at p. 17. *See, e.g.,* Classified intelligence reporting (Aug. 2001); (Jan. 2002); *see also* SSCI at p. 105.

[169] SSCI at p. 105. Moreover, IAEA inspection information indicated that Iraq had paid approximately $15-$20 for the tubes it acquired in the 1980's. *Id.*

[170] Denial refers to the ability to prevent the Intelligence Community from collecting intelligence, for example, by avoiding overhead imagery or by encrypting communications. Deception refers to the ability to manipulate intelligence with false or misleading information, for example, by disseminating "cover stories" for illicit activity, by directing controlled or "double agents" at U.S. intelligence, or by presenting decoy structures for imagery. *See* Department of Defense, *Iraqi Denial and Deception for Weapons of Mass Destruction and Ballistic Missile Programs* (Oct. 8, 2002).

[171] NGIC, *Iraq: Specialty Aluminum Tubes Are an Exercise in Deception* (NGIC-1143-7184-03) (Nov. 25, 2002) at p. 4. Similarly, the CIA noted that Iraq's claim that the tubes are intended for rockets "may be a deception effort by Baghdad to deflect attention away from nuclear-related procurements." CIA, *Iraq's Hunt for Aluminum Tubes: Evidence of a Renewed Uranium Enrichment Program* (WINPAC IA 2002-051HCX) (Sept. 30, 2002) at pp. 2-3.

[172] Senior Executive Memorandum, Title Classified (Feb. 1, 2003).

[173] To its credit, CIA WINPAC did attempt to conduct an independent review of its conclusions about the tubes by convening a panel of centrifuge experts to evaluate the relative merits of the two alternative hypotheses for the intended use of the tubes. This team's "independent" review, however, was conducted based on a review of "available documentation" on the subject, a briefing from CIA on the chronology of events surrounding Iraqi attempts to procure the

tubes, a briefing from DOE outlining DOE's views on the tubes, and sample tubes for "visual examination." CIA, Title Classified (Sept. 17, 2002). The team told the SSCI that its review was based primarily on "a stack of documents provided by the CIA" which contained the various intelligence assessments regarding the tubes, and the briefing from DOE. Notes of red team interview with SSCI prepared by CIA Office of Congressional Affairs (Nov. 13, 2003); *see also* DCI Statement for the Record at Tab 1, p. 25 & n. 98. The team concluded that the tubes were consistent with design requirements of gas centrifuge rotors, and inconsistent with design requirements of rocket motor casings. DCI Statement for the Record at Tab 1, p. 25.

[174] Interview with CIA WINPAC nuclear analysts (Oct. 8, 2004).

[175] *Id.* (noting that such a reassessment had been drafted in summer 2004 but was still being reviewed by management in late 2004).

[176] Interview with DOE intelligence analyst (Oct. 27, 2004).

[177] NIE at p. 16.

[178] Classified intelligence reporting (Sept. 2002).

[179] Interview with CIA Iraq WMD Review Group analyst (Sept. 9, 2004).

[180] *Id.* The sourcing for this report remains unclear as of 2005. *Id.* Similarly, the NIE indicated that in late August 2002, according to sensitive reporting, Iraq asked about increasing the internal diameter and wall thickness each by 1.0 mm, thus increasing the external diameter by 3.0 mm. NIE at p. 78. This information was also from the liaison service. Classified intelligence report (Aug. 2002). The procurement attempt, however, was never definitively linked to Iraq. Interview with CIA WINPAC nuclear analysts (Oct. 8, 2004); Interview with CIA Iraq WMD Review Group analyst (Sept. 9, 2004).

[181] NIE at pp. 18-19.

[182] SSCI at pp. 119-120; *see also* Interview with NIO/SNP (Sept. 20, 2004). The DCI Statement for the Record noted that this mistaken reference was traceable to an earlier CIA/NESA publication. The workers had been associated with Iraq's Electromagnetic Isotope Separation (EMIS) uranium enrichment program. Comments from NIO/SNP (March 3, 2005).

[183] DCI Statement for the Record at Tab 1, p. 32.; SSCI at p. 120. This mistake was also traced to the earlier CIA/NESA publication. Comments from NIO/SNP (March 3, 2005).

[184] NIE at pp. 18-19; DOE, Intelligence Highlights, *Iraq: Nuclear Reconstitution Efforts Underway?* (July 22, 2002).

[185] Interview with DOE intelligence analyst (Oct. 27, 2004); *see also* Interview with CIA WINPAC nuclear analyst (Aug. 11, 2004). CIA, on the other hand, was more concerned about the uranium Iraq already had in-country, as described in the NIE. Although Iraq's stockpile of low enriched uranium was inspected once per year by the IAEA, CIA was concerned that the uranium could be diverted for enrichment and weapons before anyone detected it was missing. Interview with NIO/SNP (Sept. 20, 2004); *see also* DCI Statement for the Record at Tab 1, p. 22. The NIO/SNP briefed the SSCI on October 4, 2002 and explained that the uranium information was not in the Key Judgments of the NIE and was included in the body for completeness—but only after first noting that Iraq already had uranium in country as noted above. Comments from NIO/SNP (March 3, 2005).

[186] Interview with NIO/SNP (Sept. 20, 2004).

[187] Interview with former senior intelligence officer.

[188] Interview with DOE intelligence analyst (Oct. 27, 2004).

[189] Interview with NIO/SNP (Sept. 20, 2004) (only DOE relied on the uranium from Niger information to support the case for reconstitution).

[190] The President stated that "the British Government has learned that Saddam Hussein recently sought significant quantities of uranium from Africa." President George W. Bush, Address Before a Joint Session of the Congress on the State of the Union (Jan. 28, 2003). A related problem within the Intelligence Community is that, when asked to vet the State of the Union speech, the Intelligence Community lacked a formal process to do so. Department of State and CIA, *Department of State and CIA: The Joint Report of the Inspectors General of CIA and State on the Alleged Iraqi Attempts to Procure Uranium From Niger* (Sept. 2003) (noting the lack of a formal vetting process and recommended the institution of more formalized procedures).

[191] NIE at p. 25.

[192] Classified intelligence report (Oct. 2001); Classified intelligence report (Feb. 2002); Classified intelligence report (March 2002). There was additional reporting that Iraq was seeking to procure uranium from Africa, but this reporting was not considered reliable by most analysts at the time, and it was subsequently judged not credible and recalled. Interview with CIA WINPAC nuclear analysts (Aug. 11, 2004); CIA, Memorandum for the DCI, *In Response to Your Questions for Our Current Assessment and Additional Details on Iraq's Alleged Pursuits of Uranium From Abroad* (June 17, 2003) at p. 2. For example, separate reporting indicated Iraq had offered weapons to a country in exchange for uranium. Classified intelligence report (April 1999). There were two human intelligence reports in March-April 1999 indicating that a delegation of Iraqis, Iranians, and Libyans had arrived in Somalia to discuss the possibility of extracting uranium from a Somali mine. Classified intelligence report (March 1999); Classified intelligence report (April 1999). Another report indicated further Iraqi involvement with a uranium purchase. Classified intelligence report (April 2002); *see also* SSCI at p. 47 n. 6; CIA, Memorandum for the DCI, *In Response to Your Questions for Our Current Assessment and Additional Details on Iraq's Alleged Pursuits of Uranium From Abroad* (June 17, 2003) at p. 2. There was also one report from a U.S. Department of Defense agency that indicated that a large quantity of uranium was being stored in a warehouse in Cotonou, Benin, destined for Iraq. Classified intelligence report (Nov. 2002). A Defense HUMINT officer checked the warehouse one month later and saw only what appeared to be bales of cotton. Defense HUMINT did not report these findings, however, until February 10, 2003. SSCI at pp. 59-60, 68. A CIA cable dated January 2003 had reported that a foreign liaison service claimed that the uranium stored at the warehouse in Benin was not destined for Iraq. SSCI at p. 59-60, 64.

[193] Classified intelligence report (Feb. 2002).

[194] *Id.*; Classified intelligence report (Dec. 2001).

[195] Interview with CIA WINPAC nuclear analyst (Sept. 20, 2004); *see also* SSCI at p. 38.

[196] SSCI at p. 38.

[197] *Id.* at pp. 39-42.

[198] Classified intelligence reporting (March 2002); *see also* SSCI at p. 43.

[199] Classified intelligence reporting (March 2002).

[200] *Id.*

[201] *Id.*

[202] *Iraq's Weapons of Mass Destruction: The Assessment of the British Government* (Sept.

2002) (unclassified) (also referred to as the "Dossier" or "white paper").

[203] Interview with CIA/DO officials (Sept. 3, 2004) (noting that the documents were passed to the Embassy on Oct. 9, 2004); *see also* Department of State, Rome 004988 (Oct. 11, 2002) (cable from U.S. Embassy Rome reporting receipt of the documents on October 9).

[204] Department of State and CIA, *Joint Report of Inspectors General on Iraqi Attempts to Procure Uranium From Niger* (Sept. 2003) at p. 11; CIA, *Analyses on an Alleged Iraq-Niger Uranium Agreement* (undated but prepared sometime after March 7, 2003) (attaching copies and translations of documents); *see also* SSCI at pp. 57-58 (noting that the documents were similar to the original reporting).

[205] Department of State and CIA, *Joint Report of Inspectors General on Iraqi Attempts to Procure Uranium From Niger* (Sept. 2003) at p. 12. Although the documents were made available to CPD several days after they were sent from Rome in mid-October 2002, CPD did not share the documents with WINPAC or attempt to assess their authenticity. *Id.*, Appendix, at pp. 6-7.

[206] Senior Publish When Ready, *Request for Evidence of Iraq's Nuclear Weapons Program Other Than the Aluminum Tube Procurement Effort* (Jan. 17, 2003). By January 2003, CIA WINPAC analysts had come to believe that such uranium procurement efforts, if they could be shown to be true, would bolster the case that Iraq was reconstituting its nuclear program. Interview with WINPAC nuclear analyst (Sept 20, 2004); *see also* SSCI at pp. 62-63.

[207] SSCI at pp. 63-64.

[208] President George W. Bush, Address Before a Joint Session of the Congress on the State of the Union (Jan. 28, 2003).

[209] SSCI at p. 66; *see also* Interview with NIO/SNP (Sept. 20, 2004) (noting that he never saw a draft of the speech, was not asked to comment on it, and was never contacted about releasing any information from the NIE or otherwise).

[210] Interview with CIA WINPAC nuclear analyst (Sept. 20, 2004); *see also* SSCI at p. 66. Information from the October 2002 NIE on the uranium deal was also provided to Secretary Powell in preparation for his speech to the United Nations, but no statement about uranium from Africa was included in that speech. Department of State and CIA, *Joint Report of Inspectors General on Iraqi Attempts to Procure Uranium From Niger* (Sept. 2003) at p. 26. Secretary Powell, during his meetings at CIA to vet the speech, was informed that there were doubts about the Niger reporting and did not include it for that reason. *Id.* Even after the documents were found to be forgeries, however, DIA provided memoranda to the Office of the Secretary of Defense indicating that other corroborating information still existed. But that information consisted of the report from Ambassador Wilson, and the report from the Defense Department agency regarding a warehouse in Benin. SSCI at pp. 69-71.

[211] CIA, *Congressional Notification Regarding Purported Iraqi Attempt to get Uranium from Niger* (April 3, 2003) at p. 7.

[212] IAEA, *Analysis of Relevant Documents* (March 10, 2003).

[213] CIA, *Analyses on an Alleged Iraq-Niger Uranium Agreement* (undated but prepared sometime after March 7, 2003) (appending original and translated documents); IAEA, *Analysis of Relevant Documents* (March 10, 2003); Interview with FBI (Sept. 21, 2004).

[214] CIA, *Analyses on an Alleged Iraq-Niger Uranium Agreement* (undated but prepared sometime after March 7, 2003). *See also* Senior Publish When Ready, *Iraq's Reported Interest*

in Buying Uranium from Niger and Whether Associated Documents are Authentic (March 11, 2003) (concluding the documents were forgeries). The errors in the original documents, which indicated they were forgeries, also occur in the February 2002 report that provided a "verbatim" text of the agreement, indicating that the original reporting was based on the forged documents.

[215] Department of State and CIA, *Joint Report of Inspectors General on Iraqi Attempts to Procure Uranium From Niger* (Sept. 2003) at p. 11. Although the *Inspectors General* report notes that all three reports were recalled, CIA/DO officials advised the Commission that in fact two of the reports were recalled and the third, which included information not included in the forged documents, was reissued with a caveat that the information the report contains may have been fabricated. Comments from CIA/DO (March 3, 2005).

[216] CIA, Memorandum for the DCI, *In Response to Your Questions for Our Current Assessment and Additional Details on Iraq's Alleged Pursuits of Uranium From Abroad* (June 17, 2003) at p. 1.

[217] Interview with NIO/SNP (Sept. 20, 2004). The SSCI report referenced the memorandum for the DCI, and stated that the memorandum had no distribution outside the CIA. SSCI at p. 71. This reference left the mistaken impression, however, that CIA did not inform others of its conclusions regarding the forged documents and the concomitant reliability of information about a possible uranium deal with Niger. The NIO/SNP emphasized that CIA not only recalled the original reporting as having possibly been based on fraudulent reporting, but the NIO, with CIA and other agencies in attendance, also briefed Congress on the matter. Interview with NIO/SNP (Sept. 20, 2004).

[218] It is still unclear who forged the documents and why. The Federal Bureau of Investigation is currently investigating those questions. Interview with FBI (Sept. 21, 2004); *see also* Interview with CIA/DO officials (Sept. 3, 2004). We discuss in the counterpart footnote in our classified report some further factual findings concerning the potential source of the forgeries. This discussion, however, is classified.

[219] NIE at pp. 5, 35. The Intelligence Community also judged that Iraq maintained delivery systems for its BW agents. *Id.* at p. 7. For its part, the British Joint Intelligence Committee assessed in September 2002 that Iraq "currently has available, either from pre-Gulf War stocks or more recent production, a number of biological warfare" agents and weapons. Butler Report at p. 74. The Australian Office of National Assessments judged by September 2002 that "Iraq is highly likely to have chemical and biological weapons," that "Iraq has almost certainly been working to increase its ability to make chemical and biological weapons," and, in December 2002, that many of Iraq's WMD activities were hidden in mobile facilities. Australian Parliamentary Joint Committee on Australian Secret Intelligence Organization, Australian Secret Intelligence Service and Defense Signals Directorate, *Intelligence on Iraq's Weapons of Mass Destruction* (Dec. 2003) at pp. 32, 61. With respect to mobile BW facilities, however, the Defense Intelligence Organization assessed in March 2003 that the level of evidence required to confirm the existence of such mobile facilities had not yet been found. *Id.* at pp. 61-62.

[220] NIE at p. 41.

[221] ISG, *Comprehensive Report of the Special Advisor to the DCI on Iraqi WMD,* Volume III, "Biological Warfare," (Sept. 30, 2004) at pp. 1-3 (hereinafter "ISG Report, Biological").

[222] *Id.* at pp. 11-12. Iraq continued to conduct research and development on weaponization until 1995. *Id.* at pp. 13-15.

[223] *Id.*

[224] DCI Statement for the Record at Tab 3, p. 1.

[225] *Id.* at pp. 3-5; *see also* CIA, *Iraq's Biological Warfare Program: Saddam's Ace in the Hole* (SW-90-11052CX) (Aug. 1990) at pp. 4-5.

[226] DCI Statement for the Record at Tab 3, pp. 3-5.

[227] Classified intelligence reporting; *see also* DCI Statement for the Record at Tab 3, p. 2, n. 1.

[228] Classified intelligence reporting; *see also* ISG Report, Biological, at p. 15.

[229] Classified intelligence reporting; *see also* DCI Statement for the Record at Tab 3, pp. 3-5.

[230] CIA, *Iraq's Biological Warfare Program: Well Positioned for the Future* (OTI IR 97-012X) (April 1997).

[231] NIC, *Iraq: Post-Desert Fox Activities and Estimated Status of WMD Programs* (July 1999). *See also* SSCI at p. 143.

[232] CIA, Title Classified (WINPAC IA 2002-059X) (Nov. 21, 2002). *See also* DCI Statement for the Record at Introduction, p. 1.

[233] Interview with CIA WINPAC BW analyst (Oct. 8, 2004). Analysts assessed that Iraq could restart BW production within six months. NIC, *Worldwide BW Programs: Trends and Prospects, Volume I: The Estimate* (NIE 99-05CX/I) (May 1999) at pp. 4 and 43.

[234] Interview with CIA Iraq WMD Review Group analyst (Aug. 3, 2004) ("Substantial volume"); DCI Statement for the Record at Tab 3, p. 6 (citing NIC, *Worldwide Biological Warfare Programs: Trends and Prospects, Update* (NIE 2000-12HCX) (Dec. 2000) (noting that the "new information" caused the Intelligence Community to "adjust...upwards" its 1999 assessment of the BW threat posed by Iraq. The "new information" refers to the Curveball reporting, which began in January 2000.)).

[235] Interview with Defense HUMINT official (Nov. 2, 2004). Defense HUMINT confirmed that it had disseminated 95 reports from Curveball. DIA, *Memorandum from Director, DIA Re: Curveball Background* (Jan. 14, 2005). *See, e.g.*, Classified intelligence reporting. Six reports from Curveball were disseminated in CIA channels: five in 2000 and one in March 2004. Interview with CIA/DO officials (Sept. 27, 2004). The five reports disseminated in 2000 were obtained by WINPAC analysts during meetings with foreign liaison service officials. The remaining report was disseminated when CIA finally obtained direct access to Curveball in March 2004. Comments from CIA/DO (March 3, 2005).

[236] Classified intelligence reporting.

[237] Interview with CIA/DO officials and CIA Iraq WMD Review Group analysts (Aug. 3, 2004).

[238] NIC, *Worldwide Biological Warfare Programs: Trends and Prospects, Update* (NIE 2000-12HCX) (Dec. 2000) at p. 22.

[239] CIA, DCI Nonproliferation Center, *New Evidence of Iraqi Biological Warfare Program* (SIR 2000-003X) (Dec. 14, 2000). *See also* SSCI at p. 144.

[240] CIA, *Iraq: Mobile Biological Warfare Agent Production Capability* (WINPAC IA 2001-050X) (Oct. 10, 2001) at pp. 1, 7.

[241] Senior Publish When Ready, *Iraq: Mobile BW Agent Production Capability* (Sept. 19, 2001) (sources indicate Baghdad continues to pursue a mobile BW capability to produce large

amounts of BW agents covertly).

[242] Interviews with CIA Iraq WMD Review Group analysts (Aug. 3, 2004 and Sept. 20, 2004) (citing to timeline prepared by the CIA Iraq WMD Review Group, quoting the DCI's prepared testimony). Director Tenet based this statement on information obtained from Curveball, whom he described as "a credible defector who worked in the program." The classified version of the report discusses in detail CIA's discovery that the fourth source, whose reporting the DCI stated corroborated Curveball's reporting, was not the direct source of the reporting sourced to him on BW.

[243] The President's Summary of the NIE reflected this finding, noting that "[w]e assess that most elements of Iraq's BW program are larger and more advanced than before the Gulf War" and "[w]e judge that Iraq has some BW agents." NIC, President's Summary, NIE, *Iraq's Continuing Programs for Weapons of Mass Destruction* (PS/NIE 2002-16HC) (Oct. 2002). The unclassified summary of the NIE contained the same assessment. Unclassified NIE at p. 2 ("Iraq has some lethal and incapacitating BW agents" and "[a]ll key aspects...of Iraq's offensive BW program are active and most elements are larger and more advanced than they were before the Gulf War").

[244] NIE at pp. 7, 36, 43.

[245] DCI Statement for the Record at Tab 3, p. 16; *see also* Interview with WINPAC BW analyst (Oct. 8, 2004).

[246] *See, e.g.*, Classified intelligence reporting; *see also Joint CIA-DIA Assessment of [Foreign Service] Source Curveball* (June 7, 2004) at pp. 1-2; SSCI at pp. 148-9.

[247] *Joint CIA-DIA Assessment of [Foreign Service] Source Curveball*, (June 7, 2004) at pp. 1-2; *see, e.g.*, Classified intelligence report (May 2004) (recalling Curveball report).

[248] NIE at pp. 41-43; Interview with WINPAC BW analyst (Oct. 8, 2004); *see also* SSCI at pp. 148-149; Interview with former WINPAC BW analyst (Oct. 25, 2004).

[249] Classified intelligence report; *see also* SSCI at p. 161.

[250] Interview with CIA/DO officials and CIA Iraq WMD Review Group analyst (Aug. 3, 2004); Interview with CIA/DO officials (Sept. 27, 2004). Classified intelligence report (Oct. 2003) (stating that, contrary to the information reported by the same source in June 2001, "there was no equipment for the production of biological weapons at this facility" and that the "source had no knowledge of biological weapons production at other facilities").

[251] Interview with CIA/DO officials (Sept. 27, 2004); Interview with Defense HUMINT official (Nov. 2, 2004).

[252] Interview with Defense HUMINT official (Nov. 2, 2004).

[253] Classified intelligence report (March 2002); *see also* NIC, *The Iraqi National Congress Defector Program* (NIC 1768-02) (July 10, 2002) at pp. 3-5; SSCI at p. 160.

[254] Interview with CIA/DO officials and CIA Iraq WMD Review Group analysts (Aug. 3, 2004); *see also* NIC, *Iraqi National Congress Defector Program* (NIC 1768-02) (July 10, 2002) at pp. 4-5. The NIE actually sourced its information to a *Vanity Fair* article, which quoted the INC source as an unnamed "defector." David Rose, "Iraq's Arsenal of Terror," *Vanity Fair* (May 2002) (cited in source documents to annotated NIE). Defense HUMINT issued a fabrication notice, but never recalled the INC source's reporting. The distinction between these two actions is discussed in the text below.

[255] Interviews with CIA Iraq WMD Review Group analyst (Aug. 3, 2004 and Sept. 20,

2004).

[256] CIA, *Iraq: Biological Warfare Agents Pose Growing Threat to U.S. Interests* (WINPAC IA 2002-060CX) (Nov. 13, 2002).

[257] CIA, *Iraq: Options for Unconventional Use of CBW* (WINPAC IA 2003-010HJX) (Feb. 13, 2003).

[258] Secretary of State Colin L. Powell, Remarks to the United Nations Security Council (Feb. 5, 2003) (annotated version). Referring to Curveball, Secretary Powell said that a chemical engineer who was actually present during BW production runs provided information on the mobile facilities. Referring to the second source, Secretary Powell noted that "a second source, an Iraqi civil engineer in a position to know the details of the program, confirmed the existence of transportable facilities moving on trailers." Referring to the fourth source, Secretary Powell said that a source "in a position to know" reported that Iraq had mobile production systems mounted on trucks and railway cars. Referring to the INC source, Secretary Powell noted that an "Iraqi major who defected confirmed" that Iraq has mobile BW production facilities. *Id.; see also* Interview with CIA/DO officials (Aug. 3, 2004); SSCI at p. 161.

[259] CIA, *Iraqi Mobile Biological Warfare Agent Production Plants* (WINPAC) (May 16, 2003).

[260] Interview with CIA WINPAC BW analyst (Oct. 8, 2004); Interview with former CIA WINPAC BW analyst (Nov. 10, 2004) (noting that Curveball was recontacted in April 2003 to query him about the trailers found in Iraq; Curveball was shown pictures of the trailers and he identified components on those trailers that were similar to those on the mobile BW facilities he had described in his earlier reporting). Interview with Defense HUMINT official (Nov. 2, 2004).

[261] ISG Report, Biological at p. 2.

[262] *Id.* at p. 12.

[263] *Id.*

[264] *Id.* at pp. 11-13.

[265] *Id.* at p. 13.

[266] *Id.* at p. 15.

[267] *Id.*

[268] *Id.*

[269] *Id.* at pp. 11-13, 15, 38.

[270] *Id.* at pp. 15, 18, 19, 38.

[271] *Id.* at p. 1.

[272] *Id.* at pp. 3, 73-98.

[273] *Id.* at p. 3.

[274] According to a Defense HUMINT official, when Defense HUMINT pressed for access to Curveball, the foreign service said that Curveball disliked Americans and that he would refuse to speak to them. The CIA also pressed for access to Curveball, but it was not until the DCI himself intervened in late November 2003, stating that CIA officers in Baghdad were uncovering serious discrepancies in Curveball's reporting, that the foreign service allowed U.S. intelligence officials to interview Curveball, in March 2004. Interview with Defense HUMINT official (Nov. 2, 2004); Comments from former WINPAC BW analyst (March 3, 2005); Classi-

fied cable traffic (Nov. 2003). The Senate Select Committee on Intelligence criticized Defense HUMINT for failing to demand that the foreign service provide direct access to Curveball. SSCI at p. 153. We do believe that the leadership of the Intelligence Community should have pressed harder and sooner for access to Curveball; with that said, we think it is difficult to expect that Defense HUMINT could have "demanded" access to another intelligence service's asset. Eventually, the head of the foreign intelligence service only agreed to grant CIA access to Curveball in December 2003 because of the serious discrepancies emerging from analysts' investigation in Iraq. Even then, the head of the foreign service faced significant opposition to his decision to grant access from within his service; several senior foreign service operations officers even threatened to resign if the CIA were allowed access to Curveball. Comments from former WINPAC BW analyst (March 3, 2005); Classified cable traffic (Dec. 2003).

[275] Interview with Defense HUMINT official (Nov. 2, 2004).

[276] *Id.* Defense HUMINT reiterated to Commission staff that in its view it was "impossible" to validate Curveball because Defense HUMINT, like CIA, had been denied direct personal contact with the source. Defense HUMINT, viewing itself as only the "conduit" for the information, allowed the analysts' enthusiastic response to Curveball's reporting to serve as "validation" for the source's veracity. Comments from Defense HUMINT (March 3, 2005). As explained further below, Defense HUMINT's abdication of responsibility in this regard was a serious failing.

[277] SSCI at p. 153; *see also* Interview with CIA WINPAC analysts (Oct. 8, 2004).

[278] SSCI at p. 191.

[279] Interview with CIA/DO officials (Sept. 27, 2004); *see also* CIA/DO description of the DO Asset Validation System (Sept. 2004) (prepared in response to Commission request).

[280] Electronic mail exchange between Defense HUMINT officials (Feb. 12-13, 2003).

[281] Interview with CIA WINPAC BW analyst (Oct. 8, 2004) (noting that other information indicated Curveball's information was plausible). Interviews with former CIA WINPAC BW analyst (Nov. 10, 2004, and Feb. 23, 2005).

[282] Interview with CIA WINPAC BW analyst (Oct. 8, 2004); Interview with former CIA WINPAC BW analyst (Nov. 10, 2004). According to WINPAC analysts, Curveball's reporting seemed to fit a plausible storyline of Iraq's BW efforts. Curveball claimed that Iraq's mobile BW program began in 1995, at about the same time Iraq's BW-related activities at fixed facilities such as Al Hakam were compromised. To analysts, this storyline seemed logical: Iraq had shifted its BW efforts from the compromised fixed facilities to the more easily concealed mobile units. *Id.* This rationale can also be found in CIA, *Iraq: Mobile Biological Warfare Agent Production Capability* (WINPAC IA 2001-050X) (Oct. 10, 2001) at p. 5. ("We judge that the May 1995 planning for construction of mobile BW production units allowed Iraq to admit aspects of its offensive BW program to UNSCOM starting in July 1995.").

[283] Interview with CIA/DO officials and CIA Iraq WMD Review Group analyst (Aug. 3, 2004); Interview with CIA WINPAC BW analyst (Oct. 8, 2004).

[284] Interview with CIA/DO officials and CIA Iraq WMD Review Group analyst (Aug. 3, 2004); Interview with CIA WINPAC BW analyst (Oct. 8, 2004); *see also* SSCI at p. 156.

[285] Classified cable traffic (Feb. 2001).

[286] Electronic mail from Department of Defense detailee ("question re curve ball") (Dec. 18, 2002); SSCI at p. 153.

[287] Interview with former CIA WINPAC BW analyst (Feb. 23, 2005); Interview with CIA/ DO official (Feb. 22, 2005); SSCI at p. 154.

[288] Electronic mail from CIA/DO [detailee] to Deputy Chief, Iraqi Task Force, CIA/DO (Feb. 4, 2003).

[289] Interview with CIA/DO officials (Aug. 3, 2004); Interview with CIA Iraq WMD Review Group analyst (Sept. 20, 2004). David Kay of the ISG also told the Commission that the foreign service had "warned" the CIA that the source was questionable before publication of the NIE. Interview with David Kay (May 26, 2004).

[290] Interview with CIA WINPAC BW analyst (Oct. 8, 2004).

[291] Interview with CIA/DO officials (Aug. 3, 2004); *see also* SSCI at p. 190.

[292] Classified cable traffic (April 2002).

[293] *Id.*

[294] *Id.*

[295] Interview with CIA WINPAC BW analyst (Oct. 8, 2004) (noting that operational traffic was shared with WINPAC, particularly traffic from the CIA/DO's Counterproliferation Division).

[296] Electronic mail from CIA WINPAC BW analyst (Dec. 20, 2002) (summarizing Curveball assessment).

[297] Interview with former CIA WINPAC BW analyst (Nov. 10, 2004).

[298] *Id.*

[299] As noted above, denial refers to the ability to prevent the Intelligence Community from collecting intelligence, and deception refers to the ability to manipulate intelligence with false or misleading information. *See* Department of Defense, *Iraqi Denial and Deception for Weapons of Mass Destruction and Ballistic Missile Programs* (Oct. 8, 2002). Information from 1998 indicated that the Iraqis had broken and then reconstituted part of the wall, which convinced the majority of analysts that the wall was "temporary" and would allow BW trailers through it, thus not contradicting Curveball's reporting. When United Nations Monitoring Verification and Inspection Commission (UNMOVIC) inspectors visited the site on February 9, 2003, they found that the wall was a permanent structure and could find nothing to corroborate Curveball's reporting. Comments from former WINPAC BW analyst (March 3, 2005). Further, when analysts visited the site after OIF, they discovered that, in actuality, the wall was a six foot high solid structure. Interview with WINPAC BW analyst (Nov. 22, 2004). This and other discrepancies in Curveball's information that ultimately led to the conclusion that he was a fabricator are discussed further below.

[300] *See, e.g.*, NIE at p. 41.

[301] Interview with CIA WINPAC analysts (Oct. 8, 2004).

[302] Senior Publish When Ready, *Memorandum to the Secretary of Defense* (Sept. 19, 2001) (emphasis added).

[303] NIE at p. 41.

[304] Classified cable traffic (May 2002) (fabrication notice); *see also* SSCI at p. 151.

[305] Senior Publish When Ready, *Iraq's Expanding BW Capability* (July 13, 2002).

[306] NIE at p. 43.

[307] Interview with CIA/DO chief of the regional division responsible for relations with the

foreign liaison service handling Curveball (hereinafter "Division Chief"), CIA/DO (Jan. 31, 2005).

[308] *Id.*

[309] Interview with CIA/DO Division Chief and former chief of the responsible regional group within the division (hereinafter "Group Chief"), CIA/DO (Dec. 14, 2004); Interview with CIA/DO Division Chief, (Jan. 31, 2005); *see also* Interview with CIA/DO Group Chief, (Feb. 8, 2005). The division chief could not recall the precise date of the lunch.

[310] Interview with Division Chief and Group Chief, CIA/DO (Dec. 14, 2004); Interview with Division Chief, CIA/DO (Jan. 31, 2005); *see also* Interview with CIA WINPAC analysts (Oct. 8, 2004) (stating that the DO's responsible regional division told WINPAC analysts that "even the [foreign service] didn't think Curveball was a good source"); Interview with David Kay (May 26, 2004) (noting that he believed the foreign service had "warned" the CIA about Curveball "before the NIE" was published).

[311] Interview with Division Chief and Group Chief, CIA/DO (Dec. 14, 2004); Interview with CIA/DO Division Chief (Jan. 31, 2005). Former DDO Pavitt told the Commission that he had heard that the division chief had been told by the foreign service that the foreign service lacked confidence in Curveball's reporting. Although he could not recall when he learned this information, he thought it was probably "after OIF." Interview with former CIA Deputy Director for Operations James Pavitt (Feb. 7, 2005).

[312] Interview with CIA/DO Division Chief (Jan. 31, 2005); Interview with Division Chief and Group Chief, CIA/DO (Dec. 14, 2004); Interview with CIA/DO Group Chief (Feb. 8, 2005).

[313] Interview with CIA/DO Division Chief (Jan. 31, 2005).

[314] *Id.*

[315] Interview with Division Chief and Group Chief, CIA/DO (Dec. 14, 2004); *see also* Interview with CIA/DO Group Chief (Feb. 8, 2005). Former DDO Pavitt also stated that he did not understand, prior to the commencement of hostilities with Iraq, that Curveball's reporting was a major basis for the Intelligence Community's judgments about Iraq's BW program. Interview with former Deputy Director for Operations James Pavitt (Feb. 7, 2005).

[316] At the time, DDCI McLaughlin had three executive assistants—one from the Directorate of Operations (hereinafter EA/DDCI from DO) one from the Directorate of Intelligence (hereinafter EA/DDCI from DI) and one from the National Security Agency. Interview with EA/DDCI from DO (Feb. 8, 2005).

[317] Electronic mail from EA/DDCI from DO ("DDCI Iraq WMD Brief") (Dec. 18, 2002); Electronic mail from Group Chief, CIA/DO ("Re: next steps on curve ball") (Dec. 18, 2002).

[318] *Id.*

[319] Interview with EA/DDCI from DO (Feb. 8, 2005).

[320] Electronic mail from EA/DDCI from DO ("DDCI Iraq WMD Brief") (Dec. 18, 2002); Electronic mail from Group Chief, CIA/DO ("Re: next steps on curve ball") (Dec. 18, 2002).

[321] Classified cable traffic (Dec. 2002).

[322] Classified cable traffic (Dec. 2002).

[323] Interview with EA/DDCI from DO (Feb. 8, 2005); Interview with CIA WINPAC BW analyst (Feb. 8, 2005).

[324] Interview with EA/DDCI from DO (Feb. 8, 2005) (noting that it was apparent that "a great deal was beginning to turn on this guy").

[325] Electronic mail from EA/DDCI from DO ("Meeting to Review Bidding on Curveball") (Dec. 19, 2005).

[326] Interviews with former Deputy Director of Central Intelligence John McLaughlin (Feb. 2, 2005 and March 7, 2005).

[327] Electronic mail from Group Chief, CIA/DO ("operational assessment of Curve Ball") (Dec. 19, 2002).

[328] Interview with Division Chief and Group Chief, CIA/DO (Dec. 14, 2004); Interview with CIA/DO Group Chief (Feb. 8, 2005).

[329] Interview with Division Chief and Group Chief, CIA/DO (Dec. 14, 2004).

[330] Interview with CIA/DO Group Chief (Feb. 8, 2005).

[331] Interview with Division Chief and Group Chief, CIA/DO (Dec. 14, 2004); Interview with CIA/DO Group Chief (Feb. 8, 2005); Interview with CIA WINPAC BW analyst (Feb. 8, 2005); Interview with EA/DDCI from DO (Feb. 8, 2005).

[332] Interview with CIA WINPAC BW analyst (Feb. 8, 2005). The other source was the fourth source described above.

[333] Interview with Division Chief and Group Chief, CIA/DO (Dec. 14, 2004); Interview with CIA/DO Group Chief (Feb. 8, 2005); Interview with CIA WINPAC BW analyst (Feb. 8, 2005).

[334] Interview with Division Chief and Group Chief, CIA/DO (Dec. 14, 2004); Interview with CIA/DO Group Chief (Feb. 8, 2005).

[335] Interview with CIA WINPAC BW analyst (Feb. 8, 2005).

[336] Interview with EA/DDCI from DO (Feb. 8, 2005). At the time of his interview with Commission staff, the executive assistant incorrectly remembered the analyst as actually working for the Directorate of Operations Counterproliferation Division, rather than the Directorate of Intelligence's WINPAC.

[337] *Id.*

[338] Interview with EA/DDCI from DO (Feb. 8, 2005). *See, e.g.*, Classified cable traffic (Oct. 2002) (noting that the foreign service officer responsible for Curveball "noted that CB continued to be a 'handling problem'").

[339] Interview with EA/DDCI from DO (Feb. 8, 2005).

[340] Electronic mail from EA/DDCI from DO ("Proofread") (Dec. 20, 2002).

[341] The WINPAC BW analyst replaced "parked" with "housed." Electronic mail from CIA WINPAC BW analyst ("RE: Proofread") (Dec. 20, 2002).

[342] Electronic mail from EA/DDCI from DO ("Proofread") (Dec. 20, 2002).

[343] *Id.*

[344] *Id.* The WINPAC BW analyst asked, with respect to this last sentence, "[w]hy has the DO not disseminated this information or shared it with the analytical side? Could we please see this new evaluation?" Electronic mail from EA/DDCI from DO ("Proofread") (Dec. 20, 2002).

[345] Interview with EA/DDCI from DO (March 11, 2005).

[346] *Id.*

[347] Interview with former Deputy Director of Central Intelligence John McLaughlin (Feb. 2, 2005).

[348] Interview with former Deputy Director of Central Intelligence John McLaughlin (March 7, 2005).

[349] Interview with CIA/DO Group Chief (Feb. 8, 2005); Interview with Division Chief and Group Chief, CIA/DO (Dec. 14, 2004). The division chief did not recall this meeting during his second interview with the Commission.

[350] Interview with Division Chief and Group Chief, CIA/DO (Dec. 14, 2004); Interview with CIA/DO Group Chief (Feb. 8, 2005). Electronic mail from Group Chief, CIA/DO ("operational assessment of Curve Ball") (Dec. 19, 2002).

[351] Interview with CIA/DO Group Chief (Feb. 8, 2005).

[352] Interview with former Deputy Director for Operations James Pavitt (Feb. 7, 2005).

[353] Interview with former Deputy Director for Operations James Pavitt (March 8, 2005).

[354] Interview with former Associate Deputy Director for Operations (March 8, 2005).

[355] *Id.*

[356] Interview with Division Chief and Group Chief, CIA/DO (Dec. 14, 2004); Interview with CIA/DO Division Chief (Jan. 31, 2005); Interview with CIA/DO Group Chief (Feb. 8, 2005).

[357] Interview with CIA/DO Group Chief (Feb. 8, 2005).

[358] *Id.* The Group Chief did not recall exactly what editing she did.

[359] Interview with CIA/DO Division Chief (Jan. 31, 2005).

[360] Interview with EA/DDCI from DO (Feb. 8, 2005).

[361] Interview with DO officer responsible for sources and methods protection (Feb. 22, 2005).

[362] Interview with EA/DDCI from DI (Feb. 22, 2005).

[363] Interview with Division Chief and Group Chief, CIA/DO (Dec. 14, 2004); Interview with CIA/DO Division Chief (Jan. 31, 2005).

[364] *Id.*

[365] Interview with CIA/DO Group Chief (Feb. 8, 2005).

[366] Interview with former Deputy Director for Operations James Pavitt (Feb. 7, 2005).

[367] Interview with former Deputy Director of Central Intelligence John McLaughlin (Feb. 2, 2005). There was a meeting with the division chief listed on Mr. McLaughlin's official calendar for January 28, 2003. According to Mr. McLaughlin and one contemporaneous document, however, this meeting covered another subject. *Id.*

[368] Interview with former Deputy Director of Central Intelligence John McLaughlin (March 7, 2005).

[369] Classified cable traffic (Jan. 2003).

[370] Classified cable traffic (Jan. 2003).

[371] Interview with CIA/DO Division Chief (Jan. 31, 2005).

[372] Electronic mail from Division Chief ("Re: [Foreign Service] BW Source") (Feb. 3, 2003); *see also* Electronic mail from Group Chief, CIA/DO ("curve ball") (Feb. 3, 2003).

[373] *Id.*

374 Interview with former Deputy Director of Central Intelligence John McLaughlin (Feb. 2, 2005).

375 *Id.*

376 *Id.*; Interview with former Director of Central Intelligence George Tenet (Jan. 25, 2005).

377 Electronic mail from Executive Officer of the responsible regional division, CIA/DO ("[Foreign Service] BW Source") (Feb. 3, 2003) (forwarding the memorandum).

378 *Id.*

379 *Id.*

380 Interview with former Director of Central Intelligence George Tenet (Jan. 25, 2005).

381 Interview with Division Chief and Group Chief, CIA/DO (Dec. 14, 2004); Interview with CIA/DO Division Chief (Jan. 31, 2005).

382 *Id.*

383 *Id.*

384 *Id.*

385 Interviews with former Director of Central Intelligence George Tenet (Jan. 25, 2005 and March 10, 2005).

386 *Id.*

387 Interview with former CIA WINPAC BW analyst (Nov. 10, 2004); Comments from DOE (March 3, 2005); Comments from INR (March 3, 2005).

388 Interview with former CIA WINPAC BW analyst (Nov. 10, 2004).

389 *Id.*

390 Interviews with former CIA WINPAC BW analyst (Nov. 10, 2004 and Nov. 22, 2004).

391 Interview with former CIA WINPAC BW analyst (Nov. 10, 2004). The information that Curveball had been out of Iraq during July through December 1998 and left Iraq in March 1999 traveling in true name—in contradiction to his claims—was eventually confirmed by cross-referencing pertinent travel records. The records matched the itineraries supplied by Curveball's family members. *Id*; Comments from former WINPAC BW analyst (March 3, 2005).

392 Classified intelligence report.

393 Interview with former CIA WINPAC BW analyst (Nov. 10, 2004). Interviews with Curveball's childhood friends also revealed that he had a reputation as a "great liar" and a "con artist"; his college roommate labeled him a "congenital liar." CIA analysts said that these sentiments appeared to be universal, noting that "people kept saying what a 'rat' Curveball was." *Id.*

394 Interview with former CIA WINPAC BW analyst (Nov. 10, 2004). One of the WINPAC analysts who conducted the investigations in Iraq noted that other analysts had also shared with David Kay their growing sense of unease with what they were finding (and not finding) in Iraq. According to the analyst, however, CIA management—and some analysts—were still reluctant to retreat from Curveball's information. *Id.*

395 Interview with former CIA WINPAC BW analyst (Nov. 10, 2004); CIA, Inspector General, *Inspection Report of the DCI Center for Weapons Intelligence, Nonproliferation, and Arms Control (WINPAC) Directorate of Intelligence* (IG 2004-0003-IN) (Nov. 2004) at p. 14.

396 *Id.*

[397] *Id.*

[398] *Joint CIA-DIA Assessment of [Foreign Service] Source Curveball* (June 7, 2004) at pp. 1-2; *see also* Interview with CIA/DO officials (Aug. 3, 2004); Interview with CIA WINPAC analysts (Aug. 11, 2004).

[399] According to a WINPAC BW analyst, Curveball had described a number of agricultural facilities to the foreign service when it had interviewed him in 2000, including one east of Baghdad at which he claimed to have worked. In 2001, at the request of the handling foreign service, Curveball had made a physical model and drawn detailed sketches of the facility. The sketches showed, "without a doubt," that mobile BW trailers were able to move in and out of the buildings. The facility Curveball described was subsequently identified as Djerf al-Naddaf, which Curveball then confirmed. Analysts noted, however, that there was a wall at the facility that Curveball had not identified. The Iraqis had broken and then reconstituted part of the wall, which convinced the majority of analysts that the wall was "temporary" and would allow BW trailers through it, thus not contradicting Curveball's reporting. As noted, after OIF, analysts learned that the wall was actually a solid, six foot high structure. The fact that Curveball did not know of the wall's existence provided substantial evidence that he had not been at the facility when the wall had been constructed—according to imagery in May 1997. Interview with CIA WINPAC BW analyst (Nov. 22, 2004).

[400] *See, e.g.*, Classified intelligence reporting. As discussed, by the time of CIA's first face-to-face interview with Curveball in March 2004, the Intelligence Community was aware of serious problems with his reporting. The recall notice on this report concluded that the interview with Curveball had revealed: "Discrepancies surfaced regarding the information provided by ... [Curveball] in this stream of reporting, which indicate that [Curveball] lost his claimed access in 1995. [Curveball] was unable/unwilling to resolve these discrepancies; our assessment, therefore, is that [Curveball] appears to be fabricating in this stream of reporting." Interview with CIA/DO officials (Sept. 27, 2004).

[401] As noted, Defense HUMINT had disseminated 95 reports from Curveball and six Curveball reports were disseminated in CIA channels. All of these reports were recalled after Curveball was deemed a fabricator. Also, the handling foreign service continues, officially, to stand by Curveball's reporting. Interview with CIA/DO officials (Sept. 27, 2004). Another foreign service had maintained a similar official position until late 2004. *Id.*; Interview with Division Chief and Group Chief, CIA/DO (Dec. 14, 2004).

[402] Interview with CIA/DO officials (Sept. 27, 2004); Interview with former CIA WINPAC BW analyst (Nov. 10, 2004) (noting that when Curveball first requested asylum, he was essentially told to "get in line." He feared being returned to Iraq and subsequently offered information about his work in Iraq in an attempt to speed the asylum process).

[403] Interviews with CIA/DO officials (Aug. 3, 2004 and Sept. 27, 2004); Interview with former CIA WINPAC BW analyst (Nov. 10, 2004).

[404] Interviews with CIA/DO officials (Aug. 3, 2004 and Sept. 27, 2004); Interview with former CIA WINPAC BW analyst (Nov. 10, 2004).

[405] Interview with CIA officials (Dec. 8, 2004).

[406] As described above, reporting from both of these sources was disseminated by DIA. With regard to the second source, although CIA's post-war investigation led it to conclude that the source was being directed by the INC, DIA has not recalled the reporting as of March 3, 2005. Interview with CIA officials (Dec. 8, 2004); Comments from CIA/DO (March 3, 2005);

Comments from DIA (March 8, 2005).

[407] Interview with CIA officials (Dec. 8, 2004). With respect to liaison reporting, however, the Intelligence Community is generally unaware whether those sources may be connected to the INC. *Id.*

[408] NIE at p. 43; Secretary of State Colin Powell, Remarks to the United Nations Security Council (Feb. 5, 2003) ("An Iraqi major who defected confirmed that Iraq has mobile biological research laboratories [and] production facilities.").

[409] CIA and DIA, *Congressional Notification on [the INC source]* (Jan. 27, 2004); Interview with Defense HUMINT official (Nov. 2, 2004). This problem was not discussed in the Senate Select Committee on Intelligence's report.

[410] Interview with CIA/DO officials and CIA Iraq WMD Review Group analysts (Aug. 3, 2004). Although there were other missed opportunities to prevent this information from being used in Secretary Powell's speech, if the reports had been reissued with a recall notice it is likely the error would have been caught.

[411] Classified intelligence report (May 2002) (fabrication notice); *see also* Interview with Defense HUMINT official (Nov. 2, 2004). As a consequence of this failure, reporting from the INC source remained in analysts' databases with no indication that it was considered unreliable.

[412] CIA and DIA, *Congressional Notification on [the INC source]* (Jan. 27, 2004) at p. 3; CIA, *Iraq WMD Lessons Learned* (Aug. 2004).

[413] Interview with CIA/DO officials and CIA Iraq WMD Review Group (Aug. 3, 2004).

[414] SSCI at p. 247.

[415] *Id.* The Defense HUMINT official also cleared several reports for declassification, including the report from the INC source, but told the Senate Select Committee staff that he and the declassification staff did not notice that the report was the same one on which a fabrication notice had been issued. *Id.*

[416] NIE at pp. 9, 28.

[417] *Id.* All of these assessments were made with "high confidence." *Id.* at p. 9.

[418] *Id.* at p. 28.

[419] ISG, *Comprehensive Report of the Special Advisor to the DCI on Iraqi WMD*, Volume III, "Iraq's Chemical Warfare Program" (Sept. 30, 2004) (hereinafter "ISG Report, CW") at p. 1.

[420] *Id.* at p. 2.

[421] *Id.* at p. 3.

[422] *Id.* at p. 1. At least one CIA analyst who worked extensively on pre-war intelligence and with the ISG concluded that, although he "believed" Saddam wanted to reconstitute his CW program, the analyst had seen no "evidence" of Saddam's desire to do so. Interview with CIA CW analyst (Oct. 8, 2004).

[423] Interview with CIA Iraq WMD Review Group analyst (Sept. 23, 2004); Interview with CIA WINPAC CW analyst (Oct. 8, 2004).

[424] Interview with CIA WINPAC CW analyst (Oct. 8, 2004).

[425] DCI Statement for the Record at Tab 2, p. 1.

[426] *Id.*

[427] CIA, *Iraqi WMD Programs: The Road to Reconstruction* (SW 95-40007CX) (Feb. 3, 1995) at p. 1.

[428] *Id.*

[429] CIA, *Iraq's Remaining WMD Capabilities* (NESA IR 96-40101) (Aug. 26, 1996) at p. 5; *see also* Senior Executive Memorandum (Jan. 12, 2002) (discussing the value of Kamil's information).

[430] Interview with CIA WINPAC CW analyst (Oct. 8, 2004). The ISG Report cites April 1997 as the date for this test. WINPAC and DIA have subsequently indicated that the tests were actually conducted in June 1998. Comments from DIA (citing MID-217-98 (Aug. 17, 1998)); Comments from CIA WINPAC (March 3, 2005). The discrepancy in dates does not affect the analysis.

[431] Subsequent analysis of the samples has been inconclusive. ISG, *Comprehensive Report of the Special Advisor to the DCI on Iraqi WMD*, Volume I, "Regime Strategic Intent" (Sept. 30, 2004) at p. 54. Iraq admitted in its 1996 declaration that it researched VX production routes and had produced pilot-scale quantities of VX but denied that it had conducted large scale production or weaponization of VX. The ISG concluded, however, that Iraq had "weaponized" VX by filling three aerial bombs with VX during the Iran-Iraq war. Interview with CIA WINPAC CW analyst (Oct. 8, 2004); ISG Report, CW at pp. 21, 33. For their part, WINPAC analysts now believe that the VX degradation products found on missile fragments may have been the result of cross-contamination from the filler-lines used to fill these three aerial bombs. Interview with CIA WINPAC CW analyst (Oct. 8, 2004).

[432] Interview with CIA Iraq WMD Review Group analyst (Sept. 23, 2004); Interview with CIA WINPAC CW analyst (Oct. 8, 2004).

[433] ISG Report, CW at p. 13. Both of these events contributed to Saddam's decision to stop cooperating with United Nations weapons inspectors.

[434] CIA, DCI Nonproliferation Center, *Iraq's Chemical Warfare Program: Status and Prospects* (NPC 98-10005C) (Aug. 1998) at p. iii. Two fall 1998 NIC products reached similar conclusions. NIC, *Outstanding WMD and Missile Issues* (Sept. 15, 1998) at Table 2A; NIC, *Outstanding WMD and Missile Issues* (Nov. 1998).

[435] NIC, *Outstanding WMD and Missile Issues* (Nov. 1998) at p. 2.

[436] NIC, *Iraq: Rebuilding A Chemical Weapons Production Capability* (May 24, 2000).

[437] DCI Statement for the Record at Tab 2, pp. 2-3. UNSCOM had prepared a draft survey of Iraq's chemical industry in 1999, in which UNSCOM judged that Iraq's "philosophy was to develop the chemical industry to a technical level that, in peacetime, could produce for the civilian market (*i.e.*, pesticides) but based on the technical capabilities could also easily be reconfigured to produce key precursors if needed." *Id.* (citing draft survey). The NIC noted that this survey was consistent with Intelligence Community assessments. *Id.* The motivation for Saddam's interest in CW was assessed to be based on "regime preservation, regional esteem, and retaliation capability." *See, e.g.*, CIA, WINPAC/BCG, Briefing for Ambassador Negroponte, *Status of Iraq's CW Program* (May 10, 2002).

[438] NIC, *Iraq: Rebuilding A Chemical Weapons Production Capability* (May 24, 2000); *see also* CIA, WINPAC/BCG, Briefing to John Wolf, Assistant Secretary of State for Nonproliferation, *Status of Iraq's CW Program.* (Aug. 17, 2001); CIA, DCI Nonproliferation Center, *UNMOVIC/IAEA Would Hinder Iraq's WMD Programs* (NPC SIR 2001-001X) (March 30,

2001).

[439] *See, e.g.*, CIA, Publish When Ready, *Iraq: Baghdad Anticipating US Retaliation* (Sept. 20, 2001).

[440] Senior Executive Memorandum (Oct. 23, 2001) (discounting London *Daily Telegraph* reporting that CW were being moved); CIA, *Memorandum for the Secretary of Defense* (Oct. 23, 2001) (same).

[441] Classified intelligence reporting (Nov. 30, 2001).

[442] NIC, *Iraqi Military Capabilities Through 2003* (NIE 99-04/II) (April 1999).

[443] Senior Executive Memorandum (Jan. 5, 2002). The Memorandum cautioned, however, that the Intelligence Community lacked detailed information on many aspects of the CW program. *Id.* Iraq had approximately 500 metric tons of weaponized CW stockpile at the time of Operation Desert Storm. DCI Statement for the Record at Tab 2, p. 9.

[444] Briefing by WINPAC analysts to Principals Committee (July 18, 2002); CIA Iraq WMD Review Group, *Iraq WMD/CW Production Timeline* (undated) at p. 4.

[445] NIE at p. 6. The President's Summary of the NIE did not differ from the language used in the Key Judgments of the Estimate. That summary stated that "Baghdad has begun renewed production of mustard, sarin, GF (cyclosarin), and VX. Although information is limited, Saddam probably has stocked at least 100—and possibly as much as 500—metric tons of CW agents. Iraq has experience in manufacturing CW bombs, artillery rockets, and projectiles, and we assess it has CW bulk fills for short-range ballistic missile (SRBM) warheads." NIC, President's Summary, NIE, *Iraq's Continuing Programs for Weapons of Mass Destruction* (PS/NIE 2002-16HC) (Oct. 2002).

[446] NIE at p. 6.

[447] *Id.* at p. 28. *See also* DCI Statement for the Record at Tab 2, p. 9.

[448] DCI Statement for the Record at Tab 2, p. 9 (elaborating on the factors mentioned in the NIE).

[449] *Id.* (citing NIC, *Iraqi Military Capabilities Through 2003* (NIE 99-04) (April 1999)).

[450] Interview with CIA WINPAC CW analyst (Oct. 8, 2004).

[451] NIE at p. 28.

[452] Interview with CIA WINPAC CW analyst (Oct. 8, 2004); *see also* DCI Statement for the Record at Tab 2, p. 3 (Imagery was "critical" to assessments that Iraq had restarted CW production) and *id.* at p. 5 (*"Our assessments about these transshipments became a key element of judgments that Iraq had resumed production of CW agents."* (emphasis in original)).

[453] DCI Statement for the Record at Tab 2, pp. 3, 7-8; Interview with CIA WINPAC CW analyst (Oct. 8, 2004).

[454] Interview with CIA WINPAC CW analyst (Oct. 8, 2004).

[455] DCI Statement for the Record at Tab 2, p. 8.

[456] *Id.*

[457] *Id. See also* Interview with CIA Iraq WMD Review Group analyst (Sept. 23, 2004) (noting that there were "no good sources on CW"); Interview with CIA CW analyst (Sept. 13, 2004) (noting that there were between 30 and 40 total sources that reported on the existence of CW in Iraq). Again, because of the sheer number of sources that reported on *some* aspect of CW, we do not extensively examine every source. Rather, we confine our in-depth review to

those sources described by the Intelligence Community itself as being the most significant.

[458] DCI Statement for the Record at Tab 2, p. 4 (citing classified intelligence report (Feb. 1999)).

[459] *Id.*

[460] *Id.*

[461] DCI Statement for the Record at Tab 2, p. 5.

[462] *Id.; see also* Classified intelligence report (Nov. 2001).

[463] *Id.*; Interview with CIA Iraq WMD Review Group analyst (Nov. 15, 2004). *See also* Butler Report at pp. 100 and 101

[464] Interview with NIO/SNP (May 26, 2004).

[465] *Id.*

[466] NIE at p. 32.

[467] *Id.* at p. 33.

[468] *Id.* at p. 34.

[469] *Id.* at p. 35.

[470] *Id.*

[471] *Id.*

[472] Interview with former CIA WINPAC CW analyst (Nov. 10, 2004).

[473] *Id.*

[474] NIC, *Iraq's Chemical Warfare Capabilities: Potential for Dusty and Fourth-Generation Agents: Memorandum to Holders of NIE 2002-16HC* [the October 2002 NIE] (M/H NIE 2002-16) (Nov. 2002). The *Memorandum* was prepared at the request of the U.S. Central Command as a follow-up to the October NIE and "examine[d] the CW implications for any US-led military operations against Iraq as they relate[d] to" dusty and fourth-generation CW agents. *Id.* (Impetus for *Memorandum to Holders of NIE 2002-16HC*).

[475] A dusty agent is a CW agent "that is combined with an inert carrier … and disseminated as an aerosol." *Id.* at p. 5.

[476] A fourth-generation agent is a highly toxic CW agent that is "more difficult to treat medically than the currently fielded traditional nerve agents." *Id.* at p. 3.

[477] *Id.* at p. 14.

[478] *Id.*

[479] NIC, *Nontraditional Threats to the US Homeland Through 2007* (NIE-2002-15HJ) (Nov. 2002) (published in January 2003) at p. 33.

[480] CIA, WINPAC, *2001 Intelligence Report to Congress on the Chemical Weapons Convention* (CDR 2002-002 HCX) (Dec. 2002) at pp. 51-52.

[481] *Id.* at p. 52.

[482] ISG Report, CW at p. 1.

[483] *Id.* at p. 2.

[484] *Id.* at p. 3.

[485] *Id.* at p. 1. At least one CIA analyst who worked extensively on pre-war intelligence and with the ISG concluded that, although he "believed" Saddam wanted to reconstitute his CW

program, the analyst had seen no "evidence" of Saddam's desire to do so. Interview with CIA CW analyst (Oct. 8, 2004).

[486] ISG Report, CW at p. 123. The majority of ammunition supply points searched were within the assessed "Red Line" surrounding Baghdad and, more specifically, sites which were reported to have a Samarra-type truck or to be near artillery units capable of firing 122 mm multiple rocket launcher or 155 mm CW rounds (both of which the Iraqis were known to have used in the past to deliver CW). In addition, the ISG searched numerous "captured enemy ammunition" depots that included hundreds of thousands of tons of munitions. None of these searches yielded any CW munitions. *Id.* at pp. 34-35.

[487] *Id.* at p. 37. This included the Al-Musayyib Storage Depot site. *Id.*

[488] *Id.* at p. 123.

[489] *Id.* at p. 1.

[490] *Id.* at p. 12.

[491] *Id.* at p. 14. The one exception noted by the ISG was a single scientist who said that he was approached in 2003 by "Uday's officer" with a request to make "a chemical agent." *Id.* at p. 15.

[492] NIE at p. 32.

[493] ISG Report, CW at pp. 24-25.

[494] *Id.* at p. 24. The ISG also concluded that management of chemical facilities by "previously identified CW personnel" could be attributed to Iraq's command economy and not to illicit purposes. *Id.* at p. 15.

[495] *Id.* at p. 16. In attempting to determine whether Iraq's chemical infrastructure was intended for legitimate or illicit purposes, the ISG generally considered the commercial utility of certain chemicals or processes, Iraq's historical use of chemicals and processes for CW purposes, and the availability of CW expertise necessary for CW production. *Id.* at pp. 15, 18-22.

[496] *Id.* at p. 13.

[497] *Id.* at p. 11.

[498] *Id.* at p. 29. The ISG offered several possible explanations, including unilateral destruction of CW munitions, the loss of munitions when they were forward-deployed in anticipation of a conflict, and the possibility that some pre-1991 munitions remained in storage areas. *Id.* at pp. 27-33, 97.

[499] *Id.* at pp. 29-30. The ISG recovered a total of 53 chemical munitions from various sources and military units throughout Iraq. The ISG concluded that these munitions were part of Iraq's pre-1991 CW program. *Id.* at p. 30.

[500] *Id.* at p. 107.

[501] *Id.* at pp. 109-110.

[502] *Id.* at p. 110.

[503] *Id.* at p. 43. The ISG also rejected the theory that the labs were used to maintain technical expertise because their work was limited to laboratory-scale production. *Id.* at p. 44.

[504] Interview with CIA WINPAC CW analyst (Oct. 8, 2004); *see also* DCI Statement for the Record at Tab 2, p. 3 (imagery was "critical" to assessments that Iraq had restarted CW production) and *id.* at p. 5 (*"Our assessments about these transshipments became a key element of judgments that Iraq had resumed production of CW agents."* (emphasis in original)).

505 *Id.* (citing NIC, *Iraq, Unusual Logistical Activities In Preparation for an Anticipated US-Led Campaign* (ICB 2002-09) (May 2, 2002)).

506 DCI Statement for the Record at Tab 2, p. 8.

507 *Id.* The Samarra truck, a modified Mitsubishi water tanker truck, was confirmed by UNSCOM inspections and Iraqi statements in 1991 to have been used as a decontamination truck, although it was never clear that all Mitsubishi-manufactured water tanker trucks owned by the Iraqis were used in this manner. In addition, these Samarra type trucks escorted known shipments of CW material from the Samarra CW Complex in the 1980s to places such as Kirkuk Airfield, from where Iraqi Air Force planes launched CW strikes into Kurdistan. Comments from NGA (March 3, 2005).

508 Interview with CIA WINPAC CW analyst (Oct. 8, 2004) (noting that the conclusion that the transshipments involved CW was "a kind of catalyst" for broader conclusions about the status of Iraq's CW program). Interview with CIA WINPAC CW analyst (Oct. 8, 2004).

509 NGA, *Reassessment of Activity at Al Musayyib Barracks Brigade Headquarters and Ammunition Depot, 1998-2004* (June 15, 2004) (hereinafter "NGA Reassessment"); Comments from NGA (March 3, 2005). The Al Musayyib imagery was that referred to by Secretary of State Colin Powell during his pre-war address to the United Nations Security Council; *see also* Interview with CIA WINPAC CW analyst (Oct. 8, 2004).

510 NGA Reassessment at p. 1.

511 *Id.* at pp. 3, 6.

512 *Id.* at pp. 8-9. "Grading" is the changing of the ground level to a smooth or slightly sloping surface. It can be used to facilitate the run-off of liquid from a surface.

513 *Id.* at p. 8.

514 DCI Statement for the Record at Tab 2, p. 8.

515 NGA Reassessment at pp. 5, 7-8.

516 *Id.* at p. 8.

517 *Id.* at p. 1. Although analysts also relied on a small number of human source and signals intelligence reporting, the "critical" factor in their analysis was the transshipment activity seen on imagery.

518 Interview with CIA WINPAC CW analyst (Oct. 8, 2004).

519 *Id.*

520 Collection Concepts Development Center Study, *Iraqi Weapons of Mass Destruction: Recommendations for Improvements in Collection (Study One)* (June 29, 2000) at p. 10.

521 *Id.*

522 NGA, *Analysis of Iraq's Weapons Programs* (provided to Commission Nov. 16, 2004); Interview with NGA officials (Nov. 16, 2004); Interview with CIA WINPAC CW analyst (Oct. 8, 2004) (noting that analysts saw increased activity at depots); *see also* DCI Statement for the Record at Tab 2, p. 7 (noting that the "first indication" of CW transshipments came in March 2002 based on imagery); *id.* at Tab 2, p. 8 (noting that "[t]he scope of [the transshipment] activity was far too great" to be movement of residual CW stocks).

523 Interview with NGA officials (Nov. 16, 2004); Interview with CIA WINPAC CW analyst (Oct. 8, 2004).

524 *Id.* WINPAC CW analysts explained in March 2005 that they had also seen a drop off in

activity in late 2002 despite the increased volume of imagery collection, and this drop off suggested that the apparent *increased* transshipment activity seen in spring 2002 was not "solely a function of collection frequency." Comments from CIA WINPAC (March 3, 2005).

[525] NGA Reassessment at p. 2.

[526] DCI Statement for the Record at Tab 2, p. 4.

[527] Classified intelligence report. The source reported that Saddam Hussein sought a weapon that would "combine two or more of the three capabilities: chemical, biological, nuclear into a single weapon." *Id.* According to analysts, a "combination" device was infeasible because a nuclear yield would destroy any CW or BW agent. Interview with CIA Iraq WMD Review Group analyst (Sept. 13, 2004).

[528] Classified intelligence report. The production of "tons" of agent in mobile labs was unlikely because of the estimated capacity of any possible mobile production facility. Interview with CIA Iraq WMD Review Group analyst (Sept. 13, 2004).

[529] DCI Statement for the Record at Tab 2, p. 4.

[530] Interview with CIA Iraq WMD Review Group analyst (Sept. 13, 2004).

[531] DCI Statement for the Record at Tab 2, p. 4.

[532] Interview with CIA Iraq WMD Review Group analyst (Sept. 13, 2004) (reporting recalled in February 2004); *see also* DCI Statement for the Record at Tab 2, p. 4, n. 13.

[533] Interview with CIA Iraq WMD Review Group analyst (Sept. 13, 2004) (citing classified cable traffic (Sept. 1999)).

[534] *Id.*; (noting that a CIA case officer who interviewed him in March 2003 characterized him as an "information peddler"); *see also* Classified cable traffic (Jan. 2003).

[535] DCI Statement for the Record at Tab 2, p. 4.

[536] Interview with CIA Iraq WMD Review Group analyst (Sept. 13, 2004). Despite this long history, reporting similar to the Iraqi chemist's—although not confirmed as his—appeared via DIA channels in December 2002 and July 2003, and has not since been reevaluated. While it is unclear whether the chemist is in fact the source of this information, we are not aware of any efforts by DIA to determine whether or not he is, and as a consequence, whether the reporting should be recalled.

[537] DCI Statement for the Record at Tab 2, p. 5. Comments from Iraq WMD Review Group (March 3, 2005).

[538] CIA, *Iraq WMD Lessons Learned* (Aug. 2004) at p. 25.

[539] *Id.*; *see also* Interview with David Kay (May 26, 2004) (noting compartmentation within WMD programs); Interview with representatives of the ISG (May 26, 2004) (same).

[540] In a 2004 review of this source's reporting, analysts concluded that his credibility was questionable, because of the probability that he would not have access to information on such disparate topics. DCI Statement for the Record at Tab 2, p. 5, n. 14; *see also* CIA, *Iraq WMD Lessons Learned* (Aug. 2004) at p. 25.

[541] Interview with CIA Iraq WMD Review Group analysts (Feb. 2, 2005).

[542] Classified intelligence report (March 2002).

[543] DCI Statement for the Record at Tab 2, p. 4; *see also* Interview with CIA WINPAC CW analyst (Oct. 8, 2004). Analysts should have been further alerted by the source description, which cautioned that "[w]hile source has reported reliably in the past, reporting reliability can-

not be confirmed regarding *domestic Iraqi activities.*" Classified intelligence report (March 2002) (emphasis added).

544 DCI Statement for the Record at Tab 2, p. 4.

545 Interview with CIA CW analyst (Oct. 8, 2004). An analyst who was not directly involved with Iraq WMD issues before the war said after OIF that she would have "discounted" the report because of the obvious technical inconsistency. *See* Interview with CIA Iraq WMD Review Group analyst (Sept. 23, 2004).

546 Butler Report at pp. 100 and 101.

547 Interview with NIO/SNP (May 26, 2004). This report was distributed to a very small group of senior officials prior to the publication of the NIE—including the NIE's principal author—but it was not made available to most analysts. *Id.*

548 NIE at p. 7. The NIE assessed that the UAVs could also be used for CW delivery, although that was judged less likely. *Id.* at p. 49.

549 The Air Force dissented, concluding that Iraq was developing UAVs primarily for recon-naissance rather than for BW or CW delivery. NIE at pp. 7, 52.

550 NIE at pp. 51-52.

551 Interview with CIA WINPAC UAV analyst (Aug. 11, 2004).

552 *Id.*

553 NIE, *Nontraditional Threats to the US Homeland Through 2007* (NIE-2002-15HJ) (Nov. 2002) (published January 2003).

554 CIA, Memorandum for Chairman of the House Permanent Select Committee on Intelli-gence Porter Goss, Title Classified (March 6, 2003) (cited in timeline provided by CIA Iraq WMD Review Group analyst (Sept. 9, 2004)).

555 ISG, *Comprehensive Report of the Special Advisor to the DCI on Iraqi WMD*, Volume II, "Delivery Systems" (Sept. 30, 2004) (hereinafter "ISG Report, Delivery Systems") at pp. 42, 52.

556 *Id.* at p. 51.

557 *Id.* at p. 56.

558 *Id.* at pp. 51-52, 56.

559 *Id.* at pp. 48, 50.

560 *Id.* at pp. 7, 52 (stating that Iraq had tested the liquid-propellant al-Samoud variant beyond 150 km, and that the solid-propellant Ababil-100 was capable of flying over 150 km).

561 NIE at pp. 7, 52, 54.

562 ISG Report, Delivery Systems at pp. 5, 9-10, 17-18. Because the pre-war assessments regarding Iraq's ballistic missile programs were largely accurate, this study will focus on the Intelligence Community's assessment of the role of UAVs as delivery systems.

563 Classified intelligence report; UNSCOM, *Final Inspection Report* (190/CBW-4) (June 13-18, 1997) (attached in annotated version of DCI Statement for the Record at Tab 4, p. 1); *see also* DCI Statement for the Record at Tab 4, p. 1. The converted MiG-21s would be fitted with drop tanks filled with BW agent and flown as Remotely Piloted Vehicles (RPVs). UNSCOM, *Final Inspection Report* (190/CBW-4) (June 13-18, 1997).

564 Classified intelligence report; UNSCOM, *Final Inspection Report* (190/CBW-4) (June

13-18, 1997)).

565 Classified intelligence reporting; UNSCOM, *Final Inspection Report* (190/CBW-4) (June 13-18, 1997).

566 Classified intelligence reporting; *see also* DCI Statement for the Record at Tab 4, p. 1.

567 Classified intelligence reporting; *see also* DCI Statement for the Record at Tab 4, pp. 1, 3; SSCI at p. 221.

568 Classified intelligence report; UNSCOM, *Final Inspection Report* (190/CBW-4) (June 13-18, 1997); *see also* SSCI at p. 221.

569 Classified intelligence reporting; *see also* DCI Statement for the Record at Tab 4, p. 1.

570 Classified intelligence reporting; *see also* DCI Statement for the Record at Tab 4, pp. 1, 3.

571 Classified intelligence reporting; *see also* DCI Statement for the Record at Tab 4, p. 2.

572 Classified intelligence report; *see also* DCI Statement for the Record at Tab 4, pp. 2-3.

573 SSCI at p. 216 (citing annual Intelligence Community assessments of foreign missile developments and ballistic missile threat through 2015); *see also* Classified intelligence report; DCI Statement for the Record at Tab 4, pp. 1-2.

574 *See, e.g.*, Senior Executive Memorandum, *In Response to Questions On Iraqi Efforts to Produce UAVs for BCW Delivery and On Iraqi Procurement of UAV-related Equipment* (June 15, 2002) (various sources "lead us to conclude that Iraq is trying to produce UAVs in order to deliver CBW agents").

575 DCI Statement for the Record at Tab 4, pp. 1-3; *see also* Interview with CIA WINPAC analysts (Aug. 11, 2004).

576 CIA, NPC, *Intelligence Community Assessment of Residual Iraqi Weapons of Mass Destruction* (Sept. 1992); *see also* DCI Statement for the Record at Tab 5, p. 1.

577 DCI Statement for the Record at Tab 5, p. 1.

578 *Id.*

579 *Id.* at p. 2.

580 *Id.* at p. 3.

581 NIE at pp. 7, 52. The Director of Air Force Intelligence judged that Iraq was developing these UAVs "primarily for reconnaissance rather than [as] delivery platforms for [CW or BW] agents." The Air Force noted that [CW or BW] delivery is "an inherent capability of UAVs but probably is not the impetus for Iraq's recent UAV programs." *Id.* at p. 52. While the NIE did not actually say—as the Air Force dissent suggests—that the UAVs were "primarily" for [CW or BW] delivery, this potential use was the overwhelming focus of the document's discussion on the UAVs; as the NIC would later acknowledge, "little, if any, attention was given...to missions other than those associated with WMD delivery." DCI Statement for the Record at Tab 4, p. 5.

582 NIE at pp. 7, 51-52.

583 *Id.*; *see also* Interview with CIA WINPAC UAV analyst (Aug. 11, 2004).

584 NIE at p. 52.

585 *Id.*; DCI Statement for the Record at Tab 4, p. 5.

586 Classified intelligence reporting (describing crash of L-29 in October 2000); *see also* DCI Statement for the Record at Tab 4, pp. 2-3.

[587] Classified intelligence report (noting that in 1992 Iraq had approximately 10 drones "designed and produced" to deliver BW agents).

[588] Classified intelligence reporting; SSCI at pp. 222-223 (describing five intelligence reports).

[589] Classified intelligence report (Jan. 1998); *see also* SSCI at p. 223.

[590] DCI Statement for the Record at Tab 4, pp. 1-2. This conclusion was bolstered by reporting suggesting that the UAV may have been armed with BW agents. *Id.* at p. 2 (citing classified intelligence reporting).

[591] Classified intelligence reporting.

[592] Classified intelligence report; *see also* SSCI at pp. 225-226.

[593] NIE at p. 7.

[594] SSCI at pp. 226-227 (quoting written response of CIA WINPAC to a question from the Committee about the Intelligence Community's analysis of UAVs); *see also* Interview with CIA WINPAC UAV analysts (Aug. 11, 2004).

[595] With respect to the assessments of other Western intelligence services, the British Joint Intelligence Committee assessed in March 2002 that Iraq was developing a UAV—specifically, that Iraq was modifying a small jet trainer, the L-29, to be used as a UAV—that could have BW and CW delivery applications. *See* Butler Report at pp. 84, 171. The Australian Defense Intelligence Organization (DIO), however, doubted Iraq's ability to disperse chemical and biological agents using UAVs. *See* Australian Parliamentary Joint Committee on ASIO, ASIS and DSD, *Intelligence on Iraq's Weapons of Mass Destruction* (Dec. 2003) at pp. 62-63.

[596] NIE at p. 7.

[597] Interview with CIA WINPAC UAV analyst (Aug. 11, 2004); *see also* SSCI at p. 227; DCI Statement for the Record at Tab 4, p. 4. The first indication that the UAVs might be used to target the U.S. surfaced in the summer of 2001, following the attempted procurement.

[598] NIE at p. 52.

[599] DCI Statement for the Record at Tab 4, p. 3.

[600] Interview with CIA Iraq WMD Review Group analyst (Sept. 9, 2004); Classified intelligence reporting (Sept. 2002).

[601] Interview with CIA Iraq WMD Review Group analyst (Sept. 9, 2004); Classified cable traffic (March 2002).

[602] Interview with CIA Iraq WMD Review Group analyst (Sept. 9, 2004) (citing finished intelligence pieces, *e.g.*, ICA, 2002-05HC (July 2002) at p. 19).

[603] Interview with CIA Iraq WMD Review Group analyst (Sept. 9, 2004) (citing finished intelligence); *see also* NESAF IA 2002-20113 CXH at p. 12.

[604] Interview with CIA Iraq WMD Review Group analyst (Sept. 9, 2004); *see also* Classified cable traffic (Sept. 2002); Classified cable traffic (Oct. 2002).

[605] *Id.* Moreover, when the distributor notified the procurement agent in March 2002 that he could not obtain U.S.-mapping software, he responded, "I don't think they'd be interested in that." Classified cable traffic (July 2002); *see also* Classified cable traffic (Sept. 2002); Classified cable traffic (Oct. 2002).

[606] Interview with CIA WINPAC analysts (Aug. 11, 2004); Interview with CIA Iraq WMD Review Group analyst (Sept. 9, 2004).

[607] Interview with CIA WINPAC analysts (Aug. 11, 2004).

[608] DCI Statement for the Record at Tab 4, p. 4; *see also* Interview with CIA WINPAC UAV analyst (Aug. 11 2004); Interview with CIA Iraq WMD Review Group analyst (Sept. 9, 2004).

[609] Interview with CIA WINPAC analysts (Aug. 11, 2004); *see also* Interview with NIO/SNP (Sept. 20, 2004).

[610] NIE at pp. 7, 52.

[611] The unclassified version of the NIE, however, dropped the reference to the Air Force and rephrased the assessment to state that "Iraq maintains…several deployment programs, including for a UAV most analysts believe probably is intended to deliver biological warfare agents." *See* Unclassified NIE at p. 2. According to the NIO/SNP, the unclassified paper contained alternative views but did not identify the holders thereof, following longstanding practice. The NIO/SNP noted that the practice was in the process of being revised. Interview with NIO/SNP (Sept. 20, 2004). The unclassified version of the NIE also indicated a difference of opinion about the aluminum tubes, although it did not attribute the opinions to specific agencies. Unclassified NIE at p. 1.

[612] Interview with CIA Iraq WMD Review Group analyst (Sept. 9, 2004) (citing CIA paper prepared for the NSC, *Iraq's WMD* (Jan. 16, 2003); *see also* Classified intelligence report (recalled in October 2004); Written Response by CIA Iraq WMD Review Group (Feb. 25, 2005).

[613] *Id.* (quoting testimony).

[614] Interview with CIA WINPAC UAV analyst (Aug. 11, 2004).

[615] Interview with former CIA WINPAC analyst (Oct. 25, 2004); President George W. Bush, Remarks by President on Iraq at Cincinnati Museum Center (Oct. 7, 2002).

[616] Interview with CIA Iraq WMD Review Group analyst (Sept. 9, 2004).

[617] NIE, *Nontraditional Threats to the US Homeland Through 2007* (NIE-2002-15HJ) (Nov. 2002) (published in January 2003). The President's Summary of the Nontraditional Threats NIE was also phrased in terms of capabilities rather than intent, but that summary described Iraq as having "at least one small UAV that could be launched from a ship to dispense biological agents on the U.S." NIC, President's Summary of the NIE, *Nontraditional Threats to the US Homeland Through 2007* (PSNIE-2002-15HJ) (Nov. 2002) (published Jan. 2003). The President's Summary also noted that Saddam probably would attempt clandestine attacks against the United States if "ongoing military operations risked the imminent demise of his regime, or for revenge." The INR dissent was included in the Summary, and that dissent noted that Saddam is "unlikely to conduct clandestine attacks against the U.S. Homeland even if the regime's demise is imminent." Another NIE, NIC, *Foreign Ballistic Missile Developments and the Threat Through 2015* (M/H NIE 2001 19HJ/I) (dated 2002 but published in February 2003), uses the same language.

[618] CIA, Memorandum for Chairman of the House Permanent Select Committee on Intelligence Porter Goss, Title Classified (March 6, 2003) (cited in timeline provided by CIA Iraq WMD Review Group analyst (Sept. 9, 2004)).

[619] *Id.*

[620] CIA, *Iraq's Ballistic Missiles and Long-Range Rockets* (WINPAC IA 2003-017) (March 19, 2003) at p. 3.

[621] *Id.* (describing the al-Samoud II, which had a slightly larger diameter than the al-

Samoud but was otherwise almost identical); *see also* Interview with CIA WINPAC missile analyst (Oct. 8, 2004); CIA, *U.S. Analysis of Iraqi's Declaration* (Dec. 7, 2002).

[622] ISG Report, Delivery Systems at p. 52.

[623] *Id.* at pp. 4, 44.

[624] *Id.* at pp. 5, 44.

[625] *Id.* at pp. 45-46.

[626] *Id.* at p. 46.

[627] *Id.* at p. 42.

[628] *Id.* at pp. 46-47.

[629] *Id.* at pp. 48, 51-52.

[630] *Id.* at pp. 51-52.

[631] *Id.* at p. 48.

[632] *Id.*

[633] *Id.*

[634] *Id.* at pp. 52-53.

[635] *Id.* at p. 56.

[636] *Id.*

[637] *Id.*

[638] *Id.* at pp. 48, 50. The ISG report notes that Iraq purchased four MP2000 and two 3200VP autopilots through the procurement agent. According to reporting, the procurement agent was seeking both the MP2000 and 3200VG autopilots along with the mapping software. *See* Classified intelligence report (Aug. 2001); Classified intelligence report (Sept. 2004).

[639] ISG Report, Delivery Systems at p. 50.

[640] *Id.* at pp. 10, 17-18.

[641] *Id.* at p. 9.

[642] The Intelligence Community inaccurately assessed that Iraq retained up to a dozen Scuds or Scud-variant missiles from the original force of 819 missiles, based on accounting discrepancies. NIE at p. 7. The ISG concluded, based on documentary evidence not previously disclosed, that Iraq had either expended or destroyed all of its Scud missiles by 1991. ISG Report, Delivery Systems at p. 9. The Community also learned in December 2002, from Iraq's declaration to the United Nations, that Iraq had another al-Samoud variant that also flew over 150 km. CIA, *U.S. Analysis of Iraqi's Declaration* (Dec. 7, 2002).

[643] NIE at p. 52.

[644] SSCI at pp. 235-236 (making same observation).

[645] Interview with CIA WINPAC UAV analysts (Aug. 11, 2004).

[646] Senior Executive Memorandum, *In Response to an Inquiry About What the Iraqis Are Likely to Disclose If They Use the U.S. and British "White Papers" as a Guide* (Nov. 27, 2002).

[647] NIE at p. 7.

[648] ISG Report, Delivery Systems at p. 9.

[649] Interview with CIA WINPAC analysts (Oct. 8, 2004) (noting analysts learned about the new missile from Iraq's December 2002 Declaration to the United Nations); *see also* CIA,

Iraq's Ballistic Missiles and Long-Range Rockets (WINPAC IA 2003-017) (March 19, 2003) at p. 3.

[650] Interview with National Intelligence Officer for Near East and South Asia (hereinafter "NIO/NESA") (Nov. 8, 2004); Interview with former Assistant Secretary of State for Intelligence and Research (Nov. 1, 2004).

[651] *Id.* The NIO/NESA explained that there was very little information available on the intentions of Iraq's senior leadership, and he did not know what analytical process, other than sheer speculation, could have led analysts to the conclusion that Iraq had abandoned its WMD programs. Interview with NIO/NESA (Nov. 8, 2004).

[652] ISG, *Comprehensive Report of the Special Advisor to the DCI on Iraqi WMD*, Volume I, Regime Strategic Intent (Sept. 30, 2004) at p. 46 (hereinafter "ISG Report, Regime Strategic Intent").

[653] *Id.*

[654] *Id.* at p. 34.

[655] NIC, *Prospects for Iraq: Saddam and Beyond* (NIE 93-42) (Dec. 1993); *see also* Interview with NIO/NESA (Nov. 8, 2004) (analysts were "flying blind" when attempting to characterize regime intentions); SSCI at p. 369 (lack of intelligence on Saddam's intentions was a "constant theme" among analysts after 1991).

[656] NIC, *Iraq: Saddam Husayn's Prospects for Survival Over the Next Year* (SNIE 36.2-91) (Sept. 1991) at p. v, n. 1 (INR and Treasury assessed that the Intelligence Community lacked sufficient information to support a firm judgment on Saddam's prospects for survival).

[657] *Id.* at p. viii (Key Judgments).

[658] *Id.* at pp. viii-ix.

[659] NIC, *Saddam Husayn: Likely to Hang On* (NIE 92-7) (June 1992) at pp. iii, 4.

[660] NIC, *Prospects for Iraq: Saddam and Beyond* (NIE 93-42) (Dec. 1993) at pp. 1, 2, 5, 14.

[661] *Id.* at p. 1. Another assumption underlying the analysis was that "Saddam Husayn will not alter his basic domestic and foreign policy goals: to maintain his hold on power by any means necessary,…[and] to rebuild Iraq's military might—including weapons of mass destruction programs." *Id.*

[662] NIC, *Iraq: Likelihood of Renewed Confrontation* (SE 95-8) (June 27, 1995) at p. 2; *see also* CIA, *No Rest for Iraq's Weary* (NESA IR 95-40122) (June 20, 1995) (noting that there was rampant poverty and widespread crime and corruption in Iraq, and that the government was doing little to alleviate the suffering).

[663] NIC, *Iraq: Likelihood of Renewed Confrontation* (SE 95-8) (June 22, 1995) at p. 4.

[664] *Id.*

[665] *Id.* at p. 1.

[666] *Id.* at p. 2.

[667] NIC, *Iraq: Regime Prospects for 1997* (ICB 96-3C) (Dec. 26, 1996) at p. 1.

[668] *Id.* at pp. 1, 3; *see also* NIC, Title Classified (ICB 97-16) (July 22, 1997); NIC, *U.S. Position Eroding Sharply in the Middle East* (NIC 1738-98) (March 20, 1998) (anti-American sentiment among Arab publics had caused U.S. political standing to plummet, increasing Arab expectations for a formal end to sanctions).

[669] *Id.*

[670] *Id.* at pp. 1-2; *see also* NIC, *Iraq: Regime Prospects for 1997* (ICB 96-3C) (Dec. 26, 1996) at pp. 1, 5.

[671] NIC, *Iraq: Prospects for Confrontation* (ICB 98-21) (July 18, 1998) at p. 2. *See also* NIC, *Iraq: Saddam's Next Moves* (SOCM 99-4) (March 2, 1999) (noting an increasing risk that Saddam would "act impulsively" to regain the initiative and attention in the wake of mounting frustration over unmet demands to lift sanctions).

[672] NIC, *Iraq: Prospects for Confrontation* (ICB 98-21) (July 18, 1998) at p. 3.

[673] Interview with NIO/NESA (Nov. 8, 2004).

[674] CIA, *Iraq-United States: Hardening Stance Toward UNSCOM* (NESA IM 96-20005) (Aug. 9, 1996).

[675] CIA, *Iraqi Denial and Deception Against International Inspection Regimes* (OTI IA 2002-169-CHX) (Oct. 7, 2002) ("Iraq's apparent willingness to agree to a resumption of inspections in part reflects confidence in its ability to prevent the international community from discovering the extent of its current and past weapons-related activities.").

[676] CIA, *Iraq: Saddam Maneuvering to Survive 2002* (NESAF IA 2002-20024C) (Feb. 15, 2002) at p. 1.

[677] *Id.* at p. i.

[678] *Id.* at p. 2.

[679] CIA, *Iraqi War Crimes: Saddam Husayn al-Tikriti* (NESAF IR 2001-40064JX) (April 3, 2001) (analyzing Saddam's decision making processes); Interview with NIO/NESA (Nov. 8, 2004) (noting difficulty in obtaining information on regime decisionmaking).

[680] *Id.*

[681] NIC, *Iraqi Military Capabilities Through 2003* (NIE 99-04/II) (April 1999).

[682] CIA, *Iraqi War Crimes: Saddam Husayn al-Tikriti* (NESAF IR 2001-40064JX) (April 3, 2001) at pp. 1-2.

[683] *Id.*

[684] *Id.* at p. 2.

[685] NIC, *Iraqi Military Capabilities Through 2003* (NIE 99-04/II) (April 1999); *see also* Interview with NIO/NESA (Nov. 8, 2004).

[686] NIC, *The Gulf Crisis: Implications of War, A Peaceful Solution, or Stalemate for the Middle East* (SNIE 36/39-91) (Jan. 1991) at p. iii (Saddam Hussein undeterred from his goal of regional supremacy); NIC, *Prospects for Iraq: Saddam and Beyond* (NIE 93-42) (Dec. 1993) (noting that one of the assumptions underlying the Estimate was that Saddam would not alter his long-term goal of making Iraq a dominant regional power); NIC, *Iraq: Prospects for Confrontation.* (ICB 98-21) (July 17, 1998) at p. 2 (Saddam's long-term goal of reasserting regional dominance); NIC, *Iraqi Military Capabilities Through 2003* (NIE 99-04/II) (April 1999) (Iraq's fundamental goals remained unchanged and included regional domination).

[687] NIC, *Prospects for Iraq: Saddam and Beyond* (NIE 93-42) (Dec. 1993) at p. 1.

[688] NIC, *Iraqi Military Capabilities Through 2003* (NIE 99-04/II) (April 1999) at p. 6.

[689] NIC, *Stability of the Iraqi Regime: Significant Vulnerabilities Offset by Repression* (ICA 2002-02HC) (April 2002) at p. 5.

[690] NIC, *Iraqi Military Capabilities Through 2003* (NIE 99-04/II) (April 1999) at p. 5 (noting assessment was unchanged from previous NIEs in 1994 and 1995).

[691] NIC, *Iraq: Prospects for Confrontation* (ICB 98-21) (July 17, 1998) at p. 2; *see also* NIC, *Prospects for Iraq: Saddam and Beyond* (NIE 93-42) (Dec. 1993) (achieving goal of regional dominance required rebuilding military might, including WMD).

[692] Interview with NIO/NESA (Nov. 8, 2004) (the dearth of information made any analysis of Iraqi political calculations largely speculative, and analysts therefore relied on historical information and observed behavior).

[693] ISG Report, Regime Strategic Intent at p. 42.

[694] ISG, Transmittal Message to *Comprehensive Report of the Special Advisor to the DCI on Iraqi WMD* (Sept. 23, 2004) at p. 8.

[695] ISG Report, Regime Strategic Intent at p. 34. Iraq's invasion of Kuwait led to the immediate imposition of comprehensive and mandatory trade and financial sanctions under United Nations Security Council Resolution (UNSCR) 661. These sanctions remained in place after the ceasefire of February 28, 1991. UNSCR 687 of April 3, 1991 created UNSCOM and required Iraq's WMD disarmament. UNSCR 687 explicitly linked Iraq's WMD disarmament to Iraq's right to resume oil exports; the withdrawal of wider sanctions was also dependent on this step. UNSCR 715, passed on October 11, 1991, required Iraq's unconditional acceptance of ongoing inspections to monitor and verify Iraq's compliance with UNSCR 687. *Id.*

[696] *Id.* at p. 46.

[697] *Id.* at p. 44.

[698] *Id.* at p. 46.

[699] Interview with Special Advisor to the Director of Central Intelligence Charles Duelfer (Oct. 13, 2004).

[700] ISG Report, Regime Strategic Intent at p. 1.

[701] *Id.* at pp. 7, 70.

[702] *Id.* at pp. 11, 12.

[703] *Id.* at pp. 8-9.

[704] *Id.* at p. 34.

[705] *Id.*

[706] *Id.* at p. 41.

[707] *Id.* at p. 47.

[708] *Id.*

[709] *Id.* at p. 48.

[710] *Id.* at p. 34.

[711] *Id.* at p. 49.

[712] *Id.* at pp. 57-58.

[713] *Id.* at pp. 56-57, 60.

[714] *Id.* at p. 65.

[715] *Id.*

[716] *Id.* at pp. 65-66.

[717] Although the Senate Select Committee on Intelligence's report discussed some of the pre-war analytical products regarding Iraq's threat to regional security, the Committee did not have the benefit of the ISG report and therefore did not discuss the discrepancies between the

pre-war assessments of the political dynamics within the Iraqi regime and the post-war findings in that regard. *See generally* SSCI at pp. 367-390.

[718] Interview with Special Advisor to the Director of Central Intelligence Charles Duelfer (Oct. 13, 2004).

[719] ISG Report, Regime Strategic Intent at pp. 11, 65. One senior Iraqi official told the ISG that he was not certain whether Saddam's statement that Iraq had no WMD was true, given the U.S. government's belief that Iraq did have such weapons. *Id.* at p. 62.

[720] Interview with NIO/NESA (Nov. 8, 2004); Interview with NIO/SNP (Sept. 20, 2004). The former Assistant Secretary of State for Intelligence and Research noted that he had discussed this possibility with other senior administration officials before Operation Iraqi Freedom began, but that ultimately they had rejected the possibility. They rejected it because they thought Saddam would have no reason not to come clean with the inspectors if he had truly disarmed. Although they considered the possibility that Saddam's behavior could be explained by his pride, as well as by his desire to intimidate and deter his adversaries by allowing them to think he had WMD, they ultimately rejected that theory. Interview with former Assistant Secretary of State for Intelligence and Research (Nov. 1, 2004).

[721] Interview with NIO/NESA (Nov. 8, 2004).

[722] *See, e.g.,* NIC, *Iraq: Saddam Husayn's Prospects for Survival Over the Next Year* (SNIE 36.2-91) (Sept. 1991) at p. xi (this assessment, prepared shortly after the end of the Gulf War, assumed that Saddam would not fully comply with United Nations resolutions and that sanctions would remain in effect); NIC, *Prospects for Iraq: Saddam and Beyond* (NIE 93-42) (Dec. 1993) at p. 1 (identifying as an assumption that Saddam would not fully comply with United Nations resolutions); NIC, *Iraq: Prospects for Confrontation* (ICB 98-21) (July 18, 1998) at p. 3 (stating that "Saddam does not intend to fully comply with relevant Security Council resolutions").

[723] Interview with NIO/NESA (Nov. 8, 2004) (noting the dearth of political reporting).

[724] Some reporting indicated that Iraq may have moved biological and chemical weapons stockpiles to Syria just prior to the start of the war in March 2003. CIA, Title Classified (Dec. 13, 2004) (citing one classified intelligence report (March 2003) from a foreign service). The security situation along the border between Iraq and Syria prevented the ISG from conclusively ruling out the possibility that such weapons were transported across the border. Interview with Special Advisor to the Director of Central Intelligence Charles Duelfer (Oct. 13, 2004). It is important to note, however, that, given the overall findings of the ISG, there was nothing left to move by March 2003, save possibly some pre-1991 CW shells. Therefore, the conclusion that militarily significant stockpiles of CW or BW could *not* have been moved to Syria just before the war necessarily follows from the ISG's overall findings about the state of Iraq's WMD programs after 1991.

[725] NIC, *Current Iraqi WMD Capabilities* (NIC-1848-98) (Sept. 30, 1998) at p. 1.

[726] *Id.*

[727] Interview with former senior administration official.

[728] SSCI at pp. 260-261; *see also* Interview with CIA/DO officials (Sept. 22, 2004).

[729] Interview with Defense HUMINT official (Nov. 2, 2004); Interview with CIA/DO official (June 23, 2004).

[730] Bureaucratic incentives not only affect the ability to recruit quality sources, but they may

affect the ability to obtain quality reporting from existing sources. When policymaker interest in a particular topic is high and the number of existing sources in that area is low, collectors may understandably respond by pressing an asset to report on issues going beyond his usual access, or by giving more credence to an untried source than would normally be the case. *See, e.g.*, Butler Report at pp. 105-109.

[731] Interview with Defense HUMINT official (Nov. 2, 2004); *see also* SSCI at p. 153.

[732] *See also* SSCI at p. 191 (also concluding that Defense HUMINT's performance represented a "serious lapse" in tradecraft).

[733] Interview with Division Chief and Group Chief, CIA/DO (Dec. 14, 2004). For example, the CIA attempted to validate Curveball's claim that he was present when a BW accident took place by evaluating him for signs of exposure. And when the trailers were discovered in Iraq in the spring of 2003 that were thought to be the mobile facilities reported by Curveball, CIA/DO suggested that Curveball be shown several "control" pictures along with the pictures of the actual trailers found in Iraq as a tool to test his truthfulness. Defense HUMINT and WINPAC analysts believed such "testing" was unnecessary, however, and no such testing appears to have been undertaken. *Id.*

[734] DCI Statement for the Record at Tab 6, p. 7.

[735] *Id.* at p. 2.

[736] Interview with CIA/DO officials (Sept. 22, 2004) (noting that human sources who claimed Iraq did not have WMD were viewed as taking the Iraqi "party line," and thus their information was not considered worthy of dissemination).

[737] Interview with CIA WMD Review Group Analyst (Sept. 23, 2004).

[738] Interview with CIA/DO officials (Sept. 22, 2004).

[739] CIA, *Iraq WMD Lessons Learned* (Aug. 2004) at p. 26.

[740] *Id.*; Interview with Director of the Defense Intelligence Agency Vice Admiral Lowell Jacoby (Jan. 17, 2005).

[741] Interview with NSA officials (Aug. 26, 2004); NSA, *Written Responses from NSA to WMD Commission's NSA Request No. 16* (Feb. 17, 2005) at p. 1.

[742] *See, e.g.*, NGA, *NGA Reassessment of Activity at Al Musayyib Barracks Brigade Headquarters and Ammunition Depot, 1998-2004* (June 15, 2004).

[743] Interview with CIA WINPAC analysts (Aug. 11, 2004). Biological, chemical and, to a lesser extent, nuclear programs, are potentially concealable from overhead reconnaissance, although delivery system programs are more difficult to hide. *Id.*

[744] *Id.*

[745] Even in the case of chemical weapons programs, which are more difficult to conceal than biological warfare programs, imagery alone is not determinative, as demonstrated by the October 2002 NIE's error in analyzing transshipment activity as evidence of an Iraqi CW program.

[746] NIE at p. 28.

[747] Interview with CIA WINPAC CW analyst (Oct. 8, 2004).

[748] NGA, *NGA Reassessment of Activity at Al Musayyib Barracks Brigade Headquarters and Ammunition Depot, 1998-2004* (June 15, 2004).

[749] NGA, *Matrix of NIMA/NGA Intelligence Relative to the BW and CW portions of the NIE*

on Iraq, October 2002 (June 30, 2004) at p. 13. Even outside of the dual-use context imagery can be misleading. The NIE noted that imagery that had previously been interpreted as motor cases for missiles in fact showed heat treatment ovens used in the production of motor cases. NIE at p. 59.

[750] Collection Concepts Development Center Study, *Iraqi Weapons of Mass Destruction: Recommendations for Improvements in Collection* (Study One) (June 29, 2000) at p. 13.

[751] *Id.*

[752] SSCI at pp. 266-267.

[753] *See generally* Source Documents for the October 2002 NIE.

[754] Interview with Assistant Director of Central Intelligence for Analysis and Production (Sept. 28, 2004) (noting general lack of understanding of, and respect for, MASINT).

[755] Interview with Assistant Director of Central Intelligence for Collection (July 20, 2004) (describing end-to-end review of collection approaches); *see also* SSCI at p. 259.

[756] Collection Concepts Development Center Study, *Iraqi Weapons of Mass Destruction: Recommendations for Improvements in Collection* (Study One) (June 29, 2000) at p. 18.

[757] Interview with NSA officials (Sept. 8, 2004).

[758] NSA, *Memorandum Re: Clarification Question* (Oct. 27, 2004). Somewhat contradictorily, NSA subsequently said that it had in fact "pursued" this recommendation, although it conceded that there was no "active" effort until two years after the CCDC study. NSA, *Written Responses from NSA to WMD Commission's NSA Request No. 16* (Feb. 17, 2005).

[759] Collection Concepts Development Center Study, *Iraqi Weapons of Mass Destruction: Recommendations for Improvements in Collection* (Study One) (June 29, 2000) at p. 10.

[760] Interview with NGA officials (Nov. 16, 2004); SSCI at p. 266 (quoting officials from the National Intelligence Collection Board as to doubling of collection operations).

[761] As noted, beginning in March 2002, NGA increased its coverage to include ammunition depots that had not previously been imaged on a regular basis. Accordingly, there was no "baseline" of activity for these sites on which to base an assessment that the activity level had changed.

[762] Interview with CIA WINPAC CW analyst (Oct. 8, 2004); Interview with NGA officials (Nov. 16, 2004).

[763] Although the Senate Select Committee on Intelligence's report discusses the reliance on imagery intelligence, it does not discuss the effect of the increased coverage on the ability to distinguish increased activity from increased collection.

[764] DCI Statement for the Record at Introduction at p. 2.

[765] Interview with CIA WINPAC nuclear analysts (Aug. 11, 2004).

[766] The tendency to hew to the prevailing analytical view, and to view new information exclusively through the prism of that existing paradigm, is variously described as "self-conditioning," "tunnel vision," "groupthink," "path dependency," etc. Whatever the lexicon, this phenomenon as addressed here describes a tendency to adhere to a prevailing view without sufficiently questioning the hypotheses underlying that conclusion.

[767] To be sure, denial and deception remains a significant challenge to the Intelligence Community. Educating analysts and collectors about that threat is important to ensure that the problem is neither overestimated nor underestimated.

[768] Also, one basis for the conclusion that the tubes were for centrifuges was that the specifications were excessive for rockets, yet CIA analysts did not vigorously pursue an effort to determine the specifications used in the Italian rocket from which the Iraqis had reverse-engineered theirs, reasoning that such information was unnecessary. Similarly, CIA reasoned that the tubes were intended for centrifuges because they were procured through intermediary countries, but that procurement method is equally consistent with the tubes' use in conventional weapons. NIE at p. 74.

[769] A problem with the Team B effort in the mid-1970s was not its existence, which was, in many ways, a salutary instance of outside expertise factoring into Community estimates. Rather, the flaw was that a Team C was not also created to posit that the Soviet Union might actually be *weaker* than either the Intelligence Community or Team B assessed.

[770] Interview with former Secretary of Defense and Director of Central Intelligence James Schlesinger (Aug. 25, 2004) (noting that competition among agencies can improve the product of each agency).

[771] The NIE contained dissenting views from INR, Air Force Intelligence, and DOE on several topics. In that regard, the NIE fully aired conflicting views. One potential subsidiary problem, however, is that whether the dissent appears in the final product (and how it is expressed) depends in part on the willingness and ability of individual agency representatives to present such contrary views forcefully and effectively at NIE coordination meetings. NIE at pp. 7, 14, 16, 52.

[772] *Compare* NIE at p. 14 (INR dissent noting that it saw "no compelling evidence" that Iraq had commenced "an integrated and comprehensive approach to acquire nuclear weapons") *and id.* at p. 16 (DOE agreement that reconstitution is underway but that the tubes are probably not part of that program) *with id.* (NIE assessing that Iraq "has reconstituted its nuclear weapons program").

[773] Interview with NGIC analysts (Dec. 7, 2004); DIA, *Iraq: Procuring Possible Nuclear-Related Gas Centrifuge Equipment* (MID-227-01-SCI) (Nov. 30, 2001) (NGIC assessment that the tube tolerances were excessive for rockets).

[774] SSCI at p. 22 (describing the "layering" phenomenon).

[775] NIE at pp. 28, 52; *see also* DCI Statement for the Record at Tab 2, p. 9.

[776] NIE at p. 28.

[777] *Id.* at p. 33.

[778] SSCI at pp. 22-23 (discussing the layering problem in the CW assessments).

[779] Interview with former CIA WINPAC CW analyst (Nov. 10, 2004).

[780] CIA, former Deputy Director of Central Intelligence Richard Kerr, *The Evidence and Analysis of Iraqi WMD: The National Intelligence Estimate of October 2002* (Jan. 28, 2004) (making the observation that analysts focused too much on weapons and not enough on Iraq).

[781] ISG Report, Regime Strategic Intent at pp. 7-9, 34, 46. The ISG also found that the Iraqi economy and infrastructure were collapsing under the weight of sanctions, making it difficult to restart WMD programs. ISG Report, Nuclear at p. 5. Analysts faced difficulty getting some of this information. Interview with CIA WINPAC analysts (Aug. 11, 2004).

[782] The ability to ensure that weapons analysts will factor in the effect of the social and political context on their analysis depends on meaningful interaction between the functional and regional analytic units. There is some indication that coordination and cooperation between

these units needs improvement. As one analyst noted, the functional units such as WINPAC have highly varying relations with the regional components, such as NESA. Interview with CIA WINPAC analysts (Aug. 11, 2004).

[783] Indeed, one analyst related that the demand for current intelligence became so acute that he not only gave up long-term research, but often was spending so much time preparing current intelligence and responding to policymaker follow-up questions on that current intelligence that he could not even read his daily in-box of raw intelligence reporting. That task was delegated to a junior analyst (with no expertise on Iraq WMD issues) who pulled traffic he thought might be of interest. Interview with former CIA WINPAC CW analysts (Nov. 10, 2004).

[784] NIE at p. 13.

[785] *See, e.g.*, Interviews with CIA WINPAC analysts (Aug. 11, 2004 and Oct. 8, 2004); Interview with DOE intelligence analyst (Oct. 27, 2004) (noting that "DOE didn't want to come out before the war and say [Iraq] wasn't reconstituting").

[786] CIA, *Iraq and al-Qa'ida: Interpreting a Murky Relationship* (CTC 2002-40078 CH) (June 21, 2002) at p. 5 (the scope note to the paper stated that "our approach is purposefully aggressive in seeking to draw connections, on the assumption that any indication of a relationship between these two hostile elements would carry great danger to the U.S."); *see also* SSCI at p. 304.

[787] Interview with NSA officials (July 14, 2004).

[788] Classified intelligence report (March 2002).

[789] CIA, Memorandum for the Deputy Executive Director, CIA, *DI-DO Information Sharing Status* (Sept. 28, 2004) at p. 5. CIA is coordinating this effort with Defense HUMINT. CIA, *Changes to Strengthen DO Intelligence* (Nov. 8, 2004) at p. 5.

[790] This is a problem that applies to analyst-to-analyst relationships as well. For example, CIA analysts did not share their increasing doubts about the significance of the Iraqi mapping software procurement with other analysts in the Community.

[791] CIA, *DO/EA Division Review on DI-DO Information Sharing Pilot* (Aug. 9, 2004).

[792] Interview with former Deputy Director for Operations James Pavitt (May 18, 2004); Interview with Division Chief and Group Chief, CIA/DO (Dec. 14, 2004).

[793] SSCI at p. 247.

[794] Interview with National Intelligence Officer for Intelligence Assurance (Nov. 18, 2004).

[795] SSCI at pp. 269-271.

[796] Interview with CIA/DO officials and CIA Iraq WMD Review Group analyst (Aug. 3, 2004).

[797] Interview with Assistant Director of Central Intelligence for Analysis and Production (Sept. 22, 2004).

[798] *Id.* (noting that the average NIE is 55 pages, while the average estimate of one close liaison intelligence service equivalent is about 17 pages).

[799] *Id.*

[800] *Id.* (noting that the specified liaison service presents the views of each agency where there is a difference in opinion).

[801] Interview with NIO/SNP (Sept. 20, 2004); *see also* NIC, *Everything You Always Wanted to Know About NIEs...But Were Afraid to Ask* (2004) (unclassified booklet).

[802] NIC, *National Intelligence Council* (April 2004) (unclassified booklet describing the roles and responsibilities of the NIC).

[803] *Id.*

[804] Interview with NIO/SNP (Sept. 20, 2004) (normally takes "months" to publish an NIE). Some NIEs have been produced very quickly, however. *See* CIA, Center for Studies in Intelligence, *Sherman Kent and the Board of National Estimates: Collected Essays* (1994) (noting that NIE entitled "Sino-Soviet Intentions in the Suez Crisis" was published in one day).

[805] NIC, *Everything You Always Wanted to Know About NIEs...But Were Afraid to Ask* (2004) (unclassified booklet). The Terms of Reference are reviewed by peers in the NIC and presented to the Community, and often to the NFIB, for approval. *Id.*

[806] *Id.; see also* SSCI at p. 10 (describing NIE process).

[807] Interview with NIO/SNP (Sept. 20, 2004); *see also* SSCI at p. 11.

[808] *Id.* The draft is also sometimes submitted to a panel of experts for review. *Id.*; SSCI at p. 11.

[809] Interview with NIO/SNP (Sept. 20, 2004); *see also* SSCI at p. 11.

[810] Interview with NIO/NESA (Nov. 8, 2004).

[811] Interview with NIO/SNP (Sept. 20, 2004).

[812] *Id.* (noting that the Senate demanded the NIE be completed in three weeks); *Letter from Senator Richard Durbin to Director of Central Intelligence George Tenet* (Sept. 9, 2002) (requesting that the DCI "direct the immediate production of a National Intelligence Estimate assessing the current and projected status—over the next 10 years—of Iraq's weapons of mass destruction capabilities"). Senators Bob Graham and Carl Levin also requested an NIE covering various topics related to Iraq's WMD programs. CIA, *Congressional Requests and Responses re Iraq WMD Chronology.*

[813] Interview with NIOs (May 26, 2004) (describing the October 2002 Iraq NIE process).

[814] Interview with DOE intelligence analyst (Oct. 27, 2004).

[815] *Id.*

[816] During this time period, however, the CIA Directorate of Operation's Counterproliferation Division provided the SSCI staff with quarterly briefings on its WMD covert action operations, including those directed against Iraq, according to the Chief of Intelligence for the Directorate of Operations. Comments from Chief of Intelligence, Office of the Deputy Director of Operations (March 3, 2005).

[817] Interview with NIO/SNP (Sept. 20, 2004).

[818] *Id.*

[819] *Id.*; *see also* SSCI at p. 286.

[820] Interview with NGIC officials (Dec. 7, 2004); Interview with NGIC official (Dec. 14, 2004).

[821] *Id.* (including NGIC CW analysts) (Dec. 7, 2004). A review of NGIC's published intelligence shows that as late as October 2001, NGIC estimated that Iraq had between 10-100 tons of agents in its stockpile. NGIC, *Iraq: Current Chemical Warfare Capabilities* (Oct. 23, 2001). In March 2003, NGIC published an assessment of Iraq's CW delivery capabilities that noted that the "upper limit of the assessed Iraqi CW agent stockpile [was] 500 metric tons." NGIC, *Iraq's UAV CW Delivery Capabilities—An Unlikely Threat* (NGIC-1671-7685-03) (March 25, 2003).

[823] Interview with NGIC officials (Dec. 7, 2004); Interview with NGIC official (Dec. 14, 2004).

[824] *Id.*

[825] Electronic mail from NGIC to CIA and DIA, containing NGIC's line in and line out edits on the CW section of the draft NIE (Sept. 24, 2002) (noting "[w]e are not able to come up tomorrow [to the NIE coordination meeting] so please support our points").

[826] Interview with NIO/SNP (Jan. 5, 2005); *see also* Interview with NGIC officials (Dec. 7, 2004). The NIO/SNP noted that the NIE included at least 15 pages of alternative views from different agencies, suggesting that there was not an effort afoot to quash dissent. NGIC admits that it did not convey its position to the Army G-2 representative prior to the Military Intelligence Board. Comments from NGIC (March 3, 2005).

[827] SSCI at p. 206 (quoting DIA testimony). NGIC has now retreated somewhat from its allegations, claiming that it has "reexamined this issue" and NGIC now "cannot confirm" whether the DIA representatives conveyed NGIC's position to the NIO during the coordination meeting for the NIE. NGIC asserts that DIA's concurrence with the stockpile position eventually published in the NIE indicates that DIA did not present NGIC's stockpile position at the coordination meeting. According to NGIC, DIA also did not inform them about subsequent drafts of the NIE. Comments from NGIC (March 3, 2005). In any event, NGIC also noted that DIA—and not NGIC—had the responsibility within the defense intelligence establishment to assess CW stockpiles. *Id.*

[828] Interview with NGIC officials (Dec. 7, 2004). The NGIC analyst noted that NGIC had subsequently published items that were "not in concert" with the NIE, but had not published anything to clarify its position on the 100-500 MT stockpile range. *Id.* In addition to the Military Intelligence Board, two more opportunities were available for NGIC to have provided its views. An errata sheet was published for the NIE on October 18, 2002, about three weeks after the NIE was published. NGIC notes that it "has no record of being informed" of the errata sheet. Comments from NGIC (March 3, 2005). If NGIC believed its views were mistakenly (or purposefully) omitted, it could have tried to clarify the record through this errata sheet. Also, another NIE was published in November 2002, as a follow-up to the October NIE to cover certain aspects of the tactical CW threat that the military wanted to have addressed. NIC, *Iraq's Chemical Warfare Capabilities: Potential for Dusty and Fourth-Generation Agents: Memorandum to Holders of NIE 2002-16HC* [the October 2002 NIE] (M/H NIE 2002-16) (Nov. 2002). NGIC took issue with some aspects of this NIE, but remained silent on the issue of restarted production for increased stockpiles. *Id.*

[829] *See, e.g.*, Senator Carl Levin, "Buildup to War on Iraq," *Congressional Record* (July 15, 2003) at pp. S9358-S9360; Walter Pincus and Dana Priest, "Some Iraq Analysts Felt Pressure from Cheney Visits," *Washington Post* (June 5, 2003) at p. A1; Nicholas D. Kristof, "White House in Denial," *New York Times* (June 13, 2003) at p. A33; Jay Taylor, "When Intelligence Reports Become Political Tools..." *Washington Post* (June 29, 2003) at p. B2; Douglas Jehl, "After the War: Weapons Intelligence; Iraq Arms Critic Reacts to Report on Wife," *New York Times* (Aug. 8, 2003) at p. A8; Dana Milbank and Walter Pincus, "As Rationales for War Erode, Issue of Blame Looms Large," *Washington Post* (July 10, 2004) at p. A1; Glenn Kessler, "Analyst Questioned Sources' Reliability; Warning Came Before Powell Report to UN," *Washington Post* (July 10, 2004) at p. A9; T. Christian Miller and Maura Reynolds, "Question of Pressure Splits Panel," *Los Angeles Times* (July 10, 2004) at p. A1; James Risen and Douglas Jehl,

"Expert Said to Tell Legislators He Was Pressed to Distort Some Evidence," *New York Times* (June 25, 2003) at p. A11; Robert Schlesinger, "Bush Aides Discredit Analysts' Doubts on Trailers," *The Boston Globe* (June 27, 2003) at p. A25; Seymour M. Hersh, "The Stovepipe," *The New Yorker* (Oct. 27, 2003) at p. 77.

[830] Our review has been limited by our charter to the question of alleged policymaker pressure on the Intelligence Community to shape its conclusions to conform to the policy preferences of the Administration. There is a separate issue of how policymakers used the intelligence they were given and how they reflected it in their presentations to Congress and the public. That issue is not within our charter and we therefore did not consider it nor do we express a view on it.

[831] Interview with CIA Ombudsman for Politicization (Oct. 4, 2004) (describing CIA definition of "politicization," the core of which is alteration of analytical judgments under pressure to reach a particular conclusion).

[832] Interviews with CIA WINPAC analysts (Aug. 11, 2004; Sept. 20, 2004; and Oct. 8, 2004).

[833] Interview with former Assistant Secretary of State for Intelligence and Research (Nov. 1, 2004).

[834] The CIA Ombudsman for Politicization also conducted a formal inquiry in June 2002 regarding a CIA assessment of possible Iraqi links to al-Qa'ida. This inquiry, which was discussed in the SSCI report, did not involve Iraqi WMD assessments. Rather, that inquiry focused on a paper published by the Counterterrorist Center Office of Terrorism Analysis (CTC/OTA) entitled *Iraq and al-Qa'ida: Interpreting a Murky Relationship* (CTC 2002-40078 CH) (June 21, 2002). CIA regional analysts from the Office of Near East and South Asia analysis (NESA) were upset about the paper for several reasons: because the paper went further than NESA was prepared to go with respect to possible links between al-Qa'ida and Iraq, because the paper was not coordinated with NESA, and because the consumer was not informed that the paper represented an uncoordinated assessment representing only the views of CTC/OTA. The CIA Ombudsman's investigation, based on interviews with numerous analysts involved, revealed that the root of the problem was a strained relationship between the two offices rather than any attempts at "politicization." He found no evidence that political pressure had caused any analyst to change any judgments. The Ombudsman concluded that the problem was instead a management issue. Interview with CIA Ombudsman for Politicization (Oct. 4, 2004).

[835] *Id.* (providing Charter for Ombudsman's office). That office defines politicization as "an unprofessional intrusion by intelligence officers into the policymaking process, characterized by skewing of information and judgments to support or oppose a specific policy or general political ideology." Such "unprofessional manipulation of information and judgments can be deliberate—for example, to please a policymaker or under pressure from an intelligence manager. The distortion can also be unintentional, arising from poor tradecraft practice." *Id.*

[836] *Id.*

[837] *Id.*

[838] Interview with CIA WINPAC analysts (Oct. 8, 2004).

[839] Interview with National Intelligence Officers responsible for drafting NIE (May 26, 2004). A number of analysts have pointed to the limited time allotted to complete the NIE as a species of pressure on analysts. When pressed by Commissioners and staff members as to

whether more time would have changed the NIE's assessments, however, the NIOs have answered that the Estimate would not have come to different conclusions even if more time had been available. Interview with National Intelligence Officers responsible for drafting NIE (May 26, 2004); Interview with NIO/SNP (Sept. 20, 2004).

[840] Interview with CIA WINPAC analysts (Oct. 8, 2004) (citing aluminum tubes for nuclear weapons, Curveball's reporting for biological weapons, and "transshipment activity" for CW); *see also* DCI Statement for the Record at Tab 1, p. 19; Tab 3, p. 16; and Tab 2, p. 3.

[841] Interview with CIA/DO officials and CIA Iraq WMD Review Group (Aug. 3, 2004); Interview with CIA WINPAC analysts (Oct. 8, 2004); Interview with NIO/NESA (Nov. 8, 2004). For example, the DCI Statement for the Record, which explained how analysts reached their conclusions in the NIE, noted that analysts would have required substantial new streams of information indicating that Iraq had abandoned its WMD programs to come to the conclusion that Iraq had no WMD programs or stockpiles. DCI Statement for the Record at Tab 1, pp. 34-35; Tab 2, p. 14; Tab 3, pp. 26-29; and Tab 4, p. 11.

[842] Interview with NIO/NESA (Nov. 8, 2004).

[843] *Id.*

[844] *Id.*

[845] Interview with DOE intelligence analyst (Oct. 27, 2004).

[846] Interview with former Assistant Secretary of State for Intelligence and Research (Nov. 1, 2004). The head of the Intelligence Community must constantly make judgments based on ambiguous information, and based on that information make decisions about how to strike the balance between independence and access when presenting estimates to policymakers. *For a discussion of this issue, see* Jack Davis, "The Challenge of Managing Uncertainty: Paul Wolfowitz on Intelligence-Policy-Relations," *Studies in Intelligence*, no. 5 (1996); Efraim Halevy, "In Defence of the Intelligence Services," *The Economist* (July 31, 2004) at pp. 21-23.

[847] Interview with former Assistant Secretary of State for Intelligence and Research (Nov. 1, 2004); Interview with NIO/NESA (Nov. 8, 2004). *For variations on this theme, see* Thomas L. Ahern, Jr., CIA Center for the Study of Intelligence, *Good Questions, Wrong Answers: CIA's Estimates of Arms Traffic Through Sihanoukville, Cambodia, During the Vietnam War* (Feb. 2004); Harold P. Ford, CIA Center for the Study of Intelligence, *CIA and the Vietnam Policymakers: Three Episodes 1962-1968* (1998). In one instance, Mr. Ford concluded: "In our third episode, 1967-68, a few working-level CIA officers developed and championed accurate assessments ... Many hazards, however, undercut these judgments. Political pressure from the White House [and other influential military and civilian parties] caused DCI Helms...to override the conclusions their analysts had derived from available evidence. Then Headquarters analysts themselves refused to accept new field estimates of the enemy's intentions for Tet because these did not jibe with their own published estimation of the enemy's likely conduct." *CIA and the Vietnam Policymakers* at p. 2.

[848] Interview with former CIA WINPAC analysts (Nov. 10, 2004).

[849] CIA, Inspector General, *Inspection Report of the DCI Center for Weapons Intelligence, Nonproliferation, and Arms Control (WINPAC) Directorate of Intelligence* (IG 2004-0003-IN) (Nov. 2004) (Employee Opinion Survey) at p. 9. The same survey revealed that 7 percent of WINPAC analysts had "personally experienced or observed an instance within WINPAC where [sic] an analytic judgment was changed to suit a customer's preference." *Id.*

[850] *Id.*

[851] Interview with former CIA WINPAC analysts (Nov. 10, 2004).

[852] Interview with former CIA WINPAC BW analyst (Nov. 10, 2004).

[853] *Id.*

[854] CIA, Inspector General, *Inspection Report of the DCI Center for Weapons Intelligence, Nonproliferation, and Arms Control (WINPAC) Directorate of Intelligence* (IG 2004-0003-IN) (Nov. 2004) at pp. 13-14.

[855] *Id.*

[856] *Id.*

[857] Interview with former CIA WINPAC analysts (Nov. 10, 2004).

[858] The analyst had also brought his concerns to the CIA Ombudsman for Politicization in November 2003. That inquiry focused only on whether analysts had been pressured to change their analysis, and the Ombudsman concluded there had been no such impropriety. The Ombudsman referred the matter to the DDI, who met with WINPAC analysts and explained why a reassessment was not needed. Interview with CIA Ombudsman for Politicization (Oct. 4, 2004).

[859] Interview with former CIA WINPAC analysts (Nov. 10, 2004).

[860] In another incident, a CIA/DO case officer has filed suit against the CIA, alleging that CIA officials pressured him to produce intelligence reports to support the position that Iraq had WMD, and that the CIA retaliated against him when he refused. Dana Priest, "Officer Alleges CIA Retaliation," *Washington Post* (Dec. 9, 2004) at p. A2.

[861] *See supra* Nuclear Weapons Finding 1.

[862] *See supra* Biological Warfare Findings 1 and 6.

[863] *See supra* Conclusion 28.

CHAPTER TWO
CASE STUDY: LIBYA

Summary & Findings

In accordance with our mandate, we compared the Intelligence Community's judgments concerning Libya's weapons programs before Tripoli's decision to open them to international scrutiny with current assessments, thereby providing a rare "before" and "after" study of the U.S. Intelligence Community's performance. We believe that the collection and analytic efforts on Libya's weapons represent, for the most part, an Intelligence Community success story. The Community collected good intelligence on Libya's nuclear and missile programs, and it used this intelligence to enter into well-managed discussions with the Libyans, which eventually led to on-site inspections, and, ultimately, Libyan disavowal of weapons of mass destruction. We found that:

- The Intelligence Community accurately assessed what nuclear equipment Libya possessed, but it was less successful in judging how Libya could exploit the material;

- The Intelligence Community's judgment that Libya possessed chemical weapons agents and chemical weapons bombs was correct, but Libya's actual chemical weapons stockpile proved to be smaller than estimated;

- The Intelligence Community's assessments of Libya's missile programs appear to have been generally accurate, but it is not yet possible to evaluate them fully because of limited Libyan disclosures;

- The Intelligence Community's penetration of the A.Q. Khan proliferation network provided invaluable intelligence on Libya's nuclear efforts;

- The contribution of technical intelligence to assessments of Libya's chemical, biological, and nuclear programs was limited; it provided some valuable information on Libya's missile programs;

- Analysts generally showed a commendable willingness to question and reconsider their assessments in light of new information;

- Analysts tracking proliferation program developments sometimes inappropriately equated procurement activity with technical capabilities; and

- Shifting priorities and the dominance of current intelligence production leave little time for considering important unanswered questions on Libya.

INTRODUCTION

On December 19, 2003, the Libyan government announced that it would halt all efforts to produce or acquire chemical or nuclear weapons, and pledged to eliminate any existing stockpiles of such weapons or materials.[1] To ensure compliance, Libya agreed to formally "declare" the existence of all relevant weapons, materials, and facilities, and to permit a series of inspections in Libya, commencing in January 2004. As a result of these declarations and visits, inspectors were able to speedily remove key materials related to missiles and weapons of mass destruction (WMD)—including centrifuges, an entire uranium conversion facility, nuclear weapons designs, uranium hexafluoride, and guidance packages for the Scud-C missile—and ensconce them safely in the United States. By March 2004, inspectors confirmed that Libya had destroyed its unfilled chemical munitions and secured its chemical weapons stockpile of approximately 24 metric tons of mustard gas for eventual destruction.[2] This unprecedented disarmament effort resulted in significant steps toward the normalization of U.S.-Libyan relations, including the lifting of most economic sanctions on Libya and the unfreezing of its assets in the United States.[3]

As directed by the Executive Order establishing this Commission, we have compared the Intelligence Community's judgments concerning Libya's weapons programs before Tripoli's decision to open them to international scrutiny with current assessments, thereby providing a rare "before" and "after" study of U.S. intelligence assessments. In so doing, we interviewed policy officials as well as intelligence analysts and collectors. We also consulted finished intelligence production, the written "collection requirements" sent to intelligence agencies, and other intelligence documents.

We conclude that collection and analytic efforts with regard to Libya's weapons programs and in support of the U.S./U.K.-led efforts represent, for the most part, an Intelligence Community success story. The Community collected significant intelligence on Libya's nuclear and missile programs, providing a vital lever used by policymakers to pressure Tripoli to openly declare its nuclear and chemical materials and disavow its WMD and long-range missile programs.

Some discrepancies did exist between analysts' judgments prior to 2003 and the realities found in Libya; for example, analysts overestimated certain capabilities and developmental timelines relating to Libya's nuclear program and underestimated some elements of Libya's missile program. And no evidence of an expected small-scale Libyan biological weapons program has been uncovered. However, the Community's key pre-December 2003 intelligence and assessments as to Libyan nuclear procurement and chemical production appear to have been largely confirmed by the facts on the ground.

While the discrepancies that were found did not affect the general accuracy of the judgments that Libya was actively pursuing development of a nuclear weapon and possessed chemical weapons, they do point to some weaknesses in collection and analysis. It is apparent to us that the Community is not well-postured to replicate such successes.

COMPARING INTELLIGENCE ASSESSMENTS WITH U.S. FINDINGS IN LIBYA

Nuclear Weapons

Finding 1

The Intelligence Community accurately assessed what nuclear-related equipment and material had been obtained by Libya, but it was less successful in judging how well Libya was able to exploit what it possessed.

Prior to December 2003, the strength of clandestine reporting on Libya's procurement activity provided the Intelligence Community with a fairly accurate view of what nuclear-related equipment and material Libya possessed. Intelligence suggesting that Libya was receiving nuclear equipment via the A.Q. Khan network, and reporting from the 1980s indicating that Libya had acquired yellowcake from Niger in 1978 were later validated by inspections.[4] Intelligence that Libya had received uranium hexafluoride feed material for its gas centrifuge program was also confirmed.[5] In addition, it appears that the Community correctly identified key personnel in the nuclear program.[6] Libya's declarations did reveal some surprises that are discussed in the classified report.[7]

The Community was less successful in judging how well Libya was able to exploit what it possessed. CIA and DIA had assessed that Libya could produce enough weapons grade uranium for a nuclear warhead as early as 2007.[8] However, as noted in a 2004 National Intelligence Estimate, the 2007 date was shown by the declarations and inspections to be unrealistic, and this assessment did not take into account the developmental difficulties the Libyans actually faced.[9] Indeed, the lack of sufficient progress on developing a nuclear weapon is one of the factors that may have prompted Qadafi to abandon and disclose Libya's nuclear program.

Chemical Weapons

Finding 2

The Intelligence Community's central judgment that Libya possessed chemical weapons agents and chemical weapons aerial bombs was correct, but Libya's actual chemical agent stockpile proved to be smaller in quantity than the Intelligence Community estimated.

Analysts based their estimates of Libya's chemical weapons capabilities on assessments of chemical production capabilities and access to precursors. Analysts judged that Libya had produced, at most, roughly 100 metric tons of mustard agent.[10] They also believed that Libya had produced small quantities of sarin,[11] but assessed that this would have been of very low quality and therefore would have degraded quickly.[12] Analysts generally did not believe that Libya had chemical warheads for missile delivery, but they assessed that Libya could probably weaponize existing chemical agents in some fashion.[13] They further concluded that Libya had produced approximately 1,000 250-kg aerial chemical weapons bombs.[14]

Prior to December 2003, the Intelligence Community continued to judge that Libya was pursuing a limited chemical weapons program through small-scale research efforts.[15] The CIA also assessed that Libya wanted to start development of new nerve agents.[16] Moreover, CIA analysts noted that "several hundred" Iraqi chemical and biological weapons experts had been in Libya during the decade preceding the disclosures.[17]

Although a 2004 National Intelligence Estimate correctly stated that Libya possessed chemical weapons agents and aerial bombs, Libya's actual chemical stockpile proved to be smaller in quantity than the Intelligence Community estimated. Libya declared in March 2004 to the Organization for the

Prohibition of Chemical Weapons (OPCW) that it possessed about 24 metric tons of sulfur mustard agent—considerably less than the Intelligence Community had predicted. On the other hand, Libya declared to OPCW that it had produced more than 3,500 unfilled aerial munitions, including 250-kg bombs.[18]

Biological Weapons

Finding 3

The Intelligence Community's assessment that Libya maintained the desire for an offensive biological weapons program, and was pursuing at least a small-scale research and development effort, remains unconfirmed.

In the early 1990s, analysts had strong evidence that Libya was developing a biological weapons program, and policymakers worked closely with the international community to thwart Libya's efforts in this area—including instituting sanctions that prohibited the purchase of even dual-use items.[19] Throughout that period, analysts judged that Libya maintained the desire for an offensive biological weapons program, and most assessed that Libya was pursuing at least a small-scale research and development effort.[20]

These assumptions persisted through the late 1990s and the early part of this decade. During this period, analysts observed signs of reorganization and revitalization of the program, including purchases of dual-use equipment. This pre-declaration intelligence remains unconfirmed.[21]

Libyan declarations have failed to shed light on Tripoli's plans and intentions for its biological program. In addition, the suspect facilities inspectors have visited all have legitimate civilian biotechnology uses.[22] One Libyan official stated that while Libya intended to build an offensive biological weapons program, it never went beyond the planning stage, and that Qadafi considered the biological program too dangerous and ordered its termination sometime prior to 1993.[23] A senior Libyan official, who has remained a key interlocutor on Libya's WMD programs, initially referred inspectors to another senior official who ostensibly knew the details of the biological warfare (BW) program.[24] According to intelligence, this senior official also "would not discuss any intent, offensive or defensive, for the Libyan BW program."[25] Lower-level officials have not only denied working on an offensive program, but some have also denied that Libya had even a defensive program. This group of lower-level officials, comprising the bulk of biological weapons officials with whom the inspectors have met, claims to have stopped working in the program in the early 1990s.[26] None of them admit to knowing about the possible revitalization of the program early this decade.

As a result, it is not possible to measure with certainty the accuracy of the Intelligence Community's assessments of Libya's biological weapons program, and we cannot address further reasons why uncertainty continues in this unclassified report.

Delivery Systems

Finding 4

The Intelligence Community's assessments of Libya's missile programs appear to have been generally accurate, but it is not yet possible to evaluate them fully because of limited Libyan disclosures.

Declarations and inspections appear to confirm analysts' skepticism about Libya's indigenous missile program. Libyan declarations confirm that the Intelligence Community had a comprehensive understanding of Libya's programs, its designs, and its success rate.[27] The Intelligence Community's predictive record on Libya's cooperative efforts with foreign nations is more mixed, but the Intelligence Community's forecasts were nevertheless generally accurate. The Community—despite possibly erring in assessing the scale and developmental timeline—correctly identified ongoing efforts to extend the range of Libya's Scud missiles.[28]

It is not yet possible to fully evaluate the accuracy of the Intelligence Community's pre-disclosure assessments. However, what we know at this point suggests that the Community's predictions about Libya's missile programs were generally accurate.

THE UNDERPINNINGS OF SUCCESS

This section examines the contribution of the collection and analytical disciplines to achieving the success described above. While it appears the Community was able to achieve more with regard to Libya's nuclear and missile programs than its chemical and biological programs, the Community's overall record illustrates multiple examples of ways in which intelligence can succeed. These include: seamless partnerships between analysts and collectors; the availability of a variety of reporting from human and technical collectors; and the ability of analysts to be flexible in their judgments while tracking and monitoring programs over time. These kinds of successes may be among the best the current intelligence system can offer.

Nuclear Program

Finding 5

The Intelligence Community's penetration of the A.Q. Khan proliferation network provided invaluable intelligence on Libya's nuclear efforts.

Intelligence Community analysts agree that the information obtained as a result of penetrating the Khan network was critical to their understanding Libya's nuclear efforts.

The Khan network provided "one-stop shopping" for a state seeking to develop a gas centrifuge uranium enrichment program, to procure nuclear weapons information, or to gain access to supplier contacts.[29] By 2000, information was uncovered that revealed shipments of centrifuge technology from the Khan network were destined for Libya.[30] The Intelligence Community then learned through what former DCI George Tenet correctly described as "operational daring"[31] that the Khan network was the source of Libya's procurement of a nuclear weapons design.[32] Further information about the details of these efforts is classified and cannot be discussed in an unclassified setting.

The Intelligence Community's dramatic successes with regard to Libya are further exemplified by events surrounding the seizure of the BBC China, a ship bound for Libya carrying centrifuge technology.[33] The Intelligence Community's detection of the vessel and its cargo was based on a variety of innovative collection efforts which also cannot be discussed in detail here. Nevertheless, it is apparent that the outcome of these operations—which facilitated interdiction of materials providing definitive proof that Libya was working on a clandestine uranium enrichment program—served as a critical factor in Tripoli's decision to open up its weapons programs to international scrutiny.[34]

Chemical and Biological Warfare Programs

Finding 6

The Intelligence Community's performance with regard to Libya's chemical and biological programs was more modest, due in part to the limited effectiveness of technical collection techniques against these targets.

As discussed above, the Intelligence Community possessed some limited information suggesting that Libya was continuing work on limited chemical and biological programs. The overall paucity of intelligence on these programs, however, may be attributed in no small measure to the general ineffectiveness of technical collection efforts.

That being said, it should be noted that there are few distinguishing characteristics that enable the identification of chemical or biological facilities through imagery or other technical means. Moreover, much of the technology and expertise required for chemical and biological programs is dual-use, making it easier to acquire and more difficult for the Community to track. It is also apparent that, at least with regard to biological weapons, the relatively low volume of information could be attributed to the fact that Libya may not have actually had an active biological warfare program.

Delivery Systems

Finding 7

The Intelligence Community gathered valuable information on Libya's missile programs.

In contrast to the chemical and biological programs, the Community was well-postured to support the efforts of policymakers with regard to Libya's missiles. The Community had intelligence on facility locations, personnel involved in the programs, and Libya's cooperative efforts with other nations. This broad understanding contributed significantly to the success of the U.S./ U.K. inspections.

Analysis

Finding 8

Analysts generally demonstrated a commendable willingness to question and reconsider their assessments in light of new information.

Prior to 1999, analysts were skeptical about Libya's ability to implement functioning WMD programs. While a great deal of attention was focused on Libya's chemical weapons development efforts, analysts generally viewed Libya as an inept bungler, the court jester among the band of nations seeking biological or nuclear capabilities. This skepticism was based on Libya's lack of a high-technology industrial base, the absence of a trained cadre of sophisticated scientists, and the success of international sanctions, which hampered Libya's efforts to purchase complete or partially complete WMD systems.[35]

When new information began to emerge in 1999 and 2000 suggesting that Libya was reinvigorating its nuclear, missile, and biological programs, analysts immediately began to re-examine their past assumptions and launched formal efforts to explore alternative scenarios. For example, in 2001 and 2002, CIA analysts organized simulation workshops to examine the implications of suspected changes in Libya's nuclear and missile programs.[36] These efforts, however, received only limited management support, and analysts told us that the focus on current production meant that they had little time and few resources for this analytic endeavor.[37]

The new information led technical analysts to change their views dramatically about the Libyans' abilities to integrate technologies into weapons. Analysts shifted to what amounted to a "worst case" analysis, judging in a 2001 National Intelligence Estimate that Qadafi could have a nuclear weapon as early as 2007 (down from 2015 in an Estimate two years earlier), given foreign assistance.[38] The intelligence that led to this change was from classified intelligence reporting that cannot be discussed in this unclassified report. [39]

Meanwhile, in the months leading up to this new information, the Community's political analysts observed that, given Qadafi's efforts to normalize relations with the West, renunciation of Libya's WMD programs would be a natural next step.[40] However, because good evidence showed that Tripoli was still acquiring components for weapons programs, analysts believed that they could not conclusively assess that Qadafi would open the programs for inspection. Nonetheless, analysts wanted to alert policymakers to what they saw as a likely and exploitable possibility. Analysts subsequently asked the DCI's red cell team—an office responsible for testing alternative hypotheses—to consider the theory, and the team published a paper considering this scenario.[41]

Finding 9

Analysts tracking proliferation program developments sometimes inappropriately equated procurement activity with technical capabilities, and many analysts did not receive the necessary training to avoid such failings.

The analysts who tracked Libya's proliferation program saw intelligence on Libyan attempts to procure chemical, biological, and nuclear components and technologies, but lacked detailed information on Libya's ability to produce workable weapons systems from these acquired items. Unfortunately, analysts often equated procurement activity with weapons system capability.[42] As our Iraq case study previously noted, this equation of procurement with capability is a fundamental analytical error—simply because a state can buy the parts does not mean it can put them together and make them work. In our judgment, based upon our discussions with senior analytic experts, this error was caused by multiple factors, including a lack of experience or training among technical analysts in how to incorporate the systems integration capabilities of a would-be nuclear power into their assessments. In addition, many technical analysts have a weak understanding of the scientific, academic, industrial, and economic base a country requires in order to develop and actually produce weapons.

In the case of Libya (and Iraq, as we described earlier), the propensity to equate procurement with capability was partially the result of collectors gathering a disproportionately large volume of procurement-related intelligence, which may have, in turn, led analysts to overemphasize its importance. To avoid such traps, we believe that analysts—who all too often are rewarded based upon the production of current intelligence reporting—need stronger incentives to invest the substantial time necessary to develop expertise in foreign research, development, and acquisition capabilities.

Finding 10

Analytic products sometimes provided limited effective warning to intelligence consumers, and tended to separate WMD issues from broader discussions of political and economic forces.

Finally, we note that some of the analysis produced prior to Libya's renunciation of WMD provided intelligence consumers with limited useful warning. For example, National Intelligence Estimates on Libya's nuclear program only included assessments of when Libya "could" complete a nuclear warhead, without a corresponding judgment about when such an event was likely or the probability of such an event. Equally problematic, the use of WMD-specific Estimates isolated analysis of the WMD question from discussions of the political and economic forces that could lead to significant advances or delays in a national WMD program. One of the Libya Estimates even noted this explicitly, stating that its estimates were based on the success and pace of the missile programs, international technology transfers, political motives, military incentives, and economic resources, and did not take into account the possibility of significant political and economic change.[43] This weakness is similar to that found in our Iraq case study, which found that the Intelligence Community failed to examine seriously the possibility that domestic or regional political pressures (or some other factors) might have prompted Saddam Hussein to destroy his stockpiles and to forswear active development of WMD after the first Gulf War.[44]

LOOKING AHEAD

The Intelligence Community's efforts are currently focused on supporting U.S. government efforts to assess Libyan compliance with the terms of its agreements to dismantle its chemical, biological, nuclear, and missile programs. With the establishment of an official presence in Tripoli, the United States has had, since January 2004, a standing presence in-country that will provide continuous assessment of Libya's compliance with its dismantlement commitments.[45] In addition, the United States, the United Kingdom, and Libya have established a standing trilateral mechanism called the Steering and Coordinating Committee to address future weapons-related issues.[46] As a result, many in the policy and intelligence communities believe there is an "extremely low probability of things going wrong" with regard to the Libyan agreements.[47]

These positive developments aside, the Intelligence Community bears a significant and ongoing burden relating to Libya. The Community must continue to assist in verifying Libyan disclosures.

Moreover, it is clear that Libya has been considerably less forthcoming about the details of its chemical and biological weapons efforts than about its nuclear and missile programs. The analysts we interviewed agreed that if Libya maintained any biological or chemical programs, they would be small-scale.[48] And whatever may be said about the current state of the Libyan programs and the veracity of Tripoli's disclosures, it remains true that the mercurial regime may suddenly shift its plans and intentions, leading to a covert resuscitation of these programs that the Intelligence Community will be expected to detect.

There are, moreover, other significant ongoing intelligence challenges concerning the Libya target. For instance, the policy community will look to the Intelligence Community to answer questions surrounding Libyan compliance with its pledge to renounce and cease the use of terrorism.[49] For the reasons discussed below, we have some doubts about whether the Intelligence Community is well postured to confront these challenges.

Reduced Emphasis on the Target

Finding 11

Shifting priorities and the dominance of current intelligence production leave little time for considering important unanswered questions on Libya, or for working small problems that might prove to have an impact on reducing surprise over the long term.

There is growing concern within the Intelligence Community that thinking "Libya is done" may leave collectors and analysts without the resources needed to track and monitor future change.[50] Competing priorities have reduced the focus on Libya since the 2003 declarations, and Libya may again become a low priority for collectors. Some analysts say they have already begun to feel the effects of the shift in priorities.[51]

There is little doubt that important questions remain about Libya's WMD programs. Yet given competing demands on technical analysts (tracking Libyan missile developments, for example, is only a part of the responsibilities of a single analyst at CIA), it is difficult to see how the Community will work these issues as policy priorities fluctuate.

Finding 12

This finding is classified.

CONCLUSION

The Intelligence Community should be commended for its contributions to forcing Tripoli to openly declare its nuclear and chemical materials and abandon development efforts, as well as hand over parts of its missile force and cancel its long-range missile projects. Such renunciation is, we believe, the real measure of a WMD-related intelligence success. At the same time, the Intelligence Community should recognize the ways in which it can improve its collection and analysis efforts, and how the shift of resources and emphasis away from Libya may—in the future—create difficulties.

ENDNOTES

[1] Remarks by the President, *President Bush: Libya Pledges to Dismantle WMD Programs,* White House Press Secretary (Dec. 19, 2003), available at http://www.whitehouse.gov/news/releases/2003/12/200331319-9.html (accessed March 7, 2005).

2 Interview with senior administration officials (Sept. 22, 2004). The teams did not uncover any evidence of a current biological weapons program, nor has Libya admitted the existence of biological weapons materials or facilities as part of the disclosures made under its agreement with the United States and United Kingdom. DIA, Title Classified (Feb. 24, 2004).

[3] Executive Order No. 13357 (Sept. 22, 2004) (terminating the national emergency with respect to Libya, which led to the effective end of that sanctions regime). Libya continues to be designated as a State Sponsor of Terrorism, however, and sanctions based on that designation remain in place.

[4] Reporting may have slightly understated the quantity of yellowcake. NIC, Title Classified (NIE 2004-05HJ) (May 2004) at p. 48.

[5] Interview with State Department/INR analysts (Sept. 8, 2004). Department of Energy analysts announced in February 2005 their view that the material was from North Korea. Glenn Kessler, "North Korea May Have Sent Libya Nuclear Material, U.S. Tells Allies," *Washington Post* (Feb. 2, 2005) at p. A1.

[6] NIC, Title Classified (May 2004) (NIE 2004-05HJ).

[7] *Id.* at p. 48.

[8] The CIA caveated this assessment, noting that Libya would "face significant technical challenges" to its nuclear program "that could lengthen the time needed to begin producing nuclear warheads." CIA, Title Classified (SPWR 021602-5) (Feb. 16, 2002). Moreover, an NIE cautioned that the judgments were based on the assumption that Libya would receive "foreign assistance in its fissile material production and weapon development efforts." NIC, Title Classified (NIE 2001 19HJ-I) (Dec. 2001) at p. E-37.

[9] NIC, Title Classified (NIE 2004-05HJ) (May 2004).

[10] *Id.* at p. 49.

[11] *Id.*

[12] Interview with CIA analysts (Sept. 10, 2004).

[13] NIC, Title Classified (NIE 2004-05HJ) (May 2004).

[14] *Id.* at p. 49.

[15] Interview with State Department/INR analysts (Sept. 8, 2004).

[16] CIA, Title Classified (SPWR 021602-5) (Feb. 16, 2002).

[17] CIA, Title Classified (SPWR 012203-02) (Jan. 22, 2003); Interview with CIA analysts (Sept. 10, 2004).

[18] NIC, Title Classified (NIE 2004-05HJ) (May 2004) at p. 49.

[19] Interview with State Department/INR analysts (Sept. 8, 2004).

[20] NIC, Title Classified (NIE 2004-05HJ) (May 2004) at p. 50; Interview with State Department/INR analysts (Sept. 8, 2004).

[21] CIA, Title Classified (SEIB011104-02) (Jan. 12, 2004) at p. 3.

[22] Interview with senior administration officials (Sept. 22, 2004).

[23] CIA, Title Classified (SEIB011104-02) (Jan. 12, 2004) at p. 3.

[24] *Id.*

[25] *Id.*

[26] Interview with CIA analysts (Sept. 10, 2004).

[27] *Id.*

[28] NIC, Title Classified (NIE 2004-05HJ) (May 2004).

[29] CIA, Title Classified (WINPAC IA 2004-003HCX) (Feb. 12, 2004) at pp. 14-15.

[30] Interview with CIA officials (Sept. 14, 2004).

[31] George J. Tenet, Director of Central Intelligence, Speech at Georgetown University, February 5, 2004, available at http://www.cia.gov/cia/public_affairs/speeches/2004/tenet_georgetownspeech_02052004.html (accessed Jan. 18, 2005)

[32] Interview with CIA officials (Sept. 14, 2004).

[33] CIA, Title Classified (WINPAC IA 2004-003HCX) (Feb. 12, 2004) at p. 6.

[34] Interview with CIA officials (Sept. 14, 2004).

[35] *Id.*

[36] Interview with CIA analysts (Sept. 10, 2004); *see also*, e.g., Senior Panel Review, *Mediterranean WMD Implications Game II* (Dec. 12, 2002).

[37] Interview with CIA analysts (Sept. 10, 2004).

[38] NIC, Title Classified (NIE 2001 19HJ-I) (Dec. 2001).

[39] Interview with CIA officials (Sept. 14, 2004); CIA, Submission to the Commission (March 9, 2005).

[40] Interview with CIA analysts (Sept. 11, 2004).

[41] CIA, Title Classified (July 18, 2003). Similarly, since the disclosures, analysts have asked the red cell to examine the possibility that Qadafi's agreement to abandon these programs is merely temporary. Interview with CIA ballistic missile analysts (Sept. 10, 2004). *See, e.g.,* Senior Panel Review, *Mediterranean WMD Implications Game II* (Dec. 12, 2002). Analysts have also worked closely with collectors to reassess existing sources and information in light of the revelations.

[42] Interview with CIA analyst (Nov. 14, 2004).

[43] NIC, Title Classified (NIE 2001 19HJ-I) (Dec. 2001).

[44] Chapter One (Iraq).

[45] Interview with State Department/INR analysts (Sept. 8, 2004); Interview with State Department official (Sept. 24, 2004).

[46] Interview with senior administration officials (Sept. 22, 2004); Interview with State Department/INR analysts (Sept. 8, 2004).

[47] Interview with State Department/INR analysts (Sept. 8, 2004)

[48] Interview with NGA analysts (Sept. 9, 2004); Interview with CIA analysts (Sept. 10, 2004).

[49] Policymakers are also concerned with Libyan progress on human rights, domestic political and economic modernization, and regional political developments; the Intelligence Com-

munity will be expected to provide key support on these more traditional intelligence issues. Interview with State Department official (Sept. 24, 2004).

[50] *See, e.g.,* Interview with CIA officials (Sept. 14, 2004) (noting that the priority for new sources will be to verify Libya's past disclosures).

[51] Interview with CIA analysts (Sept. 10, 2004).

CHAPTER THREE
CASE STUDY: AL-QA'IDA IN AFGHANISTAN

Summary & Findings

In accordance with the Executive Order, the Commission compared the Intelligence Community's assessment of chemical, biological, radiological, and nuclear weapons in Afghanistan before and after Operation Enduring Freedom, the U.S.-led invasion of October 2001. We believe that the Intelligence Community correctly assessed al-Qa'ida's limited ability to use these weapons to inflict mass casualties. However, the war in Afghanistan and its aftermath revealed important new information about the level and direction of chemical, biological, and nuclear research and development that was underway. Specifically, we found that:

- The Intelligence Community concluded that at the time of the commencement of the war in Afghanistan, al-Qa'ida's biological weapons program was both more advanced and more sophisticated than analysts had previously assessed;

- Analytic judgments regarding al-Qa'ida's chemical weapons capabilities did not change significantly as a result of the war;

- The Community appears to have been correct in its assessment of the low probability that al-Qa'ida had built a nuclear device or obtained sufficient material for a nuclear weapon. However, the war in Afghanistan brought to light detailed and revealing information about the direction and progress of al-Qa'ida's radiological and nuclear ambitions;

- Intelligence gaps prior to the war in Afghanistan prevented the Intelligence Community from being able to assess with much certainty the extent or specific nature of al-Qa'ida's weapons of mass destruction capabilities;

- Analysis of al-Qa'ida's potential development of weapons of mass destruction in Afghanistan did not benefit from leveraging different analytic disciplines; and

- Analysts writing on al-Qa'ida's potential weapons of mass destruction efforts in Afghanistan did not adequately or explicitly state the basis for or the assumptions underlying their most critical judgments.

INTRODUCTION

On October 7, 2001, less than a month following the September 11 attacks, the United States began combat operations over the skies of Afghanistan. Operation Enduring Freedom's initial objectives were to destroy terrorist training camps and infrastructure, capture al-Qa'ida leaders, and force the cessation of all activities by and in support of terrorists within Afghanistan's borders. As a byproduct of these operations, the U.S. Intelligence Community was able to collect documents, conduct detainee interviews, and search former al-Qa'ida facilities, assembling intelligence that shed startling light on al-Qa'ida's intentions and capabilities with regard to chemical, biological, radiological, and nuclear weapons.

As directed by Executive Order, the Commission compared Intelligence Community assessments regarding al-Qa'ida's weapons of mass destruction programs in Afghanistan prior to the war with evidence obtained as a consequence of military operations and the updated assessments that resulted. In so doing, we reviewed raw and finished intelligence products, conducted interviews with analysts, and examined collection requirements documents and other information.

We found that just prior to the war in Afghanistan in 2001, the Intelligence Community was able to correctly assess al-Qa'ida's limited ability to use unconventional weapons to inflict mass casualties. Yet when the war uncovered new evidence of WMD efforts, analysts were surprised by the intentions and level of research and development underway by al-Qa'ida. Had this new information not been acquired, and had al-Qa'ida been allowed to continue weapons development, a future intelligence failure could have been in the offing.

A note before proceeding: this unclassified review of the Intelligence Community's performance on Afghanistan is necessarily more limited than the classified version. In particular, it does not go into great detail on the Intelligence Community's continuing efforts to collect and analyze intelligence relating to al-Qa'ida and its chemical, biological, radiological, and nuclear weapons. The reason for this is that any such discussion would invariably pose too great a risk of disclosing to al-Qa'ida (and other adversaries) information that could be used to defeat our intelligence capabilities in the future. Consequently, significant portions of our classified report are simply too sensitive for public disclosure.

COMPARISON OF INTELLIGENCE: "BEFORE" AND "AFTER" SNAPSHOTS OF AL-QA'IDA'S WEAPONS OF MASS DESTRUCTION PROGRAMS IN AFGHANISTAN

Biological Weapons

Finding 1

Information obtained through the war in Afghanistan and in its aftermath indicated that al-Qa'ida's biological weapons program was further along than analysts had previously assessed.

Pre-War

Information in the Intelligence Community's possession since the late 1990s indicated that al-Qa'ida's members had trained in crude methods for producing biological agents such as botulinum toxin and toxins obtained from venomous animals.[1] But the Community was uncertain whether al-Qa'ida had managed to acquire a far more dangerous strain of agent (an agent we cannot identify precisely in our unclassified report and so will refer to here as "Agent X").[2] The Community judged that al-Qa'ida operatives had "probably" acquired at least a small quantity of this virulent strain and had plans to assemble devices to disperse the agent.[3] While the Community believed that a facility to which the group had access provided the potential capability and expertise to produce biological agents, it had no evidence that the facility was being so used.[4] Likewise, the Intelligence Community assessed that al-Qa'ida was "highly unlikely" to have acquired two other dangerous biological agents, and had no credible reporting indicating it was attempting to do so.[5]

Post-War

In fact, al-Qa'ida's biological program was further along, particularly with regard to Agent X, than pre-war intelligence indicated.[6] The program was extensive, well-organized, and operated for two years before September 11, but intelligence insights into the program were limited. The program involved several sites in Afghanistan.[7] Two of these sites contained commercial equipment and were operated by individuals with special training.[8] Documents found indicated that while al-Qa'ida's primary interest was Agent X, the group had considered acquiring a variety of other biological agents.[9] The documents obtained at the training camp included scientific articles and handwritten notes pertaining to Agent X.[10]

Reporting supports the hypothesis that al-Qa'ida had acquired several biological agents possibly as early as 1999, and had the necessary equipment to enable limited, basic production of Agent X.[11] Other reporting indicates that al-Qa'ida had succeeded in isolating cultures of Agent X. Nevertheless, outstanding questions remain about the extent of biological research and development in pre-war Afghanistan, including about the reliability of the reporting described above.[12]

Chemical Weapons

Finding 2

Analytic judgments regarding al-Qa'ida's chemical weapons capabilities did not change significantly as a result of the war.

Pre-War

Prior to the war in Afghanistan, analysts assessed that al-Qa'ida "almost certainly" had small quantities of toxic chemicals and pesticides, and had produced small amounts of World War I-era agents such as hydrogen cyanide, chlorine, and phosgene.[13] Unconfirmed reporting indicated that al-Qa'ida operatives had sought to acquire more modern and sophisticated chemical agents.[14] Training manuals used by al-Qa'ida indicated that group members were familiar with the production and deployment of common chemical agents.[15] Nevertheless, the Intelligence Community was doubtful that al-Qa'ida could conduct attacks with advanced chemical agents potentially capable of causing thousands of casualties or deaths.[16]

Post-War

The war in Afghanistan and its aftermath revealed relatively little new intelligence on the group's chemical efforts. Several miscellaneous items appeared in the wake of the war.[17] One item, for example, described work on a pesticide that used a chemical to increase absorption; the agent was apparently tested on rabbits and dogs.[18]

U.S. military teams also found glassware and chemical reagents at an al-Qa'ida training camp. CIA assesses that samples taken from the site may contain trace amounts of two common chemicals that can be used to produce a blister agent.[19] There is reporting indicating that the group was attempting to produce this blister agent, and considered using it to attack Americans.[20] In total, however, these scattered pieces of evidence have not substantially altered the Intelligence Community's pre-war assessments of al-Qa'ida's chemical program.

As with al-Qa'ida's biological weapons program, questions persist about the group's historical and current chemical weapons programs.[21]

Radiological and Nuclear Weapons

Finding 3

The war in Afghanistan brought to light detailed and revealing information about the direction and progress of al-Qa'ida's radiological and nuclear ambitions.

Pre-War

The Intelligence Community assessed that al-Qa'ida was unlikely to have built a nuclear device or obtained sufficient fissile material for a nuclear weapon, and was "significantly less likely" to have acquired a complete nuclear weapon.[22] However, the Community lacked a high confidence level in these judgments because of "substantial" information gaps.[23] Analysts were apparently most worried about the possibility that al-Qa'ida could obtain nuclear material from outside sources.[24]

Given their level of uncertainty, the Intelligence Community's concerns about al-Qa'ida's unconventional weapons capabilities grew in November 2001 when, in an interview with a Pakistani journalist, Usama Bin Laden claimed that he had both nuclear and chemical weapons.[25] In response, the CIA's Weapons Intelligence, Nonproliferation, and Arms Control Center and the DCI's Counterterrorist Center produced an assessment speculating about al-Qa'ida's nuclear options. The report judged that al-Qa'ida probably had access to nuclear expertise and facilities and that there was a real possibility of the group developing a crude nuclear device.[26]

The Intelligence Community could not ultimately reach a definitive conclusion about whether al-Qa'ida possessed radiological material that could be dispersed via conventional weaponry.[27] Considering the wide availability of radiological materials and the fact that al-Qa'ida training manuals discussed the use of such substances for assassinations,[28] the Intelligence Community concluded that such a weapon was well within al-Qa'ida's capabilities.[29]

Post-War

Documents found at sites used by al-Qa'ida operatives indicated that the group was interested in nuclear device design.[30] In addition, al-Qa'ida had established contact with Pakistani scientists who discussed development of nuclear devices that would require hard-to-obtain materials like uranium to create a nuclear explosion.[31]

In May 2002, technical experts from CIA and the Department of Energy judged that there remained no credible information that al-Qa'ida had obtained fissile material or acquired a nuclear weapon.[32] Analysts noted that collection efforts in Afghanistan had not yielded any radioactive material suitable for weapons, and that there were no credible reports of nuclear weapons missing from vulnerable countries.[33]

Among the nuclear-related documents found by U.S. forces in Afghanistan was a manual that discussed openly available concepts about the nuclear fuel cycle and some weapons-related issues.[34]

Collection by media sources also added some details to the intelligence picture surrounding al-Qa'ida's weapons of mass destruction efforts. In November 2001, CNN journalists found hundreds of documents describing al-Qa'ida's nuclear and explosive development efforts in an abandoned safe house. CNN commissioned three experts to review the documents, including David Albright, an expert on proliferation who had been a consultant to the United Nations organization investigating Iraq's weapons program. CNN published the results of this work in January 2002, concluding that al-Qa'ida was pursuing a "serious weapons program with heavy emphasis on developing a nuclear device."[35]

AWAKENING TO A NEW THREAT: COLLECTION SHORTFALLS AND ANALYTIC UNCERTAINTY

The war in Afghanistan and its aftermath confirmed two key intelligence judgments made before the September attacks: al-Qa'ida did not have a nuclear device, nor did it have large-scale chemical and biological weapons capabilities. However, information obtained in the course of the war revealed that analysts were largely unaware of the extent of al-Qa'ida's weapons of mass destruction research and development (especially with regard to Agent X) in Afghanistan. Moreover, while analysts had suspected that al-Qa'ida was interested in sophisticated weapons, including nuclear devices, the war provided real information about specific efforts to obtain these weapons.

Our study revealed a number of overarching problems that help to explain why the Intelligence Community assessed al-Qa'ida's capabilities the way it did. These problems are likely to affect the Intelligence Community's future performance with regard to assessing the unconventional weapons programs of al-Qa'ida, other terrorist groups, and rogue states.

Inadequate Collection: Little Insight into Al-Qa'ida's Capabilities and Intentions

Finding 4

Intelligence gaps prior to the war in Afghanistan prevented the Intelligence Community from being able to assess with much certainty the extent of al-Qa'ida's weapons of mass destruction capabilities.

The underestimation of al-Qa'ida's fast-growing unconventional weapons capabilities and aggressive intentions is a failure in the first instance to understand adequately the character of al-Qa'ida after ten years of its mounting attacks against us (as documented in the 9/11 Commission Report), and its aspirations to acquire highly lethal weapons. This failure led the Intelligence Community to focus inadequate resources on al-Qa'ida as a target. A post-September 11 National Intelligence Estimate, prepared as the war in Afghanistan began in October 2001, highlighted how little the Intelligence Community actually knew,[36] including the scarcity of reporting on al-Qa'ida targets.[37] The National Intelligence Estimate went on to describe further the nature of the intelligence gaps.[38]

Indeed, as one Counterterrorist Center official told us, the Intelligence Community "entirely missed" assessing the size and scope of al-Qa'ida's Agent X program: "If it hadn't been for finding a couple key pieces of paper [in Afghanistan]...we still might not have an appreciation for it. We just missed it because we did not have the data."[39] Other analysts noted that the documents and detainees accessed as a result of the war in Afghanistan combine to show that al-Qa'ida had a "major biological effort" and had made meaningful progress on its nuclear agenda.[40] Despite diligent collection efforts after 1998, it was "remarkable how much [the Community] had not identified [in Afghanistan]."[41]

Although the Intelligence Community had limited information about al-Qa'ida, it was not able to assemble a more complete picture of the group's efforts because it failed to penetrate the al-Qa'ida network. Human intelligence penetration of such highly compartmented, security-conscious groups, composed primarily of Middle Eastern males, is and will likely always be a highly difficult task.[42]

Moreover, for reasons we documented in our previous chapters on Iraq and Libya, technical collectors often have great difficulty tracking weapons of mass destruction efforts. This is especially true for non-state actors.

Analysis: Cross-Discipline Collaboration, Warning, and Evaluation

Finding 5

Analysis on al-Qa'ida's potential weapons of mass destruction development in Afghanistan did not benefit from leveraging different analytic disciplines.

Analysis of al-Qa'ida's unconventional weapons efforts in Afghanistan should bridge three different analytic disciplines—traditional regional analysis, state-focused weapons of mass destruction technical analysis, and terrorism analysis. Yet, in this case, analysts in these disciplines often did not work together. Organizational structures, information handling barriers (including data access and storage), and cultural disconnects blocked effective collaboration—including cooperation in testing analytical assumptions.

For example, traditional WMD analysts, who possess most of the Community's WMD technology expertise, focused mostly on state WMD programs—programs that often employ modern production and weaponization techniques. Terrorism analysts, on the other hand, needed to focus on lesser, often even crude, technologies more applicable to terrorists' needs and capabilities. Terrorism analysts even used a different vocabulary to describe unconventional weapons capabilities, using the term "CBRN"—chemical, biological, radiological, and nuclear—weapons programs instead of "WMD" programs. Afghanistan regional analysts focused more on political, economic, opium production, and military (Taliban) issues. In truth, credible analysis of al-Qa'ida's unconventional weapons programs required expertise from all three disciplines, but didn't get it.

This division among analysts was reflected in their competing assessments of al-Qa'ida's unconventional weapons capabilities in the year 2000. Some state-program analysts felt that terrorism analysts were overestimating the potential threat because non-state actors were technologically limited and, in their view, Afghanistan lacked the necessary resources and infrastructure for sophisticated weapons of mass destruction development. These differences in views would be re-examined after September 11,[43] but differences in analytic approach persisted. While here and elsewhere in this report we speak of the value of competitive analysis, here was an example that makes the point that competing analysis is of no use, even counterproductive, if there is no attempt at constructive dialogue and collaboration.

Finding 6

Analysts writing on al-Qa'ida's potential weapons of mass destruction efforts in Afghanistan did not adequately state the basis for or the assumptions underlying their most critical judgments. This analytic shortcoming is one that we have seen in our other studies as well, such as Iraq, and it points to the need to develop routine analytic practices for quantifying uncertainty and managing limited collection.

A lack of cooperation across disciplines was only one of the analytical shortcomings we observed. In general, the Community's analysts did not do enough to optimize the reliability of their predictive assessments. For example, analysts' most serious judgment—that Usama Bin Laden did not have a nuclear device—was made in the absence of *any* hard data. The Intelligence

Community assessed that fabrication of at least a "crude" nuclear device was within al-Qa'ida's capabilities, if it could obtain fissile material.[44] Despite the self-evident importance of the issue and the profound uncertainty surrounding it, documents we reviewed indicate that the conclusion that al-Qa'ida did not have a nuclear device was reached without in-depth technical analysis assessing potential al-Qa'ida capabilities,[45] a formal assessment of al-Qa'ida denial and deception capabilities related to Afghanistan, or tests of key assumptions underlying analytic judgments.

At the very least, analysts could have highlighted for policymakers the uncertain foundations of their key assessments. However, some analytic products on al-Qa'ida's unconventional weapons capabilities, both before and after September 11, offered highly speculative judgments without citing *any* evidentiary anchors, while others used single sources, and in some cases, dated information. As a result of these poor analytic practices, it is impossible to determine what information analysts were working with or how they weighted that information in formulating judgments. For example, a November 2001 assessment by CIA's Weapons Intelligence, Nonproliferation, and Arms Control Center pertaining to al-Qa'ida's possible nuclear capabilities offers numerous important judgments regarding the group's intentions to use nuclear weapons and its level of technical expertise. The report does not, however, explain the foundation for these assessments or cite prior reporting or finished products to support its conclusions.[46] The National Intelligence Estimates were the only products we reviewed that consistently laid out sources, collection issues, and intelligence gaps for readers, thus highlighting what the Community both did and did *not* know.

CONCLUSION

Key questions remain about al-Qa'ida and Afghanistan. There are critical intelligence gaps with regard to each al-Qa'ida unconventional weapons capability—chemical, biological, and nuclear. To address these problems, it is essential that the Community focus resources on the difficult task of increasing human intelligence collection on terrorist groups in general, and on al-Qa'ida in particular. We offer recommendations on how to improve our nation's human intelligence capabilities in Chapter Seven (Collection) of this report.

ENDNOTES

[1] National Intelligence Council (NIC), Title Classified (ICA 2001-07HC) (Oct. 22, 2001) at p. 4.

[2] *Id.* at pp. 4-5.

[3] *Id.* at p. 1.

[4] *Id.* at p. 7.

[5] *Id.* at p. 8.

[6] DCI's Counterterrorist Center, Title Classified (May 23, 2002) at p. 1.

[7] NIC, Title Classified (NIE 2004-08HC/I) (Dec. 2004) at p. 117; DIA, Submission to the Commission (March 2, 2005).

[8] *Id.*

[9] *Id.* at pp. 117-118.

[10] *Id.* at p. 118.

[11] DCI's Counterterrorist Center, Title Classified (May 23, 2002) at p. 2; DIA, Submission to the Commission (March 2, 2005).

[12] *Id.* at p. 1.

[13] NIC, Title Classified (ICA 2001-07HC) (Oct. 22, 2001).

[14] *Id.*

[15] *Id.*

[16] *Id.* at p. 1.

[17] DCI's Counterterrorist Center, Title Classified (May 23, 2002).

[18] In August 2002, CNN obtained a large archive of al-Qa'ida video. Among the 64 cassettes was material showing operatives experimenting with lethal chemical gas on three dogs. Nic Robertson, *Tapes Shed New Light on Bin Laden's Network* (CNN Aug. 18, 2002), *available at* archives.cnn.com/2002/US/ 08/18/terror.tape.main/ (accessed March 10, 2005).

[19] DCI's Counterterrorist Center, Title Classified (May 23, 2002) at p. 4.

[20] *Id.*

[21] CIA, Submission to the Commission (March 10, 2005).

[22] NIC, Title Classified (ICA 2001-07HC) (Oct. 22, 2001) at p. 8.

[23] *Id.*

[24] *Id.* The Intelligence Community was also aware that during the U.S. trial of Usama Bin Laden and others for the August 7, 1998 bombings of the East African embassies, prosecution witness Jan Ahmade al-Fadl detailed efforts to assist Bin Laden in an attempt to acquire uranium from a source in Sudan in late 1993 and early 1994.

[25] Tim Weiner, "Bin Laden Asserts He Has Nuclear Arms," *New York Times* (Nov. 10, 2001) at p. B4 (recounting Bin Laden's assertion in the Pakistani English-language daily newspaper, *Dawn*, that "[w]e have chemical and nuclear weapons as a deterrent and if America used them against us, we reserve the right to use them").

[26] CIA, Title Classified (WINPAC IA 2001-060) (Nov. 23, 2001).

[27] NIC, Title Classified (ICA 2001-07HC) (Oct. 22, 2001) at p. 8.

[28] DCI's Counterterrorist Center, Title Classified (May 23, 2002).

[29] NIC, Title Classified (ICA 2001-07HC) (Oct. 22, 2001).

[30] DCI Counterterrorist Center, Title Classified (May 23, 2002) at p. 3.

[31] *Id.*

[32] *Id.*

[33] *Id.* at p. 4.

[34] CIA, Submission to Commission (March 4, 2005).

[35] *Id.*

[36] NIC, Title Classified (ICA 2001-07HC) (Oct. 22, 2001) at p. 12.

[37] *Id.* at pp. 9, 12.

[38] *Id.* at p. 12.

[39] Interview with CIA analysts and other Intelligence Community senior analysts (Sept. 28, 2004).

[40] *Id.*

[41] *Id.*

[42] It was perhaps never more so than during much of the decade leading up to the September 11 attacks, when the Intelligence Community was only beginning to awaken to and focus in earnest on the emerging threat of non-state terrorist groups. During that time, collection and analytical emphasis remained primarily focused on state actors, rather than terrorist organizations. Concurrently, the Intelligence Community was facing a resource crisis as a part of post-Cold War budget cuts. In addition, based on our interviews with analysts from several agencies and our review of the written record, it is clear to us that between 1991 and 1996 (while Usama Bin Laden was operating in Sudan), the Intelligence Community paid little attention to collection activities in Afghanistan, or maintenance of the covert infrastructure the CIA had developed there as a result of its anti-Soviet activities in the 1980s.

[43] Interview with CIA analysts and other Intelligence Community senior analysts (Sept. 28, 2004).

[44] Title Classified (ICA 2001-07HC) (Oct. 22, 2001) at p. 12.

[45] We found one exception to the general lack of technical analysis and context, involving a Senior Executive Intelligence Memo in early 2001 in which CIA and nuclear experts speculated on why Usama Bin Laden might be seeking to use uranium with conventional explosives. Several technical scenarios were briefly examined.

[46] CIA, Title Classified (WINPAC IA 20001-060) (Nov. 23, 2001) at p. 1.

CHAPTER FOUR
TERRORISM: MANAGING
TODAY'S THREAT

Summary & Findings

As part of the Commission's charter to assess whether the Intelligence Community is properly postured to support the U.S. government's efforts to respond to the threats of the 21st century, we reviewed the progress the Intelligence Community has made in strengthening its counterterrorism capabilities since the September 11 attacks. We found that, although the Community has made significant strides in configuring itself to better protect the homeland and take the fight to terrorists abroad, much remains to be done to ensure the efficient use of limited resources among agencies responsible for counterterrorism intelligence. The U.S. government has not yet successfully defined the roles, missions, authorities, and the means of sharing information among our national and homeland security organs. Specifically, we found that:

- Information flow between the federal, state, local, and tribal levels—both up and down—is not yet well coordinated;

- Ambiguities in the respective roles and authorities of the National Counterterrorism Center and the Intelligence Community-wide Counterterrorist Center have not been resolved;

- Persistent conflicts over the roles, missions, and authorities of counterterrorism organizations may limit the Community's ability to warn of potential threats;

- Confusion and conflict regarding the roles, missions, and authorities of counterterrorism organizations have led to redundant efforts across the Community and inefficient use of limited resources; and

- The failure to manage counterterrorism resources from a Community perspective has limited the Intelligence Community's ability to understand and warn against terrorist use of weapons of mass destruction.

INTRODUCTION

Providing intelligence that facilitates the global war on terrorism and warns against terrorist use of weapons of mass destruction is currently the Intelligence Community's most vital mission. There is every reason to believe that this will remain the top priority for a generation or more. As a result, it is impossible to reach broad conclusions regarding the Intelligence Community's overall performance, and develop meaningful suggestions for improvement and reform, without an understanding of Intelligence Community capabilities with regard to countering the terrorist threat—both now and in the future.

We did not set out to study "terrorism" writ large; such an ambitious endeavor is beyond the scope and time allotted to this Commission. Rather, we chose to focus narrowly on examining several well-documented weaknesses inherent in the Intelligence Community's counterterrorism capabilities prior to the September 11 attacks, and on measures the Intelligence Community has subsequently taken to remedy those deficiencies. Our work thus focused on four primary areas:

1. The status of *information sharing* among federal agencies with foreign and domestic intelligence and law enforcement responsibilities, as well as between federal agencies and state, local, and tribal law enforcement;

2. The effectiveness of the *threat-warning* mechanism by which policymakers are kept informed of potential terror threats;

3. The ability to synthesize relevant *all-source terrorism analysis* in a timely manner; and

4. The Intelligence Community's ability to provide the intelligence necessary to interdict a planned *terrorist attack using a weapon of mass destruction.*

We conclude that although the Intelligence Community has made significant strides in each of these areas, much remains to be done. We found substantial evidence that information flows between the federal level and the state, local, and tribal levels—both upward and downward—are not yet well coordinated.

The roles and responsibilities among Intelligence Community agencies charged with primary responsibility for terrorism intelligence—both tactical and strategic—are not clearly defined. Sustained bureaucratic infighting and poor coordination prevent the Community from optimizing its resources to fight terrorism and alert policymakers to terrorist threats. Moreover, Community efforts to integrate technical and regional intelligence expertise with counterterrorism analysis do not provide sufficient focus on the threat posed by weapons of mass destruction in the hands of terrorists.

Resolving complex bureaucratic issues that transcend agency and subject-matter boundaries is usually difficult. However, three and a half years removed from the September 11 attacks, the persistence of agency coordination problems and unclear definitions of responsibility suggest to us a lack of Community leadership. The intelligence entities responsible for counterterrorism, especially terrorism analysis and threat warning, must be properly aligned, supported, and integrated for the task at hand.

SYSTEMIC FLAWS AS OF THE "SUMMER OF THREAT"

It is well-established that the Intelligence Community's structure and practices prior to the September 11 attacks were simply not up to the task of waging a global war on terror and protecting the homeland. The systemic Intelligence Community deficiencies during the "Summer of Threat" leading up to the attacks were summed up by the 9/11 Commission in two short sentences: "Information was not shared... Analysis was not pooled."[1] For present purposes, we highlight three of the specific failings identified by the 9/11 Commission in its examination of the Intelligence Community before September 11.

First, prior to September 11, there was a failure to share terrorism-related information rapidly and efficiently within agencies; among entities within the Intelligence Community tasked with producing intelligence to support counterterrorism efforts, and with state, local, and tribal law enforcement. For example, the FBI lacked basic computer capabilities, and did not share information even within its own organization. The CIA and the FBI were unwilling or unable to exchange information quickly and effectively with each other. And the Immigration and Naturalization Service and FBI did not learn from the CIA which identified terrorists were entering the United States and where they might be.[2]

Second, the Intelligence Community's analysts were ill-equipped to "connect the available dots" that might have led to advance warning of the September 11 attacks.[3] The "dispersal of effort on too many priorities" and the "declining attention to the craft of strategic analysis" were among the shortcomings identified by the 9/11 Commission's staff.[4] The CIA published many useful analytical reports on terrorism before the attack, but the Intelligence Community failed to produce a comprehensive, cross-cutting assessment of the threat. Analysts had difficulty carving out time to work on longer-term analyses that could have unified disparate elements of intelligence and pointed to the existence of a growing threat or particular vulnerability.[5]

Third, there was a lack of coordinated effort among the major federal agencies tasked with counterterrorism responsibilities, and confusion as to the roles and responsibilities of those agencies. Because the CIA and FBI lacked an optimized, cooperative analytical and operational effort, they were not well configured to detect and counter a threat, like that posed by the September 11 plotters, which "fell into the void between foreign and domestic threats." [6]

NOTABLE IMPROVEMENTS SINCE THE SEPTEMBER 11 ATTACKS

We found evidence that this grim picture has improved in many respects since September 11. In the information sharing arena, for example, consolidation of terrorist "watchlists" and expanded use of those lists for screening purposes have increased the likelihood of detecting known or suspected terrorists and obtaining additional information about them.[7] Moreover, counterterrorism information sharing has increased in quantitative terms—that is, terrorism intelligence products are disseminated more broadly, and are produced by more agencies, than before September 11.[8]

Similarly, the Intelligence Community has remedied many of the analysis-related problems it faced leading up to the September 11 attacks. In particular, the Community increased its analytic efforts on terrorism-related issues, including analytic support to operations, and at the President's direction established the Terrorist Threat Integration Center (TTIC, now the National

Counterterrorism Center, or NCTC) as the Community's center for analysis on these topics.[9] Many analysts arrive with substantial experience gained from working on terrorism accounts at the DCI's Counterterrorist Center (CTC),[10] an organization originally based at the CIA and staffed primarily by CIA officers that also includes representatives from throughout the Community. Analysts are increasingly being assigned to the NCTC for two-year rotations instead of short-term, stop-gap stints, enabling it to develop some badly-needed depth of expertise among its analytic corps.[11] Perhaps most significantly in light of the criticisms leveled by the 9/11 Commission, the NCTC is producing analytic products that integrate the comments and concerns of analysts across the Community.[12]

Moreover, the President's Terrorist Threat Report, a daily analytic publication produced by the NCTC, is truly a Community effort—with five agencies regularly contributing and a production schedule established by regular inter-agency meetings.[13] Prior to the September 11 attacks, it was far from clear that the intelligence resources of all the relevant agencies in the Intelligence Community were being tapped to create a complete picture of terror threats for senior policymakers. In contrast, the NCTC now hosts "ecumenical" meetings five days a week, in which managers representing CIA, FBI, DIA, NSA, and the Departments of State and Homeland Security[14] share and discuss intelligence regarding key terror threats.[15] The NCTC also meets five times weekly with senior representatives of CIA, FBI, DIA, and Homeland Security at a formal planning production board to divide responsibility for drafting analytical products (mainly those which will appear in the President's threat report) and to share information.[16] This process represents a level of formal and informal interaction on the terrorist threat among the primary intelligence agencies that simply did not exist prior to September 11, and that seems to clearly represent an improvement in the identification of threats and the mechanism through which threat warning intelligence is provided to senior policymakers.[17]

In our view the overall quality of finished analytic pieces on terrorism has also improved. Analysts in the Community now have access to substantially more information as the result of the Intelligence Community's heightened prioritization of the terrorism issue, the availability of intelligence from new collectors (particularly FBI and Homeland Security), and expanded access to information about human intelligence sources.[18]

Perhaps most importantly, from an operational perspective it is clear that many of CTC's efforts to disrupt terrorist networks and plots—partially enabled by its in-house analytic cadre—have been extraordinary successes. Put simply, CTC has brought the fight to the terrorists.

Finally, we have found that September 11 and the subsequent anthrax attacks not only triggered an aggressive counterterrorism response throughout the U.S. government, but also prompted the Community to reconsider its approach to the possible acquisition and use of weapons of mass destruction by terrorists, which we refer to by short-hand throughout this case study as "WMD terrorism." In December 2002, in the midst of post-September 11 bureaucratic realignment, the President announced a national strategic policy on weapons of mass destruction.[19] The President called for the application of new technologies, increased emphasis on intelligence collection and analysis, the strengthening of alliance relationships, and the establishment of new partnerships with former adversaries. The main pillars of the President's program included interdiction efforts, nonproliferation programs, and consequence management. In particular, he called for an emphasis on improving intelligence regarding weapons of mass destruction facilities and activities, expanding the interaction among U.S. intelligence, law enforcement, and military agencies, and enhancing intelligence cooperation with friends and allies.[20]

High-level attention within the policy and intelligence communities has had an important impact on the WMD terrorism issue. Our interviews suggest that the Intelligence Community now has a more extensive operational capability dedicated to the problem, has enhanced its intelligence reporting and analysis functions, and has instituted a more robust effort to address the problem domestically. Moreover, the Community appears at least to recognize the unique characteristics of unconventional weapons in the terrorism context, as other organizations have followed the CIA's lead in placing additional—although not yet sufficient—resources for WMD terrorism into the counterterrorism effort.

Since September 11, the reallocation of resources to respond to WMD terrorism has resulted in significant improvements in both foreign and domestic intelligence. We understand that within the Intelligence Community, sources have gotten better, the amount of data available has dramatically increased, and intelligence is more harmonized, consistent, and less reliant on vague "chatter." On the domestic side, there have been significant attempts to disrupt terrorist means of delivery.[21]

Despite all of these noteworthy developments, our study found that the Community still has a long way to go before it can claim to have optimized its counterterrorism capabilities or fully fixed the serious deficiencies that existed prior to September 11. We thus turn to the areas where the picture is not as promising.

We begin by focusing on needed improvements in the sharing of terrorism information with state, local, and tribal governments. Next, we examine the more general bureaucratic "turf war" between agencies, and the pronounced lack of clarity as to the roles, responsibilities, and authorities involving various entities tasked with the counterterrorism mission—particularly the NCTC and the Counterterrorist Center. Finally, we examine the continuing coordination problems between the CIA, FBI, and Homeland Security in addressing the threat posed by WMD terrorism.

INFORMATION SHARING: MUCH ROOM FOR IMPROVEMENT

Finding 1

Although terrorism information sharing has improved significantly since September 11, major change is still required to institute effective information sharing across the Intelligence Community and with state, local, and tribal governments.

For a number of years before the September 11 attacks, the Intelligence Community closely followed the al-Qa'ida terrorist threat, yet failed to adequately exploit information it had concerning several individuals who were either involved in the planning of or participated in the attacks.[22] Although the 9/11 Commission did not find that better information sharing would have prevented the attacks, at least nine of the ten "operational opportunities" that the commission identified as missed opportunities to possibly thwart the plot pertain to some form of a failure to share information.[23] These perceived failures have made "information sharing" a mantra for intelligence reform for the three and a half years since the attacks.

We have found that as a general matter, the Intelligence Community has sought to improve terrorism information sharing by modifying the structures and processes for sharing that were in place prior to September 11—rather than establishing wholly new approaches. We agree with the recent assessment of the Intelligence Community Inter-Agency Information Sharing Working Group, which found that "[a] great deal of energy...is being expended across the [Intelligence Community] to improve information sharing. However, the majority of these initiatives *will not produce the enduring institutional change required to address our current threat environment.*"[24]

The importance of effective sharing of information at all levels of the Intelligence Community is discussed in several chapters of our report, but particularly in Chapters Nine (Information Sharing) and Eight (Analysis). In this section, we specifically address the Intelligence Community's efforts, since September 11, to improve the sharing of terrorism information across the Intelligence Community and with state, local, and tribal governments. Our specific findings are categorized in four broad areas.

First, we found substantial improvement in information sharing relating to terrorist watchlisting and screening. "Watchlisting"—the process of assembling databases of known or suspected terrorists—was not well coordinated among federal agencies prior to September 11, but several effective reforms have been implemented in the wake of the attacks.[25] For example, the new Terrorist Screening Center—an interagency effort to consolidate terrorist watchlists and provide operational support for federal employees around the world, 24 hours a day, seven days a week—now administers a single database that combines international and domestic terrorism data provided by the NCTC and FBI. The database also integrates information from immigration and customs offices, the Transportation Security Administration, the U.S. Marshals Service, Department of Defense, and Interpol. The Terrorist Screening Center ensures that government investigators, screeners, and agents are working from the same comprehensive information and that they have access simultaneously to information and experience that will allow them to act quickly when a suspected terrorist is screened and stopped.

Second, we have found that the sharing of counterterrorism information has increased in quantitative terms—more terrorism information is being shared with more entities both inside and outside the Intelligence Community than before the September 11 attacks. This has largely occurred through the increased use of "tearlines"—the practice of generating intelligence reports at several different classification levels so it can be shared with a cross-section of federal, state, local, and tribal officials—which has resulted in more releasable information being provided to consumers.[26] And security-based sharing restrictions have been substantially reduced, allowing analysts and security personnel greater access to the information they need to do their jobs.[27]

All this being said, problems remain. While the Intelligence Community has reduced its use of restrictions on further dissemination of intelligence products without the consent of the originator,[28] inconsistent application of dissemination restrictions, such as ORCON ("originator controlled"), continue to impede the flow of useful terrorism information.[29] In relations with state, local, and tribal authorities, more terrorism information is being shared, but federal officials continue to have difficulty establishing consistent and coordinated lines of communication with these officials.[30] In this regard, we have found that there is no comprehensive policy or program for achieving the appropriate balance regarding what terrorism information to provide to state, local, and tribal authorities and how to provide it. Additionally, the redundant lines of communication through which terrorism-related information is passed—for example, through the Joint Terrorism Task Forces, Anti-Terrorism Advisory Councils, Homeland Security Information Network, TTIC Online, Law Enforcement Online Network, Centers for Disease Control alerts, and Public Health Advisories, to name just a few—present a deluge of information for which state, local, and tribal authorities are neither equipped nor trained to process, prioritize, and disseminate.

Our third category of findings relates to the sharing of information to ensure that analysts throughout the Intelligence Community have the widest possible access to information regardless of which agency collects the information. Today, the primary means of sharing information throughout the Community continues to be through interagency personnel exchange programs, such as the model used by the NCTC. These personnel exchanges can be quite effective, but they do nothing to improve the flow of information throughout those agencies or enable agencies to engage in competitive analysis based on access to the same set of information. Collectors of information continue to operate as though they "own" information and, in fact, collectors largely control access to the information that they generate. Decisions to withhold information are typically based on rules that are neither clearly defined nor consistently applied, with no system in place to hold collectors accountable for inappropriately withholding information.

Finally, we have found that there is currently no single entity in the Intelligence Community with the responsibility and authority to impose a centralized approach to sharing information. Although the NCTC model has certainly facilitated improved information sharing on counterterrorism issues, it lacks sufficient authority and resources necessary to provide strong leadership in this area.

COUNTERTERRORISM WARNING AND ANALYSIS: A STRUGGLE BETWEEN AGENCIES

Notwithstanding significant gains in terrorism intelligence since September 11, a number of problems remain. Our study found evidence of bitter bureaucratic "turf battles" between agencies, and a pronounced lack of clarity as to the roles, responsibilities, and authorities of various entities tasked with the counterterrorism mission. Specifically, this interagency jockeying over overlapping counterterrorism analytical responsibilities indicates that major organizational issues affecting the allocation of resources, assignment of responsibilities, coordination of analysis, and effective warning remain unresolved.

Who's in Charge of Counterterrorism Analysis and Warning?

Finding 2

Ambiguities in the respective roles and authorities of the NCTC and CTC have not been resolved, and the two agencies continue to fight bureaucratic battles to define their place in the war on terror. The result has been unnecessary duplication of effort and the promotion of unproductive competition between the two organizations.

The Community's inability to implement a "one team, one fight" strategy in the terror war may be attributed both to ongoing bureaucratic battles between agencies charged with responsibility for counterterrorism analysis and warning, as well as the failure of Community leaders to effectively resolve these disputes and clearly define agency roles and authorities. The conflict and ambiguity surrounding the role of the Terrorist Threat Integration Center during its abbreviated existence starkly illustrates both points.

After the September 11 attacks, TTIC was created for the purpose of improving the sharing of terrorist threat data and the analysis of terrorism-related information. However, as the Markle Foundation has reported, "the very fact of the TTIC's creation caused confusion within the federal government and among state and local governments" about the respective roles of TTIC and other federal agencies responsible for counterterrorism analysis and terrorist threat assessments.[31] Even today—despite being designated by the intelligence reform act as the preeminent, integrated center for threat warning and analysis—the NCTC continues to have difficulty asserting its primacy for the terrorism warning mission.

This dispute—and the potential problems to which it could lead—has been apparent since February 2003, when Senators Collins and Levin highlighted the issue in a joint letter (the "Collins-Levin Letter") to the Secretary of Homeland Security, the Director of TTIC, and the Directors of Central Intelligence and the FBI. The letter asked that the officials clarify responsibilities among counterterrorism elements of the U.S. government. In their April 2004 response, the agency heads stated that "TTIC has primary responsibility in the [U.S. government] for terrorism analysis (except analysis relating solely to purely domestic terrorism) and is responsible for the day-to-day terrorism analysis provided to the President and other senior policymakers."[32] In order to make it possible for TTIC to achieve this mission, the letter further stated that the DCI, in consultation with the other leaders of the Intelligence Community, would determine by June 1, 2004, what additional analytic resources would be transferred to TTIC from the CTC.[33]

Despite this unequivocal statement, TTIC was never able to fully perform its mission. Other entities, CTC in particular, differed over the level of support they should provide to TTIC and resisted supplying it with an adequate number of detailees—thus hampering TTIC's ability to assume the leading role assigned to it.

In May 2004, TTIC Director John Brennan sent correspondence to then-Director of Central Intelligence George Tenet, explaining how TTIC intended to carry out the responsibilities identified in the Collins-Levin letter. He warned that lacking significant new analytic resources, TTIC would not be able to carry out the mission of having "primary responsibility" for providing terrorism analysis to the President and senior policymakers.[34]

The next month, Director Brennan sent the DCI a follow-up memorandum entitled "TTIC at the Breaking Point." In this memorandum, he argued that other intelligence agencies had failed to provide sufficient numbers of analysts to TTIC, and that the personnel that had been provided possessed only limited competency or a low level of experience. He further noted that these agencies continued to insist on developing their own independent counterterrorism analytical capabilities. This organizational multiplicity, Director Brennan argued, had created not only a "dangerous shortfall in TTIC's analytic resources and mission," but also "unnecessary analytic redundancy within the intelligence, law enforcement, defense, and homeland security communities."[35] In sum, Director Brennan wrote, a general refusal by entities within the Intelligence Community to "sign on to the fundamental premise that resources and mission will migrate to TTIC" had left the Center "unable to fulfill the mission of 'primary responsibility' for terrorism analysis in the U.S. government," and had forced the U.S. government into a "retreat from the integration model" of terrorism analysis and threat warning.[36]

Approximately one week later—on July 2, 2004—then-Deputy Director of Central Intelligence John McLaughlin attempted to address Director Brennan's concerns by outlining (at the DCI's request) a "division of resources and analytical responsibilities" between CIA and TTIC.[37] In interviews with this Commission, Director Brennan repeatedly stated that he had not received an official answer to his urgent memos of May and June.[38] When later asked specifically about the July 2 response, he dismissed it as failing to provide a meaningful answer to the basic questions he had raised regarding allocation of responsibilities for counterterrorism analysis and warning—despite the fact that the July 2 memorandum does in fact deal with virtually every issue highlighted by Director Brennan.[39]

The memorandum may not have been the answer Director Brennan wanted, but it certainly constituted a clear attempt by the Community's leadership to allocate roles, responsibilities, and resources among counterterrorism organizations. Addressed to CIA's Deputy Directors for Intelligence and Operations, as well as to Director Brennan, the memorandum provided for the immediate transfer of 60 personnel to TTIC, but it did not provide the "primary responsibility" over terrorism analysis for TTIC that Director Brennan had requested.

In fact, the memorandum declined to grant TTIC sole authority over analysis pertaining to international terrorist networks, instead explicitly stating that other agencies (including CTC) would continue sharing that function. The memorandum acknowledged that this would result in redundancy, but argued that "on something as important as terrorism analysis," some overlap between agencies was to be preferred.[40]

Although we believe that excessive redundancy in Community counterterrorism efforts is wasteful of scarce resources and thus counterproductive (see our discussion below), we express no view on the overall merits of the organizational plan and division of labor outlined in the July 2, 2004 memorandum. However, it is of great significance, we think, that the Community was ultimately unable to enforce that plan—or, to date, *any* plan—and bring an end to the interagency squabbling between CTC and NCTC.

We have been told that the plan outlined in the July 2 memorandum fell victim to bureaucratic neglect and rapid change within the Community; shortly after its distribution there was turnover in the DCI's office, and ambiguities fostered by creation of the NCTC by executive order and, later, passage of the intelligence reform act, raised new questions about the designated roles of the nation's counterterrorism organizations. Our study suggests that there may have been another factor, as well: the entrenched opposition of both CTC and NCTC to effectively cooperating or consolidating aspects of their authorities.

The fact that Director Brennan did not regard clear direction from the DCI to be an "answer" to his pleas to resolve confusion over roles, resources, and responsibilities—presumably because it did not allocate the prerogatives to his organization that he had requested—speaks volumes about the hardened mindsets of the two organizations' leadership, and their desire to protect or expand their bureaucratic "turf." As the Director of the Counterterrorist Center characterized the relationship, the Center "is fighting a war with TTIC." [41]

Although recent passage of the intelligence reform act may resolve issues related to responsibilities and resources,[42] the history of the dispute tempers our optimism. Whatever the precise allocation of resources and responsibilities is to be, the DNI must act quickly to resolve the issue. Absent strong leadership, other organizations in the Intelligence Community may continue to resist providing resources to NCTC, as they did with TTIC, and may dispute its "primary" role in coordinating terrorism intelligence.[43] Alternatively,

NCTC may resist well-reasoned direction to permit CTC to continue performing several of its important functions. If so, the war between agencies that are tasked to fight the war on terror will continue. Unfortunately, such a conflict constitutes far more than a common bureaucratic dispute, the sort of administrative power struggle so common in the corridors of government. Rather, it has profound operational implications for the ability of the Intelligence Community to perform the all-important function of providing terrorism analysis and warning information to policymakers.

A Failure to Warn with One Voice

Finding 3

Persisting ambiguities and conflicts in the roles, missions, and authorities of counterterrorism organizations hamper effective warning.

The dispute between the NCTC and CTC is especially troubling in the context of threat warning—the process by which threat information is conveyed to decisionmakers in time for them to take action to manage or deter the threat. Continuing disagreements about the two offices' roles and missions have in the past led to inconsistent warning messages being conveyed to decisionmakers and—far more troubling—these warnings were conveyed in a manner that may have sowed confusion.

What Part of "Warning" Should Be Competitive?

For present purposes, we divide warning into two components: (1) the *analytic* function that produces a warning and (2) the *process of communicating* those threat judgments to decisionmakers. As a general matter, while we strongly endorse competitive *warning analysis* (*i.e.*, competition in the first component of warning), we believe that the process of communicating threats to decisionmakers (*i.e.*, the second component) should be coordinated and integrated. We say this because we do not believe decisionmakers are well-served by incoherent, uncoordinated warnings of impending threats. Rather, warning should be presented to decisionmakers in a coordinated manner that makes clear the level of certainty with which they are held.

According to NCTC officials, the NCTC must have primacy, if not exclusivity, in providing warning intelligence to the President and controlling the analytical resources required for this mission.[44] NCTC principals acknowledge that CTC needs to retain analytical capability to directly support the CIA's Directorate of Operations (DO)—and to continue the spectacular successes the DO has achieved in the war on terror.[45] However, as a general matter they assert that it is improper to "divide effort when it comes to terrorism,"[46] and have claimed as a core responsibility the "production of terrorist threat warnings, advisories, and alerts," which are to be "issued by [the NCTC] alone or as formally coordinated products of the 'Warn 7.'"[47] Moreover, in its role as coordinator of the President's Terrorist Threat Report (PTTR), the NCTC insists that it has oversight responsibility for determining what terrorism analysis is provided to the President.[48] In sum, the NCTC conceives its mission as providing coordinated threat warning and analytical reports—reflecting "diversity of viewpoint but coordination of common response"—to senior policymakers.[49]

Perhaps unsurprisingly, CTC does not embrace this division of labor. CTC views itself as the preeminent counterterrorism entity within the Intelligence Community.

In CTC's view, NCTC's main contribution to the terrorism fight lies in its access to intelligence information and databases—both foreign and domestic.[50] As a result, CTC leaders expressed to us the view that the NCTC should be responsible for generating an integrated Community view of threats, but should *not* have the dominant voice in counterterrorism analysis and warning.[51] A recent example of where this theoretical disagreement had concrete consequences is discussed in our classified report, but cannot be detailed in an unclassified format.

Ideally, a single warning vehicle (such as the President's Terrorist Threat Report, now provided daily by the NCTC) should provide a forum for ensuring that policymakers do not receive inconsistent messages. But we have seen evidence that this is not always so. It is further possible that legislation creating the NCTC may obviate such interagency conflicts in the future—but we are only guardedly optimistic.[52] In this sense, we believe that the DNI will have to create mechanisms by which competitive analysis for warning is maintained, and the dissemination of warnings is carefully coordinated. We address this issue more fully in Chapter Eight of our report (Analysis). More broadly, the DNI will have to force the nation's counterterrorism organizations to concentrate more fully on fighting terrorists, rather than each other.

Maintenance of Redundant Capabilities

Finding 4

Persistent ambiguities and conflicts in the roles, missions, and authorities of counterterrorism organizations with regard to analysis and warning have led to redundant efforts across the Community and inefficient use of limited resources.

An absence of clearly defined roles and authorities with regard to analysis and warning leads inevitably to competition in key capabilities, and redundant efforts across the Community. For example, we spoke with a senior analytic manager who recounted one incident in which a single raw intelligence report spurred five different agencies to write five separate pieces, all reaching the same conclusion. Not only were analysts' efforts redundant, but policymakers were then required to read through all five papers to look for subtle differences in perspective that could have been better conveyed in a single, coordinated paper.[53]

This phenomenon is especially troubling given the scarce analytic resources available for counterterrorism efforts. Agencies expressed serious concern about their ability to engage in long-term strategic analysis given the demands generated by customer questions and daily indicators of new threats.[54] For example, the NCTC spends roughly 70 percent of its time on immediate threats,[55] primarily because analysts have to run each potential threat to ground, even if it seems suspect from the outset.[56] Similarly, the FBI estimates that about 50 percent of analysts' time is spent on direct operational support.[57] All of these requirements tend to leave little time and resources for thoughtful, strategic work on new and emerging threats. All of this is, of course, compounded by the significant trouble agencies are experiencing in retaining qualified and experienced analysts.[58]

Despite this serious resource issue, there is ongoing evidence of an interagency failure to cooperate and efficiently divide responsibility in counterterrorism analysis. For example, NCTC WMD analysts with whom we spoke described their willingness and capability to engage in long-term, strategic analysis on behalf of the counterterrorism community.[59] But when a senior CTC official—who noted the need for such analysis and lamented the difficulty of allocating time and resources for it in the context of CTC's operationally-driven environment—was asked about the possibility of using NCTC resources for that purpose, he stated bluntly that "[NCTC] doesn't have those capabilities."[60] It is unclear whether such statements reflect a lack of understanding between the two entities concerning complementary capabilities that could be mutually leveraged, institutional resentment and an unwillingness to operate collaboratively, or simply an ongoing struggle over personnel resources.

Again, although recent passage of the intelligence reform act may resolve issues related to responsibilities and resources,[61] we are not optimistic that anything in the legislation itself resolves the dispute. We address the issues associated with managing scarce analytic resources more fully in Chapters Six (Leadership and Management) and Eight (Analysis).

THE FAILURE TO MANAGE COMMUNITY RESOURCES IN RESPONSE TO THE WMD TERRORISM THREAT

Finding 5

The failure to manage counterterrorism resources from a Community perspective has limited the Intelligence Community's ability to understand and warn against terrorist use of weapons of mass destruction.

Recognizing that the worst terrorist attack would be one involving weapons of mass destruction, some elements within the Community have begun to incorporate analytic and collection capabilities with respect to the WMD terrorism threat into their counterterrorism organizations. At the same time, the CIA's Weapons Intelligence, Nonproliferation, and Arms Control Center provides intelligence support aimed at protecting the United States and its interests from all advanced weapons threats. Our review of the relationship among these various entities reveals that some systemic weaknesses are preventing the development of a focused, integrated, well-resourced bureaucracy that can most effectively combat the worst-case threat of a homeland terrorist attack. Specifically:

■ There is no clear leadership or bureaucratic architecture defining roles and responsibilities for WMD terrorism. This adversely affects analysis, collection, and threat warning; and

■ The domestic intelligence effort on WMD terrorism is lagging behind the U.S. government's foreign intelligence capabilities.

Defining Roles and Responsibilities for the WMD Terrorism Threat

Notwithstanding the President's National Strategy to Combat Weapons of Mass Destruction promulgated in December 2002, the overriding concern of key officials whom we have interviewed is that, within the U.S. government, there is no overall direction and coordination on WMD terrorism. As the chief of the FBI's WMD Countermeasures Unit rhetorically asked, "[w]ho is ultimately responsible for preventing the use of a WMD?" [62]

The most significant consequence of the lack of coordination is that each organization appears to be defining its own mission and trying to make sure it has the resources to be self-sufficient across a broad range of responsibilities.[63] The result is predictable: duplicative roles, power vacuums where individual organizations assert their authority, and confusion within the Community. As the NCTC's head of analysis observed, it is necessary not only to clarify affirmative roles and responsibilities, but also to delineate those responsibilities for which agencies are *not* responsible.[64]

For example, despite changes since September 11, coordination problems between the FBI and the CIA continue to disrupt analysis on WMD terrorism and operations against weapons of mass destruction targets. As the FBI has expanded its overseas operations and the CTC tries not to lose its targets when they travel to the United States, coordination is essential. However, according to the head of the CTC's WMD unit, there is no sense of "jointness," or shared mission, on the part of the FBI and CTC, despite the co-location of portions of both organizations.[65]

It appears that coordination among domestic agencies responsible for responding to a potential WMD terrorist threat also suffers from confusion and a lack of coordination. For instance, the FBI told us that the Department of Homeland Security had, in response to a possible threat, taken the initiative to start moving radiation detection resources to New York during the Republican National Convention without coordinating with the Bureau. Subsequent to the move, the "threat" was revealed to be a legitimate movement of a medical isotope.[66] Had even the most elemental communication and coordination taken place—in the form of a phone call from Homeland Security to the FBI—this fact might have surfaced earlier, thereby avoiding the squandering of limited counterterrorism resources.[67]

Perhaps most alarming is the allegation that when terrorism cases move from a purely foreign focus to a domestic emphasis requiring a hand-off in primary responsibility from the CIA to the FBI, the CIA finds it difficult to obtain information from the FBI about ongoing investigations.[68] Such gaps in cooperation, occurring at the vital fault line between foreign and domestic intelligence, are reminiscent of the "void" that the September 11 attack plotters operated in to achieve their objectives.[69]

The stark division between the Intelligence Community's WMD terrorism programs and the Community's state-based weapons of mass destruction programs further hampers the WMD terrorism effort.[70] As our case study of al-Qa'ida in Afghanistan also confirms, the personnel who work the WMD terrorism issue mostly coordinate with their state program counterparts on an *ad hoc* basis. Efforts have been made to remedy this problem within CIA,[71] but we think it vital that such cooperation be greatly expanded throughout the Community.

The Domestic Intelligence Effort on WMD Terrorism

While the FBI has responded to the threat posed by WMD terrorism by increasing the resources dedicated to this issue, the FBI's efforts in this regard remain subordinated to the broader war on terror. For example, approximately a year ago, the FBI committed (on paper) to staffing its WMD Integration and Targeting Unit—the unit responsible for providing expertise on WMD terrorism—with a total of 26 staff positions. Today, the unit has only two people— the unit chief and a single intelligence analyst.[72]

Unsurprisingly, the FBI, like other agencies responsible for the WMD terrorism threat, is having difficulty finding people with the right expertise and has yet to develop a specific career track or program for developing expertise regarding the threat.[73] Other agencies having responsibility for WMD terrorism are also understaffed, and the few experts that do exist are suffering from burnout.[74] To its credit, the FBI has acknowledged its need for more resources in this area,[75] but it is clear to us that the FBI's weaknesses are not susceptible to a quick fix. We discuss our proposals addressing this and related issues more fully in Chapters Six (Leadership and Management), Eight (Analysis), and Ten (Intelligence at Home).

CONCLUSION

The Intelligence Community's capabilities with regard to current terror threats have improved significantly since September 11, 2001. Nevertheless, the continued lack of definitional clarity as to roles and responsibilities in the war on terrorism, and ongoing conflicts among key counterterrorism agencies, constitute an ongoing challenge—and one that we believe should be foremost on the mind of the new DNI.

ENDNOTES

[1] National Commission on Terrorist Attacks Upon the United States, *The 9/11 Commission Report* (2004) (hereinafter "9/11 Commission Report") at p. 353.

[2] *Id.* at p. 371.

[3] *Id.* at pp. 277, 408-09.

[4] Eleventh Public Hearing of the National Commission on Terrorist Attacks Upon the United States, *Staff Statement Number 11* (April 14, 2004) at p. 3.

[5] *Id.* at p. 5.

[6] 9/11 Commission Report at p. 263.

[7] Interview with Terrorist Screening Center official (Nov. 9, 2004).

[8] Interview with TTIC senior officials (Oct. 19, 2004); Interview with DIA (JITF-CT) analysts (Oct. 26, 2004); Interview with Department of State (INR) analysts (Nov. 3, 2004).

[9] NCTC was created on December 6, 2004 pursuant to Executive Order. The establishment of NCTC is also codified by the *Intelligence Reform and Terrorism Prevention Act of 2004* (hereinafter "IRTPA"). Under IRTPA, NCTC subsumes the primary duties of TTIC, and is intended to serve as the governmental entity responsible for counterterrorism analysis and warning and for developing strategic operational plans for counterterrorism operations conducted by the U.S. government. Nevertheless, although the name has changed, the organization and its bureaucratic challenges remain essentially the same, and the identical problems surrounding TTIC that are discussed in this report threaten to envelope the newly-created NCTC. In this report, for ease of reference, when we use the term NCTC, we refer to both NCTC and its predecessor, TTIC, unless otherwise noted.

[10] Interview with TTIC senior analyst (Nov. 5, 2004).

[11] Interview with TTIC (WMD) analysts (Oct. 19, 2004).

[12] *Id.*

[13] Interview with TTIC senior analyst (Oct. 19, 2004); Interview with TTIC senior analyst (Nov. 5, 2004).

[14] Along with NCTC, these agencies have been dubbed the "Warn 7." Interview with TTIC senior analyst (Oct. 19, 2004).

[15] Interview with TTIC senior analyst (Oct. 19, 2004). During the "Summer of Threat" prior to the September 11 attacks, the interagency Counterterrorism Security Group (CSG), headed by Richard Clarke, had access to disseminated intelligence from several agencies, but it did not have the capability to integrate intelligence from each agency on a daily basis, nor did it have access to the internal, non-disseminated information of intelligence agencies. 9/11 Commission Report at p. 255.

[16] Interview with NCTC senior official (Feb. 4, 2005); Interview with TTIC senior analyst (Oct. 19, 2004); Interview with TTIC senior analyst (Nov. 5, 2004).

[17] The PTTR is produced six days a week, usually runs three to five pages in length, and may have, on average, one to four articles. It is delivered to the President and senior policymakers by the PDB briefers. Interview with TTIC senior analyst (Nov. 5, 2004).

[18] Interview with CTC (WMD) official (Oct. 22, 2004).

[19] National Security Presidential Directive 17, *National Strategy to Combat Weapons of Mass Destruction* (Dec. 2002).

[20] *Id.*

[21] Interview with FBI (WMD) officials (Oct. 14, 2004); Interview with FBI (Counterterrorism) official (Oct. 22, 2004).

[22] The 9/11 Commission identifies several instances in which sharing of information might have led to further investigation that could have revealed the plot, but does not conclude that the sharing of any specific pieces of information actually held would have likely led to preventing the attacks. *See, e.g.*, 9/11 Commission Report at pp. 272, 276.

[23] *Id.* at pp. 355-356.

[24] *Calibration Report: Intelligence Community Collaboration and Information Sharing to Win the War on Terrorism: Phase 1* (May 2004) at p. ES-1 (hereinafter "IC Inter-Agency ISWG May 2004 Calibration Report") (emphasis in original).

[25] These watchlisting reforms were undertaken at the direction of the President, primarily under Homeland Security Presidential Directive 6, *Integration and Use of Screening Information* (Sept. 16, 2003).

[26] This finding is consistent with the conclusion of the Inter-Agency Information Sharing Working Group. *FY2004 Congressionally Directed Actions on Information Sharing, Consolidated Report of the Information Sharing Working Group* (Dec. 14, 2004) at p. 23.

[27] Interview with TTIC senior analyst (Oct. 19, 2004); Interview with TTIC senior official (Oct. 19, 2004); Interview with DIA (JITF-CT) analysts (Oct. 26, 2004); Interview with State Department (INR) analysts (Nov. 3, 2004); Interview with FBI (National Joint Terrorism Task Force) official (Nov. 5, 2004); Interview with CIA (DO) official (Nov. 8, 2004).

[28] Interview with TTIC senior official (Oct. 19, 2004); Interview with DIA (JITF-CT) analysts (Oct. 26, 2004). Between 2001 and 2003, the rate of use of originator controls on terrorism-related reporting across the Intelligence Community dropped by approximately 50 percent. Seventh Public Hearing of the National Commission on Terrorist Attacks Upon the United States (Jan. 26, 2004) (Statement of Russell E. Travers, TTIC Deputy CIO for Information Sharing).

[29] The rule of originator control, or ORCON, allows the agency that originates information to retain control over its dissemination and declassification (if it is classified) or its release to non-governmental parties. *See, e.g.*, IC Inter-Agency ISWG May 2004 Calibration Report, NRO submission, Appendix B at p. B-37 (listing ORCON as a cultural barrier that "must...be addressed"); *id.*, DIA submission, Appendix B at p. B-12 (citing FBI and NSA ORCON dissemination as constraining assembly of terrorism intelligence database).

[30] Interview with CIA (Collection Concepts Development Center) official (Oct. 7, 2004); Interview with FBI (WMD) officials (Oct. 13, 2004); Interview with emergency preparedness official of the Office of the Governor of Virginia (Nov. 10, 2004); Homeland Security Advisory Council, *Final Report: Intelligence and Information Sharing Initiative* (Dec. 2004).

[31] Markle Foundation Task Force on National Security in the Information Age, *Creating a Trusted Information Network for Homeland Security* (2003) at pp. 7-8. The Markle Foundation funds a variety of studies that analyze the potential of new technologies to address critical public sector needs, particularly in the areas of health and national security.

[32] Letter from Thomas J. Ridge, Secretary of Homeland Security; Robert S. Mueller, III,

Director Federal Bureau of Investigation; George J. Tenet, Director of Central Intelligence; and John O. Brennan, Director Terrorist Threat Integration Center; to The Honorable Susan M. Collins, Chairwoman Senate Committee on Governmental Affairs, and The Honorable Carl Levin, Ranking Member (Apr. 13, 2004) at p. 2.

[33] *Id.*

[34] Memorandum from John O. Brennan, TTIC Director, to Director of Central Intelligence (May 19, 2004) at pp. 2-4, 6-8.

[35] Memorandum from John O. Brennan, TTIC Director, to Director of Central Intelligence (June 23, 2004).

[36] *Id.*

[37] Memorandum from John E. McLaughlin, Deputy Director of Central Intelligence (July 2, 2004).

[38] Interviews with John O. Brennan, TTIC Director (Sept. 22, 2004 and Feb. 8, 2005).

[39] Interview with John O. Brennan, Interim Director of NCTC (March 15, 2005). The July 2 memorandum does not directly discuss the counterterrorism responsibilities of FBI, DHS or the Defense Department, which are mentioned briefly in Director Brennan's first memorandum.

[40] *Id.*

[41] Interview with Director of CTC (Nov. 5, 2004). Other CTC personnel expressed the same sentiment, using nearly identical language. Interview with senior CTC official (Oct. 22, 2004).

[42] IRTPA at § 1021 (adding section 119 to the National Security Act to establish the NCTC in law, provide its primary missions, and outline the reporting chain of its director).

[43] *Id.* at § 1021 (adding section 119(d) to the National Security Act to provide that one of the primary missions of the NCTC is to "serve as the primary organization in the United States Government for analyzing and integrating all intelligence…pertaining to terrorism").

[44] *See, e.g.*, Interview with TTIC senior official (Feb. 4, 2005).

[45] Interview with TTIC senior analyst (Oct. 19, 2004).

[46] Interview with TTIC senior official (Feb. 4, 2005).

[47] NCTC, CIA, FBI, DIA, NSA, and the Departments of State and Homeland Security comprise the so-called "Warn 7." *Id.*; Memorandum from John O. Brennan, TTIC Director, to Director of Central Intelligence (May 19, 2004) at ¶ 7.

[48] Letter from Thomas J. Ridge, Secretary of Homeland Security; Robert S. Mueller, III, Director Federal Bureau of Investigation; George J. Tenet, Director of Central Intelligence; and John O. Brennan, Director Terrorist Threat Integration Center; to The Honorable Susan M. Collins, Chairwoman, Senate Committee on Governmental Affairs, and The Honorable Carl Levin, Ranking Member (April 13, 2004) at p. 3; IRTPA at § 1021(f)(D).

[49] Interview with TTIC senior analyst (Oct. 19, 2004).

[50] Under IRTPA, NCTC serves not only as the governmental entity responsible for counterterrorism analysis and warning, but is also responsible for developing strategic operational plans for counterterrorism operations conducted by the U.S. government. It is our understanding that details regarding how NCTC will perform its strategic operational planning role have not fully been resolved. Accordingly, this report does not address NCTC's responsibility for this strategic planning function. IRTPA at § 1021.

[51] Interviews with CTC senior officials (Oct. 22, 2004 and Nov. 5, 2004).

[52] The law vests the NCTC with authority to "disseminate terrorism information, including current terrorism threat analysis," to senior policymakers, but does not grant it exclusive authority to do so. Moreover, the NCTC is given "primary responsibility within the United States Government for conducting net assessments of terrorist threats." But the law also states that nothing in its text "shall limit the authority of [other agencies] to conduct net assessments." IRTPA at §§ 1021(f)(1)(G), 1021(f)(2).

[53] Interview with FBI (Counterterrorism) official (Nov. 4, 2004).

[54] Interview with CTC official (Oct. 22, 2004); Interviews with TTIC senior analyst and TTIC (WMD) analysts (Oct. 19, 2004); Interview with DIA analysts and managers (Oct. 26, 2004); *see also* Interviews with former senior Intelligence Community officials (Sept. 28, 2004 and Oct. 15, 2004).

[55] Interview with TTIC senior analyst (Oct. 19, 2004).

[56] Interview with TTIC (WMD) analysts (Oct. 19, 2004).

[57] Interview with FBI (Counterterrorism) official (Nov. 4, 2004).

[58] CTC cited burnout as a critical retention problem. Interview with CTC (WMD) official (Oct. 22, 2004). DIA cited examples of analysts leaving to work fewer hours for higher salaries with contractors. Interview with DIA analysts and managers (Oct. 26, 2004).

[59] Interview with TTIC (WMD) analysts (Oct. 19, 2004).

[60] Interview with senior CTC official (Oct. 22, 2004).

[61] IRTPA at § 1021.

[62] Interview with FBI (WMD) officials (Oct. 14, 2004). *See also* Interview with former senior intelligence official (Oct. 15, 2004) (discussing Collection Concepts Development Center (CCDC) study on the active interdiction of weapons of mass destruction, which underscored that one of the main underlying problems was that no one owned the problem of WMD terrorism); Interview with CTC (WMD) official (Oct. 22, 2004) (suggesting dedicating a NSC policy staffer to the issue); Interview with FBI (Counterterrorism) official (Oct. 22, 2004) (noting how the pre-election threat is an example of how U.S. government lacks a national WMD terrorism strategy).

[63] Interview with FBI (WMD) officials (Oct. 14, 2004).

[64] Interview with TTIC senior analyst (Oct. 19, 2004).

[65] Interview with CTC (WMD) official (Oct. 22, 2004); Interview with FBI (WMD) officials (Oct. 14, 2004).

[66] Interview with FBI (WMD) officials (Oct. 14, 2004).

[67] *Id.*

[68] Interview with CTC (WMD) official (Oct. 22, 2004); Interview with FBI (National Joint Terrorism Task Force) official (Nov. 5, 2004).

[69] 9/11 Commission Report at p. 263.

[70] Even the two groups' jargon differs. Those working on state-based programs talk of "WMD;" while those working on terrorism programs talk of "CBRN" (i.e., chemical, biological, radiological, and nuclear devices).

[71] An example of positive coordination is provided in our classified report, but cannot be discussed in an unclassified format.

[72] Interview with FBI (WMD) officials (Dec. 2, 2004).

[73] *Id.*

[74] *See, e.g.*, Interview with CTC (WMD) official (Oct. 22, 2004).

[75] Interview with FBI (WMD) officials (Oct. 14, 2004).

CHAPTER FIVE
IRAN AND NORTH KOREA:
MONITORING THE DEVELOPMENT
OF NUCLEAR CAPABILITIES

The Commission carefully studied the Intelligence Community's capability to assess accurately the nuclear programs of Iran and North Korea. In doing so, we reviewed numerous intelligence reports and conducted interviews with Intelligence Community analysts, collectors, and supervisors, as well as policymakers and non-governmental regional and weapons experts. Because even the most general statements about the Intelligence Community's capabilities in this area are classified, the Commission's assessments and eleven specific findings cannot be discussed in this report. The Commission has, however, incorporated the lessons learned from its study of Iran and North Korea in all of our recommendations for reform of the Intelligence Community.

PART TWO
LOOKING FORWARD

PART TWO:
LOOKING FORWARD

Until now, this report has focused on the limitations and strengths of today's Intelligence Community. We reviewed the Intelligence Community's recent performance in assessing the unconventional weapons programs of Iraq, Libya, and Afghanistan. We also assessed the Intelligence Community's current capabilities to confront several of today's priority intelligence challenges—including Iran, North Korea, and terrorism. (As we have noted elsewhere, while classification concerns precluded us from including our Iran and North Korea findings in our unclassified report, the lessons we learned from these reviews inform our recommendations.) And we complemented the formal "case studies" that appear in Part One of this report with reviews of other important challenges the Intelligence Community faces today, including the need to share intelligence across the Intelligence Community and the difficulties of coordinating intelligence across the foreign-domestic divide.

We found an Intelligence Community that has had some significant successes, but that is, on balance, badly equipped and badly organized to confront today's threats. We found human intelligence collectors who have struggled in vain to find sources with valuable information—and often failed to vet properly the sources they did find. We found technical intelligence collectors whose traditional techniques have declining utility against threats that are increasingly elusive and diffuse. And we found an analytical community too quick to rely upon assumptions or conjecture, and too slow to communicate gaps and uncertainties to policymakers.

But above all, we found an Intelligence Community that was too disorganized and fragmented to use its many talented people and sophisticated tools effectively. There are not enough coordinated and sustained Community-wide efforts to perform critical intelligence functions—ranging from target development to strategic analysis—and critical information still too often does not get to the analysts or policymakers who need it most. On the flip side of the same coin, we found that many of the Intelligence Community's recent successes stemmed from cross-agency efforts—such as the innovative fusing of different collection capabilities to penetrate a particular intelligence target. We found, in short, an Intelligence Community that needs to be better *integrated* and more *innovative* if it is to be able to confront today's intelligence challenges.

With these lessons in mind, our report now turns toward the future. In the chapters that follow, we set forth our recommendations for change within the Community. We begin our discussion of proposed reforms with a chapter on leadership and management (Chapter 6). However, the task of transforming the Intelligence Community, if it is to be complete, must go beyond questions of organization. As a result, we make recommendations addressing several specific areas of intelligence (or challenges the Intelligence Community faces): Collection (Chapter 7); Analysis (Chapter 8); Information Sharing (Chapter 9); the challenge of uniting intelligence efforts across the foreign and domestic divide (Intelligence at Home, Chapter 10); Counterintelligence (Chapter 11); and a largely classified chapter on managing covert action (Chapter 12). Finally, we conclude with a stand-alone chapter examining our intelligence capabilities with respect to the most dangerous unconventional weapons threats the United States faces today, and offer recommendations on how to improve those capabilities (Proliferation, Chapter 13).

CHAPTER SIX
LEADERSHIP AND MANAGEMENT: FORGING AN INTEGRATED INTELLIGENCE COMMUNITY

Summary & Recommendations

Today's Intelligence Community is not a "community" in any meaningful sense. It is a loose confederation of 15 separate intelligence entities. The new intelligence reform legislation, by creating a Director of National Intelligence (DNI) with substantial new authorities, establishes the basis for the kind of leadership and management necessary to shape a truly integrated Intelligence Community. But the reform act provides merely a framework; the hard work of forging a unified Community lies ahead.

In order to surmount these challenges, the DNI will need to lead the Community; he will need to integrate a diffuse group of intelligence entities by gaining acceptance of common strategic objectives, and by pursuing those objectives with more modern management techniques and governance processes. In this chapter we recommend several structures that could demonstrate the value of such collaboration.

Specifically, we recommend that the DNI:

- Bring a mission focus to the management of Community resources for high-priority intelligence issues by creating several "Mission Managers" on the DNI staff who are responsible for overseeing all aspects of intelligence relating to priority targets;

- Create a leadership structure within the Office of the DNI that manages the intelligence collection process on a Community basis, while maintaining intact existing collection agencies and their respective pockets of expertise;

- Make several changes to the Intelligence Community's personnel policies, including creating a central Intelligence Community human resources authority; developing more comprehensive and creative sets of performance incentives; directing a "joint" personnel rotation system; and establishing a National Intelligence University.

Summary & Recommendations (Continued)

We also recommend that:

- The President establish a National Counter Proliferation Center (NCPC) that reports to the DNI. The NCPC—a relatively small organization, with approximately 100 staff—would manage and coordinate analysis and collection on nuclear, biological, and chemical weapons across the Intelligence Community, but would not serve as a focal point for government-wide strategic operational planning; and

- The Executive Branch take steps to strengthen its intelligence oversight to ensure that intelligence reform does not falter, and that the Intelligence Community strengthen its own processes for self-evaluation.

INTRODUCTION

Today's Intelligence Community is not truly a community at all, but rather a loose confederation of 15 separate entities.[1] These entities too often act independently of each other. While a "community" management staff has long existed in the Office of the Director of Central Intelligence (DCI), it has never had the authority or resources it needed to manage all these disparate components.

The diffuse nature of the Intelligence Community does have important merits—for example, the existence of different agency cultures and ways of doing business increases the likelihood that hypotheses about key intelligence issues will be "competitively" tested, and allows for the development of diverse pockets of expertise. While such advantages should be retained, they aren't a reason to tolerate the current lack of coordination. As our case studies aptly demonstrate, the old, single-agency methods of gathering intelligence are losing ground to our adversaries. And conversely, many of our recent intelligence successes have resulted from innovative cross-agency efforts—but such laudable examples are the exception, the products of *ad hoc* efforts rather than institutionalized collaboration.

Concern about the harmful impact of disunity on national security was a major factor leading to passage of the *Intelligence Reform and Terrorism Prevention Act of 2004*. In creating a Director of National Intelligence (DNI) with substantial (though not sweeping) new authorities, the act created the framework for an integrated management structure for the United States' intelligence apparatus. However, passage of the intelligence act is merely prologue; the hard work of forging a genuine Intelligence Community, linked for the purpose of optimizing its capabilities and resources, must now begin.

We are realists. We recognize that effecting such a transformation in intelligence will take years to accomplish—and, indeed, will fall short without sustained leadership from the Director of National Intelligence and continued support from the President and Congress. This chapter offers our view on the essential tasks the new DNI might prioritize—and the challenges he will confront—as he begins this effort. We also offer, at the end of the chapter, a notional organizational structure for the new Office of the DNI, which we believe would serve the DNI well in confronting these tasks and challenges.

BUILDING AN INTEGRATED INTELLIGENCE COMMUNITY

Levers of Authority: Powers and Limitations of the New DNI

First, the good news. Under prior law, the Director of Central Intelligence had three demanding jobs—he ran the CIA, acted as the President's principal intelligence advisor, and (in theory, at least) managed the Intelligence Community. Thanks to the new intelligence legislation, the new DNI is now only responsible for two; the task of running the day-to-day operations of the CIA will be left to the Agency's own Director.[2]

The bad news is that the DNI's remaining statutory responsibilities continue to be demanding, full-time jobs. The DNI's management responsibilities will be both critically important and exceedingly difficult, and there is a real risk that the obligation to provide current intelligence support to the President and senior policymakers will reduce or eliminate the attention the DNI can devote to the painstaking, long-term work of integrating and managing the Community. It would be unrealistic—and undesirable—to expect the Office of the DNI to neglect or abdicate its responsibility as intelligence advisor to the President. But it is not necessary in all instances for the DNI to be present at the briefings himself. We do believe that it is possible for the DNI to assume what is essentially an oversight rather than a direct role in fulfilling this function, and we suggest that the DNI interpret the obligation in this way.

The DNI's management responsibilities will be more than sufficient to occupy the DNI's time and talents. On the first day in office, the new DNI will not have much of a foundation to build upon. A former senior Defense Department official has described today's Intelligence Community as "not so much poorly managed as unmanaged."[3] After a comprehensive study of the Community, we can't disagree. The DNI will need to create—virtually from scratch—structures, processes, and procedures for managing this notoriously sprawling, complicated, and fragmented bureaucracy. But with this "blank slate" also comes an opportunity. The new Director will be in a position to build a leadership and management staff that is suited to today's intelligence needs, rather than accommodate and modify an inherited administrative structure.

The intelligence reform legislation gives the DNI substantial new levers of authority to perform management responsibilities, but those powers are also limited in important respects. Most of the entities within the Intelligence Community—such as NSA, NGA, and the intelligence component of the FBI—continue to be part of separate executive departments. This means that the DNI will be expected to manage the Intelligence Community, but will not have direct "line" authority over all the agencies and entities he is responsible for coordinating and integrating. NSA, to cite just one example, remains with the Department of Defense, and its employees will therefore continue to be part of the Defense Department's "chain of command."

This means that the DNI will be required to manage the Community more by controlling essential resources than by command. And the new legislation does give the DNI important new budget and personnel authorities. For example, the intelligence reform act grants the DNI a substantially stronger hand in the development and execution of the overall intelligence budget, or National Intelligence Program, than that previously given to the DCI.[4] The leverage that these budget authorities were intended to provide, however, cannot be effectively exercised without an overhaul of the Intelligence Community's notoriously opaque budget process, which obscures how resources are committed to, and spent against, various intelligence programs. The DNI could wield his budgetary authorities with far more effectiveness if he were to build an end-to-end budgetary process that allowed for clarity and accountability—a process similar to the Planning, Programming, and Budgeting System employed by the Department of Defense.

With that said, the DNI's "power of the purse" is far from absolute. Many important intelligence programs are funded in whole or in part from joint military and tactical intelligence budgets that are under the control of the Defense Department.[5] In light of these overlapping responsibilities and competing budgetary authorities, it is imperative that the Office of the DNI and the Department of Defense develop parallel and closely coordinated planning, programming, and budget processes. (Indeed, the relationship between the DNI and the Secretary of Defense is of great importance and will be discussed separately in this chapter.)

Another important (and related) management tool for the DNI is the acquisition process. If the DNI builds and drives a coherent, top-down Intelligence Community acquisition structure, he will have a powerful device for Community management, and will make an important step toward developing the coherent long-term allocation of resources that the Intelligence Community sorely lacks today—particularly with respect to evaluating and acquiring large, technology-driven systems. But, as in other areas, the DNI's role in the acquisition process is not absolute. Under the new intelligence reform act, the Secretary of Defense and the DNI will have joint acquisition authorities in many instances—another factor that weighs in favor of strong Defense Department-Intelligence Community interaction on many fronts.[6]

In addition to these budget and acquisition authorities, the intelligence act also grants the DNI significant personnel powers. The act gives the DNI a substantial staff, and it empowers the DNI to transfer personnel from one element of the Intelligence Community to another for tours of up to two years.[7] These are important new authorities; our terrorism case study sets out the difficulties the Terrorist Threat Integration Center encountered in obtaining adequate personnel support from other agencies. However, like the DNI's budgetary authorities, these powers are not unrestricted; the intelligence reform act states that the procedures governing these personnel transfers must be developed jointly by the DNI and by the affected agencies,[8] which could provide department and agency heads with an opportunity to impede the DNI's initiatives. We suggest that the DNI make the development of these procedures an early priority, to ensure that the required "procedures" become just that—processes for effecting the flexible transfer of personnel and minimizing negative impact on the affected agencies, and not vehicles that provide agencies with a veto over the DNI's personnel authorities.

The intelligence act also expressly directs the DNI to implement management-related reform measures that have long been neglected by Community managers. Among these are specific mandates to develop Community personnel policies; maximize the sharing of information among Community agencies; improve the quality of intelligence analysis; protect the sources and methods used to collect intelligence from disclosure; and improve operational coordination between CIA and the Department of Defense. This explicit congressional direction should significantly strengthen the DNI's hand as the work of creating a new management structure begins.

The DNI will likely need every bit of the leverage bestowed by these new powers and embodied in the statutory mandate for change. Few of the recommendations that follow can be implemented without affecting the current responsibilities of a particular agency, sometimes in ways that can be expected to leave the affected agency unhappy. For instance, if the DNI is going to manage the target development system—the process by which the Intelligence Community prioritizes information needs and develops collection strategies to fulfill those needs—he will, by necessity, be taking responsibilities away from the collection agencies. If the DNI is going to build a modern information sharing infrastructure for the Intelligence Community, he will need to override particular agencies' views about what information is and is not too sensitive to be placed in the shared information space.

Making hard decisions that adversely affect particular agencies will constitute a major departure from prior Community management practices. Former DCIs have brought the Intelligence Community together by consensus, a practice that left many difficult but important management challenges unaddressed. Indeed, over the course of our study we repeatedly came across important decisions that Community leaders were unable to resolve—a state of affairs that allows bureaucratic disputes and unhealthy ambiguities in responsibilities to fester. (The lengthy turf battle between the CIA Counterterrorist Center and the Terrorist Threat Integration Center (now NCTC), which we discussed in Chapter Four (Terrorism), is just one example.)

While the air is thick with talk of the need for coordination within the Intelligence Community, one can expect that the DNI's new (and sometimes ambiguous) authorities will be challenged in ways both open and subtle. In order to sustain successful integration, the DNI will need to establish processes that demonstrate by their own effectiveness the value of Community-wide cooperation. This can be achieved by securing "buy-in" on common strategic objectives, developing common practices in reviewing progress toward goals (using shared metrics whenever possible), and building a common approach to human resource management. We recommend several structures—such as the "Mission Managers" that we discuss immediately below—that could be useful in demonstrating the value of collaboration, and we also encourage the DNI to seek to emulate best practices used by large organizations both within and outside government.

Organize Around Missions

Throughout our study, we observed a lack of Community focus on intelligence missions. Each individual agency tries to allocate its scarce resources in a way that seems sensible to that particular agency, but might not be optimal if viewed from a Community perspective. The DCI's management staff is organized around intelligence functions—there are, for instance, separate Assistant DCIs for "Collection" and "Analysis"—rather than around priority intelligence targets. So while it might have been the case that an individual at the DCI level was responsible for knowing about our collection capabilities on a given country, and while it might also have been the case that an individual at the DCI level was responsible for knowing the state of *analysis* on that country, no one person or office at the DCI level was responsible for the *intelligence mission* concerning that country as a whole.

We believe it is important that the DNI develop a management structure and processes that ensure a strategic, Community focus on priority intelligence missions. The specific device we propose is the creation of "Mission Managers."

> ### Recommendation 1
>
> We recommend that the DNI bring a mission focus to the management of Community resources for high-priority intelligence issues by creating a group of "Mission Managers" on the DNI staff, responsible for all aspects of the intelligence process relating to those issues.

Under the current system, collectors, analysts, and supervisors throughout the Community working on a given target function largely autonomously, communicating and collaborating only episodically. The Mission Managers we propose would be responsible for designing and implementing a coordinated effort. As the DNI's point person for individual high-priority subject matter areas, Mission Managers would be responsible for knowing both what the Community knows (and what it does not know) about a particular target, and for developing strategies to optimize the Community's capabilities against that particular target. For any such target—be it a country like China, a non-state actor like al-Qa'ida, or a subject like "proliferation"— a Mission Manager would be charged with organizing and monitoring the Community's efforts, and serving as the DNI's principal advisor on the subject. Most importantly, and in contrast to the diffusion of responsibility that characterizes the current system, the Mission Manager would be the person *responsible* for Community efforts against the target. There would never be a question of accountability.

The Mission Manager, therefore, would have substantial responsibilities both for driving collection and identifying shortcomings in analysis in the Mission Manager's subject area. With respect to collection, Mission Managers would chair Target Development Boards, described further below and in Chapter Seven (Collection). In this capacity, the Mission Managers' role would include identifying collection gaps, working with the various collection agencies to fill them, and monitoring the collection organizations' progress in that regard. As explained in greater detail in Chapter Eight (Analysis), they would also serve as the DNI's primary tool for focusing the Intelligence Community's analytical attention on strategic threats to national security and optimizing the Community's resources against them. While they would not directly command the analytical cadre, they could—in cases where agency heads were resistant to properly aligning resources or addressing analytic needs—recommend that the DNI's personnel powers be invoked to correct the situation or quickly re-configure the Community to respond to a crisis. Because of their responsibilities for developing a coordinated approach to collection and analytic efforts, we believe that the Mission Managers would also collectively serve as an important device for achieving Community integration over time.[9]

Some might suggest that the Mission Manager function will conflict with the role of National Intelligence Officers (NIOs) within the National Intelligence Council (NIC), the Community's focal point for long-term, interagency analysis. The NIOs are granted authority under the new legislation for "evaluating community-wide collection and production of intelligence by the Intelligence Community and the requirements and resources of such collection and production."[10] We believe this role is complementary with that of the Mission

Managers. NIOs, in our view, should continue to serve as the Community's principal senior analysts. In this position, they spearhead assembly of National Intelligence Estimates and other publications that articulate Community analytic conclusions, identify differences in agency views and why they exist, and explore gaps and weaknesses in collection. But once an Estimate on a given topic is finished, NIOs move quickly to the next, perhaps not to officially revisit the subject matter for years. They have neither the time nor the authority to craft and implement strategic plans designed to improve the Community's work on a particular issue over time. This, as we see it, will be the Mission Managers' role.

Coordinate Target Development

Recommendation 2

We recommend that the DNI create a management structure that effectively coordinates Community target development. This new target development process would be supported by an integrated, end-to-end "collection enterprise."

The Intelligence Community's fragmented nature is perhaps best exemplified by the process in which its resources are directed to collect information on subjects of interest. One would expect that this vital aspect of intelligence—which we refer to as "target development"—would be among those where coordination and integration is most essential. Instead, the target development process is left primarily to individual collection agencies, operating from a general list of intelligence objectives called the National Intelligence Priorities Framework, in combination with *ad hoc* requirements generated by analysts and other intelligence "customers," such as policymakers and the military. This decentralized process is refined only episodically at the Community level, usually through the personal intervention of the Assistant Director of Central Intelligence for Collection.

This is an unacceptable status quo, and we recommend that the DNI make fixing it a top priority. As our case studies have shown, many of the recent penetrations of hard targets have been facilitated by fusing collection disciplines. Such cross-agency collection strategies cannot be systematically encouraged while the various collection platforms remain isolated within the confines of their individual agencies. The current system, in which individual agencies set their own collection priorities, also marginalizes the role of the intelligence "customers" and analysts for whom intelligence is collected.

As a result, we believe it is essential that the DNI develop a unified target development process that exists "above the stovepipes." We develop more fully our target development recommendations in Chapter Seven (Collection), but because of the importance of this issue we highlight it here. We would give the Mission Managers responsibility for driving and maintaining an over-arching collection strategy in their subject matter areas. In developing this strategy, each Mission Manager would chair, and be supported by, a standing DNI-level Target Development Board that would include experts from key "customers" and from each major collection agency, who could keep the Mission Manager informed of its agency's capabilities (and limitations) against the target. This approach would ensure that the target development process was both integrated and user-driven.

We also recommend that the target development process be supported by an integrated "collection enterprise": that is, a collection process that is coordinated and integrated at all stages, from collection management to data exploitation to strategic investment. Again, we discuss this recommendation in detail in Chapter Seven (Collection).

Facilitate Information Sharing

Recommendation 3

We recommend that the new DNI overhaul the Community's information management system to facilitate real and effective information sharing.

No shortcoming of the Intelligence Community has received more attention since the September 11 attacks than the failure to share information. There have been literally dozens of Intelligence Community initiatives in this area, with advances most apparent in the area of counterterrorism. Unfortunately, almost all of these efforts have worked around the most intractable and difficult information-sharing impediments, rather than solved them. While minor advances have been made in some areas, the ultimate objective of developing a Community-wide space for sharing intelligence information has proven elusive. In our view, the fundamental reason for the lack of success is the absence of empowered, coherent, and determined Community leadership and management.

We strongly recommend that the new DNI tackle this problem early on by overhauling the Community's information management system, including as a central component the creation of a single office responsible both for information management and information security. We also suggest that the DNI begin with a painless, but symbolically important, first step: namely, to jettison the very phrase "information sharing." To say that we must encourage agencies to "share" information implies that they have some ownership stake in it—an implication based on a fundamental (and, unfortunately, all too common) misunderstanding of individual collection agencies' obligations to the Intelligence Community, and to the government more broadly. We believe that the DNI might begin the process of building a shared information space by putting the DNI's imprimatur on a new phrase, perhaps "information access," that indicates that information within the Community is a Community asset—not the property of a particular agency. Our information sharing recommendations, which we detail in Chapter Nine (Information Sharing), begin from this premise.

Create Real "Jointness" and Build a Modern Workforce

Recommendation 4

We recommend that the DNI use his human resources authorities to: establish a central human resources authority for the Intelligence Community; create a uniform system for performance evaluations and compensation; develop a more comprehensive and creative set of performance incentives; direct a "joint" personnel rotation system; and establish a National Intelligence University.

Perhaps the most effective authorities the intelligence reform act grants the DNI are those pertaining to personnel. These new authorities come none too soon, as it is becoming increasingly apparent that the Intelligence Community cannot continue to manage its personnel system the way it always has. The Community still attracts large numbers of highly qualified people, but retaining them has become a real challenge. Today's most talented young people change jobs and careers frequently, are famously impatient with bureaucratic and inflexible work environments, and can often earn far more outside the government. The Community's personnel system is ill-suited to hire and retain people with these characteristics; merely getting hired can take over a year, and compensation is too often tied to time-in-grade, rather than demonstrated achievement.

Moreover, at precisely the moment when the Intelligence Community is facing the prospect of recruiting in this very different job market, the average experience level of the people in many elements of the Intelligence Community is declining. It is uncertain whether this is merely a transitory phenomenon, reflecting an ambitious post-9/11 hiring program. The analytical cadre may grow in experience and stabilize over the next few years. In the short term, however, it is clear that the Intelligence Community suffers from an eroding base of institutional wisdom, not to mention a lack of accumulated knowledge and expertise.

These overarching employment trends are, unfortunately, only the tip of the iceberg. Today's Intelligence Community has additional systemic weaknesses with regard to personnel. For example, the Community has had difficulty recruiting individuals with certain critical skill sets; has often failed to encourage the type of "joint" personnel assignments that are necessary to breaking down cultural barriers that exist among agencies; and has proven insufficiently adept at hiring and mainstreaming mid-career "lateral" hires from outside of the Intelligence Community. This section suggests reforms of the human resources system that would help equip the Community to confront these formidable challenges.

Establish a central Human Resources Authority for the Intelligence Community. As a threshold matter, the Intelligence Community needs a DNI-level office responsible for analyzing the workforce, developing strategies to ensure that priority intelligence missions are adequately resourced, and creating Community human resources standards and policies to accomplish these objectives. The human resources authority would also establish evaluation standards and metrics programs to assess the intelligence agencies' performance in hiring, retention, and career development.

This office would also have responsibility for developing policies to fill gaps in the Intelligence Community's workforce. Our case studies have highlighted a wide variety of these critical personnel needs. We have found that the Community has difficulty in attracting and retaining people with scientific and technical skills, diverse ethnic and religious backgrounds, management experience, and advanced language capabilities. Similarly, the Community has struggled to develop the mid-career lateral hires that will be increasingly necessary to complement a workforce that can no longer expect to depend on Intelligence Community "lifers." This authority would have responsibility for developing the Community personnel policies that can overcome these systemic shortcomings.

Direct a personnel rotation system that develops "joint" professionals in the senior ranks of the Intelligence Community. Much has been made of the need to develop "jointness" in the Intelligence Community. Study after study has cited the significance of the Goldwater-Nichols Act in transforming the U.S. military from four independent services to a single, unified fighting force.[11] The Goldwater-Nichols analogy does not apply perfectly to the Intelligence Community; as we discuss below, we do not believe that the Intelligence Community should be reorganized comprehensively around national intelligence "centers" that would serve as the equivalent to the military's joint commands. But we do believe that the personnel reforms of the Goldwater-Nichols Act, which encouraged (and in some instances required) individuals to serve "joint" tours of duty outside of their home services, should be replicated within the Intelligence Community.

We recommend, therefore, that the DNI promptly develop mechanisms to ensure that joint assignments are taken seriously within the Intelligence Community. Today, the Community's agencies vary substantially in the seriousness of their commitment to cross- and interagency assignments. It is insufficient merely to ensure that an Intelligence Community professional who works in an Intelligence Community center or at a different intelligence agency will suffer no punishment upon returning home. Instead, personnel should be affirmatively rewarded for successfully completing joint tours, and intelligence professionals should gain eligibility for promotion to senior levels only if they complete joint assignments. Jointness did not occur effortlessly in the Department of Defense. The DNI will likely find that fostering a truly "joint" culture in the Intelligence Community will require significant and persistent attention.

Create more uniform performance evaluation and compensation systems. Personnel systems across the Intelligence Community are in flux, with some agencies moving to new merit-based pay systems and others retaining but modifying the traditional federal General Schedule (GS) system. These differences have the effect of inhibiting the cross-agency movement of personnel that is so critical to building an integrated Intelligence Community. To avoid this problem, we recommend that the Intelligence Community's human resources authority adopt a common personnel performance evaluation and compensation plan. This plan would define core Community competencies and set evaluation criteria (for the entire workforce as well as for key segments, such as analysts), and establish a standard pay grade and compensation structure—while retaining the flexibility to allow agencies to evaluate performance factors unique to their organizations. We further recommend that such a unified compensation structure be based on a merit-based model. A merit-based approach is being used increasingly across the federal workforce, and more rationally links performance to organizational goals and strategies.

We also believe that this review of the compensation structure should focus in particular on ways for the Intelligence Community to recruit talented individuals from *outside* the government. Today, the Intelligence Community can promise the following to talented scientists, scholars, or businesspersons who wish to serve: a lengthy clearance process before they begin, a large pay and benefits cut, a work environment that has difficulty understanding or using the talents of outsiders, and ethics rules that significantly handcuff them from using their expertise when they seek to return to their chosen professions. It should come as little surprise that too few talented people from the private sector take the offer. The DNI should develop special hiring rules aimed at attracting such individuals, including special salary levels and benefits packages and streamlined clearance processes.

Develop a stronger incentive structure within the Intelligence Community. In addition to encouraging greater use of financial incentives, we recommend that the Community consider new techniques to motivate positive performance. A real "Intelligence Community" would reward and encourage types of behaviors that currently are not emphasized. These behaviors—a commitment to sharing information, a willingness to take risk, enthusiasm for collaborating with intelligence professionals at other agencies, and a sense of loyalty to the Intelligence Community's missions—must be reinforced if they are to become institutionalized. Government entities are severely limited in the monetary rewards they can offer to reinforce desired behavior, but there are other rewards that can serve as suitable alternatives. Advanced education and training, professional familiarization tours, coveted assignments, and opportunities to attend conferences and symposia are all rewards that might be associated with reinforcing new behaviors.

But it is not enough merely to encourage the right kinds of behavior; it is also critical that the Intelligence Community does not reward its employees for the wrong reasons. Our review found that agencies within the Intelligence Community often made personnel decisions based upon the wrong criteria. For instance, as discussed in our Iraq case study, agencies that collect human intelligence place considerable value on the number of sources they recruit—an incentive system that of course encourages its employees to recruit easier, less important sources rather than taking the time (and the risk) to develop the harder ones. A similar problem exists in the analytical community, where we were told that analysts are disproportionately rewarded for producing "current intelligence" assessments, such as articles that appear in the President's Daily Brief. If we are to expect our human intelligence collectors to take risks and our intelligence analysts to devote time to long-term, strategic thinking, agencies must have a personnel evaluation system that does not punish them for these behaviors.

Establish a National Intelligence University. The Intelligence Community has a number of well-founded and successful training programs. Individual organizations within the Community conduct various discipline-specific training programs.[12] Yet there is no initial training provided to all incoming Intelligence Community personnel that instills a sense of community and shared mission—as occurs, for example, in all of the military services. Nor is there an adequate management training program[13]—a fact that may have contributed to declining numbers in the Intelligence Community's mid-level management corps, and the low performance evaluations that this corps recently received in one major intelligence agency.

A National Intelligence University (NIU) could fill these gaps by providing Community training and education programs, setting curriculum standards, and facilitating the sharing of the Community's training resources. A progressive and structured curriculum—from entry level job-skills training to advanced education—could link to career-advancement standards for various Intelligence Community occupations and permit intelligence professionals to build skills methodically as they advance in their responsibilities. The NIU could also serve as a research center for innovative intelligence tools and a test bed for their implementation across the Intelligence Community. The development of such a university—which could be built easily and at modest expense on top of existing Intelligence Community training infrastructure—would be a relatively easy and cost-effective way to develop improved Community integration and professionalism.

Develop New Mechanisms for Spurring Innovation

Recommendation 5

We recommend that the DNI take an active role in equipping the Intelligence Community to develop new technologies.

While human intelligence has always been the most romanticized of the collection disciplines, technology has driven the course of intelligence over the past century. Advanced technology and its creative application remain a comparative advantage for the United States, but we fear that the Intelligence Community is not adequately leveraging this advantage. Elements of the Intelligence Community continue to perform remarkable technical feats, but across many dimensions, Intelligence Community technology is no longer on the cutting edge. And this problem affects not only intelligence collection; we also lag in the use of technologies to support analysis. This trend may result from a recent decline in the Intelligence Community's commitment to scientific and technological research and development.

We advise the DNI to take an active role in reversing this trend. To be sure, individual agencies will continue to develop new technologies that will serve their missions. But we recommend that the DNI encourage a parallel commitment to early-stage research and development to ensure that important new technologies that might be neglected by individual collection agencies are explored. Toward this end, we recommend that the Office of the DNI have its own significant pool of research and development money at its disposal.

It is not enough, moreover, merely to develop new technologies; it is also critical to ensure that there are effective processes in place to make sure those new technologies are actually put into practice. Like many large organizations, the Intelligence Community has had difficulty "mainstreaming" new technologies (which are often developed by outside organizations like In-Q-Tel, a private, non-profit entity that identifies and invests in new technologies for the CIA). It also often fails to build programmed funding transitions from research and development to deployment. In order to ensure that new technologies actually reach the users who need them, we recommend that the DNI require the larger agencies within the Intelligence Community to establish mechanisms for integrating new technologies, and develop metrics for evaluating each agency's performance in this regard.

In Chapter Seven (Collection), we recommend DNI-level management practices that would encourage the development of new technical collection technologies. But there is more to the problem than that. Research and development leaders within the Intelligence Community have told us that they cannot attract or retain the best and the brightest young scientists and engineers because career paths are unattractive, the Community's research infrastructure is poor, and the environment is too risk averse. We have seen similar shortfalls in technical and scientific expertise among the analytic corps and within the cadre of human intelligence collectors. As has been noted above, we advise the DNI to utilize personnel authorities to ensure that scientific and technical career tracks are adequately developed and rewarded by intelligence agencies.

A DIFFERENT KIND OF "CENTER": DEVELOPING THE NATIONAL COUNTER PROLIFERATION CENTER

Recommendation 6

We recommend that the President establish a National Counter Proliferation Center (NCPC) that is relatively small (*i.e.*, fewer than 100 people) and that manages and coordinates analysis and collection on nuclear, biological, and chemical weapons across the Intelligence Community. Although government-wide "strategic operational planning" is clearly required to confront proliferation threats, we advise that such planning *not* be directed by the NCPC.

In the preceding section we recommended that the new Director of National Intelligence take several steps aimed at forging a better integrated Intelligence Community. In this section we address whether this objective could be further advanced through the creation of a National Counter Proliferation Center (NCPC). The recent intelligence reform legislation envisions the creation of an NCPC modeled on the newly-created National Counterterrorism Center

(NCTC).[14] But the act also gives the President the opportunity to decide not to create the center—or to modify certain characteristics—if the President believes that doing so serves the nation's security.[15]

Although we endorse the idea of creating an NCPC, we believe it should look very different from the NCTC. The distinguishing feature of the NCTC is its hybrid character: the NCTC serves simultaneously as an integrated center for counterterrorism intelligence *analysis* and as a driver and coordinator of national interagency counterterrorism *policy* (the new intelligence legislation describes this latter responsibility, in rather confusing fashion, as "strategic operational planning"). As a result of these two roles, the Director of the NCTC has a dual-reporting relationship; he reports to the DNI on terrorism intelligence matters, and reports to the President when wearing his policy coordination hat. While we understand the motivations that may have led to these overlapping intelligence and policy functions in the counterterrorism area, we doubt that it is a good idea to replicate the model—and the mixed reporting relationships it creates—in other substantive areas.

We are also skeptical more generally about the increasingly popular idea of creating a network of "centers" organized around priority national intelligence problems. While we sympathize with the desire for better coordination that animates these proposals, centers also impose costs that often go unappreciated. As our Iraq case study aptly illustrates, centers run the risk of crowding out competitive analysis, creating new substantive "stovepipes" organized around issues, engendering turf wars over where a given center's mission begins and ends, and creating deeply rooted bureaucracies built around what may be temporary intelligence priorities. In most instances we believe that there are more flexible institutional solutions than centers, such as the national Mission Managers we propose.

So, while we recommend the creation of a National Counter Proliferation Center, the center we envision would differ substantially from both the NCTC and from the large analytical centers that some have suggested might serve as organizing units for the Intelligence Community. The NCPC we propose would serve as the DNI's Mission Manager on counterproliferation issues: it would not conduct analysis itself, but would instead be responsible for *coordinating* analysis and collection on nuclear, biological, and chemical weapons[16] across the Intelligence Community. As such, it would be much smaller than the NCTC (it would likely require a staff of no more than 100 people) and would not perform a policy planning function. Specifically, the Director of the NCPC would:

Develop strategies for collecting intelligence on the proliferation of nuclear, biological, and chemical weapons (and their delivery vehicles). The Director of the NCPC would manage the target-development process for nuclear, biological, and chemical weapons. Like any Mission Manager, the NCPC would develop multi-disciplinary collection strategies to attack hard targets, and would review the performance of collection agencies in gaining access to these targets. Similarly, it would have full visibility into all compartmented intelligence programs, thus ensuring that relevant capabilities are fully employed by collectors and considered by analysts.

Coordinate, oversee, and evaluate analytic production. As already noted—and in contrast to the National Counterterrorism Center—the NCPC would *not* contain a large staff of analysts working on proliferation. Rather, the NCPC would coordinate decentralized analytic efforts occurring at various agencies. This would increase the likelihood of competitive analysis of proliferation issues across the Community. In some cases, the NCPC might determine that no part of the Community is addressing a proliferation-related issue sufficiently and designate a small group of resident NCPC analysts drawn from throughout the Community to work on the issue.

With these analytic oversight responsibilities, the NCPC will fulfill several critical functions, including ensuring that appropriate technical expertise is focused on state weapons programs; that gaps in the Community's knowledge about the relationship between state actors and non-state threats (*e.g.*, black- and gray-market proliferators such as A.Q. Khan) are addressed; and that the NCTC has access to subject matter expertise on nuclear, biological, and chemical questions. We do not believe that the NCPC should take the lead on the crucial question of the terrorist procurement of unconventional weapons. That responsibility should, in our view, fall to the NCTC. But the Director of the NCPC should support the NCTC and be prepared to step in and appeal to the DNI if this crucial area is receiving insufficient resources and attention.

Participate in setting the budget associated with nuclear, biological, and chemical weapons. As the 9/11 Commission correctly noted, true management authority also must include some budget authority.[17] In line with this observation, the NCPC would make recommendations regarding counterproliferation-related budget submissions for National Intelligence Program funds. The NCPC would also support the DNI in fulfilling his statutory responsibilities to "participate" in the development of counterproliferation-related program funds in other military intelligence budgets.

Support the needs of a Counterproliferation Joint Interagency Task Force, the National Security Council, and other relevant consumers as the Intelligence Community's leader for interdiction-related issues. Counterproliferation interdiction, in a variety of forms, will remain an important part of combating the spread of nuclear, biological, and chemical weapons. The NCPC would play a vital intelligence support role both in helping to formulate U.S. interdiction strategies and in assisting in individual interdiction operations. The NCPC would also support strategic planning for interdiction efforts pursued by other government entities, including the Departments of Defense, State, Homeland Security, Commerce, and Treasury. Developing plans for and executing interdiction operations using the full capabilities of interagency, private sector, and international partners is a role appropriately played by a new Counterproliferation Joint Interagency Task Force, which we propose in Chapter Thirteen (Proliferation).

As noted above, we do not believe that, in addition to these important responsibilities, the NCPC should also be the focal point for strategic *policy* planning on countering nuclear, biological, and chemical proliferation. The Intelligence Community will inevitably be a major force in any interagency strategic planning process, but we believe it is inadvisable to "double-hat" another intelligence component with what is fundamentally a policy role, or to bifurcate the command structure overseeing it.[18]

Nevertheless, it is self-evident that *someone* should be performing strategic interagency planning on counterproliferation issues. As we will discuss in detail in Chapter Thirteen (Proliferation), the task of collecting intelligence on biological weapons and other proliferation threats is notoriously difficult; and we cannot reasonably expect intelligence alone will keep us safe. A successful counterproliferation effort will require a coordinated effort across the entire U.S. government, from the Intelligence Community to the Department of Defense to the Department of Commerce to the other agencies involved in this important work. In our more comprehensive later treatment of the counterproliferation challenge, we offer several recommendations on how to build such a sustained interagency coordination process, including the creation of a joint task force for counterproliferation.

POTENTIAL PITFALLS ON THE PATH TO INTEGRATION

Our recommendations to this point have involved management strategies and organizational structures that could support the DNI's effort to forge an integrated Intelligence Community. In this section, we briefly identify two formidable challenges that may stand in the way of this objective. They both involve potentially problematic *relationships* for the Intelligence Community's leadership: namely, with the FBI and the Department of Defense.

Working with the FBI: Integrating Intelligence at Home and Abroad

Former Director of Central Intelligence James Woolsey told us that one of the most critical jobs of the new DNI will be to fuse the domestic and foreign intelligence enterprises.[19] This objective can only be achieved if the capabilities of agencies with intelligence responsibilities in the United States, like the FBI, are both strengthened and integrated with the efforts of other intelligence agencies. The FBI has made some significant strides in creating an effective intelligence capability, and we make substantial recommendations in Chapter Ten (Intelligence at Home) that we believe would further strengthen those capabilities.

There may, however, be speed bumps ahead for the DNI in ensuring that the FBI's intelligence resources are managed in the same manner as those within other Intelligence Community agencies. As we explain in detail in Chapter Ten (Intelligence at Home), the intelligence reform legislation is ambiguous in the extent to which it brings the FBI's analytical and operational assets into the Intelligence Community and under the DNI's leadership. We advise that this ambiguity be quickly resolved and suggest ways of making the DNI's authority over the FBI comparable to that of other intelligence agencies such as NSA and NGA—subject to, of course, the ongoing involvement of the Attorney General in ensuring the Bureau's compliance with laws designed to protect privacy and civil liberties.

Working with the Defense Department: Coordinating the National Intelligence Program with the Secretary of Defense

The most controversial sections of the intelligence reform act were those relating to the relationship between the DNI and the Secretary of Defense. This is not at all surprising, given the vital importance of effective intelligence support to military operations and the fact that many of the largest components of the Intelligence Community reside in the Department of Defense. These realities create an inherent challenge for any DNI seeking to bring order and coherent management to the Intelligence Community.

Recent events have highlighted the magnitude of this challenge. Over the past few months the Department of Defense has taken several steps to bolster its own internal intelligence capabilities. These have included initiatives to remodel defense intelligence that may enable Combatant Commanders to task and control national collection assets directly;[20] establishing the U.S. Strategic Command (STRATCOM) as the Global Intelligence, Surveillance, and Reconnaissance (ISR) manager for the Defense Department;[21] assigning the DIA as the key intelligence organization to support STRATCOM's ISR mission;[22] and building up the Defense Department's human intelligence capabilities to make the Defense Department less reliant on the CIA's espionage operations.[23]

We believe that several of these Defense Department initiatives are good ones, and should be supported. However, in all instances, we think these efforts need to be closely coordinated with the DNI—and in some cases we believe steps should be taken to ensure that the Defense Department's intelligence efforts do not undermine the new DNI's ability to manage the Intelligence Community. We identify four important issues pertaining to this relationship here: the need to balance support to military operations with other intelligence requirements; the importance of ensuring that the DNI maintains collection authority over national intelligence collection assets; the need to manage Intelligence Community agencies that reside in the Department of Defense; and the importance of coordinating Defense Department and CIA human intelligence operations.

Balancing support to military operations with other intelligence needs. Balancing the high priority, and often competing, demands on the U.S. Intelligence Community resources will be a significant challenge. The DNI will need to develop processes for serving the military's requirements while preserving the ability to fulfill other national needs. Toward this end, we recommend the creation of a high level position within the Office of the DNI dedicated to military support. This individual would function as the principal military intelligence advisor to the DNI, serve as the Mission Manager for military support issues, and advise the DNI on issues of Defense Department-Intelligence Community coordination.

Ensuring that the DNI maintains authority over the tasking of national intelligence collection assets. If the Director of National Intelligence is to have any ability to build an integrated Intelligence Community, the DNI must be able effectively to manage national intelligence collection capabilities. To achieve this goal, we believe the Defense Department's requirements for national collection assets should be funneled through, not around, the DNI's integrated collection enterprise, outlined in Chapter Seven (Collection). In this process, the Defense Department's requirements for national intelligence collection in support of military operations will be represented by the DNI's principal military advisor. This individual will work closely with STRAT-COM and the Combatant Commanders to ensure their needs for national intelligence support are met, and will lead the Target Development Board responsible for creating integrated collection strategies in response to U.S. military requirements. This process maintains the DNI's authority to manage national intelligence collection assets and increases the DNI's ability to effectively meet both the military's requirements and other national intelligence needs.

Developing clear procedures for the management of Defense Department agencies within the Intelligence Community. Many of the Intelligence Community's largest agencies reside within the Department of Defense. The new intelligence legislation's push towards unified intelligence management will further complicate the lives of the heads of these agencies, who will be uncertain whether they should answer to the Secretary of Defense or to the DNI. While some ambiguity is inevitable, there are certain steps that the DNI and the Secretary of Defense could take to add clarity in this area, including developing a joint charter that specifies each agency's reporting chain and operating authorities, and combining and coordinating management evaluations and audits to avoid needless and unproductive duplication of management oversight activities.

It is also critical that the DNI and the Secretary of Defense establish effective and coordinated protocols for exercising their acquisition authorities. As we have noted, the new legislation requires the DNI to share Milestone Decision Authority with the Secretary of Defense on all "Department of Defense programs" in the national intelligence budget. This important provision is also among the statute's more ambiguous ones, as the term "Department of Defense program" is undefined. As the success of these shared acquisition authorities is crucial to the fielding of future capabilities, we believe that the President should require the Secretary of Defense and the DNI to submit, within 90 days of the DNI's confirmation, their procedures for exercising shared Milestone Decision Authority, and a list of those acquisition programs they deem to be "Defense Department programs" under the legislation.

Coordinating Special Operations Command and CIA activities. The war on terrorism, and U.S. Special Operations Command's expanded role as the Defense Department's operational lead, have dramatically increased military intelligence interactions around the world. While the Defense Department has an organic human intelligence capability, the Department must closely coordinate its operations with the DNI to ensure deconfliction of operations and unity of purpose. We offer recommendations to address these coordination issues in our detailed discussion of human intelligence reform needs (Chapter 7, Collection). Here we recommend that the DNI and the Secretary of Defense, as part of their obligation to report to Congress within 180 days on joint procedures for operational coordination between the Defense Department and CIA,[24] address this specific issue of deconfliction with U.S. Special Operations Command.

Another Potential Pitfall: Legal Myths in the Intelligence Community

Throughout our work we came across Intelligence Community leaders, operators, and analysts who claimed that they couldn't do their jobs because of a "legal issue." These "legal issues" arose in a variety of contexts, ranging from the Intelligence Community's dealings with U.S. persons to the legality of certain covert actions. And although there are, of course, very real (and necessary) legal restrictions on the Intelligence Community, quite often the cited legal impediments ended up being either myths that overcautious lawyers had never debunked or policy choices swathed in pseudo-legal justifications. Needless to say, such confusion about what the law actually requires can seriously hinder the Intelligence Community's ability to be proactive and innovative. Moreover, over time, it can breed uncertainty about *real* legal prohibitions.

We believe this problem is the result of several factors, but for present purposes we note two. First, in the past there has not been a sizable legal staff that focused on Community issues. As a result, many Community problems were addressed through *ad hoc*, interagency task forces that tended to gravitate toward lowest common denominator solutions that were based on consensus and allowed action to be stalled by the doubts of the most cautious legal shop. Second, many rules and regulations governing the Intelligence Community have existed for decades with little thought given to the legal basis for the rules, or whether circumstances have changed the rules' applicability. Under such circumstances, it is unsurprising that legal "myths" have evolved.

The recent creation of a DNI General Counsel's office will increase the probability that Community legal issues are addressed more seriously. But the existence of the office alone does not guarantee an ongoing and systematic examination of the rules and regulations that govern the Intelligence Community. We therefore recommend that the DNI General Counsel establish an internal office consisting of a small group of lawyers expressly charged with taking a forward-leaning look at legal issues that affect the Intelligence Community as a whole. By creating such an office, the DNI will help ensure that the Intelligence Community is fully able to confront the many real—and imaginary—legal issues that will arise.

SUSTAINED OVERSIGHT FROM THE OUTSIDE AND IMPROVED SELF-EXAMINATION FROM WITHIN: MAKING SURE REFORM HAPPENS

Many—perhaps most—of the recommendations contained in this report have been made before. That we find ourselves proposing several sensible changes that former Secretary of Defense and Director of Central Intelligence James Schlesinger endorsed in 1971 suggests to us either that the Intelligence Community is inherently resistant to outside recommendations, or that it does not have the institutional capacity to implement them.[25] In either case, we are left with the distinct impression that meaningful intelligence reform proposals are only likely to become reality if the Intelligence Community receives sustained, senior level attention from knowledgeable outside observers. Today the Community receives only episodic oversight from the President's Foreign Intelligence Advisory Board (PFIAB), Congress, and a thinly-stretched National Security Council. We recommend several changes to improve this state of affairs.

Recommendation 7

We recommend that the Executive Branch improve its mechanisms for watching over the Intelligence Community in order to ensure that intelligence reform does not falter. To this end, we suggest that the Joint Intelligence Community Council serve as a standing Intelligence Community "customer council" and that a strengthened President's Foreign Intelligence Advisory Board assume a more vigorous role in keeping watch over the progress of reform in the Community.

We recommend that the Joint Intelligence Community Council (JICC) serve as a "customer council" for the Intelligence Community. The JICC, which was created by the recent legislation, consists of the heads of each department that has a component in the Intelligence Community. Chaired by the DNI, the JICC will include the Secretaries of State, Treasury, Defense, Energy, and Homeland Security, the Attorney General, and other officers designated by the President.[26] Although not a perfectly representative group of consumers, the JICC should provide the DNI with valuable feedback on intelligence products.[27] We do not think, however, that the JICC is the appropriate body to perform more sustained oversight of the Intelligence Community. Since the DNI chairs the JICC, and the members of the JICC are heads of departments containing intelligence components, the body would have a "conflict of interest" that would impair its ability to play an independent oversight role.

We recommend that the President's Foreign Intelligence Advisory Board assume a more vigorous role with respect to the Intelligence Community. The PFIAB as it is currently constituted, however, is insufficiently equipped to accomplish this task. In addition to the seasoned national security policy experts now on the Board, a reinvigorated PFIAB would need more technical specialists able to assess Intelligence Community performance, as well as a larger staff to support the review and investigation tasks inherent in meaningful oversight. Such a PFIAB is not impossible to conceive, for it has existed in the past—as it should in the future.

Recommendation 8

We recommend that the President suggest that Congress take steps to improve its structure for intelligence oversight.

As a commission established by the President, we tread onto the terrain of congressional reform with some trepidation. The new intelligence legislation, however, contains a provision requiring the delivery of our report to Congress. As a result, we believe that it would not be inappropriate for us to make suggestions for reform in this area that the President could, in turn, recommend that the Congress implement.

The 9/11 Commission concluded in its final report that the Congressional intelligence committees "lack the power, influence, and sustained capability" necessary to fulfill their critical oversight responsibilities.[28] The 9/11 Commission offered two alternatives for overhauling the intelligence committees: (1) creating a bicameral committee, modeled on the Joint Atomic Energy Committee; or (2) combining intelligence authorization and appropriation authorities into a single committee in each chamber.[29] The House and Senate have not adopted either of these options. While we echo the 9/11 Commission's support for these proposals, we also recommend a number of more modest suggestions for improving Congressional oversight of intelligence.

Limit the activities of new intelligence oversight subcommittees to strategic oversight. Both the House and the Senate intelligence committees have indicated their intention to establish oversight subcommittees.[30] But these subcommittees will not improve intelligence if they simply demand additional testimony from top intelligence officials on the crisis or scandal of the day. We suggest that, if created, the oversight subcommittees limit their activities to "strategic oversight," meaning they would set an agenda at the start of the year or session of Congress, based on top priorities such as information sharing, and stick to that agenda.

Adjust term limits. The Senate has voted to remove term limits for the Senate Select Committee on Intelligence.[31] While the House may consider this too large a step, it could consider alternatives that would ensure the survival of institutional memory while also bringing in "new blood" and providing more members with exposure to intelligence issues. For example, the House could lengthen or even eliminate the term limits for some of the committee slots rather than for all of the slots. We suggest making the House leadership's authority to waive term limits explicit in the rules, and specifying that some positions on the intelligence committee would be free of term limits.

Reduce the Intelligence Community's reliance upon supplemental funding. There were good reasons for supplemental funding requests following the September 11 attacks. But for fiscal year 2005, nearly two-thirds of the key operational needs for counterterrorism were not included in the President's budget, and instead were put in a supplemental budget request later in the year.[32] This reduces the Intelligence Community's ability to plan operations and build programs. Instead of continuing to rely on large supplemental appropriations, we recommend that Congress and the President develop annual budgets that include the Intelligence Community's needs for the entire year and better allow planning for future years.

Adjust budget jurisdiction. Currently, the House and Senate oversight committees have different jurisdictions over the various components of the intelligence budget. Both committees have jurisdiction over the National Intelligence Program (NIP). The House intelligence committee also shares jurisdiction with the Armed Services Committee over the Joint Military Intelligence Program (JMIP) and Tactical Intelligence and Related Activities (TIARA) budgets. The Senate intelligence committee has no jurisdiction over JMIP or TIARA, although it provides advice to the Armed Services

Committee on both budgets. This complicates conferences on the intelligence authorization bill and reduces intelligence committee input into the JMIP and TIARA budgets. We recommend broadening the Senate intelligence committee's jurisdiction to include JMIP and TIARA in order to integrate intelligence oversight from the tactical through to the national level.

Allocate the intelligence budget by mission, rather than only by program or activity. The DNI can also take steps to streamline and professionalize the intelligence oversight process. One impediment to Congressional evaluation of the intelligence budget is the way the budget is presented. Because line items track specific technologies or programs rather than mission areas, it is nearly impossible for Congress—or the Executive Branch—to evaluate how much money is being spent on priority targets such as terrorism or proliferation. We recommend that the DNI restructure the budget by mission areas, thus permitting greater transparency throughout the budget cycle. This mission-centered budget would permit the individual Community elements to track their expenditures by mission throughout the year, affording the DNI greater flexibility in managing the Community, and the Executive Branch and Congress an increased ability to provide effective oversight.

Deter unauthorized disclosures. More substantive Congressional oversight must be accompanied by a strengthened commitment to protect sensitive information from unauthorized disclosure. The Congress has rules to protect sensitive information and a process for investigating and penalizing those who violate those rules.[33] In some instances, however, unauthorized disclosures have either been ignored or treated lightly. The Senate and House leadership should place greater emphasis on ensuring that all members understand the need to carefully protect sensitive information and the penalties for unauthorized disclosures. For example, the leadership could make clear that all unauthorized disclosures of classified information will be referred to the ethics committees. Furthermore, both Senate and House members who are read into sensitive compartments should follow the same nondisclosure procedures applicable to the Executive Branch.[34]

Improve committee mechanisms to encourage bipartisanship. Partisan politics should never be allowed to threaten national security. To foster bipartisanship, we recommend that the House intelligence committee consider adopting provisions similar to those in the Senate, such as designating the ranking member as the Vice Chairman of the committee, requiring that the majority maintain no more than a one-member advantage in membership, and ensuring that the rules provide the majority and minority leaders with equal access to committee information. The committees could also take concrete steps to reinforce close, cooperative relationships among the entire staff. For example, regular joint staff meetings could be encouraged or even required. Perhaps most importantly, the staff should consist of national security professionals focused on the objectives and priorities of the committee.

Encourage more informal discussions and collaboration between the Intelligence Community and its congressional overseers. The Intelligence Community typically interacts with Congress in formal ways, through briefings to the intelligence committees and formal testimony. However, there also have been occasional "off sites" at which senior lawmakers and Intelligence Community leaders have met in a more informal and less adversarial setting. Both sides have stressed the value of these informal sessions, both in fostering cordial cross-branch relationships and in increasing bipartisanship among lawmakers. We encourage the expanded use of these and other informal collaborative efforts.

Consider an intelligence appropriations subcommittee. While the intelligence authorizing committees are well-staffed and completely focused on the Intelligence Community, the intelligence appropriations are simply a small part of the Defense and other appropriators' jurisdiction, so staffing and attention to intelligence issues are in short supply on the appropriations committees. The resulting mismatch reduces oversight and coordination of policy within Congress. While we recognize the difficulties, we suggest that serious consideration be given to the establishment of an appropriations subcommittee focused exclusively on the intelligence budget.

Look for ways to reduce the cost of oversight in the Intelligence Community. With so many congressional committees with jurisdiction over aspects of foreign and domestic intelligence, the oversight process—between staff requests, formal testimony, congressionally directed actions, and budget reviews—imposes great demands on the resources of the Intelligence Community. Intelligence Community professionals collectively appear before Congress in briefings or hearings over a thousand times a year, and also respond to hundreds of formal written requests from Congress annually[35] —and the latter number will only increase in light of the recent intelligence reform legislation, which itself added 27 one-time and 16 annual reports to the DNI's annual congressional reporting requirements. While we recognize that congressional oversight inherently has costs, we encourage the Congress to look for ways to streamline their interactions with the Intelligence Community.

Recommendation 9

The Intelligence Community should improve its internal processes for self-examination, including increasing the use of formal "lessons learned" studies.

As important as executive and legislative oversight is, they will never be a substitute for an Intelligence Community that takes self-evaluation seriously. But the Intelligence Community has done far too little to institutionalize "lessons learned" studies and other after-action evaluations that are commonplace in the Department of Defense and other government agencies. Of course, when human resources are stretched thin, the idea of devoting good personnel to examine the past often seems a luxury that intelligence agencies cannot afford.

Understandable as it is, this view must be resisted. Over the long run, an organization with sound "lessons learned" processes will be more efficient and productive—even if those processes seem to be distracting good people and resources from the imperatives of the moment. We recommend that the DNI develop institutionalized processes for performing "lessons learned" studies and for reviewing the Intelligence Community's own capabilities, rather than waiting for commissions like ours to do the job. In a separate chapter we offer a recommendation in this regard that is specific to analysis, (see Analysis, Chapter 8)—but this is a problem that affects all areas of intelligence. While we think it advisable that organizations devoted to self-evaluation exist in all major intelligence agencies, the DNI must drive an independent "lessons learned" process as well—for it is the DNI who will have insight into shortcomings and failures that cut across the intelligence process. We also note that whatever entities at the DNI or agency level assume these after-action responsibilities—be they agency inspectors general or other offices—they should not conduct these reviews to justify disciplinary or other personnel action, but rather to identify shortcomings and successes and to propose improvements to aspects of the intelligence process.

CONCLUSION

The creation of an integrated Intelligence Community will not happen merely by improving activities within different agencies, and it will most certainly not happen spontaneously. It will take assertive leadership by the new DNI, vigorous support from senior policymakers and Congress, and sustained oversight from outside the Intelligence Community. Provided all that, and substantial time, a Community that has resisted management reform—and often management of any sort—can emerge better configured to deal with the pressing challenges of the new century.

ADDENDUM: THE OFFICE OF THE DIRECTOR OF NATIONAL INTELLIGENCE

In our discussion of management issues the DNI will confront, we have tried to eschew the "boxology" that often dominates discussions of government reform. While it is obviously important to consider what staff functions will be performed in the Office of the DNI, precise organizational questions about the structure of the office—such as, for instance, the number of deputies the DNI should have and their responsibilities—are questions to which there is no "right answer." Nonetheless, when considering the tasks that will need to be performed in the office of the DNI, we necessarily had to consider how the office might be organized to perform these functions. We offer here the result of these considerations, but we emphasize that the model we propose is a notional one that we offer only to facilitate further discussion.

The new legislation creates a number of positions in the Office of the Director of National Intelligence. The statute creates a Senate-confirmed principal deputy to the DNI, and empowers the DNI to appoint up to four deputy directors. In addition, the statute also states that the Office of the DNI shall contain a General Counsel, a Director of Science and Technology, a National Counterintelligence Executive, a Civil Liberties Protection Officer, and the National Intelligence Council. Finally, the legislation provides that the Office of the DNI *may* include "[s]uch other offices and officials as may be established by law or the Director may establish or designate in the office," including "national intelligence centers." Of these various mandated and discretionary offices, only one—the Civil Liberties Protection Officer—is required by the act to "report directly to" the DNI;[36] in our view, the remainder can therefore report to the Director through one of the four Deputy DNIs (DDNI) permitted under the legislation.

The notional model described below—and depicted on the wiring chart at the end of this chapter—is structured around four Deputy Directors: a Deputy Director for Integrated Intelligence Strategies; a Deputy Director for Collection; a Deputy Director for Plans, Programs, Budgets, and Evaluation; and the Chief Information Management Officer. We also suggest the creation of two additional positions: an Assistant DNI for Support to Military Operations, and an Assistant DNI for Human Resources. The section that follows briefly describes the responsibilities of each of these subordinate offices.

Deputy DNI for Integrated Intelligence Strategies

We have stressed the need for ensuring that the Intelligence Community's management structure be focused on missions, and propose the creation of Mission Managers to ensure that intelligence collection is driven by the needs of analysts, policymakers, and other intelligence "customers." In our proposed organizational structure for the Office of the DNI, Mission Managers would be housed in the office of a Deputy DNI for "Integrated Intelligence Strategies." This office would also perform the following functions (often through the Mission Managers):

Mission Manager coordination, support, and oversight. The Deputy Director for Integrated Intelligence Strategies would advise the DNI on the intelligence subjects that require Mission Managers, and develop processes for the periodic review of those subjects to ensure that new priority intelligence topics are not missed. He or she would also oversee the Mission Managers and resolve disputes among them in those (we expect rare) situations where they disagree among each other over the prioritization of intelligence requirements.

Customer support. Mission managers will be the primary interface for customer support on their substantive topics, but the DDNI for Integrated Intelligence Strategies would establish procedures to improve customer support across the Intelligence Community and assess new ways to improve the ways in which policymakers and other users receive intelligence support.

Analytical oversight. The office of the Deputy Director for Integrated Intelligence Strategies would be responsible for overseeing the analytical community (often through Mission Managers), reaching out to subject-matter experts outside of the Intelligence Community (and developing procedures and processes for analysts throughout the Community to do the same), and encouraging the development and mainstreaming of new analytical tools.

Current intelligence support to the DNI. In fulfilling his role as principal intelligence advisor to the President, the DNI will require a support staff. This staff would be housed in the Office of the Deputy Director for Integrated Intelligence Strategies, who would serve as the DNI's principal intelligence expert.

Deputy DNI for Collection

Both in this chapter and in our later chapter devoted to Collection (Chapter 7), we emphasize the need for Community-level leadership of vital collection functions that today are not centrally managed. We would create a Deputy DNI for Collection to perform this role. One of this official's most important functions would be to oversee the customer-driven collection requirements process managed by the Mission Managers and their Target Development Boards. The Mission Managers should provide the needed analytic input directly to collection agencies, but there must be a mechanism to ensure that intelligence collectors are responding to those requirements. The Deputy DNI for Collection would also perform the following functions:

Strategic oversight of collection. The Office of the Deputy Director for Collection would monitor the performance of collection agencies in responding to all customer needs, including, most importantly, the requirements developed by Mission Managers and Target Development Boards and those that ensure that U.S. military commanders and forces are also appropriately supported. It would also oversee the development of the "integrated collection enterprise" we recommend in Chapter Seven (Collection).

Development of new collection sources and methods. When collection requirements cannot be met because of insufficient capabilities, this office would spur the development of new sources and methods to overcome the capability gap. This office would play an especially important role in sponsoring those new capabilities whose interoperability across collection agencies is critical to Community collaboration. Efforts to identify new capabilities will include outreach to U.S. government laboratories, industry, and academia, as appropriate.

Strategic investment for Community collection. When collection requirements cannot be met because of insufficient capability, and new technologies and systems are required, the Deputy DNI for Collection would advocate innovative science and technology for collection applications, and would ensure such capability requirements are addressed in the development of the National Intelligence Program (NIP) budget, and in the DNI's inputs to the Joint Military Intelligence Program (JMIP) and Tactical Intelligence and Related Activities (TIARA) budgets.

Deputy DNI for Plans, Programs, Budgets, and Evaluation

As we have noted, the DNI's primary leverage will come not through "line" control of Intelligence Community agencies, but rather from his budgetary authorities. We would establish a Deputy DNI for Plans, Programs, Budgets, and Evaluation (PPBE) to ensure that this authority is exercised promptly and completely. The Deputy DNI for PPBE's most significant functional responsibilities would include:

Plans and policy. The DNI is responsible for developing and presenting the NIP budget and for participating in the development of the JMIP and TIARA budgets.[37] To develop a rational investment balance to meet customer needs, the DNI will have to evaluate the capabilities of the Community, develop options for resource allocations, and propose specific programs submitted for inclusion in the NIP.

Comptroller. As a financial manager, the DNI is responsible for executing the NIP and reprogramming funds within limits established in the new legislation.[38] In performing these duties, the DNI will require a staff element to fill these comptroller functions.

Acquisition. The reform legislation makes the DNI the Milestone Decision Authority for major acquisition systems funded in whole within the NIP and assigns the DNI responsibility to procure information technology systems for the Intelligence Community. Through the Deputy DNI for PPBE, the DNI would set acquisition policy, provide acquisition oversight, and act as program manager for all Community systems whose interoperability is essential to Community effectiveness. As we have noted, for the major systems over which the DNI and the Secretary of Defense share acquisition authority, joint procedures must be established with the Defense Department.

Program evaluation. The Deputy DNI for PPBE would be responsible for analyzing and evaluating plans, programs, and budgets in relation to Community objectives and requirements, and for ensuring that costs of Community programs are presented accurately and completely.

Chief Information Management Officer

One of our major information sharing recommendations is that the DNI appoint a chief information management officer (CIMO) who would manage the information sharing environment for the Intelligence Community. Given the importance of the development of such an environment, we would make the CIMO one of the DNI's Deputies. We detail the CIMO's responsibilities in our chapter on Information Sharing (Chapter 9), but we emphasize here that this individual would be responsible both for information *sharing* and information *security* across the Intelligence Community. As the attached organizational chart suggests, we would have the CIMO supported by three separate component offices dedicated to information sharing, information security and protection of sources and methods, and risk management.

Assistant DNI for Support to Military Operations

The Director of Central Intelligence (DCI) currently has an Associate DCI for Military Support—a position created in the wake of Operation Desert Storm to provide a high level military representative on the DCI's staff whose mission was to improve the Intelligence Community's support to military operations. Incumbents in this position have been three-star officers, normally with a combat-arms background. As we have noted in our management discussion, in the wake of the intelligence reform legislation the relationship between the DNI and the Secretary of Defense will assume great significance. Accordingly, we would suggest that a similar—and strengthened—military support position be created in the Office of the DNI who would act as principal advisor to the DNI on military support issues, serve as Mission Manager for intelligence support to military operations, and assist the DNI in developing joint strategies and coordination procedures between the DNI and the Secretary of Defense.

Assistant DNI for Human Resources

The intelligence legislation provides the DNI with substantial personnel authorities, and we recommend earlier in this chapter that a DNI-level Human Resources Authority be established to develop and implement appropriate personnel policies and procedures for the Intelligence Community. We would propose that an Assistant DNI for Human Resources oversee this Human Resources Authority, and oversee the substantial changes in recruiting, training, and personnel policy that we believe are necessary. The Assistant DNI for Human Resources would also oversee the National Intelligence University that we recommend in this chapter.

A Notional Organization of the Office of the Director of National Intelligence

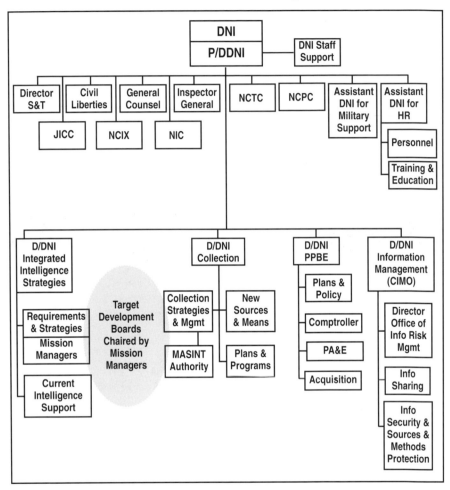

ENDNOTES

[1] While the 15 organizations within the Intelligence Community are not all technically "agencies"—some are instead designated as "bureaus" or "offices" within executive departments or military services—we at times refer to them collectively as "agencies," for the sake of simplicity and convenience. For a more detailed description of the components of the Intelligence Community, please see our Overview of the Intelligence Community at Appendix D of this Report.

[2] Intelligence Reform and Terrorism Prevention Act of 2004 at § 1011, Pub. L. No. 108-458 (hereinafter "IRTPA").

[3] Interview with senior Department of Defense official (Oct. 4, 2004).

[4] The DNI is to "determine" and guide the development of the NIP and the budgets for the Community's component agencies. IRTPA at § 1011. Moreover, in contrast to the DCI, whose formal participation in the budget process ended when the annual budget was prepared, the DNI both directs the allocation of National Intelligence Program appropriations and can "ensure the effective execution" of the annual intelligence budget. Perhaps most importantly, while the DCI could not transfer national intelligence program funds within the budget of an intelligence agency without approval of the agency's department head, the DNI can transfer up to $150 million annually (or 5 percent of a given intelligence agency's budget) without approval. *Id.*

[5] The overall budget for intelligence is divided into three separate programs: the National Intelligence Program; the Joint Military Intelligence Program (JMIP); and the programs for Tactical Intelligence and Related Activities (TIARA). The Secretary of Defense has primary authority to develop the annual JMIP and TIARA budgets, although the new legislation states that the DNI shall "participate" in the development of these processes. *Id.*

[6] The DNI has exclusive Milestone Decision Authority only for major system intelligence acquisition programs that are not in the Department of Defense. The DNI must share Milestone Decision Authority with the Secretary of Defense for systems funded by the NIP that are within the Defense Department, and lacks even joint Milestone Decision Authority over major system intelligence programs that rely in whole or in part on the Defense Department's joint military or tactical intelligence program funds. *Id.*

[7] *Id.*

[8] *Id.*

[9] Some have suggested—drawing on a loose analogy to the military's use of "joint commands"—that the best way to accomplish this task is to divide the universe of intelligence into "national intelligence centers." As we discuss later in this chapter, while we believe that centers can and should be used in certain circumstances, we are less enthusiastic about the idea of using centers as a generally applicable organizational model for tackling intelligence problems, and believe the Mission Manager concept to be superior for this purpose.

[10] IRTPA at § 1011.

[11] *See, e.g.,* James R. Locher, *Victory on the Potomac: The Goldwater-Nichols Act Unifies the Pentagon* (2002); Commission on the Roles and Capabilities of the United States Intelligence Community (i.e., Aspin-Brown Commission), *Preparing for the 21st Century: An Appraisal of U.S. Intelligence* (1996).

[12] DCI Community Management Staff, *NFIP—Funds by Selected Topic: Education and Training* (Dec. 7, 2004) (prepared at the Commission's request).

[13] Interview with senior CIA official (Dec. 9, 2004).

[14] IRTPA at § 1021 (on the NCTC) and § 1022 (on the NCPC).

[15] *Id*. at § 1022.

[16] While we believe that chemical weapons are not a threat of the same order as nuclear and biological weapons, there are sufficient areas of overlap between the processes for collecting intelligence on these three categories of weapons to justify the inclusion of chemical weapons in the NCPC's mission. It is critical, however, that resources at the NCPC be allocated among these weapons types in a manner that is proportionate to the threat.

[17] *Final Report of the National Commission on Terrorist Attacks Upon the United States* (2004) at p. 410 (hereinafter "9/11 Commission Report").

[18] We recognize that the Intelligence Community implements policy when it executes covert action, but this is done (we think appropriately) with very strict oversight and in relatively limited circumstances.

[19] Interview with R. James Woolsey, former Director of Central Intelligence (Aug. 24, 2004).

[20] Interview with senior Defense Department official (Feb. 3, 2005).

[21] Interview with senior Defense Department official (Jan. 13, 2005).

[22] *Id*.

[23] Interview with senior Defense Department official (Feb. 3, 2005).

[24] IRTPA at § 1013.

[25] James Schlesinger, A *Review of the Intelligence Community* (Mar. 10, 1971).

[26] IRTPA at § 1031.

[27] The JICC as currently composed does not include a representative from the Executive Office of the President, or other parts of the Executive Branch that do not include elements of the Intelligence Community. The President could easily solve the problem of no White House representation by making the Special Assistant to the President for National Security Affairs a member of the Council.

[28] 9/11 Commission Report at p. 420.

[29] *Id*.

[30] The U.S. House of Representatives has created a Subcommittee on Oversight for the 109th Congress. The Senate has to date not created one although there is ongoing discussion of the issue.

[31] Senate Resolution 445, 108th Congress, 2nd Session (Oct. 9, 2004).

[32] Interview with DCI Community Management Staff official (Feb. 23, 2005); CIA, *Response to Document Request # 74, Question 2*.

[33] *Rules of the Select Committee on Intelligence, Congressional Record* (Feb. 25, 2003) at pp. S2689-S2694.

[34] HPSCI staff members are required by HPSCI Rules 12(b)(2) to sign a Non-Disclosure Agreement. Both Members and staff are bound by the House Rules regarding non-disclosure of classified material. Senate Rule 10.5 also contains a requirement of a Non-Disclosure Agreement for SSCI staffers.

[35] Office of the DCI, Submission to Commission (March 2005).

[36] IRTPA at § 1011.

[37] *Id*.

[38] *Id*.

Chapter seven
collection

Summary & Recommendations

The collection of information is the foundation for everything that the Intelligence Community does. While successful collection cannot ensure a good analytical product, the failure to collect information—as our Iraq study demonstrated—turns analysis into guesswork. And as our review demonstrates, the Intelligence Community's human and technical intelligence collection agencies have collected far too little information on many of the issues we care about most.

This chapter sets forth our recommendations for improving the collection capabilities of our Intelligence Community so that it is better equipped to confront today's diffuse, elusive, and ever-changing intelligence challenges. These recommendations fall into two categories: those focused on improving the performance of particular collection agencies, and those aimed at integrating the management of collection across the Intelligence Community. Among other suggestions, we recommend that the DNI:

- Create an "integrated collection enterprise"—that is, a management structure that ensures that the Intelligence Community's decentralized collection capabilities are developed in a manner that is consistent with long-term strategic intelligence priorities, and are deployed in a coordinated way against today's intelligence targets;

- Encourage the development of new and innovative human intelligence collection techniques, and empower the CIA to coordinate the full spectrum of human intelligence activities performed in the Intelligence Community; and

- Establish an Open Source Directorate in the CIA responsible for collecting and storing open source information, and developing or incorporating commercial tools to assist users in data searches—including those in foreign languages.

INTRODUCTION

The Intelligence Community exists, first and foremost, to collect information vital to the national security of the United States. This may seem self-evident, but it bears restating—for as our case studies demonstrate, there are simply too many gaps in our understanding of too many serious national security threats. Our Iraq case study found a near complete failure across all of the Intelligence Community's collection disciplines—from those who collect human intelligence, to the technical collection agencies that take satellite photographs and intercept communications—to gather valuable information on Saddam Hussein's weapons capabilities. And our broader review found that Iraq was not an isolated case. From Iran's pursuit of nuclear weapons to the inner workings of al-Qa'ida, the Intelligence Community frequently admitted to us that it lacks answers.

The collection challenges facing the Intelligence Community are certainly daunting. In addition to maintaining the ability to penetrate closed societies— a capability that proved essential to the conduct of foreign policy during the Cold War and that remains vital today with regard to states including China, North Korea, and Iran—the Community also faces the imperative of collecting against secretive transnational organizations that operate globally. At the same time, modern warfare requires that national intelligence collectors both support strategic planning needs and offer real-time assistance to military operations. In short, the Community is facing unprecedented demands to do it all, and to do it all very well.

It is clear that the old ways of doing business will not suffice to meet these challenges. For example, the "traditional" model for collecting human intelligence is ill-suited to confront some of today's most critical intelligence challenges. And traditional technical collection techniques have been degraded by the pace of change in telecommunications technology and by our adversaries' increasing awareness of our capabilities. It therefore came as no surprise to us when we found that many recent intelligence successes resulted from more innovative collection techniques. But as these innovation efforts are still episodic and far too rare, in this chapter we offer recommendations aimed at encouraging our intelligence agencies to develop new ways of collecting information—ranging from methods for conducting human intelligence, to finding technologies for exploiting the massive amount of "open source" information now available on the Internet and in other publicly available sources.

But to focus only on developing new techniques would be to confront only half of the collection challenge. Of equal importance—and consistent with our call for greater integration throughout the Intelligence Community—we found that collectors too often operate independently. Our largely autonomous collection agencies have not been accountable to any central authority within the Intelligence Community for the investments they make or the qual ity of intelligence they collect. Moreover, because they do not coordinate their activities, opportunities for highly promising collaborative collection are often missed. Therefore, we also propose that the Intelligence Community's collection capabilities be managed as an "integrated collection enterprise"— that is, we need a collection process that is strategically managed and coordinated at every step, from investment in research and development, to the acquisition of technical systems, to the formulation and implementation of coordinated cross-agency strategies for deploying our collection resources.

Despite the difficulty and diversity of the challenges facing the Intelligence Community, the excuse "it's too hard" plainly will not suffice. We must reconfigure the Community's collection capabilities in ways that enable it to reduce uncertainty against key intelligence threats. This chapter offers our recommendations for accomplishing this objective.

THE TARGETING CHALLENGE

Our recommendations are designed to increase the Intelligence Community's ability to collect against today's targets as well as expected targets of the future. As a starting point, however, it is worth considering how our collection system got where it is today, and why the rapidly changing nature of many threats makes that system so inadequate.

The Cold War

Throughout the Cold War, the United States focused its collection efforts against monolithic Communist powers—the Soviet Union and China—and their proxy states. These targets had sizeable military and industrial complexes that our satellites could observe, and they had hierarchical institutions, predictable communications procedures, and reporting behavior that we could selectively target for eavesdropping. As a result, although penetration took time and was far from perfect, on the whole the Intelligence Community gained an impressive understanding of our main adversaries.

During this period, a number of intelligence agencies—the National Security Agency, the National Reconnaissance Office, and others—developed around the various technologies and disciplines used to collect against these targets.[1] These agencies were largely independent entities capable of determining their own strategies with only general guidance from above. As a general matter, they engaged in limited collaborative collection, and each (unsurprisingly) tended to invest in the research and development of technologies for collecting on the traditional Cold War targets. They did not (nor, perhaps, could they) anticipate the very different threats that we face today.

Today's Targets

In contrast to the Cold War, today's collection environment is characterized by a wider spectrum of threats and targets. For example, non-state actors such as al-Qa'ida present a new type of asymmetric menace. They operate globally, blending into local society and using informal networks for support. Locating and tracking dispersed terrorists and guerrilla fighters hiding in an urban environment—rather than massed armored forces on a European battlefield—typifies the type of collection problems the Intelligence Community faces today.[2] Such dispersed targets can, and often do, communicate chiefly through methods that are difficult to detect and that some of our collection systems are poorly suited to penetrate. In sum, today's threats are quick, quiet, and hidden.

Of course, state actors like Russia, China, and North Korea also continue to require attention. But for several reasons, penetrating these targets has also become more difficult than ever before. For example, authorized and unauthorized disclosures of U.S. sources and methods have significantly impaired the effectiveness of our collection systems. Put simply, our adversaries have learned much about what we can see and hear, and have predictably taken steps to thwart our efforts.[3] In addition, the changing face of weapons technology now means that certain weapons types, particularly biological and chemical weapons, can be produced in a manner that is difficult or impossible to detect.[4] All of this implies that the Community's effectiveness will continue to decline in the coming years unless concerted change occurs.[5]

Addressing Today's Collection Demands

It's not just that targets have changed; demands for collection have also shifted. Most significantly, since the first Gulf War, U.S. military requirements for national intelligence have spiked.

In the not-too-distant future, the U.S. military hopes to achieve a common operating picture of the battlefield in real time using a diverse set of tactical, national, and commercial sensors and communication technologies. This force transformation will create new requirements for collection and necessitate new approaches to fusing and integrating data to enable real-time analysis. And although the military's vision is not yet a reality, current demands have already put a strain on finite collection capabilities.

As a result, military requirements on national collection systems (such as satellites) have already diminished our effectiveness with respect to other targets important to national decisionmakers. For example, a study of why the Intelligence Community failed to warn of the surprise nuclear tests in India in May 1998 found that limited collection on India test sites was explained, in part, by its low priority owing to competing military requirements.[6] More recently, we found that support to current military operations in Iraq diverted imagery collection resources that would otherwise have been available to obtain information on nuclear developments on other priority targets in the region.

Regrettably, the Intelligence Community does not currently have a systematic process for balancing these competing interests. Today, the Assistant DCI for Collection and the Under Secretary of Defense for Intelligence meet frequently to discuss collection issues, including the allocation of national intelligence systems to support the needs of the military. However, neither individual has the requisite authority or resources to routinely develop and direct the implementation of integrated target development strategies.[7] As a result, the Intelligence Community has tended not to use its available collection systems efficiently.

This inefficiency is merely illustrative of a larger problem—the absence of methods for prioritizing and coordinating our Intelligence Community's decentralized collection capabilities. No office or individual sets long-term research and development priorities, acquires necessary capabilities, and formulates and implements an integrated collection strategy from a Community-wide perspective. Instead, each of these functions is run by a panoply of different intelligence collection organizations.

Our case study of Iraq found that such disaggregation sometimes undermined effective intelligence gathering. Other studies we conducted, including those involving Iran's nuclear program and North Korea, further concluded that the current collection system has limited ability to engage in long-term, coordinated planning on existing threats, let alone to anticipate surprises. As a result, intelligence collection appears to be consistently behind the curve in identifying change, and it is usually positioned to be reactive rather than proactive—when it needs to be both.

Many of these observations—and our associated recommendations—are not new. Several decades of studies of the Intelligence Community have identified the lack of a unified, coherent collection process as a major shortcoming of the Community.[8] These studies recognized that under the existing system, no one other than the President, who obviously lacks the time for such a detailed task, has the clear authority to direct all of the nation's collection assets. This absence of central authority has impeded the development and implementation of unified strategies that operate existing collection assets against "hard targets."[9] In today's threat environment, we cannot wait decades longer to remedy these problems.

CREATING AN "INTEGRATED COLLECTION ENTERPRISE"

Recommendation 1

The DNI should create a new management structure within the Office of the DNI that manages collection as an "integrated collection enterprise." Such an integrated approach should include coordinated target development, collection management, data management, strategic planning and investment, and the development of new collection techniques.

Intelligence collection is a massive endeavor. In order to collect effectively, the Intelligence Community must develop, buy, and operate collection systems, manage the data that the systems collect, and plan for the acquisition of future systems. It is this cradle-to-grave process that we refer to as the "collection enterprise." As the following makes clear, the Mission Managers we proposed in our chapter on management will play an integral role in nearly every facet of this integrated structure. There are five key components to this enterprise:

Target development: The process of defining collection priorities, determining existing collection gaps, and developing integrated collection strategies to address those gaps;

Collection management: Ensuring the effective implementation of the integrated collection strategies across the collection disciplines;

Data management: Supervising the processing, exploitation, movement, and analysis of data that is collected through each of the different collection disciplines;

Strategic planning and investment: Evaluating different investment alternatives, considering budgetary tradeoffs, and establishing long-term acquisition strategies; and

Developing new collection techniques: Evaluating current collection methods, designing new methods (including new platforms for human intelligence), and establishing research and development programs to fill intelligence needs.

As we have already discussed, each of the five functions we identify is currently performed primarily within individual collection agencies. The goal of our recommendation is to create an integrated collection process that performs each of these functions from the perspective of the *entire* Intelligence Community, rather than individual agencies. This is not to say that there are no benefits to the current decentralized approach to intelligence collection. We recognize, for example, that each agency understands its own capabilities best and is, in many ways, able to optimize its own efforts.

Our recommendation therefore attempts to build on these strengths. The new integrated enterprise will draw on the technical expertise possessed by each collector, but will also demand that agencies work together to ensure that all forms of collection are used where they are most needed and effective. We also do not expect the new collection enterprise to displace existing personal relationships between collectors and analysts that allow analysts to provide additional clarifications or tasking. We do expect, however, that the centralized process we propose would ensure that the resources of our collection agencies are marshaled in a more strategic, cost-effective, and coordinated way.

We consider each of the key components of this integrated enterprise in turn.

Integrated Target Development

Recommendation 2

Target Development Boards, which would be chaired by the Mission Managers, should develop collection requirements and strategies and evaluate collectors' responsiveness to these needs.

Current collection processes are unique to each collection discipline and are often supported by complex and opaque "requirements systems." This typically means that in order to ask a collection agency to gather intelligence on a particular issue, analysts must forward their intelligence needs to their organization's collection managers or to discipline-specific Community collection committees, which in turn send collection requirements to specific collection agencies. Some analysts may also submit informal, *ad hoc* requests to their working-level associates and counterparts in collection organizations. Each collection agency then works independently to satisfy the "customer"—meaning, in this case, the analyst.

This rather haphazard process is occasionally prodded or refined by the intervention of the Assistant Director of Central Intelligence for Collection and his National Intelligence Collection Board (NICB), whose members represent the collection agencies. The board members meet to discuss and review some high-priority intelligence issues and the efforts by individual collection agencies to fulfill the associated collection requirements. We believe that this process has shown itself to be inadequate to the collection challenges facing the Community today, and that a more integrated strategy—one that would consolidate information needs and collection capabilities in one forum—would be a dramatic leap forward. We recommend the establishment of standing Target Development Boards for this purpose.

In our chapter on management (Chapter 6), we recommend that the DNI establish several "Mission Managers" who would be responsible for managing both analysis and collection on a particular intelligence target. Each Mission Manager would chair a Target Development Board, which would precisely define and prioritize information needs for that Mission Manager's subject area, determine existing intelligence gaps, and develop collection strategies to address them. As this list of responsibilities suggests, the boards would comprise both analysts and collectors from all relevant agencies and the military. Board members would have full visibility into the range of collection capabilities (including, as needed, those that are especially sensitive). The boards, led by the Mission Manager, would develop collection strategies that would serve as the blueprint for the Community's collection efforts. The boards would also provide a forum for discussing the optimal way to conduct those efforts. Ultimately, Target Development Boards would assess whether collectors have fulfilled their information needs[10]—and if they determine that existing collection capabilities cannot fulfill these requirements, Mission Managers could recommend that research and development of particular new sources and technologies are needed.

We have purposely avoided addressing the question of comprehensively listing which issues should be served by Mission Managers. In our view, the new DNI will be best situated to evaluate what issues are most pressing and therefore require Mission Managers. That being said, we believe the DNI should develop clear processes for defining the scope of responsibility for new Mission Managers and for phasing out—or "sunsetting"—Mission Managers whose missions no longer warrant such attention. We think this last point is critical, for one of the advantages we see in Mission Managers, as opposed to more permanent centers, is the flexibility they offer the DNI to adjust to shifting priorities. Finally, the DNI might consider establishing a "Global Issues Mission Manager" to serve as a "catch-all" for any number of issues that require special attention yet do not require their own Mission Manager.

Strategic Management of Collection

Target Development Boards would send baseline requirements for their issue directly to collection agencies (*e.g.*, NSA, NGA, CIA). In addition, a consolidated, prioritized list of all the target board requirements—reflecting the priorities of the President, other key decisionmakers, and the military—would be developed on a periodic basis to provide strategic guidance to collectors as to the nation's most important information needs and to ensure a balance is maintained between national intelligence collection support to military operations and other national priorities.

The part of the DNI's office responsible for managing national intelligence collection resources would work with the Mission Managers to ensure that their consolidated collection strategies are executed efficiently, and would resolve conflicting requirements. This part of the DNI's office would be best suited to strategically oversee the implementation of the integrated Target Development Board strategies by guaranteeing that collection agencies were in fact targeting the identified priorities and making sure that each collection system was targeting the intelligence gaps that it is best suited to address. This same entity could monitor overall developments within the collection organizations and would assist the Mission Managers by keeping them informed of collection activities and helping to evaluate the performance of collectors.

Introducing Mission Managers, Target Development Boards, and a strategic management element to the collection process would thus address several specific, serious flaws that were identified in our case studies by providing a permanent mechanism for identifying current and future intelligence gaps and pairing those gaps with the capabilities required to fill them, a forum for developing strategies that optimize resources by reducing redundancy and maximizing opportunities to use the various collection disciplines in tandem or complimentary fashion, and a formalized system for ironing out competing collection priorities across the Community.

Targeting in an Integrated Fashion

What might the target development and strategic management components of the integrated collection enterprise mean in practice? We anticipate that the basic process might work much as described in the following scenario if the DNI were to designate a Mission Manager for Country X:

Targeting in an Integrated Fashion (Continued)

We envision that the Country X Mission Manager, in conjunction with analysts and the Country X Target Development Board, will identify the most important subject matter areas relating to Country X's nuclear program. The Target Development Board will then study all available collection capabilities against the target and craft a strategy that matches those capabilities from across the Community to the intelligence "gaps" we have in our understanding of Country X's program. If collectors come up short in filling these "gaps," the Mission Manager may recommend more aggressive collection techniques involving higher risk strategies. Because it is a standing entity, the Target Development Board will be able to quickly revisit priorities in response to changing events, and adjust the collection strategy correspondingly.

Having developed a collection strategy, the Mission Manager then will forward collection requirements to various collection agencies—NSA, NRO, CIA, DIA, and others. A collection-focused office in the DNI's office (perhaps a Deputy DNI for Collection), assisted by the Mission Manager, will work to ensure that the collection agencies implement the collection strategy, help them fine-tune it where necessary to encourage complementary collection strategies, and seek to avoid redundant efforts.

As our case studies suggest, there will likely be conflicts over resources. For instance, the Mission Manager for Terrorism may argue that more satellite time should be directed toward targets of interest in Country Y, and the DNI's designee will be forced to make hard choices. The Mission Manager and the DNI's appropriate deputy will remain involved in the day-to-day monitoring of collection efforts to coordinate with the collection agencies and ensure that Country X issues are addressed—or that an inability to collect on the Country X target, due to a need to focus collection resources elsewhere, is factored into Community-wide assessments.

Integrated Data Management

The collection enterprise does not stop with the actual collection of information. It is also about moving that information into the collection agencies, processing and exploiting the data, disseminating it to analysts and, increasingly, directly to users. All of this requires a sophisticated information infrastructure that allows for the manipulation of huge volumes of data. (Chapter 9 (Information Sharing) deals with the necessity of removing barriers to information flow *among* agencies.) But a precondition to improving Community-wide information sharing is the development of common data management infrastructures *within* individual agencies that can be integrated with the Community as a whole. Only then will different collection agencies be able to collaborate and effectively maximize the advantages of multi-discipline collection.[11]

The idea that an integrated data management infrastructure will allow collection agencies to work more closely with one another is far from new. In fact, we must commend the current Directors of NSA and NGA—Lieutenant General Michael Hayden and Lieutenant General (Ret.) James Clapper—for their visionary efforts to create interfacing data management tools and methodologies for their two agencies. Regrettably, the directors' efforts have been stymied by two problems. First, the agency bureaucracies have tended to focus on their local needs versus the more global, Community-wide needs. Second, both agencies have been unable to successfully complete the necessary large-scale acquisition contracts.[12]

The lack of progress in developing new information infrastructures, and the failure to develop common information technology standards across the Community, will continue to be a major impediment to an integrated collection enterprise. Without a Community-wide plan, we fear that individual agencies will continue to invest—and waste—large amounts of resources in underperforming information infrastructures that cannot be integrated easily with other information systems across the Community.

We therefore propose, consistent with the *Intelligence Reform and Terrorism Prevention Act's* directive,[13] that the DNI develop a strategic plan for enabling collaboration and information sharing among collection agencies. This plan would identify the requirements for a Community-wide information infrastructure, set common standards for promoting information sharing techniques such as data-tagging, and develop guidance on new tools and methods for exploiting and processing collected data.

Integrated Strategic Planning and Investment

Technical collection currently accounts for roughly half of the intelligence budget.[14] One of the obstacles to achieving an integrated collection system is the fragmented nature of the intelligence budget, which is divided along programmatic lines and largely committed to legacy systems. Previous attempts to develop Community-wide budget priorities have met resistance from individual intelligence organizations, which naturally prefer the autonomy they enjoy under the current system.

Without a single individual or office to overcome these barriers, the Intelligence Community's enormous investment in technical collection has been, in some cases, duplicative and slow to respond to changed conditions; it has also provided the United States with inadequate capabilities to penetrate targets. Integrating strategic planning and investment would give a single office authority to look across collection agencies and advise the DNI on where to invest the Community's resources.

We believe the DNI should establish an office with requisite authorities to develop a strategic investment plan for Community-wide collection capabilities. This body would:

■ Review, evaluate, and oversee National Intelligence Program (NIP) collection programs and budgets as part of the DNI's annual review process, including strategic investment for development of future collection concepts and associated processing, exploitation, and analysis capabilities;

■ Conduct evaluations of collection investment alternatives across disciplines;

■ Allocate strategic investments to develop new sources and methods;

■ Collaborate with designees of the Secretary of Defense to ensure the effective integration of collection systems in the NIP, Joint Military Intelligence Program (JMIP), and Tactical Intelligence and Related Activities (TIARA) budgets;

■ Ensure that investments in collection, processing, exploitation, and dissemination technologies are appropriately balanced; and

■ Ensure appropriate funding for strategic investment priorities and, to the extent possible, ensure that such funds are not obtained through supplemental funding.

Integrated Development of New Collection Techniques

The primary obstacle to developing and implementing a sound research and development program is the same as that which stands in the way of an integrated strategic investment plan. Today there is no single official empowered to manage the Community's overall research and development needs. A single person should have authority to assess alternative options, select among competing priorities, choose solutions, and direct appropriate research and development initiatives to solve collection problems.

To establish an integrated approach to research and development across the Intelligence Community, the DNI should create an office responsible for assessing collection technology needs and developing a unified research and development strategy. This structure should be responsible for the following functions:

- Assessing program and technology gaps and proposing solutions;

- Developing and defining collection research and development strategies and plans;

- Developing and implementing innovative approaches for technical, operational, and exploitation functions related to collection;

- Working with the Office of the DNI's Director of Science and Technology to ensure that the national technology community—including the government, national labs, academia, and the commercial sector—has effective processes to recognize future threats and opportunities, and to help develop new and effective collection approaches;

- Ensuring the development of collection sensors, platforms, systems, and architectures that show substantial promise of defeating foreign denial and deception programs; and

- Ensuring that agencies have sufficient research and development funds to take advantage of innovative new approaches in collection and analysis.

This office should also be equipped with a significant budget in order to fund independent research without first seeking consensus from the collection agencies' various research and development units. It should also be given authority to oversee and recommend modifications to the research and development budgets of those units. We believe that the DNI should determine how these collection-specific research and development needs should relate to the newly-created Director of Science and Technology. [15]

Even with the creation of an office dedicated to Community-wide research and development, we remain concerned that the DNI may have difficulty ensuring unity of effort.[16] The DNI does not have control over significant portions of the research and development budget contained in JMIP and TIARA. Nor does the new legislation resolve existing conflicts between the authorities of the DNI and Secretary of Defense for funding and managing programs within the NIP, JMIP, and TIARA. We have learned of several instances in which important efforts were stalled by conflicts of authority. For example, at least one major technical collection initiative—one that we cannot describe in our unclassified report—has been in limbo for over two years because the Intelligence Community and Defense Department cannot agree on a single set of requirements, mission scenarios, funding, operational control, and integration with other technical collection programs. Our recommendation, therefore, is only a half-step toward the needed solution; as we have noted elsewhere (see Chapter 6, Management), close cooperation with the Defense Department is also required.

IMPROVING THE PERFORMANCE OF INDIVIDUAL COLLECTION DISCIPLINES

Human Intelligence Collection

Human intelligence serves policymakers by providing a unique window into our targets' most guarded intentions, plans, and programs. During the Cold War, intelligence from GRU Colonel Oleg Penkovskiy proved critical to our management and eventual resolution of the Cuban missile crisis. Later, Polish Colonel Ryszard Kuklinsky provided us with highly secret war plans from the Soviet Union. The recent penetration of the A.Q. Khan nuclear proliferation network is another example of an impressive human intelligence achievement.

As the President himself has observed, the United States desperately needs human sources to confront today's intelligence challenges.[17] To its credit, the Intelligence Community has, since September 11, undertaken efforts to rise to the President's challenge and redirect human intelligence collection toward today's threats. But as our case studies make clear, in the context of hard targets like Iraq, Iran, North Korea, and al-Qa'ida, human intelligence is still not delivering the goods. We have identified numerous reasons for this:

Losing human intelligence resources. Since the dissolution of the Soviet Union, the loss of human intelligence resources has brought the Community well below optimal strength. In the 1990s, CIA's Directorate of Operations (DO) experienced an appreciable decline in its career service rolls, including a significant decline in operations officers.[18] Similarly, DIA's Defense HUMINT service lost hundreds of billets between 1995 and 2001.[19] The Community has suffered a hemorrhage of irreplaceable experience.

The threat has changed, but we have not adapted. Post-Cold War targets—which include numerous "denied areas" and elusive non-state terror organizations—require our human intelligence agencies to develop different skill sets. We believe that human intelligence collectors have been too slow to respond to this sea change in operational requirements.

The hardest conventional targets remain largely impenetrable. Traditional state targets remain resistant to human penetrations. Our foes tend to be police states and totalitarian dictatorships—regimes that typically excel at countering espionage against them. Closed states like North Korea and Saddam Hussein's Iraq have countered U.S. collection efforts with, among other tools, pervasive counterintelligence and security apparatuses. Our case studies—including both Iraq (Chapter 1) and our classified studies of other "closed societies"—starkly illustrate human intelligence collectors' continuing difficulty in penetrating these targets. Intelligence Community coordination issues, bureaucratic risk aversion, and highly inadequate cover diversification have all retarded progress against these key targets.

Human intelligence collection is uncoordinated and lacks common standards. Minimal coordination among elements in the past sufficed when the CIA, FBI, and the Defense Department had more distinct missions, but lines of authority have blurred due to these agencies' responses to the imperatives of the terrorist threat. Both the FBI and the Defense Department's Special Operations Forces are major new players, and DIA has expanded its existing human intelligence service. There is considerable value in the new resources and perspectives that these new players bring, but there are risks as well. These risks can only be addressed through greater coordination.

Some human intelligence agencies do a poor job of validating human sources. The story of "Curveball"—the human source who lied to the Intelligence Community about Iraq's biological weapons programs—is an all-too-familiar one. Every agency that collects human intelligence has been burned in the past by false reporting; indeed, the Intelligence Community has been completely fooled several times by large-scale double-agent operations run by, among others, the Cubans, East Germans, and Soviets. It is therefore critical that our human intelligence agencies have excellent practices of validating and vetting their sources.

We believe that these deficiencies in validating sources demonstrate that the Intelligence Community needs to change fundamentally the way it conducts the human intelligence mission. Specifically, we recommend: (1) that the Community develop and increase the use of new human intelligence collection methods; (2) that a new Human Intelligence Directorate be created within the CIA and that it be given the lead in coordinating the full spectrum of human intelligence activities performed Community-wide; (3) that steps be taken to professionalize the Intelligence Community's cadre of human intelligence officers; and (4) that human intelligence training be diversified and expanded to broaden expertise and reduce seemingly intractable training bottlenecks.

Coordinating Human Intelligence

Recommendation 3

Strengthen the CIA's authority to manage and coordinate overseas human intelligence operations across the Intelligence Community by creating a Human Intelligence Directorate outside the Directorate of Operations.

The new Act stipulates that the Director of the Central Intelligence Agency (DCIA) will "provide overall direction for and coordination of the collection of national intelligence outside the United States through human sources by elements of the Intelligence Community ... and ensure that the most effective use is made of resources."[20] Consistent with this statutory mandate, we recommend the creation of a Human Intelligence Directorate—within the CIA but separate from the existing Directorate of Operations—to serve as a national human intelligence authority, exercising the responsibility to ensure the coordination of all agencies conducting human intelligence operations on foreign soil.

The Human Intelligence Directorate would have direct "command" authority over CIA human intelligence components—which, if this Commission's recommendations are accepted, would be expanded to include not only the Directorate of Operations but also the proposed Innovation Center discussed in the following section. But its overseas human intelligence coordination responsibilities would extend more broadly across the Intelligence Community.

When most people think of human intelligence, they think about the CIA—and, more specifically, about the professional case officers in the CIA's Directorate of Operations (DO) who conduct the CIA's human espionage operations. But there are in fact a host of entities that collect human intelligence either through clandestine or overt means, ranging from long-established agencies like the Defense HUMINT service and the FBI to agencies that until recently had not viewed themselves as intelligence collectors (like immigration officials and customs officers). This range of entities conducting human intelligence activities, of course, raises serious coordination challenges—and these challenges are only becoming more formidable. As we discuss in Chapters Six (Management) and Ten (Intelligence at Home), both the Defense Department and the FBI are stepping up their own, more traditional overseas intelligence activities, as well as other, less conventional human intelligence efforts, such as those associated with the Department of Defense's special operations forces. While we believe that many of these efforts are commendable, they heighten the risk that intelligence operations will be insufficiently coordinated—a state of affairs that can, in the world of foreign espionage, have dangerous and even fatal consequences.

We propose the creation of the Human Intelligence Directorate within CIA to address this pressing need. The Directorate would coordinate the overseas operations of the DO with those of the Defense Department and the FBI. The CIA—with a network of case officers around the globe—is uniquely situated to perform this function, and its power to insist on such coordination should be reaffirmed. To accomplish this task, however, there are many issues the CIA's Human Intelligence Directorate will have to resolve with the Defense

Department and the FBI in establishing its authorities with respect to human intelligence. In order to ensure suitable attention to this process, we recommend the Director of CIA (DCIA) be required to report to the DNI, within 90 days of the DNI's confirmation, exactly what protocols have been established with the Defense Department and the FBI to ensure effective coordination among the three organizations and appropriate oversight of their respective activities.

The need for coordination is pressing and pronounced. Increasingly, for example, the FBI's intelligence operations cross national boundaries, thus requiring greater coordination with CIA and the Defense Department. The CIA, and in particular its field supervisors, should act as the focal point for overseas coordination to ensure that FBI tradecraft practices abroad reflect the hostile environment in which intelligence gathering occurs.

We emphasize three things that would *not* occur under our proposed system. First, other human intelligence collection agencies—to include DIA clandestine and overt operations, the Special Operations Command, and other human intelligence operations carried out by military services—would not surrender command authority and operational control over their human intelligence assets. Rather than "run" these components, the Human Intelligence Directorate would broadly direct and coordinate human intelligence activities overseas. Second, the DCIA's authorities as head of the Human Intelligence Directorate would not extend to directing collection against any specific target; rather, as discussed earlier in this Chapter and in Chapter Eight (Analysis), this responsibility would fall to Mission Managers. Third, we do not propose changing or stifling successful coordination efforts that already occur at "lower levels" in the field.

In addition to coordinating overseas human intelligence operations for the Community, the Human Intelligence Directorate would serve as the centerpiece for Community-wide human intelligence issues, including by helping to develop a national human intelligence strategy, integrating (where appropriate) collecting and reporting-disseminating systems, and establishing Community-wide standards for training and tradecraft. Finally, the Directorate also would have the responsibility for expanding, enriching, and diversifying the full range of human intelligence capabilities. We believe it is this task that makes it essential that the Human Intelligence Directorate be located within the CIA and under the direction of the Agency's Director—but *not* part of the

Directorate of Operations. As discussed in detail below, we believe that the DO is not ideally situated to incubate a variety of new human intelligence techniques, or to vet those developed by other agencies or entities, such as the Innovation Center.

Fostering Innovation

Recommendation 4

The CIA should develop and manage a range of new overt and covert human intelligence capabilities. In particular, a "Human Intelligence Innovation Center," independent of the CIA's Directorate of Operations, should be established to facilitate the development of new and innovative mechanisms for collecting human intelligence.

The Directorate of Operations, which conducts the CIA's human espionage operations, is one of the Intelligence Community's more elite and storied organizations. It takes justifiable pride in its ability to recruit spies and manage diplomatically delicate foreign liaison relationships. The DO has rigorous training programs—its premier training facility known colloquially as "the Farm," has become well-known through its depiction in popular movies and novels—and continues to attract some of the nation's most impressive talent.

It is a well-known rule of bureaucratic behavior, however, that when an organization does something particularly well, it is difficult to encourage that organization—or the people within it—to do things that are new and different.[21] And so it has proven with the Directorate of Operations. While the need to develop new methods of collecting human intelligence has been apparent for years, the DO has struggled to develop and "mainstream" new techniques, remaining wedded instead to the traditional model of recruiting spies.

We have seen positive indications that the new leadership of the CIA is aggressively exploring new human intelligence methods. If it is left to the DO to develop and implement these new ideas, however, we are skeptical that they will ever become more than a peripheral part of the DO's mission. Accordingly, we recommend the establishment of an "Innovation Center" within the CIA—but *not* within the Directorate of Operations—responsible for overseeing the development of new and non-traditional methods of conducting human intelligence. This center's mission would be not only to evaluate and develop new human intelligence approaches, but also to serve as a think-tank and proving ground for new human intelligence techniques and methods. [22]

We recognize that there are arguments that such an innovation center should be placed outside of the CIA entirely, in light of the historically outsized influence that the DO has held over the CIA's management. But in our view it would be inadvisable to add yet another organization to the already dispersed constellation of human intelligence collection entities. (Indeed, as we suggested in the previous section, we believe that the CIA should exercise a *stronger* hand in coordinating human intelligence collection across the Intelligence Community.) The DNI, however, should monitor the Innovation Center closely, not only to ensure that it is performing its mission well but also to encourage the implementation of its useful new ideas.

In addition to this institutional recommendation to encourage the development of innovative new human intelligence practices, in our classified report we also point to several specific methods that in our judgment should either be explored or used more extensively. Unfortunately, these specific methods cannot be discussed in our unclassified report.

Professionalizing Human Intelligence Across the Community

We have been critical of the CIA's Directorate of Operations at certain points, but it is important also to emphasize what they do well. While we have concluded that the DO is not the best place to foster innovation in human intelligence, it does continue to set the standard for traditional human intelligence operational "tradecraft." It is to the DO that the rest of the Community should look for guidelines on asset validation and ways to build productive relationships with liaison services. We recommend that the DCIA, acting in his Community leadership role as the head of the Human Intelligence Directorate, work actively to develop and further professionalize human intelligence components outside of CIA in these and other areas.

For example, our review of the Community suggests that the Defense Department's attempts to develop a clandestine strategic intelligence arm have fallen short because of the absence of a professional human intelligence career path—for both military officers and civilians—and an overall environment that historically has not fostered sufficient respect for, or investment in, human intelligence collection capabilities. While there are of course many talented Defense HUMINT clandestine case officers, the service has not developed the operational capability that it would possess if intelligence officers followed a long-term career path and passed on lessons learned.[23] We believe that the CIA—in its role as Community-wide human intelligence coordinator—should assist DIA in further professionalizing its cadre of clandestine case officers, and—in light of the Community-wide scarcity of fully-trained case officers—ensure that Defense HUMINT's clandestine service is properly leveraged and coordinated with the DO's operations.

Recommendation 5

The CIA should take the lead in systematizing and standardizing the Intelligence Community's asset validation procedures, and integrating them with all information gathering activities across the human intelligence spectrum.

The case of Curveball (described in detail in our Iraq study) illustrates the importance of integrating sound validation processes wherever possible—in all forms of human intelligence activities including unilateral collection, liaison-provided information, debriefings, and other human-acquired inputs into intelligence reporting. (By "validation processes" we mean the ways in which intelligence collectors ensure that the information provided to them is truthful and accurate.) The Pentagon's plans to increase its human intelligence capabilities make it especially important that Defense HUMINT adopt and institutionalize sound vetting and validation practices to ensure the reliability of information it disseminates to the Intelligence Community. It will be the responsibility of the Human Intelligence Directorate and the Defense Intelligence Agency to ensure that proper source validation occurs whenever possible, and that overt collectors are not simply passive conduits for human intelligence. In our classified report, we also make specific recommendations to improve the asset validation practices of human collection agencies that cannot be discussed in an unclassified format.

Collecting Human Intelligence: Custodial Interrogations

One source of critical intelligence, particularly with respect to terrorist plans and operations involving the use of nuclear, biological, or chemical weapons, is the interrogation of captured detainees. We consider it essential, and indeed have been assured that it is currently the case, that the Attorney General personally approves any interrogation techniques used by intelligence agencies that go beyond openly published U.S. government interrogation practices. While we recognize that public disclosure of Attorney General approved or forbidden techniques to be used by U.S. interrogators or by foreign personnel in interrogations in which the United States participates would be counterproductive, we emphasize that it is vital that all such practices conform to applicable laws. Where special practices are allowed in extraordinary cases of dire emergency, those procedures should require permission from sufficiently high-level officials to ensure compliance with overall guidelines, and records should be kept to provide oversight for deviation from regular practices. It is also important that notice of Attorney General approved techniques and the circumstances of any deviations from regular practices be given to appropriate congressional overseers. Interrogation guidelines should also form part of the training of relevant intelligence personnel. Compliance with approved practices should be uniformly enforced. Assurance that these steps have been taken across the Community will enhance the credibility of the Intelligence Community as a law-abiding and responsibly governed entity in the public mind, thereby enhancing its ability to perform its crucial functions.

Shaping the Force: A Larger and Better Trained Human Intelligence Officer Cadre

Recommendation 6

The Intelligence Community should train more human intelligence operators and collectors, and its training programs should be modified to support the full spectrum of human intelligence collection methods.

The reforms and initiatives discussed above would vastly improve our nation's human intelligence capabilities. But one thing will still be missing— the people necessary to do what needs to be done. We recognize the ease of saying "more money will solve the problem," and for that reason have avoided recommendations that do little more than propose an outlay of additional funds. But in the case of human intelligence, we simply need more people.

In our classified report, we offer statistics showing how badly outgunned our human intelligence collectors are, at precisely the time when the most is expected of them. Although we make few recommendations that we believe will require substantial budget increases, we do believe that this is an area where increased funding for the purpose of expanding human intelligence forces would be appropriate—and where, as we have noted elsewhere (see Management, Chapter 6), the need for long term planning militates strongly toward a shift away from unpredictable supplemental budget appropriations. In our classified report, we offer additional recommendations on how to improve human intelligence training programs within the Intelligence Community. This discussion cannot be included in our unclassified report.

Technical Intelligence Collection

Signals and Imagery Intelligence

Signals intelligence and imagery collection systems are obviously critical to the Intelligence Community's ability to collect information. Unfortunately, as our Iraq case study vividly illustrates, a combination of factors—most relating to our adversaries' increasingly effective use of denial and deception—have significantly eroded the utility of the Community's legacy signals and imagery systems. In our classified report, we specify examples highlighting the scope of the problem.

The Community is investigating and developing numerous technologies and methods that can potentially surmount some of these collection challenges. These technologies cannot be discussed in detail in an unclassified report. However, we recommend that the DNI should, as an early priority, delve into the complex technical issues that surround these innovations. The DNI should also assist collectors in developing and operationalizing the most promising innovations, while redoubling efforts to improve *existing* means of countering and reducing the distorting effects of denial and deception.

To aid him in the latter effort, the DNI will inherit a commendable roadmap previously developed by the DCI. Among other things, this strategy establishes efforts to counter-denial and deception by our adversaries as "a top priority for the Intelligence Community."[24] Yet, like many DCI strategies, we are concerned that the prose has not fully translated into practice. To ensure effective implementation, we suggest a mid-course review of the strategy's first five years: a thorough examination of accomplishments and shortfalls, an update of the principal actions that specific Intelligence Community entities have taken and should take, and a renewed effort to solicit the full backing and resources of relevant planning and acquisition professionals across the Community. The effort to overcome foreign denial and deception will be ongoing; there is no easy or quick fix for the problems that plague technical collectors.

In the short term, technical collectors' most important contributions to the Community's mission may occur when they operate in conjunction with other collection disciplines. As a result, we believe that implementation of the integrated collection enterprise we recommend in this chapter will significantly enhance the Community's ability to optimize its existing technical collection capabilities. Target Development Boards, in particular, will provide an ongoing opportunity to engage in cooperative collection efforts among collection disciplines —specifically to capitalize on the joint capabilities of technical and human collectors. Such joint activities have been at the source of some of the Community's most notable successes in recent years. In our classified report, we cite examples of types of joint efforts which we cannot discuss here.

Signals Intelligence in the United States

Recommendation 7

The President should seek to have the Foreign Intelligence Surveillance Act amended to extend the duration of electronic surveillance and "pen registers" in cases involving agents of foreign powers who are *not* U.S. persons.

The Foreign Intelligence Surveillance Act (FISA)[25] governs, in part, the manner in which the U.S. government may conduct electronic surveillance within the United States and electronic surveillance of U.S. persons abroad. NSA and the FBI have long operated within the confines of FISA and—according to NSA—the statute has not posed a serious obstacle to effective intelligence gathering. It has, however, become a growing administrative burden, because NSA (in cooperation with the FBI) must now obtain far more FISA warrants than it did when traditional communications were prevalent.[26]

The increased frequency with which NSA must obtain FISA orders, in turn, has placed a significant burden on the Department of Justice's Office of Intelligence Policy Review (OIPR), which represents the United States in the Foreign Intelligence Surveillance Court when NSA requires a FISA order.

We recommend that the President seek to have FISA amended to extend the duration of electronic surveillance and "pen register"[27] orders as they apply to agents of foreign powers who are *not* U.S. persons. We think the President might consider seeking an extension of the initial electronic surveillance period from 90 to 120 days, as well as an extension from 120 days to one year for follow-on orders. In addition, we recommend seeking an extension of the initial pen register period from 90 days to one year. Again, it is our view that each of these extensions should only apply to non-U.S. persons; by limiting the extension in this manner, the Justice Department and the FISA Court will maintain their current levels of attention when U.S. persons' civil liberties are implicated. Although these relatively modest changes to FISA procedures will not eliminate the burdens carried by NSA and the Department of Justice, we believe that they will at least lessen them and allow those agencies to focus their attention where it is most needed.

Measurement and Signature Intelligence

Recommendation 8

The DNI should appoint an authority responsible for managing and overseeing innovative technologies, including the use of technologies often referred to as "MASINT."

To its proponents, measurement and signature intelligence, or MASINT, is an unjustly overlooked specialty. A wide variety of collection techniques fall under the heading of MASINT—everything from sensors, lasers, ground-based radars, and pretty much any other technical measure that does not fit easily into the traditional intelligence disciplines.[28] Skeptics view these as a batch of unrelated technical intelligence tools, better developed and funded separately rather than under a single label.

Putting aside these definitional problems, some MASINT technical collection measures have had successes. Such technical capabilities can sometimes identify WMD programs, and can help counter denial and deception programs.

Although we are unsure of exactly how such techniques can best be supported, we are confident that the current situation is not the answer.[29] The designation of DIA—which lacks the staff, budget, and authority to control the development and deployment of MASINT systems—as the "National MASINT Manager" has failed to help these techniques prosper. These techniques are, almost by definition, some of the more innovative collection techniques in the Intelligence Community's arsenal, but they are often given short shrift as a result of DIA's neglect or disinterest.

We therefore recommend that the DNI take responsibility for coordinating new intelligence technologies, including those that now go under the title MASINT. This could be done by a special MASINT authority or as part of the DNI's Office of Science and Technology.

It is critical to note that, in our view, the MASINT coordinator should *not* directly control MASINT collection. Rather, we believe the most sensible division of MASINT responsibilities is that NGA be responsible for imagery-derived MASINT, while CIA and Defense Department elements take responsibility for their own operational sensors and other aspects of MASINT that fall naturally into their bailiwicks. At the same time, the DNI's designated representative would monitor the status of MASINT-like programs throughout the Intelligence Community to ensure that they are fully implemented and given the necessary attention.

Open Source Collection

Recommendation 9

The DNI should create an Open Source Directorate in the CIA to use the Internet and modern information processing tools to greatly enhance the availability of open source information to analysts, collectors, and users of intelligence.

Open Source information has long been viewed by many outside the Intelligence Community as essential to understanding foreign political, economic, social, and even military developments.[30] Currently, the Intelligence Community has one collection organization, the Foreign Broadcast Information Service (FBIS), that specializes in providing some of these vital elements—particularly the rapid reporting of foreign print, radio, and television news. While this service is highly valued within the Community and academia, the Community does not have any broader program to gather and organize the wealth of global information generated each day and increasingly available, if only temporarily, over the Internet.

We also believe that the need for exploiting open source material is greater now than ever before. Today, the spread of information technology—and the ever increasing pace at which it advances—is immune to many traditional, clandestine methods of intelligence collection. Whereas advanced technological research once occurred only in large facilities and within enormous government bureaucratic institutions, today it can (and does) occur in nondescript office parks or garages, and with very small clusters of people. And for these new challenges, many open source materials may provide the critical and perhaps only window into activities that threaten the United States.

Much has happened in the world of open source in the past ten years. Internet search tools like Google have brought significant new capabilities and expectations for open source information to analysts and users alike. Regrettably, the Intelligence Community's open source programs have not expanded commensurate with either the increase in available information or with the growing importance of open source data to today's problems. This is an unacceptable state of affairs. Consider the following:

- *The ever-shifting nature of our intelligence needs compels the Intelligence Community to quickly and easily understand a wide range of foreign countries and cultures.* As we have discussed, today's threats are rapidly changing and geographically diffuse; it is a fact of life that an intelligence analyst may be forced to shift rapidly from one topic to the next. Increasingly, Intelligence Community professionals need to quickly assimilate social, economic, and cultural information about a country—information often detailed in open sources.

- *Open source information provides a base for understanding classified materials.* Despite large quantities of classified material produced by the Intelligence Community, the amount of classified information produced on any one topic can be quite limited, and may be taken out of context if viewed only from a classified-source perspective. Perhaps the most important example today relates to terrorism, where open source information can fill gaps and create links that allow analysts to better understand fragmented intelligence, rumored terrorist plans, possible means of attack, and potential targets.

- *Open source materials can protect sources and methods.* Sometimes an intelligence judgment that is actually informed with sensitive, classified information can be defended on the basis of open source reporting. This can prove useful when policymakers need to explain policy decisions or communicate with foreign officials without compromising classified sources.

- *Only open source can "store history."* A robust open source program can, in effect, gather data to monitor the world's cultures and how they change with time. This is difficult, if not impossible, using the "snapshots" provided by classified collection methods.

We believe that this gap between the Intelligence Community's needs and its capabilities must be addressed on two fronts: collection and analysis. The former we discuss here; the latter is discussed more fully in Chapter Eight (Analysis).

We recommend that the DNI create an Open Source Directorate in the CIA to develop and utilize information processing tools to enhance the availability of open source information to analysts, collectors, and users of intelligence. At a minimum, such a program should gather and store many, if not most, of the digital newspapers and periodicals available over the Internet, regardless of language. (Daily storage is required because most of these newspapers and periodicals are on the Internet for only short periods of time.) We believe that this open source information will be invaluable to those charged with watching emerging threats and would provide a baseline for intelligence collectors and analysts when issues suddenly rise to national security significance. In addition, it can tip off analysts and collectors to changes that warrant more focused intelligence collection.

In the near term, we believe that without an institutional "champion" and home, open source will never be effectively used by the Intelligence Community. It is our hope that open source will become an integral part of all intelligence activities and that, at some point in the future, there may no longer be a need for a separate directorate. We acknowledge that our recommendation could create one more collection specialty. But, for now, open source is inadequately used and appreciated and is in need of the high-level, focused attention that only a separate directorate can provide.

As important as collecting open source material, however, is the task of getting the material to the analysts who need it. We were repeatedly told that analysts have difficulty accessing open source information at their desks.[31] The Intelligence Community must make a concerted effort to solve the technology and security challenges associated with getting open source information to every analyst's desktop.

PROTECTING SOURCES AND METHODS

Our case studies strongly suggest that a persistent inability to protect human and technical collection sources and methods has substantially damaged U.S. intelligence capabilities. Authorized and unauthorized disclosures have compromised critical signals interception and satellite imagery programs, as well as hard-earned human intelligence sources. Better protection of these sources and methods, which should be thought of as the Community's crown jewels, will require sustained attention by the DNI and the consideration of a range of possible approaches. We believe that the act's emphasis on the DNI's obligation to protect sources and methods will help raise the priority placed on this important issue.[32] We also believe that the institutional recommendations in our information sharing chapter (Chapter 9)—which include making a single person in the office of the DNI responsible both for information sharing and for information security—will help ensure that information sharing imperatives do not overwhelm the need to protect sources and methods.

To accompany these institutional suggestions, we offer recommendations to help address two problems that have harmful effects on sources and methods: (1) the problem of *authorized* disclosures and (2) the problem of *unauthorized* disclosures (more commonly referred to as "leaks") of classified information.

Authorized Disclosures of Sources and Methods

Recommendation 10

Efforts should be taken to significantly reduce damaging losses in collection capability that result from *authorized* disclosures of classified information related to protection of sources and methods.

Authorized disclosures often have unintended and harmful effects. One common source of such disclosures is the sharing of intelligence with foreign countries both through cooperative ventures and diplomatic demarches. The Intelligence Community should take more rigorous steps to integrate counterintelligence expertise into the sharing and demarche decisions and processes, and to formally analyze the potential costs and benefits of such disclosures. These processes would need to include methods for tracking the consequences of unauthorized disclosures, and a formal process for resolving disputes among agencies and stakeholders over the costs and benefits of particular disclosure decisions.

Another *de facto* "disclosure" of information about the technical capabilities of intelligence satellites occurs when public announcements are made concerning a satellite launch. We therefore recommend that the United States examine whether its space launch techniques can be altered to shield spaceborne collection techniques and operations more effectively.

The Problem of Media Leaks

The scope of damage done to our collection capabilities from media disclosures of classified information is well documented. Hundreds of serious press leaks have significantly impaired U.S. capabilities against our hardest targets. In our classified report, we detail several leaks that have collectively cost the American people hundreds of millions of dollars, and have done grave harm to national security. We cannot, however, discuss them in an unclassified format. These and hundreds of other leaks have been reported to the Justice Department by the Intelligence Community in the last ten years. However, to date, not a single indictment or prosecution has resulted.

According to past government studies, the long-standing inability of the U.S. government to control press leaks results from a combination of factors—the use of unauthorized disclosures as a vehicle to influence policy, the lack of political will to deal firmly and consistently with government leakers in both the executive and legislative branches, the difficulty of prosecuting cases under existing statutes, and the challenge of identifying the leaker.[33] The government's impotence in dealing effectively with this problem was well characterized by then-Deputy Assistant Attorney General Richard K. Willard, in 1982:

> In summary, past experience with leaks investigations has been largely unsuccessful and uniformly frustrating for all concerned....The whole system has been so ineffectual as to perpetuate the notion that the Government can do nothing to stop the leaks.[34]

The Commission recognizes the enormous difficulty of this seemingly intractable problem and has considered a broad range of potential solutions. We conclude that the long-standing defeatism that has paralyzed action on this topic is understandable but unwarranted. Leaks cannot be stopped, but they can be reduced. And those responsible for the most damaging leaks can be held accountable if they can be identified and if the government is willing to prosecute them.

Recommendation 11

The DNI should ensure that all Inspectors General in the Intelligence Community are prepared to conduct leak investigations for their agencies; this responsibility can be coordinated by a Community-wide Inspector General in the Office of the DNI, if such an office is established.

Coordinated leaks investigations. The DNI Inspector General, assuming one is named, should be given specific responsibility for overseeing leaks investigations within the Intelligence Community and for coordinating investigations that require reaching into multiple agencies within the Community. The DNI's Inspector General would be uniquely positioned to coordinate leak investigations across the Intelligence Community. Several intelligence agencies have explained that the Justice Department is rarely willing to open investigations of leaks when the number of possible leakers is large. Furthermore, these agencies have expressed the opinion that complaining agencies should be allowed to conduct investigations of their own employees so as to

narrow down the list of possible leakers. By heeding these concerns, this recommendation will reduce the investigative load for the Justice Department
and FBI while putting more of the burden on the agencies that often feel the
impact of leaks most directly.

Vigorous application of DNI administrative authorities. When internal CIA
leakers have been identified, the DCI's authority to impose sanctions ranging
from fines, suspension or revocation of clearances, or even firings is relatively
robust. This authority should extend to the DNI. The DNI should, in turn, vigorously enforce the 2002 DCI Directive on stemming unauthorized disclosures across the Community.[35] We hope that the 2002 Directive will acquire
greater force under the new DNI than it has had under past DCIs.

Better education and training for intelligence producers, users, and media.
Policymakers who leak intelligence to the press in order to gain political
advantage and journalists who publish leaked intelligence may do so without
fully appreciating the potential harm that can result to sources and methods.
The Intelligence Community should consider implementing a widespread,
modern-day equivalent of the "Loose Lips Sink Ships" campaign to educate
individuals about their legal obligations—and possible penalties—to safeguard intelligence information. Officers at all agencies that produce and use
intelligence should be fully briefed at the time they first sign the non-disclosure agreement and be periodically re-briefed about its responsibilities.

Internal changes at the Department of Justice. As noted more fully in Chapter Ten (Intelligence at Home), we recommend that the primary national security component of the Department of Justice be placed under the auspices of a
single Assistant Attorney General. We do so in the hope that the combined
forces of the Department can be better brought to bear on a variety of issues,
including unauthorized disclosures.

Finally, there is one point regarding leaks on which the Commission could not
come to agreement. During our work, we were repeatedly told that the greatest
barrier to prosecuting leaks was in identifying the "leaker." And many people
with whom we spoke also said that the best (if not only) way to identify leakers
was through the reporters to whom classified information was leaked. In this
vein, we thoroughly discussed the advantages and disadvantages of creating
some sort of qualified privilege for reporters, which might simultaneously protect both First Amendment interests and the government's interest in protecting

classified information. Regrettably, and despite all of our efforts, we could not reach agreement on the details of such a proposal.

ENDNOTES

[1] Although the National Imagery and Mapping Agency (NIMA)—renamed the National Geospatial-Intelligence Agency (NGA)—was established after the Cold War, it was cast from the same mold.

[2] CIA, Title Classified (OTI IA 2002-141) (Aug. 26, 2002); CIA, Title Classified (OTI IA 2002-053 (SPS)) (Oct. 2004); CIA, Title Classified (OTI IA 2003-06) (Feb. 2003); Department of Defense Joint Staff, Title Classified (Dec. 2003); Defense Science Board, *Future Strategic Strike Systems* (Feb. 2004).

[3] National Intelligence Council (NIC), Title Classified (NIE 98-04) (1998-99).

[4] For a more detailed discussion of this issue, see Chapter Thirteen (Proliferation).

[5] NIC, Title Classified (NIE 98-04) (1998-90) at Volume 1.

[6] CIA, *The Jeremiah Report: The Intelligence Community's Performance on the Indian Nuclear Tests* (June 1, 1998) (hereinafter "Jeremiah Report").

[7] CIA, *Response to WMD Commission Request # 74* (Oct. 8, 2004).

[8] House Permanent Select Committee on Intelligence, IC21: *Intelligence Community in the 21st Century* (April 9, 1996) (hereinafter "IC21"); Commission on the Roles and Capabilities of the United States Intelligence Community, *Preparing for the 21st Century: An Appraisal of U.S. Intelligence* (1996) (hereinafter "Aspin-Brown Commission"); Jeremiah Report.

[9] *See, e.g.*, IC21.

[10] Target Development Boards would not just address analysts' needs. They would also address the needs of the military commanders for intelligence support to military operations.

[11] This idea is not unlike the Department of Defense's theory of Network Centric Warfare, which allows for widespread dissemination of data to the military to provide a shared awareness of the battle space. *See generally* Congressional Research Service, *Network Centric Warfare: Background and Oversight Issues for Congress* (June 2, 2004).

[12] Here we cite an example of an NSA acquisition problem that cannot be included in our unclassified report.

[13] Intelligence Reform and Terrorism Prevention Act of 2004 at § 1011, Pub. L. No. 108-458 (hereinafter "IRTPA").

[14] This includes the tactical programs in the Department of Defense. FY2005 NFIP, JMIP, and TIARA Congressional Budget Books.

[15] IRTPA at § 1011.

[16] We recognize that some competition in research and development is desirable and should be encouraged by the DNI. At the same time, even when research and development occurs in several locations, its efforts must still be integrated in a way that minimizes unproductive redundancy.

[17] *See, e.g.*, Memorandum from the President to the Director of Central Intelligence (Nov. 18, 2004).

[18] CIA, Directorate of Operations Recruitment (Sept. 14, 2004) (briefing slides).

[19] Interview with Defense HUMINT officials (Sept. 9, 2004).

[20] IRTPA at § 1011.

[21] *See generally* James Q. Wilson, *Bureaucracy: What Government Agencies Do and Why They Do It* (Basic Books) (1989).

[22] If the innovation center proves a successful model, we believe the DNI should explore replicating it in other agencies as well.

[23] As we have already noted, we are far from the first to recognize the shortcomings in Defense HUMINT. *See, e.g.*, Aspin-Brown Commission; Council on Foreign Relations, *Making Intelligence Smarter: The Future of U.S. Intelligence* (1996); IC21; Defense Science Board *Task Force on Intelligence Support to the War on Terrorism* (Oct. 2003); House Permanent Select Committee on Intelligence, *Classified Annexes to The Intelligence Authorization Act For Fiscal Year 1998, 1999, 2003, 2004, 2005.*

[24] DCI, Title Classified (March 2000) at pp. 1-2.

[25] 50 U.S.C. §§ 1805, 1842.

[26] Interview with representatives of NSA's General Counsel's Office (Sept. 16, 2004); Interview with representatives of the Office of Intelligence Policy Review, Department of Justice (Oct. 25, 2004).

[27] A "pen register" or "trap and trace" device is roughly equivalent to using "caller identification" on a target phone (*i.e.*, it collects incoming and outgoing phone numbers).

[28] The term "MASINT" was first coined in 1970 by DIA to describe any number of disparate forms of collection and analysis such as active radar interrogation of targets, laser intelligence, optical measuring of reflected light from distant objects such as spacecraft, nuclear intelligence, acoustic intelligence, and infra-red analysis.

[29] According to DCI Porter Goss, "[p]ast efforts to manage MASINT have been hampered by an unrealistic view of MASINT as a single enterprise." Porter Goss, Director of Central Intelligence, *Cooperative Way Forward on MASINT Management* (Dec. 15, 2004) at p. 1.

[30] "Open Source" usually refers to all information that is generally publicly available and unclassified. It can include print media as well as radio and television broadcasting. With the advent of the Internet, there has been a major increase in the availability of open source textual data. This report focuses on, but is not limited to, this easily accessible open source textual data.

[31] *See, e.g.,* Interview with senior In-Q-Tel official (Feb. 3, 2005).

[32] The act states that the new DNI "shall protect intelligence sources and methods from unauthorized disclosure." It also limits the DNI's ability to delegate responsibility for protecting sources and methods, stating that the DNI "may only delegate" this authority to the Principal Deputy DNI. IRTPA at § 1011.

[33] National Counterintelligence Policy Board, *Report to the NSC on Unauthorized Media Leak Disclosures* (March 1996) at pp. C2-C4.

[34] *Report of the Interdepartmental Group on Unauthorized Disclosures of Classified Information* (March 31, 1982).

[35] DCI, Title Classified (Dec. 9, 2002).

CHAPTER EIGHT
ANALYSIS

Summary & Recommendations

The role of intelligence analysts is to tell policymakers what they know, what they don't know, what they think, and why. When analysts fail to provide adequate warnings of an impending threat, or provide incorrect conclusions to decisionmakers—as they did with Iraq—the consequences can be grave. Although there is no way to ensure against all future intelligence failures, we believe that several initiatives could improve management of analytic efforts, deepen analyst expertise, reduce intelligence gaps, and enhance the usability of existing information—all of which would improve the quality of intelligence.

Mission Managers, introduced in previous chapters, will play a critical role in this reform effort. They will encourage competitive analysis, present the views of all agencies to decisionmakers, ensure that analysts drive collection, and prepare the analytic community to meet the threats of the 21st Century.

In addition to adopting the Mission Manager approach, we also recommend—among other improvements—that the DNI:

- Emphasize strategic analysis by establishing a new long-term research and analysis unit, under the mantle of the National Intelligence Council, to serve as the lead organization for interagency projects involving in-depth analysis and expanded contacts with experts outside of the Intelligence Community;

- Institute Community-wide, career-long programs for training analysts and managers, and provide appropriate performance incentives;

- Develop and integrate into regular use new tools that can assist analysts in filtering the vast quantities of information that threaten to overwhelm the analytic process, as well as tools designed for foreign language exploitation; and

- Ensure that analysts are engaging in competitive analysis, mandate routine and ongoing examinations of finished intelligence, and require the lessons learned from "post mortems" to be incorporated into the intelligence education and training program.

INTRODUCTION

Analysts are the voice of the Intelligence Community.

While intelligence failures can certainly result from inadequate collection, recent experience shows that they can also occur when analysts don't effectively assess all relevant information and present it in a manner useful to decisionmakers. Improving the business of analysis should therefore be a major priority of the new Director of National Intelligence (DNI).

As in our chapter on collection, our recommendations—supported by vivid examples taken from our case studies—focus both on *integrating* analytical efforts across the Community and improving the overall *quality* of analysis.

The analytic effort in the Intelligence Community is hardly a monolithic enterprise; most of the Community's 15 organizations have at least one analytic component. Some of these agencies specialize in meeting the needs of particular users—notably the Defense Department's DIA and the State Department's INR. Some specialize in analyzing particular types of data—signals intelligence at NSA and geospatial intelligence at NGA. Some, such as the intelligence element of the Department of Energy, specialize in substantive intelligence topics, such as nuclear technology issues.

The separation of these analytic units serves a vital function; it fosters competitive analysis, encourages a diversity of viewpoints, and develops groups of analysts with different specialties. Any reform of the Community must preserve these advantages; our suggested move toward greater integration should not mean the homogenization of different viewpoints. Nevertheless, there is a great and growing need for Community analytic standards, interoperable and innovative technologies, access to shared information, and a common sense of mission. In many cases today, analysts in the 15 organizations are unaware of similar work being done in other agencies. Although analysts may develop working relationships with counterparts in other organizations, there is no formalized process or forum through which to do so. These dysfunctional characteristics of the current system must change; collaboration must replace fragmentation as the analytic community's primary characteristic.

Despite the fact that the analytic units are largely isolated and autonomous, we have been deeply impressed by pockets of excellence within them. The

Community is blessed with a highly intelligent, dedicated analytic workforce that has achieved significant successes. We also note that, in response to Iraq-related failures, the Intelligence Community has recently undertaken several serious (although scattered) efforts to improve the overall quality and integrity of its analytical methods and products.

We conclude, however, that these strengths and reforms are too few and far between. Our investigation revealed serious shortcomings; specifically, we found inadequate Intelligence Community collaboration and cooperation, analysts who do not understand collection, too much focus on current intelligence, inadequate systematic use of outside experts and open source information, a shortage of analysts with scientific and technical expertise, and poor capabilities to exploit fully the available data. Perhaps most troubling, we found an Intelligence Community in which analysts have a difficult time stating their assumptions up front, explicitly explaining their logic, and, in the end, identifying unambiguously for policymakers what they *do not know*. In sum, we found that many of the most basic processes and functions for producing accurate and reliable intelligence are broken or underutilized.

This Commission is not the first to recognize these shortcomings—we trod a well-worn path. Again and again, many of the same obstacles to delivering the best possible analytic products have been identified. The Church Committee's 1976 report, the House Permanent Select Committee on Intelligence's 1996 study of the Intelligence Community in the 21st Century, the 1998 Rumsfeld Report side letter to the President, the 1999 Jeremiah Report, the Markle Foundation's 2003 Task Force, and the 9/11 Commission Report all pointed to the problems created by the poor coordination and resistance to information sharing among Intelligence Community agencies. Some studies, notably the 1996 report by the Council on Foreign Relations and the 1996 study by the Aspin-Brown Commission, noted the need to systematically engage in and use competitive analysis. As early as 1949, the Hoover Commission faulted the Intelligence Community for failing to improve relations with decision-makers, and these concerns were echoed by the Aspin-Brown Commission and, most recently, the Markle Foundation Task Force.[1] Finally, the House and Senate intelligence committees have both noted the problems the Intelligence Community faces in processing the collected information available to it, as well as the difficulty analysts have engaging in long-term analysis, given the press of daily demands.[2]

In other words, many of the problems we have identified have been apparent to observers of the Intelligence Community—and to the Community itself—for decades. Nevertheless, they have remained largely unresolved, due largely to institutional resistance to change, the classified nature of the work, and a lack of political will to enforce change.

We believe the creation of the Office of the DNI offers a unique opportunity to finally resolve many of these issues by infusing the analytic culture with new processes and Community standards. We believe that this new management structure can foster a new sense of community among analysts. Until the analytic community adopts a new approach, analysts at one agency will continue to be denied access to critical reporting from others; analysts will resist collaborating and coordinating across units; managers will persist in placing the need to answer the "daily mail" over the need to develop true expertise; and new commissions will be appointed in the wake of future intelligence failures. As discussed in previous chapters, we believe that the creation of Mission Managers will be an important factor in avoiding this grim outcome.

Our recommendations, therefore, focus on exploiting the opportunity presented by the new legislation and the creation of the Office of the DNI, as well as on instituting changes to the Community's culture that will improve analytic performance. In doing so, we offer specific suggestions for how the community of analysts can be better integrated without sacrificing all-important independent analysis, and how the Intelligence Community can ensure that analysts have the tools, training, and "tradecraft" practices to ensure that the analytic community is prepared to meet today's and tomorrow's threats.

Achieving Community Integration Among Analysts

We believe that a principal goal of improving analysis should be to integrate the community of analysts while at the same time promoting independent—or competitive—analysis. In this sense, we believe a major challenge for the first Director of National Intelligence will be to foster more collaboration among analysts across the Community—that is, to bring the benefits of collaboration to daily support to the President, to strategic intelligence and warning, and to assistance to military, law enforcement, and homeland security efforts. In our view, there are five prerequisites to creating such a community:

Achieving Community Integration Among Analysts (Continued)

- *Community standards* for analysis (analytic expertise, analytic performance, and analytic presentation to consumers) so that the work of any one analytic unit can be relied upon and understood by others;

- *A common analytic work environment* (a shared network, compatible tools, and a common filing system for products and work in progress) so that a DNI can know the state of intelligence on critical issues, and so knowledge and supporting data can be shared quickly and efficiently across the Community;

- *A group of "Mission Managers,"* acting on behalf of the DNI, to oversee the state of intelligence on designated priority issues (including the state of analytic skills and resources, the gaps in existing knowledge, strategies to fill those gaps, and the effectiveness of agreed upon collection strategies)—from a Community perspective;

- *A body of "joint" analysts* to work in concert with analysts across the Community—to help fill gaps in strategic research as distinct from current reporting, to prompt collaboration on tasks that merit a Community perspective, and to help spread sound analytic methods and standards; and

- *Daily intelligence support to the President*, without which the DNI would find it very hard to impose standards and priorities on organizations free to plead the exigencies of meeting immediate needs of important clients.

MANAGING THE COMMUNITY OF ANALYSTS

As we have discussed in our chapters on management and on collection, no single individual or office in today's Intelligence Community is responsible for getting the answers right on the most pressing intelligence issues of our day. We have recommended the creation of Mission Managers to fill this role, and they will perform a variety of essential tasks—including leading the development and management of collection strategies against high-priority intelligence targets. Because we believe that analysis must drive the collection process, it will be vital that Mission Managers also act as leaders in the analytic community. First and foremost, they must assess the strengths and weaknesses of analytic production in their areas of substantive responsibility.

These assessments will enable Mission Managers to develop strategic analysis plans to guide the Community's analytic efforts over the long term. Moreover, the assessments will guide Mission Managers in their role as chairs of Target Development Boards; their understanding of the gaps in analysts' knowledge will ensure that these gaps do in fact drive collection.

Armed with a clear understanding of where expertise resides in the Community, Mission Managers will also be able to foster competitive analysis. We expect that Mission Managers will ensure that finished intelligence routinely reflects the knowledge and competing views of analysts from all agencies in the Community. In particular, we expect that Mission Managers will encourage analysts to make differences in judgments, and the substantive bases for these differences, explicit in all finished products.

Recommendation 1

Mission Managers should be the DNI's designees for ensuring that the analytic community adequately addresses key intelligence needs on high priority topics.

To accomplish this, Mission Managers must have a comprehensive view of the skills and knowledge of the Community as a whole. The DNI should call on all agencies to provide—and regularly update—information about the knowledge and skills of their analysts, including their academic backgrounds, professional experiences, military experiences, and languages. The DNI's staff should make this information accessible through an easy-to-use directory and search tool. Mission Managers and agency heads would draw on this information to identify existing gaps, develop strategies to fill them, and create long-run strategic plans to avoid gaps on critical intelligence issues.

The model we envision is in stark contrast to the status quo, in which decisionmakers and analysts have little ability to find, track, and allocate analytic expertise. Although some efforts have been made to create such a database, ironically organizations have contributed information on the condition that other agencies not have access to their data. Our interactions with various agencies strongly suggest that the Intelligence Community still lacks a full understanding of the number, type, and skill-level of analysts in the various analytic organizations.[3] Therefore it is difficult to identify the gaps in expertise for purposes of hiring, training, supervising professional development, or managing day-to-day work. Today, line managers identify the gaps in expertise in their own analytic organizations, but little is done to understand gaps from the perspective of an entire agency, much less the entire Community. With so weak a grasp of the Community's analytic resources, it is no wonder that agencies have difficulty quickly aligning their resources to respond to crises.

Even in the area of counterterrorism, which has consistently received high-level attention, agencies have struggled to establish a true Community analytic counterterrorism effort. The only way the Intelligence Community could bring together counterterrorism analytic expertise was to pull analysts away from their home agencies and house them together. From its inception, the Terrorist Threat Integration Center (now NCTC) faced fierce bureaucratic resistance in its efforts to do just this.

We believe a Mission Manager could respond to this or similar challenges more intelligently, quickly, and decisively. A Mission Manager would be able to (1) identify where analytic expertise resided and call on analysts from a variety of agencies to respond to critical questions; (2) identify and recommend to the DNI which analysts should be moved within or between agencies, if required in order to respond to a crisis; (3) "surge" on such a crisis, in the event that Community resources were insufficient, by tapping outside experts to contribute their expertise; (4) create a "virtual center" without physically co-locating analysts and without establishing a segregated and centrally-managed body to analyze a particular subject matter; and (5) clearly define organizational roles rather than letting bureaucratic dogfights, such as those surrounding TTIC, determine who has responsibility for which task. This, we believe, is how the analytical community should be managed.

Although Mission Managers would manage analysis by substantive area, they would not—in contrast to a center like the National Counterterrorism Center or the National Intelligence Council—actually *do* extensive intelligence analysis. Rather, a Mission Manager should coordinate and oversee decentralized analysis. By maintaining this separation of responsibilities, we believe that Mission Managers can prevent so-called "groupthink" among analysts. Indeed, we think fostering competitive analysis within the Community is a critical aspect of the Mission Manager's role.

We acknowledge that the Mission Managers will, if effective, interfere with the current autonomous management of analytic resources within individual organizations. But we see this as a strength, ensuring that members of the Community work together instead of at odds with one another. The risk, of course, is that a Mission Manager with a strong analytic viewpoint could reduce, rather than foster, competitive analysis. While this may sometimes happen—because Mission Managers must have substantive expertise to guide the Community's work—we expect Mission Managers to act more as facilitators of analytic products than as senior analysts. Consequently, their role most often should be to clearly present analytic viewpoints—including alternative views—to policymakers. If a Mission Manager fundamentally disagrees with the prevailing view in the Community, the Mission Manager could present his own view as an alternative, but he should not silence the perspective of other specialists in the Community.

Although not a precondition for success, our vision for Mission Managers ultimately requires a significant technological change—the creation of a "common work environment" for the community of analysts working on a topic. By "common work environment" we mean a shared information network with compatible computer tools and a common computer filing system for analytic products. Such technology is necessary to permit the Mission Manager to have full visibility into the emerging analytic work that is (or is not) being done on a topic, the basis for analytic assessments, and the degree of collaborative involvement between analysts and collectors. This common work environment will also enable greater collaboration between analysts in different agencies, as well as with the nucleus of analysts we recommend placing in the National Intelligence Council (see below).

A final note about managing the Intelligence Community's analysts: we recommend that one of the DNI's earliest undertakings be to have a senior advisor assess the Intelligence Community's medium- and long-term analytic needs, identify analytic gaps, and recommend ways to fill those gaps. And because the Intelligence Community's needs should be closely correlated with policymaker priorities, policymakers should be included in this assessment. Recommendations for correcting deficiencies might include such methods as targeted hiring, correcting national educational shortcomings, or contracting with outside experts.

TAPPING NON-TRADITIONAL SOURCES OF INFORMATION

Analysts have large quantities of information from a wide variety of sources delivered to their desktops each day. Given the time constraints analysts face, it is understandable that their daily work focuses on using what's readily available—usually classified material. Clandestine sources, however, constitute only a tiny sliver of the information available on many topics of interest to the Intelligence Community. Other sources, such as traditional media, the Internet, and individuals in academia, nongovernmental organizations, and business, offer vast intelligence possibilities. Regrettably, all too frequently these "nonsecret" sources are undervalued and underused by the Intelligence Community. To be true all-source analysts, however, Community analysts must broaden their information horizons. We encourage analysts to expand their use of open source materials, outside experts, and new and emerging technologies.

To facilitate analysts' productive use of open source information, the Intelligence Community should create an organization responsible for the collection of open source information. We discuss the need for an open source organization in greater detail in Chapter Seven (Collection). It merits emphasis here, however, that simply creating this organization is unlikely to be sufficient. Analysts who routinely receive clandestine reporting too often see unclassified reporting as less important, and they spend too little time reviewing and integrating data available through open sources. Analysts on lower priority accounts use open source materials because they have difficulty getting clandestine collectors to assist them, but even they receive little or no training on how to evaluate available open sources or find the best information most efficiently.

Recommendation 2

The DNI should create a small cadre of all-source analysts—perhaps 50—who would be experts in finding and using unclassified, open source information.

As the CIA increases its analytic workforce, a small number could be reserved and trained specifically in open source research. They could then be assigned to offices willing to experiment with greater use of open source material, where they would be expected to answer questions for and provide useful unclassified information to analysts. They would also produce their own pieces highlighting open source reporting but drawing on classified information as well.[4] We see these "evange-analysts" as essentially leading by example. They should show other analysts how to find and procure useful open source material, how to assess its reliability and biases, and how to use it to complement clandestine reporting.

We acknowledge that, given the demand for more analysts, there are real costs to designating even this small number as open source specialists. But we expect that the need for these specialized analysts will not be permanent. Over time, the knowledge this group has about open sources is likely to be absorbed by the general population of analysts—as a result both of their education outreach efforts and of the influx of younger, more technologically savvy analysts. As this happens, these open source specialists can be absorbed into the broader analytic corps.

In addition to this special cadre of analysts, the Community will need to find new ways to deal with the challenges presented by the growing availability of open source materials. Among these challenges is the critical problem of processing increasing numbers of foreign language documents.

Recommendation 3

The DNI should establish a program office within the CIA's Open Source Directorate to acquire, or develop when necessary, information technologies to permit prioritization and exploitation of large volumes of textual data without the need for prior human translation or transcription.

Information technology has made remarkable advances in recent years. The private sector (without the same kinds of security concerns as the Intelligence Community) has led the adoption of technologies that are also critical to intelligence. Two areas show particular promise: first, machine translation of foreign languages; and second, tools designed to prioritize documents in their native language without the need for translation.

The Community will never be able to hire enough linguists to meet its needs. It is difficult for the Community to predict which languages will be most in demand and to hire the necessary linguists in advance. And even an aggressive hiring and training effort would not produce an analytic workforce that can absorb the huge quantity of unclassified foreign language material available today.

Eventually, all analysts should have basic foreign-language processing tools easily available to them so that even those who are not language-qualified can pull pieces of interest and get a quick, rough translation. NSA has done pioneering work on machine translation and is pursuing a number of separate initiatives; the military services, CIA (including In-Q-Tel), and other agencies sponsor largely independent projects. There is an abundance of activity, but not a concerted, coherent effort, which has led to steady but slow development.

Advanced search and knowledge extraction technologies could prove to be even more valuable than machine translation (and of course, the two are very much related). We refer here to software that uses mathematical operations, statistical computations, and relational analyses to cluster documents and other data by subject, emphasis, and association in order to identify documents that are similar even when the documents do not use the same key words. Other types of software algorithms can discern concepts within a text; some can depict relationships between ideas or between factual statements based on an understanding of the word's meaning rather than merely searching for a word verbatim. As these tools mature, they will be invaluable to agencies that now find themselves collecting more information than they can analyze. They will also become essential to analysts caught in a similar avalanche of data.

The Intelligence Community has only begun to explore and exploit the power of these emerging technologies. The Intelligence Community's current efforts should be coordinated, consolidated where appropriate, directed, and augmented. Therefore, we suggest that the DNI establish a program office that can lead the Community effort to obtain advanced information technology for purposes of machine translation, advanced search, knowledge extraction, and similar automated support to analysis. This office would draw on the various initiatives in these areas dispersed throughout the Intelligence Community. It would work to avoid duplication of effort and would promote collaboration and cross-pollination. It would serve as a knowledge bank of state-of-the-art technology. It would also serve as a testbed, using open source information to experiment with software that has not yet been certified for classified environments. When appropriate, it would hand off successful technologies for use on classified networks. While we would place the program office in the new Open Source Directorate, where quick deployment seems most likely to occur, we recognize that NSA is a center of excellence for linguistics and technology, and it must surf a data avalanche every day. For that reason, we suggest that the program office be jointly staffed by NSA and CIA.

Context Is Critical

Many of the intelligence challenges of today and tomorrow will, like terrorism or proliferation, be transnational and driven by non-state actors. Analysts who cover these issues will need to know far more than the inclinations of a handful of senior government officials; they will need a deep understanding of the trends and shifts in local political views, cultural norms, and economic demands. For example, analysts seeking to identify geographic areas likely to be receptive to messages of violence toward the United States will need to be able to distinguish such areas from those that, while espousing anti-U.S. rhetoric or advocating policies at odds with the interests of the United States, nevertheless eschew violent tactics.

Clandestine collectors, however, are poorly structured to fill the intelligence gaps these analysts face. Imagery is of little utility, and both signals and human intelligence are better positioned to provide insight into the plans and intentions of a few important individuals rather than broader political and societal trends.

As a result, analysts are supplementing clandestine collection not only with a greater reliance on open source material and outside experts, but also with their own expertise. To enable them to do so, the Intelligence Community must expand analysts' opportunities to travel and live overseas. And it must consider reforms to the security clearance process that often hampers recruitment of those with the most experience living and working among groups of interest to the Community. Failure to think creatively about how to develop an analytic cadre with a deep understanding of cultures very different from our own will seriously undermine the Community's ability to respond to the new and different intelligence challenges of the 21st century.

Recommendation 4

The Intelligence Community should expand its contacts with those outside the realm of intelligence by creating at least one not-for-profit "sponsored research institute."

We envision the establishment of at least one not-for-profit "sponsored research institute" to serve as a critical window into outside expertise for the Intelligence Community. This sponsored research institute would be funded by the Intelligence Community, but would be largely independent of Community management. The institute would both conduct its own research as well as reach out to specialists, including academics and technical experts, business and industry leaders, and representatives from the nonprofit sector and from Federally Funded Research and Development Centers.

Free from the demands created by the events of the day that burden those within the Intelligence Community, this sponsored research institute's primary purpose would be to focus on strategic issues. It would also serve as an avenue for a robust, external alternative analysis program. Whatever alternative analysis the Community undertakes internally—and we see this as essential—there must be outside thinking to challenge conventional wisdom, and this institute would provide both the distance from and the link to the Intelligence Community to provide a useful counterpoint to accepted views. In this vein, the DNI might consider establishing more than one such institute. By doing so, competitive analysis would be further promoted and healthy competition between the research institutes would help both from being co-opted by the Intelligence Community.

This sponsored research institute would eliminate some existing impediments to more extensive outreach. The institute would have a budget that would enable it to pay top experts unwilling to work for the lower rates typically offered by Intelligence Community components. Moreover, contractors linked to the institute would be available to all Intelligence Community components, avoiding any suggestion that contractors were tasked to provide assessments to support the views of a particular agency. Further, although the staff of the research institute would take recommendations from analysts for particular people to contact outside of the Community, we expect the staff itself to pull together possible contacts in critical fields, expanding the circle of those whose knowledge would be available to the Intelligence Community. The sponsored research institute could also become a center for funding non-traditional methods of assembling open source information. In our classified report we provide an example that cannot be discussed in an unclassified format.

Such a sponsored research institute is not the only way to capitalize on expertise from outside the Intelligence Community. Although the institute would expand the Community's ongoing outreach efforts, the Intelligence Community also needs to think more creatively and, above all, more *strategically* about how it taps into external sources of knowledge. This may include recognizing that the Community may simply not be the natural home for real expertise on certain topics. While economic analysts, for example, can and do play a valuable role in the Community, economists at the Federal Reserve, World Bank, or private sector companies investing millions in emerging markets are likely to have a better handle on current market conditions. Relying on these experts might free up Community resources to work more intensely on finding answers no one else has.

Each of these proposals assumes the Community will have access to existing experts, but that will not always be the case. As a result, the Community must also find ways to support the development of the external expertise it needs. One biosecurity expert remarked that what we really need is a major effort to foster publicly-minded experts to tackle the biothreats likely to face the United States in the future.[5] Title VI of the Higher Education Act, which supports language and area studies in universities, and the National Security Education Program (the Boren Program) might also help. We believe the Intelligence Community should think even more broadly about ways to meet national information needs.

Finally, analysts also need to take full advantage of currently available and underutilized non-traditional technical intelligence capabilities, like advanced geospatial intelligence techniques and measurement and signature intelligence (MASINT). Analysts would benefit from additional training and education to increase their awareness of new and developing collection techniques, so that they are able to effectively task these sources and use the information provided.

MANAGING THE INFLUX OF INFORMATION

As countless groups both inside and outside the Intelligence Community have commented, there is a dire need for greater information sharing—or, as we prefer to put it, information *access* in the Intelligence Community. We address this topic more fully in Chapter Nine (Information Sharing).

But analysts not only need more information, they also need new ways to manage what is already available to them. Analysts today "are inundated and overloaded with information."[6] A study published in 1994 revealed that analysts on average had to scan 200 to 300 documents in two hours each day, just to discover reports worth writing about.[7] If we assume that relevant information has doubled for most analytic accounts over the past ten years (a gross understatement if open source information is considered)—and if we depend on analysts not just to pick reports to write about but instead to "connect the dots" among names, phone numbers, organizations, and events found in other documents—the typical analyst would need a full workday just to perform the basic function of monitoring new data.

The private sector is already using tools and techniques to handle the greatly increased flow of information in today's world; many of the best of these operate even before a user begins to look for relevant information. By the time an Internet user types search terms into Google, for example, the search engine has already done a huge portion of the work of indexing the information and sorting it by relevance. In fact, Google already has educated guesses about what information will be most useful regardless of the breadth of the user's search.

The Intelligence Community's widely used tools for processing raw intelligence traffic are far weaker. According to a senior official at CIA's In-Q-Tel, when analysts enter the Intelligence Community they discover that they have "left a world that was totally wired."[8] Today, an analyst looking for information on Intelligence Community computers is effectively performing a keyword search without any relevance ranking or additional context. The Community has been largely resistant to efforts to import tools from the private sector that offer new and different ways of using technology to exploit data.[9] While this resistance is often driven by legitimate concerns about security, these concerns can (and must) be overcome in the development of information technology for the Intelligence Community.

Recommendation 5

The Community must develop and integrate into regular use new tools that can assist analysts in filtering and correlating the vast quantities of information that threaten to overwhelm the analytic process. Moreover, data from all sources of information should be processed and correlated Community-wide *before* being conveyed to analysts.

The Intelligence Community is only in the beginning stages of developing effective selection, filtering, and correlation tools for its analysts, and more progress must be made. While in every case people are needed to see whether the proposed connections are real—and to be alert for intuitive but inchoate linkages—the Intelligence Community must more effectively employ technology to help draw attention to connections analysts might otherwise miss.

But better tools are not the whole answer. Time and again, tools introduced to the Intelligence Community have failed to take hold because the Community's analysts were accustomed to doing business a different way. We therefore believe there is a need to improve on the Community's long standing, but now outdated, basic approach to processing, exploiting, and disseminating information. In our view, the Intelligence Community needs processes that help analysts correlate and search large volumes of data after traditional dissemination by collectors but *before* the information overflows analysts' inboxes.

Without such a change, we are afraid that analysts will be overwhelmed by piles of information through which they have little hope of sorting.

FOSTERING LONG-TERM RESEARCH AND STRATEGIC THINKING

Managers and analysts throughout the Intelligence Community have repeatedly expressed frustration with their inability to carve out time for long-term research and thinking. This problem is reinforced by the current system of incentives for analysts, in which analysts are often rewarded for the number of pieces they produce, rather than the substantive depth or quality of their production.

Analysts are consistently pressed to produce more pieces faster, particularly those for current intelligence publications such as the President's Daily Brief (PDB). One analyst told us that if an office doesn't produce for the PDB, its "cupboard is bare."[10] But constant pressure to write makes it hard for analysts to find time to do the research—and thinking—necessary to build the real expertise that underlies effective analysis. In one particularly alarming example, an Iraq analyst related that the demand for current intelligence became so acute that he not only gave up long-term research, but also stopped reading his daily in-box of intelligence reporting. That task was delegated to a junior analyst with no expertise on Iraq weapons of mass destruction issues who pulled traffic he thought might be of interest.[11] Although this is an unusually dramatic example, we provide additional classified statistics illustrating this problem in our classified report.

The drive to fill current publications can also crowd out work on strategic military and proliferation issues. As with long-term research, work on these issues may fall by the wayside as analysts respond to immediate, tactical policymaker interests. And strategic work may be discouraged simply because presenting it in a format usable by current intelligence publications is difficult or impossible. Technical assessments are generally seen as too cumbersome for daily intelligence and more difficult for the non-technical briefers to discuss should the President choose to have a dialogue on the issue. Although some of these products reach senior policymakers separately, the fact that they are typically excluded from the publication designed to inform the President about the most important issues of the day likely suggests to analysts that this work is not as highly valued as other topics.

Managers with whom we spoke are aware of the dearth of strategic, long-term thinking, and are seeking ways to remedy the problem. However, we think that part of the solution lies within the new office of the DNI.

Recommendation 6

A new long-term research and analysis unit, under the mantle of the National Intelligence Council, should wall off all-source analysts from the press of daily demands and serve as the lead organization for interagency projects involving in-depth analysis.

We recommend placing this new unit under the National Intelligence Council where analysts would be able to focus on long-term research and underserved strategic threats, away from the demands of current intelligence production. Although some analysts in this new organization would be permanently assigned, at least half—and perhaps a majority—would serve only temporarily and would come from all intelligence agencies, including those with more specialized analysts, such as NGA and NSA. Typically, analysts would have two-year assignments in the unit; in some cases, analysts may spend shorter periods in the organization, long enough to complete a single in-depth research project of pressing need. Because we expect the topics tackled by this group to be complex, collaboration with those outside the unit should be pervasive.

We envision the analysts located in this unit leading projects that bring in experts from across the Intelligence Community, as well as from outside the sphere of intelligence. This collaboration will enable the Intelligence Community to tackle broad strategic questions that sometimes get missed as many analysts focus on narrow slivers of larger issues. DIA analysts and managers, for example, told us that the current division of key analytical responsibilities among the various Department of Defense intelligence units at DIA, the service intelligence centers, and the unified commands makes it difficult for DIA to develop an integrated, strategic assessment of emerging security issues. We expect this new organization to fill such gaps.

Some might be concerned that this new analytic unit would create unhealthy barriers between those engaged in current intelligence and those conducting long-term research. But as proposed, this office avoids that division. Using the common technology infrastructure we propose, we expect that analysts in the new office would easily be able to draw on the insight of analysts still in their home offices who are working on current intelligence. Moreover, because analysts would rotate through this office and remain only for a short period of time, they would not run the risk of veering off into studying questions that might be intellectually interesting but are unlikely to be important to decision-makers. These analysts would come to the office with an understanding of the pulse of current intelligence. Even more important, those same analysts would return to their line units, and the production of timely intelligence, with a greater depth of understanding of their accounts.

Rotations to this unit would also reinforce habits that should be second nature, but sometimes get lost in the daily press of business. Analysts would have time to think more carefully about their words, ensuring that terms used to express uncertainty or concerns about credibility were consistent over time and across accounts. We hope that this unit would also engage in alternative analysis—and that this would help to foster alternative analysis throughout the Intelligence Community. Moreover, rotations through this unit would foster a greater sense of community among analysts and spur collaboration on other projects as well.

Although this strategic analytic unit could be housed in a number of places, we believe that the NIC is best. First, the NIC remains today one of the few places within the Intelligence Community that focuses primarily on long-term, strategic thinking. Second, the NIC is already accustomed to working with analysts across the Community and is therefore likely to be seen as an honest broker—an organization that treats analysts from different agencies equally. Third, the NIC already regularly engages outside experts. Indeed, many National Intelligence Officers spend the bulk of their careers outside the intelligence field.

ENCOURAGING DIVERSE AND INDEPENDENT ANALYSIS

Throughout our case studies we observed the importance of analysts clearly identifying and stating the basis for their assessments. But good analysis goes well beyond just saying what is known, what is unknown, and what an analyst thinks. It is critical that analysts find ways of routinely challenging their initial assumptions and questioning their conclusions—in short, of engaging in competitive (or, as we prefer to call it, independent) analysis.

Recommendation 7

The DNI should encourage diverse and independent analysis throughout the Intelligence Community by encouraging alternative hypothesis generation as part of the analytic process and by forming offices dedicated to independent analysis.

We believe that diverse and independent analysis should come from many sources. In this vein we offer several recommendations that should foster diverse and independent analysis, most particularly our proposed long-term research and analysis unit in the National Intelligence Council, our proposed not-for-profit sponsored research institute, the preservation of dispersed analytic resources, and Community training that instills the importance of independent analysis.

To begin, we note ongoing efforts within the Intelligence Community that have provided valuable independent analysis. The CIA's Directorate of Intelligence, for example, currently has an organization that exclusively drafts "red cell" pieces—documents that are speculative in nature and sometimes take a position at odds with the conventional wisdom.[12] This office proved especially valuable in the context of Libya, for reasons we discuss in greater detail in our classified report but cannot discuss here.

We foresee our proposed long-term research and analysis unit augmenting such existing efforts. We envision the office conducting some of its own alternative analysis, working with analysts in their home offices to conduct independent analysis, and ensuring that analytic judgments are routinely challenged as new information becomes available. By both engaging in its own work and working in conjunction with other offices, we hope that the unit will help catalyze independent analysis throughout the Community and, in the long run, ensure that independent analysis becomes part of the standard way of thinking for all analysts.

Our envisioned not-for-profit sponsored research institute is another natural location for independent analysis to be conducted. In fact, a well-designed research institute should be ideal in that it would have close relationships with non-Intelligence Community experts, as well as easy access to large volumes of open source material. Similarly, the National Intelligence Council should further foster alternative analysis through a National Intelligence Estimate (NIE) process that promotes dissenting views. In our view, the NIE process today is designed to serve as a Community product and, as such, can sometimes become a consensus building process. We hope that the DNI will encourage the NIE drafters to highlight and explore dissenting opinions.

We must stress, however, the importance of fostering a culture of alternative analysis *throughout* the Intelligence Community, as opposed to centralizing the function in a single office (or even several offices). An office solely responsible for dissenting opinions is at risk of losing credibility over time, which would not make it an attractive place for analysts to work. Moreover, we are afraid that an office dedicated to independent analysis would—in the long run—end up having its own biases, and would not provide the diversity of views that we think is so important.

We thus recommend that the DNI give particular "red-team" or "devil's advocate" assignments to individuals or offices on a case-by-case basis, rather than trying to produce all alternative analysis through a separate office. By doing so, no individual or office would constantly bear the brunt of criticizing other analysts' work, nor would such alternative analysis be thought to be the sole responsibility of a single, stand-alone office. And while the DNI is statutorily required to assign an individual or entity responsibility for ensuring that the Community engages in alternative analysis,[13] this should not in our view artificially limit the locations in which such analysis occurs.

Perhaps most important, however, is the view that the Intelligence Community should not rely upon specialized "red team offices," or even individual "red team exercises" to ensure there is sufficient independent analysis. Rather, such independent analysis must become a habitual analytic practice for *all* analysts. The decentralization of the Intelligence Community's analytic bodies will naturally contribute to independent and divergent analysis, and we believe that the Mission Managers we propose will play a valuable role in identifying and encouraging independent analysis in their topic areas. But the Intelligence Community must also ensure that analysts across the Community are trained to question their assumptions and make their arguments explicit. Alternative analysis should be taught in the very first analyst training courses as a core element of good analytic tradecraft. It is to this topic—the training of analysts—that we next turn.

IMPROVING TRADECRAFT THROUGH TRAINING

A common theme from our case studies is that the fundamental logical and analytic principles that should be utilized in building intelligence assessments are often inadequately applied. There are several reasons for this. Key among these is a leadership failure; managers of analysts have neglected to demand the highest standards of analytic craft. This management weakness has been compounded in recent years by the lack of experience among analysts, caused by the more than 33 percent decline in the number of analysts from the latter part of the 1980s through most of the 1990s. On top of the numerical reduction, many of the *best* analysts left during this period because they were the ones who could easily get jobs outside of government. The outflow of knowledge was even greater than the outflow of people.

The Intelligence Community started slowly to hire more analysts in the late 1990s, and recent congressional and executive branch actions are now resulting in further expansion of the analytic corps. As a result, the Intelligence Community is now populated with many junior analysts and few mentors. And the focus on current intelligence has meant that few analysts are given the time to develop expertise, while managers have little time to develop management and mentoring skills.

These difficulties have reduced the quality of finished intelligence. When we reviewed finished intelligence, we found egregious examples of poor tradecraft, such as using a piece of evidence to support an argument when the same piece also supported exactly the opposite argument—and failing to note this fact. In some cases, analysts also failed to update or correct previously published pieces, which led other analysts and policymakers to make judgments on faulty or incomplete premises.

But far and away the most damaging tradecraft weakness we observed was the failure of analysts to conclude—when appropriate—that there was not enough information available to make a defensible judgment.[14] As much as they hate to do it, analysts must be comfortable facing up to uncertainty and being explicit about it in their assessments. Thankfully, we have found several instances of recent efforts by individual analysts to clearly admit what they do and do not know. In particular, a recent National Intelligence Estimate used new processes to ensure that source information was carefully checked for accuracy before inclusion in the estimate. In addition, the Estimate clearly highlighted the intelligence collection gaps on the topic and analysts' level of confidence in their judgments. In our classified report we discuss the particulars of this Estimate in greater depth. Still, these efforts have not been institutionalized, nor are they widespread. We heard many times from users of intelligence that they would like analysts to tell them up front what they don't know—something that intelligence analysts apparently do too infrequently.

Recommendation 8

The Intelligence Community must develop a Community program for training analysts, and both analysts and managers must prioritize this career-long training.

The Intelligence Community must reverse the erosion of analytic expertise that has occurred over the last 15 years. Analytic reasoning must be more rigorous and be explained in clearer terms in order to improve both the quality and credibility of intelligence. Specifically, analysts should take pains to write clearly, articulate assumptions, consistently use caveats, and apply standard approaches to sourcing. A renewed focus on traditional tradecraft methods needs to be augmented with innovative methodologies and tools that assist the analyst without inhibiting creativity, intuition, and curiosity.

This strengthening of the analytic workforce can only occur through a dedicated effort by the Intelligence Community to train analysts throughout their careers. A structured Community program must be developed to teach rigorous tradecraft and to inculcate common standards for analysis so that, for instance, it means the same thing when two agencies say they assess something "with a high degree of certainty." Equally important, managers and analysts must be held accountable for ensuring that analysts continue to develop expertise throughout their careers. The excuse, "I didn't have time for training," is simply unacceptable. This responsibility of both managers and analysts for continued tradecraft training should be made part of all performance evaluations.

Another critical element of training for analysts, and one that has been long lacking in the Intelligence Community, concerns their understanding of intelligence *collection*. Today, analysts receive too little training on collection capabilities and processes, and the training they do receive does not adequately use practical exercises to help analysts learn how to build effective collection strategies to solve intelligence problems. This fundamental ignorance of collection processes and principles can lead to serious misjudgments, and we recommend that the Intelligence Community strengthen analyst training in this area. In our classified report we point to areas in other intelligence agencies' training programs that we believe could be improved, but that cannot be discussed in an unclassified report.

What Denial and Deception (D&D) Means for Analysis

State and non-state actors either with or seeking to develop WMD materials and technologies all practice robust denial and deception techniques against U.S. technical collection. We must significantly reduce our vulnerability to intelligence surprises, mistakes, and omissions caused by the effects of denial and deception (D&D) on collection and analysis. To do so, the Community must foster:

- *Greater awareness of D&D among analysts,* including a deeper understanding of what other countries know about our intelligence capabilities, as well as the D&D intentions, capabilities, and programs of those countries.

- *Greater specification by analysts of what they don't know and clearer statements of their degree of certainty.* Analysts should also work more closely with collectors to fully exploit untapped collection opportunities against D&D targets, and to identify and isolate any deceptive information.

- *Greater appreciation for the capabilities and limitations of U.S. collection systems.*

- *Greater use of analytical techniques that identify the impact of denial and the potential for deception.* Analysts must understand and evaluate the effects of false, misleading, or even true information that intelligence targets may have injected into the collection stream to deceive the United States.

Recommendation 9

The Intelligence Community must develop a Community program for training managers, both when they first assume managerial positions and throughout their careers.

Managerial training must also be vastly expanded throughout the Intelligence Community. Although scattered training is available, the Intelligence Community currently has no systematic, serious, or sustained management training program, and none that readily allows for cross-agency training—even though management problems can be similar across agencies. CIA managers, for example, receive a small portion of the training provided to their military counterparts.[15] And we are dismayed that some in the Intelligence Community resisted programs such as merit-based pay due to a mistrust of managers' ability to accurately and fairly measure performance.

Prospective managers should be given extensive management training before assuming their responsibilities, and current managers should be enrolled in refresher training courses on a regular basis. A well-trained management and leadership corps within the Intelligence Community is vital to the health of analysis (and collection), and the Community is currently suffering the consequences of its absence. To the degree that a few individuals at the CIA have already recognized this problem, and are designing programs to address it, we commend them.

Although we hesitate to prescribe any specific level of centralization for analytic and managerial training, we do suggest that some of the training be Community-wide, perhaps housed in our proposed National Intelligence University or done through an online education program.[16] We do so in full recognition that individual agencies may want to conduct their own training because their workforce requires specialized skills, and that some resist centralized training on the grounds that training should engender a strong affiliation among analysts for their particular agency.

Notwithstanding these objections, as discussed in our chapter on Management, we believe that the creation of the DNI provides a unique opportunity to reconsider implementing some elements of Community training. The benefits will be enormous: it will teach common tradecraft standards, standardize teaching and evaluation, foster a sense of Community among analysts, and, we hope, provide analysts with a wider range of training opportunities throughout their careers. It may also create economies of scale in training costs. For these reasons, we strongly encourage joint training whenever feasible.

MAKING ANALYSIS MORE TRANSPARENT

Training analysts and managers to use better "tradecraft" is only half the battle; rigorous analytic methods must be demanded in every intelligence product. One way of doing so—and at the same time ensuring that customers are confident in the intelligence they receive—is to make the analytic process more transparent. Although we recognize that real security issues make total transparency impossible, we fear that protecting sources and methods has resulted in the shrouding of analysis itself, not just the intelligence on which it is based. This tendency must, we believe, be actively resisted.

Recommendation 10

Finished intelligence should include careful sourcing for all analytic assessments and conclusions, and these materials should—whenever possible in light of legitimate security concerns—be made easily available to intelligence customers.

We recommend forcing analysts to make their assumptions and reasoning more transparent by requiring that analysis be well sourced, and that all finished intelligence products, either in paper or in digital format, provide citations to enable user verification of particular statements. This requirement is no more rigorous than that which is required in law, science, and the social sciences, and we see little reason why such standards should not be demanded of the Intelligence Community's analysts. Analysts are generally already expected to provide sources for internal review; including this information in finished analysis would simply increase the transparency of the process.

We further recommend that customers have access to the raw intelligence reporting that supports analytic pieces whenever possible, subject to legitimate security considerations. For many intelligence customers, especially senior policymakers and operators, a general description, such as State Department "diplomatic reporting" simply does not provide the confidence needed to take quick and decisive action.[17] Where a user accesses finished intelligence electronically, he should be able to link directly to at least some portion of the raw intelligence—or to underlying finished intelligence—to which a judgment is sourced.

Requiring that citations be routinely available and linked to source documents need not preclude analysts from making judgments or inferences; rather, the availability of such materials will simply enable users to distinguish quickly between those statements that are paraphrased summaries of intelligence reporting, and those that are analytic judgments that draw inferences from this reporting. Of course, some analysts might worry that such a system would essentially sideline the analyst, making his or her work irrelevant because all of his or her hard calls could be "questioned" by returning to the original sources and performing the analysis independently. We do not, however, think this is inherently bad. Intelligence customers should be able to question judgments, and analysts should be able to defend their reasoning. In the end, such a reform should bolster the stature of good analysts, as policymakers and operators come to see their analytic judgments as increasingly accurate and actionable.

Recommendation 11

The analytic community should create and store sourced copies of all analytic pieces to allow readers to locate and review the intelligence upon which analysis is based, and to allow for easy identification of analysis that is based on intelligence reports that are later modified.

We recommend that the DNI create a system to electronically store sourced versions of analytic pieces and ensure that source information is easily accessible to intelligence users, consistent with adequate security permissions. Of course, to make such electronic storage and accessibility possible one needs first to have a truly integrated information sharing environment and shared information technology systems—a considerable challenge given the inadequacies of today's information technology environment, on which we comment more fully in Chapter Nine (Information Sharing).

The DNI should also encourage the development of a system that enables Intelligence Community personnel to update intelligence information that has been judged to be unreliable, of increased or decreased certainty, or simply retracted. These updates must be electronically flagged in the intelligence reports themselves as well as any analytic products citing to the reports. Such tracking systems have existed in other fields for decades (*e.g.*, Lexis and Westlaw for the legal world).[18]

Above and beyond the technical constraints to implementing such a system, there are several barriers that have blocked these reforms in the past. For example, CIA's Directorate of Operations maintains a close hold on its highly sensitive reporting, often with good reason. Making this raw reporting accessible to policymakers and intelligence officers across the Community raises several security and counterintelligence-related concerns. Furthermore, it is questionable to what degree *all* policymakers will need access to raw reporting.

But none of these issues explains why the Intelligence Community's efforts in this vein are still in such a stage of infancy. While there will be information that cannot be provided to intelligence customers, many decisionmakers can and do read intelligence reporting at the same time as the analysts who receive it. Further, access to an analytic product is typically limited to those who are cleared to read the intelligence reports on which it is based. The easy availability of source information, related reporting, and other finished intelligence products, along with a system to clearly identify old intelligence that has been reconsidered in one way or another, will benefit both analysts and customers. Analysts will, we believe, do their work more meticulously and accurately, while customers will be able to better understand the products they receive and know whether the Community continues to stand behind the intelligence.

IMPROVING SCIENTIFIC, TECHNICAL, AND WEAPONS INTELLIGENCE

Recommendation 12

The DNI should develop and implement strategies for improving the Intelligence Community's science and technology and weapons analysis capabilities.

A specific subset of analysts within the Intelligence Community is responsible for assessing emerging threats to U.S. interests resulting from advances in foreign science and technology (S&T) and weapons developments. Using specialized scientific and technical expertise, skills, and analytic methodologies, these analysts work on some of today's most important intelligence issues, including counterproliferation, homeland security, support to military operations, infrastructure protection, and arms control. We are therefore concerned that a recent Intelligence Science Board study concluded that the Intelligence Community's current S&T intelligence capability is "not what it could be and not what the nation needs."[19]

The Intelligence Science Board study and our own research found that the Intelligence Community's ability to conduct S&T and weapons analysis has not kept pace with the changing security environment.[20] The board's study noted the Intelligence Community was particularly vulnerable to surprise by "rapidly changing and readily available emerging technologies whose use by state and non-state actors, in yet unanticipated ways, may result in serious and unexpected threats."[21] The S&T areas of most concern include biological attacks, nuclear threats, cyber warfare, Chinese technology leapfrogging, and the impact of commercial technologies on foreign threats.[22] In addition, current analysis often fails to place foreign S&T and weapons developments in the context of an adversary's plans, strategy, policies, and overall capabilities that would provide customers with a better understanding of the implications for U.S. security and policy interests.[23] One senior Administration official interviewed by the Commission staff described the Intelligence Community's capability to conduct this kind of all-source S&T and weapons analysis as "pretty poor" and "mediocre at best."[24]

The state of the Intelligence Community's S&T and weapons analysis capabilities should be a key issue for the DNI, given the importance of these fields in providing warning and assessments of many of today's critical threats. In addition to hiring more analysts with technical and scientific skills and experience, the Intelligence Community would benefit from more contact with outside technical experts who could conduct peer reviews and provide alternative perspectives. In addition, resources should be set aside for conducting in-depth and multidisciplinary research and analysis of emerging technologies and weapon developments to help the Community keep pace with the ever-changing security environment. The use of analytical methodologies, such as red teaming, scenario analyses, and crisis simulations, to explore and understand the impact of new technologies and weapons on U.S. interests should also be encouraged to help analysts guard against technology surprise.

To ensure progress will be made in the future, we recommend that the DNI designate a Community leader for developing and implementing strategies for improving the Intelligence Community's S&T and weapons analysis capabilities. This person should report to the DNI on a periodic basis on the status of the Community's relevant capabilities and make recommendations on where further improvements are needed.

SERVING INTELLIGENCE CUSTOMERS

Analysts are the link between customers and the Intelligence Community. They provide a conduit for providing intelligence to customers and for conveying the needs and interests of customers to collectors. This role requires analysts to perform a number of functions. Analysts must assess the available information and place it in context. They must clearly and concisely communicate the information they have, the information they need, the conclusions they draw from the data, and their doubts about the credibility of the information or the validity of their conclusions. They must understand the questions policymakers ask, those they are likely to ask, and those they should ask; the information needed to answer those questions; and the best mechanisms for finding that information. And as analysts are gaining unprecedented and critically important access to operations traffic, they must also become security gatekeepers, revealing enough about the sources for policymakers to evaluate their reporting and conclusions, but not enough to disclose tightly-held, source-identifying details.

Analysts fulfill these functions through interactions with a wide range of intelligence customers, who run the gamut in terms of rank, area of responsibility, and understanding of intelligence. "Typical" customers include not only the President and senior policymakers, but also members of Congress, military commanders, desk officers in executive agencies, law enforcement officers, customs and border patrol officials, and military units in the field. We do not attempt to examine each of these relationships, but we do note some challenges in this area. Specifically, we address how the Intelligence Community might modernize some customer relationships, some components of an "appropriate" relationship between analysts and customers, and how the President—and to a lesser degree other senior policymakers—should be supported.

Modernizing the Analyst-Customer Relationship

Recommendation 13

The DNI should explore ways to make finished intelligence available to cus-tomers in a way that enables them—*to the extent they desire*—to more easily find pieces of interest, link to related materials, and communicate with ana-lysts.

The Intelligence Community must distribute its products more efficiently and effectively. Today's policymaker receives intelligence in almost the same way as his 1985 predecessor; most intelligence products from the CIA's Director-ate of Intelligence, for example, are still delivered in hardcopy. For some cus-tomers, this may remain the preferred method of receiving intelligence. For others with different needs or preferences—and we have heard from some of them—the Intelligence Community should consider ways to modernize intel-ligence distribution.

Some modernization has occurred; most notably, a limited number of Wash-ington policymakers can access some intelligence products through the Defense Department's secure networks—JWICS and Intelink—at their desk. But the "populating" of these networks varies across agencies and by product type. For example, INR and DIA routinely place their publications on these secure networks, and a large percentage of finished intelligence products related to counterterrorism can be found online. By contrast, CIA sharply lim-its the use of its finished intelligence on these networks, citing the need to protect its human sources. And even when intelligence is available on elec-tronic networks, the interfaces are clumsy and counterintuitive—far below the presentation of online publishers such as the *Washington Post*.

This state of affairs is markedly inferior to the state of the practice in private industry. Most customers of intelligence products cannot search electronic libraries of information or catalogues of existing products. They cannot query analysts in real time about needed information or upcoming products. They cannot link finished intelligence documents together electronically to create a reference trail. They cannot easily review research programs to provide sug-gestions or recommendations. They cannot explore thoughts and views with analysts in an informal online environment. They cannot read informal messages alerting them to new information which may include analysts' preliminary thoughts or judgments on an item. They cannot tailor information displays to their needs. They cannot reshape raw data into graphics and charts. They cannot access different intelligence media electronically.

This is not an area in which there is only one right answer; there are many ways to provide up-to-the-minute, in-depth information to policymakers in user-friendly formats. We also recognize that because of the dramatic effects an electronic system would have on the way the Intelligence Community does its work and because of substantial security concerns, any new program along these lines will require a great deal of additional thought and planning. Nevertheless, we believe that even in the relatively near future the benefits of an integrated electronic system will outweigh the risks, and it will become more necessary as a new generation of customers—with a preference for the flexibility of digital technology—reaches higher levels of government.

Components of the Analyst-Customer Relationship

Regardless of how customers receive intelligence, both analysts and customers have to recognize that certain exchanges between the two are appropriate and should be encouraged. Perhaps most importantly, we believe it is critical that customers engage analysts. It is the job of the analyst to express clearly what the analyst knows, what the analyst doesn't know, what the analyst thinks, and why—but if the analyst does not, the customer must insist that the analyst do so. If necessary, the customer should challenge the analyst's assumptions and reasoning. Because they are "keepers of the facts," analysts can play a decisive role in policy debates, a role that has temptations for analysts with strong policy views of their own. A searching examination of the underlying evidence for the analysts' factual assertions is the best way to reassure policymakers that the analysts' assertions are well-grounded. We reject any contention that such engagement is in itself inappropriate or that the risk of "politicizing" intelligence cannot be overcome by clear statements to analysts as to the purpose of the dialogue. When an analyst leaves a policymaker's office feeling thoroughly cross-examined and challenged to support his premises, that is not politicization; it is the system working at its best. Only through active engagement of this sort will intelligence become as useful as it can be.

Analysts also have a responsibility to tell customers about important disagreements within the Intelligence Community. We were told by some senior policymakers that it sometimes took weeks to get an answer to a question—not because the answer was difficult to obtain, but because analysts were hesitant to admit to Intelligence Community disagreement on an issue. This is not how intelligence should function. Analysts must readily bring disagreement within the Community to policymakers' attention, and must be ready to explain the basis for the disagreement. Such disagreement is often a sign of robust independent analysis and should be encouraged.

In addition to conveying disagreements, analysts must also find ways to explain to policymakers degrees of certainty in their work. Some publications we have reviewed use numerical estimates of certainty, while others rely on phrases such as "probably" or "almost certainly." We strongly urge that such assessments of certainty be used routinely and consistently throughout the Community. Whatever device is used to signal the degree of certainty—mathematical percentages, graphic representations, or key phrases—all analysts in the Community should have a common understanding of what the indicators mean and how to use them.

Finally, analysts and Intelligence Community leaders have a responsibility to take note, whenever possible, of what their customers are doing and saying, and to tell those customers when actions or statements are inconsistent with existing intelligence. We do not mean to suggest that analysts should spend all of their waking hours monitoring policymakers, or that analysts should have a "veto" over policymaker statements. Rather, when aware of upcoming speeches or decisions, analysts should make clear that they are available to vet intelligence-related matters, and analysts should—when necessary—tell policymakers how their statements diverge from existing intelligence. Having fulfilled this duty, analysts must then let politically-accountable policymakers determine whether or not a statement is appropriate in light of intelligence judgments.

Serving the President and Senior Policymakers

The new legislation designates the DNI as the person primarily responsible for ensuring that the President's day-to-day intelligence needs are met.[25] This means that the Office of the DNI, not the Director of the Central Intelligence Agency, should have the final authority over the content and production of the

President's Daily Brief (PDB)—or whatever other form intelligence support to the President may take.

We also believe that the DNI will have to work closely with the President and the National Security Council to reconsider how intelligence should best be presented to the President, because we are dubious that the PDB—in its current incarnation—is the right answer.

Our case studies, primarily Iraq, highlight several flaws indicating a need to rethink the PDB.[26] PDB pieces are typically limited by space constraints. While sophisticated, in-depth analysis can be presented in this abbreviated fashion, the task is considerably more difficult than drafting a more immediate, less research-intensive piece that updates the reader on current events and provides a more limited, near-term analytic focus. As a result, we worry that individual PDB articles fail to provide sufficient context for the reader. This view was reinforced by one senior intelligence officer's observation that policymakers are sometimes surprised to find that longer, in-depth intelligence reporting provides a different view from that conveyed by the PDB. The same individual noted that when a policymaker is given a piece of information about a certain subject, the policymaker will often ask questions about the information, leading to follow-up on that subject, thereby exacerbating the current intelligence bias.[27] Moreover, the PDB staff tends to focus on today's hot national security issues, or on issues that attracted the President's interest the last time they came up. This can lead to repeated reporting on a given topic or event; a drumbeat of incremental "hot news" articles affects a reader much differently than the same information presented in a longer, contextualized piece that explains the relationship between the various reports. Finally, the PDB sometimes includes excessively "snappy" headlines, which tend to misrepresent an article's more nuanced conclusions, and which are, in our view, unnecessary; a two or three-word indicator of the piece's subject (such as "North Korea-Nuclear") would tell policymakers which pieces were of most interest to them without obscuring the subtle contours of an issue raised in the text.

Having identified these potential problems, we are hesitant to suggest how the PDB process should be altered. Only the President can say for certain how often and in what format he prefers to receive national intelligence information. We do, however, recognize that the creation of the DNI will shift what has been a CIA-centric PDB process to more of a Community one—shepherded by the Office of the DNI.

Recommendation 14

The President's Daily Brief should be restructured. The DNI should oversee the process and ensure a fair representation of divergent views. Reporting on terrorism intelligence should be combined and coordinated by the DNI to eliminate redundancies and material that does not merit Presidential action.

Regardless of the structure of the PDB process, the DNI will need to respond to the demands of senior advisors and the President. We recommend that the DNI create an analytic staff too small to routinely undertake drafting itself, but large enough that its members would have expertise on a wide range of subjects. The staffers would task the appropriate experts and agencies to draft responses to decisionmaker requests. They could also perform last minute editing and would—in every case—ensure that the pieces reflect any differences of opinion in the Community.[28] In our view, it is simply not enough to present dissenting views from the Intelligence Community only in longer, more formal assessments like National Intelligence Estimates. Rather, because policymakers tend to be significantly influenced by daily intelligence products, we believe it is essential that those products offer as complete a perspective on an issue as is feasible. This is not to suggest that the production of each daily briefing for the President or others should recreate a mini-NIE process; in many cases, relatively few intelligence agencies need be involved. But when agencies have sharp differences, the DNI's analytic staff should be responsible for ensuring that the final memorandum clearly reflects these competing conclusions and the reasons for disagreement.

Equally important, we believe that the DNI should seek to combine—with the President's concurrence, of course—the three primary sources of intelligence that now reach the President. Currently, in addition to the PDB, the President receives the President's Terrorism Threat Report (PTTR), which is prepared by the National Counterterrorism Center and is appended to each day's PDB. The President may also be verbally briefed by the Director of the FBI who uses material from a "Director's Daily Report" prepared by his staff.

We have reviewed these materials and discussed the briefings with many regular participants. There are plainly redundancies that should be eliminated, but we are also concerned that the channels conveying terrorism intelligence are clogged with trivia. One reason for this unnecessary detail is that passing information "up the chain" provides bureaucratic cover against later accusations that the data was not taken seriously. As one official complained, this behavior is caused by bureaucracies that are "preparing for the next 9/11 Commission instead of preparing for the next 9/11." It may be difficult to stem this tide, but the new DNI is in the best position to bring order to the process. We recommend that the DNI be given clear responsibility for combining terrorism intelligence into a single, regular Presidential briefing (whether a daily briefing is required should depend on the pace of events). This briefing would resemble and would perhaps be combined into the PDB.

In the same vein, several senior officials told us that they read the PDB not so much for its content (for it often did not necessarily include especially critical information) as much as to stay apprised of matters on which the President is briefed. In this light, although the DNI and the PDB staff must be free to make a professional judgment about the intelligence to present on any given day, we recommend that the DNI encourage suggestions from policymaking agencies like State and Defense about topics that could usefully be presented in the President's briefing. By taking this step the PDB would likely become more attuned to a wider variety of pressing national security issues.

We fully recognize that the DNI's role calls for a delicate balance. It will be tempting for the DNI's analysts to become the primary drafters themselves, and analysts in individual agencies will continue to face demands from those in their chain of command to respond to requests directly. The former would turn the office of the DNI into one more analytic entity putting forward its own views. The latter problem recreates the situation we have today, which often results in a multiplicity of uncoordinated views appearing before senior decisionmakers. The DNI's analytic cadre, whose responsibility it is to understand and to put forward the views of the Community's experts, wherever located, must ensure that analytic differences in the Community are not suppressed and, equally important, are not presented to decisionmakers in a piecemeal fashion that forces senior officials to sort out the differences themselves.

RETAINING THE BEST ANALYSTS

The Intelligence Community is unlikely to have the funding necessary to rely exclusively—or even primarily—on economic incentives to recruit and retain the best and the brightest. The Community, however, has always offered analysts something more: the opportunity to play a role in shaping the decisions of the nation's top leaders and to help maintain the security of our nation. To the extent that the Community loses sight of this as a motivating factor for its employees, it loses its most valuable tool for recruitment and retention.

Recommendation 15

The Intelligence Community should expand the use of non-monetary incentives that remind analysts of the importance of their work and the value of their contributions to national security.

Recognize good performers. The Intelligence Community should look for ways to ensure that the best analysts are recognized both within the Community and by decisionmakers outside of the Community. The fact that the Community on the whole works in relative anonymity makes this recognition all the more necessary. Analysts who are viewed as experts get the opportunity to do exactly what analysts are hired to do—play a part in shaping U.S. policy. In turn, analysts who have the chance to sit face-to-face with top-level decisionmakers are motivated in a very personal way to do their best.

Provide travel, training, rotations, and sabbaticals. All analysts are not alike, and not all opportunities for professional development will appeal to all equally. But giving analysts time to do the things they most want to do, particularly when the activities also contribute to the development of their expertise, is beneficial to everyone. One DIA manager told us that fully funding a robust travel budget would be far cheaper than paying salaries on a par with those paid by contractors, and would help a great deal in keeping analysts motivated and interested.[29] Other analysts are likely to find other activities more appealing, from full-time academic training, to policy rotations, to stints in the Office of the DNI or other agencies within the Community.

Permit careers to focus on the analysts' areas of interest. Analysts also differ in their preferred approaches to their careers. Some enjoy being generalists, moving among all types of accounts and bringing a fresh perspective; others have a strong interest in a certain type of analysis—such as conventional weapons—or an area of the world, and might choose to spend time on a variety of similar accounts. Still others seek to specialize on fairly focused subject matters. The Intelligence Community benefits from all of these career paths, and in the best of all worlds, analysts would be able to follow the one best suited to their interests. The nature of the intelligence business will never allow for such a perfect fit; some specialists will need to remain on an account after their interest in it has waned, and some analysts will be pulled from where they are happiest to respond to an emerging crisis. But the goal should be to get it right for as many analysts as possible. Doing so is an enormously powerful retention tool. Managers of technical analysts explained to us that they had a great deal of difficulty retaining analysts because they came in expecting to work on areas in which they had developed expertise, but were pulled by the demands of the job into other areas that they found less interesting.[30] We expect that the Mission Managers will be able to place more focused attention on long-range planning and generate an increased understanding of where knowledge and expertise reside—and thus better position the Community to respond to emerging crises in a thoughtful way and reduce the numbers of analysts forced into jobs they dislike.

Provide tools and support. Managers also complained that analysts often find that the tools and technology available in the Intelligence Community fall short of what they use in school, at home, or in the private sector.[31] Moreover, analysts across the board face declining administrative support. Among other things, analysts typically must do desktop publishing, maintain files of classified materials not available electronically, manage contracts, and perform logistical tasks associated with travel or training. In other words, analysts often view their counterparts in the private sector as having better tools and better support that enable them to spend their time and energy on core tasks. Giving analysts what they need to do their job and ensuring that they spend their time as *analysts*, not clerks or administrative aides, would emphasize that their time and skills are valued.

LEARNING FROM PAST MISTAKES

The new intelligence reform legislation requires the DNI to assign an individual or entity the responsibility to ensure that finished intelligence products are timely, objective, independent of political considerations, based on all sources of available intelligence, and grounded in proper analytic tradecraft. In the course of conducting relevant reviews, this entity is further directed to produce a report of lessons learned.[32]

Recommendation 16

Examinations of finished intelligence should be routine and ongoing, and the lessons learned from the "post mortems" should be incorporated into the intelligence education and training program.

Iraq, Libya, and Afghanistan have offered opportunities for the Intelligence Community to compare its assessments with the ground truth and examine the sources of the disparities. We have already seen evidence that the lessons learned from Iraq are being incorporated by analysts covering other countries or intelligence topics. Analysts are increasingly careful to explain their analytical baseline in their products, and attribute the sources of intelligence underlying it. The Intelligence Community, analysts say, has adopted the "rule of elementary school math class," in that its analysts are dedicated to "showing our work" to prevent the "layering of analysis."[33]

This is an area in which the Intelligence Community should learn from the Department of Defense, which has an especially strong, institutionalized process for benefiting from lessons learned. In our classified report, we discuss a Defense Department "lessons-learned" study that we found particularly impressive, but that we cannot elaborate upon here. Intelligence Community lessons-learned efforts (such as CIA's Product Evaluation Staff) had less success, in part because they do not have sufficient resources or possess much prestige within intelligence agencies. Nor do we think that, in general, intelligence agencies should be responsible for "grading their own papers." The intelligence reform legislation recognizes the need for a separate body that conducts reviews of analysis, a welcome idea that should be fully embraced by the Community.

CONCLUSION

The changes that we recommend are significant departures from the current way in which the Community conducts the business of analysis. Some run counter to long-standing, embedded practices, and we are mindful that they may be resisted by analysts and managers alike. We believe, however, that these changes are essential to improving the Community's capability to accurately assess threats and to provide timely, relevant, thoughtful support to policymakers. Intelligence analysis faces unprecedented challenges; unprecedented measures to strengthen the analytical process are well warranted.

ENDNOTES

[1] U.S. Senate, *The Final Report of the Select Committee To Study Governmental Operations with Respect to Intelligence Activities* (April 26, 1976) (*i.e.*, Church Committee Report); Permanent Select Committee on Intelligence, U.S. House of Representatives, *IC21: Intelligence Community in the 21st Century* (1996); Commission to Assess the Ballistic Missile Threat to the United States (*i.e.*, Rumsfeld Commission), *Side Letter to the President* (March 18, 1999); CIA, *The Jeremiah Report: The Intelligence Community's Performance on the Indian Nuclear Tests* (June 1, 1998); Markle Foundation Task Force, *Creating a Trusted Information Network for Homeland Security* (Dec. 2003); National Commission on Terrorist Attacks Upon the United States, *Final Report of the National Commission on Terrorist Attacks Upon the United States* (*i.e.*, The 9/11 Commission Report) (2004); Council on Foreign Relations, *Making Intelligence Smarter: The Future of U.S. Intelligence: Report of an Independent Task Force* (1996); Commission on the Roles and Capabilities of the United States Intelligence Community (*i.e.*, Aspin-Brown Commission), *Preparing for the 21st Century: An Appraisal of U.S. Intelligence* (1996); *Report of the Commission on Organization of the Executive Branch of the Government* (*i.e.* Hoover Commission Report) (1949).

[2] Staff review of House Permanent Select Committee on Intelligence and Senate Select Committee on Intelligence Markups of Intelligence Authorization Bills, 1991-2005.

[3] Interview with senior intelligence official (Sept. 22, 2004).

[4] The CIA has had similar programs in the past whereby the agency introduced analysts who were tools experts to work alongside other analysts. These analysts were just like their analytic colleagues, except that they were also specialists in how to use analytic technologies and could help counterparts learn to use these tools to structure research problems. CIA Office of Research and Development, *Office of East Asian Analysis Testbed Project Final Report* (Sept. 30, 1994).

[5] Interview with biosecurity expert (Feb. 4, 2005).

[6] Inter-agency Information Sharing Working Group, *Consolidated Report* (Dec. 14, 2004) at p. 5. We provided an additional footnote illustrating the magnitude of this challenge in our classified report.

[7] CIA Office of Research and Development, *Office of East Asian Analysis Testbed Project Final Report* (Sept. 30, 1994).

[8] Interview with senior In-Q-Tel official (Feb. 3, 2005). In addition, a senior manager of analysis told us he knew there is a need to make better use of open sources but that this could not be achieved without assistance in the form of preliminary correlation of the data. Interview with senior CIA DI official (Feb. 10, 2005).

[9] Interview with senior In-Q-Tel official (Feb. 3, 2005).

[10] Interview with CIA analysts (Jan. 24, 2005).

[11] Interview with former CIA WINPAC analysts (Nov. 10, 2004).

[12] These formal alternative analysis programs are also reinforced by the existence of multiple analytic units in the Community, which often reach different analytic conclusions.

[13] The DNI is statutorily required to assign responsibility "for ensuring responsibility that, as appropriate, elements of the Intelligence Community conduct alternative analysis." Intelli-

gence Reform and Terrorism Prevention Act of 2004 at § 1017, Pub. L. No. 108-458 (hereinafter "IRTPA").

[14] Chapter Three (Afghanistan).

[15] Interview with senior CIA official.

[16] There currently exist several very successful joint training programs. The Joint Military Intelligence College, for example, currently operates a very successful program—a structured intermediate/advanced curriculum for Intelligence Community officers across the Community. At the same time, many similar efforts have failed for various reasons, including insufficient funding and lack of bureaucratic clout. The Defense Department Chancellor for Civilian Education's program is one such example of an unsuccessful cross-agency effort. Interview with former senior staff of the defunct Department of Defense Office of the Chancellor for Civilian Education and Development (Jan. 13, 2005).

[17] Some, but not most, of the finished intelligence provided to the Commission included lists of reference numbers identifying particular sources, but we understand that such lists are not routinely provided to policymakers. In any case, these lists provide no indication of how one could determine which specific document supported facts included in the piece.

[18] We recognize that the DCI is currently working to establish Community procedures for such a system, and we commend this development. Chapter One (Iraq) provides a detailed discussion of how analysts and intelligence users continued to use reporting considered unreliable.

[19] DCI Intelligence Science Board Task Force, *The State of Science and Technology Analysis in the Intelligence Community* (April 2004) at p. xiii (hereinafter "ISB Report").

[20] *Id.* at p. xiii; Interview with senior intelligence official (Oct. 7, 2004); Interview with senior DIA analyst (Sept. 23, 2004).

[21] ISB Report at pp. 26-27.

[22] *Id.* at p. 27.

[23] *Id.* at pp. 26, 28; Interview with administration official (Sept. 30, 2004); Interview with administration official (Sept. 10, 2004).

[24] Interview with senior administration official (Oct. 12, 2004).

[25] IRTPA at § 1011.

[26] In addition, several senior policymakers expressed concerns about the utility of the PDB in its current incarnation.

[27] Interview with senior intelligence analyst (Nov. 8, 2004).

[28] We understand that the CIA is already moving in this direction and we commend it for doing so.

[29] Interview with DIA analysts and managers (Oct. 26, 2004).

[30] *See, e.g.*, Interview with CIA WINPAC analysts (Oct. 14, 2004).

[31] *Id.*

[32] IRTPA at § 1019.

[33] Interview with DIA analysts (Nov. 22, 2004).

CHAPTER NINE
INFORMATION SHARING

Summary & Recommendations

While the imperative to improve information sharing within and beyond the Intelligence Community is widely acknowledged, it is too infrequently noted that the Intelligence Community—and the new DNI—have an additional responsibility that is often in tension with the first: the need to protect intelligence sources and methods. What therefore is needed—and what is largely absent from today's Intelligence Community—are structures and processes for sharing intelligence information that are driven by commonly accepted principles of *risk management*. While some collection agencies have greatly improved their information sharing practices since September 11, others have allowed overly stringent protective requirements to play too decisive a role in the decision whether to share information. Concern about security in a narrow sense should not crowd out actions to ensure national security in the larger sense. Sometimes—indeed, often—the right answer will be to limit access to information because of security concerns; but collection agencies, which for perfectly understandable bureaucratic reasons may systematically undervalue the need to share information, should not make this decision.

Accordingly, in this chapter we call for a consolidation of authority and the centralized management of intelligence information along the following lines:

- Resolve management ambiguities created by the recent intelligence reform legislation through two actions: (1) ensure that the newly-created Program Manager reports to the President through the DNI; and (2) expand the Information Sharing Environment envisioned by the statute to include all intelligence information, not just intelligence related to terrorism;

- Create a single position under the DNI with responsibility for both information sharing and the protection of sources and methods: a chief information management officer; and

- Break down both policy and technical barriers to information sharing by eliminating inconsistent agency practices and establishing, to the fullest extent possible, uniform standards across the Intelligence Community designed to facilitate implementation of a networked community.

	An End to "Sharing"

We begin with an important reservation about terminology. The term information "sharing" suggests that the federal government entity that collects the information "owns" it and can decide whether or not to "share" it with others. This concept is deeply embedded in the Intelligence Community's culture. We reject it. Information collected by the Intelligence Community—or for that matter, any government agency—belongs to the U.S. government. Officials are fiduciaries who hold the information in trust for the nation. They do not have authority to withhold or distribute it except as such authority is delegated by the President or provided by law. As we have noted elsewhere, we think that the Director of National Intelligence could take an important, symbolic first step toward changing the Intelligence Community's culture by jettisoning the term "information sharing" itself—perhaps in favor of the term "information integration" or "information access." But as the term "information sharing" has become common parlance, we will use it in this chapter to avoid confusion.

INTRODUCTION: THE LAY OF THE LAND

The 9/11 Commission Report depicted a number of failures by one agency to pass terrorism warning information to other agencies, resulting in missed opportunities to apprehend terrorists.[1] Although the problem of information sharing was not a central part of the Intelligence Community's failure to assess Iraq's weapons programs properly, our study of Iraq found several situations where key information failed to reach those who needed it: for example, poor information systems resulted in a failure to recall reporting from a source who was determined to be a fabricator, and early reporting raising questions about the credibility of Curveball was not widely distributed to the analytical community.[2] Our review of other aspects of the Intelligence Community—and in particular, the Intelligence Community's current capabilities to combat the terrorist threat—revealed other shortcomings in the way in which information is communicated between and among intelligence agencies.

Our study is hardly the first to identify the need for information sharing, both within the Intelligence Community and in other areas of the government.[3] The Intelligence Community has taken its own steps to address the problem internally, and has launched more than 100 initiatives since September 11 to improve information sharing.[4] While some of these steps deserve praise, progress has been uneven and sporadic. As demonstrated in our terrorism case study, the Terrorist Threat Integration Center, now absorbed within the National Counterterrorism Center, has succeeded in establishing connections to dozens of networks at its new terrorism warning center—but obstacles remain. Representatives from one agency still face legal and policy barriers that prevent them from gaining access to the databases of another.[5] Collectors of information continue to operate as though they "own" the information, and collectors continue to control access to the information they generate.[6] Decisions to withhold information are typically based on rules that are neither clearly defined nor consistently applied, with no system in place to hold collectors accountable for inappropriately withholding information.[7]

In short, while some progress has been made since September 11, we are still quite far from the goal of enabling personnel from across the Intelligence Community to access information from anywhere in the Community through their own network-based connections. In our terrorism case study, we agreed with the recent assessment of the DCI's Information Sharing Working Group, which found that "[a] great deal of energy...is being expended across the [Intelligence Community] to improve information sharing. However, the majority of these initiatives *will not produce the enduring institutional change required to address our current threat environment.*"[8]

Recognizing the incomplete nature of the Intelligence Community's efforts, the President and Congress have taken their own steps in recent months to address the problem. The new reform legislation built upon Executive Order 13356 by mandating the creation of an "Information Sharing Environment" for all "terrorism information," and created a new office—a "Program Manager" who reports to the President—to administer it.[9] The purpose of the Information Sharing Environment is to ensure "the sharing of terrorism information among all appropriate Federal, State, local, and tribal entities, and the private sector through the use of policy guidelines and technologies."[10] The new law also recast the Information Systems Council established by Executive Order 13356 as the "Information Sharing Council" with responsibility to oversee the development of the Information Sharing Environment.[11] Most everyone now "gets it"; when we asked the most distinguished leaders of the Intelligence Community to name their first priority for reform, many responded "information sharing." There is broad consensus on the big picture. But the problem is hard to fix. While some technical barriers exist, policy barriers are the real problem. One must not dismiss concerns about security or the protection of sources and methods as illegitimate; but, at the same time, such concerns must not force a stalemate, which is too often the result when interagency initiatives move from rhetoric to implementation.

The initial implementation plan of the Information Sharing Council exemplifies our concern. The President directed the Council, within 120 days, to produce a "plan, with proposed milestones, timetables for achieving those milestones, and identification of resources" to execute the plan.[12] While the initial plan proposes milestones and timetables, the plan lacks specific quantitative metrics by which to measure success or failure over time.[13] In many cases, the Council seems to have defaulted to consensus,[14] which in most cases means that many hard decisions were not made. A senior member of the Information Sharing Council described the Council's product as a "plan to make a plan,"[15] and we agree.

We recognize that, in addressing the information sharing problem, we do not write on a blank slate. Our recommendations therefore will focus on questions of implementation and enforcement. We offer recommendations on how to smooth out ambiguities in information sharing responsibilities that the intelligence reform legislation created, and more generally on how we believe the new Director of National Intelligence should manage the information sharing effort. Success will require strong, centralized leadership and an enforcement regime that is based on clearly defined milestones, carries substantial penalties for failure to meet them, and has minimal tolerance for excuses. The recommendations below offer our views on how to get there.

IMPLEMENTING THE NEW INTELLIGENCE LEGISLATION: DISENTANGLING OVERLAPPING AUTHORITIES

Recommendation 1

The confused lines of authority over information sharing created by the intelligence reform act should be resolved. In particular:

- The Information Sharing Environment should be expanded to encompass all intelligence information, not just terrorism intelligence;

Recommendation 1 (Continued)

- The Director of the National Counterterrorism Center should report to the DNI on all matters relating to information sharing; and

- The overlapping authorities of the DNI and the Program Manager should be reconciled and coordinated—a result most likely to be achieved by requiring the Program Manager to report to the DNI.

There is no shortage of officials who have been charged in recent years with ensuring information sharing across the federal government. Indeed, the intelligence reform act itself assigns substantial—and often overlapping—responsibilities to three people:

- The *Director of National Intelligence* is given "principal authority to ensure maximum availability of and access to intelligence information within the Intelligence Community consistent with national security requirements."[16] The DNI was also given overall information sharing responsibility to develop an "enterprise architecture for the intelligence community and ensure that elements of the intelligence community comply with such architecture."[17]

- The *Director of the National Counterterrorism Center* shall "provide strategic operational plans...for the effective integration of counterterrorism intelligence and operations across agency boundaries, both inside and outside the United States."[18] The Director of NCTC also has direct responsibility to "disseminate terrorism information" to all appropriate agencies within the Executive Branch and to the Congress.[19]

- The *Program Manager* is "responsible for information sharing across the Federal Government."[20]

Some of these overlapping authorities can be easily addressed. The Director of the NCTC works for the DNI, and notwithstanding the NCTC Director's theoretical right to report to the President on interagency "strategic operational planning,"[21] split authority for sharing intelligence information is a recipe for stalemate. We recommend that the DNI (and the President, if need be) make clear that the Director of the National Counterterrorism Center exercise his authority to disseminate terrorism information under the supervision of the DNI.

The harder problem concerns the relationship between the DNI and the information sharing program manager. The legislation directs the President to create an Information Sharing Environment that encompasses all terrorism information from all levels of government within the United States, plus terrorism information from the private sector and from foreign nations.[22] The intelligence reform act gives the program manager "government-wide" jurisdiction but responsibility limited to terrorism information, since the Information Sharing Environment is (at least initially) defined in terms of "terrorism information."[23] The program manager has a two-year term, without explicit provision for re-appointment or succession. For the first year, the primary duty of the program manager is to prepare a plan for submission to the President and to Congress.[24] According to the Conference Report on the legislation, Congress intended to consider extension of the program manager position beyond two years after receiving the program manager's recommendations on "a future management structure for the [Information Sharing Environment]."[25] As noted above, the intelligence reform act stipulates that the Information Sharing Council[26] shall "assist the President and the program manager in their duties" with respect to the Information Sharing Environment.[27]

Although the legislation sets lofty goals for the information sharing program manager, it is not clear that the office has the authority needed to implement even the best of plans for the Information Sharing Environment. The program manager's role is, at bottom, only advisory; the statute confers no budget or executive authority over information sharing programs.[28] In the quite likely event of conflicts that cannot be resolved by the program manager, the job of arbitrating interagency disputes will fall to the Office of Management and Budget.[29]

At the same time, the program manager may have just enough authority to interfere with implementation of information sharing throughout the Intelligence Community. The Community is unlikely to adopt one solution for sharing terrorism intelligence and another for sharing intelligence about chemical, biological, and nuclear weapons. As explained by the interim director of the NCTC, the people working the terrorism problem must be able to search all intelligence information for linkages and insights where the terrorist connection is not obvious.[30] Thus, the program manager's authority over terrorism information could drive, distort, or delay the Intelligence Community's efforts to share all intelligence more effectively.

To resolve this institutional ambiguity, we believe that the program manager's implementation of a government-wide terrorism information space needs to be coordinated with the DNI's responsibilities to drive information sharing within the Intelligence Community. Our view is that optimal coordination will result if the program manager reports to the Director of National Intelligence. With that said, we recognize that there are competing considerations.

First, the program manager was placed outside the Intelligence Community in order to extend information sharing to elements that normally do not exchange information with the Intelligence Community. These include law enforcement agencies (federal, state, local, tribal, and foreign), federal regulatory agencies (*e.g.*, Federal Aviation Administration, Commerce, and Customs) and the private sector. As our terrorism case study demonstrates, the Intelligence Community has struggled to provide terrorism information to state, local, and tribal authorities.[31] Solutions that work in a classified world cannot be used to share data with this vast new audience. Still, much of the terrorism information shared by and among these agencies will originate with or pass through elements of the Intelligence Community. In our view, the DNI is in the best position to balance the need for sharing terrorism information with the need to protect intelligence sources and methods.

A second objection is that the Intelligence Community includes some of the worst offenders where information sharing is concerned. Unfortunately, we question whether the program manager is likely to force hard decisions on the Intelligence Community if the DNI cannot. Unlike with the temporary program manager, intelligence organizations cannot easily wait out the DNI's tenure, plus the DNI has budget, acquisition, and other authorities over some of the largest agencies affected by the information sharing mandate.

In short, we are far more sure of our diagnosis, that the legislation's allocation of responsibilities is unworkable, than of our prescription—granting the DNI authority over the program manager. In the absence of a better prescription, however, we offer what we believe is the most workable approach to this messy problem.

The intelligence reform act provides that the President shall "designate the organizational and management structures that will be used to operate and manage the Information Sharing Environment."[32] This language, in our view, permits the President to incorporate the role of the program manager into the Office of the DNI in order to ensure the necessary leadership and accountability for the Information Sharing Environment.

MANAGING INFORMATION ACCESS, INFORMATION SECURITY, AND INFORMATION TECHNOLOGY

Of course, if the DNI is to exercise such authority, the DNI must demonstrate a commitment and an ability to achieve information sharing across the government. That will not be easy. So far, information sharing among intelligence agencies, even regarding terrorism, is intense but *ad hoc*. As we described in our terrorism case study, terrorism information sharing depends far too much on agency-specific workarounds. There has not been strong leadership or a centralized approach. Agencies have resisted broader solutions for two plausible reasons: first, because of technological incompatibilities; and second, because of security and privacy restrictions on sharing data. Neither of these objections is trivial, but the Community only makes matters worse by allowing them to fester for lack of decisionmaking authority. For that reason, we recommend that responsibility for security and technology issues in the Intelligence Community be combined into a single office reporting directly to the DNI or his principal deputy. This office would oversee and manage the policy, security, and technical dimensions of all information sharing within the Intelligence Community. To make clear that its responsibilities exceed those of the traditional federal government Chief Information Officer, it could be called the Chief Information Management Officer (CIMO).

Recommendation 2

The DNI should give responsibility for information *sharing*, information *technology*, and information *security* within the Intelligence Community to an office reporting directly to the DNI or to the Principal Deputy DNI.

The job of the chief information management officer is to make the difficult decisions that ensure uniform information sharing and security policies across the Intelligence Community. He or she would be responsible for issuing policies and directives for the Information Sharing Environment, empowered to enforce such policies *within* the Intelligence Community, and held accountable for the overall progress of the Information Sharing Environment both within and beyond the Intelligence Community. We also note that the Mission Managers we propose—who would have unique insight into the information that exists in their respective subject areas—could play a key role as advocates for information sharing and as advisors to the CIMO concerning the content of material in the Information Sharing Environment (and who should have access to it).

No Information Sharing Environment can succeed unless it also acts as an information security environment. The chief information management officer must assure both greater sharing of information and the protection of sources and methods. Protection of sources and methods is not only a solemn duty of the intelligence profession, but it is also a matter of survival and the foundation of the Community's success. Even inadvertent compromises can lead to dead agents or the obsolescence of technical systems that cost billions of dollars and take more than a decade to acquire. The risk is clear: adding scores of professionals to an Information Sharing Environment lacking adequate security and information access controls may compromise the Community's intelligence sources and methods.

The potential conflict between network expansion and network security leads to bureaucratic confrontations between their respective advocates. The two camps normally report through separate chains of command that converge only at high levels of institutional management. Hence conflicts of lesser importance that are not worthy of escalation remain unresolved and result in paralysis. Those of greater importance are elevated to high-level managers who typically have broad responsibilities well beyond adjudication of network or information access issues, and precious little time or attention to work the problems. Until the recent push for information sharing, the security contingent held all the trump cards. No one was held accountable for failure to share information; but the opposite was true for a security failure.

Finding the right compromise between information sharing and information security is a question of risk management. Each of these values should be accorded its proper weight, with due recognition of the increased importance of information sharing in the current threat environment. Successful execution of this risk management function requires hands-on, continuous planning and leadership—not disjointed and occasional adjudication by committee. Accordingly, we recommend that responsibility within the Intelligence Community for both information *sharing* and information *security* (protection of sources and methods) reside with the DNI, delegable to the chief information management officer. The CIMO would be held accountable for the effective development of the shared information space, using risk management to achieve the right balance between sharing and security. The dual responsibilities of this office would encourage planning and decisions based on overall mission objectives and accountability to the diverse needs of Information Sharing Environment users.

LEARNING FROM PAST INFORMATION SHARING EXPERIENCE

We do not propose to tell the DNI and the chief information management officer how to resolve all of the difficult technical and policy issues associated with creating an Information Sharing Environment that works. Nonetheless, we can offer some insights that may be of use as the DNI sets forth on this difficult endeavor. Many of these insights arise from the Intelligence Community's experience with Intelink, which functions as a kind of Internet for the secure sharing of intelligence in parts of the Intelligence Community.

Recommendation 3

In designing an Information Sharing Environment, the DNI should, to the extent possible, learn from and build on the capabilities of existing Intelligence Community networks. These lessons include:

- The limitations of "need to know" in a networked environment;

- The importance of developing mechanisms that can protect sources and methods in new ways;

- Biometrics and other user authentication (identification) methods, along with user activity auditing tools, can promote accountability and enhance counterintelligence capabilities;

Recommendation 3 (Continued)

- System-wide encryption of data can greatly reduce the risks of network penetration by outsiders; and

- Where sensitive information is restricted to a limited group of users, the Information Sharing Environment should ensure that others searching for such information are aware of its existence and provided with a point of contact who can decide quickly whether to grant access.

First, it is unrealistic to think that we can achieve our information sharing goals without departing from traditional approaches to the "need-to-know" principle. Under the current rules, each government official who holds classified information has a responsibility "to ensure that a need-to-know exists" before giving access to another person, even if that person has all the requisite clearances.[33] In practice, these individual decisions follow agency-specific policies (or unstated habits) that vary widely across the Intelligence Community. If rigidly applied, the "need-to-know" rule is incompatible with a networked environment. In a networked environment, providers of information cannot know for sure when a user "needs" a particular piece of information. Instead, as the Intelink experience demonstrates, users of this service must be given access to all information broadly available on the network within the clearance levels of the individual user, and consistent with applicable privacy and civil liberties guidelines. Intelink provides the Intelligence Community with classified services analogous to those of the World Wide Web on the Internet.[34] It provides easy user access, security and privacy safeguards, information discovery and search, collaboration through e-mail and chat rooms, and automated, personalized information delivery.[35] Other existing information sharing networks include JWICS (up to Top Secret/Sensitive Compartmented Information), SIPRNet (up to Secret/collateral information), and OSIS (Sensitive But Unclassified and For Official Use Only).

At the same time, one must not dismiss the risks of this approach. Moving to an Information Sharing Environment requires additional safeguards. Strong authentication, careful audits of user behavior, including inquiries into the reasons for accessing a particular report, will all help to safeguard the system from compromise. In addition, even in a generally open environment, information of extraordinary sensitivity will have to be restricted to limited groups or to "communities of interest" with proper clearances.[36] For example, information access controls could limit viewing privileges for a particular document to a list of named individuals, with enforcement facilitated by requiring biometric identification of each user prior to viewing the document. The CIA has already established a "trusted network" on Intelink that permits the automated distribution of highly sensitive "blue border" reports to pre-approved individuals.[37]

But the proliferation of communities of interest raises another problem. What if an analyst is searching for—and needs to know—information that is hidden in an access-controlled database? How does the analyst even know whom to ask for access? One solution proposed for this problem is to make available a catalog of all the communities of interest in the Information Sharing Environment, functioning much like a library catalog in that it provides an access number and a brief summary of the information contained in these areas (much like controlled or reserved stacks at public libraries). While such an approach may not suit all situations—sometimes even the summary descriptions will be too sensitive to share widely—it could enhance the ability of analysts to access information they need.

Similarly, Intelink has not yet reached its full potential because some agencies still do not make much of their reporting available through the Intelink system. The reluctance of some agencies to connect their information systems and databases with outside systems such as Intelink stems not simply from a lack of interagency trust. Some agencies, notably NSA, provide intelligence officers from trusted partner nations with access to their networks, while agencies such as CIA resist sharing information about human assets with any foreign nationals for fear of compromising sources and methods. The Intelligence Community can resolve this tension by requiring stronger authentication procedures for all users of Intelink and similar systems, and by enabling users to establish communities of interest—essentially, highly secure virtual workspaces—that shield particularly sensitive information from all users except those who have been admitted by name. Authentication methods using biometrics and digital certificates offer excellent protection against unauthorized information access, since they can establish with near certainty the identity of the person attempting to access a given system. Emerging software-based auditing tools that monitor the behavior of users can help security officers spot suspicious activity and further strengthen the integrity of Intelink and related information systems.

As has been recognized by the Markle Foundation in some detail, such automated accountability technologies would greatly strengthen counterintelligence capabilities as well as protecting privacy.[38] Modern encryption can provide additional security by effectively precluding the deciphering of internal communications by persons outside the network. Control checks, such as identity management systems, can check each user's access privileges and either admit them, deny them access, or provide a security point of contact to adjudicate the matter virtually. Additional security might be provided by considering greater use of "thin clients," where all data is stored on servers remote from the user, and user terminals have no interface for removable media (*i.e.*, no ability to write to a CD).

All of these technologies are available off the shelf today. Experience with Intelink suggests that sometimes the best approach is to "just do it." Without having studied the information sharing implementation plans of the agencies concerned, we cannot say that this is the only way forward. But building on the lessons learned through the use of Intelink and current networks with information sharing capabilities offers many advantages.

SETTING UNIFORM INFORMATION SHARING POLICIES

The fundamental barriers to information sharing are not a matter of technology; they arise from the legal, policy, and cultural "rules" that pervade the system. That is why information sharing cannot be a matter of issuing one edict or adopting one technology. It requires a patient sorting out of many complex policy threads and adapting systems and policies to emerging Intelligence Community and government processes. Without pretending that we have identified all of the problems, let alone all of the solutions, we have been able to isolate several of the policies that stand in the way of information sharing. In many cases we suggest solutions to these problems.

Recommendation 4

Primary institutional responsibility within the Intelligence Community for establishing clear and consistent "U.S. persons" rules should be shifted from individual collection agencies to the Director of National Intelligence. These rules would continue to be subject to the Attorney General's review and approval. To the extent possible, the same rules should apply across the Intelligence Community.

The rules governing collection and retention of information on "U.S. persons" are complicated, subject to varying interpretations within each agency, and differ substantially from one agency to the next.[39] These rules, in practice, often pose substantial impediments to analysts accessing "raw data" in the possession of particular collection agencies. We believe that practical responsibility for authoring and periodically reviewing these "U.S. persons" rules should be shifted from individual collection agencies to the DNI, subject to statutory review and approval by the Attorney General.[40] Vested with this responsibility, the DNI would ensure that these rules are consistent across agencies, that they are periodically reviewed and updated to account for new collection technologies and analytic tools, and that they accurately encapsulate statutory and constitutional privacy protections enshrined in law. As we note in Chapter Six (Leadership and Management), we suggest that the DNI vest primary responsibility for harmonizing and reviewing these rules within the Office of the DNI's General Counsel.

Recommendation 5

The DNI should set uniform information management policies, practices, and procedures for all members of the Intelligence Community.

Current agency-specific policies and practices do not suit a modern, networked environment. For example, criteria for certifying networks and software for use on networks differ from one agency to the next. The Intelligence Community lacks common standards for firewalls and network gateways.[41] Uniform standards and procedures should govern submission of documents and information to the Information Sharing Environment; submission of information to the sharing environment should be an obligation, not a choice.

To enable users from across the Intelligence Community to access quickly the information they need, the DNI will need to standardize data and meta-data formats, as well as procedures for adjudicating disputes.

Recommendation 6

All users of the Information Sharing Environment should be registered in a directory that identifies skills, clearances, and assigned responsibilities of each individual (using aliases rather than true names when necessary). The environment should enable users to make a "call for assistance" that assembles a virtual community of specialists to address a particular task, and all data should be catalogued within the Information Sharing Environment in a way that enables the underlying network to compare user privileges with data sensitivity.

At present, the Intelligence Community has no comprehensive online directory of analysts and technical experts. Our case studies—particularly Iraq, Afghanistan, and Terrorism (Chapters 1, 3, 4)—and our discussion of intelligence analysis (Chapter 8), highlight the need for ongoing communication and interaction among analysts, and for "communities of interest" that can form, adapt, and dissolve in response to specific issues or tasks. For example, a Mission Manager examining collection on biological weapons in Asia should be able to find and call on all analysts in other Intelligence Community agencies who have an expertise in biological weapons or an Asian regional specialty. Analysts' biographical profiles, previous analytic reporting output, and contact information should be readily accessible to the Mission Manager through the Information Sharing Environment.

Recommendation 7

The DNI should propose standards to simplify and modernize the information classification system with particular attention to implementation in a network-centric Information Sharing Environment.

Finally, the rules governing classification of national security information are antiquated and overly complex. As we noted in our terrorism case study, caveats such as ORCON ("originator controlled") wrongly imply that collectors of intelligence "own" the information and should control access to it.[42] The compartmentation of highly sensitive activities creates unknown islands of information under the "personalized"[43] security governance of each program manager. For understandable reasons, collectors have historically accorded paramount importance to protection of sources and methods and have given insufficient weight to information dissemination and "sharing." This culture of diffused information ownership has resulted in inconsistent information access standards and arbitrary enforcement of those standards.

The DNI should move toward a culture of "stewardship" of intelligence information instead of ownership. Federal government information belongs to the nation and is entrusted to the Intelligence Community in order to pursue the nation's best interest. Collectors of intelligence information should not control access to such information; the DNI or the DNI's designee should exercise that authority. As a baseline standard or norm, the DNI should require the submission of all intelligence information, with proper classification controls, to the Information Sharing Environment. Those who seek to exclude particular information from the environment must carry the burden of proving that such exclusion is clearly in the nation's interest.

EMPLOYING STRONG ENFORCEMENT MECHANISMS AND INCENTIVES TO DRIVE CHANGE

The Information Sharing Environment envisioned by the President and Congress faces innumerable pragmatic obstacles to speedy implementation. Transition to new technology, new data standards, and new procedures will disrupt existing agency functions, some of which may serve a vital national security role. For critical systems, it may be necessary to create a parallel infrastructure for the Information Sharing Environment, keeping legacy systems fully operational until the new one is built, tested, and ready for switch-over. Agencies will procrastinate for fear of degrading mission performance. Security apprehensions will sprout. The DNI will need to drive change relentlessly or the sharing environment will founder.

Recommendation 8

We recommend several parallel efforts to keep the Information Sharing Environment on track:

- **Collection of metrics.** The chief information management officer should introduce performance metrics for the Information Sharing Environment and automate their collection. These metrics should include the number and origination of postings to the shared environment, data on how often and by whom each item was accessed, and statistics on the use of collaborative tools and communications channels, among others. Such performance data can help to define milestones and to determine rewards and penalties.

- **Self-enforcing milestones.** Milestones should include specific and quantifiable performance criteria for the sharing environment, as well as rewards and penalties for succeeding or failing to meet them. The DNI should empower the chief information management officer to use the DNI's budget, mission-assignment, and personnel authorities to penalize poor agency performance.

- **Incentives.** The DNI should ensure that collectors and analysts receive honors or monetary prizes for intelligence products that receive widespread use or acclaim. Users should post comments or rate the value of individual reports or analytic products, and periodic user surveys can serve as peer review mechanisms.

- **Training.** The DNI should promote the training of all users in the Information Sharing Environment, with extended training for analysts, managers, and other users of the environment.

PROTECTING PRIVACY AND CIVIL LIBERTIES

No discussion of information sharing initiatives would be complete without noting that the sharing of information has raised privacy and civil liberties concerns in the wake of September 11.

Our recommendations in this chapter rest securely in the belief that all concerned will follow provisions in the new legislation and executive orders that are designed to make the protection of civil liberties an ongoing priority for the intelligence and law enforcement communities. The recent executive orders establishing the NCTC and mandating greater sharing of counterterrorism information each included the protection of "the freedom, information privacy, and other legal rights of Americans" as part of the underlying policy.[44] And on the same day the President issued these orders, he established the President's Board on Safeguarding Americans' Civil Liberties.[45]

Building on these executive orders, the legislation establishes a Privacy and Civil Liberties Oversight Board within the Executive Office of the President.[46] The Board is tasked with reviewing regulations, policies, and laws relating to counterterrorism, including those that address information sharing, to ensure that each of these takes account of privacy and civil liberties concerns.[47] The Board is also charged with regular reviews of the information sharing practices of the executive branch to address the same concerns.[48]

Further, the new law places a Civil Liberties Protection Officer in the office of the DNI,[49] who, alone among the legislatively-mandated staff, must *directly* report to the DNI.[50] The statute also recommends, although it does not require, that other entities establish similar positions.[51] The officer is specifically charged with ensuring that policies and procedures protect civil liberties, that the use of technology does not erode privacy protections, and that U.S. persons information is handled in compliance with existing legislation.[52]

Provisions of the legislation specifically calling for more information sharing also take care to address privacy concerns. Indeed, the new system must "incorporate[] protections for individuals' privacy and civil liberties."[53] Even before implementation of the new Information Sharing Environment, the President, in consultation with the Privacy and Civil Liberties Oversight Board, must issue guidelines to "protect privacy and civil liberties in the development and use" of the Information Sharing Environment.[54] And the separate implementation plan must include a "description of the means by which privacy and civil liberties will be protected in the design and operation" of the Information Sharing Environment.[55] Further underscoring the centrality of this issue, the Program Manager for this effort must "ensure the protection of privacy and civil liberties" when he sets policies and procedures for information sharing.[56] And oversight of this issue will be ongoing. The President's annual report to Congress on the status of information sharing must address, among other things, "actions taken in the preceding year to implement or enforce privacy and civil liberties protections."[57]

Thus, the law already provides the framework for appropriate protection of civil liberties in the context of information sharing. Adequate protection will, however, require detailed implementation in the development of the system itself, perhaps assisted by the oversight board and privacy experts and groups outside the Intelligence Community. In our view, an equally important protection is in the technology and the culture of the agencies that do the sharing. Much new technology can be used effectively to protect information from misuse. The intelligence reform act recognizes this possibility by calling for the use of audit, authentication, and access controls in the Information Sharing Environment.[58] These technologies impose accountability on every user of the Information Sharing Environment. They also allow agencies to know who is accessing particular files and to determine, in advance or after the fact, whether access is proper. Data can be tagged to identify which people or organizations are entitled to access it, and strong authentication can dramatically reduce the risk that an unauthorized user will gain access. Auditing techniques allow the system to find users whose access is unusual or not clearly justified and to alert supervisors or security personnel to the need for further investigation—a technique that is unavailable when information is shared by paper. All of these techniques can provide added privacy protection for Americans.

The pursuit of privacy and national security is not a zero sum game. The same technologies that protect against violations of privacy can also provide strong counterintelligence capabilities—something that will be essential if the Information Sharing Environment is to work over the long run. As the Markle Foundation plainly put it, any information sharing system must come with mechanisms designed to foster trust, "[f]or without trust, no one will share."[59]

ENDNOTES

[1] For example, CIA failed to pass names of suspected terrorists to the Federal Aviation Administration and Customs, and the FBI failed to disseminate a warning from its St. Louis Field Office to any other agency. *Final Report of the National Commission on Terrorist Attacks Upon the United States* (2004) (hereinafter "9/11 Commission Report") at p. 258.

[2] Chapter One (Iraq).

[3] *See generally* 9/11 Commission Report; Markle Foundation Task Force, *Creating a Trusted Information Sharing Network* (Dec. 2003).

[4] DCI Community Management Staff, *Calibration Report: Community Intelligence Community Collaboration and Information Sharing to Win the War on Terrorism: Phase 1* (May 2004) (unclassified excerpt) (hereinafter "IC May 2004 Calibration Report").

[5] Chapter Four (Terrorism).

[6] *Id.*

[7] *Id.*

[8] IC May 2004 Calibration Report at p. ES-1 (emphasis in original).

[9] Intelligence Reform and Terrorism Prevention Act of 2004 at § 1016, Pub. L. No. 108-458 (hereinafter "IRTPA").

[10] *Id.* at § 1016(b)(2).

[11] *Id.* at § 1016(a)(1).

[12] Executive Order 13356 (Aug. 27, 2004) at § 5(c).

[13] The failure of the Information Sharing Council to specify quantitative metrics for accountability may have resulted from the overlap in responsibilities between the Council as provided by Executive Order 13356, and those of the Program Manager as provided by the Intelligence Reform Act of 2004.

[14] The Information Sharing Council report is replete with phrases like "mutually satisfactory approach." See generally Information Systems Council, *Initial Plan for the Interoperable Terrorism Information Sharing Environment* (Dec. 20, 2004) (hereinafter "ISC Report").

[15] Interview with Department of Defense counterintelligence and security official (Feb. 8, 2005).

[16] IRTPA at § 1011 (amending § 102A of the National Security Act).

[17] *Id.*

[18] *Id.* at § 1021.

[19] *Id.*

[20] *Id.*

[21] *Id.*

[22] *Id.* at § 1016(b).

[23] While the act gives the information program manager responsibility (without limitation) for "information sharing across the Federal Government," the provisions creating this office are in the context of legislation that deals only with "terrorism information" as expressly defined. IRTPA at § 1016(a)(4).

[24] *Id.* at § 1016(f)(1).

[25] In discussion of the Conference Report, Senator Collins stated: "The legislation provides that the program manager is to serve for two years, during the initial development of the ISE, to ensure that the project gets off to a sound start. As part of the implementation plan to be submitted to Congress after one year, the program manager is to recommend a future management structure for the ISE, including a recommendation as to whether the position of program manager should continue." *Congressional Record—Senate* (Dec. 8, 2004) at p. S11973.

[26] This and future references in the text to the Information Sharing Council refer to the legislatively created body; previously the term referred to the one created by Executive Order.

[27] IRTPA at § 1016(g)(1).

[28] The legislation provides that the Program Manager will "assist in the development of policies, procedures, guidelines, rules and standards" for the ISE. *Id.* at § 1016(f)(2)(A).

[29] Executive Order 13356 established the Information Systems Council, chaired by the Office of Management and Budget, and directed it to "report to the President through the Assistants to the President for National Security Affairs and Homeland Security." Executive Order 13356 (Aug. 27, 2004) at § 5(c). IRTPA renamed the "Information Systems Council" to be the "Information Sharing Council" and gave it responsibility to "assist the President and the program manager in their duties" with respect to information sharing. IRTPA at § 1016(g)(1).

[30] Interview with senior National Counterterrorism Center official (Feb. 8, 2005).

[31] Chapter Four (Terrorism).

[32] IRTPA at § 1016(b)(1)(B). We do note, however, that in the discussion of information sharing in connection with the Conference Report on the intelligence reform act, Senator Collins stated, "It is not our intent that the DNI also assume further responsibilities of program manager." *Conference Report—Senate* (Dec. 8, 2004) at p. S11973.

[33] Executive Order 12968 (Aug. 4, 1995) at § 2.5(b).

[34] Many of the future "milestones" described in the Information Sharing Council's report have already been achieved by Intelink: "At the core of this interoperable terrorism sharing environment, is an environment resembling the Internet. The environment would have a variety of sites managed by participating organizations with tools to help link users (*i.e.*, information producers and consumers) with the information they need. Unlike the Internet, however, this is not a loose, voluntary association of parties, but rather a disciplined structure for the creation, protection, dissemination, retention, and use of actionable information across seven related communities." ISC Report at p. 24.

[35] The Information Sharing Council's report describes Intelink services on JWICS and SIPRNET as follows: "The networks provide sophisticated search and discovery capabilities, support email and collaboration, and maintain directories and other services making it easy for users to find and use information." *Id.* at p. 35.

[36] This is done by metadata tags specifically referencing the identity of individuals authorized to have access to a particular document.

[37] Interview with CIA counterintelligence officials (Jan. 27, 2005).

[38] Markle Foundation Task Force on National Security in the Information Age, *Creating a Trusted Information Sharing Network* (Dec. 2003) at p. 140.

[39] "Agencies within the Intelligence Community are authorized to collect, retain, or disseminate information concerning United States persons only in accordance with procedures estab-

lished by the head of the agency concerned and approved by the Attorney General." Executive Order 12333 (Dec. 4, 1981) at § 2.3.

[40] This might require a change to Executive Order 12333, which directs individual agencies to establish their own U.S. persons rules (subject to Attorney General approval) and does not expressly interpose the DNI in that process. As we note in Chapter Ten (Intelligence at Home), our envisioned Assistant Attorney General for National Security would be the natural office to take the lead in securing Justice Department approval of such guidelines.

[41] Interview with Department of Defense counterintelligence and security official (Feb. 8, 2005).

[42] Chapter Four (Terrorism).

[43] The program managers of Special Access Programs have wide discretion to set security rules applicable only to their program.

[44] Executive Order 13354 (Aug. 27, 2004) at § 1(b); Executive Order 13356 (Aug. 27, 2004) at § 1(b).

[45] Executive Order 13353 (Aug. 27, 2004).

[46] IRTPA at §1061.

[47] *Id.* at § 1061(c)(1).

[48] *Id.* at § 1061(c)(2).

[49] *Id.* at § 1011.

[50] *Id.*

[51] *Id.* at § 1062.

[52] *Id.* at § 1011.

[53] *Id.* at § 1016(b)(2)(H).

[54] *Id.* at § 1016(d)(2)(A).

[55] *Id.* at § 1016(e)(8).

[56] *Id.* at § 1016(f)(2)(B)(viii).

[57] *Id.* at § 1016(h)(2)(H), (I).

[58] *Id.* at § 1016(b)(2)(I).

[59] Markle Foundation Task Force on National Security in the Information Age, *Creating a Trusted Network for Homeland Security* (Dec. 2, 2003) at p. 18.

CHAPTER TEN
INTELLIGENCE AT HOME: THE
FBI, JUSTICE, AND HOMELAND
SECURITY

Summary & Recommendations

Combating chemical, biological, and nuclear terrorism, as well as other foreign intelligence challenges, will require intelligence assets both inside and outside the United States. As the events of September 11 demonstrated, we cannot afford a wall that divides U.S. intelligence efforts at the border. Although the FBI is making progress toward becoming a full member of the Intelligence Community, it has a long way to go, and significant hurdles still remain. In our view, the FBI has not constructed its intelligence program in a way that will promote integrated intelligence efforts, and its ambitions have led it into unnecessary new turf battles with the CIA.

Meanwhile, the Department of Justice has not yet put its national security components in one office; its anti-terrorism and intelligence support offices are as scattered as they were on September 10, 2001. And the Department of Homeland Security is still following a Treasury Department order from the 1980s that requires high-level approval for virtually all information sharing and assistance to the Intelligence Community.

In light of these problems we recommend that:

- The FBI create a new National Security Service within the Bureau and under a single Executive Assistant Director. This service would include the FBI's Counterterrorism and Counterintelligence Divisions and its Director- ate of Intelligence, and would be subject to the coordination and budget authorities of the DNI;

- The DNI ensure that there are effective mechanisms for preventing con- flicts and encouraging coordination among intelligence agencies in the United States;

- All intelligence activity within the United States—whether conducted by the CIA, FBI, or Department of Defense—remain subject to Attorney Gen- eral guidelines designed to protect civil liberties;

> ## Summary & Recommendations (Continued)
>
> ■ The Department of Justice consolidate its national security elements—the Office of Intelligence Policy Review, and the Counterterrorism and Counterespionage sections—under a new Assistant Attorney General for National Security; and
>
> ■ The Department of Homeland Security rescind Treasury Order 113-01.

INTRODUCTION

The events of September 11 made clear that terrorists can operate on both sides of the U.S. border. Terrorists are seeking nuclear and biological weapons outside the United States, but they long to use them here.

This new reality requires first that the FBI and other agencies do a better job of gathering intelligence inside the United States, and second that we eliminate the remnants of the old "wall" between foreign intelligence and domestic law enforcement. Both tasks must be accomplished without sacrificing our domestic liberties and the rule of law, and both depend on building a very different FBI from the one we had on September 10, 2001. It is these two tasks to which we now turn.

CHANGE AND RESISTANCE TO CHANGE AT THE FBI

It has now been three and a half years since the September 11 attacks. A lot can be accomplished in that time. Three and a half years after December 7, 1941, the United States had built and equipped an army and a navy that had crossed two oceans, the English Channel, and the Rhine; it had already won Germany's surrender and was two months from vanquishing Japan.

Change

The FBI has spent the past three and a half years building the beginnings of an intelligence service and striving to transform itself into a hybrid law enforcement and intelligence agency.[1] Field offices now routinely cull intelligence information from operations and investigations, and disseminate Intelligence

Information Reports. An intelligence official from another law enforcement agency praised the FBI's ability to extract pertinent information from cases, pointing out that "[t]hey are doing a better job than anybody could have expected."[2] The Bureau has developed new intelligence training courses, Field Intelligence Groups to supervise intelligence production, and an expanded analytic cadre. FBI headquarters has hired hundreds of analysts and agents from outside its traditional core competencies (law enforcement, accounting, and the military).[3] In 2003 Director Mueller appointed an Executive Assistant Director for Intelligence to preside over these efforts and lead the newly created Office (now Directorate) of Intelligence. These are no small accomplishments.

At the same time, determination at the top of the organization does not always translate into change in the field. FBI Directors, no less than outsiders, must contend with a bureaucratic culture that naturally resists change. We are not the first to see the problem. The 9/11 Commission noted with some concern that it had "found gaps between some of the announced reforms and the reality in the field."[4]

Past efforts to build a strong intelligence capability within the FBI have foundered on this resistance. In 1998 and 1999, similar reforms[5] failed in quick succession as a result of strong resistance from the FBI's operational divisions and an intelligence architecture that could not defend itself inside the bureaucracy.[6] Several of the obstacles FBI has faced in reforming itself stem from the Bureau's long and proud law enforcement culture. While the Bureau is making progress toward changing its culture, it remains a difficult task and one that we believe will require more structural change than the Bureau has instituted thus far.

As America's premier federal law enforcement agency, the FBI's law enforcement legacy is strong. Law enforcement work has long been the surest route to professional advancement within the Bureau. Even now, only nine of the heads of the FBI's 56 field offices come from divisions other than the Criminal Division.[7] And many field offices are still tempted to put law enforcement ahead of intelligence-gathering, betting that "Bin Laden is never going to Des Moines."[8] This is understandable—local political and other external forces often press the Bureau to focus on its criminal law enforcement responsibilities. As one Special Agent in Charge explained, when a local law enforcement agency calls for help, "you never want to say no."[9]

Resistance to Change

So, the question remains: can the FBI's latest effort to build an intelligence capability overcome the resistance that has scuppered past reforms? In our view, the effort this time is more determined, but the outcome is still in doubt.

Here we highlight three areas critical to intelligence work—analytic capability, validation of human sources of intelligence (*i.e.*, asset validation), and information technology—in which the FBI has made significant but, in our view, insufficient progress.

First, the FBI is still far from having the strong analytic capability that is required to drive and focus the Bureau's national security work. Although the FBI's tactical analysis has made significant progress, its strategic capabilities—those that are central to guiding a long-term, systematic approach to national security issues—have lagged.[10] And while the FBI maintains the ambitious goal of improving its strategic analysis—creating a Strategic Analysis Unit in the Directorate of Intelligence and a strategic analysis function in each Field Intelligence Group by 2005[11]—every indication is that the Bureau will have difficulty meeting this worthy objective, particularly at the field level. This is because the Bureau has largely been unable to carve out time for its analysts in the field to do long-term, strategic analysis. According to a 2004 evaluation of one Field Intelligence Group, "because of the current structure and manpower constraints, nearly all analysis is limited to the tactical level supporting individual cases."[12] A 2005 National Academy of Public Administration study on the FBI forecasts that "even after a larger analytical staff is built, the tendency will be for immediate operational demands to push out strategic analyses."[13] To place the Bureau's current production in context, consider that the FBI currently publishes approximately a quarter as many long-term (non-current) analytic pieces as CIA does in a given year.[14]

This is not to suggest that the Bureau should replicate CIA's model. The Bureau's field office structure makes the FBI unique. One senior official emphasized that FBI has an operational emphasis that disproportionately requires actionable intelligence.[15] But although we are sympathetic to the FBI's particular analytic needs, we remain concerned that the current structure of the FBI's intelligence program, and the relationship between analysts and field operations, will not encourage analysts to rise above individual investigations, develop subject matter expertise, or *drive*—and not merely *inform*—counterintelligence, counterterrorism, and foreign intelligence collections, investigations, and operations.

The Bureau must also overcome a long history of treating analysts as "support staff." In the field offices there have always been two main categories of personnel: agent and non-agent (or "support"), and there is little doubt that agents enjoy preeminent status. As a 9/11 Commission staff statement noted, several field analysts complained that they "were viewed as 'uber-secretaries,' expected to perform any duty that was deemed non-investigative, including data entry and answering phones."[16] Even today, there is still evidence of analysts' subordinate role. As just one example, according to a 2004 report on one field office, "due to a backlog of telephone numbers to be loaded into telephone applications, the FIG [Field Intelligence Group] has requested overtime and pulled analysts from squads to load and analyze data…[T]he use of [Intelligence Analysts] for clerical duties diminishes the analytical function of an [Intelligence Analyst]."[17] We expect the FBI will struggle to get its analytic cadre where it needs to be, in part because the Bureau must compete with other, better-established analytical entities within the Intelligence Community for analytic resources.[18]

A second area that requires further reform is the system by which the FBI attempts to validate human sources of information, commonly referred to as "asset validation." For any organization that collects human intelligence, having an independent system for asset validation is critical to producing reliable, well-vetted intelligence. Indeed, the Intelligence Community's failure to validate assets adequately and communicate fabrication notices properly proved especially costly in the Iraq WMD debacle.[19]

Over the past several years the FBI's Counterintelligence Division has instituted a sophisticated and intensive system for asset validation. This initiative deserves praise, but the FBI has not yet instituted this system in its other operational divisions.[20] Director Mueller and the head of FBI's Counterterrorism and Counterintelligence Divisions have both stated their intentions to establish comparable systems in the Counterterrorism and Criminal Divisions, but these plans have yet to be implemented.[21] When we asked agents in the field about the FBI's asset validation, we received answers indicating that asset validation remains largely controlled by the field offices.[22] Indeed, when we asked the FBI for a summary of how many assets had been terminated in the last year because they had been judged to be fabricators, we were told that an answer would take time since a request first had to go out to each of the field offices and then analyzed back at headquarters.[23] This response strongly suggests that the FBI still lacks a centrally-managed database of its human assets—an essential element of any objective and systematic approach to asset validation.

Finally, further reforms are also necessary in the FBI's information technology infrastructure, which remains a persistent obstacle to successful execution of the FBI's national security mission. We believe that the Bureau's failure to develop efficient mechanisms for information sharing both inside and outside the FBI seriously undermines the Bureau's ability to perform its intelligence work. As early as 2002, Senator Richard Shelby highlighted the FBI's failure to develop information technology tools adequate to support its national security mission as a serious shortcoming.[24] Recently the FBI declared that it will largely abandon the Virtual Case File system it had been developing for the past four years at a cost of $170 million. Although Director Mueller claimed in May 2004 that the system was expected to be completed by the end of the year,[25] at about the same time the National Research Council concluded that the FBI's information technology modernization was "*not* currently on a path to success" and that the Virtual Case File System should not be the foundation for the FBI's "analytical and data management capabilities for the intelligence process"—in part because the system was designed to serve the criminal investigative mission rather than the intelligence mission.[26]

Beyond the shortcomings of these individual intelligence capabilities, some of the FBI's achievements in gathering intelligence within the United States raise questions about its ability to focus its intelligence efforts effectively. The Bureau has a remarkable ability to amass resources for a particular task, but its efforts may be poorly tuned. For example, in 2002 the FBI undertook a large-scale effort to interview all recent Iraqi immigrants to the United States in hopes of uncovering foreign intelligence and counterterrorism information that might contribute to the war effort.[27] This huge effort did produce some useful intelligence, but it required countless FBI investigators and many months. Although the project was coordinated with other intelligence agencies in FBI's Joint Terrorism Task Forces, it is less clear to us whether the effort made effective use of strategic analysis or targeting—and the scale of the interview program produced considerable civil liberties controversy.

INTEGRATING THE FBI INTO THE INTELLIGENCE COMMUNITY

The FBI's intelligence capabilities plainly require continued attention. But strengthening the FBI's national security capabilities is not the only task at hand. The FBI must also interact effectively with the rest of the Intelligence Community. The FBI has 1,720 professional intelligence analysts,[28] more than 12,000 agents capable of collecting valuable information in the field,[29] and the primary responsibility for counterintelligence and counterterrorism in the United States.[30] As such, it is a large and critical contributor to U.S. intelligence efforts.

The need for better intelligence coordination across the foreign-domestic divide was identified by the 9/11 Commission and was a moving force behind the *Intelligence Reform and Terrorism Prevention Act*. Creating a DNI with explicit responsibility for coordinating and managing domestic and foreign intelligence agencies serves as an important step in the right direction. But the legislation cannot create a community by itself. In fact, if nothing is done, a determinedly independent FBI could largely elude the DNI's intended authorities. To understand the risk, it is necessary to understand the mechanisms by which the DNI is expected to lead the Intelligence Community.

In writing the intelligence reform legislation, Congress did not create a Secretary of Intelligence or move all of the intelligence agencies under the direct command of the DNI. Congress left the intelligence agencies where they were—the Defense Department in most cases—but it also granted the DNI substantial authority over those agencies. NSA is typical. Though it is a Defense Department agency, NSA is part of the Intelligence Community. To ensure that NSA is responsive to the DNI, Congress gave the DNI significant authority over both NSA's budget[31] and a say in the appointment of its director.[32] The intelligence reform law applies the same basic authorities to the FBI but, in the case of the FBI, the DNI's principal tools for ensuring influence remain troublingly vague.

The DNI's Budget Authority Over the FBI

As a general matter, the DNI's budget authority over parts of the Intelligence Community is significant. The DNI prepares and has reprogramming authority over the National Intelligence Program (NIP, formerly the National Foreign

Intelligence Program, or NFIP). The DNI also ensures that the NIP budget is effectively executed, and monitors its implementation.[33] This picture is, however, far less clear vis-à-vis the FBI. We fear that the DNI may find it difficult—if not impossible—to impose the level of accountability envisioned by the legislation because the FBI's budget is not configured to allow effective Intelligence Community oversight.[34] And in our view, nothing in the Bureau's internal reforms since September 11 has altered this fact.

Approximately a third of the Bureau's total budget is funded through the National Intelligence Program.[35] The vast majority of this money is allocated to the FBI's Counterterrorism and Counterintelligence Divisions.[36] In stark contrast, none of the NIP budget goes to the Bureau's Directorate of Intelligence.[37] Thus, if the current arrangement stands, the DNI will have no budget authority over the office that the Bureau has put at the center of its efforts to develop an intelligence capability.

And this curious arrangement appears even odder when one considers where NIP money goes in light of the DNI's personnel authority over the FBI. In those cases in which an FBI component *does* receive NIP money (*e.g.*, for the Counterterrorism or Counterintelligence Division budgets), the DNI has *no* say in selecting the individual who runs that component. On the other hand, in the one case in which the DNI *does* have a say over an FBI official's appointment (*i.e.*, the Executive Assistant Director of Intelligence),[38] that official's office (*i.e.*, the Directorate of Intelligence) *doesn't* get NIP money. This strikes us as a peculiar arrangement, and one that diminishes the DNI's ability to ensure that the FBI is fully integrated into the Intelligence Community.

This rather confused budgetary situation is further complicated by FBI's internal budget categories. As required by the intelligence reform act, the FBI parses its budget into four parts: intelligence, counterterrorism/counterintelligence, criminal justice services, and criminal enterprises/federal crimes.[39] There is, however, only a small overlap between the National Intelligence Program budget and the Bureau's internal intelligence budget component— what it calls its "Intelligence Decision Unit."

Thus, when the FBI says that the Executive Assistant Director of Intelligence—again, the person over whom the DNI has some personnel authority—has "full control" over the "resources" of the Intelligence Decision Unit,[40] this says very little about the Executive Assistant Director's authority over National Intelligence Program funds. This is aptly illustrated by the fact that the Intelligence Decision Unit contains less than a third of the Bureau's NIP funds, and that a significant portion of Intelligence Decision Unit dollars go to parts of the FBI that are wholly unrelated to national intelligence programs.[41] In short, simply because something is in the FBI's "intelligence" budget gives little indication of whether the money is relevant to the Intelligence Community or, more importantly, to the DNI.

Not only is the Bureau's internal "intelligence" budget unit not aligned with the Bureau's NIP appropriations, we also doubt that the head of the Directorate of Intelligence actually has even the limited budget authority claimed by the FBI over what it internally describes as the "intelligence" budget. While the FBI states that the Executive Assistant Director for Intelligence "oversees" the Intelligence Decision Unit,[42] it remains unclear whether the Executive Assistant Director will actually have direct authority to formulate, direct, or reprogram the Intelligence Decision Unit budget. This is because, according to an official at the Office of Management and Budget, the Directorate of Intelligence only has unilateral authority over that percentage of the Intelligence Decision Unit that goes directly to the Directorate of Intelligence itself.[43] This means the Directorate has direct authority over only about *four percent* of the Bureau's own "intelligence" budget.[44] Fully 96 percent of the Intelligence Decision Unit falls outside the Directorate of Intelligence, in divisions like Counterintelligence and Counterterrorism.[45]

Hence, although the FBI's Executive Assistant Director for Intelligence may provide input into policy-related decisions regarding the Intelligence Decision Unit, the Executive Assistant Director will not, for instance, control the salaries of those included in the unit, or have budget execution authority over the unit as a whole.[46] So, while the Bureau states that "[a]ll of [its] efforts to create and manage the FBI intelligence budget are directed at ensuring that the DNI is able to exercise oversight of all intelligence spending,"[47] it is rather doubtful that creating the Intelligence Decision Unit—or providing the Executive Assistant Director for Intelligence general oversight over it—accomplishes this goal.

In our view, the FBI's budget process should be organized in a way that unambiguously ensures the responsiveness of the FBI's national security elements to the DNI. This means two things. First, the National Intelligence Program budget should include the budgets of the Directorate of Intelligence—as well as the Counterintelligence and Counterterrorism Divisions (perhaps excluding purely domestic terrorism work). Second, the DNI should have personnel authority over the FBI official who is responsible for all National Intelligence Program budget matters within the FBI. The current arrangement is far from this ideal.

Instead, the confused allocation of resources, combined with the questionable budgetary authority of the one FBI official over whom the DNI exercises some personnel authority, threatens to undermine one of the DNI's critical "levers of power." If the DNI does not know how NIP funds are allocated and spent by the FBI, and if the DNI does not have some personnel authority over the FBI official responsible for managing NIP funds, then he runs the risk of losing the very authority that the legislation was intended to confer. In such a case, the DNI will have to revert to other authorities, and it is to these we now turn.

Appointment Authority and the Weakness of the Intelligence Directorate

Another important tool at the DNI's disposal is appointment authority of Intelligence Community officials. Congress grants the DNI concurrent authority over the appointment of the heads of intelligence agencies such as NSA, NGA, and CIA.[48] In the case of the FBI, however, this authority is diluted. The DNI has no say in the appointment of the Director of the FBI, presumably because the FBI is the "primary criminal investigative agency in the federal government"[49] and the FBI Director spends considerable time overseeing a large law enforcement staff involved in criminal justice matters. Rather than conferring a role in the appointment of the Director of the FBI, the statute gives the DNI a say in the appointment of the Executive Assistant Director for Intelligence.[50]

This is a workable approach if the Executive Assistant Director for Intelligence can direct the resources necessary to accomplish the Bureau's national security mission. Indeed, that seems to have been Congress's plain intent. The intelligence reform law states that the Executive Assistant Director's office (the Directorate of Intelligence) will be responsible for supervising "all national intelligence programs, projects, and activities of the Bureau" and overseeing all "field intelligence operations."[51] Additionally, the legislation states that the Directorate of Intelligence is responsible for strategic analysis, the intelligence workforce, and coordinating collection against nationally determined requirements.[52] On the other hand, if the Executive Assistant Director does *not* have authority over the FBI's intelligence-gathering activities, then the DNI's ability to influence appointments to that position becomes of minimal import.

Unfortunately, that is the case today. The Directorate of Intelligence itself has no authority to direct any of the Bureau's intelligence investigations, operations, or collections. It currently performs no analysis, commands no operational resources, and has little control over the 56 Field Intelligence Groups, which, according to the FBI, "manage and direct all field intelligence operations."[53]

Instead, the FBI's national security resources, analysts, and collection capabilities are concentrated in the FBI's Counterintelligence and Counterterrorism Divisions and in the field offices. In fact, the FBI is currently configured so that no single individual other than the Director of the FBI (and perhaps his Deputy) has the authority to direct all of the Bureau's national security missions.

Because the DNI's ability to influence the FBI's conduct depends so heavily on the DNI's ability to oversee the Directorate of Intelligence, we looked closely at what authority the directorate has. We conclude that the directorate's *lack* of authority is pervasive. We asked whether the Directorate of Intelligence can ensure that intelligence collection priorities are met. It cannot. We asked whether the directorate directly supervises most of the Bureau's analysts. It does not. We asked whether the head of the directorate has authority to promote—or even provide personnel evaluations for—the heads of the Bureau's main intelligence-collecting arms. Again, the answer was no. Does it control the budgets or resources of units that do the Bureau's collection? No. The DNI's appointment influence over the head of the directorate therefore does little to bring the FBI's national security activities into a fully functioning Intelligence Community.

Setting and enforcing intelligence priorities. The Directorate of Intelligence is responsible for assigning national intelligence priorities to the FBI's field offices. The FBI has officially stated that it both "recognizes and supports the DCI's authority to formulate intelligence collection requirements for the United States Intelligence Community and has issued FBI collection tasking directives that translate those requirements into actual tasking by the FBI."[54] Yet at the working level, we found that national intelligence requirements were not uniformly understood. As one FBI official in the Directorate of Intelligence put it, the FBI sees these requirements "more as an invitation" to fill collection gaps than as directives.[55] We spoke with agents at the field level who also expressed some confusion about whether these requirements are directive or advisory.[56] The directorate has recognized this problem in internal reports, noting that interviews with personnel in one field office "demonstrated that individuals were still generally not familiar with the published requirement sets."[57] Although a significant part of the problem is that the national requirements system itself does not demand adequate accountability, our concern is that the DNI's attenuated line of authority vis-à-vis the FBI will make this problem particularly acute.

We do not believe this state of affairs is what the 9/11 Commission envisioned when it stressed the need for the FBI "to be able to direct its thousands of agents and other employees to collect intelligence in America's cities and towns."[58] Without control of collection resources, the Directorate of Intelligence lacks the requisite authorities to direct intelligence gathering. Unlike the Counterterrorism, Counterintelligence, Cyber, and Criminal Divisions, the Directorate of Intelligence currently commands no operational resources and has no authority with respect to field operations; it cannot initiate, terminate, or re-direct any collection or investigative operation in any FBI field office or in any of the four operational divisions at FBI headquarters.[59] Additionally, the directorate has no direct authority over the heads of the field offices unless it can somehow prompt the intervention of the FBI Director or his deputy.

Although the FBI has established Field Intelligence Groups in all of its field offices to "manage and direct all field intelligence operations,"[60] the Directorate of Intelligence has little direct control over the field groups either. Nor is it clear that the Field Intelligence Groups will have a real impact on how field offices actually conduct counterintelligence or counterterrorism investigations and activities—the core of FBI's intelligence collection capabilities.[61]

Controlling analysis and related resources. The Directorate of Intelligence also lacks direct supervisory authority over the vast majority of the FBI's analysts. While there are 1,720 intelligence analysts at the Bureau,[62] the Directorate of Intelligence contains just 38 of them.[63] Although the intelligence reform act designates the Directorate of Intelligence as responsible for strategic analysis,[64] the directorate currently does no analysis itself;[65] the 38 analysts in the directorate perform a policy role.[66] (The directorate does, however, coordinate the Director's Daily Brief to the President—a compilation of analytic products that are produced by the operational divisions and packaged by the intelligence directorate for dissemination.)[67]

Furthermore, related resources that do fall under the control of the intelligence directorate may continue to fluctuate. In at least one case, resources that were initially given to the Directorate of Intelligence were later taken away. In early 2004 the Directorate of Intelligence hired a contractor to design and execute a comprehensive intelligence training program. The directorate's ownership of this intelligence training component ended, however, when the FBI's training headquarters at Quantico, Virginia asserted primacy in training matters and directed that it be given ownership of the program.[68] Quantico won the battle, and the Directorate of Intelligence, rather than being able to tailor its own program, was forced into the position of customer. Once again, this illustrates why a line of authority that only connects the DNI to the Bureau through the Directorate of Intelligence may result in the DNI having only tenuous authority with respect to the FBI's national security-related resources.

Exercising promotion and evaluation authority. Lacking significant operational and resource authority, the Executive Assistant Director for Intelligence might turn to personnel authority to manage the Bureau's national security effort. Yet the intelligence directorate has little personnel authority with respect to the Bureau's national security elements. The intelligence directorate's primary leverage comes from its semi-annual review of how headquarters and field offices have utilized intelligence resources—a so-called "program" review.[69] These evaluations do not, however, impose individual accountability for failing to fulfill headquarters-issued requirements, much less control how assets are directed. These after-the-fact reviews therefore have no direct effect on those who lead the execution of the Bureau's national security missions.

With respect to promotions and personnel evaluations, the head of the intelligence directorate is not the performance "rating official" (nor does the head of the directorate share that responsibility) for the component head in any FBI field office or headquarters division. The head of the intelligence directorate is the performance "rating official" for only four people at the Bureau—three special assistants and the Assistant Director of the office.[70] In turn, the Assistant Director rates only three people outside of the Directorate of Intelligence.[71] And unlike the Assistant Directors in the Counterintelligence, Counterterrorism, and Criminal Divisions, the Assistant Director of the Directorate of Intelligence does not rate the heads of the 56 field offices,[72] nor does anyone in the Directorate of Intelligence have any personnel rating authority (direct or indirect) over the Field Intelligence Groups or their supervisors.[73] At best, the intelligence directorate exercises a series of broken lines of authority over the Bureau's national security functions. In turn, these broken lines also represent a broken chain of influence for the Director of National Intelligence.

"Intelligence Elements" of the FBI

The DNI has one more power over the FBI's intelligence activities—in theory, at any rate. The new intelligence act empowers the DNI to lead the Intelligence Community, which it defines as including the FBI's "intelligence elements."[74] What are those elements? Neither the statute nor the FBI has defined the term. In our view, those elements should include the Bureau's principal intelligence-gathering units—the Counterterrrorism and Counterintelligence Divisions, as well as the intelligence directorate itself. Once again, because this issue has not been resolved, it is not clear that the FBI's national security-related divisions will in fact be subject to effective oversight and coordination by the DNI.

In reforming its intelligence capabilities since September 11, the FBI opted not to fundamentally reorganize its existing operational structure. Thus while the Bureau has significantly improved (and certainly has further plans to improve) many of its intelligence *capabilities*, it has not integrated these capabilities to ensure that national intelligence requirements and strategic analysis drive counterterrorism, counterintelligence, and foreign intelligence operations, investigations, and collection. And in our view, whether the DNI and the FBI will be able to direct those resources effectively and in meaningful coordination with the rest of the Intelligence Community remains in question so long as the FBI's primary national security components answer to different chains of authority outside of the DNI's aegis.

Realigning the FBI's Intelligence Elements

Recommendation 1

To ensure that the FBI's *intelligence elements* are responsive to the Director of National Intelligence, and to capitalize on the FBI's progress, we recommend the creation of a new National Security Service within the FBI under a single Executive Assistant Director. This service would include the Bureau's Counterterrorism and Counterintelligence Divisions and the Directorate of Intelligence. The service would be subject to the coordination and budget authorities of the DNI as well as to the same Attorney General authorities that apply to other Bureau divisions.

To resolve these issues of coordination and authority and to facilitate further reform, we propose a National Security Service within the FBI. This service would include the FBI's Counterintelligence and Counterterrorism Divisions, as well as its Directorate of Intelligence.

The creation of such a service would bring the FBI's operational divisions with national security responsibilities under the DNI's authority. The service would account for all of the FBI's National Intelligence Program-funded resources, thereby giving the DNI effective budget control as well. The service would be led by an Executive Assistant Director. In order to preserve the intelligence reform act's intent that the DNI have a say in the appointment of the FBI's top intelligence official, this individual would serve in the role of the Executive Assistant Director for Intelligence.

Because of the strength of the FBI's field offices, some link between the head of the service and certain field offices is also needed. For example, the National Security Service could have authority to approve and evaluate Special Agents in Charge of the 15 field offices that have an official foreign diplomatic presence. The service should also have inspection authority to evaluate the work of FBI's field offices. Through these evaluation and appointment authorities, the headquarters elements of the service (and through them, the DNI) would have a lever to ensure that the FBI is accountable for fulfilling national intelligence requirements through its investigatory, operational, and collection capabilities.

Recognizing the danger that field offices may drain National Security Service resources for more immediate law enforcement needs, we recommend the development of a process to prevent excessive diversion of the service's resources. This is not to say that National Security Service resources will never be re-allocated to other missions, but that they should be re-allocated or detailed to other divisions only temporarily, and only with the permission of the head of the National Security Service, under procedures agreed upon by the DNI.

Like the 9/11 Commission, we considered and rejected the creation of a separate agency devoted entirely to internal security without any law enforcement powers.[75] The FBI's hybrid nature is one of its strengths. In today's world of transnational threats, the line between "criminal activity" and "national security information" is increasingly blurred, as is well-illustrated by the use of illegal drug proceeds to fund terrorist activity. The FBI can quickly bring criminal justice tools, such as search warrants, to bear in its national security mission. In addition, the FBI's criminal justice role demands everyday contact with state and local officials—contact that is invaluable for obtaining information relevant to national security.

We believe it is critical that the National Security Service remain within the FBI. Personnel in the service would take advantage of its specialized career options, but agents in the service would go through law enforcement training along with their counterparts in the FBI's criminal divisions. Agents could laterally transfer between the service and the FBI's other divisions mid-career.

Because the National Security Service will remain part of the FBI, analysts will continue to work in the headquarters components of the non-service divisions and on criminal cases in the field offices. The FBI will continue to hire all of its personnel through a single office; its information technology and information sharing infrastructure will remain combined; and the support service functions will still serve the entire Bureau.

Ensuring continuing coordination between the FBI's two halves is critical for at least two reasons: such coordination is necessary to optimize the FBI's performance in both national security and criminal investigations, and—equally important—it will help ensure continued attention to civil liberties and legal limits on the power of government to intrude into the lives of citizens. Of course, all activities in the National Security Service would be performed consistent with the Attorney General Guidelines for national security investigations and foreign intelligence collection, as well as under Department of Justice and Congressional oversight.

As long as the Bureau continues to expose Special Agents to a tour of criminal work, as it should, its agents will have experience in criminal justice matters and continue to be extensively trained to uphold the Constitution and protect civil liberties. Working in the criminal justice environment sensitizes agents to civil liberties limits on a daily basis, through regular contact with Department of Justice attorneys as well as the courts. The Bureau's national security and criminal justice components can and must continue to work together.

If that is done, we see no civil liberties protections to be gained by requiring that personnel work separately in the Counterterrorism or Counterintelligence Divisions rather than a National Security Service that combines these divisions. In fact, civil liberties protections would if anything be increased if, as we suggest, investigations of purely domestic terrorism were assigned to the FBI's Criminal Division. There is no civil liberties reason to insulate National Intelligence Program funds from the oversight of the DNI. Nor do we believe that civil liberties are diluted if the head of the National Security Service sets intelligence priorities or performs personnel evaluations of Special Agents in Charge.

In short, without creating walls between the FBI's national security and criminal components, the National Security Service would establish a single focal point for the Bureau's national security mission and a series of direct lines connecting the DNI to the national security elements at FBI headquarters and in the field. The proposed service would provide a more defined and prestigious career track for agents focused on national security. It would also enhance the Bureau's intelligence capabilities, providing strategic analysis, asset validation, intelligence career planning, training, and strategic targeting for the FBI's overall national security mission—functions that are now scattered and, in many cases, undeveloped. A National Security Service would protect national security intelligence resources, demand real accountability, and ensure that intelligence requirements are met—all without fundamentally changing the structure or nature of the FBI's 56 field offices that are the hallmark of the organization. In the field offices agents will continue to do both intelligence and criminal work; collectors and analysts will continue to work side by side.

Despite all of these advantages to creating a National Security Service within the FBI, we are compelled to add a note of caution—the same that was eloquently sounded by the 9/11 Commission:

> We have found that in the past the Bureau has announced its willingness to reform and restructure itself to address transnational security threats, but has fallen short—failing to effect the necessary institutional and cultural changes organization-wide. We want to ensure that this does not happen again.[76]

Our recommendations attempt to effect this necessary institutional change, and to instill a culture that is truly consistent with the demands of national security intelligence operations. In our view, while the FBI has made steps in the right direction since September 11, it still has many miles to travel. Reform will require enormous commitment and effort within the FBI, as well as sustained outside coordination and oversight. And despite the many benefits associated with having a combined law enforcement and intelligence agency, we recommend that policymakers re-evaluate the wisdom of creating a separate agency—an equivalent to the British "MI-5"—dedicated to intelligence collection in the United States should there be a continued failure to institute the reforms necessary to transform the FBI into the intelligence organization it must become.

ENDING THE TURF WAR BETWEEN THE FBI AND THE CIA

Recommendation 2

The DNI should ensure that there are effective mechanisms for preventing conflicts and encouraging coordination among intelligence agencies in the United States.

Both CIA and the FBI have long had responsibilities for foreign intelligence collection in the United States, subject in both cases to Attorney General oversight.[77] If anything, the need for continued activity on the part of both agencies will only increase. Valuable foreign assets and lucrative targets can come and go across our borders practically as they please. The Intelligence Community must be as agile and flexible as their target's travel plans.

The past four years have witnessed many instances of exemplary and ongoing cooperation between CIA and FBI; the two agencies have, among other achievements, increased joint operations and successfully worked together against several hard target countries.[78] But clashes have become all too common as well, particularly in the context of intelligence gathered in the United States. When sources provide information to both agencies, the FBI complains that conflicting or duplicative reports go up the chain, causing circular or otherwise misleading streams of reporting.[79] In response, CIA claims that FBI headquarters is more concerned about credit for intelligence production than the quality of its reporting.[80] If the agencies' fight were limited to disputes about who gets credit for intelligence reports, it would be far less alarming. Unfortunately, it extends beyond headquarters and into the field, where lives are at stake.

Overseas, lack of cooperation between CIA and FBI has resulted in clashes over interaction with foreign liaison services and over coordination of other activities.[81] Both agencies agree that lack of coordination has jeopardized ongoing intelligence activities.[82]

Moreover, officials from CIA's Counterterrorist Center told us that they have difficulty tracking and obtaining information about terrorist cases after they hand them off to the FBI—as they must do when the focus of a case shifts from overseas to the territorial United States.[83] The failure of CIA and FBI to cooperate and share information adequately on such cases could potentially create a gap in the coverage of these threats, like the one the September 11 attack plotters were able to exploit.[84]

These conflicts between agencies that should regard each other as compatriots signal the need for a strong Intelligence Community leader with effective, acknowledged authority over both CIA and FBI—for a DNI, in fact.

In our view, the primary source of friction concerns the FBI's desire to expand its current authorities relative to intelligence activities and production within the United States. The FBI is, of course, the largest and most active collector of intelligence inside the United States, but the CIA has long had officers collecting intelligence in the United States as well. In December 2004, the FBI proposed a new Memorandum of Understanding to govern intelligence coordination between the FBI and CIA.[85] The FBI's proposed guidelines exhibit the Bureau's desire for new controls over other agencies' activities and intelligence production in the United States. At least some in CIA have interpreted the FBI's recent initiatives as an attempt by the Bureau to gain control over CIA operations in the United States.[86]

The Commission asked the FBI to identify significant risks or problems associated with continuing to allow CIA to carry out non-intrusive foreign intelligence activities inside the United States under existing guidelines and authorities. The Bureau responded that lack of coordination has occasionally resulted in different agencies identifying the same targets, recruiting the same sources, and disseminating circular reporting.[87] The FBI's draft Memorandum of Understanding appears, however, to be an extreme reaction to these concerns. While we cannot discuss the details of the FBI's proposed Memorandum in an unclassified report, we believe that the Bureau's proposal establishes procedures that are overly burdensome and counterproductive to effective intelligence gathering.

The FBI's generalized statements about the need for coordination do not justify the kinds of restraints that it is seeking to impose. To the extent that the FBI is seeking to impose constraints on the CIA that parallel those that the CIA imposes on FBI operations abroad, the analogy is misguided. Foreign operations often occur in a hostile environment where lack of coordination can be fatal and U.S. embassies provide a logical focal point for coordinating intelligence activities in that country. Neither is true of activities inside the United States.

In claiming new territory, the FBI has argued that it is too hard to define assets or to place them in counterintelligence, counterterrorism, or foreign intelligence "boxes."[88] We think this is all the more reason to have a fluid system for coordination—where both agencies are involved in the collection of foreign intelligence in the United States and conflicts are resolved by the DNI (or the Attorney General if it is a question of what U.S. law permits). Only increased cooperation, better procedures to accomplish it, and responsiveness to strong national leadership will help to resolve conflicts when they occur. The days of negotiated treaties among sovereign intelligence agencies are over, or should be. This dispute should be resolved by the DNI and monitored to ensure consistent improvement.

Bringing the FBI's national security elements under the direction of the DNI will be a significant step towards achieving this increased agility and simultaneously ensuring that the Intelligence Community agencies act in concert against foreign intelligence targets. In addition to developing effective mechanisms for coordination, the DNI will need authority to arbitrate between agencies in instances of conflict, an authority the DNI will only have if the FBI becomes a fully responsive and accountable member of the Intelligence Community.

A final, and critical, point: in exercising this authority, we expect the DNI to require scrupulous adherence to Attorney General Guidelines designed to protect civil liberties. Nothing in our call for greater coordination between the FBI and CIA is meant to alter *in any way* existing civil liberties protections. The best way to protect civil liberties is not by favoring one agency over another but by ensuring that every agency adheres to the law. That is the purpose of the Attorney General's Guidelines, which establish rules both for FBI national security investigations and foreign intelligence collection,[89] and for the CIA's foreign intelligence and counterintelligence activities in the United States.[90] The Guidelines strictly delineate the manner in which each agency can conduct operations, providing the clarity necessary to protect civil liberties. Perhaps most importantly, both sets of Guidelines make clear that the CIA must turn to the FBI, which must in turn obtain either Justice Department or court approval, for *any* remotely invasive or non-consensual activity, such as searches, electronic surveillance, or non-consensual interviews within the United States.[91] Coordination will not change any of these rules; indeed, giving the DNI coordinating authority without revising the Guidelines will likely enhance the protection of civil liberties, for it will ensure that all domestic collection is carefully supervised, coordinated, and directed.

THE DEPARTMENT OF JUSTICE: THE REMAINING REORGANIZATION

Recommendation 3

The Department of Justice's primary national security elements—the Office of Intelligence Policy and Review, and the Counterterrorism and Counterespionage sections—should be placed under a new Assistant Attorney General for National Security.

In the wake of September 11, much criticism rightly focused on legal and procedural impediments to information sharing—the proverbial "wall"—between U.S. law enforcement agents and intelligence officers. As a result, all three branches of government dismantled the dividing elements between these two functions. Major changes were made at the CIA, FBI, and Department of Homeland Security. The core organization of the Justice Department, however, did not change at all.

The Justice Department's three primary national security components are located in different divisions, with no individual below the Deputy Attorney General who can supervise all three. The Office of Intelligence Policy and Review (OIPR) is responsible for FISA requests, representing the Department of Justice on intelligence-related committees, and advising the Attorney General on "all matters relating to the national security activities."[92] It is independent of any division and reports directly to the Deputy Attorney General. In contrast, both the Counterterrorism and Counterespionage sections are located in the Criminal Division, but they each report to two *different* Deputy Assistant Attorneys General. If there is method to this madness, neither we, nor any other official with whom we spoke, could identify it.

There is reason to believe that this awkward (and outdated) organizational scheme has created problems between the Justice Department and the Intelligence Community. In our classified report we describe one such problem that cannot be discussed in our unclassified report.

We believe that bringing the Office of Intelligence Policy and Review closer to its operational counterparts like the Counterespionage and Counterterrorism sections would give the office better insight into actual intelligence practices and make it better attuned to operational needs. Attorneys in the Counterterrorism and Counterespionage sections routinely work alongside FBI agents and other intelligence officers. By contrast, OIPR is largely viewed within the Department as an "assembly line operation not requiring any special grounding in the facts of a particular matter."[93] OIPR's job is to process and adjudicate FISA requests—not to follow a case from start to completion. One of the advantages of placing all three national security components under a single Assistant Attorney General is that they will see themselves as acting in concert to serve a common mission.[94]

In our view, a more effective construct would place an Assistant Attorney General for National Security in charge of all three national security elements (OIPR, Counterespionage, and Counterterrorism).[95] This Assistant Attorney General would serve as a single focal point on all national security matters. The Assistant Attorney General would be responsible for reviewing FISA decisions and determining what more can be done to synthesize intelligence and law enforcement investigations. In an era when it is becoming increasingly incumbent upon organizations like the FBI to balance both their law enforcement and intelligence responsibilities, more thoughtful, innovative, and constructive legal guidance is in high demand.

A further possibility would be to create a new Associate Attorney General position that was responsible for both the Criminal Division and our recommended National Security Division.[96] This construct has the advantage of ensuring that criminal and national security measures are "merged" prior to reaching the Deputy Attorney General, who is responsible for operations within the entire Department of Justice extending far beyond criminal and national security matters. This structure also has the added benefit of providing the Justice Department with management levels more closely aligned with those of other departments (*i.e.*, the cabinet Secretary, a Deputy Secretary, and Under Secretaries).

Furthermore, this construct would align the Justice Department's national security elements with the Intelligence Community. It would create a structure that is parallel to the one proposed for the FBI, and would highlight that Department of Justice attorneys are not just there to advise the Bureau if a matter becomes a criminal investigation. We believe this integration would make Justice more responsive to the FBI's needs and perhaps better able to allocate resources to the national security mission in general.

THE DEPARTMENT OF HOMELAND SECURITY: MORE WALLS TO BREACH

The Department of Homeland Security is the primary repository for information about what passes in and out of the country—a critical player safeguarding the United States from nuclear, biological, or chemical attack. Yet since its inception Homeland Security has faced immense challenges in collecting information efficiently, making it available to analysts and users both inside and outside the department, and bringing intelligence support to law enforcement and first responders who seek to act on such information.

Although we have included Homeland Security in our discussion of intelligence collection within the United States, we have not completed a detailed study of the Department's current capabilities. We will therefore make only one formal recommendation with respect to Homeland Security. Nonetheless, it is plain that Homeland Security faces challenges in all four of the roles it plays in the Intelligence Community—as collector, analyst, disseminator, and customer.

The Department of Homeland Security has no shortage of intelligence collectors. With 22 agencies, Homeland Security commands more than 180,000 personnel from the U.S. Coast Guard, Customs and Border Protection, Secret Service, Immigration and Customs Enforcement (ICE), Transportation Security Administration, and Office of Infrastructure Protection.[97] ICE has more than 3,000 employees.[98] ICE collects reams of data on foreigners entering the United States and manages the Student and Exchange Visitor Information System database, which includes information on foreign students studying in the United States. However, whether agencies like ICE are equipped to make this information available to the Intelligence Community in useable form remains unclear. ICE officials explained that they would not give other agencies unfettered access to their databases (despite those agencies' wishes) because of unspecified legal constraints.[99] We find this September 10th approach to information sharing troubling; it deserves careful scrutiny from the DNI and the new Secretary of Homeland Security, to ensure there is full information sharing consistent with intelligence needs and valid civil liberties concerns.

A critical Homeland Security function is disseminating threat information to law enforcement and other officials at the federal, state, local, and tribal level. The Department of Homeland Security currently faces many difficulties in this regard. According to one Homeland Security official, local law enforcement officials are currently "shotgunned" by the information flow coming from a variety of federal sources, and confused as to who has the lead in supporting their information and intelligence needs.[100] Senior officials at Homeland Security emphasize that the process of declassifying information takes too long and frequently prevents the department from quickly sharing concrete, actionable information with law enforcement.[101] Instead, law enforcement officials often receive a steady steam of vague threat reporting, unsupported by adequate sourcing, and incapable of serving as a basis for action.

Homeland Security's problems with sharing national security information do not end there. Like many other intelligence organizations, Department of Homeland Security officials expressed concerns about the lack of procedures for sharing intelligence across agencies. As an example, Homeland Security officials have expressed concern that they have no mechanism for getting answers to "hot questions" they pose to the FBI and the National Counterterrorism Center.[102] Some of the obstacles to interagency collaboration are even more basic. As one senior Homeland Security official in the Information Analysis section remarked about the FBI, "I still can't send them an e-mail, and they can't send one back."[103] Finally, in a variation on a familiar theme, some law enforcement agents at Homeland Security have expressed unwillingness to share operational information out of concern that other agencies might seek to "steal" their cases.[104]

Recommendation 4

The Secretary of Homeland Security should rescind Treasury Order 113-01 as it applies to Department of Homeland Security elements.

Homeland Security's approach to information sharing unfortunately draws sustenance from rules that Immigration and Customs Enforcement inherited from the Treasury Department. ICE currently operates under an old Treasury order (T.O. 113-01) regarding requests for assistance from the Intelligence Community.[105] Established in the wake of the Iran-Contra affair, this order requires that all requests by the Intelligence Community for assistance be reduced to writing and submitted for approval to the Secretary or Deputy Secretary of the Treasury. The order provides an exception only for "routine exchange between the Intelligence Community and the Department of the Treasury of substantive intelligence information and recurring reports."[106] It leaves the interpretation of what constitutes a "routine" exchange up to the head of the agency involved. The order apparently applies to all information sharing agreements between former Treasury elements of Homeland Security and the Intelligence Community, since they are not considered "routine."[107] When the Department of Homeland Security was created and Immigrations and Customs Enforcement was transferred to its jurisdiction, the order remained in effect, although oversight was shifted to the Under Secretary for Border and Transportation Security.[108]

We find it highly disappointing that such a barrier to communication between law enforcement and intelligence agencies has survived in a department created to avoid the mistakes and miscommunication that led to the September 11 attacks. It should be rescinded, not extended. The default policy for personnel within Homeland Security component agencies should be to cooperate with requests for assistance and information sharing coming from the Intelligence Community, not to refer such requests to a lengthy and bureaucratic process practically designed to deter collaboration. We strongly recommend that the Secretary of Homeland Security promptly rescind Treasury Order 113-01 and replace it with a new order that ensures greater information sharing and collaboration between all entities of Homeland Security and the Intelligence Community. Similarly, we believe that the Department of the Treasury should evaluate whether its successor to Treasury Order 113-01 (Treasury Order 105-18) should be modified to effect smoother cooperation within the Intelligence Community.

ENDNOTES

[1] The FBI refers to itself in these terms. According to the FBI, "now that the Intelligence Program is established and developing, we are turning to the next stage of transforming the Bureau into an intelligence agency." FBI, *The FBI's Counterterrorism Program Since September 2001, Report to the National Commission on Terrorist Attacks upon the United States* (April 14, 2004) at p. 31. Director Mueller also refers to the FBI as "both a law enforcement and an intelligence agency." *Testimony of Robert S. Mueller, III, Director, Federal Bureau of Investigation, Before the United States Senate Committee on the Judiciary* (May 20, 2004).

[2] Interview with U.S. Immigration and Customs Enforcement official (Feb. 28, 2005).

[3] According to Director Mueller, in 2004, 30 percent of new hires had accounting, law enforcement, and military backgrounds. Interview with Robert Muller, FBI Director (Oct. 20, 2004).

[4] *Final Report of the National Commission on Terrorist Attacks Upon the United States* (2004) at p. 425 (hereinafter "9/11 Commission Report").

[5] As a result of the FBI's strategic plan of 1998, the Bureau created an Office of Intelligence. One year later, in November 1999, the FBI created an Investigative Services Division that subsumed the Office of Intelligence and was designed to "house a new Information, Analysis and Assessments Branch." FBI, *Press Release* (Nov. 11, 1999). According to a 1999 FBI press release, the aim of the Investigative Services Division was to extract information from case files "and other existing sources to identify future trends and means of preventing crime and threats to national security. The FBI intends to increase its reliance on information analysts and to devote additional efforts to recruiting highly qualified persons to perform this function." *Id.*

[6] According to a 9/11 Commission staff statement, at the time that the Investigative Services Division was set up, an internal FBI review "found that 66 percent of the bureau's analysts were not qualified to perform analytical duties....The new division did not succeed. FBI officials told us that it did not receive sufficient resources, and there was ongoing resistance to its creation from senior managers in the FBI's operational divisions. Those managers feared losing control. They feared losing resources. They feared they would be unable to get the assistance they wanted from the new division's analysts." 9/11 Commission Staff Statement # 9, *Law Enforcement, Counterterrorism, and Intelligence Collection in the United States Prior to 9/11* (April 13, 2005) at pp. 5-6; *see also* Alfred Cumming and Todd Masse, *FBI Intelligence Reform Since September 11, 2001: Issues and Options for Congress* (CRS Report RL 32336) (updated Aug. 4, 2004) at p. 58.

[7] Interview with FBI Directorate of Intelligence official (Jan. 19, 2005).

[8] Interview with FBI Special Agent in Charge (Dec. 8, 2004) (using this example to describe how the demands on field offices may vary, in part, according to location).

[9] *Id.*

[10] Simply in quantitative terms, the majority of FBI's reporting comes in the form of Intelligence Information Reports (IIRs), unfinished intelligence products. In recent years the Bureau has dramatically increased the number of IIRs it produces. Further details are provided in our classified report that we cannot reference here.

[11] FBI Directorate of Intelligence, *Report to the President of the United States: Comprehensive Plan for the FBI Intelligence Program with Performance Measures* (Feb. 16, 2005) at p. 28

(hereinafter "FBI, Comprehensive Plan").

[12] FBI Directorate of Intelligence, *Cincinnati Division Field Intelligence Group On-Site Review* (Oct. 13, 2004) at p. 6.

[13] National Academy of Public Administration, *Transforming the FBI: Progress and Challenges* (Jan. 2005) at p. xv. The report notes that "[i]n-depth strategic collection and analysis efforts tend to be deferred at the FBI." *Id.*

[14] Further details are provided in our classified report that we cannot reference here. In Fiscal Year 2004, the FBI published 250 Intelligence Assessments. FBI, *Office of Intelligence Response to Request # 15* (Jan. 5, 2005).

[15] Interview with FBI official (Oct. 22, 2004).

[16] 9/11 Commission Staff Statement # 9, *Law Enforcement, Counterterrorism, and Intelligence Collection in the United States Prior to 9/11* (April 13, 2004) at p. 9.

[17] FBI Directorate of Intelligence, *Office of Intelligence On-Site Review of Field Intelligence Groups* (Sept. 10, 2004) at p. 6.

[18] Currently 25 percent of the Bureau's analytic cadre has an advanced degree. Interview with FBI Directorate of Intelligence official (Oct. 18, 2004). In comparison, 60 percent of analysts in CIA's Directorate of Intelligence have an advanced degree. Interview with CIA Directorate of Intelligence Human Resources official (Jan. 10, 2005).

[19] The failure to communicate fabrication notices properly was, specifically, a problem for Defense HUMINT Service. Chapter One (Iraq).

[20] Interview with FBI counterintelligence official (Feb. 18, 2005).

[21] *Id.*

[22] *See, e.g.*, Interview with FBI Field Intelligence Group official (Feb. 3, 2005).

[23] Interview with FBI official (Jan. 24, 2005).

[24] Senator Shelby wrote, "The FBI has never taken information technology very seriously, and has found itself left with an entirely obsolete information technology infrastructure that is wholly inadequate to the FBI's current operational needs, much less to the task of supporting sophisticated all-source intelligence fusion and analysis." Richard C. Shelby, Vice Chairman, Senate Select Committee on Intelligence, *September 11 and the Imperative of Reform in the U.S. Intelligence Community* (Dec. 10, 2002) at p. 72.

[25] *Testimony of Robert S. Mueller, III, Director, Federal Bureau of Investigation, Before the United States Senate Committee on the Judiciary* (May 20, 2004) ("Our goal is to deliver Virtual Case File capabilities by the end of this year").

[26] National Research Council of the National Academies, James C. McGroddy and Herbert S. Lin (Eds.), *A Review of the FBI's Trilogy Information Technology Modernization Program* (2004) at pp. 3-4, 26.

[27] Interview with FBI official (Dec. 15, 2004).

[28] FBI Directorate of Intelligence, *Response to Commission FBI Request # 15* (Jan. 5, 2005).

[29] The FBI has a total of 12,254 Special Agents. Interview with FBI Directorate of Intelligence official (Jan. 19, 2005).

[30] Executive Order No. 12333 (Dec. 4, 1981) at § 1.14(a).

[31] Intelligence Reform and Terrorism Prevention Act of 2004 at § 1011, Pub. L. No. 108-

458 (hereinafter "IRTPA").

[32] *Id.*

[33] *Id.*

[34] *See, e.g.,* Interview with FBI official (March 7, 2005).

[35] *See, e.g.,* Interview with Office of Management and Budget officials (Feb. 8, 2005). While the FBI's NIP dollars are *appropriated* through the House Subcommittee on Science, State, Justice, and Commerce, and Related Agencies and the Senate Subcommittee on Commerce, Justice, and Science, these dollars are *identified* as part of the NIP budget.

[36] FBI, *National Foreign Intelligence Program FY 2005 President's Request* (Jan. 27, 2004).

[37] Interview with Office of Management and Budget officials (Feb. 8, 2005).

[38] IRTPA at § 1014(b)(2)(H).

[39] *Id.* at § 2001(f); *see also* 9/11 Commission Report at p. 426 (recommending that the FBI "align its budget structure according to its four main programs...to ensure better transparency on program costs, management of resources, and protection of the intelligence program").

[40] FBI, Comprehensive Plan at p. 9.

[41] *Id.* at p. 10 (noting that the FY 2005 Intelligence Decision Unit Budget is $819,108,658 and that 39 percent of the Intelligence Decision Unit Budget goes to the Directorate of Intelligence, Criminal program, and Administrative Support combined). The Directorate of Intelligence, Criminal Division, and Administrative Support are not included in the National Intelligence Program budget. FBI, *National Foreign Intelligence Program FY 2005 President's Request* (Jan. 27, 2004); *see also* Interview with Office of Management and Budget official (March 16, 2005).

[42] FBI, Comprehensive Plan at p. 9.

[43] Interview with Office of Management and Budget official (March 8, 2005).

[44] FBI, Comprehensive Plan at p. 10.

[45] *Id.*

[46] Interview with Office of Management and Budget official (March 8, 2005) (suggesting, nevertheless, that several of the Executive Assistant Director's various specific budgetary authorities relative to the Intelligence Decision Unit may be currently undetermined). FBI states that the only individual with budget execution authority is the Director of the FBI. Interview with FBI official (March 7, 2005).

[47] FBI, Comprehensive Plan at p. 10.

[48] IRTPA at § 1014.

[49] *The Attorney General's Guidelines on General Crimes, Racketeering Enterprise and Terrorism Enterprise Investigations* (May 30, 2002) at p. ii.

[50] IRTPA at § 1014(b)(2)(H).

[51] *Id.* at § 2002(c).

[52] *Id.* at § 2002(c)(1) & (3).

[53] FBI, Comprehensive Plan at p. 15. The Directorate of Intelligence indicates that field intelligence operations constitute the process of "identify[ing]" intelligence gaps, "lev[ying]" requirements as "tasks," providing "support" to the intelligence cycle, "conduct[ing] intelli-

gence assessments" and "know[ing] and report[ing] the scope and extent of [Field Office] collection capabilities." *Id.* at pp. 3-4. In some cases, Field Intelligence Groups are like other FBI field office components, or "squads" (*e.g.,* counterterrorism, counterintelligence, criminal, and cybercrime). In other cases, they are more nascent and embedded in existing operational squads. FBI Directorate of Intelligence, *FBI Field Office Intelligence Operations: Concept of Operations* (Aug. 2003) at p. 2.

[54] FBI, *Response to Commission FBI Request # 16-1 through 16-10* (Feb. 3, 2005) at pp. 3-4.

[55] Interview with FBI Directorate of Intelligence officials (Nov. 18, 2004).

[56] Interview with FBI official (Jan. 18, 2005); Interview with FBI Field Intelligence Group official (Feb. 3, 2005).

[57] FBI, Directorate of Intelligence, *Columbia Division Field Intelligence Group On-Site Review* (Jan. 3, 2005) at p. 12.

[58] 9/11 Commission Report at p. 423.

[59] Interview with Directorate of Intelligence official (Jan. 19, 2005). In contrast, the FBI's operational divisions are explicitly given authorities to task field offices as well as initiate and terminate cases.

[60] FBI, Comprehensive Plan at p. 15.

[61] As defined, the Field Intelligence Groups do not have authorities to drive counterintelligence and counterterrorism investigations, collections, and operations. Interview with Directorate of Intelligence official (March 8, 2005).

[62] FBI Directorate of Intelligence, *Response to Commission FBI Request # 15* (Jan. 5, 2005).

[63] FBI Directorate of Intelligence, *Response to Commission FBI Request # 10* (Sept. 30, 2004).

[64] IRTPA at § 2002(c)(6).

[65] Interview with Directorate of Intelligence official (Jan. 19, 2005). As noted earlier, the Bureau has stated that it plans on adding a strategic analysis unit to the Directorate of Intelligence. However, it is not clear whether this unit will conduct strategic analysis or instead provide guidance for the field offices on how to produce such reporting. FBI, Comprehensive Plan at p. 28.

[66] Interview with Directorate of Intelligence official (Jan. 19, 2005).

[67] *Id.*

[68] *Id.*

[69] *Id.*

[70] *Id.*

[71] They are a Deputy Assistant Director in the Counterterrorism Division (an evaluation that is then reviewed by the head of the Counterterrorism Division) and two section chiefs in the Criminal and Counterintelligence Divisions. In the first case, the Deputy Assistant Director is rated by one component of the FBI and reviewed by another. Even more peculiar, while the Directorate of Intelligence has rating authority for a Deputy Assistant Director in Counterterrorism, in the Criminal and Counterintelligence Divisions the Assistant Director of the Directorate of Intelligence is the rating official for a Section Chief. *Id.*

[72] Interview with Directorate of Intelligence official (March 8, 2005). Although the Assistant Director of the Directorate of Intelligence does not rate the heads of the field offices like the Assistant Directors in these other divisions, the Assistant Director does provide *input* into these evaluations. *Id.* The Assistant Directors in FBI's Counterintelligence, Counterterrorism, and Criminal Divisions rate the heads of FBI's 56 field offices on a rotating basis.

[73] *Id.*

[74] IRTPA at § 1073.

[75] This was one proposal that the 9/11 Commission considered. According to the 9/11 Commission Report, "we have considered proposals for a new agency dedicated to intelligence collection in the United States....We do not recommend the creation of a new domestic intelligence agency. It is not needed if our other recommendations are adopted—to establish a strong national intelligence center, part of the NCTC, that will oversee counterterrorism intelligence work, foreign and domestic, and to create a National Intelligence Director who can set and enforce standards for the collection, processing, and reporting of information." 9/11 Commission Report at p. 423.

[76] *Id.* at p. 425.

[77] According to Executive Order 12333, CIA shall "[c]ollect, produce, and disseminate foreign intelligence and counterintelligence, including information not otherwise obtainable. The collection of foreign intelligence or counterintelligence within the United States shall be coordinated with the FBI as required by procedures agreed upon by the Director of Central Intelligence and the Attorney General." Executive Order 12333 at § 1.8(a). The FBI shall "[c]onduct within the United States, when requested by officials of the Intelligence Community designated by the President, activities undertaken to collect foreign intelligence or support foreign intelligence collection requirements of other agencies within the Intelligence Community, or, when requested by the Director of the National Security Agency, to support communications security activities of the United States Government; produce and disseminate foreign intelligence and counterintelligence." *Id.* at § 1.14 (c)(d). According to the Intelligence Reform and Terrorism Prevention Act of 2004, the CIA shall "provide overall direction for and coordination of the collection of national intelligence outside the United States through human sources by elements of the Intelligence Community authorized to undertake such collection." *Id.* at § 1011. The act is silent on CIA's domestic responsibilities for foreign intelligence.

[78] Classified CIA report.

[79] Interview with senior FBI officials (Dec. 22, 2005).

[80] Classified CIA report.

[81] *Id.*

[82] *Id.*; FBI, *Response to Commission FBI Request # 16* (Feb. 3, 2005).

[83] Interview with Counterterrorist Center WMD Unit official (Oct. 22, 2004).

[84] 9/11 Commission Report at p. 263.

[85] FBI, *Draft Memorandum of Understanding Between the Central Intelligence Agency and the Federal Bureau of Investigation Concerning the Coordination of CIA Activities in the United States and FBI Activities Abroad* (Dec. 13, 2004) (hereinafter "FBI Draft MOU").

[86] Classified CIA report.

[87] FBI, *Response to Commission FBI Request # 16* (Feb. 3, 2005).

[88] Interview with FBI official (Dec. 22, 2004).

[89] *The Attorney General's Guidelines for FBI National Security Investigations and Foreign Intelligence Collection* (Oct. 31, 2003).

[90] CIA, *Guidance for CIA Activities Within the United States* (HR 7-1) (Dec. 23, 1987) at Annex B.

[91] *Id.* In a submission to the Commission, the Center for National Security Studies expressed serious concerns about the degree to which the CIA's domestic activities were regulated. *See generally* Letter to the Commission from Kate Martin, Center for National Security Studies, *Re: Intelligence Activities in the U.S.: Current Proposals' Risks to Civil Liberties* (Feb. 16, 2005). More specifically, the Center recommended that the CIA's activities "be carried out pursuant to guidelines that are written by the Attorney General." *Id.* at p. 8. As we have just noted, this is already the case. And although we cannot, due to classification, discuss details of the current Attorney General-approved guidelines that regulate the CIA's activities in the United States, we can say that the guidelines are highly detailed and significantly *more* restrictive than those applicable to the FBI. Furthermore, the Department of Defense is subject to similar Attorney General guidelines for Defense Department intelligence activities affecting U.S. persons. Department of Defense, DoD Regulation 5240.1-R, *Procedures Governing the Activities of DoD Intelligence Components that Affect United States Persons* (Dec. 1982).

[92] Department of Justice, *Office of Intelligence Policy and Review* (Dec. 12, 2003) *available at* http://www.usdoj.gov/oipr (accessed March 12, 2005).

[93] *Final Report of the Attorney General's Review Team on the Handling of the Los Alamos National Laboratory Investigation* (May 2000) at p. 767 (hereinafter "Bellows Report").

[94] The Bellows Report identifies a further reason to have a single individual below the Deputy Attorney General to supervise OIPR: the need to have a single individual who is knowledgeable about FISA to review FISA applications that are rejected by OIPR. *Id.* at pp. 767-768. The lack of such an individual in the Wen Ho Lee investigation caused serious problems. An Assistant Attorney General for National Security would fit the bill perfectly.

[95] Prior to the Church and Pike investigations, the Department of Justice had such a unit. Since September 11, Justice officials have considered, but not pressed forward, with such a reorganization. Interview with former Assistant Attorney General (Nov. 30, 2004).

[96] The Department currently has a single Associate Attorney General who supervises the Civil Rights, Antitrust, Tax, Civil, and Environmental Divisions, along with several other smaller offices. Department of Justice Organizational Chart (July 14, 2003). There is no such intermediary between the Criminal Division (and several other offices) and the Deputy Attorney General.

[97] Interview with Department of Homeland Security Information Analysis and Infrastructure Protection official (Oct. 7, 2004).

[98] *Id.*

[99] Interview with Immigration and Customs Enforcement officials (Sept. 27, 2004).

[100] Interview with Department of Homeland Security Office of State and Local Coordination official (Dec. 9, 2004).

[101] Interview with Department of Homeland Security Information Analysis and Infrastructure Protection official (Jan. 6, 2005).

[102] Interview with Department of Homeland Security Information Analysis and Infrastruc-

ture Protection official (Dec. 17, 2004)

[103] Interview with Department of Homeland Security Information Analysis and Infrastructure Protection official (Oct. 7, 2004).

[104] Interview with Department of Homeland Security official (Jan. 6, 2005).

[105] Treasury Order 113-01 (Dec. 19, 2002) (superseding provision of same order).

[106] *Id.* at § 4.

[107] Interview with Department of Homeland Security Office of General Counsel official (March 2, 2005).

[108] Homeland Security Act of 2002 § 1512, Pub. L. No 107-296 (providing that the orders of an agency transferred to DHS shall remain in effect according to their terms until lawfully amended, superseded, or terminated).

CHAPTER ELEVEN
COUNTERINTELLIGENCE

Summary & Recommendations

Even as our adversaries—and many of our "friends"—ramp up their intelligence activities against the United States, our counterintelligence efforts remain fractured, myopic, and marginally effective. Our counterintelligence philosophy and practices need dramatic change, starting with centralizing counterintelligence leadership, bringing order to bureaucratic disarray, and taking our counterintelligence fight overseas to adversaries currently safe from scrutiny.

We recommend that:

- The National Counterintelligence Executive (NCIX)—the statutory head of the U.S. counterintelligence community—become the DNI's Mission Manager for counterintelligence, providing strategic direction for the full breadth of counterintelligence activities across the government. In this role, the NCIX should also focus on increasing *technical* counterintelligence efforts across the Intelligence Community;

- The CIA create a new capability dedicated to conducting a full range of counterintelligence activities outside the United States;

- The Department of Defense's Counterintelligence Field Activity assume operational and investigative authority to coordinate and conduct counterintelligence activities throughout the Defense Department; and

- The FBI create a National Security Service that includes the Bureau's Counterintelligence Division, Counterterrorism Division, and the Directorate of Intelligence. A single Executive Assistant Director would lead the service subject to the coordination and budget authorities of the DNI.

INTRODUCTION

Enthusiasm for spying on the United States has not waned since the Cold War. Quite the reverse. The United States is almost certainly one of the top intelligence priorities for practically every government on the planet. Faced with overwhelming American military and economic might, our adversaries increasingly rely on intelligence to gain comparative advantage. A wide range of intelligence activities are used to attack systematically U.S. national security interests worldwide. Yet while our enemies are executing what amounts to a global intelligence war against the United States, we have failed to meet the challenge. U.S. counterintelligence efforts have remained fractured, myopic, and only marginally effective.

Today, we mostly wait for foreign intelligence officers to appear on our doorstep before we even take notice. The lion's share of our counterintelligence resources are expended inside the United States despite the fact that our adversaries target U.S. interests globally. Needless to say, the result is that we are extremely vulnerable outside of our borders.

The losses the United States has sustained within its borders are formidable as well. Spies such as Walker, Ames, Hanssen, and Montes have significantly weakened our intelligence and defense capabilities. Hanssen alone compromised U.S. government secrets whose cost to the nation was in the billions of dollars, not to mention the lives of numerous human sources. Our adversaries have penetrated U.S. intelligence agencies (by recruiting spies) and operations (by running double agents).[1] The theft of some our most sensitive military and technological secrets allows states like China and Russia to reap the benefits of our research and development investments.[2] And while our defense is lacking, our current counterintelligence posture also results in the loss of offensive opportunities to manipulate foreign intelligence activities to our strategic advantage.

Moreover, while stealing our secrets, our adversaries also learn *how* we spy, and how best to counter our efforts in the future, which in turn renders our remaining sources and methods even less effective and more liable to compromise and loss—a cycle of defeat that cannot be indefinitely sustained. As former Director of Central Intelligence Richard Helms once said, "No intelligence service can be more effective than its counterintelligence component for very long."[3]

We believe that U.S. counterintelligence has been plagued by a lack of policy attention and national leadership. We hope this is now coming to a close with the signing of the first national counterintelligence strategy, approved by the President on March 1, 2005. The National Counterintelligence Executive (NCIX)—the statutory head of the U.S. counterintelligence community—has characterized the new offensive counterintelligence strategy as part of the administration's policy of pre-empting threats to the security of the United States.[4]

But a new strategy alone will not do the job. As in the old—and clearly unsuccessful—approach to homeland security, U.S. counterintelligence is bureaucratically fractured, passive (*i.e.*, focusing on the defense rather than going on the offense), and too often simply ineffective.[5] But unlike homeland security, counterintelligence is still largely neglected by policymakers and the Intelligence Community. In fact, counterintelligence has generally *lost* stature since September 11, eclipsed by more immediate counterterrorism needs. While not denigrating it outright, our top policymakers and Intelligence Community management have traditionally paid lip service to counterintelligence. Until, that is, a major spy case breaks. Even then, bureaucratic defensiveness tends to win out. Senior officials have largely addressed counterintelligence issues *ad hoc*, reacting to specific intelligence losses by replacing them with new technologies or collection methods, without addressing the underlying counterintelligence problems.

We offer four recommendations to improve counterintelligence. First, that the NCIX serve as the planner, manager, and supervisor for all United States counterintelligence efforts. Second, that CIA create a new capability dedicated exclusively to attacking intelligence threats outside the United States—a capability our nation currently does not have. Third, that the Department of Defense's Counterintelligence Field Activity be given operational and investigative authority to execute department-wide counterintelligence activities. Fourth, and as discussed more fully in Chapter Ten (Intelligence at Home), that the FBI establish a National Security Service that is fully responsive to the DNI.

Counterintelligence efforts across the Intelligence Community must be better executed in support of the foreign intelligence mission. At the heart of our recommendations is the belief that an integrated and directed U.S. counterintelligence effort will take advantage of intelligence collection opportunities;

protect billions of dollars of defense and intelligence-related investments, sources, and methods; and defend our country against surprise attack.

THE COUNTERINTELLIGENCE CHALLENGE

Spies have always existed, but currently our adversaries—and many of our "friends"—are expanding and intensifying their intelligence activities against U.S. interests worldwide. They target virtually all of our nation's levers of national power—foreign policy and diplomatic strategies, strategic weapon design and capabilities, critical infrastructure components and systems, cutting edge research and technologies,[6] and information and intelligence systems.[7] Our rivals use a range of sophisticated human and technical intelligence techniques, including surveillance, spies, attempts to influence the U.S. media and policymakers, economic espionage, and wholesale technology and trade secret theft. Further, there are indications that foreign intelligence services are clandestinely positioning themselves to attack, exploit, and manipulate critical U.S. information and intelligence systems.

The United States has not sufficiently responded to the scope and scale of the foreign intelligence threat. The number of foreign agents targeting the United States is disturbing—and the majority of them are targeting U.S. interests *outside* the United States. Despite this fact, a very large proportion of U.S. counterintelligence resources are deployed inside the United States[8]—a percentage that has changed very little since the end of the Cold War.

Although we cannot discuss details at this level of classification, suffice it to say that a number of sophisticated intelligence services are aggressively targeting the United States today. These include traditional players such as China and Russia, both of whom deploy official and non-official cover officers to target American interests.[9]

But it is not only major nation states which employ aggressive intelligence services. Terrorist groups like Hizbollah and al-Qa'ida also conduct intelligence operations within the United States. The 9/11 Commission Report, for instance, detailed how the al-Qa'ida hijackers targeted U.S. sites, cased them, and otherwise engaged in classic intelligence activities such as reconnaissance.[10] According to a senior counterintelligence official at CIA, the Agency is only just beginning to understand the intelligence capabilities of terrorist organizations.[11]

Then there are adversaries who attempt to undermine the United States in more subtle ways—through covert influence and perception management efforts. A 1997 Senate investigation found that as many as six individuals with ties to the People's Republic of China sought to channel Chinese money covertly into the 1996 U.S. presidential campaign in order to influence the American political process.[12]

The sum total of these foreign intelligence efforts is striking. During the Cold War, every American national security agency—with the possible exception of the Coast Guard—was penetrated by foreign intelligence services. Moreover, in just the past 20 years CIA, FBI, NSA, DIA, NRO, and the Departments of Defense, State, and Energy have all been penetrated. Secrets stolen include nuclear weapons data, U.S. cryptographic codes and procedures, identification of U.S. intelligence sources and methods (human and technical), and war plans. Indeed, it would be difficult to exaggerate the damage that foreign intelligence penetrations have caused.

THE STATUS QUO

While our rivals have become ever more imaginative and aggressive, our own counterintelligence services remain fractured and reactive. Each U.S. counterintelligence agency pursues its own mission from its own vantage point, rather than working in concert guided by nationally-derived strategies. Our counterintelligence effort has no national focus, no systematic way to coordinate efforts at home and abroad.[13]

Among United States agencies, the FBI dominates counterintelligence within the homeland.[14] Until recently the Bureau focused its resources and operational efforts on foreign spies working out of formal diplomatic establishments—classic official-cover intelligence. The *covert* foreign intelligence presence was largely unaddressed. Today, despite bolstering its counterintelligence resources in all field offices, the FBI still has little capacity to identify, disrupt, or exploit foreign *covert* intelligence activities.[15]

Outside the United States, the CIA has primary responsibility for counterintelligence,[16] a task which, in practice, it defines very narrowly. CIA does not systematically or programmatically undertake the counterintelligence mission of protecting the equities of other U.S. government entities, nor does it mount significant, strategic offensive counterintelligence operations against rival intelligence services. Its focus is mostly defensive; the CIA's Counterintelligence Center and the counterintelligence elements within the Directorate of Operations aim primarily to protect CIA operations.[17] CIA's current approach to counterintelligence is in contrast to its approach during the Cold War, when CIA case officers routinely targeted Warsaw Pact officials, an effort that led to a considerable number of successful counterespionage investigations.[18]

The Department of Defense, with its component counterintelligence units located within the military services, principally focuses on protecting the armed forces.[19] But no counterintelligence organization has the operational mission for the Department as a whole, leaving large swaths of unprotected areas, including highly sensitive policymaking, technology, and acquisition functions. The current system assigns each of the armed services responsibilities for counterintelligence activities in other agencies that lack their own internal capability. The services, however, do not have the range of capabilities necessary to perform this role. While the Department's Counterintelligence Field Activity (CIFA) has taken steps towards implementing a more comprehensive approach to counterintelligence, CIFA currently does not have adequate authority or resources to take on this Department-wide operational mission.[20]

As if agency-level concerns are not enough, the absence of effective and adequately empowered national counterintelligence leadership makes the situation even worse. The National Counterintelligence Executive (NCIX) is the theoretical "head" of counterintelligence,[21] but NCIX has little control over the scattered elements of U.S. counterintelligence. NCIX has only advisory budget authority, little visibility into individual agencies' counterintelligence operations, and no ability to assign operational responsibility or evaluate performance.[22] The recent intelligence reform act did not alter this situation, but it did take what we believe is a useful step—placing the NCIX in the Office of the DNI.[23]

INSTITUTIONALIZING LEADERSHIP

Recommendation 1

The National Counterintelligence Executive should become the DNI's Mission Manager for counterintelligence, providing strategic direction for the whole range of counterintelligence activities across the government.

Organizational change is not a panacea for counterintelligence, but it is necessary. Today there is no individual or office that can impose Community-wide counterintelligence reform or hold individual agencies accountable for fulfilling national counterintelligence requirements. This should change, and we believe that the obvious candidate for leadership is an empowered NCIX.

The recent intelligence reform legislation situated the NCIX in the Office of the DNI, thereby placing counterintelligence near the Intelligence Community's levers of power. To make this more than window dressing, the NCIX needs all of the DNI's authorities for counterintelligence—particularly authority over the FBI's counterintelligence operations. As the Mission Manager for counterintelligence,[24] the NCIX would build collection plans with prioritized targets and provide strategic direction to operational components. Unlike other Mission Managers, the NCIX would also be responsible for the production of strategic counterintelligence analysis.[25]

To this end, we recommend that the NCIX assume the power and the responsibility to:

- Prepare the National Intelligence Program's counterintelligence budget and approve, oversee, and evaluate how agencies execute that budget;

- Produce national counterintelligence requirements and assign operational responsibilities to agencies for meeting those requirements;

- Evaluate the effectiveness of agencies within the Intelligence Community in meeting national counterintelligence requirements;

- Direct and oversee the integration of counterintelligence tradecraft throughout the Intelligence Community;

- Establish common training and education requirements for counterintelligence officers across the Community, and expand cross-agency training;

- Identify and direct the development and deployment of new and advanced counterintelligence methodologies and technologies;

- Ensure that recommendations emerging from counterintelligence damage assessments are incorporated into agency policies and procedures;

- Deconflict and coordinate operational counterintelligence activities both inside and outside of the United States; and

■ Produce *strategic* counterintelligence analysis for policymakers.

These powers would bring the NCIX on par with the other Mission Managers discussed in Chapters Six, Seven, and Eight (Leadership and Management, Collection, and Analysis).[26]

> ## Recommendation 2
>
> The National Counterintelligence Executive should work closely with agencies responsible for protecting U.S. information infrastructure in order to enhance the United States' technical counterintelligence capabilities.

One area we believe is especially critical for the NCIX to address is the absence of a systematic and integrated technical counterintelligence capability. Historically, counterintelligence has been almost exclusively devoted to countering foreign services' human intelligence efforts. At the same time, other organizations like NSA have focused on protecting the U.S. information infrastructure.[27] We therefore recommend that the NCIX devote particular attention to working with agencies that already devote substantial resources to protection of the information infrastructure, looking beyond traditional "counterintelligence" agencies to NSA, other parts of the Department of Defense, the Department of Homeland Security's Information Analysis and Infrastructure Protection Directorate, and the National Institute of Standards and Technology.

INSIDE THE AGENCIES

Primary responsibility for carrying out counterintelligence activities should remain with CIA, FBI, and the Department of Defense. These agencies, however, need to change the way they fulfill their missions. Under stronger NCIX leadership, they must become the core of the U.S. counterintelligence community—a community with common purpose, focus, and unity of effort.

> ## Recommendation 3
>
> The CIA should create a new capability dedicated to mounting offensive counterintelligence activities abroad.

The CIA should expand its current counterintelligence focus beyond the protection of its own operations to conduct a full range of counterintelligence activities outside the United States. This will require that CIA adopt the mission of protecting the equities of other U.S. government agencies overseas and exploiting opportunities for counterintelligence collection.

We recommend that CIA pursue this mission by establishing a new capability that would—along with the Agency's existing Counterintelligence Center—report to the Associate Deputy Director of Operations for Counterintelligence. This new capability would mount counterintelligence activities outside the United States aimed at recruiting foreign sources and conducting activities to deny, deceive, and exploit foreign intelligence targeting of U.S. interests. In short, the goal would be for the counterintelligence element to track foreign intelligence officers *before* they land on U.S. soil or begin targeting U.S. interests abroad. In doing so, the new capability would complement the Agency's existing defensive operations, and would provide the Intelligence Community with a complete overseas counterintelligence capability. And as with all intelligence activity, the CIA's actions—to the extent they involved U.S. persons—would continue to be subject to the Attorney General's guidelines designed to protect civil liberties.

We must stress that our recommendation is not intended to downplay the importance of continuing to protect CIA operations. These counterintelligence activities must continue, and resources currently allocated to asset validation or other operational counterintelligence capabilities should not be diminished. In this vein, we believe that case officers devoted to the new, offensive activity should be "fenced off" so that they cannot be directed to execute other tasks.

Recommendation 4

The Department of Defense's Counterintelligence Field Activity should have operational and investigative authority to coordinate and conduct counterintelligence activities throughout the Defense Department.

While our intelligence foes strategically target our defense infrastructure, the Department of Defense's counterintelligence response remains hardwired to the 1947 framework in which it was created, with each armed service running its own counterintelligence component. In 2002, the Defense Department began to address this deficiency by creating the Counterintelligence Field Activity (CIFA), which has the authority to oversee Department of Defense "implementation support to the NCIX," complete counterintelligence program evaluations, conduct operational analysis, provide threat assessments, conduct counterintelligence training, and "oversee Defense-wide CI investigations."[28]

There is, however, one very significant hole in CIFA's authority: it cannot actually carry out counterintelligence investigations and operations on behalf of the Department of Defense.[29] Rather, Defense-wide investigations and operations are left to the responsibility of the individual services—which are, at the same time, also responsible for investigations and operations *within* their own services.[30] Perhaps unsurprisingly, the result of this arrangement is that intra-service investigations are given priority by the services, and no entity views non-service-specific and department-wide investigations as its primary responsibility. What this means is that many Defense Department components (*e.g.*, Combatant Commands, the Defense Agencies, and the Office of the Secretary of Defense) lack effective counterintelligence protection.

We believe this serious shortcoming would be best addressed by giving CIFA the authority and responsibility to provide Department-wide counterintelligence functional support by conducting investigations, operations, collection, and analysis for the Combatant Commands, Defense Agencies, and the Office of the Secretary of Defense, both inside and outside of the United States. The counterintelligence elements within each military service would be left in place to focus on their department's counterintelligence requirements. CIFA would acquire new counterespionage and law enforcement authorities to investigate national security matters and crimes including treason, espionage, foreign intelligence service or terrorist-directed sabotage, economic espionage, and violations of the National Information Infrastructure Protection Act. Specific authorization from the Secretary of Defense and a directive from the DNI can implement this change. And, as with the CIA and service elements, all of CIFA's activities that relate to U.S. persons should be performed in accordance with Attorney General-approved guidelines.

Giving CIFA additional operational authorities will make it a stronger organization better able to execute its current management responsibilities. Today the armed services are not constituted to perform the full range of counterintelligence functions that the Department of Defense requires. CIFA will gain greater visibility across the Department and relieve the service counterintelligence components from a responsibility that dilutes resources and effort away from their primary mission—to protect their services from foreign intelligence activities.

Recommendation 5

The FBI should create a National Security Service that includes the Bureau's Counterintelligence Division, Counterterrorism Division, and the Directorate of Intelligence. A single Executive Assistant Director would lead the Service subject to the coordination and budget authorities of the DNI.

With respect to the FBI, we are convinced that a number of significant changes need to take place, largely as part of our recommended creation of a new National Security Service within the Bureau. We address this proposal in detail in Chapter Ten (Intelligence at Home). For current purposes, we merely identify the key reasons why this reform is especially necessary in the counterintelligence field. In our view, bringing the FBI's national security elements under a single Executive Assistant Director responsible to the DNI, and therefore also to the NCIX, would improve the overall effectiveness and strategic direction of FBI counterintelligence and effectively empower analysts to direct collections, investigations, and operations.

CONCLUSION

Since the passage of the National Security Act of 1947, counterintelligence has been treated as a kind of second-class citizen in the intelligence profession. The result is that the subject is pushed to the periphery, our adversaries take advantage of our neglect, and American national security suffers. It is all too easy to forget counterintelligence because, other than periodic spy controversies, there is little public sign that we are doing it poorly. But we are. And our adversaries know it. Our recommended changes—centralizing management and planning, expanding our overseas efforts, and integrating and directing the counterintelligence components of the CIA, Department of Defense, and FBI—are long overdue and will help to stanch the hemorrhaging of our secrets and take the fight to our adversaries.

ENDNOTES

[1] A double agent is a person pretending to work as a spy for one government while actually working as a spy for another government.

[2] Christopher Andrew, *The Sword and Shield: The Mitrokhin Archive* (1999) at pp. 215-220.

[3] Richard Helms, *A Look Over My Shoulder* (2003) at pp. 34-35.

[4] Interview with National Counterintelligence Executive (March 10, 2005).

[5] Interview with National Counterintelligence Executive (Sept. 13, 2004).

[6] FBI, Title classified (Nov. 2004) at pp. 17-18.

[7] Classified intelligence report.

[8] Interview with Office of the National Counterintelligence Executive staff (March 9, 2005).

[9] In our classified report, we include statistics on the estimated Russian and Chinese intelligence presence that we cannot include in our unclassified report.

[10] *Final Report of the National Commission on Terrorist Attacks Upon the United States* (hereinafter "9/11 Commission Report") (2004) at p. 158 & nn. 54, 56; pp. 244-245 (noting al-Qa'ida's casing activities).

[11] Interview with Terrorist Threat Integration Center official (Oct. 6, 2004).

[12] Senate Committee on Homeland Security and Governmental Affairs, *The China Connection: Summary of the Committee's Findings Relating to Efforts of the People's Republic of China to Influence United States Policies and Elections* (1997) at pp. 5-9.

[13] Congress acknowledged this in 2002 when it created the NCIX and, disappointingly, not much has changed. S. Rep. No. 106-279 (2002) at p. 16 (noting inadequate coordination, cooperation, and information-sharing among agencies; a lack of strategic threat analysis; the lack of a national plan to integrate information and analysis; an inadequately prepared workforce with insufficient, diffused resources; and the lack of a national advocate and program for resources, policies, and proactive initiatives).

[14] Executive Order No. 12333 at § 1.14(a).

[15] Interview with FBI Assistant Director for Counterintelligence (Oct. 7, 2005).

[16] Executive Order No. 12333 at § 1.5(e).

[17] Interview with CIA counterintelligence official (Nov. 19, 2004).

[18] *See, e.g.,* Interview with senior official from the Office of the National Counterintelligence Executive (March 9, 2005).

[19] Interview with Department of Defense Counterintelligence and Security official (Oct. 14, 2004); Interview with Department of Defense Counterintelligence Field Activity official (Dec. 14, 2004). "The primary problem is that [Department of Defense] counterintelligence is assigned, under Title X of U.S. law, to the military services as their responsibility, controlled and conducted by them. The military services limit their counterintelligence routinely to support their own missions." Walter Jajko, "The State of Defense Counterintelligence," *Journal of U.S. Intelligence Studies* (Winter/Spring, 2004) at pp. 7-9.

[20] Department of Defense Directive No. 5105.67 (Feb. 19, 2002) at § 6.2.

[21] 50 U.S.C. at § 402b.

[22] Intelligence Authorization Act for Fiscal Year 2003 at §§ 902, 904.

[23] Intelligence Reform and Terrorism Prevention Act of 2004 at § 1011, Pub. L. No. 108-458.

[24] The concept of a Mission Manager is defined more fully in Chapter Six (Leadership and Management), Chapter Seven (Collection), and Chapter Eight (Analysis).

[25] The other exception is the director of the National Counterterrorism Center, the DNI's Mission Manager for Terrorism, who will also be responsible for producing strategic analysis.

[26] We examined other options for improving counterintelligence, but decided that a strengthened NCIX was the best and least disruptive option. Creating a separate national counterintelligence agency, for instance, would involve new legislation, a significant outlay of organizational effort and funding, and disruption of current operations.

[27] *See generally* National Intelligence Council, *Cyber Threats to the United States Infrastructure* (NIE 2004-01D/I) (Feb. 2004).

[28] Department of Defense Directive No. 5105.67 (Feb. 19, 2002) at §§ 6.2.4.1 & 6.2.9.

[29] *Id. at* § 6.2.

[30] Within the Department of Defense, counterintelligence functional support includes investigations, operations, collection, analysis, and functional services. Currently, only the Army, Navy, Air Force, and Marine Corps have authority to do all five activities.

CHAPTER TWELVE
COVERT ACTION

Most U.S. presidents have made use of covert action as an instrument of foreign policy; under appropriate and limited circumstances, it serves as a more subtle and surgical tool than acknowledged employment of U.S. power and influence. In the future, when the threats of proliferation and terrorism loom large, covert action may play an increasingly important role. The Commission conducted a careful study of U.S. covert action capabilities, with attention to the changing national security landscape and the special category of missions that involve both CIA and U.S. Special Operations Forces. Because even the most general statements about the Intelligence Community's capabilities in this area are classified, the Commission's assessments and four specific findings cannot be discussed in this report. The Commission has, however, incorporated the lessons learned from its study of covert action in all of our recommendations for reform of the Intelligence Community.

CHAPTER THIRTEEN
THE CHANGING PROLIFERATION THREAT AND THE INTELLIGENCE RESPONSE

Summary & Recommendations

The threat of chemical, biological, and nuclear weapons proliferation has transformed over the past two decades. The technical expertise required to produce these weapons has become increasingly widespread, while many of the materials needed to make them are widely available on the open market. Meanwhile, terrorists have expressed a growing demand for these weapons and demonstrated their willingness to use them. The Intelligence Community has not kept pace with these events.

Rather than attempt a top-to-bottom assessment of the chemical, biological, and nuclear weapons threat, here we focus on relatively new aspects of the threat that present specific intelligence challenges, and that—in our view—require additional Intelligence Community reforms beyond those discussed in our other chapters.

We recommend that:

- The DNI take several specific measures aimed at better collaboration between the intelligence and biological science communities;

- The National Counter Proliferation Center develop and ensure the implementation of a comprehensive biological weapons targeting strategy. This entails gaining real-time access to non-traditional information sources; filtering open source data; and devising specific collection initiatives directed at the resulting targets;

- The Intelligence Community, along with other relevant government bodies, support a more effective framework to interdict shipments of chemical, biological, and nuclear proliferation concern; and

- The Intelligence Community better leverage existing legal and regulatory mechanisms to improve collection and analysis on chemical, biological, and nuclear threats.

INTRODUCTION

We live in a world where the most deadly materials created by man are more widely available than ever before. Over the past decade or so, the proliferation of nuclear, biological, and chemical materials, and the expertise to weaponize them, has become a global growth industry.

Grim evidence of this abounds. For instance, the Soviet Union may have been relegated to the dustbin of history, but its nuclear materials—under uncertain control, and sought by rogue states and terrorists alike—still imperil our present. At the same time, terrorists who have already demonstrated their intent to attack us with anthrax seek more advanced biological and nuclear weapons. Perhaps worst of all, the biotechnology revolution is rapidly making new, previously unimagined horrors possible, raising the specter of a modern-day plague, spawned from a back room or garage anywhere in the world.

There is no single strategy the Intelligence Community can pursue to counter the "proliferation" menace. As we discuss in this chapter, any weapon capable of causing mass casualties presents a unique set of challenges. Our study of this subject indicates, however, that there are themes common to all. First, the Intelligence Community's efforts with regard to the spread of nuclear, biological, and chemical weapons have not kept up with the pace of proliferation, and urgently require improvement. We believe that catching up will likely require prioritizing counterproliferation over many other competing national security issues. It will also require more aggressive and innovative collection techniques, and the devotion of resources commensurate to the seriousness of the threat and the difficulty of the collection challenge.

Second, the Intelligence Community must reach outside its own confines to tap counterproliferation information, authorities, and expertise resident in the government and nation at large. The Community cannot expect to thwart proliferators on its own; counterproliferation is a team sport, and our squad must draw on the rest of the U.S. government and the full weight of its regulatory and diplomatic powers, as well as on scientific and technical experts from academia and private enterprise.

We begin our discussion of the proliferation problem by examining these themes within the context of the threat posed by biological weapons. Of all the potentially catastrophic threats facing the United States, those related to biological substances are changing the most quickly, metastasizing in recent years to include a variety of new potential users and substances. Unlike nuclear or chemical weapons, a biological weapon has actually been used to attack the United States, in the form of the anthrax attacks of 2001. In our view, biological weapons are also the mass casualty threat the Intelligence Community is least prepared to face. We therefore have focused on developing recommendations that can immediately improve our capabilities in this area—by bringing into the Community much-needed scientific experience, sharpening collection techniques, and harnessing regulatory authorities to bolster intelligence efforts.

We then survey the threat landscape with regard to nuclear and chemical weapons, and follow this with a series of recommendations designed to improve overall Intelligence Community support to the interdiction of materials of proliferation concern. We close with recommendations that recognize the importance of more generally leveraging legal and regulatory mechanisms to aid in the service of intelligence.

The stakes for the Intelligence Community with regard to all weapons of mass destruction are self-evidently high. It is not hyperbole to suggest that the lives of millions, and the very fabric and fate of our society, may depend on the way in which the Community is configured, and the powers it can bring to bear against the challenges posed by proliferation. Our recommendations do not purport to solve the proliferation problem; no commission can claim to do that. We do hope, however, that the recommendations can help better configure the Community to cope with an increasingly fluid and volatile threat environment.

BIOLOGICAL WEAPONS

Introduction: "The Greatest Intelligence Challenge"

For many years, the U.S. intelligence and policy communities did not take the biological weapons threat as seriously as the dangers posed by nuclear weapons. Many felt that states might experiment with biological weapons, but would not use them against the United States for fear of nuclear retaliation. Similarly, terrorists who promised to bring "plagues" upon the United States were thought to be merely indulging in grandiose threats; they lacked the technical expertise to actually develop and deploy a biological weapon.

These views changed suddenly in September and October of 2001 when anthrax attacks in the United States killed five people, crippled mail delivery in several cities for over a year,[1] and required decontamination efforts costing more than $1 billion.[2] The still-unsolved attack was striking in its asymmetry: the anthrax could have been produced for less than $2,500.[3]

Even more striking is how lucky we were. A determined terrorist group could do far worse with only a little more effort and a bit of luck. Even allowing for imperfect dissemination techniques, if a gram of the same anthrax used in the 2001 attacks had been disseminated outdoors in an urban area, between 100 and 1,000 people would likely have been infected, and many would have died.[4] A kilogram might infect tens of thousands of people.[5] And because biological weapons have a delayed effect, terrorists could execute multiple or campaign-style attacks before the first attack is even noticed and the warning sounded.[6]

We are concerned that terrorist groups may be developing biological weapons and may be willing to use them. Even more worrisome, in the near future, the biotechnology revolution will make even more potent and sophisticated weapons available to small or relatively unsophisticated groups.

In response to this mounting threat, the Intelligence Community's performance has been disappointing. Its analyses of state and non-state biological weapons programs often rest on assumptions unsupported by data. This is in large part because traditional collection methods do not work well, or at all, against biological threats. Even though scientists, academics, and government officials routinely describe an attack with biological weapons as one of the most terrifying and probable disasters the United States faces, the Intelligence Community is lagging behind in looking for new collection strategies, and has not sought sufficient help outside the halls of intelligence agencies. The Community cannot defeat what one senior policymaker told us was "the greatest intelligence challenge" by itself.[7]

We recommend three ways of changing the Intelligence Community's overall approach to biological weapons: (1) better coordination with the biological sciences community; (2) more aggressive, targeted approaches to intelligence collection; and (3) effective use of new regulatory mechanisms to create collection opportunities.

Biological Threats[*]

Terrorism

Despite the possibility that terrorists have gained access to biological weapons, a large bioterrorist attack has not yet occurred. Why not? First, executing a large-scale biological attack is still fairly difficult as a technical matter; it requires organization and long-term planning. Second, biological agents can be highly infectious; working with them is dangerous. Finally, the war on terrorism may have derailed nascent attack plans. But these thin lines of defense are rapidly eroding. Some terrorist groups may have the financial resources to purchase scientific expertise. Even without sophisticated expertise, a crude delivery system would be sufficient to inflict mass disruption and economic damage.[8] Moreover, extremists willing to die in a suicide bombing are not likely to be deterred by the dangers of working with biological weapons. As a result, a senior intelligence official told the Commission that we should consider ourselves "lucky" we have not yet suffered a major biological attack.[9] And the terrorist threat will only grow, as biological weapons are rapidly becoming cheaper, easier to produce, and more effective.

States

States pose another biological weapons threat, and the weapons they produce are potentially more sophisticated—and therefore more lethal—than those made by terrorists. We can only speculate as to why countries have not yet used biological weapons on a large scale. In part, there is the risk of blowback—infection could spread to the state's own population. The United States may also be protected by the threat that it will respond violently to a biological attack. As President Nixon said when he terminated the United States biological weapons program and embraced an international ban, "We'll never use the damn germs, so what good is biological warfare as a deterrent? If somebody uses germs on us, we'll nuke 'em."[10]

Covert use, however, is an entirely different matter. If the United States is attacked with biological weapons and cannot identify the attacker, the threat of nuclear retaliation will be of little use. States might attack the United States or its military installations overseas and avoid retaliation by posing as terrorists. If the spread of illness is the first sign that such an attack has taken

---

[*] The classified version of this section contains a more detailed discussion of the nature of the biological weapons threat, and also provides examples that could not be included in an unclassified report.

place, the U.S. government may have difficulty responding effectively. In many attack simulations, U.S. biodefense capabilities struggle to simultaneously administer medical countermeasures, quarantine infected individuals, and decontaminate large areas.[11]

Biotechnology

A third biological weapons threat lies not far in the future. Terrorists may soon be able to cause mass casualties that are now possible only for state-run biological weapons programs. Scientists can already engineer biological weapons agents to enhance their lethality either through genetic engineering or other manipulations.[12] Such weapons of science fiction may soon become a fact. Given the exponential growth in this field and access to its insights through the Internet, our vulnerability to the threat might be closer at hand than we suspect.

The Intelligence Gap: What We Don't Know

The Intelligence Community has struggled to understand the biological weapons threat. According to a senior official in CIA's Counterproliferation Division, "We don't know more about the biological weapons threat than we did five years ago, and five years from now we will know even less."[13]

Analysis: Assumptions Abound

Assessments of state and non-state programs rely heavily on assumptions about potential biological weapons agents, biological weapons-adaptable delivery systems, and fragmentary threat reporting. Unsurprisingly, this leads to faulty assessments. For example, in October 2002, the Intelligence Community estimated with "high confidence" that Iraq had an active biological weapons program.[14] Yet the Iraq Survey Group's post-war investigation "found no direct evidence that Iraq had plans for a new biological weapons program or was conducting biological weapons-specific work for military purposes" after 1996.[15] In Afghanistan, the story is the reverse. Despite suspicions that al-Qa'ida had biological weapons intentions, the Intelligence Community was unaware of the ambitious scope of its efforts.[16]

Biological weapons analysis also suffers from the litany of problems we have identified elsewhere in our report, including insufficient outreach to technical experts in the CIA's Directorate of Science and Technology and the Department of Energy's National Labs, as well as those in the business community,

public heath sector, and academia.[17] With limited interaction between technical experts and political analysts, the Intelligence Community "does a poor
job of matching capabilities with intent" to develop realistic biological attack
scenarios for state and non-state actors alike.[18] As one National Intelligence
Officer told us, biological weapons analysts have an "institutional bias against
creative war-gaming" and rarely engage in systematic testing of alternative
hypotheses.[19]

Collection: Continued Frustration and a Glimmer of Hope[**]

The weaknesses of analysis, however, pale beside the Intelligence Community's inability to collect against the biological weapons target. We found that
the Community's biological weapons collection woes result from both the
technological limits of traditional collection methods and a poorly focused
collection process that is ill-equipped to gather and sort through the wealth of
information that could help alert the Community to crucial indicators of biological weapons activity. In our classified report, we discuss these intelligence
collection limitations at length; unfortunately, these details cannot be included
in our unclassified report.

At bottom, the gap in collection on the biological threat is largely attributable
to the fact that the Community is simply not well configured to monitor the
large stream of information—much of it publicly available—relevant to biological weapons. In our classified report, we illustrate how considerable information about al-Qa'ida's pre-war biological weapons program in Afghanistan
could have been known through public or government sources; we cannot,
however, provide these details in an unclassified format. We emphasize here
simply that the Community must focus on doing a better job of collecting and
connecting similar indicators of biological weapons personnel and activity in
the future. Moreover, as we point out in our Chapter Eight (Analysis), it is
essential that the Community improves its access to and use of open source
intelligence—the challenges posed by the biological weapons threat reinforce
that conclusion.

However, before the Community can begin to effectively monitor such vital
indicators of biological activity, it must develop a basic understanding of the
threat landscape. We were disappointed to discover that, three-and-a-half

---

[**]A considerable majority of information contained in this section of our classified report
could not be discussed in an unclassified format.

---

years following the anthrax attacks, the Intelligence Community has still not taken many of the most rudimentary steps necessary for this sort of collection. In our classified report, we offer examples of how particular intelligence agencies have failed to take these steps, but these details cannot be discussed in an unclassified format. We also describe a (classified) nascent effort at CIA that we believe to be worthy of praise. In all events, the Intelligence Community must ensure that any new efforts support a comprehensive collection effort across different regions, groups, and biological threats. Just as in other areas of intelligence, agencies at times jealously guard their most sought-after information. This fragmentation and parochialism highlights the importance of integrating the government's efforts against proliferators as well as the need for naming a deputy to the Proliferation Mission Manager, as recommended below, to focus exclusively on biological weapons issues.

The United States Response: The Biodefense Shield

Although resources have flowed freely into biodefense since the 2001 anthrax attacks, only a fraction of these resources has gone to funding new intelligence collection strategies.[20] A senior official at the National Security Council laments that, with regard to biological weapons intelligence, "there's still a sense that it's too hard to do."[21] Although future biodefense technologies and medical countermeasures may allow the United States to neutralize the effects of biological attack, intelligence is one of the few tools today that holds out hope of avoiding attack, rather than just limiting the damage. Biodefense is critical, but it should not be our first line of defense. As a senior Centers for Disease Control and Prevention (CDC) official states, we "need to move upstream from the event"—a reactive biological weapons posture will not suffice.[22]

One positive outgrowth of U.S. biodefense programs is that they have bred new intelligence customers, beyond the traditional military and foreign policy users. Technical experts, who include the CDC, Department of Homeland Security, the United States Army Medical Research Institute for Infectious Diseases (USAMRIID), the National Institute for Allergies and Infectious Diseases (part of the National Institutes of Health, or NIH), and the Department of Agriculture, now need biological weapons threat information to inform their biodefense efforts.[23] The existence of these customers presents an opportunity to encourage more focused biological weapons intelligence, and in turn to provide the Intelligence Community with much needed expertise.

Regrettably, new biodefense customers are largely unaware of what intelligence can bring to the table. A senior NIH official, for example, expressed frustration with the quality of biological weapons intelligence that NIH receives, as well as the lack of a structured venue for receiving and assessing such information. This has made the effort to set vaccine research and development priorities more difficult and, worse yet, may have divorced vaccine research from what is known about the current threat.[24] Yet at the same time, demonstrating the cultural gap that still divides the biodefense and intelligence communities, this same official expressed immediate reluctance when told that NIH could perform its own intelligence analysis of open sources to identify the most likely biological threats.[25]

CIA analysts observe that their agency in particular does a poor job of interacting with outside experts,[26] but there are promising initiatives elsewhere within the Community. One effort aimed at increasing such interaction is the Defense Intelligence Agency's Bio-Chem 2020, a small-scale attempt at discussing emerging biotechnology threats with outside experts, usually at the unclassified or secret level. These scientists publish periodic papers on general biological threats rather than reviewing specific biological weapons analysis.[27] A senior National Security Council official praises Bio-Chem 2020 but is quick to note that it is a "cottage program," not part of a broader Intelligence Community endeavor.[28] Another useful initiative is a plan for a National Interagency Biodefense Campus at Fort Detrick, Maryland, with personnel from USAMRIID, NIH, and the Departments of Agriculture and Homeland Security. The campus, which is designed to coordinate biodefense research and serve as a central repository for expertise, will not be complete until 2008.[29] In our view, the culture gap between the biological science and defense communities is so large that housing them together is essential to fostering a common strategy. The extent of Intelligence Community participation at the campus, however, remains undetermined.[30]

Going Forward: Improving Biological Weapons Intelligence Capabilities

If the Intelligence Community does not improve its foreign and domestic collection capabilities for biological weapons, the risk of catastrophe will only grow. We see a need for three broad changes: (1) tighter Intelligence Community coordination with the biological science community both inside government and out; (2) far more emphasis on integrated and aggressive intelligence targeting; and (3) stronger regulatory efforts to control potential biological weapons technologies, which would enable more intelligence collection than any go-it-alone effort by the Intelligence Community.

Working with the Biological Science Community

Recommendation 1

The DNI should create a Community-wide National Biodefense Initiative to include a Biological Science Advisory Group, a government service program for biologists and health professionals, a post-doctoral fellowship program in biodefense and intelligence, and a scholarship program for graduate students in biological weapons-relevant fields.

When an intelligence analyst wants to understand a foreign nuclear weapons program, the analyst can draw on the expertise of thousands of Americans, all of whom understand how to run a nuclear program—because that is what they do, day in and day out. If an analyst wants the same insight into biological weapons programs, working bio-weaponeers are simply not available. The last offensive American biological weapons program ended 35 years ago.

The United States faced a similar dilemma in the late 1950s with regard to nuclear physics. The World War II physicists at Los Alamos were aging, and the younger generation did not have strong ties to the U.S. government. In response, the Defense Department founded the JASONs, an elite group of distinguished nuclear scientists that interacts with senior policymakers, receives intelligence briefings, and provides classified studies on pressing national security issues.[31] Considering the number of Nobel laureates in the group, the opportunity for rising stars to interact with leading scientists in their field, and the financial compensation that members receive, membership to the JASONs remains highly coveted.

According to a CIA report summarizing a conference of life science experts, "a qualitatively different relationship between the government and life sciences communities might be needed to most effectively grapple with the future biological weapons threat."[32] Although DIA's Bio-Chem 2020 is a successful interaction mechanism with academia and the private sector, it is insufficient compared to what is required. The Intelligence Community needs more consistent advice than that provided by unpaid professionals, and more contemporary advice than that provided by intelligence scientists who have not published research in over a decade.

We therefore recommend that the new DNI create a National Biodefense Initiative composed of several programs aimed at strengthening the Intelligence Community's biological weapons expertise. Such an initiative could be composed of the following four components:

■ An elite Biological Sciences Advisory Group, administered by the DNI's Director of Science and Technology, which would be composed of the nation's leading life science experts. The group would be compensated for their work and asked to examine and advise the DNI on biological threats;

■ A part-time government service program for select biologists and health professionals to review biological weapons analysis and answer Community queries;

■ A post-doctoral fellowship program that funds scientists for one to two years of unclassified research relevant to biodefense and biological weapons intelligence; and

■ A scholarship program that rewards graduate students in the biological weapons-relevant hard sciences in exchange for intelligence service upon completion of their degrees.

Recommendation 2

The DNI should use the Joint Intelligence Community Council to form a Biological Weapons Working Group. This Working Group would serve as the principal coordination venue for the Intelligence Community and biodefense agencies, including the Department of Homeland Security's National Biodefense and Countermeasures Center, NIH, CDC, the Department of Agriculture, and USAMRIID.

In addition to reaching *outside* the government to develop a more robust and mutually beneficial relationship with the biological science community, the Intelligence Community needs more effective links with biological experts and authorities inside the government. Nurturing this relationship will help ensure that relevant science is informing actual intelligence collection and better serving new customers. We believe that the DNI could utilize the Joint Intelligence Community Council, established by the intelligence reform legislation, to convene a working group of agencies with interest in biological weapons intelligence to serve as a kind of "consumer council."[33] This working group would have the added benefit of helping both sides—the intelligence and biological science communities—understand the needs of the other so that they can more effectively work in parallel. The DNI might consider moving the biological weapons working group, or other biological weapons intelligence units, to the National Interagency Biodefense Campus once it is completed in 2008.

Targeting Biological Weapons Threats

Recommendation 3

The DNI should create a deputy within the National Counter Proliferation Center who is specifically responsible for biological weapons; this deputy would be responsible to the Proliferation Mission Manager to ensure the implementation of a comprehensive biological weapons targeting strategy and direct new collection initiatives.

As our previous discussion of the Community's collection woes starkly illustrates, the Intelligence Community needs more aggressive, targeted approaches to intelligence collection on biological threats. Systematic targeting of potential biological weapons personnel and programs is critical. CIA's Directorate of Science and Technology is funding some promising efforts, but they remain in their initial stages, and the Directorate lacks the authority to implement a program across the Community. Much more needs to be done.

First, the Intelligence Community needs a targeted, managed, and directed strategy for biological weapons intelligence. We strongly suggest designating an office within the NCPC to handle biological weapons specifically. It is also essential that this designee (or deputy) for biological weapons work in tandem with his or her counterparts at the National Counterterrorism Center.

With visibility across the Intelligence Community, the biological weapons deputy in the National Counter Proliferation Center (NCPC) could draw on different pockets of relevant expertise. But if CIA's Directorate of Operations

(DO) is any kind of microcosm of the biological weapons intelligence world, then a daunting task lies ahead. Within the DO, the Counterterrorist Center collects against bioterrorism; the Counterproliferation Division collects against most state biological weapons programs, and the geographic area divisions collect against the remainder.[34] Such fragmentation leaves serious potential gaps.[35]

Devising and implementing a biological weapons targeting strategy will require not only that the Intelligence Community begin to think as a whole, but also that the Intelligence Community think beyond itself. Part of the challenge involves drawing on personnel and databases housed in non-Intelligence Community agencies such as Commerce's Bureau of Industry and Security and Homeland Security's Customs and Border Protection. Data from non-intelligence sources needs to be cross-referenced with the Intelligence Community's biological weapons databases, and filtered through a set of developed biological weapons indicators to direct intelligence collection. FBI and Homeland Security personnel need training in intelligence targeting and access to this system to identify homeland threats.

A comprehensive and strategic approach to biological weapons targeting will also involve open source exploitation to drive collection and warning strategies, and a multi-year research and development plan for the development and deployment of emerging collection technologies. In our classified report, we offer several suggestions for improving the Intelligence Community's capabilities which cannot be discussed in an unclassified format. Elements within the Community deserve praise for having taken steps to implement these suggestions.

It is our hope that through a Target Development Board, the NCPC's deputy for biological weapons can drive the Intelligence Community to pursue the necessary multifaceted collection approach. We encourage the Community to continue to explore and develop new approaches to collection, and we expect that these efforts would be dramatically furthered by the Mission Manager and Target Development Board devices.

Leveraging Regulation for Biological Weapons Intelligence

Recommendation 4

The National Security Council should form a Joint Interagency Task Force to develop a counter-biological weapons plan within 90 days that draws upon all elements of national power, including law enforcement and the regulatory capabilities of the Departments of Homeland Security, Health and Human Services, Commerce, and State.

The United States should look outside of intelligence channels for enforcement mechanisms that can provide new avenues of international cooperation and resulting opportunities for intelligence collection. The National Counter Proliferation Center will be able to do a great deal to expand outreach to the biological science, biodefense, and public health sectors, but an even broader effort is required to draw on departments and agencies outside of the Intelligence Community. We believe the National Security Council or perhaps the Homeland Security Council is the most appropriate venue for convening different national security elements to devise such national-level strategies. Intelligence will be able to most effectively operate in a national security environment that is organized around and cognizant of its combined efforts to work against the biothreat.

We suggest that the Joint Interagency Task Force consider, as part of its development of a counter-biological weapons plan, the following two recommendations—which involve developing beneficial relationships with foreign states and applying regulatory powers to foreign entities that do business with the United States.

Recommendation 5

The State Department should aggressively support foreign criminalization of biological weapons development and the establishment of biosafety and biosecurity regulations under the framework of the United Nations Security Council Resolution 1540. U.S. law enforcement and intelligence agencies should jointly sponsor biological weapons information sharing events with foreign police forces.

Developing close relationships with foreign governments on the biological weapons issue will be imperative if the United States is to better achieve its goals of monitoring and containing biological threats. Perhaps most importantly, the United States can bring its powers of suasion to bear on states to adopt domestic legislation that criminalizes biological weapons and establishes domestic controls to prevent proliferation—as they are obligated to do under the terms of United Nations Security Council Resolution 1540.

Criminalization will facilitate cooperation from liaison services, which are more likely to assist the United States in contexts where their domestic laws are violated. U.S. law enforcement and intelligence agencies should make cooperation with foreign officials a priority, and should establish regular information sharing events with foreign police forces to assist them in honing their awareness of the biological weapons threat and encouraging cooperation.

Recommendation 6

The United States should remain actively engaged in designing and implementing both international and regulatory inspection regimes. It should consider extending its existing biosecurity and biosafety regulations to foreign institutions with commercial ties to the United States, using the possibility of increased liability, reduced patent protection, or more burdensome and costly inspections to encourage compliance with appropriate safeguards.

International inspections will—at least with respect to state programs—remain an important counterproliferation tool in the future.[36] Arguably, designing effective inspection regimes will become all the more critical in a future where proliferation increasingly involves countries with small (and therefore difficult to detect) chemical, biological, and nuclear weapons programs. The benefits to having on-the-ground access to suspect facilities could be substantial.

There is little prospect in the near future for an international biological weapons inspection regime, however. The United States should therefore seek to obtain some of the benefits of inspections through the use of creative regulatory approaches. One such approach would involve a traditional regulatory model of imposing obligations on international businesses. The approach would build on Executive Order 12938 as amended,[37] which directs the Secretary of Treasury to prohibit the importation into the United States of products produced by a foreign person or company who "materially contributed or attempted to contribute to" the development, production, stockpiling, or acquisition of weapons of mass destruction.[38] More vigorous enforcement of this order would begin to reduce the biological weapons proliferation vulnerabilities that arise through lax internal controls in the private sector.

How might such a regime work? All companies that handle dangerous pathogens could be required to meet security standards and provide data about their facilities, as is already being done inside the United States. This need not be a unilateral undertaking. Objections from major trading partners could be reduced through cooperative inspection agreements with, for example, the United States, the European Union, and Japan. Compliance by individual companies could be ensured with a mix of carrot and stick—such as "fast lane" border controls, whereby companies that adhere to United States standards are granted speedier customs processing at our ports and airports; with the possibility of reduced liability protections and patent protections for the uncooperative.

Conclusion

Improvements in intelligence are no guarantee against a successful biological attack, but they could make such an attack substantially less likely to succeed. There are no perfect solutions, but there are better solutions than the ones we have today. For now, better is all we can do. Given the potential costs of a biological weapons attack, better is what we must do.

NUCLEAR WEAPONS

Introduction

For the Cold War-era Intelligence Community, the challenge of nuclear proliferation was menacing but manageable. The Community focused primarily on intelligence collection against a few states seeking to join the "Nuclear Club"—with an especially watchful eye directed toward states aligned with the Soviet Union.

Although tracking proliferation developments was an important and large-scale enterprise, the world's accumulated storehouse of nuclear material and knowledge was relatively well accounted for (at least internally) by nuclear states. Moreover, the number of potential nuclear proliferators and their prospective state clients were relatively few, and the potential pathways for transferring nuclear material were reasonably well known and could be monitored—in theory at least—by traditional collection platforms.

Today's nuclear proliferation threat is much more diverse, and the challenges are more difficult. The state-based threat remains, and has been joined by the nightmarish possibility that non-state actors like terrorist groups could obtain a nuclear weapon or a "dirty bomb" and detonate it in the heart of a major American city.[39] Simultaneously, the sources of nuclear materials and expertise have themselves dramatically proliferated. The breakup of the Soviet Union has left a large body of poorly secured, dubiously inventoried nuclear materials and weapons, about which the Community knows precious little. Meanwhile, shadowy, non-state proliferation networks have appeared, quietly peddling their products to the highest bidder. These new nuclear proliferators and their customers operate under a veil of secrecy, including the use of front companies to mask their intentions and movements. It is the misfortune of our age to witness the globalization of trade in the ultimate weapon of mass destruction.

There are many facets to the nuclear proliferation problem; here we focus on but two of the most important—the availability of unsecured nuclear weapons and materials, or "loose nukes," and the appearance of non-state nuclear "brokers." We believe that the Intelligence Community must do much more to improve its collection capabilities with regard to both, for the purpose of halting nuclear proliferation at the *source*. That said, we recognize the inherent difficulty of both targets, as well as the limitations on our ability to contribute much in the way of concrete operational recommendations as to how the community can improve in this regard (other than the understandable, but rather unhelpful, advice, to "try harder" and "spend more" on the endeavor). Consequently, as we discuss later in this chapter, our recommendations focus on improving the process for interdicting nuclear materials once they are in transit from the proliferators or, as a last resort, on their way to the United States.

Loose Nukes: The Great Unknown

The single greatest hurdle to a terrorist's fabrication of a nuclear device is the acquisition of weapons-usable nuclear material.[40] If terrorists are able to procure such material intact, they can skip this most difficult part of the nuclear weapons development cycle. Just as Willie Sutton robbed banks "because that's where the money is," terrorist groups are most likely seeking nuclear material from the former Soviet Union because that is where the most material is available.[41] (Additional information concerning terrorist efforts to obtain nuclear material is presented in the classified report but cannot be discussed here.) Tracking this nuclear material in the former Soviet Union is exceedingly difficult. However, we would like to emphasize that the United States has not made collection on loose nukes a high priority.

In our classified report we discuss in greater detail the reasons why our efforts to collect intelligence in this area have struggled, and we offer suggestions for improvement that cannot be discussed in an unclassified format. While we have generally shied away from simply recommending "more" effort or funding, we believe that some of these techniques may require additional funding.

The loose nukes problem is in many ways indicative of problems facing the Intelligence Community as a whole. Analysts and collectors are too consumed with daily intelligence requirements to formulate or implement new approaches. The war on terrorism and ongoing military operations have distracted the Community from longer-term threats of critical importance to national security. The perception is that there is no "crisis" until a weapon or fissile material is stolen. The problem, of course, is that we might not know this was the case until we are jolted by news of a catastrophe in Washington, D.C. or midtown Manhattan.

Established Nuclear Powers: China & Russia

While the discussion in this section has focused on the emerging intelligence challenges resulting from the proliferation of nuclear weapons and related materials, we recognize that the traditional threat of nuclear weapons in the hands of determined state adversaries remains alive and well and requires the continued attention of policymakers and the Intelligence Community. The nuclear arsenals and emerging capabilities of China and Russia, in particular, pose a challenge to the United States—a challenge about which the Intelligence Community today knows too little. In our classified report we detail some of the struggles the Intelligence Community has had in developing information about these more traditional targets—but we cannot elaborate upon our findings in this area in this report.

The Khan Network: "One-Stop Shopping" for Proliferation

Private proliferators and the "grey market" for nuclear trafficking pose another emerging threat. States no longer have a monopoly on sophisticated nuclear technology, materials, and expertise. The insecurity of nuclear materials, combined with diffusion of the technical knowledge necessary to construct or assemble a nuclear device, has resulted in a burgeoning industry for entrepreneurial middlemen. As demonstrated in our Libya case study, this threat requires new intelligence approaches.

Former Director of Central Intelligence George Tenet has spoken publicly about the "emerging threat" posed by private proliferators like A.Q. Khan.[42] As the father of Pakistan's atomic bomb, Khan helped pioneer the practice of clandestine nuclear procurement. Through front companies, subsidiaries, and a network that stretched from Pakistan to Europe,[43] Khan sought to provide countries with "one-stop shopping" for nuclear goods. We now know that Khan's network supplied nuclear equipment and expertise that "shav[ed] years off the nuclear weapons development timelines of several states including Libya."[44] Among other things, Khan's network supplied Libya with nuclear centrifuge technology.[45]

Working alongside British counterparts, CIA's Directorate of Operations was able to penetrate and unravel many of Khan's activities through human spies. They deserve great credit for this impressive success. However, the effort dedicated to bringing down the network demonstrates how rare and hard-fought future successes may be. It is possible, although unlikely, that Khan is unique. Private dealers, after all, control many of the materials needed for nuclear weapons production.

The A.Q. Khan achievement also suggests that the Intelligence Community will meet with limited success if it acts alone. Combating proliferation networks requires insight into the networks' modes of operation; for example, understanding the front companies through which they operate. As we discuss more fully in the interdiction section below, the Intelligence Community must reach out to non-traditional partners elsewhere in the government to augment its own capabilities.

Conclusion

There is little more frightening than the thought of terrorists detonating a nuclear device within the United States. And events of the past decade—including the questionable security of former-Soviet nuclear material, the emergence of private proliferation threats like A.Q. Khan, and the rise of terrorist groups determined to strike U.S. territory—have added to the threat. Furthermore, there is no good reason to expect that North Korea and Iran will be the last states to try to acquire nuclear weapons. Indeed, acquisition by these two countries might set off a cascade of efforts by others in East Asia and the Middle East. (Nor is there a good reason to expect that states of concern will only be the neighbors of these two countries and others possessing nuclear weapons. It is worth remembering that South Africa, remote in many ways from the central regions of the Cold War, made them.) We believe that our recommendations for reform discussed elsewhere in the report, in combination with this chapter's discussion of intelligence support to interdiction and leveraging regulatory mechanisms for intelligence, will at least help the Intelligence Community be as prepared as it can be.

CHEMICAL WEAPONS

Even when unintentionally released, poisonous chemicals can have terrible effects. An accidental release of poisonous gas from a chemical plant in Bhopal, India, killed thousands in 1984.[46] Deliberate chemical attacks, of course, have the potential to be even worse. In 1995, the Japanese cult Aum Shinrikyo released the chemical nerve agent sarin on the Tokyo subway, killing twelve people, sending more than 5,500 to the hospital, and sowing fear throughout the city.[47] Commentators attributed the relatively low number of fatalities to the poor quality of the agent and Aum Shinrikyo's inefficient dispersal devices.[48] In our classified report, we offer further examples of suspected chemical weapons plots that cannot be discussed in an unclassified format.

While biological and nuclear weapons could cause the worst damage, terrorists could kill thousands of Americans by simply sabotaging industrial chemical facilities. And, due to the large volume and easy accessibility of toxic chemicals in the United States, a chemical attack causing mass casualties may be more likely than a nuclear or biological attack in the near term.

As with biological and nuclear threats, the Intelligence Community is poorly positioned to meet the challenges posed by chemical weapons. Historically, it has focused on state programs and has only recently turned its attention to potential uses of chemical weapons by terrorist groups. The Community's task is complicated by the ubiquity of toxic chemicals—which are available for sale across the United States and the world—and the relative ease with which other, even more deadly substances can be manufactured from common chemical precursors. Moreover, given the increasing sophistication of the chemical industry and the various dual uses of its products, the Community will face an increasingly difficult task in differentiating legitimate from potentially hostile manufacturing efforts. Finally, as is the case with biological weapons, many small-scale chemical production facilities can be concealed in nondescript facilities that are not easily detectable through conventional collection means, such as imagery.

The Intelligence Community certainly needs to do everything possible to collect on the plans and intentions of those terrorist groups that would use chemical weapons in an attack on the United States. Moreover, because of the easy accessibility of toxic chemicals and chemical precursors, it is essential that the Community develop strong links with the FBI, which may be better suited to monitor and respond to suspicious purchases of chemicals on the state and local level and to interface with local law enforcement for the same purpose.

Such traditional intelligence activities are necessary. But as our discussion about nuclear proliferation above demonstrates, traditional methods of intelligence collection have not proved particularly adept at monitoring "loose nukes," and there are serious questions as to whether the Community will be able to detect and disrupt new, diffuse proliferation networks that acquire and traffic in nuclear materials. Without admitting defeat, we must acknowledge the possibility that nuclear materials and perhaps nuclear weapons will find their way into the international transportation stream; bound for terrorists or rogue states, who will in turn attempt to bring them to the United States. A similarly disturbing state of affairs exists with regard to chemical weapons— as the sheer volume and availability of chemicals at home and abroad indicate that it is likely such weapons or materials will come into the hands of those who would do us harm.

As a result, it seems clear that in addition to improving its traditional collection capabilities, the Intelligence Community should also focus on improving its capabilities with regard to directly supporting interdiction activities, both inside and out of the United States, and to fully utilizing the regulatory and legal mechanisms at our disposal for controlling proliferators. It is to these tasks that we now turn.

THE INTERDICTION CHALLENGE: INTELLIGENCE FOR ACTION

Introduction

The United States has articulated a broad and aggressive policy that emphasizes the seizure or disruption of proliferation-related materials bound for states or individuals.[49] However, the Intelligence Community is currently ill-equipped to support this policy. As one senior national security official told the Commission, counterproliferation interdiction requires "a whole intelligence support mechanism...that we don't have."[50]

First, the Intelligence Community must collect information from a wide variety of non-traditional sources, ranging from customs officials to private parties. Second, the Community must provide information to a wide variety of non-traditional customers, ranging from foreign partners to law enforcement. But perhaps most importantly, the intelligence process—collection, analysis, and dissemination—must be much faster and more action-oriented than has traditionally been the case. If intelligence officials detect information about an illicit nuclear shipment, they cannot wait weeks for their analytical units to produce "finished intelligence," or for policy entities to approve an interdiction response. In this regard, support to interdiction must resemble counterterrorism or counternarcotics intelligence support; it must be quick, integrated, and accurate.

In this section we will address the broad theme of intelligence support to the interdiction of weapons of mass destruction, and make recommendations designed to address these basic requirements. We propose a new model for coordinating and executing interdiction, as well as several specific suggestions that could improve the Community's collection efforts and help to protect our borders.

Although the discussion below could apply to any weapon of mass destruction, in the near-term it is likely to pertain primarily to nuclear devices and chemical materials; detection and interdiction of biological substances is particularly difficult given the dual-use nature of biological equipment and the lack of discernible signatures attributed to biological materials. As was demonstrated in 2001, a biological weapon can be effectively delivered, undetected, in an envelope.

Improving the Flow of Information

To support interdiction, the Community must tap into a wide variety of information networks that are, in many cases, outside of the Intelligence Community. Counterterrorism and counternarcotics intelligence have already taken significant steps in this regard. Counterproliferation intelligence must follow suit.

One critical information source is the Department of Homeland Security, which controls several databases that can help tip off analysts and operators looking for proliferation targets. For example, two main components of Homeland Security—Immigration and Customs Enforcement (ICE) and Customs and Border Protection (CBP)—operate a variety of databases that follow flows of people and goods across U.S. borders. These databases provide a rich source of data for relationship mapping and link-analysis among foreign companies and individuals. Yet our interviews with operators have revealed serious information sharing problems between Homeland Security and the Intelligence Community that dramatically limit their usefulness. Our classified report offers examples of these information sharing difficulties and of one successful program run by the Office of Naval Intelligence.

Developing Tools to Do It in Real Time

Effective interdiction also requires that policymakers and operators have new analytical tools that can extract information from the Intelligence Community in real time.[51] Ships carrying nuclear material will not wait for a lengthy analysis to run its course before delivering their cargoes.

For example, to support counternarcotics interdictions Joint Interagency Task Force-South has link-analysis tools that, if shared on a government-wide basis, would permit operators to quickly establish connections among terrorist organizations, proliferation networks, and other dubious international activities.[52] Rather than starting with such existing assets, nearly every intelligence, law enforcement, or military entity involved in counterproliferation is also developing similar tools. A National Security Council-commissioned report by the Community's Collection Concepts Development Center concluded in November 2003 that these efforts composed a "'Balkan gaggle' of sometimes redundant programs with little coordination and incomplete operational integration."[53] The DNI should use his authority to encourage development of these tools and coordinate agency efforts.

Carrying out effective interdictions also requires real time awareness of activities in the sea and the air.[54] The Coast Guard's Maritime Domain Awareness program and the recent National Security Presidential Directive articulating a Maritime Security Policy are steps in the right direction.[55] There is also an urgent need to share at least some portion of our air and maritime domain awareness information, and our computer-based tools, with international partners who will assist the United States in carrying out interdictions.

The scope of these activities demonstrates that successful interdiction requires a vision that stretches far beyond the Intelligence Community. To restate one of the primary themes we found in our study of proliferation: the Intelligence Community cannot win this battle on its own. Coordination and integration will be necessary.[56]

Going Forward: A Different Model

Currently, interdiction efforts are not sufficiently coordinated across agencies. This is particularly true with respect to operational planning and execution. We do not believe that the National Security Council is the proper locale for managing daily operations—counterproliferation or otherwise. Although the National Security Council plays a critical role in helping to develop government-wide counterproliferation policy, it should not become the center for interagency operations as the United States ramps up its interdiction capability.

Recommendation 7

The President should establish a Counterproliferation Joint Interagency Task Force to conduct counterproliferation interdiction operations; to detect, monitor, and handoff suspected proliferation targets; and to coordinate interagency and partner nations' counterproliferation activities.

A new Joint Interagency Task Force for counterproliferation would fill the role of planning and executing interdiction operations, drawing on the full range of military, law enforcement, and intelligence capabilities of the United States. Ideally, a Counterproliferation Joint Interagency Task Force would be flexible enough to support the operational needs of U.S. Strategic Command[57] or any other entity tasked with stopping, seizing, or destroying a given cargo.[58] The Task Force would contain diplomatic, military, intelligence, law enforcement, and other representatives from across the government. We recommend that it:

- Plan and execute the full range of overt and clandestine interdiction operations;

- Seek approval from the National Security Council for interdiction operational plans through the real-time decisionmaking process described below;

- Provide tactical and operational intelligence, air, and sea support to the Department of Defense Unified Commands to carry out particular operations;

- Establish the legal basis for all interdiction operations, including through agreements with consenting private sector actors and partner nations that have signed ship-boarding agreements;

- Coordinate country team and partner nation initiatives in order to defeat the flow of materials of proliferation concern; and

- Conduct regular interdiction gaming exercises with international partners to develop new operational plans and concepts.

Recommendation 8

The DNI should designate the National Counter Proliferation Center as the Intelligence Community's leader for interdiction-related issues and direct the Center to support the all-source intelligence needs of the Counterproliferation Joint Interagency Task Force, the National Security Council, and other customers.

As described in Chapter Six (Leadership and Management), our proposed National Counter Proliferation Center (NCPC) will serve a variety of functions. With regard to interdiction, the NCPC will fulfill the requirements of the Counterproliferation Joint Interagency Task Force, the National Security Council, and a growing body of counterproliferation intelligence users. Through a Target Development Board, the NCPC would prioritize and target for interdiction those proliferation networks of greatest strategic concern. Finally, the NCPC would ensure that the Intelligence Community provides the Task Force and the National Security Council with real-time proliferation intelligence support.

Recommendation 9

The President should establish, probably through a National Security Presidential Directive, a real-time, interagency decisionmaking process for counterproliferation interdiction operations, borrowing from Presidential Directive 27, the interagency decisionmaking process that supports counternarcotics interdictions.

The National Security Council currently holds a weekly interdiction sub-Policy Coordinating Committee meeting to identify potential interdiction targets and determine courses of action.[59] Since counterproliferation interdiction targets may often involve sensitive diplomatic and legal issues, the National Security Council will want to approve operational interdiction plans prior to execution. The time sensitivity of certain interdiction operations suggests that the National Security Council should adopt a virtual decision-making process—one in which parties can consult remotely—to accomplish this oversight function.

To streamline and clarify the counterproliferation interdiction process, we recommend a set of procedures similar to those established by Presidential Directive 27 for dealing with counternarcotics interdictions and other "types of non-military incidents."[60] Because interdictions may involve military operations that would conflict with covert activities, we recommend a separate National Security Presidential Directive that outlines the National Security Council process for supervising the planning and execution of interdiction operations. To make these decisions, National Security Council staff and senior policymakers will need intelligence to answer a range of questions.

Unlike the existing intelligence paradigm, which is heavily reliant on the production of "finished" intelligence products, interdiction may require, for example, that military commanders or customs officials communicate directly with collectors and analysts.

Recommendation 10

The State Department should enter into additional bilateral ship-boarding agreements that also help to meet the tagging, tracking, and locating requirements of the Intelligence Community and its users.

The State Department is currently charged with responsibility to secure bilateral ship-boarding agreements in support of the Proliferation Security Initiative.[61] To date, the Department has secured three important agreements.[62] We do not believe, however, that sufficient strategic thought has been directed toward how these agreements can be structured to serve intelligence purposes.

Through such bilateral agreements or related customs regulations, the State Department could, for example, require ships and aircraft to declare their locations through GPS and satellite uplink. Failure to report location information could be viewed as the rough equivalent of driving with a broken taillight, and might establish reasonable suspicion to conduct an interdiction. Such agreements and the imposition of other tracking requirements would enable intelligence to draw on new sources of data to monitor potential cargoes, vessels, and aircraft of proliferation concern.[63]

Protecting our Borders: The Department of Homeland Security

Recommendation 11

The DNI should ensure that Customs and Border Protection has the most up-to-date terrorism and proliferation intelligence. In turn, Customs and Border Protection should ensure that the National Counterterrorism Center and National Counter Proliferation Center have real-time access to its databases.

It may not be possible in all cases to identify and halt biological, nuclear, or chemical weapons shipments before they reach the United States. In such cases, our last line of defense is detecting and stopping these shipments as they cross our border. The Department of Homeland Security, through Customs and Border Protection, collects information on incoming cargo shipments that the Intelligence Community must learn to exploit. The flip side of this equation is equally important—Customs and Border Protection needs threat information from the Intelligence Community to target shipments of concern headed to the United States. Plainly, Homeland Security and the Intelligence Community need to strengthen their relationship. A discussion of ways in which this relationship can be improved is in the classified version of our report, but cannot be discussed in an unclassified format.

If we are to increase our chances of detecting proliferation materials before they enter the United States, it is critical that Homeland Security work closely with the Intelligence Community in developing its plans for screening materials coming into the United States. Moreover, once the plans are instituted, Homeland Security and the Intelligence Community must maintain a close relationship to ensure that homeland security policies reflect the Intelligence Community's most current assessments.

Recommendation 12

The DNI and Secretary of Homeland Security should undertake a research and development program to develop better sensors capable of detecting nuclear-related materials. The effort should be part of a larger border defense initiative to foster greater intelligence support to law enforcement at our nation's borders.

The Intelligence Community's collaboration with the Department of Homeland Security should not stop at targeting cargoes. A comprehensive border defense initiative would employ an array of advanced technologies to protect our borders. For example, reconnaissance satellites, unmanned aerial vehicles, nuclear detection technologies, and biometric identification cards could all play a role in border protection.

Many critical technologies to protect the border, are still in their infancy. A senior official at the Department of Homeland Security laments that the sensors deployed at our borders are "way below ideal."[64] Customs and Border Protection officials complain that some detectors are imprecise and prone to false alarms.[65] A concerted research and development effort is necessary to bring these technologies to maturity. A new sense of urgency is required.

ENLISTING COMMERCE AND TREASURY TO COMBAT PROLIFERATION

Introduction

The Intelligence Community will be most effective at combating chemical, biological, and nuclear threats if it works in concert with non-traditional government partners. Legal and regulatory regimes can help enable better intelligence gathering and disrupt proliferation-related activity.

On several occasions throughout our inquiry, departments and agencies outside of the Intelligence Community asked why our Commission was interested in their work. These comments illustrate the lack of connection between the Intelligence Community and large parts of the government. The Community often sees itself as a world apart, and it is viewed by outsiders as an unapproachable exotic.

In the area of proliferation in particular, such a failure to see beyond the Intelligence Community's borders—and a failure to acknowledge what intelligence can and cannot do—has deprived the country of anti-proliferation levers that it badly needs. As we saw with biological weapons, the lack of an effective (and truly reciprocal) relationship between intelligence and biological sciences has limited the Community's efforts. Similarly, the Community has not sufficiently harnessed the power of legal and regulatory regimes, and the synergies that could result from working more closely with them. While we did not seek to reach beyond the scope of our mandate, which is to study the Intelligence Community, the Commission did look at some ways in which legal and regulatory regimes might enhance intelligence collection specific to the counterproliferation issue.

We do not pretend to have weighed fully every non-intelligence interest at work in many of these regimes. For that reason, many of our recommendations only suggest areas for possible action by both the affected agency and the Intelligence Community. But regardless of whether specific regimes are instituted, we believe that closer cooperation between the Intelligence Community and the Departments of Commerce and Treasury could result in many mutually beneficial relationships and improved collection against difficult proliferation-related targets. The Intelligence Community will be most effective at combating chemical, biological, and nuclear threats if it works in concert with non-traditional government partners.

Department of Commerce: Enforcing the Export Control Regime

The Department of Commerce's Bureau of Industry and Security (BIS) administers and enforces the Export Administration Regulations, which govern the export of dual-use items. BIS's law enforcement authorities place it in a position to collect large amounts of information that could be of great use to the Intelligence Community.

In order to obtain the cooperation of export control violators, however, BIS needs stronger law enforcement powers, something it has lacked in recent years, mainly because some of BIS's law enforcement authorities lapsed when the Export Administration Act expired. BIS could also assist the Intelligence Community more fully if it had authority to impose increased penalties for export violations and more authority to conduct undercover activities of potential intelligence value. The Administration has supported a renewal of the act that would confer these authorities, and congressional action on renewal would make cooperation between BIS and the Intelligence Community more productive.

The Export Administration Regulations provide additional opportunities to support counterproliferation efforts. Specifically, BIS inspections, the conditions BIS imposes on export licenses, and BIS's possible access to corporate records may provide valuable intelligence and counterproliferation opportunities. We discuss these and other related matters, including two classified recommendations, more fully in our classified report.

Recommendations 13 & 14

These recommendations are classified.

Department of the Treasury: Stopping Proliferation Financiers

The Treasury Department can also provide more support to counterproliferation than it does today. The Department currently has two powerful authorities with respect to terrorism that do not now apply to proliferation. The first is the authority to freeze the assets of terrorists and their financiers; the second is the authority to take action against foreign financial institutions that allow their services to be used to support terrorism. We see no reason why these same authorities should not be enhanced to also combat proliferation.

Recommendation 15

The President should expand the scope of Executive Order 13224 beyond terrorism to enable the Department of the Treasury to block the assets of persons and entities who provide financial support to proliferation.

Pursuant to the International Emergency Economic Powers Act, the President authorized the Department of the Treasury to block the assets of persons who sponsor terrorism.[66] However, Treasury lacks a similar tool to block the assets of proliferators. To fill this gap, we recommend the President take steps to allow the Secretary of the Treasury to take the same action against persons "who provide financial or other material support to entities involved in the proliferation of weapons of mass destruction." In light of the virtually universal recognition that the greatest threat the United States faces is the intersection of terrorism and proliferation, we see no reason why Treasury's authority should extend to only half of this potentially catastrophic combination.

Recommendation 16

The President should seek to have Congress amend Section 311 of the USA PATRIOT Act in order to give the Department of the Treasury the authority to designate foreign business entities involved in proliferation as "primary money laundering concerns."

Currently, section 311 of the USA PATRIOT Act authorizes the Secretary of the Treasury—in consultation with other federal officers, including the Secretary of State and the Chair of the Board of Governors of the Federal Reserve System—to designate a foreign jurisdiction or financial institution a "primary money laundering concern," and to require that U.S. financial institutions take certain measures against the designee.[67] This power can be used when the Intelligence Community determines that a foreign financial institution is involved in proliferation-related activity. And by doing so, the Department can effectively cut the foreign institution off from the U.S. banking system. This authority is limited, however to financial institutions that assist proliferation. It would be more effective if it could also be applied to *non-financial* business entities involved in proliferation.

The reason for this suggested change is simple—many aspects of proliferation involve non-financial institutions, such as pharmaceutical, petrochemical, and high-tech companies. By limiting the Treasury Department's designation authority to financial institutions, the current law effectively addresses only one part of the business-related proliferation challenge. Expanding Treasury's authority would thus allow the U.S. government to also take action against the very businesses that supply the materials that make proliferation possible.

Specifically, we believe the Secretary's authorities should extend to the designation of individual businesses involved in proliferation as "primary money laundering concerns." Once a business was so designated, U.S. financial institutions could be required by the Treasury Department to take certain steps to avoid engaging in business transactions with the designated companies. The Secretary of the Treasury might also be able to affect whether foreign financial institutions are willing to conduct business with business entities involved in proliferation. If so, the Secretary of the Treasury could help cut off proliferators from their financial lifeblood.

Conclusion

Legal and regulatory mechanisms are valuable tools the Intelligence Community should use to their full extent. But proper use of these mechanisms requires extensive interagency cooperation. This will not be an easy task. But we believe it is a worthwhile endeavor, and one that may—in the long run—prove invaluable in combating the proliferation of nuclear, biological, and chemical weapons.

ENDNOTES

[1] Center for Counterproliferation Research, *Anthrax in America: A Chronology and Analysis of the Fall 2001 Attacks* (Nov. 2002) at p. 2.

[2] Interview with FBI official (Nov. 19, 2004).

[3] Interview with Dugway Proving Ground official (Dec. 30, 2004); *Final Report of the National Commission on Terrorist Attacks Upon the United* States (authorized edition) (2004) at p. 172 (hereinafter "9/11 Commission Report").

[4] The anthrax letter mailed to Senator Patrick Leahy had 1 trillion spores per gram. Interview with FBI special agent (Nov. 19, 2004). Inhalation of 8,000 to 10,000 spores is generally regarded as lethal, but this figure derives from studies of healthy "middle-aged" primates. Thomas V. Inglesby et al., "Anthrax as a Biological Weapon, 2002: Updated Recommendations for Management," *Journal of the American Medical Association*, vol. 287 (May 1, 2002) at pp. 2236-2252. If we accept this lethality estimate, a gram perfectly disseminated under optimal weather conditions could theoretically kill 100,000 people. Optimum weather conditions and highly efficient dissemination are unlikely, however, since weather patterns and aerosolization efficiency, among numerous other factors, would significantly alter lethality figures. National Research Council, *Making the Nation Safer* (2002) at p. 81. It is a reasonable assumption, however, that liquid or powder dissemination could kill one-thousandth to one-hundredth of those people (*i.e.*, 100 to 1,000 people). Richard Danzig, *Catastrophic Bioterrorism—What Is To Be Done?* (Aug. 2003) at pp. 1-2.

[5] In this example, a kilogram would contain 1,000 trillion anthrax spores.

[6] Richard Danzig, *Catastrophic Bioterrorism—What Is To Be Done?* (Aug. 2003) at p. 2; Brad Roberts, Institute for Defense Analyses, *Defining the Challenges of Campaign-type Responses to Campaign-type Terrorism* (Jan. 2, 2004).

[7] Interview with senior administration official (Dec. 16, 2004).

[8] NIC, Title Classified (NIE 2004-08HC/I) (Dec. 2004) at p. 24.

[9] Interview with senior intelligence official (Oct. 14, 2004).

[10] Tom Mangold and Jeff Goldberg, *Plague Wars: the Terrifying Reality of Biological Warfare* (2001) at p. 61.

[11] Tara O'Toole, Michael Mair, and Thomas Inglesby, *Shining Light on 'Dark Winter'* (2002).

[12] For example, in 2002, researchers at the University of Pittsburgh identified key proteins in *variola* (smallpox) that contribute to its virulence and demonstrated how to synthesize the virulence gene via genetic modification of smallpox's less deadly cousin *vaccina*. A. M. Rosengard, Y. Liu, Z. P. Nie, and R. Jimenez, "Variola Virus Immune Evasion Design: Expression of a Highly Efficient Inhibitor of Human Complement," *Proceedings of the National Academies of Sciences of the United States of America* (Vol. 99) (June 25, 2002) at pp. 8808-8813.

[13] Interview with senior intelligence official (Dec. 6, 2004).

[14] NIC, *Iraq's Continuing Programs for Weapons of Mass Destruction* (NIE 2002-16HC) (Oct. 2002) at pp. 5, 35. The Intelligence Community also judged that Iraq maintained delivery systems for its biological weapons agents. *Id.* at p. 7.

[15] Iraq Survey Group, *Comprehensive Report of the Special Advisor to the DCI on Iraqi*

WMD, Volume III, "Biological Warfare" (Sept. 30, 2004) at p. 1.

[16] NIC, Title Classified (NIE 2004-08HC/I) (Dec. 2004) at p. 59.

[17] Interview with senior intelligence officer (Nov. 18, 2004).

[18] Interview with senior analyst, Institute for Defense Analyses (Jan. 28, 2005).

[19] Interview with senior intelligence officer (Nov. 18, 2004).

[20] The United States spent about $14.5 billion on civilian biodefense between FY 2001 and FY 2004, and there is an additional $7.6 billion requested for FY 2005. The funds have primarily gone to the Departments of Health and Human Services (HHS) and Homeland Security (DHS), and have supported numerous initiatives to develop vaccines, environmental sensors, and emergency response capabilities. Ari Schuler, "Billions for Biodefense: Federal Agency Biodefense Funding, FY2001-FY2005," *Biosecurity and Bioterrorism: Biodefense, Strategy, Practice, and Science* (Vol. 2) (2004) at p. 86. Interview with CIA senior scientist (Jan. 18, 2005); Interview with CIA DS&T official (Jan. 19, 2005).

[21] Interview with senior administration official (Jan. 5, 2005).

[22] Interview with senior CDC official (Nov. 19, 2004).

[23] Observation made by Seth Carus, National Defense University, as related in NIC, Title Classified (NIE 2004-08HC/I) (Dec. 2004), at pp. 60-61.

[24] Interview with senior NIH official (Feb. 4, 2005).

[25] *Id.*

[26] Interview with senior intelligence official (Nov. 18, 2004); CIA has one promising effort that is in its nascent stages.

[27] Interview with CIA senior scientist (Jan. 25, 2005); Interview with biosecurity expert (Feb. 4, 2005).

[28] Interview with senior National Security Council official (Jan. 5, 2005).

[29] Interview with the Department of Homeland Security's Directorate of Science and Technology official (Nov. 15, 2004).

[30] *Id.*

[31] Ron Southwick, "Elite Panel of Academics Wins Fight to Continue Advising Military," *The Chronicle of Higher Education* (June 7, 2002). Today, the JASONs include experts from other scientific specialties as well. *Id.*

[32] CIA, Title Classified (OTI SF 2003-108) (Nov. 3, 2003)

[33] The legislation designates the Joint Intelligence Community Council as responsible for advising the DNI on "establishing requirements...and monitoring and evaluating the performance of the Intelligence Community." Intelligence Reform and Terrorism Prevention Act of 2004 at § 1031, Pub. L. No. 108-458.

[34] Classified examples concerning the Intelligence Community's collection efforts are contained in our classified report, but could not be included in an unclassified discussion.

[35] Interview with CIA senior scientist (Jan. 25, 2005).

[36] *See, e.g.*, International Atomic Energy Agency, Staff Report, *UN General Assembly Backs IAEA's "Indispensable Role"* (Nov. 2, 2004) (noting the IAEA's role in conducting inspections of nuclear programs in Iraq, Iran, and North Korea).

[37] Executive Order 12938 (amended July 28, 1998).

[38]*Id.* at § 4(a).

[39]For current purposes, we define a "dirty bomb" as a radiological dispersal device that uses the force of conventional explosives, such as TNT, to scatter radioactive material.

[40] Interview with Department of Energy intelligence analysts (Jan. 10, 2005).

[41] Interview with DIA analyst (Jan. 18, 2005).

[42] George Tenet, Remarks as prepared for delivery at Georgetown University (Feb. 5, 2004). We discuss the specifics of the A.Q. Khan story in greater detail in our classified report.

[43] *Id.*

[44] *Id.*

[45] Interview with CIA DO official (Sept. 14, 2004).

[46] Satinder Bindra, Bhopal marks chemical tragedy: 20 years since gas leak killed thousands in Indian city (Dec. 3, 2004), *available at* http://edition.cnn.com/2004/WORLD/asiapcf/ 12/02 /india.bhopal.mark (accessed Feb. 7, 2005).

[47] CIA, Title Classified (CTC 2003-30079H) (Aug. 7, 2003) at p. 4.

[48] *Id.*; Senate Government Affairs Permanent Subcommittee on Investigations Staff Statement, *Global Proliferation of Weapons of Mass Destruction: A Case Study on the Aum Shinrikyo* (Oct. 31, 1995), *available at* www.fas.org/irp/congress/1995_rpt/aum/part05.htm (accessed Feb. 7, 2005).

[49] National Security Presidential Directive-17 (also designated Homeland Security Presidential Directive-4) presents a broad national strategy for countering chemical, biological, and nuclear weapons proliferation that emphasizes interdiction of illicit proliferation transfers. In addition, the Proliferation Security Initiative provides a framework under which the United States and its allies have created agreements to authorize the tracking and interdicting of weapons-related shipments.

[50] Interview with senior administration official (Dec. 17, 2004).

[51] Collection Concepts Development Center, Title Classified (Nov. 21, 2003) at p. 4.

[52] *Id.* at pp. ii-iii.

[53] *Id.* at p. 46.

[54] *Id.* at p. 5.

[55] In particular, the Maritime Security Policy emphasizes the importance of a "robust and coordinated intelligence effort [that] serves as the foundation for effective security efforts in the Maritime Domain." NSC, *NSPD-41/HSPD-13: Maritime Security Policy* (Dec. 21, 2004) at pp. 5-6.

[56] A short classified section concerning how best to coordinate the government's interdiction efforts is omitted from this version of the report.

[57] The Department of Defense has recently named U.S. Strategic Command the lead Unified Command for the interdiction and elimination of weapons of mass destruction. Interview with senior Department of Defense official (Jan. 13, 2005).

[58]Officials from Special Operations Command and the Office of the Secretary of Defense for Policy have faulted the Intelligence Community for not gearing collection requirements toward sufficient levels of operational specificity, and for not quickly sharing the intelligence that is collected. Covert platforms must find an appropriate means to share ("push") information quickly to users, and users must have the capability to "pull" intelligence from the infor-

mation sharing environment with appropriate permissions and standards established by the DNI. OSD/SOLIC, *Nuclear Terrorism Intelligence: A Special Operations Perspective* (briefed on Oct. 26, 2004).

[59]Interview with former administration official (Feb. 7, 2005).

[60] Presidential Directive-27 was designed to enable expeditious decisionmaking, consider views of "concerned Departments and agencies," coordinate public statements, and "keep the White House fully informed throughout." *PD-27: Procedures for Dealing with Non-Military Incidents* (Jan. 19, 1978).

[61] The Proliferation Security Initiative is a framework under which the United States and its allies have created agreements to authorize the tracking and interdicting of weapons and materials of proliferation concern.

[62] Each of the three—Liberia, Panama, and the Marshall Islands—is significant because of the large number of vessels that are flagged there.

[63] Office of Naval Intelligence analysts confirm that this would indeed be helpful. Interview with National Maritime Intelligence Center officials (Feb. 14, 2005).

[64] Interview with Department of Homeland Security official (Oct. 7, 2004).

[65] Interview with Customs and Border Protection officials (Feb. 18, 2004). Interview with Customs and Border Protection officials (Jan. 21, 2005).

[66] Executive Order 13224 at § 1(d).

[67] 50 U.S.C. § 5318A.

CONCLUSION

CONCLUSION

We have approached our task mindful of its historical context. In truth, looking to the past, we find cause for discouragement. Many of the ideas and recommendations that we have made in this report were advanced with compelling reasoning by previous commissions. After ceremonious presentations to the President and to Congress, the previous recommendations were ignored or implemented weakly. Most of them failed to take hold. The question is inescapable: why should this Commission be different from the others?

Nevertheless, we are hopeful. The Intelligence Community is at the juncture of a number of powerful historical forces: the end of the Cold War, the first catastrophic attacks in the United States by international terrorists, the proliferation of nuclear weapons, the failure of U.S. intelligence in Iraq, the broad-based demand for change by the American people, and enactment by Congress of the most sweeping legislative reform since the creation of the existing Intelligence Community in 1947. These are reasons enough to believe that our work may be put to good purpose.

Perhaps the single most prominent and recurring theme in our recommendations is a call for *stronger and more centralized management* of the Intelligence Community, and, in general, the creation of a *genuinely integrated Community* instead of a loose confederation of independent agencies. This is not a new idea, but it has never been successfully implemented.

Part of the solution is to put more power and authority in the hands of the DNI. This was a principal purpose of the intelligence reform act of 2004. As we have noted elsewhere, however, the DNI's authorities under the new legislation are far from absolute. In many instances, the DNI will require the support and concurrence of the Secretary of Defense. He will need, as well, the commitment of the Federal Bureau of Investigation to become a part of the Intelligence Community and to be subject to DNI oversight. The DNI will need to use his new authorities swiftly to overcome the barriers that have plagued previous efforts. The new Intelligence Community leadership will also need to cross the old boundaries. The Mission Managers, as we have described them in our report, show how a new approach to management can bring together previously isolated activities and orchestrate an effort that embraces the entire Community.

But it is also incontrovertible that the Intelligence Community's flaws cannot be cured by top-down management alone. Reform must rise from the bottom too, and it must involve true cultural change within the Community. We make a number of specific suggestions along these lines in our report. To state just a few: processes to support analysts working long-term strategic topics; an innovation center to incubate new concepts in human intelligence; an open-source directorate that can freely experiment with new information technologies; a sizeable, uncommitted research and development budget that is available to quickly infuse funding; entirely new approaches to gathering intelligence on biological weapons; and incentives to promote the behaviors that lead to better intelligence (and discourage those that don't). Some of these challenges—especially support for long-term analysis, for innovative collection, and for aggressive research and development—will require greater resources. We are not in a position to make a precise estimate of the costs, but we believe that budget is less likely to be a constraint than culture and tradition. At every level, new and better ways of doing business should be encouraged, nurtured, and protected.

Throughout our work, we have been struck by the range of opinions on reform of the Intelligence Community. Some former and current leaders with impressive experience believe that most of what needs to be done has already occurred. We respectfully disagree. We have unquestionably seen a break with the past and many brave initiatives. We have heard of stunning successes, many of which are too sensitive to mention even in an unclassified report. But too many of these efforts are "more of the same," and many of those that break with past practices are only timid forays into new territory that could easily end in retreat.

There is another group of highly respected individuals, also with long and deep experience, who are fundamentally pessimistic about the recent legislative changes. They foresee new layers of bureaucracy with little value added weighing on institutions that are already overloaded with formalities. We also disagree with this group, but we understand their concern.

Every person with whom we spoke was unanimous on one point: there is nothing more important than having the best possible intelligence to combat the world's deadliest weapons and most dangerous actors. We agree, wholeheartedly; indeed, our survival may well depend upon it. Of course, even the most improved intelligence process is no guarantee against surprise or against weapons of mass destruction. Biological and nuclear weapons are becoming too easy to obtain for any intelligence reforms to provide absolute protection from catastrophe. But in the face of such staggering risks, we must do all we can to avoid danger. That means building an integrated, innovative, and agile Intelligence Community. Despite the uncertainties, we have done our best to chart a course that will take us to the Intelligence Community that our nation deserves.

POSTSCRIPT

POSTSCRIPT: FUTURE INTELLIGENCE CHALLENGES

No commission could examine every important issue facing the Intelligence Community. Our Commission encountered issues that were tangential to our mandate but that are likely to be crucial to the Intelligence Community and the DNI in coming years. We record in this postscript three of the issues that fall into this category.

SECURITY, COUNTERINTELLIGENCE, AND INFORMATION ASSURANCE

This country's security policies—considered in their broadest form to include physical security, infrastructure security, personnel security, and information and cyber security—are in need of serious review. Today we face new threats and vulnerabilities that are in many ways more encompassing, complex, and subtle than those we confronted in the past century. We begin with several broad observations:

■ Security is a highly decentralized government function. Today there is no single advisor to the President who deals with the full spectrum of security-related issues.

■ Effectively addressing security generates costs that must be balanced against risk and threats.

■ Security, as a discipline, has historically been dominated by "police" type management, processes, and enforcement approaches. Although the police function is still required, today's security vulnerabilities are increasingly technical in nature and related to information technology systems, software, and hardware.

Several contemporary security challenges threaten to undermine not only intelligence sources and methods, but also the national security at large. These include: unauthorized leaks, which are now beginning to rival espionage in frequency, scope, and cumulative damage; the deterioration of the concept of need-to-know, and an increasing need to balance security concerns against the need for more robust information sharing; the particular vulnerability of communication and information sharing systems; foreign information warfare programs; and the persistent incentives for overclassification of information. To respond to these challenges, the Intelligence Community must harness the power of digital and biometric "identity"; improve the efficiency of the investigation, clearance, and adjudication process; develop mechanisms designed to protect sources, methods, and capabilities; effectively manage compartmentation; and certify secure spaces and improve physical security for people, facilities, and critical infrastructure.

Intelligence analysts have been placed in a difficult position. On the one hand, analysts must protect new and extremely sensitive sources and methods. On the other hand, analysts are expected to facilitate the broadest possible forms of information sharing, both amongst fellow analysts and with outside customers who increasingly want direct access to raw data and want to collaborate directly with the most knowledgeable and credible analysts.

We have considered many of these issues and offer recommendations that we believe will help address aspects of the security challenge, including our recommendations on Information Sharing (Chapter 9), and on authorized and unauthorized disclosures (Chapter 7, Collection). Yet we know we have only scratched the surface of this complex problem. The issue of security writ large requires a separate inquiry. Accordingly, this Commission recommends early action to define new strategies for managing security in the 21st century.

RETHINKING OVERHEAD COLLECTION

Some of the most difficult issues for the Intelligence Community in the next few years concern satellite surveillance systems. These systems are extremely costly, so that cost overruns in satellite systems tend to suck resources from the rest of the intelligence budget. Increasingly, too, there are air-breathing alternatives to satellite surveillance. Satellites can sometimes gather weapons of mass destruction intelligence not available in any other way, but sometimes satellites provide little assistance in targeting other WMD activities. They also play a crucial role for the military. Choosing which satellite systems are best in this evolving environment is an enormous challenge.

The DNI will need to make tough choices about our future imagery capabilities; doing so will require a strong Planning, Programming, and Budgeting

Execution System capable of comparing the marginal values of the respective collection disciplines. We did not believe that it was within our competence to make specific judgments about whether and how to overhaul future satellite intelligence plans, although we have offered recommendations that we believe will better enable the DNI to make these judgments. Given the importance of the issue, we recommend that the DNI specifically visit this issue early in his tenure.

MAXIMIZING INTELLIGENCE SUPPORT TO PUBLIC DIPLOMACY AND INFORMATION WARFARE

We live in an information age, and the United States needs an Intelligence Community willing and able to support the demands of our public diplomacy efforts. Moreover, we need a sophisticated capability to defend our own information environments and infrastructures from attack. The Intelligence Community has already developed some capabilities of this sort, but they require further investment and attention in order to address our current weaknesses. Our computer network defense capabilities lag considerably, making us vulnerable to countries with growing offensive capabilities.

Our intelligence organizations collect information about adversaries to enable public diplomacy. They also seek information on hostile intentions and possible attacks on U.S. and allied systems. Intelligence must be able to support all of these activities. Some aspects of the Intelligence Community's capabilities in this area cannot be discussed in an unclassified format.

Although our information warfare capabilities are still evolving, this large and complex subject merits further inquiry. Many components of the discipline are also controversial. But intelligence has a major role to play in this job.

The United States, as well as the entire modern global economy, is utterly dependent on its information systems as well as the sources that move, store, and display that information. The Intelligence Community must be focused and well-postured to address any vulnerabilities to these systems.

We did not fully explore these issues; they cut across government and private sector interests, and we believe that the Intelligence Community needs to: participate in initiatives designed to define the country's information warfare policies and doctrine; fund its activities; establish appropriate oversight; and provide for better integration, coordination, and collaboration across agencies. This is an appropriate job for a Presidential Task Force.

APPENDICES

APPENDIX A
Authorizing Executive Order

Executive Order 13328
Commission on the Intelligence Capabilities of the United States Regarding Weapons of Mass Destruction

By the authority vested in me as President by the Constitution and the laws of the United States of America, it is hereby ordered as follows:

Sec. 1. Establishment. There is established, within the Executive Office of the President for administrative purposes, a Commission on the Intelligence Capabilities of the United States Regarding Weapons of Mass Destruction (Commission).

Sec. 2. Mission. (a) The Commission is established for the purpose of advising the President in the discharge of his constitutional authority under Article II of the Constitution to conduct foreign relations, protect national security, and command the Armed Forces of the United States, in order to ensure the most effective counter-proliferation capabilities of the United States and response to the September 11, 2001, terrorist attacks and the ongoing threat of terrorist activity. The Commission shall assess whether the Intelligence Community is sufficiently authorized, organized, equipped, trained, and resourced to identify and warn in a timely manner of, and to support United States Government efforts to respond to, the development and transfer of knowledge, expertise, technologies, materials, and resources associated with the proliferation of Weapons of Mass Destruction, related means of delivery, and other related threats of the 21st Century and their employment by foreign powers (including terrorists, terrorist organizations, and private networks, or other entities or individuals). In doing so, the Commission shall examine the capabilities and challenges of the Intelligence Community to collect, process, analyze, produce, and disseminate information concerning the capabilities, intentions, and activities of such foreign powers relating to the design, development, manufacture, acquisition, possession, proliferation, transfer, testing, potential or threatened use, or use of Weapons of Mass Destruction, related means of delivery, and other related threats of the 21st Century.

(b) With respect to that portion of its examination under paragraph 2(a) of this order that relates to Iraq, the Commission shall specifically examine the Intelligence Community's intelligence prior to the initiation of Operation Iraqi Freedom and compare it with the findings of the Iraq Survey Group and other relevant agencies or organizations concerning the capabilities, intentions, and activities of Iraq relating to the design, development, manufacture, acquisition, possession, proliferation, transfer, testing, potential or threatened use, or use of Weapons of Mass Destruction and related means of delivery.

(c) With respect to its examination under paragraph 2(a) of this order, the Commission shall:

(i) specifically evaluate the challenges of obtaining information regarding the design, development, manufacture, acquisition, possession, proliferation, transfer, testing, potential or threatened use, or use of Weapons of Mass Destruction, related means of delivery, and other related threats of the 21st Century in closed societies; and

(ii) compare the Intelligence Community's intelligence concerning Weapons of Mass Destruction programs and other related threats of the 21st Century in Libya prior to Libya's recent decision to open its programs to international scrutiny and in Afghanistan prior to removal of the Taliban government with the current assessments of organizations examining those programs.

(d) The Commission shall submit to the President by March 31, 2005, a report of the findings of the Commission resulting from its examination and its specific recommendations for ensuring that the Intelligence Community of the United States is sufficiently authorized, organized, equipped, trained, and resourced to identify and warn in a timely manner of, and to support United States Government efforts to respond to, the development and transfer of knowledge, expertise, technologies, materials, and resources associated with the proliferation of Weapons of Mass Destruction, related means of delivery, and other related threats of the 21st Century and their employment by foreign powers (including terrorists, terrorist organizations, and private networks, or other entities or individuals). The Central Intelligence Agency and other components of the Intelligence Community shall utilize the Commission and its resulting report. Within 90 days of receiving the Commission's report, the President will consult with the Congress concerning the Commission's report and recommendations, and will propose any appropriate legislative recommendations arising out of the findings of the Commission.

Sec. 3. Membership. The Commission shall consist of up to nine members appointed by the President, two of whom the President shall designate as Co-Chairs. Members shall be citizens of the United States. It shall take two-thirds of the members of the Commission to constitute a quorum.

Sec. 4. Meetings of the Commission and Direction of Its Work. The Co-Chairs of the Commission shall convene and preside at the meetings of the Commission, determine after consultation with other members of the Commission its agenda, direct its work, and assign responsibilities within the Commission.

Sec. 5. Access to Information. (a) To carry out this order, the Commission shall have full and complete access to information relevant to its mission as described in section 2 of this order and in the possession, custody, or control of any executive department or agency to the maximum extent permitted by law and consistent with Executive Order 12958 of April 17, 1995, as amended. Heads of departments and agencies shall promptly furnish such information to the Commission upon request. The Attorney General and the Director of Central Intelligence shall ensure the expeditious processing of all appropriate security clearances necessary for the members of the Commission to fulfill their functions.

(b) Promptly upon commencing its work, the Commission shall adopt, after consultation with the Secretary of Defense, the Attorney General, and the Director of Central Intelligence, rules and procedures of the Commission for physical, communications, computer, document, personnel, and other security in relation to the work of the Commission. The Secretary of Defense, the Attorney General, and the Director of Central Intelligence shall promptly and jointly report to the President their judgment whether the security rules and procedures adopted by the Commission are clearly consistent with the national security and protect against unauthorized disclosure of information required by law or executive order to be protected against such disclosure. The President may at any time modify the security rules or procedures of the Commission to provide the necessary protection.

Sec. 6. General Provisions. (a) In implementing this order, the Commission shall solely advise and assist the President.

(b) In performing its functions under this order, the Commission shall, subject to the authority of the President, be independent from any executive department or agency, or of any officer, employee, or agent thereof.

(c) Nothing in this order shall be construed to impair or otherwise affect the authorities of any department, agency, entity, officer, or employee of the United States under applicable law.

(d) Nothing in this order shall be construed to impair or otherwise affect the functions of the Director of the Office of Management and Budget relating to budget, administrative, or legislative proposals.

(e) The Director of the Office of Administration shall provide or arrange for the provision of administrative support and, with the assistance of the Director of the Office of Management and Budget, ensure funding for the Commission consistent with applicable law. The Director of the Office of Administration shall ensure that such support and funding meets the Commission's reasonable needs and that the manner of provision of support and funding is consistent with the authority of the Commission within the executive branch in the performance of its functions.

(f) Members of the Commission shall serve without compensation for their work on the Commission. Members who are not officers or employees in the executive branch, while engaged in the work of the Commission, may be allowed travel expenses, including per diem in lieu of subsistence, as authorized by law for persons serving intermittently in Government service (5 U.S.C. 5701 through 5707), consistent with the availability of funds.

(g) The Commission shall have a staff headed by an Executive Director. The Co-Chairs shall hire and employ, or obtain by assignment or detail from departments and agencies, the staff of the Commission, including the Executive Director.

(h) The term "Intelligence Community" is given the same meaning as contained in section 3(4) of the National Security Act of 1947, as amended (50 U.S.C. 401a(4)).

(i) The term "Weapons of Mass Destruction" is given the same meaning as contained in section 1403(1) of the Defense Against Weapons of Mass Destruction Act of 1996 (50 U.S.C. 2302(1)).

Sec. 7. Judicial Review. This order is intended only to improve the internal management of the executive branch, and is not intended to, and does not, create any right or benefit, substantive or procedural, enforceable at law or in equity, against the United States, its departments, agencies, or other entities, its officers or employees, or any other person.

Sec. 8. Termination. The Commission shall terminate within 60 days after submitting its report.

GEORGE W. BUSH

THE WHITE HOUSE,

February 6, 2004.

APPENDIX B
List of Findings and Recommendations

PART ONE: Looking Back

Chapter 1: Iraq

Iraq Findings

Overall Commission Finding: The Intelligence Community's performance in assessing Iraq's pre-war weapons of mass destruction programs was a major intelligence failure. The failure was not merely that the Intelligence Community's assessments were wrong. There were also serious shortcomings in the way these assessments were made and communicated to policymakers.

Nuclear Weapons Summary Finding: The Intelligence Community seriously misjudged the status of Iraq's alleged nuclear weapons program in the 2002 NIE and other pre-Iraq war intelligence products. This misjudgment stemmed chiefly from the Community's failure to analyze correctly Iraq's reasons for attempting to procure high-strength aluminum tubes.

1. The Intelligence Community's judgment about Iraq's nuclear program hinged chiefly on an assessment about Iraq's intended use for high-strength aluminum tubes it was seeking to procure. Most of the agencies in the Intelligence Community erroneously concluded these tubes were intended for use in centrifuges in a nuclear program rather than in conventional rockets. This error was, at the bottom, the result of poor analytical tradecraft—namely, the failure to do proper technical analysis informed by thorough knowledge of the relevant weapons technology and practices.

2. In addition to citing the aluminum tubes, the NIE's judgment that Iraq was attempting to reconstitute its nuclear weapons program also referred to additional streams of intelligence. These other streams, however, were very thin, and the limited value of that supporting intelligence was inadequately conveyed in the October 2002 NIE and in other Intelligence Community products.

3. The other indications of reconstitution—aside from the aluminum tubes—did not themselves amount to a persuasive case for a reconsti-

tuted Iraqi nuclear program. In light of the tenuousness of this other information, DOE's argument that the aluminum tubes were not for centrifuges but that Iraq was, based on these other streams of information, reconstituting its nuclear program was a flawed analytical position.

4. The Intelligence Community failed to authenticate in a timely fashion transparently forged documents purporting to show that Iraq had attempted to procure uranium from Niger.

Biological Warfare Summary Finding: The Intelligence Community seriously misjudged the status of Iraq's biological weapons program in the 2002 NIE and other pre-war intelligence products. The primary reason for this misjudgment was the Intelligence Community's heavy reliance on a human source—codenamed "Curveball"—whose information later proved to be unreliable.

1. The DIA's Defense HUMINT Service's failure even to attempt to validate Curveball's reporting was a major failure in operational tradecraft.

2. Indications of possible problems with Curveball began to emerge well before the 2002 NIE. These early indications of problems—which suggested unstable behavior more than a lack of credibility—were discounted by the analysts working the Iraq WMD account. But given these warning signs, analysts should have viewed Curveball's information with greater skepticism and should have conveyed this skepticism in the NIE. The analysts' resistance to any information that could undermine Curveball's reliability suggests that the analysts were unduly wedded to a source that supported their assumptions about Iraq's BW programs.

3. The October 2002 NIE failed to communicate adequately to policymakers both the Community's near-total reliance on Curveball for its BW judgments, and the serious problems that characterized Curveball as a source.

4. Beginning in late 2002, some operations officers within the regional division of the CIA's Directorate of Operations that was responsible for relations with the liaison service handling Curveball expressed serious concerns about Curveball's reliability to senior officials at the CIA, but these views were either (1) not thought to outweigh analytic assessments

that Curveball's information was reliable or (2) disregarded because of managers' assessments that those views were not sufficiently convincing to warrant further elevation.

5. CIA management stood by Curveball's reporting long after post-war investigators in Iraq had established that he was lying about crucial issues.

6. In addition to the problems with Curveball, the Intelligence Community—and, particularly, the Defense HUMINT Service—failed to keep reporting from a known fabricator out of finished intelligence on Iraq's BW program in 2002 and 2003.

Chemical Warfare Summary Finding: The Intelligence Community erred in its 2002 NIE assessment of Iraq's alleged chemical warfare program. The Community's substantial overestimation of Iraq's chemical warfare program was due chiefly to flaws in analysis and the paucity of quality information collected.

1. The Intelligence Community relied too heavily on ambiguous imagery indicators identified at suspect Iraqi facilities for its broad judgment about Iraq's chemical warfare program. In particular, analysts leaned too much on the judgment that the presence of "Samarra-type" trucks (and related activity) indicated that Iraq had resumed its chemical weapons program.

2. Analysts failed to understand, and collectors did not adequately communicate, the limitations of imagery collection. Specifically, analysts did not realize that the observed increase in activity at suspected Iraqi chemical facilities may have been the result of increased imagery collection rather than an increase in Iraqi activity.

3. Human intelligence collection against Iraq's chemical activities was paltry, and much has subsequently proved problematic.

4. Signals intelligence collection against Iraq's chemical activities was minimal, and much was of questionable value.

Delivery Summary Finding 1: The Intelligence Community incorrectly assessed that Iraq was developing unmanned aerial vehicles for the purpose of delivering biological weapons strikes against U.S. interests.

Delivery Summary Finding 2: The Intelligence Community correctly judged that Iraq was developing ballistic missile systems that violated United Nations strictures, but was incorrect in assessing that Iraq had preserved its Scud missile force.

1. The Intelligence Community made too much of an inferential leap, based on very little hard evidence, in judging that Iraq's unmanned aerial vehicles were being designed for use as biological warfare delivery vehicles and that they might be used against the U.S. homeland.

2. The Intelligence Community failed to communicate adequately to policymakers the weak foundations upon which its conclusions were based.

3. The Intelligence Community failed to give adequate consideration to other possible uses for Iraq's UAVs or to give due credence to countervailing evidence.

4. The Intelligence Community was generally correct in assessing that Iraq was continuing ballistic missile work that violated United Nations restrictions, but erred in many of the specifics.

Regime Decisionmaking Summary Finding: The Intelligence Community, because of a lack of analytical imagination, failed even to consider the possibility that Saddam Hussein would decide to destroy his chemical and biological weapons and to halt work on his nuclear program after the first Gulf War.

Iraq Conclusions

1. Saddam Hussein's Iraq was a hard target for human intelligence, but it will not be the last that we face. When faced with such targets in the future, the United States needs to supplement its traditional methodologies with more innovative approaches.

2. Rewarding CIA and DIA case officers based on how many assets they recruit impedes the recruitment of *quality* assets.

3. The CIA, and even more so the DIA, must do a better job of testing the veracity of crucial human sources.

4. Iraq's denial and deception efforts successfully hampered U.S. intelligence collection.

5. In the case of Iraq, collectors of intelligence absorbed the prevailing analytic consensus and tended to reject or ignore contrary information. The result was "tunnel vision" focusing on the Intelligence Community's existing assumptions.

6. Intercepted communications identified some procurement efforts, but such intelligence was of only marginal utility because most procurements were of dual-use materials.

7. Signals intelligence against Iraq was seriously hampered by technical barriers.

8. Other difficulties relating to the security and counterintelligence methods of the Iraqi regime hampered NSA collection.

9. Traditional imagery intelligence has limited utility in assessing chemical and biological weapons programs.

10. Measurements and signatures intelligence (MASINT) collection was severely hampered by problems similar to those faced by other intelligence methods. Analysts' lack of familiarity with MASINT also reduced its role in analysts' assessments of Iraq's WMD programs.

11. Recognizing that it was having problems collecting quality intelligence against Iraq, the Intelligence Community launched an effort to study ways to improve its collection performance. This process was hampered by haphazard follow-up by some agencies; in particular, NSA failed to follow-up promptly on the Intelligence Community's recommendations.

12. Analysts skewed the analytical process by requiring proof that Iraq did not have WMD.

13. Analysts did not question the hypotheses underlying their conclusions, and tended to discount evidence that cut against those hypotheses.

14. The Community made serious mistakes in its technical analysis of Iraq's unconventional weapons program. The National Ground Intelligence Center in particular displayed a disturbing lack of diligence and technical expertise.

15. Analysis of Iraqi weapons programs was also flawed by "layering," with one individual assessment forming the basis for additional, broader assessments that did not carry forward the uncertainties underlying each "layer."

16. Analysis of Iraq's weapons programs took little account of Iraq's political and social context. While such a consideration would probably not have changed the Community's judgments about Iraq's WMD, the failure even to *consider* whether Saddam Hussein had elected to abandon his banned weapons programs precluded that possibility.

17. The Community did not adequately communicate uncertainties about either its sources or its analytic judgments to policymakers.

18. The Community failed to explain adequately to consumers the fundamental assumptions and premises of its analytic judgments.

19. Relevant information known to intelligence collectors was not provided to Community analysts.

20. Relevant information known to intelligence analysts was not provided to Community collectors.

21. Inability to obtain information from foreign liaison services hampered the Community's ability to assess the credibility of crucial information.

22. The President's Daily Brief (PDB) likely conveyed a greater sense of certainty about analytic judgments than warranted.

23. The National Intelligence Estimate process is subject to flaws as well, and the Iraq NIE displays some of them. The length of the NIE encourages policymakers to rely on the less caveated Key Judgments. And the language of consensus ("most agencies believe") may obscure situations in which the dissenting agency has more expertise than the majority.

24. The Iraq NIE was produced to meet a very short deadline. The time pressure was unfortunate and perhaps avoidable, but it did not substantially affect the judgments reached in the NIE.

25. The shortened NIE coordination process did not unfairly suppress the National Ground Intelligence Center's slightly more cautious estimates of Iraq's CW stockpile.

26. The Intelligence Community did not make or change any analytic judgments in response to political pressure to reach a particular conclusion, but the pervasive conventional wisdom that Saddam retained WMD affected the analytic process.

27. The CIA took too long to admit error in Iraq, and its Weapons Intelligence, Nonproliferation, and Arms Control Center actively discouraged analysts from investigating errors.

Iraq Recommendation

The Director of National Intelligence should hold accountable the organizations that contributed to the flawed assessments of Iraq's WMD programs.

Chapter 2: Libya Findings

1. The Intelligence Community accurately assessed what nuclear-related equipment and material had been obtained by Libya, but it was less successful in judging how well Libya was able to exploit what it possessed.

2. The Intelligence Community's central judgment that Libya possessed chemical weapons agents and chemical weapons aerial bombs was correct, but Libya's actual chemical agent stockpile proved to be smaller in quantity than the Intelligence Community estimated.

3. The Intelligence Community's assessment that Libya maintained the desire for an offensive biological weapons program, and was pursuing at least a small-scale research and development effort, remains unconfirmed.

4. The Intelligence Community's assessments of Libya's missile programs appear to have been generally accurate, but it is not yet possible to evaluate them fully because of limited Libyan disclosures.

5. The Intelligence Community's penetration of the A.Q. Khan proliferation network provided invaluable intelligence on Libya's nuclear efforts.

6. The Intelligence Community's performance with regard to Libya's chemical and biological programs was more modest, due in part to the limited effectiveness of technical collection techniques against these targets.

7. The Intelligence Community gathered valuable information on Libya's missile program.

8. Analysts generally demonstrated a commendable willingness to question and reconsider their assessments in light of new information.

9. Analysts tracking proliferation program developments sometimes inappropriately equated procurement activity with technical capabilities, and many analysts did not receive the necessary training to avoid such failings.

10. Analytic products sometimes provided limited effective warning to intelligence consumers, and tended to separate WMD issues from broader discussions of political and economic forces.

11. Shifting priorities and the dominance of current intelligence production leave little time for considering important unanswered questions on Libya, or for working small problems that might prove to have an impact on reducing surprise over the long term.

Chapter 3: Al-Qa'ida in Afghanistan Findings

1. Information obtained through the war in Afghanistan and in its aftermath indicated that al-Qa'ida's biological weapons program was further along than analysts had previously assessed.

2. Analytic judgments regarding al-Qa'ida's chemical weapons capabilities did not change significantly as a result of the war.

3. The war in Afghanistan brought to light detailed and revealing information about the direction and progress of al-Qa'ida's radiological and nuclear ambitions.

4. Intelligence gaps prior to the war in Afghanistan prevented the Intelligence Community from being able to assess with much certainty the extent of al-Qa'ida's weapons of mass destruction capabilities.

5. Analysis on al-Qa'ida's potential weapons of mass destruction development in Afghanistan did not benefit from leveraging different analytic disciplines.

6. Analysts writing on al-Qa'ida's potential weapons of mass destruction efforts in Afghanistan did not adequately state the basis for or the assumptions underlying their most critical judgments. This analytic shortcoming is one that we have seen in our other studies as well, such as Iraq, and it points to the need to develop routine analytic practices for quantifying uncertainty and managing limited collection.

Chapter 4: Terrorism Findings

1. Although terrorism information sharing has improved significantly since September 11, major change is still required to institute effective information sharing across the Intelligence Community and with state, local, and tribal governments.

2. Ambiguities in the respective roles and authorities of the NCTC and CTC have not been resolved, and the two agencies continue to fight bureaucratic battles to define their place in the war on terror. The result has been unnecessary duplication of effort and the promotion of unproductive competition between the two organizations.

3. Persisting ambiguities and conflicts in the roles, missions, and authorities of counterterrorism organizations hamper effective warning.

4. Persistent ambiguities and conflicts in the roles, missions, and authorities of counterterrorism organizations with regard to analysis and warning have led to redundant efforts across the Community and inefficient use of limited resources.

5. The failure to manage counterterrorism resources from a Community perspective has limited the Intelligence Community's ability to understand and warn against terrorist use of weapons of mass destruction.

Chapter 5: Iran and North Korea

The eleven findings in this chapter are classified.

PART TWO: Looking Forward
The Recommendations

Chapter 6: Leadership and Management

1. We recommend that the DNI bring a mission focus to the management of Community resources for high-priority intelligence issues by creating a group of "Mission Managers" on the DNI staff, responsible for all aspects of the intelligence process relating to those issues.

2. We recommend that the DNI create a management structure that effectively coordinates Community target development. This new target development process would be supported by an integrated, end-to-end "collection enterprise."

3. We recommend that the new DNI overhaul the Community's information management system to facilitate real and effective information sharing.

4. We recommend that the DNI use his human resources authorities to: establish a central human resources authority for the Intelligence Community; create a uniform system for performance evaluations and compensation; develop a more comprehensive and creative set of performance incentives; direct a "joint" personnel rotation system; and establish a National Intelligence University.

5. We recommend that the DNI take an active role in equipping the Intelligence Community to develop new technologies.

6. We recommend that the President establish a National Counter Proliferation Center (NCPC) that is relatively small (*i.e.*, fewer than 100 people) and that manages and coordinates analysis and collection on nuclear, biological, and chemical weapons across the Intelligence Community. Although government-wide "strategic operational planning" is clearly required to confront proliferation threats, we advise that such planning *not* be directed by the NCPC.

7. We recommend that the Executive Branch improve its mechanisms for watching over the Intelligence Community in order to ensure that intelligence reform does not falter. To this end, we suggest that the Joint Intelligence Community Council serve as a standing Intelligence Community "customer council" and that a strengthened President's Foreign Intelligence Advisory Board assume a more vigorous role in keeping watch over the progress of reform in the Community.

8. We recommend that the President suggest that Congress take steps to improve its structure for intelligence oversight.

9. The Intelligence Community should improve its internal processes for self-examination, including increasing the use of formal "lessons learned" studies.

Chapter 7: Collection

1. The DNI should create a new management structure within the Office of the DNI that manages collection as an "integrated collection enterprise." Such an integrated approach should include coordinated target development, collection management, data management, strategic planning and investment, and the development of new collection techniques.

2. Target Development Boards, which would be chaired by the Mission Managers, should develop collection requirements and strategies and evaluate collectors' responsiveness to these needs.

3. Strengthen the CIA's authority to manage and coordinate overseas human intelligence operations across the Intelligence Community by

creating a Human Intelligence Directorate outside the Directorate of Operations.

4. The CIA should develop and manage a range of new overt and covert human intelligence capabilities. In particular, a "Human Intelligence Innovation Center," independent of the CIA's Directorate of Operations, should be established to facilitate the development of new and innovative mechanisms for collecting human intelligence.

5. The CIA should take the lead in systematizing and standardizing the Intelligence Community's asset validation procedures, and integrating them with all information gathering activities across the human intelligence spectrum.

6. The Intelligence Community should train more human intelligence operators and collectors, and its training programs should be modified to support the full spectrum of human intelligence collection methods.

7. The President should seek to have the Foreign Intelligence Surveillance Act amended to extend the duration of electronic surveillance and "pen registers" in cases involving agents of foreign powers who are *not* U.S. persons.

8. The DNI should appoint an authority responsible for managing and overseeing innovative technologies, including the use of technologies often referred to as "MASINT."

9. The DNI should create an Open Source Directorate in the CIA to use the Internet and modern information processing tools to greatly enhance the availability of open source information to analysts, collectors, and users of intelligence.

10. Efforts should be taken to significantly reduce damaging losses in collection capability that result from *authorized* disclosures of classified information related to protection of sources and methods.

11. The DNI should ensure that all Inspectors General in the Intelligence Community are prepared to conduct leak investigations for their agencies; this responsibility can be coordinated by a Commu-

nity-wide Inspector General in the Office of the DNI, if such an office is established.

Chapter 8: Analysis

1. Mission Managers should be the DNI's designees for ensuring that the analytic community adequately addresses key intelligence needs on high priority topics.

2. The DNI should create a small cadre of all-source analysts—perhaps 50—who would be experts in finding and using unclassified, open source information.

3. The DNI should establish a program office within the CIA's Open Source Directorate to acquire, or develop when necessary, information technologies to permit prioritization and exploitation of large volumes of textual data without the need for prior human translation or transcription.

4. The Intelligence Community should expand its contacts with those outside the realm of intelligence by creating at least one not-for-profit "sponsored research institute."

5. The Community must develop and integrate into regular use new tools that can assist analysts in filtering and correlating the vast quantities of information that threaten to overwhelm the analytic process. Moreover, data from all sources of information should be processed and correlated Community-wide *before* being conveyed to analysts.

6. A new long-term research and analysis unit, under the mantle of the National Intelligence Council, should wall off all-source analysts from the press of daily demands and serve as the lead organization for inter-agency projects involving in-depth analysis.

7. The DNI should encourage diverse and independent analysis throughout the Intelligence Community by encouraging alternative hypothesis generation as part of the analytic process and by forming offices dedicated to independent analysis.

8. The Intelligence Community must develop a Community program for training analysts, and both analysts and managers must prioritize this career-long training.

9. The Intelligence Community must develop a Community program for training managers, both when they first assume managerial positions and throughout their careers.

10. Finished intelligence should include careful sourcing for all analytic assessments and conclusions, and these materials should—whenever possible in light of legitimate security concerns—be made easily available to intelligence customers.

11. The analytic community should create and store sourced copies of all analytic pieces to allow readers to locate and review the intelligence upon which analysis is based, and to allow for easy identification of analysis that is based on intelligence reports that are later modified.

12. The DNI should develop and implement strategies for improving the Intelligence Community's science and technology and weapons analysis capabilities.

13. The DNI should explore ways to make finished intelligence available to customers in a way that enables them—*to the extent they desire*—to more easily find pieces of interest, link to related materials, and communicate with analysts.

14. The President's Daily Brief should be restructured. The DNI should oversee the process and ensure a fair representation of divergent views. Reporting on terrorism intelligence should be combined and coordinated by the DNI to eliminate redundancies and material that does not merit Presidential action.

15. The Intelligence Community should expand the use of non-monetary incentives that remind analysts of the importance of their work and the value of their contributions to national security.

16. Examinations of finished intelligence should be routine and ongoing, and the lessons learned from the "post mortems" should be incorporated into the intelligence education and training program.

Chapter 9: Information Sharing

1. The confused lines of authority over information sharing created by the intelligence reform act should be resolved. In particular:

- The Information Sharing Environment should be expanded to encompass all intelligence information, not just terrorism intelligence;

- The Director of the National Counterterrorism Center should report to the DNI on all matters relating to information sharing; and

- The overlapping authorities of the DNI and the Program Manager should be reconciled and coordinated—a result most likely to be achieved by requiring the Program Manager to report to the DNI.

2. The DNI should give responsibility for information *sharing*, information *technology*, and information *security* within the Intelligence Community to an office reporting directly to the DNI or to the Principal Deputy DNI.

3. In designing an Information Sharing Environment, the DNI should, to the extent possible, learn from and build on the capabilities of existing Intelligence Community networks. These lessons include:

- The limitations of "need to know" in a networked environment;

- The importance of developing mechanisms that can protect sources and methods in new ways;

- Biometrics and other user authentication (identification) methods, along with user activity auditing tools, can promote accountability and enhance counterintelligence capabilities;

- System-wide encryption of data can greatly reduce the risks of network penetration by outsiders; and

- Where sensitive information is restricted to a limited group of users, the Information Sharing Environment should ensure that others searching for such information are aware of its existence and provided with a point of contact who can decide quickly whether to grant access.

4. Primary institutional responsibility within the Intelligence Community for establishing clear and consistent "U.S. persons" rules should be shifted from individual collection agencies to the Director of National Intelligence. These rules would continue to be subject to the Attorney General's review and approval. To the extent possible, the same rules should apply across the Intelligence Community.

5. The DNI should set uniform information management policies, practices, and procedures for all members of the Intelligence Community.

6. All users of the Information Sharing Environment should be registered in a directory that identifies skills, clearances, and assigned responsibilities of each individual (using aliases rather than true names when necessary). The environment should enable users to make a "call for assistance" that assembles a virtual community of specialists to address a particular task, and all data should be catalogued within the Information Sharing Environment in a way that enables the underlying network to compare user privileges with data sensitivity.

7. The DNI should propose standards to simplify and modernize the information classification system with particular attention to implementation in a network-centric Information Sharing Environment.

8. We recommend several parallel efforts to keep the Information Sharing Environment on track:

- *Collection of metrics.* The chief information management officer should introduce performance metrics for the Information Sharing Environment and automate their collection. These metrics should include the number and origination of postings to the shared environment, data on how often and by whom each item was accessed, and statistics on the use of collaborative tools and communications channels, among others. Such performance data can help to define milestones and to determine rewards and penalties.

- **Self-enforcing milestones.** Milestones should include specific and quantifiable performance criteria for the sharing environment, as well as rewards and penalties for succeeding or failing to meet them. The DNI should empower the chief information management officer to use the DNI's budget, mission-assignment, and personnel authorities to penalize poor agency performance.

- **Incentives.** The DNI should ensure that collectors and analysts receive honors or monetary prizes for intelligence products that receive widespread use or acclaim. Users should post comments or rate the value of individual reports or analytic products, and periodic user surveys can serve as peer review mechanisms.

- **Training.** The DNI should promote the training of all users in the Information Sharing Environment, with extended training for analysts, managers, and other users of the environment.

Chapter 10: Intelligence at Home

1. To ensure that the FBI's *intelligence elements* are responsive to the Director of National Intelligence, and to capitalize on the FBI's progress, we recommend the creation of a new National Security Service within the FBI under a single Executive Assistant Director. This service would include the Bureau's Counterterrorism and Counterintelligence Divisions and the Directorate of Intelligence. The service would be subject to the coordination and budget authorities of the DNI as well as to the same Attorney General authorities that apply to other Bureau divisions.

2. The DNI should ensure that there are effective mechanisms for preventing conflicts and encouraging coordination among intelligence agencies in the United States.

3. The Department of Justice's primary national security elements—the Office of Intelligence Policy and Review, and the Counterterrorism and Counterespionage sections—should be placed under a new Assistant Attorney General for National Security.

4. The Secretary of Homeland Security should rescind Treasury Order 113-01 as it applies to Department of Homeland Security elements.

Chapter 11: Counterintelligence

1. The National Counterintelligence Executive should become the DNI's Mission Manager for counterintelligence, providing strategic direction for the whole range of counterintelligence activities across the government.

2. The National Counterintelligence Executive should work closely with agencies responsible for protecting U.S. information infrastructure in order to enhance the United States' technical counterintelligence capabilities.

3. The CIA should create a new capability dedicated to mounting offensive counterintelligence activities abroad.

4. The Department of Defense's Counterintelligence Field Activity should have operational and investigative authority to coordinate and conduct counterintelligence activities throughout the Defense Department.

5. The FBI should create a National Security Service that includes the Bureau's Counterintelligence Division, Counterterrorism Division, and the Directorate of Intelligence. A single Executive Assistant Director would lead the Service subject to the coordination and budget authorities of the DNI.

Chapter 12: Covert Action

The four recommendations in this chapter are classified.

Chapter 13: The Changing Proliferation Threat and the Intelligence Response

1. The DNI should create a Community-wide National Biodefense Initiative to include a Biological Science Advisory Group, a government service program for biologists and health professionals, a post-doctoral fellowship program in biodefense and intelligence, and a scholarship program for graduate students in biological weapons-relevant fields.

2. The DNI should use the Joint Intelligence Community Council to form a Biological Weapons Working Group. This Working Group would serve as the principal coordination venue for the Intelligence Community and biodefense agencies, including the Department of Homeland Security's National Biodefense and Countermeasures Center, NIH, CDC, the Department of Agriculture, and USAMRIID.

3. The DNI should create a deputy within the National Counter Proliferation Center that is specifically responsible for biological weapons; this deputy would be responsible to the Proliferation Mission Manager to ensure the implementation of a comprehensive biological weapons targeting strategy and direct new collection initiatives.

4. The National Security Council should form a Joint Interagency Task Force to develop a counter-biological weapons plan within 90 days that draws upon all elements of national power, including law enforcement and the regulatory capabilities of the Departments of Homeland Security, Health and Human Services, Commerce, and State.

5. The State Department should aggressively support foreign criminalization of biological weapons development and the establishment of biosafety and biosecurity regulations under the framework of the United Nations Security Council Resolution 1540. U.S. law enforcement and intelligence agencies should jointly sponsor biological weapons information sharing events with foreign police forces.

6. The United States should remain actively engaged in designing and implementing both international and regulatory inspection regimes. It should consider extending its existing biosecurity and biosafety regulations to foreign institutions with commercial ties to the United States, using the possibility of increased liability, reduced patent protection, or

more burdensome and costly inspections to encourage compliance with appropriate safeguards.

7. The President should establish a Counterproliferation Joint Interagency Task Force to conduct counterproliferation interdiction operations; to detect, monitor, and handoff suspected proliferation targets; and to coordinate interagency and partner nations' counterproliferation activities.

8. The DNI should designate the National Counter Proliferation Center as the Intelligence Community's leader for interdiction-related issues and direct the Center to support the all-source intelligence needs of the Counterproliferation Joint Interagency Task Force, the National Security Council, and other customers.

9. The President should establish, probably through a National Security Presidential Directive, a real-time, interagency decisionmaking process for counterproliferation interdiction operations, borrowing from Presidential Directive 27, the interagency decisionmaking process that supports counternarcotics interdictions.

10. The State Department should enter into additional bilateral shipboarding agreements that also help to meet the tagging, tracking, and locating requirements of the Intelligence Community and its users.

11. The DNI should ensure that Customs and Border Protection has the most up-to-date terrorism and proliferation intelligence. In turn, Customs and Border Protection should ensure that the National Counterterrorism Center and National Counter Proliferation Center have real-time access to its databases.

12. The DNI and Secretary of Homeland Security should undertake a research and development program to develop better sensors capable of detecting nuclear-related materials. The effort should be part of a larger border defense initiative to foster greater intelligence support to law enforcement at our nation's borders.

13. *This recommendation is classified.*

14. *This recommendation is classified.*

15. The President should expand the scope of Executive Order 13224 beyond terrorism to enable the Department of the Treasury to block the assets of persons and entities who provide financial support to proliferation.

16. The President should seek to have Congress amend Section 311 of the USA PATRIOT Act in order to give the Department of the Treasury the authority to designate foreign business entities involved in proliferation as "primary money laundering concerns."

APPENDIX C
An Intelligence Community Primer

INTRODUCTION

The U.S. Intelligence Community is a federation of executive branch agencies and organizations that work—both together and separately—to conduct intelligence activities necessary for the conduct of foreign relations and the protection of the national security of the United States. While the U.S. Intelligence Community is a large and complex organization, its primary mission is clear-cut: to collect and convey essential information needed by the President and other members of the U.S. policymaking, law enforcement, and military communities for the performance of their duties and responsibilities. This includes collecting and assessing information concerning international terrorist and narcotic activities; other hostile activities by foreign powers, organizations, persons, and their agents; and foreign intelligence activities directed against the United States. The President also may direct the Intelligence Community to undertake special activities, including covert action, as needed to support intelligence collection activities and to protect against foreign threats to U.S. security interests.

The purpose of the following discussion is to provide an overall picture of the U.S. Intelligence Community today and how it functions. It is intended as a primer for readers who may be unfamiliar with the subject.

MEMBERS OF THE U.S. INTELLIGENCE COMMUNITY

The U.S. Intelligence Community comprises 15 federal agencies, offices, and elements of organizations within the Executive branch that are responsible for the collection, analysis, and dissemination of intelligence. These include fourteen departmental components—eight in the Department of Defense, two in the Department of Homeland Security, one each in four other departments (State, Energy, Treasury, and Justice) and one independent agency, the Central Intelligence Agency. Each member of the Community provides a unique set of capabilities to bear upon the intelligence challenges facing the U.S. government. The members of the Intelligence Community are:

Independent Component

Central Intelligence Agency (CIA): CIA collects intelligence, principally through human means, and provides comprehensive, all-source analysis related to national security topics for national policymakers, defense planners, law enforcement officials, and the military services. CIA also conducts counterintelligence overseas and undertakes special activities at the direction of the President.

Department of Defense Components

Defense Intelligence Agency (DIA): DIA provides comprehensive, all-source, foreign-military intelligence for the military services, policymakers, and defense planners.

National Security Agency (NSA): NSA collects and processes foreign signals intelligence information for members of the policymaking and military communities and protects critical U.S. information systems from compromise.

National Geospatial-Intelligence Agency (NGA): NGA provides geospatial intelligence (described below) in support of national security and Department of Defense missions.

National Reconnaissance Office (NRO): NRO designs, builds, operates, and maintains the nation's reconnaissance satellites.

Army, Navy, Air Force, and Marine Corps intelligence organizations: Each service collects and processes intelligence relevant to its particular needs.

Non-Defense Departmental Components

Department of State/Bureau of Intelligence and Research (INR): INR provides analysis of global developments to the State Department and contributes its unique perspectives to the community's National Intelligence Estimates.

Department of Justice/Federal Bureau of Investigation (FBI): FBI takes responsibility for intelligence issues related to counterespionage, terrorism and counterintelligence inside the United States, threats to homeland security, and data about international criminal cases. Because of its law enforcement mission, the FBI is not, in its entirety, part of the Intelligence Community.

***Department of Homeland Security/Directorate of Information Analysis and Infrastructure Protection*:** This component of DHS monitors, assesses, and coordinates indications and warnings of threats to the U.S. homeland; gathers and integrates terrorist-related information; and assesses and addresses the vulnerabilities of the nation's critical infrastructures.

***Department of Homeland Security/U.S. Coast Guard Intelligence*:** Coast Guard Intelligence assesses and provides information related to threats to U.S. economic and security interests in any maritime region including international waters and America's coasts, ports, and inland waterways.

***Department of Energy (DOE)/ Office of Intelligence (IN)*:** The Department of Energy's Office of Intelligence performs analyses of foreign nuclear weapons, nuclear nonproliferation, and energy-security related intelligence issues in support of U.S. national security policies, programs, and objectives.

***Department of Treasury/Office of Terrorism and Financial Intelligence (INF)*:** Treasury's intelligence component collects and processes information that bears on U.S. fiscal and monetary policy and threats to U.S. financial institutions.

All the responsibilities of the CIA, DIA, NSA, NRO, and NGA are related to intelligence, and therefore each of these organizations in its entirety is considered a member of the Intelligence Community. The other departments and military services listed above are concerned primarily with business and missions other than intelligence and therefore only parts of their organizations are considered part of the Intelligence Community. For example, in the case of the U.S. Navy, only the Office of Naval Intelligence (ONI) is considered a member of the Intelligence Community.

In addition to the fifteen organizations listed above, the Intelligence Community also has established a number of *national centers* such as the Counterterrorist Center (CTC); Weapons Intelligence, Nonproliferation, and Arms Control Center (WINPAC); and the Crime and Narcotics Center (CNC). There is also a national center created by statute—the National Counterterrorism Center (NCTC), created by the *Intelligence Reform and Terrorism Prevention Act of 2004.* These centers are staffed by personnel from organizations across the Intelligence Community and are responsible for developing collaborative approaches to collection and analysis of intelligence on specific issues.

WHAT IS INTELLIGENCE?

Intelligence is knowledge about the world around us that will help our civilian and military leaders make more informed decisions and prepare for and counter potential and emerging threats to U.S. interests. Intelligence starts with information obtained in response to known or perceived requirements from senior policymakers, defense and law enforcement officials, and military commanders. While some of this information may be available to the public, much of it is concealed by those governments or organizations (such as terrorists) who wish it to remain secret. Thus, such information derives typically from human or technical sources gathered in a clandestine manner. Collecting such denied information is a key responsibility of the Intelligence Community.

There are five primary categories or "disciplines" of information that the Intelligence Community seeks to collect to satisfy the needs of senior policymakers, decisionmakers, and military officials. Sometimes also referred to as collection techniques, these disciplines are:

Human intelligence, or HUMINT, consists of information obtained from individuals who know or have access to sensitive foreign information that has implications for U.S. security interests. The CIA and the Defense HUMINT Service, an element of the Defense Intelligence Agency, and, more recently, the FBI, are the primary collectors of HUMINT for the Intelligence Community.

Signals intelligence, or SIGINT, is information derived from intercepted communications and electronic and data transmissions. NSA is the primary collector of SIGINT for the Intelligence Community.

Imagery intelligence, or IMINT, which is also referred to as geospatial intelligence or GEOINT, is the exploitation and analysis of imagery and other geospatial information to describe, assess, and visually depict physical features and geographically referenced activities on earth. NGA has the primary responsibility for coordinating the collection and processing of IMINT data for the Intelligence Community.

Measurement and Signature Intelligence, or MASINT, describes a category of technically derived information that provides distinctive characteristics of a specific event such as a nuclear explosion, or locates, identifies, and describes distinctive characteristics of targets through such means as optical, acoustic, or seismic sensors. The intelligence organizations within the Department of the Defense—especially DIA, NGA, and the military services—are the primary collectors of MASINT.

Open source intelligence, or OSINT, refers to publicly available information appearing in print or electronic form.

Collected information is often described as *raw intelligence* until it can be sorted, integrated, and evaluated by intelligence analysts who seek to derive meaning and understanding from the information regarding its implications for U.S. interests. Often such information can only provide an incomplete picture of the threats facing the United States. Some collected information may also be contradictory and even deceptive, planted by foreign powers intent on masking their true intentions. Analysts therefore have to supplement the collected information with their own skills, experiences, and expertise to make judgments as to the validity and likely meaning of all the information available to them. Their analysis and judgments are then conveyed to policymakers, defense and law enforcement officials, and the military services in the form of *finished intelligence* reports and briefings.

THE INTELLIGENCE CYCLE

The process of tasking, collecting, processing, analyzing, and disseminating intelligence is called the *intelligence cycle.* The intelligence cycle drives the day-to-day activities of the Intelligence Community. It starts with the needs of those who are often referred to within the Intelligence Community as intelligence "consumers"—that is, policymakers, military officials, and other decisionmakers who need intelligence information in conducting their duties and responsibilities. These needs—also referred to as intelligence requirements—are sorted and prioritized within the Intelligence Community, and are used to drive the collection activities of the members of the Intelligence Community that collect intelligence. Once information has been collected it is processed, initially evaluated, and reported to both consumers and so-called "all-source" intelligence analysts at agencies like the CIA, DIA, and the State Department's Bureau of Intelligence and Research. All-source analysts are responsible for performing a more thorough evaluation and assessment of the collected information by integrating the data obtained from a variety of collection agencies and sources—both classified and unclassified. This assessment leads to a finished intelligence report being disseminated to the consumer. The "feedback" part of the cycle assesses the degree to which the finished intelligence addresses the needs of the intelligence consumer and will determine if further collection and analysis is required. The cycle, as depicted in the figure below, is thus repeated until the intelligence requirements have been satisfied.

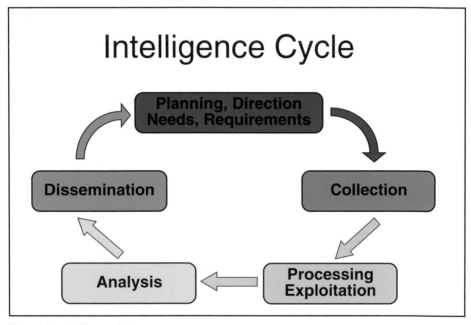

Figure 1. The Intelligence Cycle

OTHER INTELLIGENCE ACTIVITIES: COUNTERINTELLIGENCE AND COVERT ACTION

Counterintelligence encompasses actions taken to detect and counteract foreign intelligence activity that adversely affects U.S. national security interests. The FBI is the government's primary organization responsible for counterintelligence within U.S. borders, and addresses foreign intelligence services operating within the United States. CIA has the primary responsibility for conducting counterintelligence abroad. A number of other departments and agencies maintain counterintelligence elements to protect their own operations and activities within their own organizations, including the Army, Navy, and Air Force, and the Department of Energy. The Counterintelligence Field Activity (CIFA) has broad responsibilities for counterintelligence across the Department of Defense, while the National Counterintelligence Executive (NCIX) is responsible for coordinating and overseeing counterintelligence across the Intelligence Community.

Covert action is defined as activity undertaken by the U.S. government that is designed to influence foreign governments, events, organizations, or persons in support of U.S. policy and security interests in a manner that is not attributable to the United States. Typically, covert actions are carried out by CIA with such assistance as may be necessary by other elements of the Intelligence Community as directed by the President. U.S. law requires that all covert actions be approved prior to their execution by the President in a written *"finding"* and that notification be provided to the two intelligence committees in Congress. Covert actions may involve political, economic, propaganda, or paramilitary activities.

A NEW MANAGEMENT STRUCTURE FOR THE INTELLIGENCE COMMUNITY: THE INTELLIGENCE REFORM AND TERRORISM PREVENTION ACT OF 2004

The *Intelligence Reform and Terrorism Prevention Act of 2004* established the position of the Director of National Intelligence (DNI) to serve as head of the Intelligence Community and act as the principal adviser to the President on intelligence matters related to national security. The creation of the DNI separates the responsibilities of leading the Intelligence Community from heading the CIA, which had been combined in the position of Director of Central Intelligence (DCI) previously. As we discuss in our report, the legislation gives the DNI new authorities and responsibilities that the DCI did not possess under prior law.

The DNI will be assisted in his responsibilities by the Principal Deputy Director for National Intelligence and up to four Deputy Directors for National Intelligence. The Intelligence Reform and Terrorism Prevention Act also established that the Office of the DNI (ODNI) will contain the following components to assist the DNI in his leadership of the Intelligence Community:

The National Counterterrorism Center (NCTC) serves as the primary organization in the U.S. Government for analyzing and integrating all intelligence possessed or acquired by the U.S. Government pertaining to terrorism and counterterrorism, excepting intelligence pertaining exclusively to domestic terrorists and domestic counterterrorism. The NCTC also conducts strategic operational planning for counterterrorism activities, integrating all instruments of national power, including diplomatic, financial, military, intelligence, homeland security, and law enforcement activities within and among agencies. Other national centers that may be created in addition to NCTC (for example, a new *National Counter Proliferation Center*) would also be part of the ODNI.

The National Intelligence Council (NIC) is responsible for producing National Intelligence Estimates (NIEs) for the U.S. government and evaluating community-wide collection and production of intelligence by the Intelligence Community.

The National Counterintelligence Executive (NCIX) is responsible for improving the performance of the counterintelligence community in assessing, prioritizing and countering intelligence threats to the United States and providing integration of counterintelligence activities of the U.S. government.

The Director for Science and Technology (DST) is to act as the chief representative of the DNI for science and technology and to assist the DNI in formulating a long-term strategy for scientific advances in the field of intelligence.

A Civil Liberties Protection Officer will ensure that the protection of civil liberties and privacy is appropriately incorporated into the policies and procedures developed by the ODNI.

A General Counsel will serve as the chief legal officer for the ODNI.

The statute also establishes the *Joint Intelligence Community Council*, which consists of the heads of each Department that contains a component of the Intelligence Community (*e.g.*, Secretary of Defense), and which will assist the DNI in developing and implementing a joint, unified national intelligence effort to protect national security.

U.S. INTELLIGENCE RESOURCES

The intelligence resources of the United States—including manpower and funding—are grouped primarily into three categories: the National Intelligence Program, the Joint Military Intelligence Program, and Tactical Intelligence and Related Activities.

The National Intelligence Program (NIP): The *Intelligence Reform and Terrorism Prevention Act of 2004* provides the DNI with the authority to develop the budget and allocate resources under the NIP. NIP resources support national intelligence priorities and are applied to intelligence activities outside the Department of Defense and a sizable portion of the intelligence activities of the military departments and defense agencies. The agencies and organizations whose resources are included as part of the NIP include the CIA, NSA, DIA, NGA, NRO, and the intelligence elements of the Department of State, Department of Justice, Department of Energy, and Department of the Treasury.

The recent legislation provides a role for the DNI in transferring and reprogramming funds and personnel within the NIP. The Act provides the DNI with the authority to transfer funds within the NIP to an intelligence activity that is of a higher priority or in support of an emergent need, to improve program effectiveness, or increase efficiency. Such transfers or reprogramming of funds must have the approval of the Director of the Office of Management and Budget and be made in consultation with the heads of the affected department and agencies with the Intelligence Community. In addition, the transfer or preprogramming of funds for these purposes out of any agency or department funded in the NIP in a single fiscal year is not to exceed $150 million annually—or five percent of an agency or department's budget under the NIP—without approval of the head of the department or agency affected. The DNI is also authorized to transfer up to 100 people to a new intelligence center within the first twelve months of the establishment of that center, with the approval of the Director of the Office of Management and Budget and in consultation with the appropriate congressional committees. Intelligence resources under JMIP and TIARA (described below) will continue to be managed by the Department of Defense and the military services; however the DNI will participate in the development of the JMIP and TIARA budgets.

The Joint Military Intelligence Program (JMIP): The JMIP encompasses military intelligence activities that support Defense-wide objectives, as opposed to a single military service. The JMIP falls under the authority of the Secretary of Defense. JMIP resources support multiple defense organizations across functional boundaries and mission areas. Many of the programs under JMIP parallel those in the NIP. As a result, some agencies, like NGA, receive funding from both the NIP and JMIP budgets. The Deputy Secretary of Defense oversees the day-to-day activities of the Defense Department, which include the Defense Department's intelligence efforts. The Under Secretary of Defense for Intelligence serves as the JMIP Program Executive and provides policy, substantive, and programmatic guidance for the programs, projects, and activities within the JMIP.

Tactical Intelligence and Related Activities (TIARA): TIARA also falls under the authority of the Secretary of Defense and represents an aggregation of intelligence activities funded by each of the military services and the Special Operations Command to meet their specific requirements.

THE BUDGET PROCESS

Managing the annual intelligence budget can be a lengthy and complex process. As provided for in the *Intelligence Reform and Terrorism Prevention Act*, the process starts with the DNI providing guidance to the heads of agencies and organizations within the Intelligence Community for developing the NIP budget based on the priorities set by the President. The DNI will also participate in the development of JMIP and TIARA budgets managed by the Secretary of Defense including providing budget guidance to those elements of the Intelligence Community not within the NIP. This new participatory role has yet to be clearly defined. After the heads of the agencies and organizations within the Intelligence Community respond with their budget proposals and, as appropriate, after obtaining the advice of the Joint Intelligence Community Council, the DNI develops and determines the annual consolidated NIP budget. The DNI then presents the consolidated NIP budget, along with any comments from the heads of the agencies and departments containing organizations within the Intelligence Community, to the President for approval. After the NIP budget is approved and authorized, the DNI will manage the appropriations for the NIP by directing the allocation of such appropriations through the heads of the departments containing agencies or organizations within the Intelligence Community and the Director of the Central Intelligence Agency. The DNI also will monitor the implementation and execution of the NIP by the heads of the elements of the Intelligence Community that manage programs and activities that are part of the NIP, which may include audits and evaluations.

OVERSIGHT OF THE INTELLIGENCE COMMUNITY

The Intelligence Community is subject to both Executive and Legislative oversight.

The National Security Council (NSC) is the senior Executive Branch entity that provides guidance for and direction to the conduct of national foreign intelligence and counterintelligence activities. The statutory members of the NSC are the President, the Vice President, the Secretary of State, and the Secretary of Defense.

The President's Foreign Intelligence Advisory Board (PFIAB) reviews the performance of all Government agencies involved in the collection, evaluation, or production of intelligence or in the execution of intelligence policies. The PFIAB also assesses the adequacy of management, personnel, and organization in the intelligence agencies and makes recommendations to the President for actions to improve U.S. intelligence efforts. The Intelligence Oversight Board is a standing committee of the PFIAB and is the White House entity with oversight responsibility for the legality and propriety of intelligence activities.

The Office of Management and Budget, as part of the Executive Office of the President, reviews intelligence budgets with respect to all presidential policies and priorities.

The Senate Select Committee on Intelligence (SSCI) and ***the House of Representatives Permanent Select Committee on Intelligence (HPSCI)*** are the two committees of Congress with primary jurisdiction for oversight of the Intelligence Community. These committees, along with the House and Senate Armed Services, Senate Foreign Relations, House International Relations, House and Senate Judiciary, and House and Senate Homeland Security Committees, are also charged with authorizing the programs of the intelligence agencies and overseeing their activities. The appropriation committees, by virtue of their constitutional role to appropriate funds for all U.S. Government activities, also exercise some oversight functions over the Intelligence Community.

APPENDIX D
Common Abbreviations

BIS	Bureau of Industry and Security (Department of Commerce)
BW	Biological Weapons *or* Biological Warfare
CBP	Customs and Border Protection (Department of Homeland Security)
CBRN	Chemical, Biological, Radiological and Nuclear Weapons
CCDC	Collection Concepts Development Center
CDC	Centers for Disease Control and Prevention
CIA	Central Intelligence Agency
CIFA	Counterintelligence Field Activity (Department of Defense)
CPD	Counterproliferation Division (CIA)
CTC	Counterterrorist Center
CW	Chemical Weapons *or* Chemical Warfare
D&D	Denial and Deception
DCI	Director of Central Intelligence
DCIA	Director of Central Intelligence Agency
DHS	Department of Homeland Security
DIA	Defense Intelligence Agency
DNI	Director of National Intelligence
DO	Directorate of Operations (CIA)
DOD	Department of Defense
DOE	Department of Energy
DOJ	Department of Justice
DS&T	Directorate of Science and Technology (CIA)
FBI	Federal Bureau of Investigation
FBIS	Foreign Broadcast Information Service
FIG	Field Intelligence Group (FBI)
FISA	Foreign Intelligence Surveillance Act
HPSCI	House Permanent Select Committee on Intelligence
HUMINT	Human Intelligence
IAEA	International Atomic Energy Agency
IAEC	Iraqi Atomic Energy Commission

ICE	Immigration and Customs Enforcement (Department of Homeland Security)
INC	Iraqi National Congress
INR	Bureau of Intelligence and Research (Department of State)
INS	Immigration and Naturalization Services
IRTPA	Intelligence Reform and Terrorism Prevention Act of 2004
ISB	Intelligence Science Board
ISE	Information Sharing Environment
ISG	Iraq Survey Group
ITIC	Intelligence Technology Innovation Center
JAEIC	Joint Atomic Energy Intelligence Committee
JICC	Joint Intelligence Community Council
JITF-CT	Counterterrorism Joint Intelligence Task Force
JMIP	Joint Military Intelligence Program
JTTF	Joint Terrorism Task Force
MASINT	Measurement and Signature Intelligence
NCIX	National Counterintelligence Executive
NCPC	National Counter Proliferation Center
NCTC	National Counterterrorism Center
NGA	National Geospatial-Intelligence Agency
NGIC	National Ground Intelligence Center
NIC	National Intelligence Council
NIE	National Intelligence Estimate
NIH	National Institutes of Health
NIO	National Intelligence Officer
NIP	National Intelligence Program
NIU	National Intelligence University
NRO	National Reconnaissance Office
NSA	National Security Agency
NSC	National Security Council
ODNI	Office of the Director of National Intelligence
OIPR	Office of Intelligence Policy Review (Department of Justice)
PDB	President's Daily Brief
PFIAB	President's Foreign Intelligence Advisory Board

PTTR	President's Terrorism Threat Report
SEIB	Senior Executive Intelligence Brief
SEVIS	Student and Exchange Visitor Information System
SIGINT	Signals Intelligence
SOF	Special Operations Forces
SSCI	Senate Select Committee on Intelligence
STRATCOM	U.S. Strategic Command
TDB	Target Development Board
TIARA	Tactical Intelligence and Related Activities
TTIC	Terrorist Threat Integration Center
UAV	Unmanned Aerial Vehicles
UNMOVIC	United Nations Monitoring, Verification, and Inspection Commission
UNSCOM	United Nations Special Commission
USAMRIID	U.S. Army Medical Research Institute for Infectious Diseases
UNVIE	U.S. Mission to International Organizations in Vienna
WINPAC	Weapons Intelligence, Nonproliferation and Arms Control Center (CIA)
WMD	Weapons of Mass Destruction

APPENDIX E
Biographical Information for Commissioners and List of Commission Staff

Commission Co-Chairmen

Charles S. Robb is a former Virginia Governor and U.S. Senator. As a Marine Corps officer during the 1960s, he commanded an infantry company in combat in Vietnam and, as a senator during the 1990s, he became the only member ever to serve simultaneously on all three national security committees. Robb received his law degree from the University of Virginia, clerked on the U.S. Court of Appeals for the Fourth Circuit, and practiced law with Williams and Connolly in the 1970s and Hunton and Williams in the 1980s. Since leaving public office he has been a Professor of Law and Public Policy at George Mason University, served as a Fellow at the Institute of Politics at Harvard and at the Marshall Wythe School of Law at The College of William & Mary, and Chaired the Board of Visitors at the U.S. Naval Academy.

Judge Laurence H. Silberman is a senior circuit judge on the U.S. Court of Appeals for the District of Columbia Circuit. He was a member of the U.S. Foreign Intelligence Surveillance Court of Review. The intelligence court, created in 1978, is charged with overseeing sensitive law enforcement surveillance by the U.S. government. Judge Silberman has served as Under Secretary of Labor, Deputy U.S. Attorney General, and Ambassador to Yugoslavia. From 1981 to 1985 he was a member of both the General Advisory Committee on Arms Control and the Department of Defense Policy Board. Judge Silberman was appointed to the bench by President Reagan in 1985.

Commissioners

Richard C. Levin, the Frederick William Beinecke Professor of Economics, was appointed the twenty-second President of Yale University in 1993. Before becoming president, he chaired the economics department and served as dean of the Graduate School. Dr. Levin was a member of the President's Commission on the United States Postal Service and currently is a director of the Hewlett Foundation, Lucent Technologies, Satmetix, and the National Academy of Sciences' Board on Science, Technology and Economics Policy. He also chairs the board of AllLearn, a joint venture of Yale, Oxford, and Stanford Universities.

Senator John McCain of Arizona is the senior senator from his state and has served in that chamber since 1986. He began his political career in 1982 as a U.S. Congressman from Arizona. In 2000, he sought the Republican presidential nomination. Senator McCain serves as chairman of the Commerce, Science, and Transportation Committee, and he is a member of the Armed Services and Indian Affairs committees. In January 2004, Senator McCain called for an independent inquiry into pre-war intelligence on Iraq.

Henry S. Rowen is a senior fellow at the Hoover Institution. He is also Director emeritus of the Asia/Pacific Research Center at Stanford University and Professor of Public Policy and Management emeritus at the university's Graduate School of Business. He is currently doing research on regions of innovation and entrepreneurship throughout Asia and on economic and political topics in Asia. From 1989 to 1991, Rowen was the Assistant Secretary of Defense for International Security Affairs in the U.S. Department of Defense. He was Chairman of the National Intelligence Council from 1981 to 1983, served as President of the RAND Corporation from 1968 to 1972 and was Assistant Director of the U.S. Bureau of the Budget from 1965 to 1966.

Walter B. Slocombe has held several high-level positions in the Department of Defense, including Under Secretary of Defense for Policy from 1994 to 2001; Principal Deputy Under Secretary for Policy from 1993 to 1994; Deputy Under Secretary for Policy Planning from 1979 to 1981; and Principal Deputy Assistant Secretary for International Security Affairs from 1977 to 1979. During May-November 2003 he was Senior Advisor to the Coalition Provisional Authority in Baghdad for National Security and Defense. Mr. Slocombe is currently a member of the Washington, D.C. law firm Caplin & Drysdale, chartered.

Admiral William O. Studeman (Ret.) was Deputy Director of the Central Intelligence Agency from 1992 to 1995. He has held several high-level intelligence positions, including Director of the National Security Agency and Director of Naval Intelligence. He is a former Vice President and Deputy General Manager for Intelligence and Information Superiority at Northrop Grumman Mission Systems, a $5 billion global defense contractor. He retired from the Navy in 1995 and Northrop Grumman in 2005.

Charles M. Vest served as president of MIT from 1990 to 2004. He chaired the U.S. Department of Energy Task Force on the Future of Science Programs from 2002 to 2003. From 1993 to 1994, Dr. Vest chaired the President's Advisory Committee on the Redesign of the International Space Station, and from 1994 to the present he served as a member of the President's Council of Advisors on Science and Technology. He is a director of DuPont, IBM, and the Kavli Foundation.

Judge Patricia Wald served from 1999 to 2001 as a judge of the International Criminal Tribunal for the Former Yugoslavia at the Hague, Netherlands. An expert in international humanitarian law, she served 20 years on the U.S. Court of Appeals for the District of Columbia Circuit, including five years as chief judge. She was appointed by President Carter in 1979. Prior to her service on the bench, she served as Assistant Attorney General for Legislative Affairs from 1977 to 1979.

Lloyd Cutler *(Of Counsel)* is a founding partner of Wilmer Cutler Pickering Hale and Dorr LLP and served as counsel to Presidents Clinton and Carter. Mr. Cutler was a member and chairman of the Quadrennial Commission on Legislative, Executive, and Judicial Salaries, and a member of the President's Commission on Federal Ethics Law Reform in 1989.

Executive Director

Vice Admiral John Scott Redd (Ret.) served 36 years in the U. S. Navy, commanding eight organizations at sea from a destroyer to a fleet. He founded and commanded the Navy's Fifth Fleet in the Middle East in 1995 and served in several high-level policy positions in the Pentagon, including Director of Strategic Plans and Policy (J-5) on the Joint Staff. Since retiring in 1998 he has served as CEO of a high-tech education company and as Deputy Administrator/Chief Operating Officer of the Coalition Provisional Authority in Iraq.

General Counsel

Stewart A. Baker is a partner with the Washington, D.C. law firm of Steptoe and Johnson, LLP. He served as general counsel to the National Security Agency, deputy general counsel, Department of Education, law clerk to U.S. Supreme Court Justice John Paul Stevens, law clerk to the Honorable Frank M. Coffin, U.S. Court of Appeals, First Circuit, and the Honorable Shirley M. Hufstedler, U.S. Court of Appeals, Ninth Circuit. Mr. Baker also served on the

Markle Foundation Task Force on National Security in the Information Age, a Defense Science Board panel on Information Warfare, and the President's Export Council Subcommittee on Encryption.

Deputy Directors

Michael F. Munson *(Director for Plans)* is the former Deputy Director of the Defense Intelligence Agency. He has served as a Deputy Director for the National Reconnaissance Office and Director of Intelligence Program Review for the office of the Assistant Secretary of Defense, Command, Control, Communications, and Intelligence. Mr. Munson was also the study director for the Congressionally chartered National Defense Panel. He has 35 years of intelligence experience.

Gordon C. Oehler *(Director for Review)* served for 25 years at the Central Intelligence Agency in a variety of technical and managerial positions. From April 1992 through October 1997, Dr. Oehler directed the DCI's Non-Proliferation Center and is recognized as one of the nation's leading experts on technology, proliferation, and weapons of mass destruction.

Professional Staff

John E. Antonitis
Intelligence Professional

Margaret K. Baldwin
Information Technology Specialist

Orrie B. Bayliss
Information Technology Specialist

Shaba T. Bedney
Administrative Assistant

Shelley Lea Bennett
Intelligence Professional

James B. Bruce
Intelligence Professional

B. Belinda Canton
Intelligence Professional

Thomas G. Chappell
Executive Assistant

Felix J. Ciarlo
Consultant

Elbridge A. Colby
Intelligence Professional

Sean J. Coleman
Intelligence Professional

Joan L. C. Comtois
Administrative Assistant

Jeffrey R. Cooper
Consultant

Dylan D. Cors
Intelligence Professional

Michael R. Davis
Intelligence Professional

Sean B. Davis
Intelligence Professional

Diana L. Dieckhoff
Document Control Officer

Marsha L. Dimel
Human Resources Liaison

Harvey Dixon
Information Technology Specialist

Sarah S. Erwin
Executive Assistant

Andrew M. Fialdini
Intelligence Professional

Daniel J. Flynn
Intelligence Professional

Kenneth M. Geide
Intelligence Professional

Brett C. Gerry
*Deputy General Counsel &
Assistant Director*

Ashley Godwin
*Director of Staff Operations
and Finance*

Irvin Gray
*Director of Staff Operations
and Finance*

John A. Hartford, Jr.
Intelligence Professional

Kate Heinzelman
*Intelligence Professional & Special
Assistant to the General Counsel*

Robert A. Herd
Intelligence Professional

R. Evans Hineman
Consultant

John C. Hoffman
Intelligence Professional

Joseph H. Holthaus
Security Manager

William C. Hopkins
Intelligence Professional

Penelope S. Horgan
Intelligence Professional

Darrin A. Hostetler
*Associate General Counsel &
Intelligence Professional*

Paul M. Johnson
Intelligence Professional

Arthur Jones
Chief of Staff

Tiffany N. Kennedy
Document Control Officer

James C. King
Intelligence Professional

Armad J. Kittrell
Information Technology Specialist

Timothy R. Kochman
Information Technology Manager

Carl J. Kropf
Public Affairs Officer

Allen L. Krum
Intelligence Professional

Philip H. Kunsberg
Deputy Director for Plans

Thomas D. Lehrman
Intelligence Professional

Michael E. Leiter
*Deputy General Counsel &
Assistant Director*

George Lemus
Information Technology Specialist

Justin B. Longcor
Facilities and Logistics Manager

Jerry D. McEntire
Intelligence Professional

Laurence J. McQuillan
Consultant

Robert P. Morean
Deputy Director for Review

Brandon J. Murray
Information Technology Specialist

Lori E. Murray
Consultant

Peter Christopher Murray
Intelligence Professional

Dennis M. Nagy
Intelligence Professional

Julia Nesheiwat
Intelligence Professional

Robert A. Pattishall
Intelligence Professional

William R. Piekney
Intelligence Professional

Lois E. Ponikvar
Executive Assistant

Glenn D. Preston
Intelligence Professional

John J. Quattrocki
Intelligence Professional

Paul J. Redmond
Intelligence Professional

Keith E. Rice
Information Technology Specialist

Doreen G. Romero
Executive Assistant

Beth N. Sauter
Document Control Officer

Abe Schachter
Information Technology Specialist

Steven T. Schanzer
Intelligence Professional

Andrew M. Shepard
Intelligence Professional

Teresa L. Smetzer
Consultant

Kelley Brooke Snyder
Associate General Counsel &
Intelligence Professional

Suzanne E. Spaulding
Consultant

Michael K. Stransky
Intelligence Professional

John K. Strother
Intelligence Professional

Robert J. Surrette
Intelligence Professional

Patrick T. Toohey
Intelligence Professional

Monica D. Trachsel
Intelligence Professional

George Tsakiris
Information Technology Specialist

Marc A. Viola
Intelligence Professional

Samuel S. Visner
Consultant

Nancy M. Wheeler
Intelligence Professional

William Wilber
Security Officer

Edward M. Wittenstein
Intelligence Professional & Special
Assistant to the General Counsel

Shirley Cassin Woodward
Associate General Counsel &
Chief Iraq Investigator

Donald J. Wurzel
Intelligence Professional